Rethinking India's Oral and Classical Epics

Rethinking India's Oral and Classical Epics

Draupadī among Rajputs, Muslims, and Dalits

Alf Hiltebeitel

The University of Chicago Press
Chicago and London

Alf Hiltebeitel is professor of religion and director of the Human Sciences Program at The George Washington University. He is the author or editor of several books on Indian religion, anthropology, and literature.

The University of Chicago Press, Chicago 60637
The University of Chicago Press, Ltd., London

08 07 06 05 04 03 02 01 00 99 1 2 3 4 5

ISBN: 0-226-34050-3 (cloth)
ISBN: 0-226-34051-1 (paper)

Library of Congress Cataloging-in-Publication Data

Hiltebeitel, Alf.
Rethinking India's oral and classical epics: Draupadī among Rajputs, Muslims, and Dalits / Alf Hiltebeitel.
p. cm.
Includes bibliographical references (p.) and index.
ISBN 0-226-34050-5 (alk. paper). —ISBN 0-226-34051-1 (pbk.: alk. paper)
1. Draupadī (Hindu mythology) 2. Mahābhārata—History. 3. Rajputs—Religious life. 4. Untouchables—India—Religion. 5. Hinduism—Relations—Islam. 6. Islam—Relations—Hinduism. I. Title.
BL 1138.4.D72H57 1999
294.5'923046—dc21 9-8762
CIP

♾The paper used in this publication meets the minimum requirements of the American National Standard for Information Sciences—Permanence of Paper for Printed Library Materials, ANSI Z39.48-1992.

To Madeleine Biardeau

Contents

Maps and Tables

Plates

Plates follow page 192.

plaque) visited by young women and girls for immediate rewards

12. Satī platform of Rāṇiyammāḷ, wife of Rāja Desing, below the Gingee Fort. Steps in back of the platform lead down to the Ceṭṭikuḷam, a tank surrounded by crags and boulders.
13. Kalki on horseback with rider; or Desing's father Dhana Singh (Taṉciṅku), left, and uncle Tēraṇi Singh, right, as protectors of Gingee Fort. Mantaiveḷi or grazing ground, Gingee town below the fort.
14. Belā becomes satī. Elliot *Ālhā* illustration.
15. Memorial stone showing the Gingee king and his satī concubine at the Tī Pañcaṉ Kōvil; Mēlaccēri or "Old Gingee"
16. Belā's satī chabūtrā, Bairāgarh
17. Śāradā Devī Temple, Bairāgarh, with votive spears (sangs) outside entrance
18. Branching votive spear (sang) outside Bairāgarh Śāradā Devī Temple, showing the beheaded Chauṉṛā filling Śāradā's bowl with his blood (as on plate 8) and, opposite to the right, a hand holding a bloody sword

Acknowledgments

This book, more than any other I have written, has benefited from stimulating exchanges with, and helpful leads from, colleagues and friends. For that, I especially thank all the following: Anand Akundy, Ines Azar, P. Ranjan Babu, Brenda E. F. Beck, Madeleine Biardeau, Stuart H. Blackburn, Heidrun Brückner, Gyan Chaturvedi, Jayati Chaturvedi, Peter J. Claus, Paul B. Courtright, Wendy Doniger, Richard Eaton, James L. Fitzgerald, Joyce B. Flueckiger, Robert P. Goldman, Stuart Gordon, Richard Grinker, Lindsey Harlan, Balaji Hebbar, J. Kattalaikailasam, Dominique-Sila Khan, Randy Kloetzli, Frank J. Korom, Pon Kothandaraman, M. V. Krishnayya, Joel Kuipers, S. D. Lourdu, Philip Lutgendorf, Aditya Malik, Eveline Masilamani-Meyer, Barbara D. Miller, Joseph C. Miller, Seyyed Hosein Nasr, Laurie L. Patton, Indira V. Peterson, J. Rajasekaran, N. Ramachandran, A. Ramanathan, A. K. Ramanujan, Velcheru Narayana Rao, S. Ravindran, William S. Sax, Karine Schomer, John D. Smith, Jonathan Z. Smith, David Dean Shulman, G. Stephen, Sanjay Subrahmanyam, Romila Thapar, R. Venkataraman, Dewey D. Wallace, Catherine Weinberger-Thomas, David Gordon White, Harry E. Yeide, Jr., Abby Ziffren, and Claus Peter Zoller. All have made thoughtful and timely contributions to my understanding of this book's unfolding subject. For mistakes, the responsibility is my own.

Along with such exchanges, many of the above have helped me in distinctive ways with Hindi, Sanskrit, Tamil, and Telugu texts, and in conducting fieldwork. I indicate this at the appropriate points in this book.

For his editorial encouragement, I thank T. David Brent.

For help with preparing the text for camera-ready copy, thanks to Ian Gilbert.

For help with the Index, thanks to S. Ravindran.

For the maps, I thank Simon Hiltebeitel.

To my sons Adam and Simon, thanks for listening so often and for my best running commentaries.

Conventions

Tamil and Sanskrit terms generally follow the transcriptions of the standard cited dictionaries. Where terms from other South Asian languages are cited, I generally follow the transcriptions of other translators, though sometimes, perforce, selectively. The same applies to Persian and Arabic names and terms. Names of Indian districts, cities, taluk towns, and informants are given in conventional anglicized transcriptions such as one usually finds on maps or in the way people ordinarily spell their names using the English alphabet. No names of places or individuals have been disguised. Where names and terms occur in both Sanskrit and vernacular languages, I try to give both for as long as they might be helpful.

1 Introduction

This book grows out of an ongoing study of the south Indian Draupadī cult, whose projected final volume has now been reconceived. *The Cult of Draupadī, volume* 3, was first planned to have the subtitle "A *Mahābhārata* retrospective." I intended to contrast modern Indological interpretations of the epic with the Draupadī cult's folk interpretation, such as I was able to reconstruct it as a "Draupadī cult *Mahābhārata*" in volume 1, and to catch its ritual sense in volume 2. My idea was that a "living" Indian folk interpretation of the epic would provide a counterweight, and even correctives, to some of the prevailing views of the *Mahābhārata* held since the 1850s by a predominantly western, classically oriented scholarship. I intended especially to rethink the classical epic from the standpoint of the Draupadī cult's vision of it as centered on a heroine identical with the Hindu goddess.

I made some of the arguments in articles with the idea of working them into that book.[1] But gradually a new project took over the old plan. New arguments and insights pointed in other directions, and undercut earlier intentions. A one-to-one confrontation of the "Draupadī cult *Mahābhārata*" and the classical Sanskrit *Mahābhārata* is arbitrary and artificial. Both are multiple:[2] the Draupadī cult *Mahābhārata* has major regional variations (which I explore in my second Draupadī cult volume), and the Sanskrit epic exists in a southern recension that, as one would expect, is often closer to the south Indian Draupadī cult *Mahābhārata* than is the northern recension. And there are other regional folk *Mahābhāratas* to consider beside the Draupadī cult's.[3]

[1]See Hiltebeitel 1980a and b, 1981, 1984a, 1985b, 1993.

[2]As pointed out for the *Mbh* by Sutherland 1990.

[3]Most intriguing now is Mayaram's announcement that she is "completing a translation (in progress) of the Mewati Mahabharata, called the *Pandūn kā karā*" (1997, vi)—from Mewat in eastern Rajasthan. It looks, from a few references, to be fascinating for its infusion of Nāth lore, reference to fairs, accent on the Pāṇḍavas' dispossession, and coincidence in the repertoire of one Meo performer with "a rare narrative called *Hasan Husain*," drawing on

Moreover, because that project began with the confrontation of classical and folk *Mahābhāratas*, it included branching comparative studies of certain Indian folk epics which seem, despite their telling different kinds of stories, to be related to a folk *Mahābhārata* that has much in common with the Draupadī cult *Mahābhārata*. Still attempting to keep the "retrospective" and "Draupadī cult" studies together, I thus began to announce the third volume under a second subtitle: "Rethinking India's epics." But a closing volume on the Draupadī cult should be more focused on the cult itself than is possible in a study that considers the cult a reference point for questions about epic. Moreover, the "rethinking" project grew and required a new format. Material written under this impulse mainly about the *Mahābhārata* will now form another book: *Rethinking the Mahābhārata: A reader's guide to the education of Yudhiṣṭhira*. The present book was written in tandem with that one (referred to in the Bibliography as "forthcoming"). The third volume of *The cult of Draupadī* will thus be redefined again, and what I now intend is a book that will look at changes in the Draupadī cult over the years I have studied it, and consider the project of "writing about goddesses" that has become no less a fashion in current cultural and feminist studies (see Erndl and Hiltebeitel forthcoming) than it was in classical and medieval India. Nonetheless, Draupadī remains very much a force in this book and in *The education of Yudhiṣṭhira*.

This book argues that to understand how the Draupadī cult *Mahābhārata* and regional martial oral epics rethink India's classical epics, one must explore Rajput culture, and, as the study develops, Rajput-Muslim cultures, as lending a major impetus to these rethinking projects. I will often pare this general interface down by using the phrase "Rajput-Afghan culture," though not with any strict attempt to hold this usage to what is usually meant by either Rajput or Afghan separately. At other points, South Asian Nizārī or Satpanth Ismā'īlī Shī'ism will be the central Muslim configuration to consider. The argument will proceed first by analogy, marking out similarities and differences between the ways the Draupadī cult *Mahābhārata* and certain regional oral epics rethink India's classical epics. Yet, as the argument develops, we will observe that the Draupadī cult *Mahābhārata* and the *Mahābhāratas* that are reenplotted in regional oral martial epics also have significant things in common that neither of them shares with the Sanskrit *Mahābhārata*. And indeed, we will also notice a similar relation between the Sanskrit *Rāmāyaṇa* and a

---

a suppressed Shī'ite tradition (42-47, 139, 258-60). See also J. D. Smith 1990 and n.d. on another Rajasthani folk *Mbh*; Sax (cited articles) on Pāṇḍav Līlā; Flueckiger 1996, 156-76 on the Chhattisgarhi *Paṇḍvānī*; and chap. 10, n. 3, and chap. 13 below on works by Zoller and others.

popular *Rāmāyaṇa* reenplotted into a regional oral epic in which the popular *Rāmāyaṇa* is akin to the reenplotted popular *Mahābhāratas*. We will thus have to ask whether the features such regionalized *Mahābhāratas* and *Rāmāyaṇas* appear to hold in common—and note, it is not a question of the Sanskrit epics themselves but of regional and vernacular reworkings of them—have a history. To answer this, the comparisons will be carried out with an eye to the possibility of missions, migrations, and modes of transmission and diffusion.

As the argument advances, so, it is hoped, does a richer understanding of South Asian regional oral martial epics, and of India's classical epics at least in terms of what regional oral martial epics make of them. In thinking through the historical relation between the classical epics and Rajput culture, I have found C. V. Vaidya a clever pathfinder. Although his historiography is often hopeless,[4] he is the only scholar I know of to write extensively about both the classical Sanskrit epics (n.d. and 1966; [1906] 1972; 1907) and Rajputs (1924, 1926), to see interesting things in their relationship, and to see the relationship as an important problem.[5]

As to Rajputs and Muslims, I start from Kolff's insistence (1990, 1995) that prior to the "new Rajput Great Tradition" of sixteenth-century Rajasthan, there was an older, lower status medieval Rajput culture of soldiering with Afghans: one that *Ālhā* in particular recalls. Both soldiering and sects are part of this study, and in the latter case, Kassam's and Khan's writings on the Nizārī or Satpanth Ismā'īlīs, also called Khojās, have been especially eye-opening: Kassam (1994, 1995) for a largely persuasive historical reading of the double Hindu and Muslim registers found in the narratives and teachings of Satpanth songs called *ginān*s, and her beautiful translation of the ginā̄ns of Pīr Shams; Khan (1993, 1994, 1995, 1996, 1997a, 1997b) with regard to the impact of these double registers, especially as they intertwine with Nizārī messianism, on low status Rajputs and Dalits (I see no reason not to start using the term Dalit in scholarly writing for so-called "former Untouchables"). To be sure, Afghans and Nizārīs must ordinarily be thought of separately. Nizārī missions penetrated India mainly through Sind, and had less success in Afghanistan. Moreover, whereas Afghans constantly interact with Rajputs in the soldiering sphere, Nizārīs, once their history is detached from the militant Ismā'īlism of the Persian Alamūt period,[6] tend, after experiencing massacres and persecutions, to "seek camouflage and sanctuary" and to "find inconspicuous ways by which to survive" (Kassam 1995, 71-72). Yet some Afghans did bring

[4]See MacLean 1989, 26; Chattopadhyaya 1994, 161.

[5]See further Hiltebeitel in press-g.

[6]The Alamūt fort fell to the Mongols in 1256 A.D.

their own experiences of Ismā'īlī missions into Sind and Hind (or India).[7] And the militant vision of the Nizārīs did not die with its concealment. As elsewhere, Sufism often provided a cover for Ismā'īlīs within Sunnī-controlled regimes,[8] and would have enabled transmission of suppressed Ismā'īlī ideas among other unfavored populations. Moreover, regarding Shī'ism generally, the "armies of the kings and emperors of the north, up to the time of the Mughuls, were largely recruited from foreign countries," and "were mostly Shī'ahs" (Titus 1959, 89). Meanwhile, in the south such troopers were employed by the Bahmanīs and their successor states of Bijapur, Ahmadnagar, and Golconda. All the Deccan sultanates also had Shī'ī rulers who made ties with the Safavid Shī'as of Persia, and under the three successor states, Shī'ism was established through much of the Deccan (89-92). Thus, although Nizārī missions were limited mainly to northwest India, one may suspect that their camouflaged ideas had wider currency under both Sufi and Shī'ite covers.

Kolff, Khan, and Kassam thus bring us to the examination of the political and religious characteristics of a mixed culture, and point us toward exploration of its extensions beyond north India to south India. To make the roundabout argument brief, I believe one can trace elements of this Rajput-Muslim culture traveling south after Rajput culture has itself been girded by forms of south Indian goddess worship under the Pallavas, Chalukyas, and Rashtrakutas that first travelled north. We will thus begin with south Indian regional oral martial epics for which Rajput-Muslim issues seem barely on the horizon, then look north where they are central, and return south to look north and south again.

I cannot discuss all, or even a representative sample, of India's folk epics, which are found in many languages. The main ones I do discuss are indicated on map 1. A valuable attempt to introduce such a subject is the book *Oral epics of India* (Blackburn et al. 1989). I develop two arguments with this book's main editorial stance. I suggest that its scholarship on India's oral epics, in its treatment of textual and religious matters, tends to replicate the same Western "historically effected consciousness" as the scholarship on India's classical epics.[9] And I argue for a rethinking of the book's taxonomy of oral epics to single out the distinctive features of what I call "regional martial oral epics."

I will discuss four of these regional martial oral epics for their analogies with the Draupadī cult *Mahābhārata* and their allusions to the

[7]Daftary 1990, 349, 383, 404, 436, 468-70.

[8]Daftary 1990, 325, 329, 412, 435-37, 451-54, 461-67; Khan 1997b, 36. But see Kassam 1995, 72-73, 83, 377-78, on Sufi opposition to the Nizārī mission in post-Alamūt Sind.

[9]See Gadamer 1993, 300-7; Pollock 1991, 17, on the *Rām*; Hiltebeitel 1995a; in press-c.

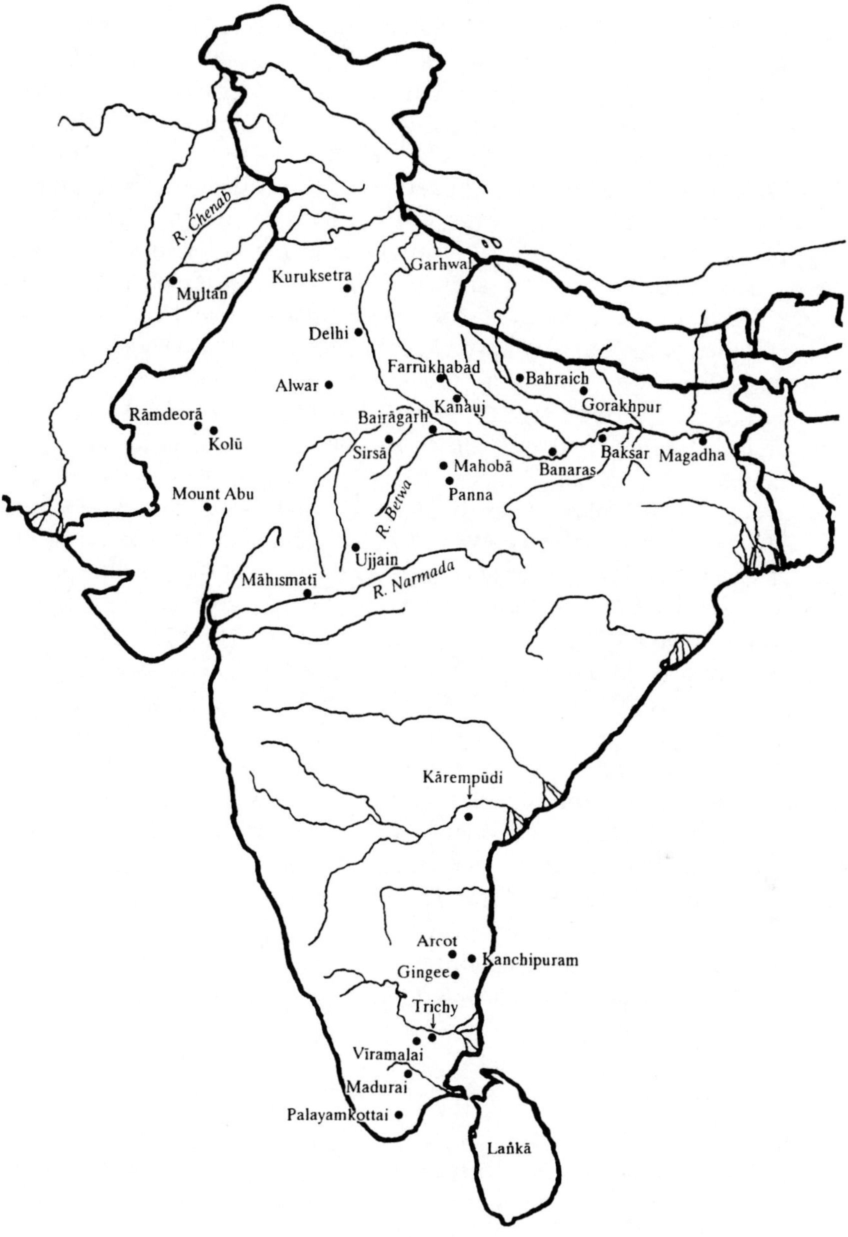

Map 1. Major oral epic and related sites

classical epics.[10] There are other south Asian regional martial oral epics that could be instructively studied as limit cases, but space forbids it.[11] The four are distinguished from all others I know of by *strong* reenplotment from either the *Mahābhārata* or the *Rāmāyaṇa*. I consider not only how each is regionally and historically grounded, but, as mentioned, the possibilities of interregional transmission. Two are south Indian: the Tamil *Elder brothers story* (Beck 1992) and the Telugu *Epic of Palnāḍu* (Roghair 1982). Two are from the north: the Rajasthani *Pābūjī* (J. D. Smith 1991), and the Hindi *Ālhā* (Waterfield and Grierson [W&G] 1923). Fortunately, all are translated from oral texts, and recorded or taken down from oral performances, although not in unaffected settings. They are variations on what J. D. Smith calls "'studio' recordings."[12] Unfortunately, Waterfield's translation of oral *Ālhā*—the so-called Elliot *Ālhā*—is rather free, and is not complete; for large sections of the Elliot *Ālhā*, I rely mainly on Grierson's summaries that are ample but never fully satisfactory. This means that generalized statements about what is and is not "in the Elliot *Ālhā*" must all be qualified by an acknowledgment that the statement is made mainly on the basis of this translation and summary. I do make such qualifiers sometimes, when it seems worth a reminder. In any case, the Elliot *Ālhā* is too vast for my very limited Hindi. But I believe the risks are worth taking. What scholarship there is on these oral epics is for the most part disappointing. And what scholarship there isn't shows a massive failure by mythologists, folklorists, historians, and scholars of Indian literature, religion, and anthropology to take them seriously.

I argue that regional martial oral epics are a distinctive genre within the larger class of India's oral epics. They are all formed in the same unsettled medieval period (twelfth to fifteenth centuries). They all make similar linkages between regionality, the peripherality of "little kingdoms," land, landed dominant castes, and the goddess of the land. *All* of these features are shared with the "Draupadī cult *Mahābhārata*," as is

[10]On allusion and analogy as optional strategies in literary interpretation, see Quint 1993, 14-15.

[11]See Hiltebeitel in press-e for such a study of the Tulu epic of Koti and Cennaya, which has much in common with the Tamil *Elder brothers story*, and 1991a, 186-206, 302-8, 373-75, 391-93, on the Bengali epic of Lausen. Both have *weak Mbh* associations, and are studied as just such limit situations. The Rajasthani oral epic *Devnārāyan* (or *Bagarāvat*) could be instructively compared for its similarly reenplotted associations with the Krsna cycle (*Harivamśa*, etc.) rather than with one of the epics; see Miller 1980, Malik 1993 and forthcoming, and B. Singh 1980, 1993. See also Lapoint 1978, 294, 301-5, on reenplotted *Mbh* themes and inversions in the north Indian *Guga* epic involving Janamejaya (whom Guga reincarnates) and his snake sacrifice in the *Mbh*.

[12]J. D. Smith 1986, 53; cf. 1991, 25-30.

a distinctive rapport between the goddess and the "little kings" who embody the classical epics' Kṣatriya ideal as it is translated into rajputized regional dominant-landed-caste idioms. Moreover, the "little kings" and divine heroines have indispensable low status (often Dalit or Muslim) sidekick-protectors who have no equivalents in the Sanskrit epics. But my interest in these oral epics begins with a point that others have treated as insignificant. In each, central characters are reincarnated heroes and heroines (sometimes including Draupadī) of the Sanskrit epics: in *Elder brothers*, *Palnāḍu*, and *Ālhā* from the *Mahābhārata*; in *Pābūjī* from the *Rāmāyaṇa*. I will approach these connections as part of the formative inner workings, the primary process cultural work, that these regional oral martial epics attempted and achieved.

In other words, each of these oral epics "rethinks" one of the classical epics. And so does the Draupadī cult. But here there are also contrasts. For the Draupadī cult, it is a case of seeing how one of the classical Sanskrit epics is "iconically" "re-presented" as a "whole" and ritually reenacted as it is "translated" into vernacular and regional terms (see Ramanujan 1991b). For oral regional martial epics, it is rather a matter of studying texts that draw only on selected themes from the classical epics in ways that play out strategic "indexical" reenplotments into a region's locational peripherality and historical dislocations. As the heroes and heroines of the classical epics veer into their new lives, things are turned inside out; winners lose, losers win.

Such considerations have required me to attempt different interdisciplinary crossovers for this book, and for *The education of Yudhiṣṭhira*, than those demanded for *The cult of Draupadī*, for which my primary leap was into anthropology. Although I have done new fieldwork for this book, and although it continues to explore anthropology itself as a discipline, rethinking India's epics has meant thinking more about literature and history than doing anthropology. No matter how important I continue to think they are for the study of Hinduism and South Asian religions, and indeed for the anthropological study of South Asia, India's classical epics are above all works of literature. This has meant recalling some of the reasons I was once an English major for my first three years of college, and giving some attention to recent studies in literature and literary theory. I describe this turn more fully in *The education of Yudhiṣṭhira*, where it bears on the Sanskrit epics directly. But for this book I must mention that I consider the Sanskrit epics to have been composed as written texts whose fictional authors make little sense if the works are the products of anonymous oral bards.[13]

[13]Cf. Bonazzoli 1979b, 142.

In this book, I extend this perspective, mutatis mutandis, to India's other epics, written and oral. For as we shall see, Indian oral epics are intertextual with both written and oral texts. They frame themselves by what seem to be literary conventions, reenplot what seem to be literary schemes, and sometimes make telling allusions to writing. To be sure, South Asian oral bards make use to varying degrees of oral formulaic verse. But this does not mean that "oral theory" can tell us how the Sanskrit epics were composed, much less recover a pristine state of pure oral tradition either behind the Sanskrit epics, or in regional oral epics themselves. I consider efforts to find oral bardic poetry and oral formulaic verse behind the Sanskrit epics prone to inflated claims, and to have little productive to say about the texts themselves that does not need correction.[14] And I regard efforts to seal off India's oral epics from a meaningful relationship to the Sanskrit epics, and more generally the drive to find the preliterate and purely oral in oral epics sung in writing cultures, as a failed attempt at scholarly exorcism.[15] No Eurasian oral epic I have read about has been persuasively elevated to the realm of the "preliterate."

In rethinking India's oral epics in relation to its classical ones, and oral versions of the classical epics themselves, I have barely indicated some of the comparative implications of Quint's study (1993) of "winners's epics" and "loser's epics," of imperial epics and epics of resistance, in his examination of western epics from Homer through Virgil and Lucan, to Tasso and Milton, and on to Eisenstein. Wherever I use such terms in this book, I am in Quint's debt, and I have reserved comparative discussion of western and Indian epics on such points for a separate essay (in press-g). Since all the texts under study in this book are stories about empires, kingdoms big and small, Kṣatriyas, Rajputs, and little kings, it has been necessary to study the different kinds of history made by the texts themselves—imagined pasts, background history reflected in the texts, history of the texts (oral, written)—and by historians who make further history out of these kinds of history. The four regional oral martial epics under study are all about little kings whose kingdoms are overrun, in one case (*Ālhā*) by an opponent who has imperial designs

[14]See especially Benson [1966] 1990, showing that "literate poets could quite easily write in a formulaic style" (230), using phrases that are "clearly oral in origin" yet "now just as clearly a literary convention," including "the poets' own conventional references to oral tradition" (235). Cf. Foley 1981, 70-72, 75-77, 88-89, on other similar challenges to "oral theory"; also Olsen 1987. For preceding discussion on oral formulas in classical Sanskrit works, see Hiltebeitel 1993, 9-12, 18, 27-28, 40; 1995a, 25-27, and especially Narayana Rao's discussion (1993) of purānic composition, making a similar point to Benson's, which applies as well to at least the *Mbh*. See further Hiltebeitel forthcoming.

[15]On scholarly exorcism, see J. Z. Smith 1990, 41, 52-53, 115, 142-43.

himself, and in all cases by larger "empires" (Muslim in the north; Chola in Tamilnadu [Beck 1978, 169-75]; Kākatiya in Andhra) that swallow the former kingdoms once they have self-destructed through the final wars that end their stories.

I have also found recent work in colonial and postcolonial studies,[16] and in trope theory,[17] helpful in contrasting metaphoric strategies of totalization, continuity, and transparency with metonymic strategies of displacement, mimicry, resistance, and localization. I see the former as useful in characterizing the replication of the *Mahābhārata*'s "whole story" in the Draupadī cult, as well as in the use of the classical epics by the Pāṇḍav Līlā and Rām Līlā in north India, and the latter as useful in thinking about ways in which regional martial oral epics disjoin the classical epics and turn them inside-out.

Such contrasts come full circle when I compare oral *Ālhā*, the most important regional oral martial epic for this study, with the very different "*Ālhā*" told in the Sanskrit *Bhaviṣya Purāṇa*. In the latter, *Ālhā*'s *Mahābhārata*-interlinkages multiply, and are highly Brahmanizied, Sanskritized, and "purāṇicized." The folk epic is "re-metaphorized" into a Brahmanical imperial history. The *Bhaviṣya Purāṇa* provides both a "mediating text" through which to gauge the stylistic, thematic, and political differences between classical and regional martial epics, and a text that forces clearer rethinking of the relation between written Sanskrit and oral vernacular epics. It will be one of the arguments of this book that while a Sanskrit reworking tends to do more metaphoric smoothing down, vernacular traditions, and especially regional martial oral epics, tend to innovate just from darker areas that the Sanskrit epics leave open, often by reenplotting their metonymic fragments. Further, whereas the Sanskrit epics and the *Bhaviṣya Purāṇa*'s version of *Ālhā* center their stories on imagined empires of the past and turnings of imperial eras, regional oral martial epics are not imperial at all. They are anti-imperial. At a time when there were no "Hindu" emperors, they reenplot the classical epics into regional pockets of Rajput or rajputized resistance, seasoned with Muslim and especially Afghan and Ismā'īlī flavors, where losing could become a new kind of winning. Empires and eras are not unimportant, but they are less important than local history, regional land, and matters of survival.

I also discuss the *Tēciṅkurājaṉ katai* or "Ballad of Rāja Desing," a martial epic from the late Mughal and colonial periods, which is anti-imperial to the core. *Desing* allows us to study a folk epic—in both written and oral form (S. Ravindran and I were fortunate to find an oral

[16]Bhabha 1994a and b; Pollock 1994.

[17]Bhabha (see n. 15), Fernandez 1986 and 1991, T. Turner 1991.

singer who knew a distinctive version)—about Rajputs and Afghans who die defending the Gingee Fort, which for some time dominated the Draupadī cult's core area. As an "historical epic," *Desing* differs from the four regional oral martial epics in that its two lone heroes made documented history, and in its near total indifference to the region's own landed caste traditions. The conflict it tells of is not one between historically unidentifiable heroes and heroines from populations long settled in a region. Rather, telling of a conflict between historically identifiable newcomers to a region, it gives its two heroes the outline and elements of an *Ālhā*-like story adapted to patterns of "indexical" remembrance typical of south Indian oral epics and hero cults. While the *Bhaviṣya Purāṇa* translates *Ālhā* "whole" into the cosmological rhythms and "icons" of a Sanskrit purāṇa, *Desing* sustains its *Ālhā*-like story on an intriguing Hindu-Muslim double register, and provides us with the key text on which to bring this book's discussion of Rajputs, Afghans, and Ismā'īlīs to a close.

The last three chapters then trace more distinctively Rajput strains back to narrative formations concerning fire-born warriors and modes of heroic self-sacrifice by males and females. Such formations would seem to antecede Muslim-Hindu interactions, and provide glimpses of some of the earliest features and conditions in the development and dissemination of *Mahābhārata* and *Rāmāyaṇa* folklores. Studying south and north Indian regional oral martial epics together with the Draupadī cult and its *Mahābhārata* thus, hopefully, points up the need to reground some of our thinking about Rajputs, Muslims, and Dalits, to relocate some of our thinking about south and north India, and to stop thinking about the *Mahābhārata* and *Rāmāyaṇa* simply as contaminating Sanskrit texts when it comes to studying South Asian oral epics.

2 Oral Epics

The study of South Asian folk epics confronts one at the outset with methodological choices. I will not stress epic as an analytic genre, or look for commonalities with classical, folk, or oral epic traditions outside of India. But I do regard epic as a sufficiently useful analytic and comparative term to allow us to continue to classify by it not only the two Sanskrit texts but a number of South Asian oral traditions. Within this broad class of South Asian epics, my initial goal will be to reconsider currently prevalent taxonomies so as to allow a better sense of what is comparable among Indian epics, and to enable better comparison on three fronts: features of India's oral epics that link certain of them strongly with the Sanskrit epics, features that disconnect these same oral epics from the Sanskrit epics, and analogies between these specific oral epics with each other.

The last two options and the option of extra-Indian comparison and analysis have the attraction of lifting the weight of Sanskrit and Brahmanical tradition off the backs of regional and vernacular creations, and of examining distinctive features of Indian oral epics either in relation to extra-Indian domains, or as alternative traditions. Among extra-Indian comparisons, John D. Smith's work on formulaic verse and "epic moments" in the *Pābūjī* epic of Rajasthan involves a successful application and rethinking of Albert B. Lord's theories on oral epic.[1] Less persuasively, Beck draws on de Vries in generalizing beyond the Sanskrit epics to "Indo-European" themes such as twinship, heroic life cycle, and status relations, and on C. S. Peirce in examining "core triangles" to identify what "types of character patterns typify epics in general and what subtypes among these are found especially well developed in India."[2] Smith, Beck, and Roghair all see India's regional

[1]Smith 1977; 1986; 1991, 18-30; Lord 1964.

[2]See Beck 1982, 18, 56 122-23, 126-28, 132, on Indo-European themes, supposedly including the *Gilgamesh Epic*, and 1989, 155 (quote). Some of Beck's branching triangles

vernacular epics as oppositional to forms of pan-Indian Brahmanical dominance conveyed (at least in part) through the Sanskrit epics: Smith in terms of "little tradition" verses "great tradition" processes of Sanskritization and Brahmanization (1991, 6, 90); Beck in terms "glorif[ying] a kind of counter culture" that allows for the critical expression of ambivalent and even negative attitudes toward Brahmans and orthodox values (1982, 11-12, 35, 136, 169); and Roghair in terms of a holistic "local world view" or regional integrative process that provides "an alternative to Brahman elite ideology" (1982, 2, 92-93, 136-37).

These three authors have each recorded, translated, and studied one of the epics I will examine. Each appreciates that south Asian oral epics, and notably the one each has studied, have problematic relationships with the Sanskrit epics. I will argue that although the oppositions they see have some heuristic value, they have overstressed them and underestimated and misunderstood the nature of the connections between Indian classical and oral epics. To put it bluntly, the relationship between Indian oral epics and the Sanskrit epics is indirect, and not susceptible to such immediate oppositions. Moreover, the significance and complexity of that relationship cannot be appreciated by explanations that sidetrack it to formalisms, sociology, or ideology. Although these authors and others have attempted to understand the relationship, I will argue that it remains ill-defined.

A. Classical and Oral Epics

While "epic" retains its usefulness as a cross-cultural analytic genre, analytical classification and definition are highly problematic in the treatment of India's wealth and variety of epic traditions. In their prevalent classification for south Asian oral epics, Blackburn and Flueckiger provide two overlapping typologies. The first, derived in part from Beck (1978) and Narayana Rao (1986), distinguishes three epic types: martial, sacrificial, and romantic (Blackburn and Flueckiger 1989, 4-5). The second, presented separately by Blackburn, contrasts multistory and single-story oral epic traditions. Multistory traditions (the Tamil Bow Song [*vil pāṭṭu*], Tulu *pāḍdana*, and *teyyam* in Kerala) include "narrative songs of heroes" performed over a limited geographical area. They consist of "as many as fifty to a hundred separate stories" that are related as a repertoire. To some degree they are also related thematically and intergenerationally, but they are "not centered on a single story," and

---

are rather fanciful: e.g., male "single fighter : gang loyalist"; female "visionary : informer" (ibid., 173-74); Daśaratha, Hanumān, and Lakṣmaṇa (166: the first two never meet).

none are "of 'epic' length."[3] This second typology raises interesting issues. The first, I believe, lends itself to confusion and distortion.

While setting the tone for the book *Oral epics of India* that they helped to edit, Blackburn and Flueckiger admit, "Some contributors to this volume have grouped the martial and sacrificial epics together as 'historical' epics because their key events and characters can be traced to identifiable historical events and personages."[4] Blackburn uses the term "historical epics" himself (1989, 26). I would argue that while the categories "martial" and "romantic" serve well for certain oral epics, the terms "historical" and "sacrificial" are less satisfactory. "Historical" is unsatisfactory when it begs the question of history, which authors who use the term are often inclined to resurrect from the barest bones, and all too easily invent.

Smith, for instance, sets out "to track down the historical Pābūjī" (1991, 73), comparing the oral *Pābūjī* he recorded with the *Vāta Pābūjī rī*, part of the seventeenth-century *Khyāta* (*Chronicle*) of Muhato Naiṇasī.[5] Smith thinks both sources "inflate" facts and history, but that the *Khyāta* is "likely to be less inflated." But it turns out that "most of the named figures in Naiṇasī's version of the story appear nowhere else in the literature" (73), and that "the obscurity" of those who do appear elsewhere "is hardly lessened, for the information varies between the tantalising and the self-contradictory" (74). "Anachronisms" and "synchronisms" abound (72): "telescoping and artificial lengthening of genealogies" (75), "extreme paucity of information" (75), likelihood that the chronicler himself relies on an oral epic tradition (72, 75-76; 78), elements that "cannot be accepted as credible history," multiple uses of single names ("no agreement at all as to how many Dodos there were" [77]), "obscurities and inconsistencies" (77). These are what Stig Wikander has called the mythic elements of an "heroic age."[6]

But Smith, undeterred, speaks of a "process which has transformed the earlier [chronicle] story into the later [epic] one. . . . an *inflation* [Smith's italics] of the story, an almost systematic exaggeration of all its most important aspects" (1991, 72). Some of his points are clearly slanted. The supposed transformation of Naiṇasī's Dalit hero Cādo into a high caste Rajput in *Pābūjī* discounts the oral epic's double portrayal

[3]Blackburn 1989, 15-16; cf. Claus 1989, 56, 73.

[4]Blackburn and Flueckiger 1989, 5, n. 17. Thus *Pābūjī* and *Devnārāyan* (or *Bagarāvat*) are interchangeably "martial" and "historical" (Kothari 1989, 102-8); *Ālhā* is "martial-historical" (Schomer 1989, 142). Cf. Beck 1982, 7: "epic-like" refers to stories that "describe genuine historical events."

[5]Tessitori 1916, 110-14; Smith 1991, 71-88, 481-96.

[6]See my reconstruction of Wikander's views in Hiltebeitel [1976] 1990, 48-59.

of this hero (and his brother Ḍhēbo) as linked with both castes. And the drift from Naiṇasī's "ordinary human beings (with, in some cases, supernatural origins and powers)" into "incarnations of figures from orthodox Hindu mythology" misleadingly suggests that "orthodox" Sanskritic deities are absent from Hindu folk religion (73-74).[7] The attempt to find an historical Gogo Cauhāṇ (or Chauhān) is even more fantastic than the search for the historical Pābūjī. Maybe there was a historical Gogo Cauhāṇ, who does have a grave site (*samādhi-dargāh*) marking his swallowing by the earth.[8] But Smith, saying "we can do no better than quote the conclusions" of D. Sharma, "the best historian of the early Cauhāṇs," allows that Gogo could originally have been a contemporary of Mahmud of Ghaznā (d. 1030 A.D.), and that a 1409 allusion to a "Goga" in a list of deities whom Jain Śrāvakas should refrain from worshiping suggests a sufficient interval for his deification.[9] On this basis, Smith considers Gogo an anachronism in both the epic and chronicle, and takes up what he considers the double anachronism of Gogo and Guru Gorakhnāth, who also appears in both versions. Despite recognizing that it is "impossible to build up serious history on the basis of such tales," Smith turns them into textual history to recover just this impossibility. In chapter 4, I will discuss features of Naiṇasī's account that make it virtually certain that his primary source is "epical," and cannot inform us about remembered or recorded history.

The term "historical epics" should thus be reserved for epics that can be profitably discussed in relation to solid and documentable historical evidence *about the story's key figures*. This is not the case for *Elder brothers*, *Palnāḍu*, *Pābūjī*, or *Ālhā*; nor is it the case for the *Mahābhārata* or *Rāmāyaṇa*. The "Ballad of Rāja Desing" is the best example of historical epic discussed in this book.

Sacrificial epics are said to "center on a heroic act of self-sacrifice, or even suicide, by a woman" (Blackburn and Flueckiger 1989, 5). Blackburn discusses only two examples: *Kanyakā Ammavāri Katha* and *Ellamma*.[10] Narayana Rao mentions *Kanyakā* and two others (1986, 136-63),

[7]Roghair, similarly seeking elements of the "local" that aren't "overlapped," attempts to recuperate an un-"Hindu" or un-"Brahmanized" local tradition which "sometimes . . . overlaps with the brahmanical view; more often it diverges." Thus a verse, which appears in both oral and written versions, is "misleading" when it asserts that the Palnad "Heroes are Śivalingas; Visnu is Cennuḍu; Pōta Rāju is Bhairava; Ankama Śakti is Annapūrna, etc." (1982, 92-93, 137).

[8]See Khan 1997b, 66, 232.

[9]J. D. Smith 1991, 74, citing D. Sharma 1959, 327.

[10]Blackburn 1989, 18. Blackburn and Flueckiger also mention *Ellamma* as an example of a "fourth type of oral epic in India [that] might be called 'miracle-cycle'" (1989, 4-5 n. 16). Insufficiently described in *Oral epics in India*, *Ellamma* is presumably the story of the

and Kothari, perhaps noting that all three are *satī* (or suttee) stories, suggests that Rajasthani satī stories could also roughly fit the category.[11] But other than gender focus and self-sacrificial versus military means of resolution, Blackburn and Flueckiger's definition of sacrificial epics does not distinguish them sufficiently from martial epics: they "are similar in that both are concerned with power, social obligation, and social unity; they turn on the themes of revenge, regaining of lost land, or restoring lost rights" (1989, 5). This collapsing distinction does not even retain the important (at least for south India) attribution of sacrificial epics to left hand castes (traders), and martial epics to right hand castes (landowners), by Narayana Rao (1986, 42), who coined both terms.[12] To my mind, "sacrificial" is a misnomer, one that is inadequate to the intended contrast, since martial epics are laden with sacrificial symbolism.

Multistory traditions could just as well be called ballads as epics, and the tragic "death stories" among them are reminiscent of sagas. Romantic epics are better considered romances. This would leave us with only historical and martial epics, which could then be called simply "epic."

Granted that Indian languages do not supply their own emic terms for epic, oral epic, and oral epic subtypes (Blackburn and Flueckiger 1989, 2-4), but that workable analytic definitions are indispensable, I will continue to use all the terms cited so far except for "sacrificial" epics, which I will use only in quotes. The latter are really not epics. They are stories about heroine-goddesses that emerge out of the genre of *purāṇa*: Sanskrit purāṇa and *sthala purāṇa* (stories about a sacred place) in the case of Reṇukā-Ellamma-Māriyammaṉ,[13] caste purāṇa in cases like *Kanyakā* and others described by Narayana Rao.[14]

The term "epic" is also loose in its application to the two Sanskrit works, which in some respects it fits less well than many south Asian oral epics. As is well known, the Sanskrit works have no term like "epic" to define them, but rather define themselves by way of several genres:

---

goddess Ellamma-Reṇukā, whose myths and cult are now best treated in Assayag 1992.

[11]1989, 111-12; cf. Roghair 1982, 132-33.

[12]Narayana Rao develops a more extensive set of oppositions between martial and sacrificial oral epics in Andhra (1986, 140-62). Perhaps Blackburn and Flueckiger ignore his contrasts and additional examples because their features are not generalizable beyond south India. Rajasthani satī stories, for instance, would not be typical of left hand castes.

[13]See Biardeau 1969; Assayag 1992.

[14]Cf. Ramanujan 1993, 106-20, on a "folk purāna" about the goddess. The story of the retreat from a king, sometimes with a river-parting reminiscent of Exodus, occurs in other south Indian caste purāṇas (Thurston and Rangachari [1904] 1965, 1:139; 4:344 (trading caste); 3:215; 4:118-19; 408-9 (cultivating castes); 5:73-74 (Dalit subcaste); 1:212; 2:277; 4:328-29; 7:407-9 (variants of Kōmati Kanyakamma myth [3:311-22]). Cf. Whitehead's Ammavaru cycle (1921, 126-38), bringing this type close to the "miracle-cycle" (see n. 10).

kāvya, refined poetry; *itihāsa*, accounts of what is said about the past (often unnecessarily called "history"); and *purāṇa*, "stories of old."[15] What I am concerned with is finding the best terms to proceed with an investigation of the relation between India's Sanskrit epics and regional martial oral epics, which, I argue, is a highly significant one. I take both Sanskrit epics as mainly martial, but with romantic subtales (such as "Nala and Damayantī"), interludes, and underlying themes that combine with the martial features. I agree with Blackburn and Flueckiger that "the Rāma story . . . approximates a romantic epic" (1989, 5, n. 18). Indeed, Arjuna is a romantic hero in the *Mahābhārata*,[16] and elsewhere I have tried to say the same even of Yudhiṣṭhira, and, of course, Draupadī (Hiltebeitel forthcoming). In fact, we could say that while they are mainly martial, the two Sanskrit epics are romantic and even multistory epics (though in a different sense from the one mentioned above, since they do center on a main story) as well. Similarly, there are romantic features (quests, wandering minstrels, miracles, suspended amorous longings) in regional oral martial epics.[17]

How then have the connections between Sanskrit classical epics and oral epics been interpreted? Let us begin with the most dismissive statements. According to Blackburn and Flueckiger, links through reincarnations are "not necessarily evidence of a common history for the Sanskrit and folk epics, nor do the resemblances always represent an imitation. . . . Rather, references to the *Rāmāyaṇa* and the *Mahābhārata* or their heroes are often simply a means of legitimizing the folk epics."[18] These authors cite *Pābūjī* as an example, and the testimony of Smith, whose personal communication to them favors performers who know the least about the classical epics, and who says in his own article in Blackburn and Flueckiger's edited volume that when northern oral epics explain how classical heroes come to figure in a story, "in most

[15]While *kāvya* is thought of especially in relation to the *Rām* as the *Ādikāvya* or "first kāvya," the *Mbh* also describes itself as *kāvya*. See Shulman 1991 for discussion.

[16]See Hiltebeitel 1988a, 282-86; Katz 1989, 60-66.

[17]Kothari suggestively links Sufism with romantic epics (1989, 108). For Blackburn, *Ālhā* is more martial than romantic, but anomalous in this category (1989, 29; see below). One could say that the Kṛṣṇa cycle in the *Harivaṃśa* and purāṇic tradition is romantic, and that there is a link between the romantic/martial and cowherd/Kṣatriya oppositions; but cowherd themes are also martial in *Ālhā*, *Palnāḍu*, *Pābūjī*, and the *Mbh* (with regard to the Yādavas). Cf. Hiltebeitel 1988a, 17-18, 32-34, 58-59, 91, 185-86, 220-21; 1989a, 5-7, 12; Flueckiger 1989, 35, 46, contrasting two versions of the Lorik-Candā epic, both drawn from local cowherding castes: one more romantic (Madhya Pradesh), one more martial (Uttar Pradesh). On romance narrative in epic comparatively, see Quint 1993, 9, 34-39, 92-93, 120-21, 136-51, 179-82, 248-56, 282-83, 302-24.

[18]Blackburn and Flueckiger 1989, 8. Cf. Katz 1989, 13, 30, 94: a historical Pariksit "legitimizing" himself by claiming Pāndava ancestry; Hiltebeitel 1995a, 24.

cases it amounts to no more than the taking up of a loose end" (1989, 182). I will address Smith's evaluation of *Pābūjī*'s *Rāmāyaṇa* connections in chapter 4. Let me just say at this point that it is more (or at least just as much) a case of delegitimization as it is of legitimization, since the oral epics treat the classical epics as incomplete, and since the *Rāmāyaṇa*s and *Mahābhārata*s they invoke are not the Sanskrit epics anyway, but oral folk versions thereof. Keeping the usages "Sanskrit epics" and "classical epics" distinct, we may thus say that although oral epics have indirect relations to the Sanskrit epics, they have direct relationships to (mainly) oral versions of the classical epic stories.

For Blackburn and Flueckiger, it is also not clear what "common history" and "imitation" are meant to rule out. The first could hardly mean common or interlinked historical events. Perhaps Blackburn means to clarify this when he says elsewhere that the developmental patterns he proposes "do not necessarily imply direct evolution because epic traditions found at different stages are not always historically related" (1989, 16). In any case, it would seem we are left to disimagine a "common history" as a context in which these texts (written and oral) would be linked. But such a history cannot simply be dismissed. As to "imitation," on the surface, this sounds like an acclamation of the independent creativity of folk traditions, which everyone applauds. But classical-oral epic linkages are hardly matters of imitation. They are powerful and in many ways consistent reenplotments and what might be called disenplotments and dislocations. The statement seems designed to argue against taking the classical epics as *prior* to the oral epics. But I do not see how we can avoid this. It is straining to imagine a South Asian history in which the classical epics do not have "informative" priority. The point driven home repeatedly by Blackburn and Flueckiger is that oral epics have an integrity independent of the Sanskrit epics. Thus, "character-based commonalities between folk and Sanskrit epics are admittedly superficial." And, "even where there are extensive borrowings from the Sanskrit epics, folk epics carry new meanings because they live in new social settings" (Blackburn and Flueckiger 1989, 8). The closing point should win universal agreement.[19] But the generalizations about classical and oral epic linkages discourage reflection by dubbing the process "superficial" and one of "borrowing."[20]

Yet the strangest theory to account for classical-oral epic rapports

[19]Cf. Roghair, Beck, and Smith, as cited above; Kothari 1989, 115-118; Schomer 1989, 152-54.

[20]See J. Z. Smith 1990, 31, 46-47, 51, on notions of borrowing, dependence, filiation, genealogy, genetic connection, etc., as being "uninteresting" while disguising and obscuring the scholar's actual interests.

comes curiously from the one oral epic scholar who also works on the Sanskrit epics: J. D. Smith. Drawing from the workshops of biblical and Homeric textual criticism, Smith supports his "loose ends" explanation by treating what he calls "doubtful" aspects of *Pābūjī*'s connections with the *Rāmāyaṇa* as non-"literal" formulae and accretive interpolations. More than this, beneath the "loose ends" that oral epics pick up from the Sanskrit epics lies a deeper unity on the level of "ideology."[21] Smith's "picture" is of a "remarkably consistent" ideology that "differs radically from conventional bhakti theology" (1989, 176), and is especially "found in the Sanskrit and martial epics," while less so in romantic and multi-story ones (178, 193). Both classical and oral martial epics attribute human suffering to the gods, "who pass evil into the world in order that they should be free from it in heaven" (176). "Epic heroes—and by extension we ourselves—are the gods' scapegoats." This ideology is "in essentials a single, coherent" one that "varies remarkably little from time to time and place to place" (193). Smith draws support from O'Flaherty's argument that Hindu myths often "portray mankind as no more than 'a convenient dump for celestial moral garbage.' Indeed, Kṛṣṇa himself is recognized as one of the most prolific dumpers."[22] We shall find some support for this theodicy.[23] But the argument leaves nothing in the gods' "defense."[24] "The gods, say the epics, are not averse from mixing in human affairs; but when they do so it is entirely for their own benefit" (193). They are treacherous in imposing fate onto man, and cannot be trusted in what they say, since they act from the very basest of motives. When Kṛṣṇa tells Arjuna to act without desire for the fruits of his actions, it seems we must imagine he has base desires of his own in championing the self-interest of the gods. By lumping all gods together in this charge, Smith overlooks the hierarchies and puzzles of bhakti and dharma that the classical epics unfold, and which oral epics selectively reenplot. In so doing, he ignores problems that the epics seek to resolve and the complexity of the values he attempts to expose as hypocritical.[25]

[21]As with Pollock (1991, 66-68), a usage of this term to disclose a dark underside of the ostensibly religious.

[22]J. D. Smith 1989, 176, citing O'Flaherty 1976, 141, 260-71.

[23]If the *Mbh* myth of the former Indras can be interpreted as a divine "Vrātya" raid into the human world to restore the "distinction" of the gods, as I argue in Hiltebeitel forthcoming, it does fit Smith's picture.

[24]See Matilal 1991 for a rounder picture on the question of what a Hindu god can and cannot do with this messy world. By implication, such judgments as Smith's arise from a faulty comparison of Hindu gods (the target domain) with a privileged notion of monotheistic omnipotence (source domain). See Poole 1986 for this terminology on comparison as metaphoric mapping.

[25]J. D. Smith softens this argument in his *Pābūjī* book, mentioning fate without blaming the

Of the contributors to these debates, only Kothari sees that danger lies in comparing the Sanskrit epics *directly* with oral epics. He argues that although there "certainly . . . are commonalities between the folk and Sanskrit epics, the search for a pan-Indian epic tradition might require a route other than that of direct comparison with the *Rāmāyaṇa* and the *Mahābhārata*" (1989, 115). Going further, he argues that although either of the two classical epics can "exist as both a sophisticated literary tradition and simultaneously as a village oral tradition," a folk or tribal *Rāmāyaṇa* or *Mahābhārata* "functions differently . . . because it is connected to a different social reality and mythological system" (115-16). Yet the distinctions are designed to discourage scrutiny of the "direct" and indirect relations which Kothari accurately perceives. His point is that there are incommensurable features between Sanskrit and oral epics. On the one side, there is "the life history of the classical epics," which he defines entirely through the results of higher criticism: the "continuous additions, alterations, different philosophical and mythical manipulations, narrow sectarian interpretations of the main characters and episodes, and the impact of time and changing values . . . [that] left their marks" on them (ibid.). On the other, folk epics have a "very different value system" (115) motivated by "belief systems and group identity. Thus we need to know more about the mythology of the lower castes and must avoid interpreting them as versions of classical mythology" (117). Though the closing point is true, Indian religions abound in cases of different value systems reworking common mythologies. Kothari also attributes "some of the influences or similarities between oral and classical epics" to "Sanskritization, that is, the desire to achieve a higher status by imitating the Sanskrit epics" (117). Such upward Sanskritization is equivalent to legitimization.

In brief, connections with the classical epics are consistently dis-esteemed. Roghair notes a tendency to over-associate *Palnāḍu* with the *Mahābhārata* (1982, 13 and nn. 18 and 30). Blackburn tells us that although most Bow Song singers are "only minimally literate," the lead singer and his or her teacher (*aṇṇāvi*) "are often self-educated in the Tamil versions of the *Rāmāyaṇa*, *Mahābhārata*, and the *purāṇas*" (1988, 14). But he does not ask why Bow Song singers are so motivated, or how epic material from these sources is integrated into their repertoire.[26] Indeed, one soon finds that rather than examining the links between the

gods (1991, 96), and suggesting only that when goddesses in folk epics destroy evil beings, "it is difficult to accept that so much human blood is shed entirely for the benefit of mankind" (97).

[26] I have begun studying with J. Kattalaikailasam a four-day *Mbh* Bow Song festival at a temple for Aravāṉ in Tirunelveli District (now V.O.C. District), Tamilnadu.

classical and oral epics that they trivialize, most oral epic specialists only repeat the tired generalizations of scholars who have written about the Sanskrit epics.[27]

The only recent authors to pursue the relation of oral and classical epics in depth are Beck and Schomer. Although Beck has, I feel, gotten sidetracked by "Indo-European" and triadic formulations, she begins with the sound instinct of listening to *Mahābhārata* allusions rather than explaining them away. She is attentive to the nuances of her oral bard's opening invocations of *Elder brothers*. First he invokes Vināyakar (Gaṇeśa) as the god who "used his tusk to write the *Mahābhārata* on palm leaves," who thus assisted Vyāsa, "the ascetic who had immortal power derived from penance to re-establish the Vedas." Then the bard invokes Sarasvatī (Vāṇiyammāḷ):

> Oh Vāṇiyammā, oh Vāṇiyammā! Bless me with your right hand
> I am searching, searching for your blessings
> Your sweet-versed lady, my teacher who taught me the Mahabharata
> I will never forget her, never (even) for a day
> The lady who taught me
> I will never forget her (even) for a day
> I am searching, searching for the god's counsel-chamber
> (And for) the sweet words (contained in) the Mahabharata.

From these lines, as Beck says, "it is clear that the bard wishes the epic story he will tell to be linked to the great story of the Mahabharata."[28] Indeed, I would suggest that the bard searches for sweet *Mahābhārata* words with which to tell *Elder brothers*, and emphasize that the words he seeks are *written*.[29] This is not a matter of loose ends.

As to Schomer, her primary subject of investigation is *Ālhā*, an epic that "is actually thought of and referred to as 'a *Mahābhārata* of the Kali Yuga'" (Schomer 1989, 141-42, 143). Schomer takes this self-understanding of *Ālhā* seriously, and thinks through some of its implications not only for *Ālhā* and *Mahābhārata*, but for South Asian folk and classical epics more generally. Her starting point is comparative: "The first feature shared by most Indian oral epics is that of linkage to the pan-Indian classical epics by means of structural parallelisms" that "are to be

[27]See Hiltebeitel 1993, 1995a for further discussion of convergent theories about classical and oral epics, relying on original kernels, interpolation, accretion, textual strata, divinization, and oral formulaic verse. Cf. chap. 1 at nn. 13 and 14.

[28]Beck 1992, 3 and nn. 2 and 6; cf. 1978, 179-80.

[29]Like the Ṛsis of Naimisa Forest, he finds them from Sarasvatī (see Hiltebeitel in press-h and forthcoming).

found at all levels: theme, plot, characters, settings, imagery, motifs, etc." (140-41). This is a bold statement: "at all levels" means that we must begin to think not about isolated features or loose ends, but about interplay. I will return to her analysis in chapters 5 and 6.

B. Epic Development and the "Real Hero"

Blackburn and Flueckiger offer a conspectus: "Epic performances ritually protect and cure, while epic narratives express local ideologies and form pathways between regional and pan-Indian mythologies. But most important, oral epics in India have that special ability to tell a community's own story and thus help to create and maintain that community's self-identity" (1989, 11). Our concern is with the notion of "pathways," which encodes a diachronic developmental theory that requires some scrutiny.

Blackburn proposes a "'nucleus' model of development" (1989, 16) for Indian oral epics, and distinguishes two developmental patterns, both of which work by "adding motifs to the core story," "either by grafting independent stories onto the core or by accumulating motifs."[30] Pattern one goes through three stages: 1. death and deification; 2. supernatural birth; 3. pan-Indian identity. Pattern two skips stage 1 and has only stages 2 and 3. The first pattern is more typical of martial (including some figures of multistory traditions) and "sacrificial" heroes and heroines; the second of romantic ones. The pair "death and deification," found only in pattern one, posits a violent "death event" as the "generative point" from which oral epics and their cults develop.[31] Both patterns, however, tell how single heroes become the stuff of epics.

Blackburn usefully correlates the two patterns with an epic's range of diffusion and its location on a ritual-entertainment continuum.[32] Multistory traditions are all local (range 10-100 miles), *Elder brothers* and *Palnāḍu* are subregional (100-200 miles), *Pābūjī* is regional (200-300 miles), and *Ālhā* is supraregional (400+ miles). As Blackburn observes, "martial epics, significantly, exist at all four geographical ranges" (20). *Elder brothers*, *Palnāḍu*, and *Pābūjī* thus join all the "sacrificial" and most of the single-story martial epics in the midranges, while *Ālhā* anomalously joins all the romantic epics in the supraregional category. This, combined with *Ālhā*'s place on the recreational side of the ritual-

[30]Blackburn 1989, 21, 16; cf. 1988, 215-16.

[31]Blackburn 1989, 31; 1988, 216.

[32]Nagy deploys Blackburn and Flueckigers' treatments of range and spread to good comparative ends in his discussion of diffusion, itinerancy, occasionality, and the pan-Hellenic in the "evolution" of the Homeric epics (1996, 44-63), but is uncritically accepting of too much of Blackburn's death and deification model (see below).

entertainment continuum, creates some problems.

According to this model, nothing diffuses between oral epic regions. Location and region are sealed concepts.[33] Oral epics exhaust themselves each within their own circumscribed areas. Yet as they develop outward to such fuzzy geographical limits, they are supposed to take on their secondary and tertiary features of extended deification through supernatural birth and pan-Indian identity. This would lead one to expect that such mythologically deep (or deepening, to adopt a developmental perspective) features would be found more readily at the fringes of an oral epic's expansion than in its core area. But this is not the case. As we shall see in each of the regional oral martial epics under study, such deep features are best known in the stories' heartlands. In the case of *Ālhā*, we shall also find that such links are least known in flanking areas beyond the heartland.[34]

Blackburn's thinking on phases two and three is, however, less crucial to him, and admittedly more speculative, than his thinking on phase one: "My own bias is to look at oral epic traditions from the bottom up, from the vantage point of the early stages of their development." As he registers, this derives "in part" from his fieldwork on one of the multi-story traditions, the Tamil Bow Song (1989, 15-16). It is to these traditions and others like them that he looks for examples of what occurs at phase one of pattern one—the death and deification of the hero or heroine—where the "critical distinction between the two patterns occurs."[35] In pattern two, a hero begins "without deification or ritual context, and may spread to the supra-regional range." But in pattern one, "if the death motif is present, the hero is deified" and "the context is ritualistic." With cultic patronage, the hero's story may move beyond the local level. But if it spreads beyond "the small group that originally worshiped the dead hero," the death motif will be "insufficient" to attract "new patronage" from "social groups with whom [the hero] is not related by either kinship or history." This weakening of the death motif will, however, be compensated for by two new "added" means of deification at "the next two successively larger geographical ranges." At the subregional level, "a supernatural birth provides the basis for worshiping the new god." And at the regional level, he or she becomes further

[33]Like "tribe" and "village," according to earlier comparative anthropological models.

[34]Nagy, building on Blackburn's formulations, even supposes that epics would become fixed at the edges of their spread (1996, 39-40), as well as in their eventual historical fixation in writing (41). The latter may be true for Homeric epics, but not for the *Mbh* or *Rām* which, contrary to Nagy, did not reach a written "final form" or "text-fixation" (45). What the critical editions of the Indian epics shows us is a fluidity of *written* forms.

[35]Like Katz (1989, 41), Blackburn wants to begin with mortality and a corresponding a priori definition of the "human" as the fount of epic. See further Blackburn 1988, 216.

"conflated with a preexisting god." Phase three in pattern one, the taking-on of a pan-Indian identity, is "the functional equivalent of the first motif: both are means of deification, but each is appropriate (or possible) at different geographical ranges" (21-22, 27). Curiously, this is not the case in pattern two, since the mostly nonmartial heroes and heroines in this track may take on a pan-Indian identity while remaining undeified.

By Blackburn's reckoning, the "overall effect" of pattern one's three-phase process is to "obscure the human origins of the hero/god with a prior divine existence" (1989, 22). As with so many Sanskrit epic scholars, one or another Western notion of the human is then taken as the basis for a theory of deification—a term general enough for Blackburn to cover three variations: local worship of a deceased hero, divine birth, and linkage with a pan-Indian deity. The further that ritual-based oral epics develop beyond local community bonds, "the greater the chance that they will be swallowed whole by some form of Vaiṣṇava, Śaiva, or Śakta [sic] worship" (27). Katz advances a similar notion that "various vested interest groups" capture segments of the *Mahābhārata* in the service of the same gods.[36]

All of this presupposes that multistory traditions develop into single-story ones. Blackburn is cautious here, insisting only that "local multistory traditions are clearly related to the long single-story traditions." It is not possible to confirm that any epic ever underwent such a transformation.[37] Blackburn claims only to account for "potential stages of epic development" and "not necessarily a direct evolution," since "there is no 'need' for any epic tradition to expand" (1989, 16). Nonetheless, the model is posed as a developmental one, and applied to all the epics that chiefly concern us in this book.

To critique this theory, it is clearly not enough to look at "developed" martial epics. We must consider the "bottom" from which Blackburn works "up." Let us examine his treatment of Claus's study of caste and regional variants of the story of Kordabbu, a hero of the Mundalas, a Dalit caste, in the Tulu pāḍdana tradition. In one Mundala account, says Blackburn, Kordabbu "is a *bhūta* (the deified dead)"; in another he has a supernatural birth in which "he becomes a *dēvaru* (a deity of divine origins)" (1989, 23). From what the hero "is" (dead turned divine), he "becomes" otherwise (divine to begin with). Blackburn cites Claus as noting that these variants are "significant enough to be a matter for

[36]Katz 1989, 149, 220-21, 245, 251, 253-69.

[37]Blackburn makes a good case that the story of Muttuppattaṉ has been given a new second-phase background of divine birth, but, as he demonstrates, this is related to its festival performance "slot" (see below) and not to geographical spread or detachment from its original community (1988, 142-43).

theological debate among the Mundala" (ibid.). But Claus does not use quite the same terms.

In areas where "the Mundala are most numerous," Kordabbu, worshiped generally as a "caste champion," "has become a deity (*bhūta*) worshiped by the village community as a whole and patronized by prominent members of all the major castes" (1989, 57). From Claus to Blackburn, the *bhūta* as "deity" has "become" a "deified dead"! Blackburn has made the term *bhūta* fit his theory. Moreover, the new "southern" position involved insisting that Kordabbu "was not a mere human and should therefore be regarded as a *dēvaru* (god), not a *bhūta*" (1989, 68). It is doubtful that the northern opponents wanted to insist that Kordabbu *was* a "mere human." The theological debate would seem to be over the nature and proper terminology for the formerly human hero's *double* divine nature. The difference seems to be between two groups of Mundala, one of which has chosen to emphasize the higher of the two words for "deity" over the lower one, whose ambiguities could not claim for Kordabbu the degree of respect that the innovating group felt was his due. Not surprisingly, this group develops its theology in an area where Mundala are less numerous, and thus more outspoken in claiming a respect for their deity that would also reflect on them.

Bhūta in South Kanara does not carry the connotation of "deified dead" in any generalizable sense. *Bhūta*s are deities of many types, many of whom have surely never had human lives or deaths of any kind.[38] Brückner makes such a point when she emphasizes that the Tulu deity (both *bhūta* and *dēvaru*) Jumādi is "not to be classed among deified humans" (1987, 22), but rather "deifies" human heroes into their appropriate rank in the *bhūta-dēvaru* pantheon.[39]

Claus does support Blackburn's argument for the validity of development from multi- to single-story traditions (1989, 57, 70-71). But he is more noncommittal on the primacy of "death and deification." That is, for Claus it is apparently possible to have a multistory tradition transformed into a single-story one without starting from death and deification.[40] Rather than singling out death as the necessary starting

[38]On types of Bhūtas, see Claus 1973, 232-33; Prabhu 1977.

[39]Brückner 1993, 287-88. On usages and distinctions between *bhūta*/*būta* and *dēvaru*/*dēveru* or *daiva*, see idem 1987, 17 and n. 3; 1993, 289, 301, 323, with variations on the recurrent phrase, "To you I [shall give a position] one step smaller than a god (*dēveru*) [and] one step bigger than the *būtas*" (323; my brackets), here describing a hero's deification; cf. 1987, 17 and n. 3; Brückner and Poti 1992, 40; Claus 1975, 48, 53.

[40]Cf. Claus and Korom 1991, 70-72, concluding that Blackburn "has no documentary proof of this development. His evidence is limited and indirect. But his method is an acceptable one. His conclusions are hypotheses, and additional evidence may or may not confirm them. As it stands, he and others would regard the hypotheses as extremely tentative, but ones that

point, he relates the issue of variants to "performance contexts," and discusses divine and human birth as "options" within a "repertoire of stock images" that provides "a matter of constant negotiation over long periods of time" (72-73). I think the position is sound.

Blackburn cites de Vries (1963, 243) and Bowra (1952, 9-27) on the death lament as "a kind of 'pre-epic' poetry" (1989, 22, n. 13). There certainly are local violently slain heroes of this type, and songs and stories about them, in India and elsewhere. Our problem lies in imagining the *transition* required by Blackburn's theory of development from this "bottom up." Let us look at how he and others agreeing with him have done this for the epics discussed in this book. I will then consider whether Blackburn's own Bow Song material presents factors that would require us to disimagine death and deification as the ground for a general theory of epic development.

Blackburn finds corroboration from Kothari and Smith in theorizing about the development of *Pābūjī*, but for *Elder brothers*, *Palnāḍu*, and *Ālhā*, he sets forth on his own. For both Kothari and Smith, the death and deification model combines with the multi- to single-story model.[41] For Kothari, "the Rajasthani ethos in which concern for propitiating the powerful spirits of those who died untimely deaths continually feeds the epic traditions of the area. The two major Rajasthani historical epics, *Pābūjī* and *Devnārāyaṇ*, appear to have developed out of a tradition of honoring powerful spirits of the dead" (1989, 102). In particular, these epics draw on a Western Rajasthan tradition connected with *bhomiyā* or *māmā*, "the generic names for warriors who died in pursuit of robbers or cattle" (110). When these heroes are killed, shrines are built for them, and priests (*bhopās*) attend them. From this vantage point, "[i]t appears the epic of *Pābūjī* is an elaborated story of a *bhomiyā* god" (110). Kothari pulls together *Pābūjī*'s further connections with ancestral cults (106), pastoral society (111), and other cults of the deified dead (*jhūjhars* and satīs), which "demonstrate the fact that cultural ideas about death give rise to an army of gods and goddesses" (112). The resulting complex forms an implicit explanation of how a pastoral hero such as Pābūjī could

would help us to understand Indian epics as a group, and the relationships between their forms." Claus does, however, suggest a similar developmental model: "The actions and events of the hero's life have gradually taken on symbolic significance" (1989, 59); "As the Mundala develop the Kordabbu story into an epic . . ." (61).

[41]For J. D. Smith, see 1989, 177-78 on multi- to single-story development, and 1991, 90-91, 110, n. 10, agreeing with and developing Kothari and Blackburn's views on *bhomiyās* (see below). In a formulation that precedes his contribution to *Oral epics in India*, Smith argues that narratives such as *Pābūjī* "acquire successive accretions of heroic, mythic, and deific elements"—although he concedes that "it is by no mean easy" to keep these terms distinct (1980, 54-56).

be divinized on the one hand, and surrounded by his army of epic companions and other contemporaries on the other.

Yet the move is made with reservation. Kothari admits that the relation between bhopā rituals for the deified dead and "narration in epic performance in Rajasthan is not yet clear to me." He insists that it has something to do with possession (1989, 112). This is persuasive if one stays with his notion that this combination "feeds the epic traditions of the area." But it is not sufficient to account for a development of *Pābūjī from* this base. For this, one seems to need the added "legitimization" of "loose ends" from the *Rāmāyaṇa*, supplied by the arguments of Smith. This is the combination Blackburn goes with: *Pābūjī* "clearly demonstrates the historical development from local to regional tradition. Underneath the accretions of supernatural birth and identification with Lakṣmaṇa lies evidence of growth from a local tradition called *bhomiyā*" (1989, 25).

As to *Elder brothers* and *Palnāḍu*, Blackburn takes them on together, as I will do in chapter 3. They supply him with examples of "grafting" to the core: these "two major south Indian oral epics grew by adding events from the political history of adjacent regions and by absorbing shorter folk narratives" (1989, 17). In *Elder brothers*, "the episode involving the heroes' births follows the standard sequence of motifs until evil threatens at the moment of their births. Then the supernatural element appears" when Viṣṇu intervenes to rescue them, and "the human origins of the heroes disappear when their story spreads and they become gods" (23-24). Similarly for *Palnāḍu*, the prenatal miracles and avataric themes at the birth of Brahma Nāyuḍu indicate that "geographical spread of a story opens it up to supernatural elements, especially in the birth episode" (24). This supernatural connection is then explained away: "although Brahma Nāyuḍu is sometimes made an avatar of Viṣṇu in the Palnāḍu epic, this only occurs in those variants with the greatest geographical diffusion, that is, the literate retellings" (25). Blackburn cites Roghair (1982, 109-10) on this point. Yet Roghair does not say that Brahma Nāyuḍu's avatar status derives from literate retellings, but rather that he is Viṣṇu's avatar in the *oral* version he has collected in Palnāḍu![42] As indicated above, it is a matter of the story's heartland.

Blackburn's theory also creates further problems when he tries to

[42]Roghair does strain to argue that Brahma Nāyudu was originally an historical social reformer, and that his identification as an avatar of Visnu is a result of superficial deification (1982, 82, 91, 107-10). But there are at least thirty-two mentions of Brahma Nāyuḍu as Viṣṇu incarnate in Roghair's oral text, and two points where being Visnu incarnate also implies his being the incarnation of Krsna (142 [4 times], 229-30 [twice]). We shall see in chap. 3 that they are not superficial.

identify this epic's "real hero." Having problematized Brahma Nāyuḍu's candidacy, he turns to the impetuous Bāluḍu as "perhaps the real hero of this epic" (1989, 24). The phrase registers that it is Bāluḍu who fits most closely Blackburn's violent death-and-deification model. But to pick out from a whole epic one "real hero" on the basis of a certain type of death event, or, as with the next case, because his name appears in the title, is to miss the point that there are all kinds of heroes, male and female, and that epics deal with the complex rapports that exist between them—and between them and other beings, including deities, who might, as J. D. Smith senses, want to maintain their "distinction" from humans. As a monogenetic theory, Blackburn's "real hero" is a variation on the Raglan-Campbell "monomyth."[43]

As to *Ālhā*, Blackburn sees it as a pattern-two type of oral epic, since it is not, he thinks, based on the death of a hero. Such epics tell stories of heroes who do not die, but are still given supernatural birth.[44] As noted, he clusters them in the supraregional range of distribution, and finds that other than *Ālhā*, they are all romantic epics rather than martial ones. To readjust the lens on *Ālhā*'s singularity in this company, Blackburn says, "In Pattern 2 the hero may be a warrior (like Ālhā), but if he is he does not die in battle." Thus "martial epics can follow Pattern 2 if (like Ālhā) the hero does not die" (28). Blackburn acknowledges that *Ālhā* is "closer" to martial than romantic epic since it tells a story of battle (29). But "the hero" Ālhā's nondeath presents a puzzle: "having received a boon of immortality, he simply wanders off into a mysterious forest and disappears. Without a warrior's death, this martial hero is neither deified nor worshipped and thus his story does not follow the pattern of other martial epics" (ibid.). A "further problem" is that while a third-phase pan-Indian connection is secure through *Ālhā*'s *Mahābhārata* ties, the second-phase motif of supernatural birth is "oblique. The only supernatural aspect of the heroic brothers' origin is that their mothers appear as amazons, pulling apart buffaloes locked in combat" (ibid.).

Blackburn continues to call attention to an important difference between *Ālhā* and *Elder brothers* and *Palnāḍu*: unlike the latter pair, whose core stories focus on a "closely bonded local community," *Ālhā*'s core story concerns "political relations between three major kingdoms in

[43]Raglan [1945] 1979; Campbell [1949] 1956. Katz shares the "real hero" construct in her argument that it must originally have been Arjuna who ascended to heaven at the *Mbh*'s end rather than Yudhiṣṭhira (1989, 206)! See my reservations on Campbell's "Oedipal Bodhisattva" type in Hiltebeitel [1976] 1990, 40 and n. 34.

[44]Blackburn 1989, 28. This nondying is rather opaque, and even for romantic epics Blackburn strains for a "death event" explanation, as with *Gūgā*, whose titular hero "dies not in battle (though he fights in one), but simply enters *samādhi*." Blackburn says, "This ending may be a later accretion" (26), but of course there is no evidence for this.

north India—Delhi, Kanauj, and Mahoba" (1989, 29-30). In this, as he says, *Ālhā* is closer to the *Mahābhārata*, whose "core story also marked out a wide area" (30). But it is hard to see how this "lack" of local bondedness explains why *Ālhā*'s warrior heroes "had little need of violent death, a supernatural birth, or an association with a pan-Indian god to facilitate the spread of their story" (30). And it is even more baffling how this same explanation is extended to the *Mahābhārata*, whose heroes, "like the heroes of the Ālhā, do not die in battle, are not deified, and are not widely worshiped. They, too, lack both the conditions and the need for deification" (30). Actually, *Ālhā* is full of heroes who die in battle; and so, of course, is the *Mahābhārata*, whose heroes are, to be sure, not "deified," but are, at least if one listens to the texts, most of them "incarnations" and "portions" of deities.

It is, however, the "real hero" construct that gives Blackburn many of his most insoluble problems. J. D. Smith seems to have foreseen the difficulties before joining the *Oral epics* project by noting with regard to *Pābūjī* and the classical epics that it "is not east to see why the 'choice' of the deified figure should vary thus" (1980a, 72). It is hard to see why Blackburn does not just say that instead of a single death event, *Ālhā* would have begun with a multiple death event: that of a cataclysmic great battle. From this base, multiple deifications would then be a logical possibility. But Blackburn is stuck with the single death event of the deifiable real hero, and the centrality of the undying Ālhā as the chief hero of the epic that bears his name. As we shall see in chapter 5, Ālhā's nondeath is not a slip from martial epic to pattern two-ness. It is one of his links with the *Mahābhārata*'s Yudhiṣṭhira.

Schomer follows Blackburn, letting his formulation become a problem for her in making it one of the points of her *Oral epics in India* essay to suggest how *Ālhā* "speaks to" and "holds" its audience "even though its central hero is not deified" (1989, 142-43). Like J. D. Smith, who poses a similar "strong resemblance" between Kṛṣṇa and the goddess Deval in *Pābūjī*, where neither, however, is the story's main "deified" hero (1980, 72), Schomer's explanation is that both stories include "cult deities"—the goddess Śāradā in *Ālhā*, Kṛṣṇa in the *Mahābhārata*—who, despite their playing an "active role," "are not central figures" (146). The historical priority of their cults and the seeming preemtiveness of their divinity account for the nondivinization of the heroes, who thereby "remain human figures" (ibid.). This explanation has at least four flaws: (1) other regional martial epics have similar (usually female) "cult deities" (Cellāttā and Periyakkaṇṭi in *Elder brothers*, Ankālamma in *Palnāḍu*, Deval in *Pābūjī*) who do not preempt divinity to the exclusion of the heroes; (2) evidence of a Kṛṣṇa "cult" prior to the *Mahābhārata* is uncertain; (3)

Kṛṣṇa is hardly "noncentral" in the *Mahābhārata*;[45] (4) in all these epics, heroes have links with divinity that not only strain but unsettle any divine/human "distinction." Ālhā's supposed nondeification has become a red herring.[46]

C. Against Death and Deification

This brings us to question whether the material Blackburn researched himself, the southern Tamil Bow Song tradition, has features that would actually prevent its serving as the ground for a "bottom up" developmental theory. Elsewhere, Blackburn has called attention to Bow Songs of a "violation-death-deification-revenge" type as evidence for what lies "at the base of many local cults in India," and prominent particularly in the south. Bow Song performance is commonly demarcated into two ritually distinct segments. In the first, "the birth, youth, and (optionally) the marriage of the main figure" builds up to a violation: "sexual . . . if the main character is a woman, or a violation of land or social rights if the main character is a man." The outcome is then the hero or heroine's "cruel, undeserved death" by either murder or suicide. In segment two, the victim is then "deified and often taken to [Mount] Kailāsa to receive boons from Śiva," after which he or she returns to earth to take revenge on those responsible for the death, provoking others to "appease the dangerous spirit with worship, build a temple, and celebrate a festival in its honor."[47]

There appear to be several important differences between these "local" hero cult patterns and "regional" ones. First, as Blackburn emphasizes (1986, 171), "violation-death-deification-revenge" heroes are linked with hero and lineage cults that are typically confined to a small geographical area and to specific and often disparate family groups within caste communities who regard the hero as an ancestor and maintain largely independent temples and festivals in his or her honor. Indeed, if the Tulu pāḍdanas are of this type, within one region a whole range of different castes may have distinctive versions of what is much the same story, each telling variants about heroes from their own ranks, and without acknowledged awareness of the others (Claus 1982, 1989). In such a fragmented case, no one variant can take on the character of a regional

[45] Indeed, Kṛṣṇa is central even when he is absent; see Hiltebeitel [1976] 1990, 86-102, and 1979, 75-83, 87-92.

[46] Schomer (1989, 154) builds further upon Blackburn's premises, giving the misleading scheme of "nondivinization" an unnecessary explanation.

[47] Blackburn 1986, 169-70. Of the three folk epics translated in Nirmala Devi and Murugan 1987 from palm leaf manuscripts, two—"Ciṉṉattampi" and "Kuṟukkulanci"—fit this description, the former in particular as a classic example.

epic as such. In contrast, as Beck has observed (1982, 109-10), a regional epic can be transmitted from one region to another without the story changing appreciably, so long as the caste identity of the main heroes remains at the same level. Thus *Elder brothers* is about Vēḷāḷar Kavuṇṭars in Kongunad and Kaḷḷars in Madurai District, both being what can be called regionally dominant landed castes.

Regional oral epics thus not only concern wider territories than violation-death-deification-revenge type stories; they do so in distinctive ways, centering on heroes of regionally dominant castes whose dominance they represent as intentionally embracing all castes and other peoples of the region, most often, notably, Muslims. Development from a local multistory tradition to a regional single-story tradition would thus probably have to be centered on the martial traditions of a dominant landed caste. Moreover, since regional epics concern conflicts *over* such wider territories, a local multistory tradition would have to expand its geography. These are possibilities, but not ones for which there is any evidence.

Second, in contrast to the deaths of Bow Song type heroes, the deaths of the heroes in regional single-story epics, however cruel they may be, cannot be called "undeserved," since the heroes themselves participate willingly in agonistic battles in which neither side has absolute claim to good or ill. The "violation-death-deification-revenge" type of hero attains divine status precisely through a death that calls and allows for the hero or heroine's revenge against the living, who then institute his or her cult by way of propitiation.[48] Deceased heroes of regional oral epics require no such return. They are already divine at birth, and death leaves no aftertaste for revenge, since, through divine intervention—usually that of Viṣṇu, sometimes of Śiva, and always in conjunction with the goddess—their deaths are "appeased" and without rancor. Heroes and heroines of oral regional martial epics do not carry on postmortem hostilities themselves. Rather, their births are the result of the unresolved animosities of heroes and heroines of the classical epics!

The contrasts in hero and story type just outlined do, however, allow for crossover figures. Most clearly straddling the border are heroes (or gods) linked with symbolisms of possession, sexuality, and violent sacrificial death. According to Blackburn, Bow Song performances at festivals in the deep south of Tamilnadu enact "god stories" (*cāmi katai*) about figures of two types: "birth stories" (*pir̲anta katai*) about gods and

[48]Cf. Kothari 1989, 109-10, but observing that spirits who have died violently and remain powerful on earth are worshipped only "by a limited group, usually a family," whereas "[s]pirits worshiped by a whole village or region are in a different category" (109-10). One wonders why he does not see Pābūjī in the latter.

goddesses of "divine descent" (*teyva vamcam*) or "divine birth" (*teyva piṟavi*) (type A), and "death stories" (*iṟanta katai*) about "spirits who were killed" (*iṟantuppaṭṭa vātai*) or "cut-up spirits" (*veṭṭuppaṭṭa vātai*) (type B), corresponding to heroes of the violation-death-deification-revenge type.[49] Blackburn regards the distinction as "key to the entire bow song tradition" (1988, 32). Normally Bow Song festivals have three main performance phases. Performances of type A stories are scheduled in the first and third slots. These stress other-worldly or "supernatural" pan-Indian "mythic" themes, and provide "auspicious borders" around performances of central slot type B stories.[50] The featured central stories heighten ritual intensity with down-to-earth themes of pain and tragedy (usually involving sexual conflicts or land rights), and cut short their "legendary" or "historical" narratives at the point of death, when the hero or heroine is "cut up."[51]

But one also finds what Blackburn implies are the somewhat unusual cases when type A "divine descent" stories occur in the central slot instead of the "cut-up spirit" type B stories. Such cases occur when the festival is at a temple of a deity of "divine birth" or "divine descent." Such a temple will choose between performing its deity's story in the central slot, in which case it will emphasize high intensity themes in that story, or moving it to the third slot to keep the central slot for a "death story"—the first slot being reserved for the village-guarding god Aiyaṉār Śāstā.[52] Or, as in the one such Bow Song performance I saw, at a Cuṭalai Māṭaṉ festival at Mēlakuḷam village near Tirunelveli (July 15, 1994), a temple may hold a one-day festival featuring the divine descent story as a central-slot equivalent.

Some uncertainty arises, however, from a brief discussion in a 1981 article that Blackburn does not follow up in his "death and deification" article (1985) or his book (1988). This concerns the intensification of "cut-up" themes in the bow songs of the cremation ground god Cuṭalai Māṭaṉ and the goddess. In the book, Blackburn provides no discussion of central-slot birth stories. He says only that death stories in the central slot are "more ritually elaborated than the performances of birth stories in the same slot; they are considerably longer and marked by the intense possession dances" (1988, 45). In 1981, however, he does discuss central-slot type A stories of "divine descent," and indicates that they occur in two forms that are distinguished by the gender of the deities. Goddess stories culminate in the goddess's slaying of the Buffalo Demon:

[49]Blackburn 1981, 211-15; 1985, 267-68; 1988, 31-32.
[50]Blackburn 1981, 212-14; 1988, 32-33, 218-19.
[51]Blackburn 1981, 216-18; 1988, 33-34, 43-45.
[52]Blackburn 1981, 220; 1988, 45.

an episode that "is present in all textual versions of these stories" where it is "expanded into the central conflict" (1981, 222). Among male "divine descent" deities, however, only one, says Blackburn, ever has his story performed in the central slot, and that is Cuṭalai Māṭaṉ. In both cases, when these stories are performed in the central slot, their narratives are modified to culminate at a point of ritual depth, accenting sexual conflict, "cut-up" death, and possession, analogous to the points at which type B stories culminate.

Upon inquiring into these matters at the Mēlakuḷam festival, and making allowances for local differences, it appears that Blackburn's statement is a good generalization or at least approximation. Complexity arises from the fact that Bow Song performers often correlate their singing at festivals with Dalit singers of another genre known as Kaṇiyāṉ Kūttu (Reiniche 1979, 203), and that the Kaṇiyārs can have different versions of the myths. According to the Kaṇiyār singer Shankanarayana, the destruction of the Buffalo Demon Mahiṣāsura (*Makiṭācuraṉ saṃhāram*) is sung for Kāḷi and for her eight avatāras: Muppiṭātiyammaṉ, Muttārammaṉ, Pattirakāḷiyammaṉ, Māriyammaṉ, Celliyammaṉ, Cantaṉa Māriyammaṉ, Akkiṉi Māriyammaṉ, and Ankāḷaparamēṣvari.[53] It is not included in the Bow Song for the regionally prominent Icakkiyammaṉ.[54] The lead Bow Song singer P. A. Subhalakshmi concurred on these points, and mentioned Kāḷi, Muttārammaṉ, and Māriyammaṉ as examples of the "many ammaṉs" for whom "the destruction of Mahiṣāsura" is performed. Subhalakshmi insisted, however, that the main possession scene at such goddess festivals could take place at any major point; it happens spontaneously, she said, and while it could be correlated with the death of Mahiṣāsura, it could also occur at other climactic moments, and is in any case not precisely scripted by the story. She insisted that the Bow

[53]Muttār Ammaṉ and Kāḷi are two of five gods (along with Aiyaṉar Śāstā, Cuṭalai Māṭaṉ, and the Brahman-become-Dalit Muttuppaṭṭaṉ) whose Bow Song stories are "most widely performed" (Blackburn 1988, xxii). On the split image of the child-devouring/ child-protecting Nīli-Icakki, also a Bow Song subject, see 92-93. Muttār Ammaṉ, from *muttu*, "smallpox, sweat, pearl," is the most popular Bow Song goddess; in twelve different births and seven separate scenes, her myths identify her with pan-Indian goddesses and relate her to Śiva (34-35). She is the local equivalent of Muttu Māriyammaṉ, whose links with the "smallpox-pearl" have the same semantic range. A mother/daughter double-death story also yields the figures of "White (Veḷḷai) Māriyammaṉ" and "Yellow (Mañcal) Mārayammaṉ," about whom Blackburn says, "they have no connection with the popular goddess Māriyammaṉ (Renukā)" (1988, 232, n. 8). This may be true of their Bow Song stories, but not of their place within Māriyammaṉ traditions.

[54]Icakki, who gives and devours children, has many temples in the Bow Song area, but seems to receive mainly private offerings rather than festivals (*kotai*) that would include Bow Song performance, although there is a Bow Song for her (Arunachalam 1976, 209-10; Reiniche 1979, 184).

Song troupe sings without noticing what is happening among the local people, other than to pause when the possession scene (which occurs along with sacrificial offerings and other rituals) interrupts.

Such variability was in evidence at the Mēlakuḷam Cuṭalai Māṭaṉ festival. According to Blackburn, the point in Cuṭalai Māṭaṉ's myth that is intensified for the central ritual slot is "when Cutalai Matan coerces a woman to sleep with him and later forces her father to serve his pregnant daughter to him as a sacrifice" (1981, 223). While this is often the case,[55] the intense possession at Mēlakuḷam occurred before this, at the point where Cuṭalai Māṭaṉ arrives in Kerala disguised as a mendicant and lures the people out to see his magic. The father, a black magician (*mantiravāti*) named Kāḷippulaiyaṉ, and his daughter Māvu Icakki ("Flour Icakki": one of "many Icakkis"), come out to see Cuṭalai Māṭaṉ, who asks them for food. This demand is the pretext for a series of offerings—including animal sacrifices to Cuṭalai Māṭaṉ and his attendants, and blood offering from the elbow by one of the members of the Kaṇiyāṉ Kūttu troupe—which now occasions the chief possession dance. Only when the Bow Song resumes does the story continue with the seduction of Māvu Icakki and a draught, caused by Cuṭalai Māṭaṉ, which provokes Kāḷippulaiyaṉ to agree to sacrifice his daughter, now pregnant from Cuṭalai Māṭaṉ, to Cuṭalai Māṭaṉ. There are, moreover, variations in the story as to whether or not it is Cuṭalai Māṭaṉ who makes Māvu Icakki pregnant. The version in which he does so seems to be specifically associated with the Kaṇiyāṉ Kūttu, while the Bow Song performances may also perform a version in which Kāḷippulaiyaṉ wants to sacrifice Māvu Icakki because her unwed condition, which has resulted from a different union, offends him.[56]

It is instructive that the two types of "divine" figures brought into rapport with "cut-up spirits" have Draupadī cult analogs. One is the multiform of Mahiṣāsura. Just as various Bow Song goddess stories include variations on "the destruction of Mahiṣāsura," one of Draupadī's two guardians is a multiform of the Buffalo Demon himself: the "Buffalo King" Pōttu Rāja. The "cut-up" demon Mahiṣāsura "becomes" the guardian deity Pōttu Rāja who brings Draupadī her "cutting" or piercing

[55]As confirmed by N. Ramachandran and G. Stephen, Folklore Research Centre, Palayamkottai, who have studied Bow Song festivals; when Cuṭalai Māṭaṉ kills the pregnant daughter, it can be the occasion for the possession and the sacrifice of a pregnant goat (personal communication, July 1994).

[56]As recounted by N. Ramachandran (see n. 55). For variants in different genres, see Reiniche 1979, 205-7 (a Bow Song text); Arunachalam 1976, 191-92 (a ballad); Blackburn 1981, 223 (Bow Song); cf. Hiltebeitel 1988a, 107. For a comparable rite in Maharashtra involving bloodletting by Dalits, see Hiltebeitel 1991a, 391-92.

weapons.[57] And the other, Cuṭalai Māṭa̱n, has affinities with Draupadī's other guardian, Muttāl Rāvutta̱n: both are black magicians with predilections for the sacrifice of pregnant females, and, in the larger corpus of their stories, are associated with Muslims.[58] What is sensed in the Bow Song as a performance-level rapport between "cut-up" (or violation-death-deification-revenge) type heroes on the one hand and these two type A counterparts—multiforms of the demon cut up by the goddess and the deity who cuts up pregnant women—on the other, thus has a precise counterpart in the Draupadī cult *Mahābhārata*. But instead of only an implicit rapport with the story's heroes at the level of performance, Draupadī's two guardians are, to varying degrees, incorporated into her cult's folk *Mahābhārata* itself as battle companions of the Pāṇḍavas.[59] As I will demonstrate, their place is analogous to that of the low status ritual service companions of the (primarily) dominant caste heroes of single-story regional oral martial epics.

Bow Song performances thus make divine-human connections of some similarity to those in regional oral epics, and in the Draupadī cult *Mahābhārata*. But they have a different vector, which I would like to call horizontal rather than vertical. By vertical, I refer to movements of descent by incarnation or divine parentage, divine intervention from above, and final ascent by the heroes to the highest heaven. Such movements permeate our regional oral martial epics.[60] Some of them—incarnation, identification with a pan-Indian deity—also appear in Blackburn's theory of development, which makes them vertical by placing them on a line that moves from the "bottom up." The first verticality derives from the structure of the stories themselves and the vertical bhakti cosmology in which their heroes live. The second derives from an evolutionary theory.

By horizontal, I mean that the Bow Song tradition makes one of its connections with divinity by performative framing. Central slot type B stories (about cut-up heroes and divinities who cut-up) are framed by type A stories (about gods and goddesses of "divine descent"). For the most part, such deities descend into the flanking stories rather than directly into the "death story." The heroes' connections with type A descending deities

[57]Hiltebeitel 1988a, 368-93; 1991a, 117-65.

[58]See Hiltebeitel 1988a, 105-10; 1989a, 357-58; 1989b, 357; 1991a, 93-94, on parallels with Muttāl Rāvutta̱n; 136 on similar Bow Song cult iconography for Cuṭalai Māta̱n and "cut-up" deities.

[59]The central slot also features possession dancing, sword-pressing, sacrifice, oracles (*kuṟi*), flour lamps (*māvilakku*), and offering of poṅkal (Blackburn 1988, 41-47, 95), all of which have Draupadī or Kūttāntavar cult parallels in connection with such "cut-up" heroes as Pōttu Rāja and Aravā̱n.

[60]J. D. Smith (1989, 180-81) also uses the term vertical in this sense and connection.

are thus lateral rather than direct. The same seems to be the case for allusions to the *Mahābhārata* and *Rāmāyaṇa*. In the examples that emerge from Blackburn's translations of first, second, and third-slot stories, there are resonant references to both epics (and to Viṣṇu and Śiva) in the more free-form birth stories in the first and third slots, but not in the tightly fixed death stories in the second.[61] Such laterality is another factor that inhibits the Bow Song from being a basic ground for a theory of oral epic development.[62] In its horizontal traversals, we might better think of it as generating movement from the "bottom out" than from the "bottom up."[63]

I thus find no explanatory power in the half of Blackburn's developmental model that proceeds from death and deification, but some in the half that proceeds from multi- to single-story traditions. "Deification" covers too many variations in divine-human interactions, and generalizes from euhemerist principles. There can be no doubt that deaths are nodal points in epics, especially martial ones. But it is fruitless to single out one death in a "multideath" epic as the "real" one, and unsound to posit that oral epics are *generally* or *necessarily* about heroes who actually lived.[64] I do not agree that "to trace the development" of an epic "we must read it backward" from "death event" to supernatural birth to a "state that is prior even to that (divine existence through association with a god)," with boons, vows, curses, and intergenerational depth as parts of the added mix that enters into this "backward-building technique" (1989, 31). This "backwards" linearity does not speak to the recursiveness and intertextuality that are among the ways Indian epics make deaths interesting by weighting them with fatality, cyclicity, and divinity, or the ways they interrelate so many memorable characters.

On the other hand, one of the reasons that the multistory to single-story half of the theory remains interesting is that it requires one to imagine the transition from the one to the other as involving multiple

[61] 1988, 59-60: the demon Vallarakkaṉ "surpass[es] even the tapas of Arjuna" on a 60-foot tapas pole (cf. Arjuna's ideally 60-foot tapas pole at Draupadī festivals, and the tapas pole on which Tāmarai surpasses Arjuna in *Elder brothers* [Beck 1992, 330-31]); Blackburn 1988, 154: when Muttuppattaṉ doesn't know what story to tell, his Brahman brothers say, "What do you mean 'what story'? There's only *one* story—forget the others. Read us the *Rāmāyana*!"; "The Death of the Little Brothers" does, however, "localize" Ayodhyā as the birthplace of the heroes' mother (97) and a site linked with the Pāṇdavas' exile (100, 126).

[62] J. D. Smith also observes these patterns, but takes the "rare" or "coda" appearances of higher deities in multistory traditions as nonessential or peripheral (1989, 181-82).

[63] This horizontal reading can be extended to Blackburn's graphing (1981, 219) of the three-phase rhythm of the Bow Song performance, with the point of deepest intensity—the point of "cutting-up"—at the "bottom" in the middle.

[64] Cf. Blackburn 1989, 27, n. 20, on the contrasting theory of Lord (1964, 201).

heroes. As far as I can see, Blackburn does not do this: perhaps because the connections between Bow Song heroes are more thematic than intertextual. Claus, however, does make such a case plausible, arguing that this could potentially happen in the Tulu pāḍdana tradition. There, he says, "there exists in the minds of the performers and audience a larger sense of the story framework from which the particular versions are drawn. Paradoxically, perhaps, this larger 'epic' never exists as a performance event."[65] It would appear to need a connecting narrative centered on dominant caste heroes, and a Tulu Vyāsa as "arranger"-poet.

Blackburn and Claus are both tentative on the possibility of grander syntheses that would apply such a theory to the Sanskrit epics. Claus asserts only that a "similar process might have produced the *Mahābhārata*" (1989, 71, n. 11), while Blackburn hints that death and deification (not multistory origins) could lie at the roots and "similar process of development" of the "cults" (not specifically epics) linked with Rāma and Kṛṣṇa (1989, 26). Not so cautious is Smith, who sees the same "paradigm" of "achieved respectability as a god" behind the deification of Kṛṣṇa, Rāma, Pābūjī, Rāmdeo, and a mid-twentieth-century western Indian brigand named Ompurī (not yet deified but . . .) (1980, 55). Smith attempts to show that the multi- to single-story process has worked similarly in the development of both oral and classical epics through Brahmanization and Sanskritization. His notion that the Sanskrit epics are the "only two thoroughly Sanskritized epics . . . known in India, composed, appropriately enough, in Sanskrit" (1989, 178), is, however, obviously tautological. And his supportive arguments that they "stand at the end of a process of development from oral 'originals,'" and that "the *Mahābhārata* was originally a non-brahmanical text" in which "'mixed-caste' Sutas" "put forward a 'new,' Kshatriya mythology which was not to be reconciled with brahmanism for some centuries,"[66] are in the main unconvincing (see Hiltebeitel in press-g). The relation between multistory and Sanskrit epic traditions in India remains an interesting tension that cannot be solved without recognizing that the Sanskrit epics were composed and written by Brahmans for whom the Sūta narrator is a literary fiction.[67]

[65]Claus 1989, 57; cf. 70-71.

[66]J. D. Smith 1989, 178, 180; cf. 1980, 49-50.

[67]See Hiltebeitel forthcoming. Nagy, despite many insights and arguments of comparative value (see n. 32), walks into the same circularity as Smith, taking back into Homeric studies from Blackburn and Smith's formulations received ideas that actually begin in, or are inspired by, Homeric studies, Biblical studies, and/or Christian apologetics (see Hiltebeitel 1995a and in press-g): the idea that the India's classical epics were originally the "'property' of the Ksatriyas" and were belatedly given their divinizing superstructure by Brahmans (Nagy 1996, 45-46); "the actual process of accretion" (47); uncritical acceptance that the

Accordingly, while there is some explanatory power in a multi- to single-story model, it is best to admit that one can posit nothing comparable to the Bow Song or the Tulu pāḍdana at the source of the Sanskrit epics. Of course the Sanskrit epics draw on multistory traditions, and so, no doubt, do all epics, whether oral or written. But then, as Haroun Khalifa discovered on the moon Kahani, so do all stories.[68]

D. Bhakti, Regionality, and the Goddess

One thing that distinguishes our main group of regional martial oral epics and related hero cults (and the Draupadī cult and its folk *Mahābhārata*) is the period of their early development, on which there is basic consensus that they all came into being from the twelfth to fifteenth or sixteenth centuries.[69] The twelfth century is also the period to which Pollock (1993) traces the incorporation of the *Rāmāyaṇa* into the political imaginary of medieval India.

It is safe to say that oral epics of the twelfth to fifteenth centuries registered the impact of Islam and that all are influenced by the "bhakti movement." But it is not enough to think of the bhakti movement that emerges into sectarian and "popular" vernacular forms from the time of the A<u>l</u>vārs, Nāya<u>n</u>ārs, and the *Bhāgavata Purāṇa*. On the one hand, one must look to earlier bhakti sources in the *Mahābhārata* and *Rāmāyaṇa* themselves, because that is precisely what is done when the classical epics are rethought in regional martial oral epic terms. On the other hand, one must also consider the relation of the bhakti movement's more normative strains, generally, to more hybrid movements like the Sants, Nāths, and Satpanth Ismā'īlīs.

But to start from bhakti as it figures centrally amid these component factors, such a background leads to questions about regionality and the goddess. Regional epics show special intensifications of their heroines' and goddesses' links with regional land. If, for instance, both Draupadī and Sītā are born in the classical epics from the earth, and represent aspects of its prosperity, neither has the intensified association with a

---

"cults" of Rāma and Kṛṣna may have developed like those of oral epic heroes (49, n. 89) — that of "death and deification of local heroes" (51); *bhūtas* as "deified dead" "just one step removed from the status of deities proper" (53); and the exceptionalism of *Ālhā* whose heroes "do not die in battle" (53). Nagy even posits a "peculiarly Indian" "semantic shift from hero to god" to account for Greek differences (49); but both cultures have both distinctions and fluidities in the hero/god relation. More positively, Nagy makes it clear that he is against "monogenetic theories" (61, n. 151).

[68]Rushdie 1990; cf. Irwin 1995, 63-102.

[69]Late twelfth for *Ālhā* (Schomer 1989, 142) and *Palnāḍu* (Roghair, 80-81), early fourteenth for *Pābūjī* (Smith 1991, 78), twelfth to mid-fifteenth for *Elder brothers* (Beck 1978, 171; 1982, 27-29), and so on (Schomer, ibid.). Such datings will be discussed further.

region's land that belongs to Draupadī in her "Gingee avatāra." Surprisingly, however, this point has not been sufficiently appreciated.

Scholarship on martial oral epics is virtually unanimous on one point: females are the primary instigators of destruction. No matter how many forces are at work driving the heroes toward wars of annihilation, central among them are the motivations of goddesses and heroines.[70] Most explanations have focused on gender relations and sexual fantasies. For Smith, drawing explicitly on psychoanalytic interpretations of Indian culture (especially Carstairs 1961), and implicitly on the "marriage and malevolence" model that attributes the "taming" of the goddess to controlling her by marriage, the "epic world is essentially a male world" reflecting "men's attitudes" that reveal "a powerful sexual fear"; although even mothers cannot be trusted, "the greatest threat" comes not from "sexually active" women but from widows and virgins.[71] Kothari, caught up in an argument that classical epic heroes and heroines supply role models for society but oral epic heroes do not, asks, "But why does Śakti appear in oral epics to destroy figures like Pābū and Tejā, who, though not comparable to Rāma and Yudhiṣṭhira, are not evil or cruel either?" His answer suggests that the image of the dominating female is part of the oral epic heroes' disadvantage in becoming role models: "Perhaps the fact that these folk *sagatīs* [Śaktis] control the heroes like Pābū and Tejā is one reason why neither are models for society: the women are dominant and cruel; the men are weak and fated" (1989, 115). Beck sees some positive modeling in female instigative roles, which emphasize not only rivalries between men over woman but between women, and female independence (1989, 169). These arguments all have their merits, but raise problems as generalizations.

Part of the problem is that they isolate gender, sexuality, goddesses, and heroines as if they pose a set of problems unique to themselves, but secondary, in the "developmental" sense, to the primary martial epic world that is thought to be about males and death.[72] These authors, along with Roghair and Schomer, seem to build upon Blackburn's formulations, which situate female figures as contributors to only secondary and tertiary processes of deification and epic formation.[73] For

[70]Beck 1982, 182 ("instigator"); Kothari 1989, 114; Roghair 1982, 135 ("it might well be argued that a woman is responsible for virtually every destructive act which is perpetuated in the epic"); Schomer 1989, 147; Smith 1986, 59; 1989, 182, 190; 1991, 96-98; Malik 1993, 380.

[71]J. D. Smith 1989, 188-89. On the "marriage and malevolence" model, see Babb 1975, 215-30; for critical discussion, Kurtz 1992, 21-23, 99, 269-70.

[72]Katz similarly imagines a primary "heroic level" to the *Mbh* with Draupadī invented to connect the originally separate Pāṇḍava and Pāñcāla cycles (1989, 38, 57, 159)!

[73]See Blackburn (1989, 24, 21) on the feminine contribution to deification in connection

Kothari, stating the matter most baldly, the heroine-goddess's great importance lies in placing "the epic on a different plane than the historical reality of the male heroes" (1989, 115). Heroines and goddesses mythicize historically real men. Beck (1982, 32) and Roghair (1982, 125-26) take the same premise to the position that the introduction of heroines and the goddess is the last stage in a series of oral epic mythologizations. For Schomer, the goddess Śāradā Devī comes into *Ālhā* from an originally separate status as the heroes' "cult deity" (146). Smith also transposes this schema back on the classical epics: Whereas Viṣṇu and Śiva remain pretty much their same selves from classical to oral epics, it is different with goddesses, who "are relatively unimportant in the *Mahābhārata* and *Rāmāyaṇa*, but they play a major role in many vernacular epics" (1989, 182). Needless to say, I do not agree. By moving goddesses and heroines to secondary and tertiary levels of a presumed order of development, scholars of India's oral epics, like scholars of her classical epics, have bewilderingly continued to treat these texts as if they originally did without females of any kind.[74]

Among these authors, however, Beck and Schomer do look beyond the deification model to disengage some of the play between classical and oral epics. In studying *Elder brothers*, Beck treats an epic in which there is direct transposition of *Mahābhārata* heroes. Interested in interlinking dyads and triads, she develops some helpful insights into the story's incarnational scheme. As table 1 indicates, she finds descending correlations at five levels between three intersecting lines of force: opposed males from the widest to the narrowest levels of social order, single females, and "degrees of localization" that move from the divine to the human. "At each social level," Beck says, there is "a role for a powerful, semimagical female. . . . Each woman blends into others, both above and below her in rank. Ultimately each is a more- or less-localized form of the great goddess herself."[75] For our purposes, what is most important are this principle of descent through female mergings,[76] and

with the hero's divine birth (phase 2) and the "identification" of heroines with pan-Indian goddesses (phase 3). Other authors actually extend Blackburn's argument.

[74]Cf. Lord 1964, 187: a comparable fanciful argument that it was "the element of the length of the Trojan War, itself an apparently historical fact, which drew unto its story the bride-stealing theme" from the myth of Persephone—a mythically prior "story pattern . . . [that] requires the element of length of time."

[75]Beck 1982, 27. At a sixth level, that of ritual, prepubescent girls (ages 10-12) replicate the role of the "chaste and powerful 'sister'" in attending to the men who impersonate the heroes in the cult's *patukaḷam* rituals in the Viramalai hills (46).

[76]Beck (1982, 51, 53) uses the notion of "merging" to extend to other goddesses in the elder brothers cult as well: Taṅkāḷ's rapports with the ascetic Periyakkāṇṭi, and with the seven virgins (Kaṉṉimār). Cf. 139 and 228, n. 1: Cellāttā, who can be called Īśvarī (Icuvari), "is

the linkages of each female with a descending order of "protectors of the land," by which Beck signifies Kṣatriyas (artisans are equivalent to Vaiśyas) at the topmost level of "abstract social (varna) theory" (ibid.). From top to bottom, the Kṣatriya function of protection of the land extends primarily, but with rivalry at each opposition, to the next lower party or individual: from "farmers" (Vēḷāḷar Kavuṇṭars) as the landed dominant caste, in their rivalry with the hunters, to the little-kingly "elder brother" Poṉṉar in his tensions with his impetuous twin Caṅkar. Clearly, protection of land and protection of the goddess-heroine are interlinked and highly charged issues: concrete, emotional, sexualized, and theoretical at every turn.

Table 1. Descending orders in *Elder brothers* (modified from Beck 1982, 26, chart 4)

Male oppositions	Corresponding females	Localization scale
1. Protectors of the land/Artisans	Great Goddess (Pārvatī)	Cosmic divine female
2. Farmers/Hunters	Goddess of the region (Cellāttā)	Regional Kuladevatā
3. Parallel relatives/ Cross relatives	Goddess of the locale (Kālī)	Local
4. Brothers/Cousins	Heroes' mother (Tāmarai)	Human females: Parent
5. Elder brother/ Younger brother	Heroes' sister (Taṅkāḷ-Parvati)	Sister

Beck also sees that these relationships work both ways: at each level, the goddess or heroine also offers protection to the males. Pivotal in terms of cult are her favor at the local and regional level, where she protects lineages, villages, and regional territories. The climactic ritual events of the elder brothers cult entail "sacrificial events" that "emphasize the men's transformation into male guardians who will act like protective brothers. All sexual overtones must be eliminated through sacrifice. Metaphors of the female goddess as a 'mother' or 'sister' to her guardians take their place."[77] In shrines of the cult, the temple layouts show that "the heroes are portrayed as servants of the goddess," and "reinforce one more general cultural assumption: that divine females (just like human ones) need the service and protection of strong males" (1982, 49). As we will see, the twins protect their sister's chastity to extreme.

These insights apply, mutatis mutandis, to other regional oral epics

thought to be a form of Śiva's wife, Pārvatī."

[77]Beck 1982, 50; cf. 52-54, 56.

and to the Draupadī cult *Mahābhārata*. They also unfold in relation to regionally cross-cutting features of bhakti, and the relation between goddesses and regions themselves. On these matters, let us take our bearings from north India. Having mentioned seven catastrophic heroines in Rajasthani oral epics alone (including Deval in *Pābūjī*), Kothari comments: "It is explicitly stated in the texts that these women were born in a supernatural realm (Indra's or Viṣṇu's heaven) and their purpose is to eliminate or annihilate (*chaḷāṇo* or *khapāṇo*) the heroes and their shrines. This folk vision of the goddess even affects the performers' versions of the classical epics: they say Sītā was born to destroy Rāma and that Draupadī appeared to kill the Pāṇḍavas" (1989, 114). We will encounter this vision again. For now, Kothari raises an interesting issue: the goddess-heroine's determination to destroy the heroes *and their shrines*. He theorizes on her destruction of the heroes but not that of their shrines, which he mentions without elaboration. But the theme seems to reflect some important realities.

Why should the goddess want to destroy the heroes' shrines? As north Indian epics, *Pābūjī* and *Ālhā* both fit this scheme quite literally. The Pābūjī cult has only two "conventional temples," both in Pābūjī's desert-home village of Koḷū, while *Ālhā* performance seems virtually shrineless.[78] Yet the minimal situation is not all that exceptional. *Palnāḍu* and *Elder brothers* each have one main shrine complex at their ritual battlefield sites of Kārempūḍi and Vīramalai, and elsewhere only subsidiary or local shrines in what appear to be rather modest numbers. At the central sites, the main temples are not shrines to the heroes but shrines to the goddess: Periyakkāṇṭi in the Vīramalai of the Tamil

[78]J. D. Smith 1991, 6, contrasts Pābūjī's two Koḷū temples with "small shrines, commemorative stones etc. [which] abound . . . outside Koḷū." Cf. Tessitori 1916, 106: "little shrines devoted to him throughout the country, he being most commonly represented on horseback and the seven Thorīs [his Dalit companions] on foot arranged in a line behind him, all in the attitude of shooting an arrow from their bows"; Srivastava 1997, 56: outside Koḷū, only in Rebārī hamlets, small Rebārī temples or platforms with tablets for Pābūjī on his mare with Rūpnāth, smaller and before him to his left, and sometimes with Pābūjī flanked by his retainers Dhēbo, Cādo, Saljī Soḷaṅkī, and Harmal. Schomer locates an "actual *mūrti* or icon of Ālhā" in a "small shrine," "little frequented," "at the foot of the hill in Maihar [Madhya Pradesh] on which the temple of Śāradā Devī is located" (Smith 1989, 180, citing Schomer, personal communication, 1982). The temple is an "important pilgrimage center" (a *Śakti Pīṭha*) where one of the breasts of Satī fell (Schomer 1989, 142, n. 2). The chief heroes of *Ālhā*, Ālhā and Ūdal, have their wrestling ground (*akhāḍā*) outside the temple (personal communication, Jayati Chaturvedi, December 1995), and coconuts litter the area representing Ālhā's head-offering to Śāradā, which won him her boon of immortality (Griffiths 1946, 156). According to Crooke ([1896] 1968, 1:283), Ālhā, said to be "still alive," "makes regular visits on the last day of the moon to Devî Sârad's temple on Mahiyâr Hill, where he has been repeatedly seen and followed." See further chap. 14, § D, on Bairāgarh.

Kongunad area, and Ankālaparamēśvarī (Ankamma, Ankālamma) at the Palnāḍu battlefield site of Kārempūḍi in Andhra. As "hero cult" stalwarts, the function of the heroes is to protect the goddess. But what is noteworthy is that this charge comes after they have died ultimately failing to protect certain heroines, the land, the region itself, and the goddess in their human lives. It is here, I think, that we find an answer to Kothari's problem about the goddess wanting to destroy the heroes and their shrines. It is because, having failed to protect her and the land, she must now protect it herself—with them (and their story) to guard her.

Here we may note that the Draupadī cult has things somewhat differently. Draupadī has many shrines, and although Gingee is a central one in the central region, it is unknown beyond it. As a goddess herself, Draupadī has the advantage of having temples of her own, and although the primary heroes, her husbands, protect her, they mainly marry her and share her sanctum as divinities themselves. The analogy here lies again not with the Pāṇḍavas but with such heroes as Pōttu Rāja-Pōrmaṉṉaṉ and Muttāl Rāvuttaṉ, who become Draupadī's guardians at her temples' boundaries. They are the figures who make the Draupadī cult a hero cult analogous to others, including, as we have seen, the Bow Song.

There is also something distinctive to be said of the regions in which most of these regional oral epic hero cults have been found. Beck and Roghair have called attention to the geographical marginality of the areas in which *Elder brothers* and *Palnāḍu* originated and thrived. Each story is set in a relatively barren area between three zones of traditionally powerful kingdoms.[79] Beck notes the similarity, extends it to the setting of *Pābūjī*, and remarks that "any number of local Indian epic legends probably share" such a "geographical understructure" (1982, 148, 221, n. 5). She appreciates the sand desert of *Pābūjī*, and her point applies as well to the forsaken kingdom of Mahobā in *Alhā*, and the rough rural splendors of Gingee (Hiltebeitel 1988a, 3). One can detect in all these cases the evocative power of the rituals of regional dominant castes and the "shatter zone" mythologies of little kingdoms.[80] Such oral epics leave in their wake not only the ends of heroic ages, but a kind of wasteland. But it is one that can be replenished by the imagery of oral epic bards, whether by a Tamil evocation of the flowering of the five landscapes in the rocky kingdom of the elder brothers (Beck 1982, 138), or the Rajasthani affection for the sand desert, with its she-camels and cows, that echoes through *Pābūjī*. Whether or not their shrines were

[79]Beck 1978; 1982, 7-8, 27-32, 147-50; Roghair 1982, 20-22, 120.

[80]On "little kingdoms," see Schnepel 1995, 145-46, tracing the term to 1959 and 1962 essays now in Cohn 1990, 554-74 and 483-99; cf. Dirks 1979, 1982. On "shatter zones," see Eaton 1978, 4-5. Cf. Hiltebeitel 1988a, 20.

destroyed, the heroes once made the land prosper.

We must thus continue to appreciate Beck's insights into the relation of mutual protection between heroes and the heroine-goddess. What is striking through all these regional epics, but nowhere, as we shall see, clearer than in *Pābūjī*, is that the heroes have failed to protect her. Their failure is poignant and always complex. As much as she motivates their destruction, she does not override their own accountability; and no matter how magical or divine she may be, she cannot protect them from themselves. The goddess's mythic devastation of hero cult shrines in north India has probably stronger echoes than the southern hero cults do of the shock of Islamic dominance, and is probably accentuated as a judgment on the heroes' inability to protect the land and the goddess, who must henceforth protect the land herself. Yet there are also repeated images of fusion and justice for the land and its marginalized peoples. And in all these cases, the precedent of the two classical epics is evident. In the *Mahābhārata* and *Rāmāyaṇa*, it is precisely at the points where the heroine-goddess is left unprotected—at Draupadī's disrobing and the abduction of Sītā—that all hell breaks loose.

E. Back to the Frames

This question of the precedence of the Sanskrit epics is, however, bedeviling. There is a danger of implying a master narrative: one that is all the more problematic and even "politically dangerous" because it seems to "privilege" two Sanskrit texts.[81] Let us repeat that regional oral epics develop in the medieval period in regions where it is probably never the Sanskrit epics themselves, but folk versions of the epics, that supply—to borrow a metaphor from Ramanujan[82]—their regional pools of classical epic signifiers. But this insistence on a distinction between an indirect relationship to the Sanskrit epics and a direct relation to medieval versions of their stories will probably not content those who have put forward such notions as "legitimization," "loose ends," "borrowing," "mere metaphor,"[83] and the "superficial" to the service of defending folk creativity against the "great tradition" constructions of Brahmans and Sanskrit. Yet I think there is a satisfying solution. It is not, however, to be found in reworkings of "theme, plot, characters, settings, imagery, motifs, etc." (Schomer 1989, 140-41): that is, reworked matter from the

[81]I thank S. D. Lourdu for his remarks to this effect. Cf. Richman 1991, 5.

[82]See Ramanujan 1991a, 441-42, and 1991b, 44-46, for his development of this metaphor in relation to that of the crystal, and my discussion in Hiltebeitel in press-f.

[83]J. D. Smith calls aspects of *Pābūjī*'s connections with the *Rām* "doubtful," dismissing them as "metaphoric" or non-"literal" formulae, as accretive interpolations, and as unhelpful in finding the historical Pābūjī (1991, 83-84, 91-94). See chap. 4, § A.

classical epics' central stories, such as the unprotected heroine theme just mentioned. Vital as such reworkings are, the solution lies in appreciating that regional oral martial epics use the classical epic convention of the frame story to frame their own stories with the main stories of one or the other of the classical epics.[84] This will be especially clear for our two north Indian oral epics.

Two things about this solution should be satisfying to any who want to defend folk creativity. First, in making the main stories of the *Mahābhārata* or *Rāmāyaṇa* into frame stories, regional oral epic bards display great creativity that deserves admiration rather than trivialization of that achievement. Second, their continuity is at the same time a discontinuity. For as I have mentioned, the births of their regional heroes and heroines can result from what Smith (1991, 93) usefully calls the "unfinished business" of classical epic heroes and heroines. Clearly this is a matter for great ingenuity, including adroit and often ironic "readings" of what the classical epics leave open, and clever "fits" and "misfits" that open new and further questions and narrative pathways.[85] One may also appreciate that another way of looking at the difference between Bow Song martial epics and regional martial epics is that whereas the former flank or frame their central-slot stories with performances of stories from the pan-Indian tradition, including allusions to the *Mahābhārata* and *Rāmāyaṇa*, the latter actually frame their central stories with lead-ins from these classical epics themselves.

In the next three chapters, I will thus discuss four regional oral martial epics, in each case beginning with these "frame stories." And since something beyond the "bottom up" linearity of death, divinization, and pan-Indian legitimization is needed to envision the complexity of "developmental patterns" behind these oral epics, I sound out the metaphor of "primary process" to describe this poetic and cultural work of framing by stories which are never "read . . . for the first time," but "are there, 'always already.'"[86] The term and its first unfolding derive

[84]See Minkowski 1989; Hiltebeitel forthcoming. Beck is the first to see such a relation, taking the Mbh as "a kind of frame" for *Elder brothers* (1978, 179; cf. 180-81, 185.)

[85]This is a point about Indian classical epics and their reenplotment in oral epics which Bakhtin, with his emphasis on the "absolute conclusiveness and closedness" of the past via "epic distance" ([1981] 1990, 14-16), makes impossible to imagine: "Outside his destiny, the epic and tragic hero is nothing; he is therefore a function of the plot fate assigns him; he cannot become the hero of another destiny or another plot" (36). India's regional oral martial epics are obviously exceptions. But Bakhtin's emphasis on irony and laughter at the national myth in the novel (21-36) does offer ways to rethink the relationship between Indian classical and oral epics.

[86]Ramanujan 1991b, 44-46. For an interpretation of why Ramanujan says, "No Hindu ever reads the *Mahābhārata* for the first time" (1991a, 419), and not "hears" it, and why he sets

of course from Freud,[87] but I adopt them through intermediary readings of V. Turner, Ricoeur, and Obeyesekere to argue that the *Mahābhārata* and *Rāmāyaṇa* are primary process for the cultural work that produces regional martial oral epics.[88]

We may thus relate Ramanujan's "pool of signifiers" to a bottom of a different kind. But Ramanujan proposes this metaphor to discuss retellings of the classical epics. Unlike retellings, regional oral epics pose problems that cannot be resolved by a notion of translation. Rather than being "translations" of the classical epics, regional oral martial epics are "reenplotted" ruptures from them. To use Ramanujan's Peircian terminology for three different types of "translation" (1991b), each regional epic has selected its own limited set of "iconic" continuities, but, far more extensively, has worked out its patterns of "indexical" relocation and vernacularization, and its themes of "symbolic" inversion or subversion. What I call primary process images from the classical epics are reworked into them, but at a culturally decisive "symbolic remove."[89]

Moreover, the rupture that is achieved by this remove makes for something analogous to secondary process "reality testing" (Freud 1961, 566-67). It is here that the primary process classical epic material runs up against local realities of "cultural ideas about death" (Kothari 1989, 112), regionally embedded obduracies of caste, the hard realities and dislocations of medieval history, sectarian rivalries, ancestral landscapes, regional pride, custom, kinship patterns, family dramas, and so on.[90] To be sure, regional epics are also "fed" from these "secondary process" directions. South Indian oral epics typically accentuate cross-cousin and mother-son relations in their reenplotments (where there were none in the classical epics), and intensify cross-cousin and mother-son relationships,[91] whereas north Indian oral epics typically raise the stakes on

this reading in a cultural process of "translation," see Hiltebeitel in press-f.

[87]As Freud says, primary process has "chronological priority": it is what is there "from the first (*von Anfang an*)" (1961, 603), "indestructible" and "immortal" (533, 577), the "indestructibility of one's earliest desires" (Ricoeur 1970, 268; cf. 104-5, 112-14).

[88]For fuller discussion, see Hiltebeitel in press-f.

[89]On this notion, which Obeyesekere regards, along with what he considers to be the lack of a censor, to be the main complexities that the work of culture adds to dreamwork "mechanisms," see Obeyesekere 1991, 19-20, 49-51, 56-58, 201, 212, 271, 282.

[90]Cf. Schomer 1989, 149-50.

[91]See Beck 1982, 174; cf. the Draupadī cult *Mbh* figures of Caṅkovati (the Pāṇḍavas "new" younger sister: Hiltebeitel 1988a, 344-49; 1991a, 29, n. 26, 405-6, 418-23), the multiple "mothers" who weep for Aravāṉ (Hiltebeitel 1991a, 328), and the importance of the *maittuṉaṉ* relationships of the sister's husband and wife's brother that deepens the significance of Jayadratha-Caintavaṉ and Pōrmaṉṉaṉ-Pōttu Rāja (1988a, 348-49 and n. 20, 397-98, 404-6). Cf. Obeyesekere 1990, 146, 160-63, on the prominence of the these same three themes in Sri Lankan "Oedipal" myths.

daughter/father and mother-in-law/daughter-in-law tensions.[92]

Discontinuity also enhances a revolutionary potential, emphasized in different contexts by Obeyesekere (1990, 187-88, 213-14) and V. Turner (1974, 72, 110-12, 122-23), that can be found when classical epic primary process material is reshaped toward new political ends. And in terms developed by Dunham and Fernandez (1991) and T. Turner (1991), and sounded out from different perspectives by Bhabha (1994a), the politics of discontinuity can find its most expressive figuration in a poeisis of "creative metonymy" that "buries metaphors" and darkens the "transparency" and "complicity" of metaphoric continuities of resemblance. One may draw a useful analogy between regional oral epics and what Bhabha calls "counternarratives" in colonial and postcolonial discourse, especially in terms of his discussion of their "metonymic strategies." Like "counter-narratives of the nation that continually evoke and erase its totalizing boundaries," regional oral epics "disturb those ideological manoeuvres through which 'imagined communities' are given essentialist identities" (1994a, 149). In its own way, each of the Sanskrit epics is a totalizing (and, one might add, "colonizing") text,[93] and each reinforces the same totality from different angles, and with similar metaphoric transparencies, including what Kothari has called "role models." The *Mahābhārata* totalizes outspokenly in its boast of containing "the entire thought" of Veda-Vyāsa (perhaps a metaphor for its own *Vedic* primary process), in its instruction about all four "goals of human life," and through its narrative frames and textual boundaries that keep turning in on themselves as text, while opening out to embrace infinity and exclude only that which "is not found elsewhere." The *Rāmāyaṇa* totalizes through its image of the perfect man, the perfect kingdom, the perfect dharma, and the perfect world for Brahmans.

In contrast, regional oral epics test the transparencies and "reality-effects" of these prior harmonizations. They are partializing discourses in which metaphors can be buried or generatively reintrenched in new metonymic domains, or, in Bhabha's terms, can be "disavowed" in a "metonymy of presence," a "partializing process of hybridity," "at once a mode of appropriation and resistance" that employs mimicry, irony, and camouflage in "an agonistic space."[94] Yet one must recognize that to the extent that regional oral martial epics have such a revolutionary potential,

[92]See Lapoint 1978, 296-97, 301-3, and below, chap. 14.

[93]Cf. Spivak 1988, 183: "we might consider the *Mahabharata* itself in its colonialist function in the interest of the so-called Aryan invaders of India." Spivak, however, situates this function in part in the dubious area of textual development ("an accretive epic"). Cf. Hiltebeitel in press-g.

[94]Bhabha 1994a, 120; cf. Mayaram 1997, 31.

and it would be a mistake to exaggerate it, it is for imagining worlds split off not only temporally from the transparencies of their reimagined classical pasts, but geographically and politically from the imperial centers of mainly Sunnī Muslim rule. It is here that we may consider ways in which the political life of India's regional oral martial epics overlaps, between the twelfth and sixteenth centuries, with that of the Satpanth Ismā'īlīs. For, as we shall see, drawing on their own early ties with oppressed populations and their recurring resistances to imperial politics,[95] Nizārī Ismā'īlīs in India developed their own new discordant and harmonizing manner of relating Indian epic and purāṇic stories in accord with their theology of *taqiyya* or "precautionary dissimulation."[96] It is such simmering strategies as these that leave regional oral martial epics to appear and sometimes be countercultural, non-Brahmanical, and anti-imperial at the same time that they draw from primary sources of the cultural mainstream—not only as they were fashioned in medieval times, but as they have continued to be told through periods of colonial and post-Independence national rule.

[95]See Daftary 1990, 52-64, 123-25, 254-55, 261-62 on early proto-Ismā'īlī associations with oppressed and peripheralized populations; on their varied resistances to imperial politics, see 306 (persecuted by the Mughal Aurangzīb), 340-52 and 418-28 (opposing the Saljūks and Mongols from Alamūt), 404 (Ghurids), 452 (Timurids), 472 (Safawids).
[96]Kassam 1995; Khan 1996, 1997a, 1997b; Daftary 1990, 566.

3 The Elder Brothers and the Heroes of Palnāḍu

Two south Indian oral epics were translated in 1982: the *Elder brothers story* by Beck,[1] and the *Epic of Palnāḍu* by Roghair. Both translators demonstrate that these oral versions reflect the cult-related backgrounds of these oral epics better than written texts of the same stories available in chapbook editions.[2]

I have discussed similarities between these two epics, and of both with the Draupadī cult *Mahābhārata*.[3] Just after their 1982 publication, I wrote a long (unpublished) ten-point comparison of them, and then a double-book review (Hiltebeitel 1984b). My sense of the comparison's value revived with additional study since 1987 of the two other oral epics that I will discuss in the next chapters.[4] Although the initial comparison is superseded, I leave its hypothesis as a point of departure: the thought that the two south Indian folk epics may be "versions of the same story."[5] The hypothesis can be expected to inspire some disbelief, so something must be said about why it remains worth proposing.

[1]Beck 1982 was preceded by the privately circulated Beck 1975, which is now revised as Beck 1992 with facing Tamil text.

[2]Beck 1982, 36-57; Roghair 1982, 7-17. Both epics are known in numerous versions. Roghair was unable to record a version by the elusive Piccaguntlu (see below), and observes that such an account might have been interesting for its variations (1982, 38, 112).

[3]See Hiltebeitel 1988a, 342, n. 13, 360; 1991a, 166-69, 223, 239, 308-10, 355-70, 379. On each epic separately, see also the indexed in the same volumes.

[4]A study of the Tulu folk epic of Koti and Cennaya was also part of this study as a "limit case." See now Hiltebeitel in press-e.

[5]I use this phrase recalling Stig Wikander's description of his midnight read one New Year's Eve, while visiting Columbia University from Sweden, of Saxo Grammaticus' account of the "Battle of Bravellir." Working through its four-generational crisis and a glass of scotch, he suddenly realized, "I've read this story before"—by which he meant "in the *Mbh*" (personal communication, 1967). The discovery led to his groundbreaking comparisons of these two "epics" (1960a, 1960b, 1978), in which, following the model he set in comparing Indian and Iranian epic (1950), he treats noncomittally the options of explaining the similarities (see Hiltebeitel [1976] 1990, 58-59, 109-13). Of course, one can never "enter the same story twice." Cf. J. Z. Smith 1982, 22, on scholarly moments of *déjà vu*.

The two folk epics are closest in the culminating segments that are most deeply integrated into their respective hero cult rituals. These portions contain comparable narrative threads and details. Each epic also contains narratives of events prior to these segments, most notably episodes preceding the births of the main heroes and stretching back into previous generations. These earlier segments have no overall narrative parallels, and only scattered correspondences in detail.[6]

As J. Z. Smith has underscored, "in comparison a magic dwells" (1982, 19-35). Smith cautions against using "genealogical" comparison to buttress theories of borrowing, diffusion, and dependency,[7] which are all too often among the "reality effects" that comparativists' magic seeks to achieve.[8] At every point, comparison raises questions of selectivity, resemblance, and difference. Because a magic dwells in it, the comparativist, and especially the comparative mythologist, can all too easily find a magic wand that turns everything into his or her special brand of stardust.[9] Yet the comparability of *Elder brothers* and *Palnāḍu* requires that we begin to look carefully at diffusion, think through diffusions of different kinds, and admit the possibility of circulating diffusion, and diffusion in different directions (see Hiltebeitel 1997). One must be able to envision kinds of diffusion that do not imply the purity of origins or genealogies of borrowing and dependency. The problem will remain with us through the rest of this book. I propose that in narrowing comparison to regional oral martial epics, we can begin by limiting propositions of diffusion to three areas:

1. Comparison related to regional landed dominant castes
2. Comparison related to mythology and ritual of South Asian hero cults
3. Comparison related to "primary processing" of *the Mahābhārata* and Rāmāyaṇa

This means that other kinds of comparison—for instance of theme, tale,

[6]Beck (1982, 32) regards the earlier generation stories in *Elder brothers* as probable late additions.

[7]1978, 243; 1982, 22; 1990, 31, 47, 53, 115, and especially 51: "'genealogy' disguises the scholar's interests and activities allowing the illusion of passive observation (what Nietzsche has termed [*Zarathustra* 2.15], 'the myth of the immaculate perception')."

[8]Smith relates Frazer's twofold typology of magic to "the enterprise of comparison in the human sciences," and finds the curious "magical" combination of a "procedure" operating on a principle of homeopathic similarity and a "theory" built on a principle of contiguity used to demonstrate contagion (1982, 21). The combination leaves historical criticism free to "exorcise" infected or even "diabolical" elements (1990, 9, 14, 41, 115).

[9]See Smith 1990, 41, on Rudolph Bultmann. As Strenski's critique of four mythologists (1988) shows, no field is more prone to aggrandizing one's own theories, belittling "ancestors'" theories, and ignoring those of contemporaries.

or hero type—will not necessarily imply diffusion, or do so only in relation to these areas. As to the carriers of such diffusion and the contexts of transmission, which will emerge as a fourth area of comparison, this chapter opens with some preliminary considerations, but leaves the subject to be taken up more fully beginning in chapter 10.

As regards type 1, one must consider Telugu Velamas and Tamil Vēḷāḷars, the main dominant landed castes who patronize these two epics and supply their chief heroes. Manuals on south Indian castes speak of tendencies of these two castes to differentiate themselves from each other, but in terms that acknowledge affinity. "The Velamas seem to have come south with the Vijayanagar kings, and to have been made Menkāvalgars ["superintendents"], from which position some rose to be Poligars. . . . To distinguish them from the Vellālas in the southern taluks, they call themselves Telugu Vellālas." Or, "Vellālas are sometimes called Arava (Tamil) Velamalu."[10] As Subrahmanyam shows, "Between the mid-sixteenth century and the 1640s, the entire space between the rivers Krishna and Kollidam [Coleroon] in south-eastern India . . . was a heavily contested region. In the years before 1550, the area had been under Vijayanagara domination, and towns such as Kondavidu, Venkatagiri, etc. . . . came to be fortified . . . and were the places of residence of a variety of Velama and Reddi lineages from Andhra. . . . In the second half of the sixteenth century, a realignment took place in the region," marked by the recentering of political power in Candragiri, Gingee, and Velur (1995, 3-4). Here, "Velama notables" were given jāgīrs (titled land) by the Mughals in the late seventeenth century; in the early eighteenth, "the Karnatak was still a frontier area, not only on account of the Marathas, but because Velama, Reddi and other warrior clans of the region remained unsubdued" (7).

Our two oral epics are rooted at the far edges of this "heavily contested region": *Palnāḍu* just within it at its most northeastern reach in Guntur District, Andhra, just south of the Krishna; and *Elder brothers* just beyond its southwestern-most reach, in its Vīramalai heartland of the Trichy-northern Kongu area not far from the Coleroon. Contacts and crossovers from Vijayanagar times are sufficient to consider possibilities of transmission between these two boundary regions. Similarities between the two epics lie only with Vēḷāḷars and Velamas, not with their opponents: in *Elder brothers*, Vēṭṭuva forest hunters who are not a dominant landed caste; in *Palnāḍu*, the above-mentioned Reḍḍis, who in

[10]Thurston and Rangachari [1904] 1965, 7:337-38, citing earlier manual authors Cox and H. A. Stuart; cf. also 17, s.v. Telugu. Both Cox and Stuart insist on the unlikelihood that there was "ever any connection" (338) between the two castes, but this refers to "racial" connections, not ones that would bear folklore transmission. Cf. Hiltebeitel 1988a, 34.

Andhra compete with Velamas as landed dominants.[11] Roghair identifies the late twelfth century as the period of the Velamas' rise to landlord and *zamindar* status in Andhra (1982, 121). If this also provides the historical background of *Palnāḍu* (76-80), it may point to formative impulses behind the crossover themes that connect Velamas and Vēḷāḷars in these two epics, and explain why their opponents have competitive status as landed dominants only in *Palnāḍu* and not in *Elder brothers*.

As regards hero cults (type 2), one must consider their bardic performances. The Piccaguṇṭlu provide a suggestive case. In Palnad, they are "a caste of itinerant narrative singers," one of the two who sing *Palnāḍu*. They do this not for the Velamas, who patronize Dalit Māla singers local to the region, but for the Velamas' Reḍḍi rivals (Roghair 1982, 38, 112, 375). Thurston notes that in more southern Andhra, in Nellore and Kurnool districts, Piccaguṇṭlu are herbalists, "beat the village drums, relate stories and legends, and supply the place of a Herald's Office, as they have the reputation for being learned in family histories." They are also "servants" of Vēḷāḷar and "Palli" (Vaṉṉiyar) cultivators in Salem District, Tamilnadu. There they work the fields of Vēḷāḷars, or live by begging—a way of life reflecting their usual name, which is taken to mean "assembly of beggars." Thurston relates their alternate name, Pinchikuntar, to a myth of their lame male ancestor, brother of a hundred Vēḷāḷars. The latter marry him to a Telugu woman of different caste (no doubt evoking the community's Telugu connections). The cripple's descendants are treated as inferior by the hundred brothers' descendants, but still relate genealogies for them at marriages and festivals (Thurston and Rangachari [1904] 1965, 6:196). The Piccaguṇṭlu are thus itinerant storytellers who serve landed dominant castes from Palnad to Kongunad. There is nothing to indicate that they recite *Elder brothers*, but they do transmit heroic mythologies that have ritual uses for Vēḷāḷars in areas that include the region of *Elder brothers*. It is not, however, just bards who would transmit and reshape hero cult myths and rituals, but castes that would espouse and relocate such stories' ideology.

As regards *Mahābhārata* primary processing (type 3), we have already noted that both oral epics tie in with the *Mahābhārata* and share affinities with the Draupadī cult *Mahābhārata*. *Palnāḍu* has a story of Pōta Rāju and the Śivanandi Fort that is an unmistakable variant of the Draupadī cult's "epicized" story of Pōttu Rāja-Pōrmaṉṉaṉ. Each has corresponding

[11]The only common conflictual element of note is that both wars are precipitated by a cockfight, but the two episodes are dissimilarly weighted. In *Palnāḍu* the cockfight is pivotal (Roghair 1982, 216-42); in *Elder brothers*, it occurs a year prior to events actually described, and is barely integrated into the story (Beck 1992, 530-33).

instigatory roles for Kṛṣṇa and Brahma Nāyuḍu, incarnations of Viṣṇu.[12] Each has similar mythologies connecting Garuḍa and Ādiśeṣa with heroes (Aravāṉ, Bāluḍu) who begin the great battles, again with corresponding roles for Kṛṣṇa and Brahma Nāyuḍu (1991a, 308-10). *Palnāḍu* situates its narrative at the juncture of the Dvāpara and Kali yugas, appropriating that pivotal time from the *Mahābhārata*, which it defers to a priority *within* the Dvāpara yuga (Roghair 1982, 87, 108, 154, 320). As we saw in chapter 2, K. Rāmacāmi Nāvitar bows to the *Mahābhārata* as he searches within it for "sweet words" to recite *Elder brothers*.

Plainly, the Draupadī cult *Mahābhārata* gets us closer to the *Mahābhārata* that Rāmacāmi "rethinks" than any classical one does. The twins' future mother Tāmarai's hair is pulled by a "black watchman (*karupput talaiyāri*)," loosening it and causing blood to flow, upon which she calls down a divine fireball (*akkiṉi centu*) into her hands, afflicts the watchmen, lets her *kūntal* (chignon) fall loose in a thousand strands, circles the fortress[13] of her birth, beats her breasts, curses her kinsmen, kills her fourteen nephews, visits Kālī, and, at Kālī's instigation, revives the fourteen children (Beck 1992, 230-51). These moments remind one of Draupadī only in her cult: her hair-pulling, dishevelment, control of fire, fort-and-battlefield circulations, Kālīrūpa, vows affecting her kinsmen, and powers of revival (Hiltebeitel 1991a, *passim*). Tāmarai also does penance where Arjuna did, "on Śiva's dancing ground in Banaras."[14] But as indicated in chapter 2, it is not just themes and episodes that define these oral epics' relation to the *Mahābhārata*, but their use of it as a frame story. I thus turn to the lives of the chief youthful heroes. The main points will be developed under eight headings, which in Proppian terms I will call "functions": actions that move the stories along in the same way, even though the actions and stories differ.[15] Where the narratives parallel each other sufficiently, the sequences will be aligned.

1. Births of the Heroes

A. Tāmarai is childless. She goes to Banaras to do 21 years of penance to Śiva to obtain the boon of a son.	A. Aitamma is childless. She "prays to many gods, visits many temples, and gives gifts to holy men" (Roghair 1982, 243).

[12]Hiltebeitel 1988a, 336-61, cf. 445; 1991a, 109-10, 145, 356.

[13]*Kōṭṭai cūttip pattiṉi*; *aval kōṭṭaiyaic cūṟṟi*; Beck 1992, 238, 246.

[14]Beck 1992, 330-47; 1982, 159-60, 166—which is likewise identified as Mount Kailāsa.

[15]Propp [1968] 1994; 1984, 69-76 (critiquing Lévi-Strauss's use of his term). In Dundes' terms, these are instances of "the symbolic equivalence of allomotifs" in which "the contents of a given motifemic slot (or Propp's function) are evidently regarded as equivalent by the folk insofar as the story line is advanced in the same fashion no matter which allomotif is employed" (1989, 139).

B. Visnu helps Tāmarai through trials, getting his sister Pārvati to intercede on her behalf with Śiva, who thus grants Tāmarai two sons and a daughter.

B. Aitamma, wife of Brahma Nāyudu (Visnu incarnate), goes to her mother-in-law Śīlamma, who advises her to call on their patron god Cennakēśvara (Viṣṇu).

C. Śiva puts the spirits/lives for all three siblings into a lemon or lime and has Tāmarai swallow it to become pregnant.

C. Śīlamma puts a lime on Cennakēśvara's icon's head. He empowers the lime. Aitamma swallows a portion and gets pregnant.

D. Tāmarai "shares" her boon: her *tapas* in Banaras secures not only her own children, but boons of offspring for (1) two barren black cows; (2) two blue horses; (3) a black childless Paṟaiyar woman; (4) an earless dog; separately, en route to Banaras, a cobra king. Her own children will be served by the others (Beck 1992, 308-57).

D. Aitamma shares her boon with women from six different castes, variously listed, but always including a Brahman. The other five women are from a group of six castes: another Velama (like Aitamma) and the five principal artisan castes of the region: barber, potter, washerman, goldsmith, and blacksmith.

Each boon thus produces seven or eight children, with species and caste features that clearly differ.[16] The boon, divine intervention, and lime-birth are conventional tale types that find parallels in folktales from all over South Asia and beyond.[17]

E. Thus are born: Poṉṉar, the older brother, incarnation of Arjuna (or Yudhisthira); Caṅkar, the younger brother, incarnation of Bhīma (or Abhimanyu); Taṅkāl, the younger sister, incarnation of the youngest of the Seven Virgins (or Draupadī); Cāmpukā, the brothers' Paṟaiyar "first minister," incarnation of Aśvatthāman (or Bhīma); Poṉṉācci, the earless bitch, and other animals.

E. Thus are born: Bālacandrudu (Bāludu), son of Aitamma and Brahma Nāyuḍu; Anapōtu Rāju, son of the Brahman woman, and five others from different artisan castes. All seven (or eight) are "born out of one fruit . . . on the same day . . . under the same stars, . . . alike in form, beauty, grace, and perfection" (Roghair 1982, 313). Bāluḍu is sometimes considered a reincarnation of Abhimanyu.

F. Before their conception, Śiva grants the brothers and Taṅkāl 120 years, but Visnu says the goddess Earth will not be able to stand such a long period, and gives them 16 years. Or at age 14 it is said that their life is now ninety percent finished (Beck 1992, 352-53).

F. Brahma Nāyuḍu, troubled at Bāludu's birth, insists on having his almanac read. Cennakēśvara, disguised as an old almanac-reading Brahman, says the child, born on the same hour and day as Krsna, is destined by Cennakēśvara to destroy all of Palnādu at age 14 (245).

Tāmarai asks Śiva for sons with the strength of twelve elephants, for

[16]See Roghair 1982, 251-52, n. 5; 295, n. 2: in one list of six the Velama and barber are both omitted (244). Elsewhere the goldsmith (309, 354) is omitted. Once all eight are mentioned (293).

[17]Tāmarai's pregnancy from swallowing the lime follows oral versions mentioned by Beck (1982, 126, 181). This detail is not, however, included in Beck 1992.

which Śiva finds the lives of Bhīma and Arjuna; a daughter with a fireball (*akkinic centu*) in her breasts, for which Śiva supplies the youngest of the Seven Virgins (*kannimār*); and for the Paraiyar woman a child with the strength of sixteen elephants, for which Śiva supplies the life of Aśvatthāman and tells him to serve the brothers as their "first minister."[18] Yet only the younger brother Cankar seems to have the strength of twelve elephants, obtained from Bhīma (Beck 1992, 450-51, 508-9).

These births recall not only the *Mahābhārata*, but also hero cult rituals, considering that impalement of limes is connected with heroes' deaths and swallowing of limes with heroic impregnation.[19] In fixing the destinies at fourteen or sixteen years, Viṣṇu indicates that both sets of lives will end in battles of destruction. The goddess Earth's (Pūmi tēvi's) impatience in *Elder brothers* surely draws from the *Mahābhārata*, where the Earth enlists Viṣṇu and the gods to take birth upon her to defeat the incarnate demons who oppress her. The complicity of Brahma Nāyuḍu, Viṣṇu incarnate, in forecasting the destruction of Palnāḍu is likewise reminiscent of Kṛṣṇa's foreknowledge of Kurukṣetra. In the Draupadī cult *Mahābhārata*, Kṛṣṇa plays devious roles to prevent the Pāṇḍavas' children—Aravān, Abhimanyu, Ghatoṭkaca, the Upapāṇḍavas, with the first two, at least, at the conventional age of sixteen (Hiltebeitel 1988a, 328)—from slaughtering the Kauravas singlehandedly lest the Pāṇḍavas, whom he protects, fail to fulfill their vows.

Each list also represents the range of castes that would be concerned with hero cult myths and rituals and espouse their ideology, although *Palnāḍu* fills in its list with humans and *Elder brothers* extends the list to animals. In Beck's oral version, the twins are Vēḷāḷar farmer-"kings," and are served by a Dalit. In *Palnāḍu*, Bāluḍu, a Velama (farmer-warrior), is joined by six brothers, four or five of whom come from different artisan castes, while the sixth—Anapōtu Rāju—is a Brahman, but one who disguises the Dalit (or again, Dalit-Brahman) identity of Pōta Rāju. Pōta Rāju has his own Dalit-Brahman mythology, and, with it, a quite prominent place in the Palnad epic.[20]

As to *Mahābhārata* incarnations, each epic has its complexities. In Beck's oral version, Ponnar-Periyacāmi-Periyaṇṇacāmi is the

[18] *Mutal mantiri*; Beck 1992, 350-55; cf. 310-11.

[19] Hiltebeitel 1991a, 524, indexing "Lemons, limes."

[20] On Pōta Rāju as a Brahman in *Palnāḍu* but generally a Dalit in Andhra, see Roghair 1982, 211; Hiltebeitel 1988a, 348, cf. 353-55; 1991a, 124-25. At Kārempūdi battlefield rituals, he is impersonated by Dalits who are offered huge amounts of food (personal communication, V. Narayana Rao, November 1987), probably representing the feeding of Brahmans. Here as elsewhere in Andhra, Karnataka, and Maharashtra, it is usually Dalits who bear the title Potrāj; see Hiltebeitel 1985a, 174-79; 1988a, 336, n. 3, 349, nn. 19, 21; 379, 408-9; 1991a, 103, n. 37, 150, 472-73.

reincarnation of Arjuna; Caṅkar-Ciṉṉacāmi-Ciṉṉaṇṇacāmi is that of Bhīma; Taṅkāḷ is the incarnation of the youngest of the Seven Virgins (Kaṉṉimār); and their Dalit first minister Cāmpukā is an incarnation of the Brahman Aśvatthāman (see Beck 1982, 15, 183-86). Alternately, in literary versions, in which Beck detects effects of Brahmanization, Poṉṉar reincarnates the Brahman-like Yudhiṣṭhira instead of Arjuna, and Taṅkāḷ reincarnates Draupadī rather than the youngest Virgin. Beck sees the latter variation as one that allows Taṅkāḷ to become "the most Brahman-like figure in the heroes' family," her rebirth from Draupadī supporting her in a "role as spokesperson for upper-class values in these versions consistent with that link," rather than in the "more visionary, less moralizing role" that connects her in bardic versions with the youngest virgin (Beck 1982, 182).

Beck may be right about the literary motivations. But there is no reason to divide the youngest virgin and Draupadī variants between classes, or between oral and written sources, or between Brahman values and lower status groups' valuations of clairvoyance. The pūcārī and other informants at the cult's paṭukaḷam ("battlefield") temple grounds in the Vīramalai Hills, where I inquired in March 1990, identified Taṅkāḷ as the reincarnation of Draupadī, not of one of the Seven Virgins, who are represented by icons in the front of the temple.[21] We should not forget that where oral versions, close to the cult, link Taṅkāḷ with Draupadī, they are likely to link her not with a Brahmanical Draupadī, but with the *virginal*, *clairvoyant*, and "less moralizing" Draupadī known through Tamil popular culture not only via the Draupadī cult itself, but through numerous *Mahābhārata* ballads. Draupadī is a virgin in her cult, and there is an important drama and ballad about her as a clairvoyant Kuṟavañci or "gypsy."[22] Similarly, to say Yudhiṣṭhira is Brahman-like risks missing his darker associations with Yama, which are evoked in classical and popular Tamil *Mahābhārata* traditions alike.

At the Vīramalai paṭukaḷam, I learned further that Poṉṉar is the reincarnation of Dharma (Yudhiṣṭhira), Caṅkar of Apimaṉṉaṉ (Abhimanyu), and Cāmpukā, known preferentially as Vīrapāhu (Heroic Arms), is said to have been born into a Vēḷāḷar Kavuṇṭar family as the reincarnation of Bhīma. It is no doubt Abhimanyu's impetuosity and violent youthful death that links him with Caṅkar and Bāluḍu (in *Palnāḍu*). These two are the exemplary reckless youths of these epics.

[21]This was also the version familiar to several participants from Kongunad at the 1994 workshop on folk religion at St. Xavier's College, Palayamkottai.

[22]See Hiltebeitel 1988a, 8, 214, 220, 222-23, 291-93; 1991a, 363-64 (Draupadī as a virgin); 1988a, 301-9 (Draupadī as clairvoyant gypsy). On Tamil *Mbh* ballad literature, including *Turopataikuṟam* (*kuṟam* = *kuṟavañci*), see Arunachalam 1976, 95-109.

Cāmpukā's upgrading to Vēḷāḷar standing, on the other hand, can be suspected as an incomplete "Kṣatriyazation" by the paṭukaḷam's Vēḷāḷar Kavuṇṭar informants, since his paṭukaḷam icon still shows him playing the drum (see plate 1) that is one of his most important epic traits and feats as a Paṟaiyar or Dalit.[23]

As to *Palnāḍu*, again sources differ. According A. Siva Prasad, the Palnāṭi Vīrāchāra Pīṭhādhipati (head of the temples of the Palnad hero-cult at Kārempūḍi),[24] Brahma Nāyuḍu is Palnāṭi Kṛṣṇayya, "Kṛṣṇa of Palnāḍu," Śakuni is compared to Nāyakurālu (the female minister of the Gurujala faction opposed to the Macerla faction which Brahma Nāyuḍu serves as minister), and Bāluḍu to Abhimanyu. Professor Y. Kumaraswamy (Department of History, Nagarjuna University, Guntur), however, recalls that Kannama Dāsu, the great Māla (Dalit) warrior adopted by Brahma Nāyuḍu, is the "prototype of Ghatoṭkaca because of his tribal affinities";[25] again, Bāluḍu is Abhimanyu, but Nalagama Rāju (leader of the Gurujala faction) is Droṇācārya, and Nāgamma (Nāyakurālu) is Kṛṣṇa playing the part of the "real politician." Chandra Sekhar (1961, 181-83) says identifications are made between Abhimanyu and Bāluḍu, Uttarā (Abhimanyu's wife) and Māncāla, Dharmarāja (Yudhiṣṭhira) and Nalagama Rāju, Śalya and Nāyakurālu,[26] and Kṛṣṇa as Ala Rācamallu in his ill-fated peace mission to Gurajāla. From Roghair's oral version, one also finds Anapōtu Rāju comparing his death with that of Droṇa and Kṛpa (Roghair 1982, 351, 356), while Bāluḍu is said to be Kṛṣṇa himself, and Brahma Nāyuḍu is, like Kṛṣṇa, Viṣṇu incarnate. More context-sensitive research is needed, but it looks like connections based on similarity contend with others that invert prior epic alliances. It is a fascinating glimpse of primary process variation.

Yet the first thing that is noticeable about these two south Indian epics is that, although they entail such reenplotments, they tell only fragments of a frame story as such to account for them: certain Pāṇḍavas are reborn

[23]See Beck 1982, 54-56: Cāmpukā beats the drum over Caṅkar's body at the patukalam; Beck's lower photo p. 91 shows the paṟai drum played at patukalam death rites as distinct from the uṭukkai drum played by bards.

[24]Interviewed January 1997. The Pīṭhādhipati is an Āruvēla Niyogi Brahman; see Roghair 1982, 26, 31-33, 112, 128 on his control of the festival and functions in relation with the mainly Dalit Māla singers. According to Gordon, Telugu Niyogi Brahmans commanded "all the large fortresses of crucial importance to Vijayanagar" (1994, 202).

[25]Professor Kumaraswamy (interviewed January 1997) comes from the Māla community, for whom (he says) Kuntī, as Guntelamma, is tutelary deity, with offerings to her at the December-January samkrānti with the new crop. Kumaraswamy supervised Ranjan Babu 1996, a thesis on *Palnāḍu* to be mentioned later.

[26]Similar stories are told about how each makes way-station pavilions and gratifies kings en route (Śalya with Duryodhana [*Mbh* 5.8], Nāyakurālu with Alagu Rāju [Roghair 1982, 217-18]) resulting in story-turning boons.

because Śiva uses their "lives" to fulfill a boon; the goddess Earth is overrun; the war launches the Kali yuga. . . . Fuller frame stories are found only in the north. Nonetheless, the "primary process" mythology of both folk epics includes "human" heroes of the *Mahābhārata*.

Moreover, in *Palnāḍu*, as in the Draupadī cult *Mahābhārata*, the reenplotted mythology extends beyond the "classical" epic to include Viṣṇu, Pōta Rāju, and a form of the regional "village goddess." Meanwhile, in *Elder brothers* the system of reenplotments differs in two ways. First, *Elder brothers* splits its Brahman-Dalit ambivalence between a Brahman who incarnates (Aśvatthāman) and a Dalit whom he incarnates (Cāmpukā) rather than having two figures who exhibit the same Brahman/Dalit ambivalence.[27] Or, in terms of three formalized statements:

In *Elder brothers*, Aśvatthāman/Brahman reincarnates [>] in Cāmpukā/Dalit.

In *Palnāḍu*, Pōta Rāju (Dalit/Brahman) has an affinity in name ["-"] with Anapōtu Rāju (Brahman/crypto-Dalit)

In the Draupadī cult *Mahābhārata*, Pōttu Rāja (Brahman/Rāja/Dalit) is an alter ego [=] of Pōrmaṉṉaṉ (Brahman/Rāja/Dalit).

Second, Viṣṇu himself, rather than his human incarnation, is the determining divine presence on the battlefield. Together, these similarities and differences can be represented as shown in table 2:

Table 2. Primary incarnational patterns in three epic folklores

Elder Brothers:	*Palnāḍu*:	*Draupadī cult Mbh*:
Various *Mahābhārata* heroes	Various *Mahābhārata* heroes	Gods and demons
Viṣṇu-Māyavar	Viṣṇu-Cennakēśvara	Viṣṇu
Goddess	Goddess	Goddess
Aśvatthāman	Pōta Rāju	Pōttu Rāja

Indeed, the Brahman Aśvatthāman who incarnates himself in the Paṟaiyar Cāmpukā is one of the chief figures in the Draupadī cult *Mahābhārata* to have his mythology crossed with that of Pōttu Rāja-Pōrmaṉṉaṉ.[28] In demonstrating the connections between Anapōtu Rāju,

[27]Cf. the two Bow Song versions of the double Brahman/Dalit traits of Muttuppaṭṭaṉ: one identifying him as a Brahman who becomes and dies as a Dalit; the other a Brahman who seems to become a Dalit but really doesn't (Blackburn 1988, 142-43).

[28]See Hiltebeitel 1988a, 374-75, 419-31, 444-46: the crossings include their connections with Śiva; mixed Brahman-Ksatriya nature; possession; army marshalship for armies opposing the Pāndavas; head-holding at close of war (Pōttu Rāju-Pōrmaṉṉaṉ holding a head

Cāmpukā, and Pōttu Rāja-Pōrmaṉṉaṉ, we are thus only closing a circle that relates Brahmans to Dalits on a ritual service arc:

Anapōtu Rāju

Palnāḍu

Pōta Rāju

Pōttu Rāja-Pōrmaṉṉaṉ

Draupadī cult *Mahābhārata*

Aśvatthāman

Aśvatthāman

Elder brothers

Cāmpukā

At this point, however, I differ from Beck, who uses the term "low status ally" to link Cāmpukā with other epic figures, including Brahma Nāyuḍu's Golla (Shepherd) allies (Beck 1982: 23, 56). The key is not low status, although that is frequent, but a distinctive type of low ritual service. Although it is not elegant, I propose the term "low status ritual service companion," and will use its abbreviation, LSRSC, to follow this thread through our regional martial oral epics. The hero in question may be a Dalit or a Brahman, or, more to the point, he may combine Brahman and LSRSC traits, from one perspective Brahman, from another Dalit.[29] As a case in point, one may cite the parody of Anapōtu Rāju's Brahman status at his death. When his Brahman castemates see his blood-soaked body, they at first refuse to handle it for his funeral, but eventually do so out of "greed for gifts" (Roghair 1982, 104, 335). His death thus generalizes the implications of his own ambiguous Brahmanhood: Brahmans become corpse handlers, a role for Dalits. It is apparently by looking only for "low status allies" rather than LSRSCs that Beck has overlooked Anapōtu Rāju's relation to Bāluḍu as the decisive analog to Cāmpukā.

We also, unlike Roghair, cannot ignore Anapōtu Rāju's affinity in

---

for Draupadī; Aśvatthāman's head demanded by Draupadi).

[29]See again Blackburn 1988, 205-7 (and n. 22) on Muttuppaṭṭaṉ's combination of these traits at the point where Brahmans' and Dalits' distinctive ritual services converge, or overlap, despite their theoretical distance on the level of purity. Certain LSRSC traits are also sometimes extended to Muslims, but in the cases treated in this book, it would be a mistake to identify the Muslim figures as LSRSCs equivalent to those on the Brahman/Dalit axis. Muslim heroes like Mīrā Tālhan (*Ālhā*) and Mōvuttukkāraṉ (*Desing*) have only a few LSRSC traits. Muttāl Rāvuttaṉ, however, could be considered an LSRSC once removed: an even lower LSRSC to the LSRSC Pōttu Rāja.

name with Pōta/Pōtu Rāju. According to V. Narayana Rao (personal communication, November 1988), the *ana-* in Anapōtu means "elder brother," at first glance a surprising name since Anapōtu Rāju is one of Bāluḍu's younger brothers.[30] Pōta Rāju too serves Andhra village goddesses as their younger brother: younger to the Seven Sisters—the seven village goddesses whose names vary in different villages and regions (Elmore 1915, 18-30). But whereas the god Pōta Rāju is junior to the goddesses he serves, his human counterpart affects seniority to the heroes he serves because of his superior but ambiguous Brahman status. The seven lime-born brothers also have a true Dalit as their adopted elder brother: Kannama Dāsu (or Kannama Nīdu), from the Māla community that sings the epic for Velamas. Brahma Nāyuḍu adopts him before the seven are born, making *him* the "elder brother of the elder brother." Bāluḍu calls Kannama elder brother, and is saved by him at birth (Roghair 1982, 105, 245-48). Tellingly, whereas the Dalit is adopted but a true elder brother, the Brahman is a true brother (born from the same lime) but a false elder brother. Anapōtu Rāju's real design (the design the text has for him) is to serve the seven brothers, himself included, to Ankālamma, chief and implicitly "eldest" of the Seven Sisters, and goddess of the Kārempūḍi battlefield. In this, he is like his namesake Pōta Rāju, who is typically (in Andhra) embodied in the form of a sacrificial post as a medium of sacrificial offering to *his* Seven Sisters.[31]

Anapōtu Rāju and Cāmpukā are thus related to the main warrior heroes of these two epics through similar roles of ritual service. This underlying rapport is handled, however, through different and even opposite strategies of caste and familial ranking. In *Elder brothers*, the Brahman Aśvatthāman takes a "downward" birth as the Dalit Cāmpukā, and is *not* lime-born. In *Palnāḍu* it is the reverse: Anapōtu Rāju (like

[30]On this point I simply follow Roghair's oral version. The Kārempūḍi Pīṭhādipati A. Siva Prasad knew Anapōtu Rāju as the oldest brother: "As the Brahman brother, he is the eldest" (oral communication, January 1997). I take it that the Pīṭhādipati speaks for a Brahmanical variant (see n. 24). Roghair's Māla (Dalit) bard Āliśetti Gāleyya's version could not be clearer that Bāluḍu is the eldest, and that taking Anapōtu Rāju to be eldest is a mistake made *in the story* (see items 4-6 below).

[31]Anapōtu Rāju is also called Manubōtu Rāju, the first part of which Sewell identified as "bison" (Sewell 1882, iv and n. 2). Sewell's source was "a copy of the latest poem on the subject" by one Mudigonda Vīrabhadra, 1862. Velcheru Narayana Rao comments: "I am not sure if *anapotu* and *manubotu* are related, but they look close. The word *anapotu* appears in written versions pretty consistently. As a matter of fact, the name Anapotu appears among Reddy families who ruled Andhra during 1300-1500 A.D. and is therefore recorded both in literary texts as well as inscriptions. *Manbotu* is a very well known word and is used in the Telugu *Mahabharata*, where it seems to mean male deer rather than bison. *Enubotu* (*enumu* + *potu*) definitely means 'he-buffalo.' *Enumu* also means 'buffalo' and is used without the suffix *potu*" (personal communication, August 1983).

Pōta Rāju in the same epic) is accorded Brahman status, and *is* lime-born. The two epics thus agree on the impossibility of intercaste consanguinity with Dalits. To be born from the same lime as the chief landed-caste heroes, the LSRSC must be a Brahman. For the companion to be an Outcaste, his "brotherhood" must be nonconsanguineous, as is so not only for Cāmpukā but Kannama Dāsu. What is central, however, is the relationship between LSRSCs and the dominant caste heroes. The primary service is repeatedly to the most hotblooded among them: Cañkar in *Elder brothers*; Bāluḍu in *Palnāḍu*.[32] These two act out the warrior machismo that draws out the low and violent acts of ritual service that Cāmpukā and Anapōtu Rāju provide.

2. Marriage and Virginity

A. The brothers marry two mother's brother's daughters whom Tāmarai (with Visnu's help) turns into stone statues (Beck 1992, 240-53) for over 21 years to keep them for the sons she hopes to have. The twins' age at marriage is uncertain, but they have grown enough since rejoining their parents at age 5 for their father Kunnuṭaiya to entrust them with ruling the kingdom.

A. Bāluḍu marries his mother's brother's daughter Māncāla. Of the other brothers, one knows only that Anapōtu Rāju marries Citlinga Mahādēvi (Roghair 1982, 335). When Bāluḍu goes to see his wife for the first time since their marriage, he tells his mother he "knows nothing" of her; "they were married like two ceremonial idols" (307), he at age 7, she at age 6.

B. Tāmarai calls on Visnu to perform the fire ceremony for the wedding, and to change the two girls from stone back to flesh (438-39).

B. Cennakēśvara, disguised as a Brahman, intervenes between Aitamma and her brother to tell them how the marriage should be performed (251).

C. Cañkar insists that the brothers safeguard their "virility" (*vīriyam*) by having silver and gold finger extensions made so they don't have to link pinkies with the girls in the ceremony. Cañkar does not even look at his bride's face while he garlands her, requiring a curtain between them, or after the wedding either (436-45).

C. After a splendid nine-day marriage, the children spend five days together in each of their natal homes and then go to live separately with their parents. "From that time on, the children go on with their children's games, but they never see each other again" (252)—until Bāluḍu seeks Māncāla's leave before battle.

D. Cañkar has the brides imprisoned, and says of his: "If she comes to me I will kill her." When all return home, the brides are held captive in a separate palace from the royal palace, where they live in finery but

D. Māncāla lives in her parents' home: a remarkable structure with seven stories and a jasmine bower. At sunrise it radiates a green light because when it was built by Viśvabrahma (Viśvakarma), he inlaid an

[32]In *Elder brothers*, where Vēḷāḷar twins act as local kings, it is only as a junior brother that Cañkar can be so impetuous and hotheaded. The moral restraints of kingship thus fall upon the elder, Ponnar. In *Palnāḍu*, where the Velamas subordinate themselves to local Rājus, Bāluḍu leads his hotheaded brothers as their elder.

"locked like prisoners" (Beck 1992, 436-37, 444-45, 734-35).

emerald elephant and a sapphire horse in the walls (314).

The typical (for south India) marriages to mothers' brothers' daughters are no surprise,[33] but the unusual virginal bridal residences will deserve further notice.[34] Māncāla's marital virginity is paralleled, however, not only by that of the twins' wives, but by Taṅkāḷ. Before Tāmarai and Kuṉṉuṭaiya die soon after their sons' wedding, Tāmarai gives the twins her parting instructions, most of which will be violated. Her last concern is Taṅkāḷ: They should be "father and mother to her"; and "when you find a good place for her see to her marriage" (Beck 1992, 446-47). It remains a failed duty for the brothers to see "the chaste girl [married] with a garland around her neck" (ibid., 446-47, 488-89, 504-5).

The two epics thus take different routes to assure the same end: the chastity and virginity of the heroes and heroines. All except Bāluḍu will remain virgins. But in his case the symbolism will be retained by his relation with his virgin bride, who will make him the virgin "bridegroom of battle." The two stories contrast psychologically: whereas the twins, through Caṅkar, show great hostility toward their brides, and hold them under suspicion, the relationship between Bāluḍu and Māncāla is couched in tenderness and endearment. Nonetheless, Māncāla's relation to Bāluḍu has two counterparts in *Elder brothers*: the "virginal" husband-wife relation, safeguarded by the wives' detainment in each epic in a "palace of prosperity," a sort of Vestal annex (or a "sealed shrine": Shulman, 1980, 192-211), and the equally virginal brother-sister relation. The twins' brides are seldom heard from, and everything of importance hinges on the sibling relationship, which is filled with great affection, especially between Caṅkar and Taṅkāḷ. When she finally laments her brothers' deaths, Taṅkāḷ even cries, "I have lost my gold, my fame, my lord of the land (*pūmipati*), and land (*maṇ*)"—a cry that probably does not, however, admit Beck's translation of "husband" for *pūmipati* (1992, 752-73)—suggesting that Taṅkāḷ laments her brothers as a wife.[35]

[33]In Sewell's summarized account, Māncāla's father is called Kannama Dāsu; he demands gold as the brideprice for her marriage to Bāludu (1882, vii). Chandra Shekhar's summary indicates, however, that her father, whom he calls "Gandakannamaneedu," is different from "Malakannamadasu." The latter is the Dalit Kannama who here "became the General of Macherla" (1961, 182). In Roghair's version, Māncāla's father Gaṇḍa Bhīma Nāyuḍu is Bāludu's mother's elder brother (1982, 248, 252). She is thus Bāludu's cross cousin and in all versions a Velama.

[34]Roghair 1982, 361, n. 27, says the structure's radiant green light "probably simply means a large amount of precious stones." In Sewell's version (1882, vi-vii), Māncāla's residence in the beautiful palace on a hilltop above Mācerla, where her father Kannama Dāsu (see n. 33 above) keeps her with him after her marriage, arouses Nāyakurālu's jealousy.

[35]But the metaphoric resonance is probably there; cf. Beck 1992, 294-95, 318-19: similar

Unconsummated marriages, unwished-for virginities, and doomed send-offs of the hero (our next theme) occur elsewhere, and are an important mytheme for this book.[36] They are not unique to South Asian regional martial epics, although such epics were probably among the first sources in India to tell such stories.

3. The Virgin's Blessing

Whether overaffectionate sister or disaffected wife, the virgin is called upon for protective blessings that, because of her clairvoyance, she must withhold.

A. Before they set out with Cāmpukā for war, the twins must seek the blessing of "the chaste girl," Taṅkāḷ, who prays to Viṣṇu. With Viṣṇu's grace the two "firm swords rose up" and "came to rest" in her hands (Beck 1992, 544-47).

B. Taṅkāḷ warns the brothers that if they fight, "there will be a sacrifice." But she won't discourage them. To see if they will return, she puts them to a test with swords, cutting up peppers in the air before they drop. She checks the pieces in her winnow and finds one whole pepper, meaning her brothers will die. But she doesn't tell them, since if she did they would lose their elephant strength (640-43).

C. Taṅkāḷ tells her brothers (Caṅkar in particular): "Today I myself will cook for you, and with my own hand I will serve you. I know if you go you will not be able to return." She cooks and serves rice.

D. After they have eaten, Taṅkāḷ says: "I want to see you two sitting handsomely in a palanquin and carried through town." The palanquin is decorated, and as she views the procession, she sings of her brothers' beauty and golden faces (1982, 654-55); that is, she sees them as if they were icons.

A. Aitamma reluctantly gives Bāludu leave for war, but says he must first ask leave of Māncāla: "Without a wife's blessing there is no hope of heaven." Bāludu is ashamed; involved with the courtesan Sabbai, he would rather see her.

B. Aitamma goes to Māncāla, who is beautiful, and asks her to "receive" Bāludu "and do all she can to keep him away from the battlefield." Māncāla only agrees to see him. She resents his seeing Sabbai. Māncāla agrees to interpret Aitamma's dream, which is full of bad portents. Māncāla swoons and says the dream foretells the deaths of Bāluḍu and many other heroes (Roghair 1982, 308-9).

C. Māncāla distances Bāludu, then feeds him. Dazed by her beauty, he chews only the betel for the meal's end. She prays over his rice and Śiva makes it uncooked for her to offer at Bāluḍu's first victory.

D. After serving him, she takes him to her father's jasmine grove. Enjoying the grove's beauty, a pomegranate held between them prevents their touching. As "they were married, like two ceremonial idols," so they appear now, surrounded by jasmine as they await their separation (307, 329).

---

phrasings in which the twins' mother Tāmarai, thinking all is lost, laments, "I have lost my king (*mannavar*, *korravar*, *purusan*)," implying in these terms both king and husband.

[36]Recall for now the Draupadī cult drama *Karna mōtca* with its portrayal of the folklore-inspired episode of Karnan's departure from his wife Ponnuruvi (Hiltebeitel 1988a, 399, 410-13; de Bruin 1994 with *Supplement*).

E. Saying they will "go and return," the twins ask Taṅkāḷ for her magical blessings. But she says they have come with their swords in their scabbards; they should have asked her to lift the swords and hand them to them. She takes the swords and cries. Caṅkar kisses her, but she says, "This is my last kiss. I shall not see you again" (658-61).

E. Bāludu hears his brothers beat the war drum, says he must go to war, and asks Māncāla's leave. She asks his escort to her house. There she predicts his death in battle, and in precise detail foresees how he will fight and die. Finally, making only one request, she gives betel to Bāludu, and he departs (329-31).

What does Māncāla request? "It is really nothing," she says. "It concerns your little brother, the Dēva Brāhmaṇa, Anapōtu Rāju. You must send Anapōtu Rāju to me" (Roghair 1982, 330). This little last favor provides our entrée to episodes that reveal the underlying relationships between the heroes, heroines, and LSRSCs of these two epics.

4. Cāmpukā's and Anapōtu Rāju's Stratagems

Cāmpukā and Anapōtu Raju do four things in common. The two LSRSCs perform four identical Proppian "functions," which come into play precisely where these epics are most deeply fleshed out by themes of caste, sexuality, ritual, and myth. They draw the heroes toward their deaths by isolating them from their armies, interfere with their relations with female sources of positive power, position themselves to replace the heroes in battle, and bring ill effects upon them from female sources of negative (and probably polluting) power. Thus, while the narratives do not parallel each other, their underlying motivations do.

In *Elder brothers*, the scene is the battlefield. Having reached their limit-age of sixteen (Beck 1992, 605), the twins enter the Vīramalai to launch their war-opening combat with the gigantic boar Kompaṉ, "the horned" or "the tusked."[37] Cāmpukā follows them, leading their army of five *koṭis* (500,000,000) of soldiers, including a crore of resident soldiers (one from every house in the kingdom's thousand revenue villages). This "resident army" (*kuṭipaṭai*) has fought for the twins in a prior war and returned home safely (543-61, 658-59, 676-77). Cāmpukā also brings five thousand dogs, but forgets the bitch Poṉṉācci, who alone has the boon to help the twins kill Kompaṉ. Poṉṉācci curses the brothers to be unable to lift their swords. A curse given by Kālī that "goes and hovers" (*kaṭakkapōy niṉṟu*) in the Vīramalai reinforces Poṉṉācci's curse (664-65, 686-87), and both curses confirm Taṅkāḷ's warnings about the swords, which she left unblessed. But according to Viṣṇu, it is Poṉṉācci's curse that causes Caṅkar's fever (687).

[37]Kompaṉ's name can also mean "clever man, used ironically" (*Tamil Lexicon*). See Hiltebeitel in press-e for a comparison of the Tamil twins' boar fight with that of the Tulu twin heroes Koti and Cennaya.

The twins must face Kompan̲ in three days, so Caṅkar sends Cāmpukā to scout out the boar. Cāmpukā returns with nine hairs as evidence of its immensity. Caṅkar says it is no time to fight so huge a boar. He must go home, rid his fever, and only then return. But Cāmpukā says Caṅkar should remain in the tent while he goes to kill the boar now, with the five crores of soldiers and five thousand dogs, so they can go home tonight. Caṅkar reluctantly consents: "If the resident soldiers die, we cannot return to our country. We will (have to) take our (own) lives here" (Beck 1992, 676-79). Kompan̲ obliviously kills the thousands of dogs while turning over in his sleep. Cāmpukā tells the vast army to flee, but he alone escapes "without looking out for the resident soldiers." Kompan̲ squeezes the army to "orange juice" and stains himself with the blood. Caṅkar receives Cāmpukā in despair: "Oh Paṟaiya! You villain.[38] Not listening to my words, you took so many resident soldiers and gave them as tribute to the boar, you sinner." The brothers cannot go home and face the wives and mothers of the slain. "It is best that we die hẹre in the Vīramalai mountains," says Caṅkar (665-83). He thus lays the blame for not inviting Poṉṉācci and the resulting death of the army on Cāmpukā (696-97). Taṅkāḷ later extends the blame for the death of Caṅkar to Poṉṉācci and her wilful curse (758-59).

In *Palnāḍu*, the scene is Māncāla's bedroom. Rather than heed his mother Aitamma and go directly for Māncāla's blessing, Bāluḍu, on Anapōtu Rāju's advice, goes first to Sabbai. Expecting Bāluḍu, Māncāla spends the night waiting on her rooftop. She sends her five parrots (one named Draupadī) to Sabbai's. They report that Sabbai is feeding Bāluḍu betel (*tāmpūlam*) and the two are touching thighs. Come morning, Bāluḍu gives Sabbai expensive gifts, and emerges shorn of his splendor: "like a mango tree plucked of its fruit . . . a serpent without its fangs. . . . like blighted millet. His turban was askew" (Roghair 1982, 309-12).

As Bāluḍu and his brothers then come to Māncāla's, it is further revealed that Anapōtu Rāju has sought to keep the couple apart for some time, having told Bāluḍu that Māncāla is hideously ugly: "like rocks that goats tread upon, . . . skinny arms, a corpselike face, . . . spindly legs, a wart on her chin, a mustache, and nasal hair. There is certainly nothing about her that would make you want to leave the courtesan, Sabbai. Furthermore, she is pop-eyed, flap-eared, and big-bellied." Now, seeing Bāluḍu's awe at her beauty, Anapōtu Rāju admits his colossal deception. Bāluḍu forgives him: "What stratagem is without its falsehood . . . ? Whatever be the reason, the dictates of Brahma cannot be avoided" (Roghair 1982, 318). Yet when Bāluḍu determines to spend the night with

[38]*Cantālan̲* = *Cāṇḍāla*, an old Sanskrit words for Dalits.

Māncāla, Anapōtu Rāju "flame[s] up," violently angry, and taunts Bāluḍu to fight his "virginal battle" lest he, Anapōtu Rāju, fight it himself: "Elder Brother, if you are overcome with desire, you stay here. Your virginal battle will be mine. I will fight both your virginal battle and my own" (319). Anapōtu Rāju withdraws only when he has obtained Bāluḍu's pledge to answer the morning war drum. Knowingly or not, Anapōtu Rāju has accomplished three things. Māncāla will use the pretext of Bāluḍu's prior night with Sabbai to divert his desire. She will safeguard what remains of Bāluḍu's "virginity" while also retaining her own. And she will harbor designs of revenge against Anapōtu Rāju himself.[39]

In each epic, these events thus precede the heroes' great battles, and involve the unheroic prospect of their LSRSCs fighting their opening battles for them. Cāmpukā actually does so; Anapōtu Rāju announces the impropriety as a challenge. Each sets things in train through a double stratagem. First, they disrupt the proper relationship between the chief heroes and their armies. Anapōtu Rāju sees to it that Bāluḍu will perform his virginal battle, but he will be "like a serpent without its fangs" because of his tainted contact with Sabbai. And Cāmpukā destroys the twins' resident army, cutting them off irrevocably from their lands and people. Second, the two seeming scoundrels nullify whatever protection the heroes might obtain from the blessings of a powerful virgin of their own caste by drawing onto them the ill effects of their relations with two lower status and indeed polluting females: a prostitute and a dog. Cāmpukā "forgets" the bitch Poṉṉācci, provoking her to curse the twins. And Anapōtu Rāju lies about Māncāla's beauty to lure Bāluḍu into his affair with Sabbai. Yet each case is still more complicated. It is also the twins' failure to honor Poṉṉācci by asking her to accompany them, taking leave only of Taṅkāḷ, that contributes to their downfall. And in reverse, Bāluḍu will die because he takes leave of the courtesan first, even leading her to suspect that he wants her to accompany him to battle (Roghair 1982, 310), which is the very thing that would have satisfied Poṉṉācci. We have seen Bāluḍu forgive Anapōtu Rāju for his mysterious "stratagem," and Caṅkar vent a momentary anger at Cāmpukā. More enduring is the anger of the virgin.

[39]Chandra Sekhar's summarized version entirely exonerates Anapōtu Rāju, attributing all the strategizing to Nāyakurālu. She contrives to break Bāludu's celibacy by introducing him to Sabbai (Syamangi), contravening Anapōtu Rāju, whom Brahma Nāyudu, before going into exile after the cock fight, leaves in charge of guarding the harem and seeing to the celibacy of Bāluḍu and other heroes (1961, 182)! This appears to be an example of the Brahmanizing process Roghair describes in connection with an edited version favored by Telugu literati and attributed to the Brahman poet Śrīnātha (1982, 7-17). Cf. n. 30 above.

5. The Virgin's Anger

Māncāla's designs against Anapōtu Rāju run to something even deeper than his lie about her looks. Just before she learns of this, she and Bāluḍu meet for the first time since their child marriage. She cannot tell Bāluḍu and his six brothers apart. At her mother Rēkhamma's advice, she approaches the seven brothers with a water basin, thinking to recognize Bāluḍu as the only one who will remain seated when his brothers rise to pay respects to their elder brother's wife. All seven look alike, "but the Brāhmaṇ was more lustrous than Bāluḍu," who had lost his lustre from his night with Sabbai. Five brothers rise, but Anapōtu Rāju remains seated, piously reflecting that since he is a Brahman, if he rises for a lower caste woman, she "will be the sinner." Seeing the two seated, Māncāla hesitates. Then, seeing the Brahman's lustre and thinking he must be her husband, she approaches him and takes hold of his feet. Anapōtu Rāju's heart breaks. He swoons and falls. Then he explains who he is and weeps "like a girl" while Māncāla washes his feet. Realizing her mistake, she goes to Bāluḍu and washes only his right foot, telling her "silly brother-in-law" Anapōtu Rāju that "one soiled foot is my portion"; the other belongs to Sabbai. When Anapōtu Rāju rebukes her, she washes Bāluḍu's other foot and touches the water to her head. Then she goes behind a glass pillar to take a full look at her husband. Her exchange with Anapōtu Rāju "went unnoticed by Bāluḍu," since he was "overcome with love-dizziness" (Roghair 1982, 316-17).

While Māncāla listens, Bāluḍu's dizziness passes and he asks Anapōtu Rāju how he could have called Māncāla ugly. As above, Anapōtu Rāju admits his monstrous falsehood and Bāluḍu forgives him. Let us then compare Māncāla's anger at Anapōtu Rāju with Taṅkāḷ's at Cāmpukā.

When Caṅkar learns (from Visnu) that his debility is caused by Poṉṉācci's curse, he sends Cāmpukā to tell Taṅkāl what has happened, and to return with the dog. When Taṅkāl sees that Cāmpukā is alone and her brothers slain, she says: "Hey, villain! Paṟaiya! Having taken and killed five crores of soldiers, have you made the women of the ten thousand revenue villages widows?" She then finds Poṉṉācci, rebukes her, gets her to halt her curse, and sends her back with Cāmpukā to her brothers, warning Cāmpukā not to insult the dog (Beck 1992, 684-95).

Realizing that Bāluḍu is "not responsible for this crime," it is "this Dēva-Brāhmana, Anapōtu Rāju, who kept me and my husband apart," Māncāla vows that Anapōtu Rāju will not live long to rejoice: "'Now as you came between me and your elder brother, so I am coming between you and your elder brother. If you do not fall a lone hero . . . , my name is not Māncāla.' This was the vow that the maiden, Māncāla, swore in her heart. In her heart was Hari's noose; in her mind was poisoned rice. Māncāla left the hall" (Roghair 1982, 318-19).

Taṅkāḷ's anger at Cāmpukā focuses entirely on the inadequacy with which he has served as the twins' minister and army leader, and by extension as Taṅkāḷ's protector. There are no sexual overtones. By contrast, Māncāla's anger erupts from her sudden awareness that her unasked-for virginity has resulted from Anapōtu Rāju's deceptions and his supposedly pious and pedantic resolve not to rise at her approach. Māncāla is thus doubly soiled by the sexually implicit contacts he provokes. She is tricked into washing his feet and thereby treating him as her husband. And she takes water tainted by Bāluḍu's night with Sabbai on her head.

The pious casuistry by which Anapōtu Rāju justifies his sitting is of course a sham. We know this because his deception of Bāluḍu is oriented to the same outcome. It is here that we may see the fitting ambiguity in Anapōtu Rāju's name: the "Pōtu Rāju" ("Buffalo King") who, though he is really a younger brother, acts like an elder brother. Indeed, this could be the episode that gives him his name, since it makes his "seniority-act" literal.[40] Moreover, the Brahmanhood that reinforces his ambiguous seniority is also a ploy. What we have here is a variant of the "myth of the outraged Brāhmaṇī," the charter myth for village goddess cults found widely in south India, including Andhra, in which a Dalit, pretending to be a Brahman, tricks a Brahman woman into marrying him. When the Brāhmaṇī discovers his treachery, she kills him with a sword and becomes a satī in the flames of their house; then she becomes the village goddess, and her sham Brahman husband becomes the prototype for the sacrificial buffalo. Anapōtu Rāju (like Pōta Rāju) is a Brahman disguising a thematic untouchability: not by his own design, however, but by the subtle design of the myth. He protects the heroine's virginity doubly. Overtly a Brahman, he motivates her vows. Covertly a Dalit, he insinuates the impurities that motivate her to remain a virgin. The heroine is not an outraged Brāhmaṇī, however, but an outraged Velama. In keeping with *Palnāḍu*'s focus on regional rather than village themes, it is not a question of village ideology, where the highest purity is that of a Brahman wife, but of a regional ideology, where it is that of a dominant landed caste virgin.[41]

As soon as Māncāla formulates her deadly vow, Bāluḍu determines to spend the night with her. We have seen Anapōtu Rāju flame up, taunt Bāluḍu, and offer to fight his "virginal battle" for him. Stung by Anapōtu Rāju's rebuke, Bāluḍu says he will do what Anapōtu Rāju says: either sleep with Māncāla or leave with his brothers. "As he spoke, Bāluḍu rose

[40]See n. 30 on this question of seniority.

[41]See Hiltebeitel 1988a, 266-77; 1982b, 81-82; Elmore 1915, 118-20, provides an example from Andhra. One wonders what the role of Brahmans might have been in the wide dispersal of the outraged Brāhmaṇī myth, with its accommodation of village buffalo sacrifices to the Brahman concern for caste purity. In contrast, the Dalit/Velama myth, with its darkly ironic treatment of Brahmans, is purely regional.

up, shining with heroism. But the Brāhmaṇ blocked his path. 'Stand where you are! I am only saying what has to be said'" (Roghair 1982, 319). In the same epic, Pōtu Rāju attempts to block the path of Brahma Nāyuḍu when the latter seeks to enter the Śivanandi Fort.[42] Like Pōta Rāju, Anapōtu Rāju sets limits, marks boundaries, portends sacrifices, and seems to evoke a large path-blocking animal.[43]

Anapōtu Rāju's intrigues have moved the story to a momentous turn. He has provoked "the vow that the maiden, Māncāla, swore in her heart" to bring him to his doom as a "lone hero." As in Draupadī cult mythology, it is implied that a virgin who makes a vow will keep her chastity at least until she finishes it. By provoking this vow, Anapōtu Rāju thus reinforces all the other "strategies" by which he guarantees Bāluḍu's "virginal battle." But Anapōtu Rāju has also worked it out, by introducing Bāluḍu to Sabbai, that Bāluḍu cannot really fight a "virginal battle" at all. The only person who will be able to fight a "virginal battle" is Māncāla. And her sworn victim will be Anapōtu Rāju himself: the "elder brother Buffalo King" who has supplied the very strategies, whether knowingly or not, by which her virginity is retained, and who has tricked her into treating him as her husband. It is thus Anapōtu Rāju's actions that will leave Māncāla a virgin after the death of Bāluḍu, just as it is Cāmpukā's that will leave Taṅkāḷ a virgin after the deaths of the twins.

In *Palnāḍū*, one thus has a myth within a myth: a situation much like the Draupadī cult mythology in which the "Buffalo King," who yields his fort and weapons to the virginal Draupadī, is also the "Battle King" Pōrmaṉṉaṉ who is tricked into yielding his fort and weapons to Vijayāmpāḷ, "Mother Victory"—that is, to Arjuna in a disguise that evokes the virgin Durgā-Vijayā ("Lady Victory"), slayer of the Buffalo Demon Mahiṣāsura.[44] Pōrmaṉṉaṉ and Anapōtu Rāju are epic doubles for the Buffalo King who serves south Indian regional and village goddesses, while the Buffalo King is himself the form taken by the Buffalo Demon Mahiṣāsura as the victim of Durgā transformed into the guardian of such village and regional goddesses (Hiltebeitel 1988a, 77). Anapōtu Rāju and Pōrmaṉṉaṉ, as epic doubles of the demon-convert Buffalo King, perform

[42]Roghair 1982, 212; Hiltebeitel 1988a, 354.

[43]Taxi drivers refer to water buffalo shambling along narrow country roads in South Arcot and Madurai Districts as "break inspectors."

[44]See Hiltebeitel 1988a, 368-72; 1989b, 348-5. I can only say of Das's failure (1991, 258-62) to see these connections that it results from his refusal to take in the significance of Pōttu Rāja's Andhra origins and a selective censorship of his otherwise rather free scholarly imagination in favor of one-dimensional philological and historicizing self-strictures. His "little knowledge of Telugu (and Tamil)" (739) makes it unclear why he attempts his etymological improvements.

ambiguous services that recall the Buffalo King's primary demon identity as Mahiṣāsura, with similar but differently handled "trace elements." Just as Mahiṣāsura lusts for Durgā, so does Anapōtu Rāju insinuate a passion for Māncāla, and Pōrmaṉṉaṉ a lust for Vijayāmpāḷ. Just as Anapōtu Rāju's collaboration with the low status Sabbai safeguards Māncāla's virginity, Pōrmaṉṉaṉ's lust for Vijayāmpāḷ is deflected onto the low status Caṅkuvati, sister of the Pāṇḍavas, so that Pōrmaṉṉaṉ can be an unthreatening guardian of the virgin Draupadī. There is, however, a major difference in the opposite evocations of the Buffalo Demon's death. In Pōrmaṉṉaṉ's case the killing of Mahiṣāsura is the precondition of the implicit rebirth that allows Pōrmaṉṉaṉ to undertake ongoing services to the virgin Draupadī. But Anapōtu Rāju draws the virgin's ire directly onto his own person. His death reenacts that of the Buffalo Demon himself, slain by the angry but beautiful virgin Durgā.

Now, as we have seen, when Māncāla feeds Bāluḍu betel and gives him leave to pursue his doom, she makes her one small request: that he send his "little brother" (she sets things right on this score) Anapōtu Rāju to her. Bāluḍu resists, but Māncāla explains that if Anapōtu Rāju "should die in battle, we would be guilty of the death of a Brāhmaṇ" (Roghair 1982, 330-31). Like the goddess with Mahiṣāsura, Māncāla has her subterfuges too. Bāluḍu joins his brothers at the gaming place where they have spent the night, and says he wants one of them to go back to Māncāla for her pearl necklace and his signet ring, which he pretends he has forgotten. All make excuses except Anapōtu Rāju, who "immediately agrees" and departs. Bāluḍu leaves messages for him and goes with his other brothers to the battlefield. Meanwhile, "Anapōtu Rāju hurries to Māncāla's house." Seeing her asleep, he calls her "using many flattering and affectionate words such as jasmine bud, perfect gold, musk." When he asks for the necklace and ring, she becomes "very angry." She weeps when he presents proof that he comes from Bāluḍu, and then tells him "she is now separating him from his elder brother as he had . . . come between her and her husband." She foretells the manner of his death, and "is surprised by his ignorance of destiny" (Roghair 1982, 332).

Although *Elder brothers* accentuates chastity at every turn and gives Cāmpukā no sexually explicit scenes, it is curious that on the only two occasions when virginal heroines—first Vīrataṅkāḷ, Taṅkāḷ's counterpart among the Vēṭṭuvas, and then Taṅkāḷ herself (Beck 1992, 528-29, 690-91)—take care to cover their nakedness, it is before Cāmpukā and outside their palaces. The contrasts are striking. Instead of seeing Māncāla chastely covered, Anapōtu Rāju finds her asleep. Instead of being met outside her house, she has invited him within. Instead of addressing her with formulae of deference and respect (as between Cāmpukā and Taṅkāḷ), he flatters her with endearments. All this is not, of course, to say that she is trying to seduce him, or he her. That is just the subtext, welling up from the seduction and Liebestod mythology of the goddess and the buffalo, and providing profound and ironic motivations for their immediate exchange. Anapōtu Rāju's strange fascination for Māncāla's virginity is never overt. Does he want her? Does he want to protect her virginity? Does she lure him sexually? Out of her fury? For the stated purpose of preventing Brahmanicide? Or to cause just that! Her actions are calculated, but his mixed: some deliberate, others seemingly unconscious. Is he a clever Brahman or another reflex of the stupidity and ignorance of the buffalo?[45] Māncāla herself is "surprised at his ignorance of destiny."

6. Impalements

The two wars could hardly be more different, but the motivations underlying them are similar. Throughout each epic, the "destined" momentum is maintained by the youthful heroes' interactions with Viṣṇu, the goddess, and their LSRSCs. Viṣṇu provides the higher guiding hand, the goddess acts through heroines and other female figures, and the LSRSC implements (whether knowingly or unknowingly) fate's deep and ritually inevitable design. Māncāla implies such a collaboration in *Palnāḍu* when she credits Anapōtu Rāju's death (which precipitates all the others) to Ankālamma and Cennakēśvara (Roghair 1982, 335).

In *Elder brothers*, Viṣṇu determines the time and manner of the brothers' deaths, first appearing as an almanac-bearing mendicant to tell them how they are cursed; then, after Poṉṉācci has finally helped them slay Kompaṉ, exhausting the twins by creating the illusory Vēṭṭuvas with his māyā; at last revealing his hand in all this to the twins; and finally shooting a jasmine-flowered arrow that cuts a thread from Caṅkar's garment (or sacred thread), bringing him to realize that the end has come (Beck 1992, 686-723). In *Palnāḍu*, Brahma Nāyuḍu, "the seer of the human world, Viṣṇu incarnate," who "knew what was to happen," prepares a fateful intercaste meal (see chapter 10) during which the war breaks out, and then sets up the contest to determine whom the war (or its first battle) will "belong to": that is, to Bāluḍu in his "virginal battle" as the "bridegroom of war" (Roghair 1982, 348-9).

There is, however, one asymmetry. Anapōtu Rāju's death precedes those of Bāluḍu and the other brothers, whereas Cāmpukā's comes after the deaths of the twins. To keep parallel developments in view, I recount

[45]Let us recall that these are traits specifically of Pōta Rāju in *Palnāḍu*; see Hiltebeitel 1988a, 343, 358, 369; Roghair 1982, 210-213.

events as they occur in *Elder brothers* and reverse the order for *Palnāḍu*.[46] Here I violate a good canon of comparative scholarship: the insistence on "parallel sequence" in the narratives compared.[47] My argument will have to be one of overriding considerations.

A. Visnu, hiding on a nearby hillock in a *suma* tree's hollow, shoots a jasmine arrow that cuts Cañkar's thread. Reaching the spot, his "whole body shaking," Cañkar explains to Cāmpukā and Ponnar that the broken thread means he must die. Calling on Visnu, he plants his sword handle in the rock: "it sunk up to the depth of one cubit and stood itself." From a short distance he runs, falls forward, and impales himself. Seeing his bravery, Ponnar follows and falls on the same sword (Beck 1992, 718-27).	A. Bāludu rebukes Brahma Nāyudu for treacheries behind the war. He scares the enemy leaping a *yojana* in the air. Seeing them flee, he says, "'There is nothing for you to fear. Bring your weapons and plant them in the ground. I am about to depart for Vaikuṇṭha.'" They "planted them in the earth with their tips pointing upward. Bāluḍu circumambulated the weapons. Then he leaped a yojana in the air and came down on all the points. Full of bravery he was stabbed" (Roghair 1982, 360).

As we now come to the deaths of Cāmpukā and Anapōtu Rāju, we must pick up Anapōtu Rāju's story where we left it.

During Bāluḍu's night with Māncāla, Anapōtu Rāju speaks for all six brothers when he says, "We will beat the war drum," though he never explicitly plays it himself.[48] It is a decisive Dalit trait of Cāmpukā's to sound the war drum for the twins, and numerous Paṟaiyar traits are evoked when he orchestrates a vast sacrifice to raise the drum from the bottom of a tank to call the resident soldiers for the opening "war against the boar."[49] The spot where Bāluḍu's brothers beat the drum is the boys' gaming place, where they have formerly played tops.

Although it is marked by groups of three, four, or five trees, one tree distinguishes the spot: a *jammi*.[50] The jammi is the Sanskrit *śamī* tree, as is the suma from which Viṣṇu shoots Cañkar's (sacred) thread in *Elder brothers*.[51] The grove, with its jammi, lie "on the way" to Kārempūḍi or Kāryamapūḍi, the battlefield (Roghair 1982, 318). It thus marks a boundary between the battlefield and the town of Mēḍapi, where the

[46]Bāludu's impalement is foreshadowed in the scene of his birth; see Roghair 1982, 249.

[47]See Dumézil 1969, 80, 84; J. Z. Smith 1990, 88.

[48]After Anapōtu Rāju's death, the other Velama brother besides Bāluḍu is the one to play the drum (Roghair 1982, 338).

[49]Cāmpukā uses a *paṟai* drum in a massive "village"-type sacrifice (Beck 1992, 644-53) with features reminiscent of those in "Pōrmannan's Fight" (Hiltebeitel 1988a, 345-70).

[50]The spot is frequently identified by the jammi tree alone (Roghair 1982: 318, 331, 332, 335, etc.), but sometimes along with other trees (318-19, 330, 336, 346-47). Cf. 292, n. 41; 363, n. 49.

[51]Beck 1992, 719, n. 1: "tree which is associated with many rituals and also with fire. It is called a sami tree in Sanskrit."

Macerla faction of kings (favored by Brahma Nāyuḍu) resides awaiting war. On its boundary site between the capital and the battlefield, it marks an appropriate spot for the ritual worship of the śamī, or *śamīpūjā*, in its combination with the rite of boundary-crossing (*sīmollaṅghana*) as part of the ceremonial of Vijayādaśamī or Dasarā by which kings, at the end of the rainy season, open military campaigns (cf. Hiltebeitel 1991a, 152-53). In effect this jammi marks the site as one that will evoke a prewar śamīpūjā—although we should insist, as elsewhere, that the Dasarā and śamīpūjā being evoked is a folk Dasarā and śamīpūjā rather than a Brahmanical royal one of the type performed at major capitals.[52]

Māncāla's silent vow, which brings Anapōtu Rāju to this spot, must now be quoted more fully: "On the way to Kāryamapūḍi is a jammi tree. Do you know the place? It is . . . where you and your elder brother [Bāluḍu] played happily together. At that tree, at seven in the morning, on your way to Kāryamapūḍi, your fate awaits you. . . . If you do not fall a lone hero [there], . . . my name is not Māncāla" (Roghair 1982, 318-19). We have seen how Māncāla brings Anapōtu Rāju before her, and followed their meeting to her surprise at his "ignorance of destiny": that he will die a lone hero by the jammi.[53] He now cries out, reproaching Bāluḍu for deceit in sending him to her. Recalling that Droṇa and Kṛpa, fighting Brahmans in the *Mahābhārata*, "died in battle with no one being blamed" (333), he rues the noncombatancy being forced upon him. But Kṛpa never dies in battle, and Droṇa's killing is the Brahmanicide that epitomizes the blame that the Pāṇḍavas—and especially Yudhiṣṭhira—must accept at the end of the *Mahābhārata* war and even at the end of the epic. Has the bard made a telling slip or a knowing misrepresentation? The latter is tempting, since Anapōtu Rāju epitomizes "ignorance."

What is striking in *Palnāḍu*, in any case, is a theme hinted at in the Draupadī cult *Mahābhārata*: that the goddess-heroine is the one who requires the Brahman's head. Draupadī's brother Dhṛṣṭadyumna is the true Brahmanicide, severing the head of Droṇa, but Draupadī then demands the head of Droṇa's son Aśvatthāman, and accepts his tiara as a substitute (Hiltebeitel 1988a, 422-31, 443-46). When Māncāla demands the death of Anapōtu Rāju, she gets both a Brahmanicide and a beheading. The volatile "madness of Brahmanicide" (idem)—which hereby

[52]Cf. Hiltebeitel 1991a, 93-96, 152-56, 225, 239-43, 315-19.

[53]Note that this scene is momentous for Roghair's bard Āliśeṭṭi Gāleyya, who "breaks down and cries at this point, anticipating what is about to happen" (Roghair 1982, 362, n. 46). Gāleyya "repeatedly described it as 'tearing out his guts'" to "hand over the epic" by reciting it whole to Roghair (129). His emotions and language suggest that he feels most intensely those moments where the story's underlying design, as seen by the clairvoyant Māncāla and, later, Brahma Nāyudu (see below), comes into view.

triggers the battle of Kārempūḍi—is thus a theme in both the Palnad and Draupadī cult "folk epics," although not in *Elder brothers*, one reason for which may be that Cāmpukā, incarnation of Aśvatthāman, is no longer a Brahman but a Dalit.[54]

"Resigned to the fate" that he does not truly understand, Anapōtu Rāju "goes sorrowly to his horse," and the horse "goes straight to the jammi tree." Bāluḍu has left to fight his "virginal battle." Finding no trace of him, Anapōtu Rāju despairs. He mounts his horse again but it won't budge. He whips it and curses it until the horse "tells him what a foolish Brāhmaṇ he is for abusing it so." Then the horse points to a message that Bāluḍu left hanging in a banyan tree. It commands Anapōtu Rāju "to remain in Mēḍapi to guard the womenfolk while the men are gone," which reminds us that Pōta Rāju is the guardian of the goddess. It also "draws proscriptions in the names of Pōtarāju, Brahma Nāyuḍu, Akka Pinakka, and Ankālaparamēsvari." As a "son" of Brahma Nāyuḍu and a devotee of Ankālamma and Pōta Rāju, Anapōtu Rāju can ignore three of the proscriptions. "But he is stopped by the proscription on Akka Pinakka. . . . She must not be violated" (Roghair 1982, 332-33). Clearly this personage, whom I have not mentioned till now, is important.

Akka Pinakka and her brother Lankanna are adopted by Brahma Nāyuḍu after he has tricked Pōta Rāju into letting him enter the Śivanandi Fort. The youngsters' real parents have left them there and escaped into the serpent world.[55] *Akka* means "elder sister or mother" and is "also applied to Goddesses"; *Pinakka* means "younger of two or more elder sisters" (Roghair 1982, 292, n. 44). Akka Pinakka is called the "elder sister to all the men of Palnāḍu" (333). This includes Bāluḍu and Anapōtu Rāju. Let us remember that Pōta Rāju is widely represented in Andhra as the village goddesses' younger brother. Anapōtu Rāju is an "elder brother" (by name) who is not only a younger brother of Bāluḍu, but of Akka Pinakka. He thus bears the same relationship to Akka Pinakka that Pōta Rāju does to village goddesses. Whereas Anapōtu Rāju's seniority and juniority are ambiguous in the scenes of his sexual overtures toward Māncāla, they are utterly unambiguous in his relation to Akka Pinakka, whose virginity and seniority "must not be violated." I suspect that Akka Pinakka is the "elder sister who is the younger of two or more elder sisters" because she is younger sister to Ankālamma, the Palnad epic's "village goddess" in her aspect as regional goddess of the Kārempūḍi

[54]The closest things in *Elder brothers* are the slaying by impalement of cows by the twins' grandfather (Beck 1992, 14ff.), which has lasting repercussions, and Caṅkar's threats to kill the Chola king (ibid., 485ff.).

[55]Roghair 1982, 213. On Lankanna, revived in the Palnad hero cult's battlefield revival rituals, see Roghair 1982, 253-58; Hiltebeitel 1991a, 356-57.

battlefield and "senior" (in this context) among the Seven Sisters.

Anapōtu Rāju has thus been led to the śamī tree by Māncāla and cannot leave it because of Akka Pinakka. He goes to a well, sharpens the weapon he would have used in battle, and discards it as useless. Then he jumps into the well after it and emerges with three lingams. These he sets up before an *āre* tree to perform a pūjā. Meanwhile, Akka Pinakka passes by, bringing food for the men at Kārempūḍi. He tells her he will go with her after he finishes eating, but he does not mention the proscriptions. While she waits by the banyan, Anapōtu Rāju performs his pūjā, calling on Viṣṇu (Cennayya) and Bāluḍu and asking what he should do. As he resigns himself to his fate, he is finally ready to perform the act that parallels the last act of Cāmpukā.

B. Cāmpukā, "seeing the two lords hanging on the sword like tamarind fruits, thought, 'The two kings have died. What reason is there for me to exist?' (So) Cāmpukā broke off a large branch from the Suma tree, came running, and set it on the stone outcropping. (Then) he stood facing north and thought of Viṣṇu. The branch began to sink into the stone. It went down to a depth of one cubit and stood upright. Cāmpukā ran to the East, turned West, and thought of Viṣṇu. He came back running and fell forward on the Suma branch. The branch pierced Cāmpukā's chest. The pulse stopped in his legs and movement left his eyes." (Beck 1992, 726-27)

B. Anapōtu Rāju determines to die by the jammi. Proving "that a Brāhman is not without heroic wrath," he calls on Bāluḍu to observe him, and "raises his writingstyle and puts it to his throat. He stabs, but the blade turns aside." He curses it and sharpens it. Making a cup from a leaf, he fills it with his blood, and puts into it his sacred thread and his "Badge of Kāḷi" ("his medals"). He invokes Ankālamma, Cennayya, and Pōtarāju and "blames them for their lack of mercy." He blames Bāluḍu for listening to Māncāla. Then he "carves off his own head and falls to the earth . . . flooding everything with red blood," into which he falls. (Roghair 1982, 334)

At the Vīramalai paṭukaḷam, I was told that Cāmpukā (Vīrapāhu) impales himself on one of his drumsticks (see plate 1), thus retaining a Paṟaiyar-drummer trait despite being regarded there as a Vēḷāḷar Kavuṇṭar. But informants interviewed at the 1994 festival identified Cāmpukā as a Paṟaiyar, and Paṟaiyars reenact his death at a separate paṭukaḷam.[56] In any case, Beck's oral version brings to the fore the features that allow us to connect Cāmpukā's impalement on a śamī branch with pointed Pōta Rājus or Pōttu Rājas and related impalement practices in both Andhra and the Tamil Draupadī cult.[57] It is probably the śamī's

[56]Information from Mr. G. Stephen, Folklore Resources and Research Center, St. Xavier's College, Palayamkottai, who covered the festival in 1994. Cf. Beck 1982, 39-41; Hiltebeitel 1991a, 355.

[57]Ankālamma/Ankamma is one of several goddesses associated with impalement rituals in Andhra; see Elmore 1915, 92 (here the stake, for the king of a folk epic, is made from a palm tree, and replaced at the king's request by an iron spike); Whitehead 1921, 68-69. In

associations with both blood sacrifice in the popular worship of "village" goddesses and with Vedic sacrifice that explains these Dalit-Brahman condensations. As to Anapōtu Rāju, the final signifier for this dubious Brahman by the non-Brahman bards of this non-Brahman epic is death at the jammi by his own writing stylus: well befitting a Brahman-as-scribe. It is perhaps even an indictment of written as opposed to oral epic.

In each epic, it is thus a death by or beside a śamī by the LSRSC that provides the ritual reflex to the battlefield deaths of the "martial caste" heroes, which alone take place through impalement *by actual weapons*. Considering the connection between the śamīpūjā and the āyudhapūjā or "honoring of weapons," it may thus be seen that each hero's death is a mode of honoring a weapon specific to his caste:[58] the putative Brahman by his stylus, the martial heroes by swords and spears, and the Dalit by the śamī branch as a real impalement stake, or alternately by a drumstick.

7. Satīs, Revivals, Salvation

These śamī tree deaths and impalements foreshadow further unfoldings that relate ultimately, through the heroines, to the goddess, and to the ensemble of hero cult rituals that these epics reflect. First, each epic follows the deaths of the LSRSCs by a series of satīs.

A. Seeing signs that her brothers have died, Taṅkāḷ goes to their "jailed" widows in the "Palace of Prosperity." She says they should join her for the funeral. The wives rue their lot and refuse to come until they learn the deaths are certain. Taṅkāl tells them their tālis have fallen, their pearl necklaces have scattered. They go inside and ignore her. Taṅkāl calls on Viṣṇu and Agni to burn the palace with them in it, making them involuntary satīs (Beck 1992, 730-39).

A. Akka Pinakka goes to Mēdapi to tell Citlinga Mahādēvi her husband Anapōtu Rāju has fallen by the jammi. Citlinga Mahādēvi prepares to become satī. Akka Pinakka says she should think of herself as a "bride going to her marriage." Māncāla tells her she too, after Bāluḍu's death, will become satī in a few days. Citlinga Mahādevi "leaps into the flames," crediting Ankālaparamēśvari and Cennakēśvarasvāmi for what has happened (Roghair 1992, 335).

Anapōtu Rāju, unlike Cāmpukā, is married; his wife can be the first satī just as her husband can be the first victim. But Māncāla, like Taṅkāḷ and Draupadī, motivates the action: these chief virginal heroines guarantee the satīs.[59] Neither Draupadī nor Taṅkāḷ becomes a satī herself,

---

the Draupadī cult, see Hiltebeitel 1991a, 104-6, 111, 140-60.

[58]It is the convention of the āyudhapūjā at Dasarā for all communities to honor their "weapons" of trade: farmers their tractors, accountants their books, delivery boys their bicycles, etc.

[59]Māncāla along with Akka Pinakka, on whose virginity see Roghair 1982, 123, 131-32, 281, 292 n. 44. On the core area Draupadī cult myth, see Hiltebeitel 1988a, 440-42; 1991b, 420 and chap. 14 below.

whereas Māncāla's case is uncertain, despite her own prediction just cited. She is both virginal and married, making her a potential satī, unlike Taṅkāḷ who is virginal but unmarried or Draupadī who is virginal with still living husbands.[60] Māncāla's last days are curiously amorphous. Unlike the twins' wives who hear that their necklaces have scattered, she scatters and strings her own necklace.[61] Roghair's bard leaves her final story incomplete. A. Siva Prasad, the Kārempūḍi Pīṭhādhipati, says she is famed for fighting and leaving her life on the battlefield. She put on battle dress after her husband's fall, yet she didn't kill anyone in particular, and did not become a satī. Similarly, in Chandra Sekhar's summary she seems to die a warrior's death: in "the last scene of the great Palnati war" she embraces the slain Bāluḍu only after she has continued the fight disguised as a male warrior on horseback, and has fallen beside him. Yet according to Babu, "All the war-widows of Palnadu committed suttee, setting an example of a virtuous wife, or sādhvī" (1996, 96).

In each epic the heroines also conclude their roles in a scenario of revivals. *Elder brothers* provides Taṅkāḷ with a senior virginal counterpart akin to Akka Pinakka. This is Arukkāṇṭi (or Periyakkāṇṭi),[62] goddess of the Vīramalai hills, who yields her place so that Taṅkāḷ can carry out the revivals. In reverse, in *Palnāḍu* it is Māncāla who yields her place in the revivals to Akka Pinakka.

B. Seeking a boon to revive the twins to talk to them briefly (for three *nālikais*: 72 minutes), Taṅkāḷ goes to Arukkaṇṭi's "pillar of penance." Coming on Garuḍa, Viṣṇu gets Arukkaṇṭi's permission for Taṅkāḷ to mount the pillar and ask Śiva for the boon. Viṣṇu gets Śiva's agreement and tells Taṅkāḷ to think of Śiva and a "golden wand will descend from the heavens." Using the wand and a water pot, she speaks briefly with her brothers, and also with Cāmpukā, by the śamī tree (Beck 1992, 740-69).

B. Māncāla has a necklace from Brahma Nāyudu that can revive the dead. After the war is over, and Māncāla has died, Brahma Nāyuḍu and Akka Pinakka raise the slain heroes and warriors (Roghair 1982, 321: Roghair's summary does not say how they do this). In Sewell's version, the Māla (Dalit) Kannama gathers the bodies together and Brahma Nāyuḍu appoints two unnamed women to "procure all kinds of herbs and drugs." With these, and "solemn incantations," he revives the slain (1882, x).

In the versions recorded by Beck and Roghair, the revivals require

[60] Taṅkāḷ, having finished the funeral rites for her satī sisters-in-law, sets forth to find her slain brothers, "letting loose the strands of her hair" so that her "kūntal hangs in tangles" (Beck 1992, 740-41). Draupadī enters the fire usually with her hair rebound as part of the restoration of her marriage(s). I trace the stories only through a conventional satī logic. There are, of course, unmarried satīs in Rajasthan. See Courtright 1995.

[61] A comparison with Taṅkāl's description here underscores the ominousness of the scattering of Māncāla's necklace.

[62] The first name is used in Beck 1992, the other in Beck 1982.

collaboration between Viṣṇu (or Viṣṇu incarnate) and two virgins: in one case Taṅkāḷ and Periyakkāṇṭi, in the other Māncāla and Akka Pinakka. Taṅkāḷ's golden wand (*poṉ perampu*) and water pot actually condense certain other revivifying instruments, since, while the golden wand and water pot are all that she seems to use, she has also asked for Śiva's *pācupatam* (the "doomsday weapon" that Arjuna obtains from Śiva by his tapas), and "the golden thread with the golden needle."[63] A similar concatenation is found in *Palnāḍu*. Before the war, Brahma Nāyuḍu revives Akka Pinakka's twin brother Lankanna. After it, he helps her revive her adoptive younger brothers (headed by Bāluḍu) and her metaphoric younger brothers (the men of Palnāḍu). Taṅkāḷ's role is central and Māncāla's only secondary to Akka Pinakka's. But Māncāla's contributory role is of the highest interest.

Brahma Nāyuḍu had revived the dead in an earlier war using a water pot, a pearl necklace, and a five-colored lotus-shaped diagram. He then determined that the necklace should be reserved for his future daughter-in-law Māncāla (Roghair 1982, 186-87 and 192, n. 106). Considering his failed attempt to have Bāluḍu killed at birth, Brahma Nāyuḍu's future-shaping role is nowhere clearer than in this provision for his still unborn daughter-in-law. This necklace appears at many points in the story. It is also called a *tulasi* necklace (tulasi or basil "beads" are sacred to Viṣṇu, while Tulasi is also a goddess attached to Viṣṇu) when it is used for the revival of Lankanna (257). It is "golden"; and it is used for other revivals, including that of Bāluḍu after his initial self-impalement at age seven.[64] Moreover, it resonates with, and may even be the same as, the necklace that Māncāla breaks to distract Bāluḍu from making sexual advances during their only night together. This necklace protects her virginity and allows Bāluḍu to be the "bridegroom of war." As Māncāla's mother says, "there will be no pathway to heaven" if they give way to desire. The restringing of the necklace safeguards their night of sexual restraint and the revivals that open the way to heaven.

Finally, each epic ends in an image of reunion and salvation.

C. Visnu takes the twins' and Cāmpukā's lives (*uyir*) to the "God's counsel chamber," presided over by Śiva. There Taṅkāl joins

C. When Bāluḍu asks his mother's final leave, he warns her that he must join his elders at Kārempūḍi, or "there will be no

[63]Beck 1992, 762-63. Note also the earlier use of red and gold needles, red and gold yarn, and "the gold wand of God" (*cāmiyuṭa poṉpirampu*; 250; cf. 272-73: gold thread at birth), obtained from Visnu; cf. Hiltebeitel 1991a, 377-83. On pācupatam, see Hiltebeitel 1988a, 372-79, 434-48. That it has powers of revival is new to me.

[64]Roghair 1982, 249; see also 143, 145 (Brahma Nāyuḍu wagers the pearl/tulasi necklace); 264 and 278 (golden tulasi necklace). Cf. Sewell 1882, ix (a tulasi necklace); Hiltebeitel 1991a, 355-66.

them after she has instituted shrines for them at the Vīramalai patukalam with Visnu's grace. Viṣnu then leaves them with Śiva, while he himself goes to the milk sea, from whence he has come so many times to aid the heroes in the course of the story (Beck 1992, 726-27, 768-71).

battle and no liberation for the heroes" (Roghair 1982, 296). When the heroes are revived, their "liberation" consists in being led by Brahma Nāyudu to the Guttikonda Cave (not only the heroes and heroines of the Mācerla faction but Nāyakurālu and her followers as well) (Sewell 1882, xi).

Śiva shares a central place in the Tamil oral epic with Viṣṇu. Thus Taṅkāḷ sings that her brothers "have joined the feet of Śiva" and "arrived at Viṣṇu's heaven" (Beck 1992, 730-33). Probably due to Lingāyat and Srī Vaiṣṇava forms of exclusivism, *Palnāḍu* reflects more sectarian opposition.[65] But while its soteriological core centers on Viṣṇu, there is a deeper inclusiveness that takes in not only Viṣṇu, Śiva, the goddess, and Pōta Rāju,[66] but Muslims. According to the Kārempūḍi Pīṭhādhipati, during the time of Aurangzīb, two Muslim warriors, Jaffar and Farīd, came to Kārempūḍi with an army. If we open the possibility that Jaffar and Farīd are Ismā'īlīs, the "time of Aurangzīb" could refer to a period in which Ismā'īlīs practiced *taqiyya* or "precautionary dissimulation" (Daftary 1990, 566), since Aurangzīb was the only Mughal emperor to launch persecution campaigns against them, both during his governorship in Gujarat, from Ahmedabad (1644-46), and upon ascending the throne at Delhi in 1646 (ibid., 306). Jaffar and Farīd took three of the stones which the sixty-six heroes of Palnāḍu had gathered from the Nāgalēru river before dying in battle and made an oven with them to cook for their army. The army was completely "stuck down; they swooned and died."[67] Lord Cennakēśvara then came to the two Muslims in the guise

[65]See Roghair 1982, 91-92. 109-10, 123-24. Numerous incidents reflect opposition between Viṣnu and Śiva, but the two gods also sometimes cooperate, as in the revivals (289).

[66]See Roghair 1982: "the epic as a whole favors Vaiṣṇavism" (125) but is sung for an *acaramu* (defined as "the Cult of the Heroes" [374]) that is not a sect but a sacred tradition with gurus and disciples dedicated to Ankālamma, Cennakēśvara, and heroes represented by lingams (120). Roghair interprets the multiple deity feature as a "now prevailing custom" that results from a Kakatiya period (thirteenth century) syncretism following prior formative sectarian rivalries. I am doubtful of Roghair's stress on the goddess and Pōta Rāju as latecomers to the epic from "different" and "popular" traditions, respectively (124-25). Such inclusiveness is found in other oral epics.

[67]In my fieldnotes, "the army was completely upset," but the tape recorder was off and S. Ravindran could not recall the Telugu term he translated. I thus borrow the quoted passage from Roghair 1982, 127, who also tells this story, with the Pīthādhipati as one of his sources. In Roghair's account the Brahman is not identified with Cennakēśvara; the army is revived through the Brahman's advice; and Jaffar and Farīd are alive at the end of the story. Roghair suggests an dubious explanation: the tombs were added in the seventeenth or eighteenth century when, under a "Muslim-Brāhmaṇ coalition," Palnad was under the nawāb of Arcot (128). Cf. Sewell 1882, xiii: "It is a curious fact that, while the Palnād Heroes worshipped indiscriminately Vishnu and Śiva, and while this mixture of worship is

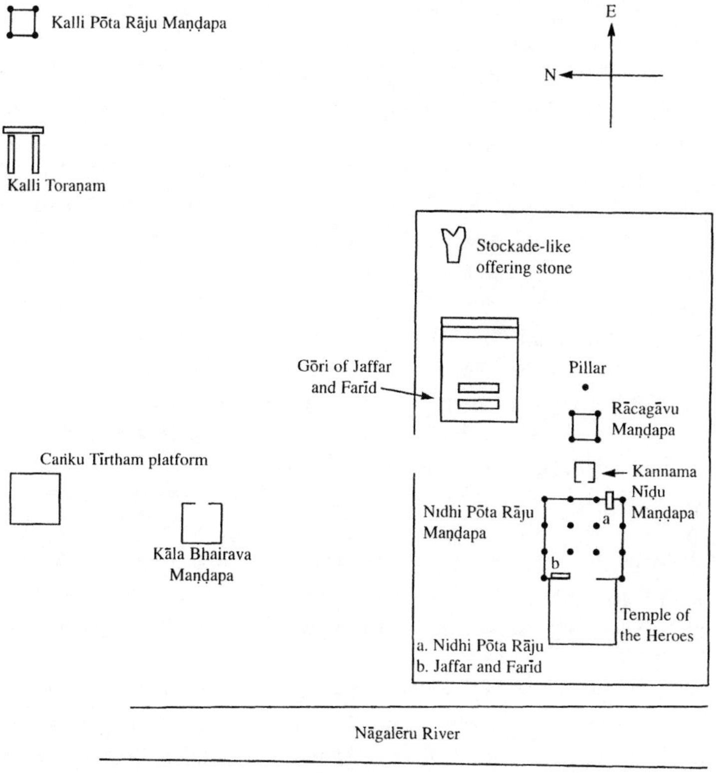

Map 2. Temple of the Heroes and Kārempūḍi battlefield (not to scale)

of an old Brahman to explain how the stones were used for worship, and they respected this. Jaffar and Farīd then installed the sixty-six stones around the inner wall of the temple of the heroes, and were portrayed "during their time" on a standing hero stone facing out from the northeast corner of the temple (see plate 2). There one finds them in the same spatial position as Draupadī's Muttāl Rāvuttaṉ (Hiltebeitel 1988a, 121-22), and, like him at Draupadī festivals, they receive worship during the festival of the heroes. Moreover, Jaffar and Farīd then buried themselves alive because they wanted to worship with these warriors, and their two tombs (*gōri*) in the temple courtyard, further out on the same north-eastward line, mark the spot where they did this (see map 2). As we shall

still largely observed in this out-of-the-way part of the country, we have in this Heroes' temple a sort of Mussulman coalition into the bargain. The Mussulmans take part in the annual festival and pay their devotions to the souls of the Heroes." See further ibid., i, xiv.

see in chapter 10, burial by taking "living *samādhi*" is found in some of the Ismā'īlī-influenced sects that appealed to low status Rajputs and Dalits in north India.[68] Jaffar and Farīd's self-burial to "worship with" the heroes presumably allows them to join the heroes and their army beyond the grave. It thus seems to be the heavenly counterpart to their being worshiped with the heroes in their earthly cult, and, more specifically, at their temple in a ritualized spatial arrangement to which the two Muslims themselves are said to have made the final contribution. Although Muslims are among the "people of Palnāḍu" who migrate there with the heroes from the north,[69] they are not mentioned as participants in the battle of Palnāḍu, and thus had to wait, at least according to the Pīṭhādhipati's story, until "the time of Aurangzīb" to become part of the cult. One would like to know if there are Muslim versions of this story.

Ultimately, however, both epics yield the major action not only to Viṣṇu, but, at important turning points, to Viṣṇu in the disguise of an almanac-bearing mendicant from (or connected with) Kāśī (Vārāṇasī). This stock figure, who has just reappeared in the story of Jaffar and Farīd, clearly reads the action into the stars, evoking a form of Viṣṇu mysteriously controlling the workings of time.[70] In his association with Śiva and Śiva's city, he further harbingers death with a promise of liberation.

In *Elder brothers*, Viṣṇu appears as a mendicant or devotee (*tācaṉ*) eight or nine times, often calling on Śiva, and either coming from or going to Kāśī, bearing three Vaiṣṇava nāmams (sectarian marks) on his forehead, carrying a conch and a sacred box called *kōpāla peṭṭi* (Gopāla's box), and sprinkling magical sacred ash (*vipūti*) that would normally belong to Śiva.[71] His last such appearance, only the second in the twins' lifetime, comes after the slaughter of their resident army. He comes to the Vīramalai and tells the twins they must have the help of Poṉṉācci to kill the boar (Beck 1992, 687). Then he returns, as always, to the milk

[68]Khan 1997b, 186, 210, 212, 229, 232; cf. 63, 93, 177, 216-18.

[69]Roghair 1982, 162; see chap. 10.

[70]In *Kāttavarāyacuvāmi Katai*, Viṣṇu appears as a tottering Purohita-Brahman bearing an almanac eaten by white ants to facilitate the quasi-Dalit Kāttavarāyaṉ's marriage to the Brāhmaṇī Āryamālai that will end in Kāttavarāyaṉ's impalement (Masilamani-Meyer in press-b, 89, 96-97). Kāttavarāyaṉ soon dons the same disguise himself, explicitly coming from Kāśī (idem, 121). In *Āravalli Cūravalli Katai*, Viṣṇu comes as a poor almanac-bearing Brahman from Kāśī at a revival scene and to officiate at the final wedding (Hiltebeitel 1991a, 419-20; Pukaḻēnti Pulavar N.d.-b, 75-76, 93). "Pañcaṅka Aiyar," "the Almanac Brahman," is a stock character in Terukkūttu dramas (S. Ravindran, personal communication), and is one of the wooden icons in some Dharmapuri District Draupadī temples.

[71]See Beck 1992, 104-5, 118-25, 179-83 (questionably), 269 and 300 in a continuous episode (269-305), 321-33, 345, 505-9, and 683-87. Tāmarai, "Lotus," who has affinities with Lakṣmī, recognizes him, in one case when she looks into his eyes (125; cf. 269).

sea. Throughout this episode the brothers call on Viṣṇu and he protects them (682-87, 698-99, 704-5). Then, after his last appearance to them as a washerman, he withholds his favor from the hollow of the śamī, and ends their sixteen-year lives (709-27).

In *Palnāḍu*, Viṣṇu (Cennakēśvara) appears three times disguised as an almanac-bearing Brahman named Nārāyaṇadās of the Vaikuṇṭha clan, or Nārāyaṇa Dāsulu with the surname Vaikuṇṭham (Viṣṇu's heaven)—*Dāsulu* and *-dās* being Telugu and Sanskritic equivalents of Tamil *tācaṉ*. In the first appearance he is identified only as Cennayya-Cennakēśvara, but it is clearly the same form as the other two. Each appearance comes at a pivotal juncture: Bāluḍu's birth (Roghair 1982, 244-45), his wedding to Māncāla (251), and before his final battle (336). In this last (as also in the first), the connection with Kāśī is explicit. He comes to the brothers at their gaming place, saying he is on the way from Kāśī to Kānci. Before disappearing, he tells them how to purify themselves for battle. Bāluḍu says that as long as their patron god Cennakēśvara protects them, all will go well. As in *Elder brothers*, Viṣṇu protects them through this episode only (Roghair 1982, 336-39).

Surely these almanac-bearing forms of Viṣṇu, the old Brahman, foreshadow the images of salvation and theological fusion with which these epics end. *Elder brothers* leaves Viṣṇu in Nārāyaṇa's abode on the milk sea, while Viṣṇu himself leaves the heroes' lives with Śiva. And in *Palnāḍu*, Brahma Nāyuḍu gathers the heroes into the Guṭṭikoṇṭa Cave, suggesting an image of resorption into Nārāyaṇa as the heroes' liberation. More than this, there is the old Brahman's subsequent visit to Jaffar and Farīd to bring these two Muslims into the worship of the heroes as well, both here and in the world beyond. Perhaps the old Brahman is an image of the primal Brahman that lifts our horizon beyond sects, religions, and the stars.[72]

8. Transformations of Dasarā

In closing, let us look back from an angle that has already shed some light in earlier studies, and has the promise of shedding more. As references to śamī trees and multiforms of Pōttu Rāja suggest, the angle is that of Vijayādaśamī or Dasarā: the royal ritual that includes among its recurrent features variations on the śamīpūjā, boundary crossings, buffalo sacrifices, and the opening of military campaigns. For *Elder brothers*, it will suffice to recall a suggestion made in the second volume of *The cult*

[72]Cf. Kassam 1995, 185: "Primordial Brahman has come in the form (*avatār*) of Pīr Shams./ If you recognize him, you will attain the other shore." Pīr Shams also comes disguised as the "poor mendicant (*faqīr*)" (302).

of Draupadī. Viṣṇu's shooting of an arrow *from* the hollow of a śamī tree at the heroes is a likely inversion of the Vijayādaśamī ritual of shooting an arrow *into* a śamī.[73] Instead of the śamī (or its substitute: often a plantain) representing a demon (ultimately Mahiṣāsura) shot at by the king or deity, in *Elder brothers* the śamī is the point from which the twins (kings and deities) are shot *at*. The śamī here does not represent a demon, or conceal the twins' weapons, as it does for the Pāṇḍavas. But it is linked with dark counter-heroic forces. It is where Māyavar-Viṣṇu has gone after he has used his māyā to produce the illusory Vēṭṭuva army that his proved the twins' final undoing; and its hollow conceals "that notorious Viṣṇu" (*antap pollāta māyavar*; 720) whose shot signals Caṅkar's death.

Pollāta, which Beck translates as "notorious," has such connotations as "wicked," as in "bad" or "evil," and "naughty" or "mischievous," as in the phrase *antap pollātap pāyaṉ*, "that naughty child," said with affection—which makes the present usage highly evocative for Viṣṇu, who is also repeatedly identified in *Elder brothers* with (or as) Kṛṣṇa. In the same epic, one hears, "It's that sneaky fellow Gopāla."[74] The usages are similar to one in a 1996 performance of the Terukkūttu drama *Karṇa mōṭca* at Madurantakam (Chingleput District), recalled by S. Ravindran (personal communication, January 1997). When Karṇa has fallen from his chariot, his *puṇṇiyam* (merit) still protects him and turns Arjuna's arrows into flowers. Kṛṣṇa disguises himself as a Brahman and asks the proverbially generous Karṇa for these merits as Karṇa's last gift. Arjuna then shoots the deadly weapon. As Karṇa lies dying, Kṛṣṇa tells Arjuna that it wasn't his arrow that killed Karṇa, but a whole series of fatalities: Indra (also disguised as a Brahman) begged Karṇa's armor and earrings; Paraśurāma cursed him to forget his Brahmāstra weapon; Karṇa promised Kuntī that he would use his snake-arrow only once; Śalya refused to drive Karṇa's chariot; and now Kṛṣṇa took all Karṇa's merits. The Kaṭṭiyaṅkāraṉ (joker) then repeats all this to Karṇa and concludes, "That mother-fucking cowherd (*māṭu mēykkira tāyōli*) is responsible for the whole thing."[75]

In *Elder brothers*, there are only four references to Viṣṇu as "notorious," and all in the scene of the god's arrow-shooting from the śamī-tree hollow (cf. Beck 1992, 718, 722, 768). The phrase supplies the theologi-

[73]Hiltebeitel 1991a, 225; cf. 94-96, 239-42; Meyer 1986, 244-47; Oppert 1893, 53, 100.

[74]*Tiruṭṭup payal kōpālaṉ vēlaiyāka irukkum* (Beck 1992, 340-41). Cf. 68-69: "the shepherd Perumāl"; 188-89, 538-39: Gopāla who climbs trees; 112-113, 32-33.

[75]For a translation of another performance of this episode, but without such a remark, see de Bruin 1994, *Supplement*, 130-33. Cf. Hiltebeitel 1988a, 410-13, especially 411, n. 23, on the appearance of impalement.

cal nub of the epic, tapping into a conception of Viṣṇu-Māyavar that evokes the god's presence at mysterious crossings of life and death, good and ill, protection and abandonment, killing and grace, death and salvation. Fittingly, Viṣṇu hides in the hollow of a śamī, a tree that marks crossings of boundaries and evokes the similarly uncanny site of the śamī in the cremation ground outside Virāṭa's city in the *Mahābhārata*, where the Pāṇḍavas conceal their weapons before donning their disguises.[76] Indeed, in a Draupadī cult folkloric variant, this śamī has a hollow in it that conceals Kālī, who is entrusted to guard the weapons. This Kālī surely emerges from the story the Pāṇḍavas tell in the Sanskrit epic to deflect the curious after they tie their weapons in the śamī: that the smelly corpse of a man which they bind up with the weapons is really, following a family custom, that of the their one hundred and eighty year old mother.[77]

The śamī in *Elder brothers* also provides the means of impalement for the twins' "villainous (*caṇṭāḷaṉ*) Paṟaiyar" companion, who impales himself with a śamī branch. Henceforth, as the temporarily revived Caṅkar soon says to his sister, "the Vīramalai will be our funeral land"—*uttirapūmi*: their *mayāṉam*, "burning or cremation ground," according to the Tamil gloss (Beck 1992, 768-69). It is at this funeral ground that Taṅkāḷ, with Viṣṇu's help, has two beautiful pavilions (*maṇṭapa*s) built for her elder brothers at the site she makes into the paṭukaḷam. And, "So that no one could perform pūjā directly in front of" Caṅkar, Taṅkāḷ had a big stone placed there, and beyond it, "at a distance," a maṇṭapa for Cāmpukā holding his drum with Poṉṉācci, facing west toward Caṅkar (Beck 1992, 768-71; see plate 1). Having established the pavilions, Taṅkāḷ performs the first pūjā there, after which Śiva calls her by chariot to the god's counsel chamber, and Rāmacāmi Navitar's *Elder brothers* ends. Here in 1990, a small vaṉṉimaram (śamī) sapling had been recently planted behind another small maṇṭapa for Mahāviṣṇu to replace one said to have been there before (see plate 3). And inside this shrine, a blue Māyavar, poised to shoot, stands beside the (four-branched) vaṉṉi that conceals him, foregrounded by what can only be a sacrificial post (see plate 4). It is thus through the collaboration of Taṅkāḷ and Viṣṇu that the Vīramalai paṭukaḷam-with-śamī becomes a ritual battlefield site for a popularly transformed śamīpūjā. There, men reenact the impalement

[76]Note that in the Tirunelveli area's crematorium mythology of Cuṭalai Māṭaṉ, the god, after his depredations, takes up residence in a śamī tree where he joins company with the dangerous goddess Brahmaśakti who lives in its summit (Reiniche 1979, 206; Hiltebeitel 1991a, 93).

[77]Hiltebeitel 1991a, 315; see *Mbh* 4.5.27-28; 180 = 18 x 10: an identification of this female corpse with the signature number of the *Mbh*. If "the gods love the cryptic," the Pāṇḍavas love not only the cryptic but the weird.

deaths by falling on the weapons of the heroes, just as the heroes did themselves (see plate 5).[78]

Śamīpūjā allusions run just as deep in *Palnāḍu*. The people of Palnāḍu begin their migration from the north leaving an incomplete Dasarā at which the Brahmans refuse the elders' Dasarā-day gifts because the house of Alagu Rāju "is guilty of murdering children, sages, and cows." For absolution, say the Brahmans, all four castes must go on pilgrimage, taking with them images of Viṣṇu-Cennakēśvarasvāmi and Lakṣmī along with "conch, gong, mendicants' pouch, and banner pole," and sing "Hari Rām" through the "holy places of the south." Not until they complete this pilgrimage by making an image of a golden cow and passing through its womb,[79] and then placing their silk on the back of a Brahman and taking audience with him, will they be absolved (Roghair 1982, 162).

The story of the people of Palnāḍu thus begins with a penitential pilgrimage procession on a Dasarā day. "In the city was a *jammi* tree. They dug up the *jammi* tree along with its roots and tied it to a serpent pillar. In this way they set forth." Numerous heroes and groups are named, each warrior bearing his weapon, and the whole army carrying "shield, dagger, lance, club, mace, blowdart, axe, and battleaxe." Seeing them set out fully armed and foreseeing that this will lead to fighting and dying, Cennakēśvara refuses to come with them until Alugu Rāju agrees to have the whole army "bundle up its weapons and tie them on to this *jammi* tree." They do this and fix a seal (Roghair 1982, 162). The weapons bound to the jammi are further joined in the procession by ritual implements (conch, gong, pouch, banner pole, serpent pillar). This bundling of weapons with the śamī is a precise analog to the "bundling" of ritual weapons connected with Pōttu Rāja in Draupadī cult ritual.[80] Moreover, the weapons that the people of Palnāḍu bundle up for their migration are ultimately linked with the Dasarā festival that they are performing when they depart. Instead of offering a śamīpūjā at the boundary of Pālamācāpuri, they dig up the jammi that is "in the city" to bring with them, and then, as they are about to set forth from Pālamācāpuri and presumably *cross* its boundary, they heed the command of Cennakēśvara and tie their weapons to it. In all this, we may detect allusion to the combined śamīpūjā, boundary-crossing, and *āyudhapūjā* of Vijayādaśamī as a foreshadowing of military campaigns (including

[78]See Hiltebeitel 1991a, 355: possessed by the twins and other heroes' spirits, males get possessed, grasp weapons, fall on the ground, and are revived. Cf. ibid., 167, 239, 316-17.

[79]On "the ceremony of the golden cow's womb" as "an important Hindu dynastic ritual" called Hiraṇyagarbham performed in south Indian warrior kingdoms to confirm, enhance, or restore "the powers of a martial ruler," see S. Bayly 1989, 66-67, 291; 1993, 456 n. 1.

[80]Hiltebeitel 1988a, 386-93; 1991a, 25-28, 78-165, 448-51.

ultimately the battle of Kārempūḍi). The migrants first major stop is at Gaya to offer "boiled rice as high as a haystack," "boiled millet as high as a hill," and a "bull buffalo" to Durgā (163-66). Such offerings figure in the same epic's story of Pōta Rāju and the Śivanandi Fort, where they are fed to Pōta Rāju as part of Brahma Nāyuḍu's scheme to bring him into the cult of the Palnad heroes (Roghair 1982, 213-14)—all of which is retold in the Draupadī cult mythology of Pōttu Rāja-Pōrmaṉṉaṉ (Hiltebeitel 1988a, 353-55).

At Kārempūḍi, the heroes weapons actually represent them (see plate 6), and are carried to the festival-and-battlefield site in processions from surrounding and distant villages. Together, the weapons and processions recall both the battle of Kārempūḍī and the people's pilgrimage-migration to Palnāḍu. From the Temple of the Heroes itself, the festival procession goes to four stations (see map 2). To the north, the ritual warriors first reach a small maṇḍapa of Kāla Bhairava, which Brahma Nāyuḍu is said to have installed to mark Kārempūḍi as the site where seven wars had been fought before the battle of Palnāḍu, and to appease the spirits who died in those wars.[81] Further north, they next go to the Caṇku (Conch) Tīrtham, a stone platform where the Pīṭhādhipati gives them all *tīrtha* water. Then they go eastward through a double-pillar-and-cross-stone arch, the Kalli Toraṇam, "as in the story." And finally, further east, they come to the Kalli Pōta Rāju Maṇḍapa, which represents the battlefield, although the battlefield, about the size of a soccer field as presently seen, lies beyond it. The battlefield is called *kallipāḍu* or *kallipaḍu*, probably "the horror and desolation" or "horror and falling," and resembles the Tamil paṭukaḷam not only in function and (partially) in name, but in being represented by "Kalli Potharaju." At this stone Pōta Rāju, the ritual warriors fall on their weapons like the heroes of the epic. According to the Pīṭhādhipati, they place their weapons down on *tangela* saplings which grow around Kalli Pōtu Rāja, and lie down there.[82] Two days later, when the ritualists return, the Pīṭhādhipati and a man from Brahma Nāyuṭu's clan sacrifice a goat, mix the blood with boiled rice, and throw it in the air. People who come to the festival take the saplings home and tie them to their doorsills to ward off evil.[83]

[81]It is tempting to relate Kārempūḍi/Kāryamapūḍi etymologically to Kurukṣetra, implying for both a "field of action." The Pīṭhādhipati, however, calls Kārempūḍi the "Andhra Kurukṣetra," but derives the name from Kāra, a Rākṣasa defeated by Rāma in the *Rām*, who "ruled this village" (*pūḍi* from *puri*). Kurukṣetra also becomes a cremation ground (see chap. 14).

[82]The Pīṭhādhipati says that "Pōta Rāju can replace a jammi tree in rituals." The Kalli Pōta Rāju, a site short of the battlefield, may thus recall the jammi where the youthful heroes gathered before the war.

[83]Other than the discussion of the name *kalli pādu/padu*, on which see Hiltebeitel 1991a,

There is thus an evident isomorphism between these battlefield rituals and two stories: the Palnad people's procession from Pālamācāpuri and the story of Pōta Rāju and the Śivanandi Fort. Looking at the two stories together, we see how Viṣṇu (Brahma Nāyuḍu, Cennakēśvara) doubly guarantees that Pōta Rāju or his jammi multiform is brought with ritual weapons from a distant fort-city (Pālamācāpuri, Śivanandi Fort) to Palnāḍu, to serve in the Palnad heroes' cult at the battlefield site of Kārempūḍi, much as Kṛṣṇa brings Pōttu Rāja with his cultic implements from the fort city of Śivānandapuri to serve the Pāṇḍavas and Draupadī at Kurukṣetra and the Draupadī cult at its paṭukaḷam (ritual battlefield). Thus even though Brahma Nāyuḍu has nothing explicit to do with the jammi tree death of Anapōtu Rāju, the scene is overdetermined by his rapports with Cennakēśvara the "old Brahman" and the bringing of Pōta Rāju, without whom Anapōtu Rāju is inconceivable.[84]

Brahma Nāyuḍu too works in strange and hidden ways. Having just readied the leaf plates for the intercaste meal that will signal peace and avoid war, he tells Kannama Dāsu to see if anyone is coming "with blessed food." Between the plate-setting and the request, the bard says, "Brahma Nāyuḍu is beyond description, the seer of the human world, Viṣṇu incarnate. He knew what was about to happen." What he foresees, and tells the Dalit Kannama to look for, is the arrival of Akka Pinakka, who will come with the food that wives have prepared for their husbands, the assembled heroes. After handing out home-cooking to many heroes, but telling Brahma Nāyuḍu that Māncāla has prepared nothing for Bāluḍu, Akka Pinakka serves up on Bāluḍu's leaf-plate what Māncāla has really prepared: "the leaf cup of blood" from Anapōtu Rāju's death at the jammi (344-46). Instantly, Bāluḍu goes crazy and the war erupts.

Let us recall that Brahma Nāyuḍu is not only Viṣṇu's avatar, but is identified with Kṛṣṇa. Here we must finally reject Roghair's strained insistence that "No stories in the epic cycle connect [Brahma Nāyuḍu] with the Viṣṇu of Hindu mythology"; that "Nothing important that Brahma Nāyuḍu does is specifically connected with any stories of Viṣṇu from outside the epic tradition" (1982, 108, 109-10). Brahma Nāyuḍu fights with no weapon (evoking Kṛṣṇa) other than a boar's tusk (evoking the Boar avatāra) (180); like Kṛṣṇa, he brings on the climactic war of

---

167-68, citing Roghair 1982, 29, and V. Narayana Rao, personal communication 1988, the description here follows that of the Pīṭhādhipati (January 1997).

[84]Not surprisingly, the Brahmanical variants which make Anapōtu Rāju the senior brother and eliminate his complicities with Māncāla (see nn. 30, 39), efface his ambiguous rapport with Pōta Rāju. I consider them secondary. Predictably, the Brahman Pīṭhādhipati maintains there is "no connection" between Pōta Rāju and Anapōta Rāju. In Āliśeṭṭi Gāleyya's version, sung by one of the authoritative Māla singers of *Palnāḍu* (the *Vidyavantulu*) whom the Pīṭhādhipati officially supports (Roghair 1982, 26), this is untenable.

destruction, and is rebuked, like Kṛṣṇa, for his treacheries, which include behind-the-scenes manipulations to bring about the deaths of menacing young heroes.[85] When the "old Brahman" at last withdraws his favor from Bāluḍu, so does Brahma Nāyuḍu.[86] Brahma Nāyuḍu's evocations of Kṛṣṇa and his rapports with Viṣṇu-Cennakēśvara are at the theological nub of this epic. He is as "notorious" and "mischievous" as Māyavar in *Elder brothers*, and as Kṛṣṇa in the *Mahābhārata*.

[85]Most notably, the death of Ala Rācamallu, which becomes the pretext by which he provokes the war (Roghair 1982, 273-90, 296, 319, 344-45, 359-60).
[86]When Bāludu fights Narasinga Rāju, Visnu not only shapes the outcome as Brahma Nāyudu incarnate, but is symbolically omnipresent in the combat: Bāluḍu, born on Kṛsna's birthday, reminds Narasinga of Kṛṣṇa (Roghair 1982, 351, 356), and Narasinga, evoking Viṣṇu's Narasimha avatar, disembowels his foe, but this time as one who is the hero rather than a demon. When Narasinga disembowels him, Bāluḍu, still protected by Viṣṇu and Ankālamma, continues fighting after removing all his out-hanging guts, leaves them on a tree for Garuḍa, and replaces them with tulasi leaves until he pulls off Narasinga's head "along with the veins and tendons" (354, 358). Only after this does Brahma Nāyuḍu provoke an argument with Bāluḍu, indicating the point at which Visnu ceases to protect Bāludu's life (as he ceases to protect the lives of the twins). One is reminded of Visnu's omnipresence in the *Mbh* war: through Kṛṣṇa on the Pāṇḍava side and his Gopa-Nārāyana warriors on the Kaurava side (Biardeau 1978, 205-9; cf. Hiltebeitel 1989a, 95).

4 The Epic of *Pābūjī*

Pābūjī, a north Indian regional martial oral epic, allows us to substantiate in some detail our analysis of *Palnāḍu* and *Elder Brothers*. They are clearly of the same species, having the same skeleton. To further flesh it out, I will run *Pābūjī* through the same eight "functions" that carried the stories along in chapter 3, asking the reader to bear in mind that I am not, in this case, suggesting direct transmission between the stories but rather some deeper problems to investigate in later chapters. *Pābūjī* introduces two new issues. Its primary process epical matter comes from the *Rāmāyaṇa* rather than the *Mahābhārata*. And it "feeds" from a northern climate of themes and tale types. We will need to ask whether it makes a difference for an oral epic to be framed by one classical epic or the other, and to think through the differences between northern regional martial oral epics and southern ones.

I rely on the recited oral version of the epic sung by Parbū Bhopo, recorded, transcribed, and translated by J. D. Smith (1991). *Bhopo* is the title for "scheduled caste" (Dalit) Nāyak Bhīls who sing *Pābūjī*, reciting it mainly for dominant caste Rajputs and Rebārī camel herders. The three castes form the primary group that worships Pābūjī in connection with the goddess Deval (1991, 4). One should note, however, that although all Rajasthan Rajputs claim royal descent, there are high or royal, middle or noble, and "little brother" or "village Rajput" classes among them (Harlan 1992, 6-9). Pābūjī is a god primarily of the latter, but one whose story links him with the higher ranks as well.

As Smith has shown, the oral text is highly regularized and formulaic.[1] He finds evidence from the seventeenth century chronicler Mūhato Naiṇasī "that *bhopos* of Pābūjī were established as early as the sixteenth century" (1991, 30). Although different bhopos know different portions, and none ever recites the whole epic sequentially, as Parbū did for Smith, the material has a high consistency. The bhopo, travelling with

[1]Smith 1977, 144-52; 1989, 5-7; 1991, 21-25, 266-67.

another family member, usually his wife (6, 14), performs the epic itinerantly using a cloth painting called a *paṛ* to depict the story along with its telling.

The paṛ, which extends the "boundaries of the text" through this visual and fluid form, sometimes varies narratively from the sung epic. It is set up as a semi-enclosure that defines the performance space as a "portable temple" for Pābūji that is centered on his court at Koḷū village.[2] In the epic, this "small desert village" is frequently "dignified as *Koḷūmaṇḍa*, 'Koḷū the religious centre'" (Smith 1991, 284, n. 42). Today it supports Pābūjī's only two "conventional temples," both on a single plot of land where Pābūjī has been worshiped since the beginning of the sixteenth century (6, 100, n. 5). The paṛ, as Pābūjī's "portable temple," thus brings his court and sanctum into the countryside. But Pābūjī's village, palace, and temple are also his fort, known as the "great village fortress of Koḷū" (430). As such, it includes the "fortress" of the lady Deval (the goddess), whose cows Pābūjī must protect (406-9). One may suspect that the goddess's "fortress" is an extension of Pābūjī's (they are adjacent on the paṛ; 56-57), or, even more suggestively, that Deval is the living embodiment of the goddess of his fort or palace.[3] As the Rāṭhoṛ (Rathaur) king, Pābūjī is lord of the "fifty-two forts" (298), implying his dominion over numerous other kings whose forts are mentioned in the story. But in real life, Koḷū "was and is a tiny and insignificant desert village" (2). Even to the epic's heroes, it is always "Koḷū in the barren sand desert." And by the end of the epic, it is a palace-fort no more.[4]

1. Births of the Heroes

Parbū Bhopo begins *Pābūjī* with an *āratī* song, "an invocation to open the performance," called *Jalampatrī*, "Horoscope" (Smith 1991, 106, 269). The story is thus framed not only by *Rāmāyaṇa* but set in the stars, and the two settings are probably not unrelated.[5] The stars also frame

[2]Smith 1986, 53; 1991, 6, 15-16, 55-68.

[3]A Rajasthani lineage deity (*kuldevī*) temple is normally in the men's quarters or *mardana* (Harlan 1992, 86-89, 101-2). Pābūjī's two Kolū temples "are evidently converted Vaisnava temples," with stones in the courtyard for his companions and Rūpnāth, but "nothing for Deval" (J. D. Smith, personal communication, February 19, 1998). Cf. chap. 2, n. 78.

[4]At the end, Pābūjī's bride inspects his empty palace (Smith 1991, 457). Some years later, his sole descendant Rūpnāth, growing up elsewhere, makes toy forts (464) until Deval tells him, "Kolū in the barren sand-desert is known as your village" (466). The boy learns that "Kolū in the barren sand-desert is known as my house and home" (467), but after exacting revenge, he becomes a wandering *jogī* (from Sanskrit *yogin, yogī*).

[5]See Smith 1991, 333-80: the she-camel quest follows the "unseen" road to Laṅkā, which is "beyond the seven seas" from which none return. This recalls Hanumān's starry leap to Laṅkā in *Rām* 4.66-5.1, whose "path will resemble the milky way" (4.66.15-16; see Lefe-

virtually every journey in *Pābūjī*, as the heroes formulaically set out and return on a road "past midnight, shining with stars." Such journeys include a pilgrimage to lake Pushkar, an expedition to Laṅkā for she-camels, and recurrent episodes of rustling, rescuing, finding, and driving cows.[6] Framing epic stories with allusion to a setting in the stars is, I argue elsewhere, a convention established in the *Mahābhārata*, and familiar to the *Rāmāyaṇa*.[7] It is also a purāṇic convention which we shall meet again in discussing the *Bhaviṣya Purāṇa*'s version of *Ālhā*.

The first verse is, "In the Saṃvat year thirty-seven Lord Pābūjī took incarnation in a plot of saffron."[8] The next three verses tell us how his nymph-mother took the form of a tigress to suckle him, and that he grew into "a strong young man." The fifth completes his introduction by invoking his "standard epithet" and royalty: "Lakṣmaṇa, the ascetic deity of the sand-desert, sat on the throne" (Smith 1991, 269 and n. 5). Although Parbū does not incorporate them into his recorded narrative, he knows stories that supply Pābūjī with the genealogy shown in table 3.[9]

---

ber 1994, 193, 362; cf. 5.1.157-63). It is probably from this that *Pābūjī* gets the idea that Laṅkā, to which it no doubt adds the she-camels, is an astronomical conundrum. According to Alberuni, Hindu astronomers "determine the longitude of the inhabitable world by Lanka, which lies in its center on the equator"; they "say that Lanka is between the two ends of the inhabitable world and without latitude," and further that it is "30 *yojana* above the earth," a southward point "foreboding evil" and "impious actions," and on the "line on which the astronomical calculations are based (as 0 degrees longitude)" which runs straight from Laṅkā to Meru through Ujjain, Multan, Kurukṣetra, the Yamunā, and Himavat (Sachau 1962, 408-9, 413-15). This cosmological Laṅkā would thus be due south on the equator from the elliptical north pole, well to the southwest of Sri Lanka, which is north of the equator and east of such a line on the equatorial north pole; cf. fig. 4.1 in Sullivan 1996.

[6]Among numerous usages, see Smith 1991, 289-91, 294-96, 333, 333-80 (journey to Laṅkā: see n. 5), 381-98, 409, 425, 435, and especially 397 and 415: Pābūjī's mare [his mother] can "ride up into the night (sky) with its constellations" and "break the stars from the sky to bring you; I shall introduce you to the court of the innocent (god) Rāma"; there are also many usages in the Laṅkā journey (333-80).

[7]See Hiltebeitel forthcoming and in press-h with reference to Naimiṣa Forest, setting of the *Mbh*'s outermost frame, as the "twinkling forest." At *Rām* 7.82.13; 83.2-4, Vālmīki's ashram at Naimiṣa Forest on the Gomatī is the site of Rāma's Aśvamedha, where Rāma hears his own story from his sons Kuśa and Lava—a usage like the *Mbh*'s of the narrative convention of linking Naimiṣa Forest with collapsible stories in frames.

[8]The Saṃvat era date, Smith explains (1991, 269, n. 1), is a "37" without the prior two digits; "Interpretations favoured by *bhopos* are 1237 (=1180 A.D.) and 1337 (=1280 A.D.)."

[9]Smith 1991, 493, n. 2, supplies Parbū's variant of the account by the seventeenth-century Naiṇasī, from whom I infer that Sonā is Pābūjī's older sister. Their mother has evidently already had Sonā, and (as a lioness) is suckling Pābūjī, who is thus her baby, when she leaves him and her husband (ibid., 481).

Table 3. Genealogy of Pābūjī

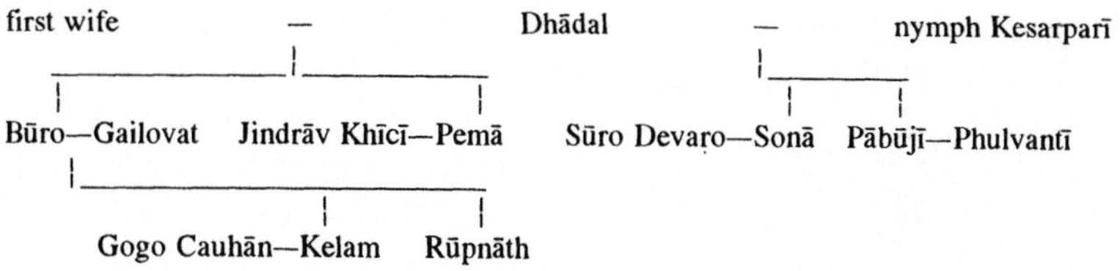

We shall meet them all, and for the moment need only note that Pābūjī's "plot of saffron" birthplace has two extensions related to his mother Kesarparī, who leaves Pābūjī as a baby because her husband sees her suckling him as a tigress.[10] Her name means "the nymph Saffron," and the form in which she promises Pābūjī to return is as his mare Kesar Kāḷamī, "Black Saffron" (Smith 1991, 269, n. 2).

After the "Horoscope's" opening five lines about Pābūjī, the next thirteen tell us that his four chief companions are also incarnations. In order of mention, the first three (dealt with in eight lines) are incarnations of goddesses. Cādo "the chieftain, king" (Rajput by birth, Nāyak-Bhīl by upbringing), the shepherd-camel herder Harmal Devāsī (a Rebārī), and the augurer Saljī Soḷaṅkī are avatāras of Mother Cāmuṇḍā, Mother Bhaisāḍ (whose "name clearly contains a reference to the buffalo-demon," Mahiṣāsura), and Mother Vīsot (Parbū's family deity), respectively.[11] The fourth companion, Cādo's brother Ḍhēbo, demarcated from the other three, gets a fuller description of five verses like Pābūjī's: "What man shall we commemorate next? Ḍhēbo used to dissolve a twelve-maund ball of bhang [hashish] (to drink); he used to eat thirteen maunds of opium. Ḍhēbo was known as an incarnation of Hanumān; he was called a chieftain of Pābūjī" (Smith 1991, 271-72). Ḍhēbo is this epic's LSRSC, and will reward our continuing attention.

For the moment, this prologue makes one thing apparent. The group of five chief heroes is composed of three backgrounded incarnations of goddesses and two foregrounded incarnations from the *Rāmāyaṇa*. Other incarnations in *Pābūjī* largely replicate and reinforce this goddess-*Rāmāyaṇa* scheme, the only one not to do so being Gogo Cauhāṇ, incarnation of the serpent Vāsuki.[12] Smith, however, tries to pick this texture apart: "Putting aside 'doubtful' incarnations such as Pābūjī's mare and his

[10]Or lioness; see n. 9.

[11]Smith 1991, 269-70, verses 6-12 and nn. 7-9 on the goddesses; 391, n. 227 and below on the double-caste identity of Cādo and Ḍhēbo.

[12]Smith 1991, 298-9, 307. On Gogo, see discussion in chap. 2.

companions, it is generally agreed that four figures in the epic story are *avatāras*. Pābūjī himself . . . ; Jindrāv Khīcī is said to be an avatāra of Rāvaṇa; Pābūjī's bride Phulvantī is said to be an *avatāra* of Rāvaṇa's sister Surapañkhā [Śūrpaṇakhā]; and Deval the Cāraṇ lady is said to be an *avatāra* of the goddess. The reason for the reincarnation of these figures is that the Rāma-story leaves them with unfinished business" (1991, 93). The last point is nicely made. But what is at stake is the nature of the unfinished business. The notion that Rāvaṇa and Lakṣmaṇa renew their opposition in a second birth looks to be a variation on a theme known in Jain traditions that they oppose each other as "hero and antihero" through a series of many lives and ages (Ramanujan 1991b, 34). *Pābūjī's Rāmāyaṇa* frame story is an artful bardic handling of primary process folklore.

Smith's distinction between "doubtful" and "generally agreed" upon incarnations is artificial. Among the companions, he has trouble with Ḍhēbo, conceding in a footnote that, "*avatāra* or not, Ḍhēbo does behave very much as though he were an incarnation of Hanumān."[13] The distinction also glosses over important questions. If, as it appears, the main criterion for genuine incarnation is unfinished business that carries the four "generally agreed" upon incarnations from one epic to the other, what is the implied unfinished business of the goddess in the Rāma-story that motivates her incarnation as Deval? Does Deval incarnate a *Rāmāyaṇa* goddess? If so, who is she? And, whatever her associations, how "human" is this goddess's incarnation in *Pābūjī*? She is everywhere so thoroughly a goddess that it seems misleading to contrast her "human motive" with her "cosmic motivation" (94). If the goddess has "unfinished business" that carries over from the *Rāmāyaṇa* to *Pābūjī*, there is no reason to dismiss her triple incarnation among Pābūjī's companions any more than her incarnation as Deval. The same goes for Kesar Kāḷamī, Pābūjī's mare, being an incarnation of his "nymph" mother.[14]

Smith is not, however, only arguing that some *Pābūjī* incarnations are "doubtful," but—supporting Blackburn's views (see chapter 2)—that incarnation in *Pābūjī* is part of a belated process of "deification," which can be deconstructed by deducing a trail back to the "historical Pābūjī": a deified brigand, cattle raider, and small Rajput chief.[15] Despite admitt-

[13]1991, 100-1, n. 15. I mention the footnoting practice because Smith peripheralizes important mythological considerations consistently in this way, especially in the chapter "Pābūjī the god."

[14]A Parī, or Apsaras according to Nainasī (Smith 1991, 481 and 493, n. 2).

[15]Smith types Pābūjī as a Robin Hood (1991, 89-91) and deified dacoit or brigand (1980, 53-55, 76, n. 10), but, if so, he is just as much a residual Vrātya: a Vedic cattle rustling type that collapses the distinction between Kṣatriya and Brahman and anticipates early Rajput vagabondage of the type described by Kolff (1990; see below, chap. 10).

ing Pābūjī's diverse cult and a "developed mythological account of his position in the universe," these "probable reasons" buttress Smith's determination to explain incarnations away (91). The "probable reasons" do not pass scrutiny.

First, the category of "doubtful" avatāras is designed to cover several variations. One is nonliteralness. Some bhopos, Smith says, take the "doubtfuls" as "literally true," while "others say it is merely a way of explaining that these heroes had received the blessing of the deities in question"—for example, "that 'Hanumān had placed his hand on Ḍhēbo's head'" (1991, 91). The notion of literalness is introduced here as a way of turning a metonymic connection of blessing that links deity and hero into something "mere." Literalness is then taken to imply exaggeration. Some bhopos, in calling Pābūjī's mare Kesar Kāḷamī a Sagatī, "take the word literally" and regard her as an "incarnation of the Goddess" (*Sagatī* = Śakti), while for others, including Parbū, it "simply means that Pābūjī's mount is 'powerful'" (*śakti*) and is "not literally" a reference to the goddess.[16] Smith discounts here a conventional resonance in favor of a likely rationalization.[17] Literalness is also buttressed by metaphor, which Smith turns to advantage by noting that Parbū accounts for some "doubtful" avatāras (270, n. 7) and certain *Rāmāyaṇa* themes as metaphoric. Thus he is "conscious" (like Smith) that Laṅkā is a "metaphor" (83-84). Parbū's account of Pābūjī's raid of Laṅkā is a "confessedly 'untrue' story" (96); Pābūjī had gone not to Laṅkā but to a village called Laṅkesariyo "located across the water in Sindh or Kutch" (83). "Sindh or Kutch" is pretty vague: Parbū's historicizing looks more like remythicization.[18] But Smith, despite admitting that his information from

[16]Smith 1991, 91; 323, n. 125; cf. 285, n. 43.

[17]Cf. Kothari 1989, 114-15 on the leading heroines of numerous Rajasthani folk epics, including folk *Rām* and *Mbh*: "These negative heroines and goddesses are known in Rajasthan by the word *sagatī*, which means Śakti (power or energy)."

[18]Laṅkā, on which see n. 5, seems to be an "othering" trope in Indian folk epics. The *BhvP* version of *Ālhā* gives Ālhā's son Indula a brief first marriage to a Laṅkā princess named Padminī, daughter of Āryasiṃha (*BhvP* 3.3.19), before his second to the Bāhlīka-Balkh princess Citrarekhā (3.3.23; W&G 212-14). Cf. Muhammad Jayasī's *Padmavat*, whose heroine Padmini comes from Simhala [Laṅkā]. The purānic author could have been influenced by the Padminī myth, which Qanungo credits the mid-sixteenth century Jayasī with inventing (1969, 1-20). Concerning this "Simhala," Qanungo chides a colleague disturbed by the "dark-skinned" features this Rajput paragon would have were she really from Laṅkā: "'If we accept Simhala as correct,' says [Ramchandra] Shuklaji, 'this must be some place in Rajputana'" (17-18). See McGregor 1984, 67-70 on this text and author, and White 1996, 198-99, 236, 260-62 on alchemical allegory in this story which locates the paradisal Plantain Forest in the "heavenly" seven-storied fortress of Laṅkā that is itself attainable only by yoga. Sankalia (1973, 48-53) and others unconvincingly locate Laṅkā in north India to suit an "originally" local Rāma story; cf. Kibe (1939) with supportive photos

different bhopos "is limited and uneven" (1991, 91), generalizes this understanding: "the performers explain that the attack on Rāvaṇa is a piece of narrative exaggeration, a 'metaphor' for a relatively minor local exploit" (1986, 64, n. 6).

For Smith, literalization, exaggeration, and metaphor are tools to recover a presumed historical original and an unembellished prior text. In insisting on a fixed text, Smith treats myth and metaphor as if they have somehow permeated this prior text's membrane. He peripheralizes epic-related mythology that Parbū knows—for example, about Kesar Kāḷamī[19]—and makes no more than passing mention of variations between the oral epic and the visualized paṛ.[20] Similarly, he marginalizes the avatar mythology about Viṣṇu's gatekeepers Jaya and Vijaya, which frames *Pābūjī*'s *Rāmāyaṇa* frame as the story behind the "generally agreed upon" incarnations. Some bhopos know it, but others "are not well informed about this background mythology, and could contribute little on the subject" (1991, 91). Here, where Parbū is on the side of the knowledgeable, Smith favors the uninformed, and downgrades Parbū's evidence: "Parbū's version of the standard mythological frame-story" is "not performed as part of the epic" (1986, 54). Smith dismisses Indological comment on it as "not particularly enlightening."[21]

We have here, in short, a strategy for treating "doubtful" aspects of *Pābūjī*'s incarnational scheme as formulaic (read: nonliteral, exaggerated, metaphoric, mere, and simple) and interpolated (read: not performed as part of the main recited text). As so often with scholarship on India's classical epics, formula and interpolation overlap in sustaining a rationalized and historicized hermeneutic.[22] One thing needed here is an appreciation of intratextual and intertextual allusion, and the play of tropes. One cannot unravel a process of textual development in *Pābūjī* by showing that particular avataric links have different associational principles (literal, figurative; metaphor, metonym; doubtful, consensual). Multivalence and ambivalence are to be expected. Ambivalence is itself

---

of humans with tails; Thapar 1978b, nn. 11, 51, and 96, seeming to favor this view with other citations. Rāja Desing's horse tries to shake him while flying to Laṅkā; from Laṅkā according to Alberuni comes the ill wind that brings smallpox (Sachau 1962, 415-16).

[19]Smith 1991, 493, n. 2; cf. 498-500.

[20]On variance between paṛ and epic, see especially Smith 1991, 427 (scene 74), 436 (78), 438 (79), 451 (86), 456-59 (88-91), all discussed below.

[21]Smith 1991, 92 and n. 17. Roghair argues similarly against *Palnādu*'s treatment of Brahma Nāyudu as an avatar, favoring his "own experience," which "suggests that few residents of Palnādu who are interested in the Heroes but not directly involved in the cult are more than marginally acquainted with or interested in the equation of Brahma Nāyuḍu with Visnu. He is known as a Visnu bhakta; that is sufficient" (1982, 109-10).

[22]See chap. 2 at n. 21.

an ironic trope within *Pābūjī*. Characters sometimes have their own doubts about incarnations. Guru Gorakhnāth, seeing Pābūjī's nephew Rūpnāth, thinks, "This little boy is some incarnation" (Smith 1991, 467). He is wrong, but only so far as we know from Parbū. Harmal Devāsī, disguised as a jogī, seems to the cameleers of Laṅkā "like some incarnation" or to be Guru Gorakhnāth (355, 360). Here they are right that he is an incarnation, but haven't guessed whose "doubtful" incarnation he is. And at the crucial moment when Phulvantī announces her determination to marry Pābūjī, her mother suspects that either she is a goddess incarnate, or that she has received a secret letter from Pābūjī. Phulvantī says neither is true (387), but the listener knows that Phulvantī's mother has intuitively grasped one of the nondoubtful incarnational threads of the epic: that her daughter incarnates Śūrpaṇakhā, reborn for her fateful marriage with the incarnation of Lakṣmaṇa. As in the classical epics, when someone asks, "Who are you? A goddess, an Asurī, a Yakṣī, A Rākṣasī, or a Mānuṣī?" it is a cat-and-mouse game for all concerned, whether they are inside the epic as characters, or into it as performers, audience, or readers.

Finally, Smith agrees with Blackburn (1989, 110) and Kothari (1989, 110) that, quoting the latter, *Pābūjī* "is an elaborated story of a *bhomiyā* god," a type of local hero in Rajasthan commemorated and divinized for having died defending cattle.[23] But Smith must override an informant to say this: "I was able, by a sequence of admittedly leading questions, to elicit from one *bhopo* a direct statement that Pābūjī was 'like a *bhomiyo*'; but once he realized what he had said, he insisted that Pābūjī was far more powerful than any *bhomiyo*" (1991, 100, n. 10). Now a scholar may see things informants do not, and try to elicit confirmation of a would-be insight. But the bhopo's cautionary note reflects a sense of hierarchy that the epic itself unfolds, as when a bhomiyo god comes at an appropriately low niche among the deities in the divine processions to Gogo's and Pābūjī's weddings (313, 402).[24] Smith (again, in a footnote) delineates *Pābūjī*'s divine hierarchy himself: "above" the "little gods of the present age (Pābūjī, Rāmdev etc.)" are "the greater gods of the previous age (Rāma, Kṛṣṇa etc.)"; above them are "the great gods themselves (Viṣṇu, Śiva and the Goddess)," and above them "exists a being—God—to whom Parbū refers indiscriminately as *bhagavān*, *īśvar* and

[23]See chap. 2, § B. The *bhomiyā/bhumiyo* is a type of divinized hero found widely in India in connection with hero stones, which also often commemorate heroes slain defending cattle. Ḍhebo, however, is more "like a *bhomiyo*" than Pābūjī.

[24]On the hierarchy relevant to *Pābūjī*, see Srivastava 1997, 80-88. That Pābūjī is "like a *bhomiyo*" is at best a forced folk analogy, a typology recognizable to the bhopo for some parallels but not evidence of a developmental process, much less of prior historicity.

qudrat, the connotations of which are, respectively, Vaiṣṇava, Śaiva and Islamic" (101, n. 22). Considering, as we shall in chapter 10, that Rāmdev (Rāmdeo, Rāmshāh Pīr) and Gogo (Guga Pīr) also have Muslim identities, this hierarchy twice has a double Islamic and bhakti register. At no point is the bhomiyo commensurate with Rāmdev or Pābūjī.

But for Smith, there is a kind of ascending scale of divinization that runs from slain hero to bhomiyo to Pābūjī and on up the ladder. Thus he wonders whether Pābūjī "will ever meet with [the] similar success" of Rāma and Kṛṣṇa, whose "devotees . . . also employed epic for the same purpose": that of providing "a mythological background" to their story because they were "originally motivated by the desire to secure a higher status for the god by linking him to the gods of the 'Great tradition'" (1991, 99). Apparently there was a "Great tradition" before the divinization of Rāma and Kṛṣṇa! In invoking their supposed epical divinization, Smith is reiterating the euhemerist arguments of Hopkins, who finds this route to explaining the "deification" of Kṛṣṇa in his epic studies,[25] and of both Rāma and Kṛṣṇa in his apologetically Christian comparative religion studies.[26] Rather than such a tiresome and anachronistic developmental legitimation scheme, I would say that *Pābūjī* poses a different issue. Rāma is not a type of deity Pābūjī might become. He is the central figure in *Pābūjī*'s incarnational drama. Where is Rāma in this scheme? The answer is obvious. He is in heaven, where the heroes—specifically Ḍhēbo, Pābūjī, Būṛo, and Rūpnāth—go at the epic's end, having passed on to meet again in "the court of the innocent (god) Rāma."[27] Why is Rāma the absent avatar in this story? Because the *Rāmāyaṇa*'s "perfect man" has no unfinished business. He does not descend. But he is the center and goal of *Pābūjī*'s devotional universe.[28] This is indeed one of the ways that it makes a difference whether it is *Rāmāyaṇa* or *Mahābhārata* that is linked with a regional folk epic: in *Mahābhārata*-linked regional folk epics, there is nothing to inhibit the avatar's re-descent. Kṛṣṇa's devious business seems to be unending.

2. Marriage and Virginity

An unconsummated marriage, generated by leftover business from the *Rāmāyāṇa*, lies, as we have now seen, near the heart of this tale. Smith summarizes Parbū's account, which forms part of the frame story. When Rāvaṇa's sister Surapaṅkhā saw Rāma, Sītā, and Lakṣmaṇa in the forest,

[25]Hopkins [1901] 1969, 215-16, 376, 397-98.

[26]Hopkins 1918, 209-17; 1923, 310-12.

[27]On this recurrent formula, see Smith 1991, 415, 440-41, 452-56, 460.

[28]A similar conundrum, and distinctively North Indian answer, will be found in *Ālhā*.

she "became infatuated with the beauty of the two young men." Rāma refused her, saying he was married already, and told her to try Lakṣmaṇa. Lakṣmaṇa also rejected her, "saying he was an ascetic who could have nothing to do with women" (1991, 92-93). Smith does not annotate this exchange, which has the possibility of relieving Rāma of a lie and passing it on to Lakṣmaṇa, since, at least in the *Vālmīki Rāmāyaṇa*, when Rāma passes Śūrpaṇakhā along, it is only he who says Lakṣmaṇa is unmarried, which is untrue.[29] In any case, commotion erupts, and Lakṣmaṇa, as one expects from *Vālmīkī* 3.17.21, cuts off Surapaṅkhā's nose and ears. But now in *Pābūjī* he promises that he will "marry her in another birth—but would not then live with her after the wedding" (Smith 1991, 93). Thus Lakṣmaṇa and Śūrpaṇakhā are reincarnated as Pābūjī and Phulvantī.

Phulvantī's arousal of passion for Pābūjī is suitably momentous. Stringing pearls, she hears him driving the she-camels he has plundered from Laṅkā into Ūmarkoṭ, her father's fort. The earth trembles from the hoofbeats of Kesar Kāḷamī. By the shaking of the pearls in her tray, Phulvantī sees that "either total famine will strike the land, or a king will arise to rule the earth." One of Pābūjī's epithets is "the Hindu king" (Smith 1991, 294, 323). Through her lattice window she sees Pābūjī enter the barren garden of the Soḍhos (her Rajput patriline), and falls in love: "Lord Pābūjī's brilliance is like that of the sun; Pābūjī appears to me spotless like the moon." His magic makes the garden turn green after twelve years of barrenness. The seventeenth-century chronicler Naiṇasī, surely drawing on a mythological tradition but one that Parbū does not mention, says Pābūjī is only twelve at this point (489).

Phulvantī is with her *tījaṇī* sisters, her cohort of girls who celebrate reaching menarche with the swinging festival of Tīj in the month of Sāvaṇ (Śravaṇa).[30] Beautifully adorned, they go out to the garden, fashion a swing, and observe the heroes. Phulvantī makes a chaplet for Pābūjī's head and sends it to him by the gardener's wife. Pābūjī resists, saying, "drive back this gardener's wife! she will bring ill-repute to Lakṣmaṇa, the ascetic deity of the sand-desert. I took incarnation in a plot of saffron, in a lotus-flower; I am called an incarnation of Lakṣmaṇa the ascetic. I cannot look at the face of a woman as she comes towards me, nor at the

[29]See Erndl 1991 for an excellent discussion of some of this episode's variants; see also Goldman 1997, 194-95.

[30]Although it is probably implied, it is not indicated that Phulvantī has celebrated only her first Tīj, which would follow her first menstruation. But she is clearly a young maiden. Parbū introduces Tīj and tījaṇī sisters in connection with Kelam, daughter of Pābūjī's brother Būṛo (Smith 1991, 298-99, nn. 75, 78).

back of a woman as she goes away from me."[31] He recognizes the chaplet as "the work of a clever and skilful hand," but rather than ask who made it, he leaps back to the mission of delivering the she-camels to Kelam (372-80).

Rāmāyaṇa primary process is at work here in evoking Lakṣmaṇa's famous (even if interpolated) line that he recognizes Sītā's anklets, but not her upper-arm bracelet or earrings, because he worshiped only her feet:[32] an astounding ascetic achievement for the "ascetic deity of the sand desert" to emulate from his former life, easily implying that Lakṣmaṇa never saw Sītā's face or back. Lakṣmaṇa is never supposed to be an ascetic in *Vālmīkī*, but it would appear that this "ankle verse" marks an early tendency in this direction, and that folklores of his asceticism build upon it. Lakṣmaṇa tells the "ankle verse" to Rāma after Sītā has been abducted by Rāvaṇa, and the brothers have found some of the jewels she dropped while Rāvaṇa flew her to Laṅkā. It is all Lakṣmaṇa ever says that might allude to the sexually charged exchange he had with Sītā by which she left him little choice but to leave her unprotected, accusing him of wanting her as the reason he was not rescuing Rāma while Rāma was chasing the golden deer (3.43). Lakṣmaṇa's asceticism is thus grounded on the anger of Sītā and his denial—in every sense—of any attraction to her.

Pābūjī clearly intensifies Lakṣmaṇa's status as "the celibate ascetic (*bāljattī*)" (Smith 1991, 93). In Parbū's *Rāmāyaṇa* prologue, when Rāma questions Lakṣmaṇa's ability to shoot an arrow at the nose of one of the Sun-chariot's horses to enable the killing of Rāvaṇa, Lakṣmaṇa says his matted hair is full of fruit. Every day for fourteen years in the forest Rāma gave him fruit, but he forgot to command him to "Eat," so Lakṣmaṇa kept the fruit in his hair.[33] Ascetic power, encapsuled as semen, is stored in the head. *Pābūjī* builds here and elsewhere on a well-attested notion, heightened in Rajasthan, "that celibacy confers strength, whilst the expenditure of semen weakens a man."[34] Pābūjī's asceticism is no

[31]Smith 1991, 379. Pābūjī has said the same thing earlier when telling Gogo Cauhān not to ask him about marrying his brother's daughter Kelam, adding, "O righteous Gogo, I have no dealings with girls" (295). But he does arrange this wedding, and it is to Kelam that he promises the wedding gift of she-camels from Laṅkā.
[32]*Rām* 4,147*; see Goldman 1980, 167-70, on this oft-recalled verse, and a similar one interpolated at 7,890*, amid Lakṣmaṇa's "anti-sexual" moments in *Vālmīki*, including Rāma's "joke" about his celibacy to Śūrpaṇakhā, and Sītā's provocation in the golden deer episode.
[33]Smith 1991, 93, 101, n. 20. Cf. Ramanujan's story from a northern Karnataka folk play about the eunuchs of Ayodhyā (1986, 67-68).
[34]Smith 1991, 93, 101 n. 19; 1986, 62; citing Carstairs 1961, especially 78-88. Caṅkar's concern to safeguard the elder brothers' "virility" (*vīriyam*) by spurning their brides has a

doubt a factor in his alliance with the snake deity Gogo Cauhāṇ,[35] and in his hazardous adventures with she-animals (his mare, the she-camels, and Deval's cows).

Pābūjī gets away from this first entanglement with Phulvantī to deliver the she-camels to Kelam. The disconsolate Phulvantī reveals her choice to her mother, who suspects, as remarked, that she is a goddess incarnate. Her mother instantly sends a Brahman to arrange the wedding (Smith 1991, 387-88). The ascetic Pābūjī says that marriage would bring him ill-repute. Phulvantī should be given to his older brother Būṛo: "If I marry and become a householder what good would it do me? I shall not marry today, nor marry tomorrow. O brahmin, I have an elder brother (named) Būṛo; take this garland and go to his palace" (390). Again we must recall the *Rāmāyaṇa*. As with the passing-around of Śūrpaṇakhā by two brothers, so it is now with her incarnation Phulvantī, only with two inversions: the initial rejection is motivated by asceticism rather than monogamy, and the deferral is from younger brother to older.

At this point, Pābūjī's chieftains intervene and tell him he should marry and have offspring to perform ancestral rites, lest he become a wandering spirit (Smith 1991, 390 and n. 226). Pābūjī agrees, but only if saffron is obtained for his wedding procession. Cādo takes charge, and tells lady Deval that "without saffron Pābūjī will not become a bridegroom!"[36] From here on, we see that this incarnation of the goddess not only wants this marriage, but wants it unconsummated. Deval tells Cādo that saffron can be obtained from the gardens of the (Afghan) Muslim Lakkhū Paṭhāṇ, and Pābūjī and his chiefs obtain it in "the battle of the saffron" (399). Deval brings the wedding invitations to all the gods (400-3). But when Pābūjī sets out for his wedding, he is beset by bad omens, the first of which is Deval herself, blocking the way of his "virgin wedding-procession" and demanding that he leave someone behind to protect her fortress (which, we have seen, is an extension of Pābūjī's own fort) and her cows. Pābūjī says he has left the fifty-two heroes of the village and the sixty-four village yoginīs, but he refuses to leave any of his chieftains behind. Yet, although Deval is angered, Pābūjī asks for her "blessing" and promises her that if "any danger befalls" her, he will

---

Rajput look, considering that *vīriyam* can mean semen (see chap. 3, § 2C).

[35]It is when Gogo asks Pābūjī for Kelam, Pābūjī's brother's daughter, that Pābūjī first says the line about never seeing a woman's face or back, which he later says about Phulvantī (see n. 31). As with Śiva, the ascetic's association with snakes is probably an alliance with generative forces.

[36]Smith 1991, 391. On ambiguities in the use of saffron (*kesarīya*) for both the warrior facing death in battle and in women's songs in allusion to men's sexual potency, see Weinberger-Thomas 1996, 37. In bringing saffron into this conflict, Pābūjī evokes his mother.

come himself, "(even) if he is seated in the wedding pavilion!" (406-9).

The series of omens now continues to be quite fantastic: a snake god (to whom they give milk), vultures (who get raw goat organs), partridges (calling at midnight at the brightness of Pābūjī's spear), jackals (howling at the hoofbeats of Kesar Kāḷamī), and last, a tiger. When Ḍhēbo beheads the tiger, Pābūjī tells Ḍhēbo he has "done ill in the land; you have spilt drops of blood in my wedding procession!" Ḍhēbo, "distressed and sad," then asks Pābūjī to right things with his magic, and Pābūjī revives the tiger, rejoining its head and body (Smith 1991, 409-13). Ḍhēbo thus defiles the procession, despite his best intentions.

At last the Soḍhos greet the procession and escort it to Ūmarkoṭ. Girding his mare, Pābūjī prepares to honor the *toraṇ*, a "brightly coloured wooden emblem fastened on the door of the bride's house," which the groom honors on arrival "by touching it with a stick or sword" (Smith 1991, 319, n. 14). The Soḍhos have placed it on the battlements of their fort. But Pābūjī pauses. He tells Ḍhēbo he has not brought a proper stick to touch it with. "Ḍhēbo the opium-drinker went and stood by a *khejaṛī* tree; . . . [he] gave a roar like Hanumān; with a jerk he picked up the *khejaṛī* tree and returned with it on his shoulder. . . . He brought it and set it up in the ruby courtyard of the fortress" (417). The khejaṛī as "stick" is immediately identified further as a *tulasī* or "sacred basil," and a "gold stick," both of which are honorific, since the khejaṛī is a "highly prized" tree, to which we must return.[37] For now, Pābūjī uses it as his stick to strike the toraṇ and break off the seven wooden birds that the Soḍhos have placed on it.

Finally, at the highpoint of the wedding, before the circumambulations of the fire are complete, Pābūjī's mare Kesar Kāḷamī whinnies. As we have seen, she is his nymph mother. Pābūjī tells Cādo to "reassure" Kesar Kāḷamī lest he strike her with his whip (Smith 1991, 421). Cādo says Pābūjī should save his whip for enemies; it "would be painful for Kesar's spotless body." At this very moment, the mare breaks her chains and Deval appears as a gold bird to "bitterly" tell Pābūjī that while he is "rejoicing" in his nuptials, Jindrāv Khīcī has stolen her cows (421-22). Pābūjī interrupts the wedding to recover them. Phulvantī curses Khīcī with the death of his eldest son, but since Khīcī is Pābūjī's sister's husband, Pābūjī says she should soften the curse. Then Pābūjī cuts the bridal knot with his sword. As he mounts his mare, Phulvantī clings to his stirrup and rebukes Kesar Kāḷamī for spoiling her marriage: "as you brought Pābūjī, so you have taken him back!"

[37]Smith credits the *tulasī* identification as honorific, but says that Parbū uses the designation "gold stick" as "merely . . . a different formula containing a different colour-word" (1991, 418, nn. 264, 265). We will see that this latter association is not so "mere."

Unbeknownst to her, and probably also to Pābūjī, Phulvantī is cursing her mother-in-law, who, in league with Deval, is wrecking her marriage while typically problematizing the tensions of their daughter-in-law/mother-in-law relationship.[38] Pābūjī tells Phulvantī not to curse Kesar Kāḷamī, since he is fated to a short life. He makes "a little gold parrot from the bridal ointment on his back" for her to "hold in her hand," and tells her it will inform her whether he survives the battle (Smith 1991, 423-24). This gold parrot, colored no doubt by the turmeric or saffron in the ointment, has surely some metonymic connection with Pābūjī's black saffron mother Kesar Kāḷamī, but also with Deval's appearance as a gold bird.

3. The Virgin's Blessing

It is not hard to see that Pābūjī's asceticism is in tension with the contending motivations of Deval, the Sagatī Kesar Kāḷamī, and the virgin heroine Phulvantī, and that the motivations of these three females contend with each other only in appearance. Their deeper conflicts are with Pābūjī, who, in just one moment, breaks faith with two of them (Kesar Kāḷamī, Phulvantī) to make up for having broken faith with the third (Deval). It is also not hard to recognize the recurring folk epic icons of the heroine-goddess stringing pearls (cf. Smith 1991, 453) and holding parrot in hand. Recalling Taṅkāḷ and Māncāla, we may call Phulvantī here an icon of blessing, in that leave-giving always implies or denies a blessing. But Phulvantī gives no blessing other than her seeming agreement not to curse Jindrāv Khīci and Kesar Kāḷamī, and her acceptance, parrot-in-hand, that Pābūjī's departure likely means his death (424). Deval, however, has given a blessing out of anger. When Pābūjī refused her request to supply a guardian of her fort and cows, but told her he would leave even in the middle of his wedding to come himself, she answered him: "O Pābūjī, may your name remain immortal in the land; may your brave leading warriors remain immortal!" (409). This is a blessing that implies her revenge and the heroes' deaths, as is presaged by the immediate sequel of omens. Deval continues to give ambiguous curses and blessings, as we shall see.

4. Ḍhēbo's Intervention

It is in Ḍhēbo the opium-eater that we find *Pābūjī*'s LSRSC. In the seventeenth-century chronicle version of Naiṇasī, the brothers Cādo and

[38]The relationship, in its starkest undercurrents, destines Pābūjī to be celibate with his wife while "riding" his mare-mother. Cf. n. 36.

Ḍhēbo (variously spelled) are two of seven Thorī or Nāyak brothers—that is, Dalits—who become Pābūjī's servants (Smith 1991, 480-81). In the folk epic, Smith seems to regard them as Rajputs, but Tessitori describes Thorīs as "a wild tribe of pillagers of the desert" (1916, 106). A Dalit aspect also surfaces in a story that Parbū Bhopo tells, but outside his recited text. After Cādo and Ḍhēbo were born, their father learned they would bring him misfortune, put them in a box, and floated then down a river. A fisherman found the box and brought it home, "where there was a Nāyak (the Untouchable caste from which the bhopos of Pābūjī are drawn). The fisherman laid claim to the box, the Nāyak to its contents; then they opened it and found Cādo and Ḍhēbo inside. Thus the two brothers were Rajputs by birth but Nāyaks by upbringing" (Smith 1991, 391, n. 227). The brothers seem to split this double patrimony: the royal Cādo (268 and n. 6), Pābūjī's trusted confidante and emissary, exemplifies Rajput refinements, and the gigantic and impetuous Ḍhēbo the impure ritual services of the Dalit Nāyaks.[39]

This birth story recalls that of Karṇa, who was born a Kṣatriya, set floating down a river, and raised by the Sūta (chariot driver) couple who found him. Karṇa is the only *Mahābhārata* character invoked in Parbū's text, and is a powerful presence in *Pābūjī*. One reason may be that he is the son of the Sun, Sūrya, who constantly "disposes of (serious) business" (Smith 1991, 275, 303, 304, etc.). Since Pābūjī as a Rāṭhoṛ Rajput would share the Rāṭhoṛs' claimed solar dynasty or Sūryavaṃśa descent from Rāma (Tod [1829] 1984, 82-83), one may suspect that Karṇa is invoked as a solar kinsman. More clearly, he is linked with Deval, who is known as "the Cāraṇ lady" and one of the two "Cāraṇ sisters" along with her sister Karṇī. This latter, whose name resonates with Karṇa's, at least in *Pābūjī*, seems to have a wider recognition in Rajasthan than her sister as a lineage deity (*kuldevī*) not only of Cāraṇs but of Rāṭhoṛs, with a major shrine in Bikaner (Harlan 1992, 49, 71; Srivastava 1997, 66). As Cāraṇs, the two sister-goddesses belong to the bardic caste that composed poetry eulogizing Rajputs (Smith 1991, 19, 503), just as Sūtas—a "mixed caste" who, like the Nāyaks, performed as "epic bards" and encomiasts—eulogize and share a mixed identity with Kṣatriyas in the *Mahābhārata*. At mysterious moments in *Pābūjī*, the sister-pair appears

[39]Smith virtually ignores this double background (see only 1991, 450, n. 303), and sees Cādo and Ḍhēbo, like Poṉṉar and Caṅkar, Ālhā and Ūdal, Rāma and Laksmaṇa, Yudhiṣṭhira and Bhīma, and others, as representatives of a "split hero" dyad-type contrasting a passive hero aligned with *daiva*, fate, and a more violent hero who defies fate through *pauruṣa*, "manliness" (1989, 190-93; 1991, 95-96; cf. Goldman 1980; 1984, 54; Biardeau 1976, 143). Yet Nāyaks have their own myth of double identity, regarding themselves as "fallen Rajputs," having once been Rajputs themselves (Smith 1991, 18-19).

to "sing songs of praise of King Karṇa" and "parvāṛos (narrative episodes in *Pābūjī*) of Pābūjī" (334-35, 392, 394, 464)—the latter, evidently, prescient stories within the story.[40] Karṇa and Pābūjī give these goddesses gifts (335). These invocations of Karṇa allude to his proverbial generosity and caste ambiguity, and probably also evoke a tension between Dalit Nāyak epic bards and high status Cāraṇ eulogists. Nāyaks who sing *Pābūjī* would seem to honor Deval as their link with the more prestigious Cāraṇs, who eulogize Rajputs as scions of the Solar, Lunar, and Agni Vaṃśas. Thus when Cādo and Ḍhebo are floated down-river, mixed-caste resonances with Karṇa are probably textured into the story as markers of the aspirations of its bards.

Ḍhēbo supplies a rich concatenation of LSRSC traits, some already met. As an incarnation of Hanumān, he carries on in the spirit of Hanumān's services to Rāma and Lakṣmaṇa. All Rajputs and chieftains take opium in *Pābūjī*, including Pābūjī himself (Smith 1991, 374, 419), but Ḍhēbo does so to excess. He has an opium box so big that Deval's one-eye bull calf can be hidden in it (442). The Soḍhos amass camel-trains of opium for six months and store it in wells to shame Pābūjī at his wedding with more than he and his men can consume. Coming to Pābūjī's rescue, Ḍhēbo "gave a roar like Hanumān; Ḍhebo swallowed the opium in a single gulp."[41] Ḍhēbo's reputation also carries to other forms of "substance abuse": he "eats opium, he drinks bhang, he drinks datura" (326); he offers "opium, tobacco or datura" to a foe before killing him (383).[42] Only Ḍhebo, even in his last words, envisions continuing his habit in heaven: "I shall take my next opium in the court of the innocent (god) Rāma" (440, 441). His intake is similar to that of Cāmpukā, who takes opium, and of Muttāl Rāvuttan̲, who receives many drugs. It is a ritual service not only for Pābūjī, whom Ḍhēbo stands in for at Pābūjī's wedding, but for Rāma, whose heavenly court, like a Draupadī temple or the court-fort-temple of Pābūjī, keeps a place for such practices.

As with our other LSRSCs, however, Ḍhēbo's most decisive services to the hero are also, and more profoundly, ritually ambiguous acts that serve the goddess. When Ḍhēbo defiles Pābūjī's wedding procession by

[40]Cf. Roghair 1982, 197: In the course of the episode of the Birth of Ankamma in *Palnāḍu*, "A story-teller must come and sing the *Epic of Palnāḍu* and the birth of Ankamma." In both cases the epic is recited "within itself" in connection with its chief goddess.

[41]Smith 1991, 408, 419; for passage to Laṅkā, he similarly offers to "swallow up the sea," or "take the water in my cupped hand and throw it into the desert land of Marwar" (367).

[42]Smith (1991, 326, n. 130) notes on datura: "The juice of the thorn-apple, a powerful narcotic which, according to *Hobson-Jobson*, causes 'temporary alienation of mind, and violent laughter' (citing Yule and Burnell 1903 [= (1886) 1986], s.v. DATURA)." Khan 1997b, 200, thinks Indian references to tobacco cannot be earlier than the eighteenth century.

shedding the tiger's blood, and supplies the khejarī tree that Pābūjī uses to honor the toraṇ for his wedding, the goddess is evoked by two of her most powerful symbols: two mentioned at the beginning of the eerie swinging song that Parbū sings to the goddess as invitation to Gogo and Pābūjī's weddings:

> Mother, your swing is fastened to a hollow *khejaṛī* tree.
> Jagadambā, your swing is fastened;
> swinging it, I have become worn out.
> Jagadambā, you gave birth to the 52 Bhairūs [Bhairavas],
> and you remained an intact virgin.
> To the beat of a drum
> you ride upon your tiger. (Smith 1991, 97)

We will find that the tiger Ḍhēbo kills and the khejaṛi tree he uproots for Pābūjī are at a deeper level violations of the goddess. But they are also inadvertent services to her that serve her design by further entangling Pābūjī in the web of breaches that he enters, also on his own, with his marriage to Phulvantī.

This brings us to Ḍhēbo's exit from the story: his intervention before the beginning of Pābūjī's last battle. Like Cāmpukā and Anapōtu Rāja, he will draw the heroes to their deaths by disrupting their armies, interfering with their sources of female power, and replacing the heroes in battle.

When Pābūjī leaves his young bride at their interrupted wedding and gives her the gold parrot that will tell her his fate, he sets off with his companions to recover Deval's cows from Jindrāv Khīcī, incarnation of Rāvaṇa. Pābūjī goes through the night to his court at Koḷū, where, it seems, he must make preparations for the campaign against Khīcī. There, as we shall see, Deval coaxes Pābūjī and others with curses and blessings. Finally, ready to ride, he says, "Cādo my chieftain, take the other chieftains in pursuit of the cows; leave behind sleeping only Pābūjī's warrior Ḍhēbo. Ḍhēbo the opium-drinker has a great belly; Ḍhēbo will not look good to the army of my sister's husband" (Smith 1991, 433). Says Smith: "This rather lame excuse . . . conceals Pābūjī's real motive for leaving Ḍhēbo behind, which is that he fears that Ḍhēbo will kill Khīcī" (433, n. 283). Were he to do so, it would widow Pābūjī's sister Pemā, and also prevent Khīcī from completing his unfinished *Rāmāyaṇa* business: revenge, as the reincarnated Rāvaṇa, for his former slaying by Lakṣmaṇa (94).

So Pābūjī sets out, leaving Ḍhēbo behind asleep. But Deval "reflected in her mind," and at once calls her maidservant to see from the palace walls who has left and who has remained behind. The maidservant says,

"Lady Deval, I can see four men mounted on horses; alone I cannot see Pābūjī's warrior Ḍhēbo!" Deval searches Ḍhēbo out at dawn, and considers how to wake him. If she touches him with her hand, her "vow is damaged" (according to Smith, her "virtue as a woman");[43] should she call him, he might be angry. So she stands at his bed-head and wakes him with her "cold tears." Answering why she awakened him, she replies, "O opium-drinker Ḍhēbo, you are sleeping peacefully; (but) the great lord Pābūjī has gone in hot pursuit of the cows!" Ḍhēbo rises in fury, bursting his bed, and threatens to seize Deval's arm and dash her against the "wall of the fortress" for calling him only after Pābūjī has left. Like Anapōtu Rāja, he is embittered at being left out of the fight. Then he promises to drive back the cows and asks for her blessing to defeat Khīcī in battle, and she blesses him to drive back the cows.[44] From here on it is clear that he is acting in her service, as he has implicitly been doing all along. He sets out riding his horse until it tires, and, with "a roar like Hanumān," he "seized the horse and thrust it under his arm" to continue his march (Smith 1991, 433-35).

5. The Virgin's Anger

When Pābūjī stops at Koḷū on his way to recover Deval's cows, the goddess, as mentioned, goads various residents into action by curses and blessings.[45] Her first encounter is with Būṛo and the last with Ḍhēbo, both approached while they sleep. She rouses Būṛo by calling to him, with no reflections about touching him.[46] He awakens, ignoring her plight, and asks her to speak "more softly and sweetly" since his left eye is throbbing. She tells him he has ruined her joy in thinking he would join in recovering the cows, and curses his eye to remain bandaged. He asks her not to curse him, and tells her he heard Pābūjī's return in the night. But the words provoke her. Deval dishevels her hair, sets out for Pābūjī's palace, and spits drops of blood (Smith 1991, 425-27). I take it that she has turned her anger toward Pābūjī for his delay, and perhaps for failing to bring Būṛo into the expedition. The curse and blessing sequence turns Deval into a disheveled goddess who spits blood and sheds cold tears.

[43]Smith 1991, 434, n. 285. She also refrains from touching him because he is a "brave hero," perhaps anticipating his show of violent anger that erupts when she does wake him. Perhaps his quasi-"untouchability" is also at play.

[44]Unless "defeat" means "kill" here, the incongruity between request and blessing is curious. Perhaps it means that defeating Khīcī and returning the cows is, cumulatively, one act.

[45]On curses (*śarāpa*, *shrap*), especially of satīs, see Harlan 1992, 139-46. Here again, Deval may speak for Phulvantī, who will "become satī."

[46]See above, n. 43.

After Būṛo, Deval goes to Pābūjī, by herself. But on the paṛ, she is shown approaching Pābūjī with her sister Karṇī. Each holds in her left hand a trident set over her left shoulder, and brandishes another implement in her right: Deval a churning-rope, showing that without her cows there is no milk to churn; Karṇi a dagger, threatening suicide unless Pābūjī rescues the cows.[47] Thus behind the violent side of Deval is an even more violent and threatening sister. This is borne out in the oft-repeated formula that when Deval swings into action, she takes up "the trident of Mother Karṇī" (Smith 1991, 339, 392, 425, 430, 434). Elsewhere in *Pābūjī*, the trident-bearing goddess is identified as slayer of the buffalo-demon (312, 402). So in her dual portrayal in song and paṛ, as she approaches Pābūjī, the disheveled, blood-spitting Deval takes on the additional, or doubled, aspect of a bearer of ritual weapons: the trident and the suicide dagger. The latter, which appears in the story here for the first time, is shown in several paṛ pictures with its open-bar grip perpendicular to the blade. It is of a type known as *alaku* or *kaṭṭāri* in the Draupadī cult, where it is one of the goddess's important ritual implements, often used for the rite of *alaku-niṟuttal*, the standing of sword-upon-pot.[48]

The wrought-up Deval finds Pābūjī seated with a look of slumber in his eyes. She complains about the cows, and the joy she has lost of thinking Pābūjī would be chasing after them. Like Būṛo, Pābūjī stalls. He asks her to speak "a little softly and sweetly," and explains that "the bridal threads dyed with turmeric are (still) fastened to my hands and feet." Deval grows "very angry" and curses him: "may the bridal threads be unfastened with the point of a spear." Pābūjī asks her not to curse him so hard, and reminds her of the scene at his wedding: he interrupted the ceremony to come at her call, and "left behind the weeping Soḍhī girl, my young bride." The goddess seems attentive when he says, "Place your trust in Pābūjī; Pābūjī will drive back your missing cows!" (Smith 1991, 427-28). But she never withdraws the curse, as Pābūjī eventually reminds her when he tells her his death has fulfilled her "oath" or "word" (*vacana*; 451). Deval only goes on leveling curses and blessings at others, and ultimately overrides Pābūjī's plan of leaving Ḍhēbo behind, blessing *him* to rescue her cows.[49]

[47]Smith attributes the explanation of this and many other par scenes to Joseph C. Miller, Jr. (1991, 427, scene 74; xii).

[48]See Hiltebeitel 1991a, 27, 276 (plate 32), 280 (plate 36), 448-49, 452-58 (including fig. 15A, and nn. 35 and 36). There is also one in the Temple of the Heroes of Palnāḍu (observed January 1997).

[49]This sequence in Naiṇasī is one of the closest in epic dimensions to Parbū's version; see Smith 1991, 490-91. Here, too, a second Cāraṇ sister is the most destructive in the final battle.

Why is the goddess so angry? Ostensibly, because of Būṛo's and Pābūjī's procrastination (Smith 1989, 90). Only Ḍhēbo arises without stalling, and even angrily threatens the goddess for her delay in not waking him sooner. He alone receives her blessing—an ambiguous one, since he will die on the expedition—without a prior curse. Ḍhēbo's impetuosity in her service typically overrides his service to Pābūjī.

But I think we must also suspect that the goddess is angry at Pābūjī about his wedding: ambivalently angry. On the one hand, she has clearly aligned herself with Pābūjī's mare-mother when the latter bolts from the wedding; on the other, she seems to begin to align herself with Phulvantī as if she were angry on her account. To be sure, it is Deval who interrupts Phulvantī's wedding and curses Pābūjī to have his bridal threads fully, and, one must assume, irrevocably severed. But Deval is only seeing to it that the ascetic deity of the sand desert gets to fulfill Lakṣmaṇa's promise that he would marry Surapaṅkhā in their next birth but not live with her after their wedding. It is for this that Pābūjī is accountable, and Deval (rather than Viṣṇu or Śiva) seems to be the one who keeps the accounts. Not only, however, is Pābūjī accountable for Lakṣmaṇa's rash promise, and the cruel treatment of Surapaṅkhā behind it; Phulvantī must be accountable too for Surapaṅkhā's overtures of seduction, directed not only at Lakṣmaṇa but Rāma, and her threatening insults of Sītā. Deval seems softer on Phulvantī than she is on Pābūjī, showing a positive interest in her when she tells Pābūjī that if he had returned her one-eyed bull calf, she would either have made it her Sun-bull, or an ox for Phulvantī's carriage (Smith 1991, 442). Phulvantī is softer on Deval than she is on Kesar Kāḷamī, whom she curses.[50]

In any case, Phulvantī has less play in dealing with her plight than the heroines of *Palnāḍu* and *Elder brothers*. In particular, unlike Māncāla with Anapōtu Rāju, she has no subterranean interactions with Ḍhēbo.[51] She has only the moment of clinging to Pābūjī's stirrups, cursing his mare, being left with her parrot, and, as only Pābūjī reports, weeping, to represent her youthful feelings at being left a virgin doomed to likely widowhood on the day of her wedding. The virgin's anger, and agency, belongs rather to the goddess.

[50] Smith 1991, 423. It may be that at their wedding Deval appeared only to Pābūjī, leaving Phulvantī unaware of her appearance as a golden bird. Cf. 59 on Deval in connection with other fate-motivating heroines (Gahlotan and Kelam).

[51] In Nainasī's chronicle version, "Dābō" is the only Thorī brother to go with Pābūjī on the wedding procession, and faces unnamed "omens of battle" with him. They go to Ūmarkot, and return *with* Sodhī (= Phulvantī). Then Dābō "went to his own home" (490 and 493-94 nn. 8, 12, 44). Again, no undercurrents.

6. Impalements

Ḍhēbo marches toward Khīcī's army, his horse under his arm. Vultures circle above him. Parbū Bhopo, outside his text, told Smith that the vultures are Jindrāv Khīcī's sisters in bird form, intent on Ḍhēbo's destruction, since he is Pābūjī's best warrior (Smith 1991, 436, n. 287). They would seem to oppose the more auspicious, yet equally ominous bird-forms the goddess assumes on Pābūjī's side.[52] South Indian folk traditions know something similar in the *Garuḍadarśana*, the "seeing" of Viṣṇu's "eagle" mount, in which Garuḍa is sighted as a bird of prey at epic scenes and ritual sites of sacrificial death.[53] What is striking in *Pābūjī* is that the vultures are female. We shall see that, like the parrot, they are forms of the goddess.

Ḍhēbo, who has attracted she-vultures to his previous slaughters (Smith 1991, 281, 371; cf. 448), calls only these his "vulture sisters," and asks them to be patient until he feeds them "fresh vital organs of the Khīcīs." But they say no:

> 'O Ḍhēbo, you are a hero in the land, and we are vultures; for this reason first give us a meal of your own flesh!' Then what did Ḍhēbo the opium-drinker say?
> 'O vulture-sisters, stay alert in your mind!
> Ḍhēbo will give you a meal of his own flesh!' . . .
> Ḍhēbo cut open his belly and drew out his entrails.
> Half the entrails he fed to the vultures;
> half the entrails he cast on to a *khejaṛī* tree. (Smith 1991, 436)

Ḍhēbo then "considered and reflected": as a "sign" that he would "remain immortal in this age," he pronounced that his entrails would make the khejaṛī tree "bear small reddish pods." Tightening his belt, he is ready to fight disemboweled.[54] He mounts his horse and calls the vulture-sisters to follow him "to the bloody battlefield" for their next course, "the fresh vital organs of the Khīcīs" (436-37).

When Ḍhēbo catches up with Khīcī, Khīcī taunts him, asking how it is that he comes alone: did Pābūjī send him and stay home to sleep? He

[52]Four birds are shown in the paṛ portrayal of this episode. They are not vultures, and probably not parrots either (Smith 1991, 436, scene 78).

[53]See Biardeau 1989a, 156; Hiltebeitel 1991a, 223, 309-10, 449, 468; 1988a, 330-32, 412-13.

[54]Like Bāluḍu in *Palnāḍu*, who puts his intestines on an *unnamed* tree to give them to Garuḍa (Roghair 1982, 354-60). Māncāla, whose instructions he follows in this disembowelment, is also left behind with parrots (315).

threatens to kill Ḍhēbo "painfully like a goat!" Angered, Ḍhēbo tells his vulture-sisters that it is time for their meal, and launches a torrent of arrows—intriguingly depicted on the paṛ.[55] As Pābūjī approaches, he hears the bow's twang and wonders if "Ḍhēbo has gone on ahead." Disbelieving Cādo that Ḍhēbo is still "sleeping in Koḷū," he says, "'see these vultures, and reflect; without a battle vultures do not wheel overhead!' Ḍhēbo the opium-drinker slew Khīcī's excellent army; alone Ḍhēbo drove back the cows." Ḍhēbo tells the cows he will take them back to Koḷū, but his time has run out. The bard reemphasizes that Ḍhēbo has made his name "immortal in the land; alone Ḍhēbo began the battle against Khīcī" and "slew his excellent army," leaving "only Khīcī alive." Ḍhēbo duels with Khīcī, but Pābūjī stays his hand, saving Khīcī's life for the reasons mentioned earlier. Ḍhēbo is displeased, but Pābūjī honors him for having "arrived before me and halted the army of Khīcī" and "driven back the cows without your lord!" (Smith 1991, 337-40).

On the way back to Kōḷu, Pābūjī tells Cādo to spread rugs on the green grass so they can give Ḍhēbo opium. Pābūjī offers it in a golden bowl, but Ḍhēbo says he lacks nothing: having "taken opium in your court at Koḷū; I shall take my next opium in the court of the innocent (god) Rāma." He opens his belt, shows he has no entrails, says he will next meet Pābūjī in Rāma's court, and becomes "a heaven-dweller" (Smith 1991, 440-41). Pābūjī then returns the cows to Deval (440-44).

With no forces left, Khīcī now seeks asylum with his maternal uncle Jaisingh Bhāṭī of Jaisalmer, who hears Khīcī's tale and determines to make the cows his own by attacking Koḷū. This is Pābūjī's final battle: one in which he faces the far greater forces of a prestigious and powerful high Rajput court without Ḍhēbo. It is also the only battle in *Pābūjī* where Koḷū itself is under attack.[56] Here, not only do she-vultures "circle over" the battlefield; so does the goddess: "Lady Deval, you took the form of the goddess Karṇī; Deval came and circled about the battle" (Smith 1991, 448). It is in the form of her sister Karṇī that, vulture-like, she at last presides.[57]

[55]The illustration (Smith 1991, 438, scene 79) shows Ḍhēbo on bent knee, bow drawn, and shooting left-handed. At the tip of his arrow is a severed human head with an arrow-like topknot, suggesting a *brahmaśiras*-type weapon, while five more outward-pointing arrows are drawn within the arc of the bow. The bent-knee posture is found in south Indian "front-runner" deities, betokening low (often Dalit) status and sometimes lameness (Masilamani-Meyer, personal communication, 1990; Hiltebeitel 1991a, 289, n. 12). Ḍhēbo is literally "front-running" for Pābūjī.

[56]Cf. Smith 1986, 62. Nainasī's version includes no preliminary venture by Dhēbo, but is otherwise quite close to Parbū's version, especially regarding the goddess.

[57]The vulture identity of Karnī is assured by her iconographic depiction as a "kite on the battlefield," a trait she shares with the Rāthor kuldevī Naganecha Ji (Harlan 1992, 71, n.

Pābūjī exchanges his sword for Khīcī's whip, knowing that Khīcī's sword cannot kill him. He tells Khīcī it is time to fulfill the vows they took (as Lakṣmaṇa and Rāvaṇa) in their previous births, and finally hits Khīcī with the whip. At last roused to anger, Khīcī "struck at Pābūjī," who ends his life by his own sword like Caṅkar and, as we shall see, like Rāja Desing. But it does not seem that he is actually killed by this blow:

Jindrāv Khīcī struck at Pābūjī with his sword;
a heavenly palanquin came up to Pābūjī.
Pābūjī entered the palanquin;
Pābūjī travelled away in the heavenly palanquin. (Smith 1991, 449)

The palanquin carries Pābūjī—and, according to the depiction on the paṛ, he rides his mare mother on the palanquin (450, scene 85)—toward Rāma's heaven. Indeed, it would seem that Pābūjī, like Ālhā, leaves the battlefield unslain. Blackburn and J. D. Smith have apparently overlooked the opportunity this scene offers to consider whether Pābūjī should be considered the "real hero" of his story, or, if not, whether *Pābūjī* is another martial epic like *Ālhā* that is anomalously romantic (see chap. 2 § B).

Left to fight on, Pābūjī's three retainers, incarnations of goddesses, "could not die, and nobody could kill those chieftains" either. The three then reflected that with Pābūjī gone to heaven and with "nobody in the land, in this village, Koḷū," there is no more to fight for: "If we fight these (enemies), nobody will be able to kill us and we shall not obtain release. So let us take up our swords against each other, and cut off each other's heads!" Cādo first beheads Salji Soḷankī, and we don't get to hear how it befalls the remaining two. Finally Khīcī beheads Būṛo (Smith 1991, 449-51).

It is this sequence that brings *Elder brothers*, *Palnāḍu*, and *Pābūjī* to their most decisive ritual convergence. The khejaṛī is a śamī.[58] The tree with the hollow that the goddess Jagadambā swings from, the tree Ḍhēbo

44; 29, fig. 10). In *Ālhā*, Ālhā's wife Sunwā undergoes a similar transformation into a battlefield-hovering magical ladyhawk (W&G 1923, 257-58), as also in *Ālhā*'s *BhvP* retelling, where she does it twice (3.3.23.105-16; 28.41-77), the first time with Ūdal's wife, jointly offering the flesh of their witch-adversary to vultures, jackals, and crows. The two heroines are thus portrayed like royal *kuldevīs*.

[58]See Biardeau 1989a, 302 and 306 (*khejra*), citing Tod (= [1829-32] 1972, 1,467 [*kaijri*]), and Sleeman 1915, vol. 1 (*cheonkul*), with note of Tod's "editor" Smith, all discussing forms of śamīpūjā, Navarātra, Dasarā, and Vijayādaśamī in high Rajput court traditions of Rajasthan. Cf. Khan 1997b, 190: a magic Rajput kingdom-guarding sword is made of a dry branch of "*khejrā*" and blessed by Jambha Pir, founder of the Rajasthani Bishnoi sect and a figure in whom Khan finds similarities to Rāmdev (see chap. 10).

uproots for Pābūjī's wedding, and the tree under which he disembowels himself are the same tree that defines Cāmpukā and Anapōtu Rāju's deaths by impalement. Only Cāmpukā is fully and unequivocally a Dalit, but Anapōtu Rājū and Ḍhēbo have familiar Dalit affinities. All three impale themselves, each in an innovative way: Cāmpukā with the śamī branch, the other two beneath a śamī—Anapōtu Rāju with a stylus, Ḍhēbo with a dagger. The three LSRSCs all die alone, their mode of self-impalement carrying implications of extreme subaltern heroism while denying to themselves the death by sword of their higher status "little king" heroes and masters.

Ḍhēbo also has separate affinities with each of the other two. Like Anapōtu Rāju, his "lone hero" death under a śamī precedes those of the other heroes. Like Cāmpukā, he goes into battle ahead of the heroes, overturning their intention: Cāmpukā by fighting Kompan̠ before Caṅkar overcomes his fever; Ḍhēbo by refusing to be left behind asleep. Yet Ḍhēbo's interventions do not directly affect the heroine. Unlike Cāmpukā, he does not return from his foray for a virgin to upbraid him. His preliminary suicide, unlike Anapōtu Rāju's, is unmotivated by the virgin heroine's designing, although it is prompted by the virgin goddess. But Ḍhēbo's death beneath the khejaṛī does leave Pābūjī unprotected in his last fight with Jaisingh Bhāṭī. This affects Phulvantī's widowhood and indirectly safeguards her virginity no less than the actions of Anapōtu Rāju guarantee the virgin widowhood of Māncāla.

How then do we see the goddess behind this design? Looking at text and paṛ together, the type of dagger Ḍhēbo uses has a revealing recurrence in *Pābūjī*'s closing scenes. Just after Deval dishevels her hair and spits blood, it appears for the first time, as noted, in a paṛ illustration, brandished by Karṇī when she joins her sister to demand the cows' return. While both sisters bear tridents, Karṇī threatens suicide with the dagger should Pābūjī fail to recover the cows. Next, in both text and paṛ, it serves as Ḍhēbo's suicide dagger.[59] After that, a more ornate dagger of the same cross-grip type is brandished by Deval. Having just taken on "the form of the goddess Karṇī" to "circle about" the battlefield, she subsumes Karṇī's iconography in the solemn paṛ scene of the end of the final battle. Now holding both dagger and trident herself and filling her drinking gourd with the blood of the slain, Deval is reminded by Pābūjī that he has fulfilled her word in bringing his own life and that of the Khīcīs to an end. As he passes over her in the palanquin on his way to heaven, he makes the final request that she heeds: she will not separate out the

[59]See Smith 1991, 436 and scene 78. Dhēbo also uses it in a *sāyl* story (see below) to open a crocodile and retrieve a necklace of Pābūjī's sister Pemā (Smith 1991, 499-500 and *par* scene 104).

blood of his Rajput, Rebārī, and Dalit Nāyak Bhīl warriors, but rather let it mingle (Smith 1991, 450-51 and *paṛ* scene 451). Finally, such a dagger is used by Queen Gailovat, Būṛo's wife, to self-deliver her baby Rūpnāth before she becomes a satī (458-59, text only), and by Rūpnāth in his revenge-slaying of Khīcī.[60]

Clearly Ḍhēbo impales himself with the weapon of the goddess. His extreme action is a form of dedication to her. Here we may finally address a sort of pending question or *praśna*:[61] Why did Ḍhēbo disembowel himself at the sole insistence of a bunch of she-vultures? If we accept by now that it is because the she-vultures are multiforms of the two sister-goddesses Deval and Karṇī, we find a parallel in *Palnāḍu*, when Anapōtu Rāju accepts his suicide by the jammi because he cannot ignore the proscription on Akka Pinakka. Like Anapōtu Rāju's death as "a lone hero by the jammi," Ḍhēbo's evokes images of a "popular Dasarā." Again, it is a question of a folk epic version of a royal śamīpūjā and boundary crossing, the two Dasarā subrites that combine worship of the śamī as an embodiment of the virgin goddess Aparājitā, the Unvanquished, with the opening of military campaigns.[62] This time the śamī is garlanded in suitable low status ritual fashion, by Ḍhēbo's guts.[63] The khejaṛī also seems to denote a boundary, since it spatially marks Ḍhēbo's entry into Khīcī territory, and temporally precipitates the beginning of the final war. It clearly defines the opening of Pābūjī's last military campaign.

If we recall Ḍhēbo's cutting of the khejaṛī outside Ūmarkoṭ for Pābūjī's wedding, the impression now grows that this cutting is a violation of the goddess and her tree. Moreover, we have noted *Pābūjī*'s eerie

[60]Smith 1991, 470-75 and scenes 95-98. Here we learn that the churning rope, held earlier by Deval when Karnī held the dagger, is not so innocent either. As Rūpnāth appears before Pemā holding the dagger in one hand and Khīcī's head in the other, Pemā uses a churning rope to churn her hated husband's blood, which she had caught in a butter churn beneath his bed (473-75 and scene 97).

[61]I use this term as it is employed in the Tulsidas *Rāmcaritmānas* tradition of asking questions of the text that reaffirm its design by posing loopholes and alternate possibilities: e.g., "Why didn't Sītā run away from Rāvana when Jatāyus knocked down his chariot? At least she could have gotten a hundred yards!" (Linda Hess, oral presentation, 1992, American Academy of Religion).

[62]On the royal śamīpūjā in Rajasthan, see Biardeau 1989a, 302, 305-8, and n. 58 above.

[63]For garlands of intestines, cf. Hiltebeitel 1991a, 332, 334; Meyer 1986, 129-34 and *passim*; Kinsley 1975, 98, 138. Cf. also n. 54 above (does Bāluḍu also hang his guts on a śamī?). That the śamī will henceforth "bear small (reddish) pods" reminds one of the early seventeenth-century *Nirnayasindhu*'s description of "the śamī of reddish thorns (*lohitakaṇṭakā*), which bore Arjuna's arrows and possessed the benevolent words of Rāma" (following Biardeau 1989a, 301; cf. Kane [1930-62] 1975,5,1:190). In *paṛ* depictions, the khejaṛī usually shows spiky leaves (Smith 1991, 417, 436, 499).

reference to the *hollowed* khejaṛī of the goddess. The śamī with the hollow now appears not only in Tamil *Mahābhārata* folklore to hold the Pāṇḍavas' weapons, and in *Elder brothers* to conceal the "notorious" Viṣṇu, but in *Pābūjī* as the tree that bears the world-wearying swing of the virgin World-Mother Jagadambā. In both *Pābūjī* and *Elder brothers*, fate's designing deity thus operates from the hollow of such a tree. From this third instance, however, it would appear that the śamī with the hollow is not primarily an allusion to the weapon-concealing scene in the *Mahābhārata*. As Biardeau has shown, the śamī's *Mahābhārata* associations are themselves rooted in Vedic ritual, where the śamī is a source of fire, and of Agni's connection with ritual weapons. According to different Vedic—and eventually popular—texts and interpretations, the Vedic firesticks have two explanations. Either they are both made of pipal wood that is said to be *śamīgarbhāt*, "from the womb of the śamī," or else the vertical male stick is of pipal and the horizontal female one of śamī. In one case, the firesticks come from the "womb of the śamī"; in the other, fire itself comes from the feminine śamī's drilling notch or hole.[64] In either case, the śamī as source of fire implies a hole or hollow that is considered a "source" or "womb." In *Pābūjī*, it evokes the fiery womb of the virgin World Mother.[65] This image of the fiery womb as source of ritual weapons may remind us that the Draupadī cult has two equivalent myths of the origin of the cult's ritual weapons. In one, they are born together with Draupadī from the fire-womb of her birth; in the other, they come ultimately from the śamī tree as personified by Pōttu Rāja.[66]

7. Satīs and Salvation

As in the two south Indian epics, the deaths of the heroes are followed by sātīs: Būṛo's queen Gailovat, Phulvantī, and "other satīs" (chieftains' wives). Phulvantī's golden parrot, having come to life, informs Phulvantī of Pābūjī's death, tells her to "become *satī*," and dies in her hand.[67] Phulvantī goes home to Ūmarkoṭ to tell her kinsmen and seek their bless-

[64]See Biardeau 1989a, 50-62; 1984, 4; Hiltebeitel 1991a, 104-5.

[65]In the Draupadī cult instance, however, Kālī seems to identify the hole in the tree either with herself or as a metaphor for her womb or vagina, saying that when the Pāṇḍavas left the weapons in the tree, they left them "in me," or "in my place" (*ennitattil*). This "garbled" folk text (see Hiltebeitel 1991a, 315) seems to make a fascinating correlation between the concealment of weapons in the goddess's fiery womb and the disguise theme of eunuchhood that comes with loss of identity.

[66]See Hiltebeitel 1988a, 382-93; 1991a, 155-56, 235-40, 422-29 on Pōttu Rāja's Draupadī cult connections with the śamī, which go back to an explicit connection between Pōta Rāju and the śamī in Andhra, on which see above, chap. 3.

[67]Smith 1991, 455; or, in the paṛ, it accompanies her as she approaches and enters the pyre (357, scene 89: her inspection of Pābūjī's empty palace; 456-59, scenes 88-91).

ing, and says she will return to Koḷū alone, with no need for an accompanying army (Smith 1991, 455-56). One of her brief reflections is interesting: "I (must have) committed a sin at the (very) gate of the blessed Lord" (456). As suggested, this is probably an allusion to her attempted seduction of Rāma and Lakṣmaṇa in her previous life. Her satī is not described.

There are no revivals of heroes in *Pābūjī*. Pābūjī has no last words with his wife. But, as already noted, he does have important last words with Deval. Having not exactly died on the battlefield but "met his end," Pābūjī, riding his mare in the heavenly palanquin, says to Deval: "O goddess, let this blood mingle! . . . If their blood remains separate then (in future) Bhīls will not protect Rajpūts and Rajpūts will not protect Bhīls, and nobody in the world will recognize Pābūjī. Honor my words and let the blood of my warriors mingle!" (Smith 1991, 450-51). The mixing of Rajput, Bhīl, and Rebārī blood in the goddess's gourd guarantees cooperation between these communities, and secures the future of Pābūjī's cult. The vision of Deval may remind us of Aravāṉ's closing vision of Kurukṣetra, in which he completes his eighteen-day vigil by telling Kṛṣṇa, Draupadī, and the Pāṇḍavas what he truly saw: Kṛṣṇa's discus severing all the armies' heads, his conch containing the heads, and Kālī's skull-bowl collecting the blood.[68]

Finally, salvation is closure on all the unfinished business of the *Rāmāyaṇa*. One gets the sense that the exodus of our heroes and heroines is complete, and that they have all "passed on to the court of the innocent (god) Rāma."

8. Transformations of Dasarā

In chapter 3, we found that the people of Palnāḍu's migration from their northern homeland required that they dig up a śamī tree to bring with them, bundled with their weapons. This story was preliminary to the central epic narrative. Its allusions not only to a popularized form of śamīpūjā and boundary crossing, but to buffalo sacrifices, served to confirm and clarify Anapōtu Rāju's solitary heroic death "by the *jammi*" as a Dasarā subplot. We find similar supporting evidence on the boundaries of *Pābūjī* for much the same complex.

According to Smith, bhopos (Parbū included) regard "the complete text" of Pābūjī as consisting of "episodes of two different types": parvāṛos and *sāyls*. So far we have been considering only parvāṛos,

[68]This vision, familiar in both the Draupadī and Kūttāṇṭavar cults, can also combine the cakra with either of the other two; see Shideler 1987, 86; Hiltebeitel 1988a, 445; 1991a, 45 n. 15; 1995b, 469 and n. 13; and chap 12 below.

literally "battles" (Smith 1991, 19). These are the main episodes of Parbū's text. Smith, in his glossary, defines a sāyl, literally a "petition" or "prayer," as "a narrative episode not forming part of the epic story, dealing with help given supernaturally by the divine Pābūjī."[69] If we were to reconcile Smith's statement with what he learned from the bhopos, we could say that sāyls are part of the "complete text," but not "part of the epic story." Or we might propose that sāyls form part of the text's boundary or frame. This is precisely how they are depicted on the paṛ, along with mythical animals and—not surprisingly—scenes from *Rāmāyaṇa* (497-502).

Parbū estimated that there are as many as twenty-four sāyls but thought most bhopos knew only from zero to four (Smith 1991, 19). It is unclear how many Parbū knew himself. At one point Smith says he knew only one (ibid.), but later he cites Parbū's accounts of two others (494, n. 26, 500). By the first statement, Smith seems to mean that Parbū knew only one in metrical form (500). Most sāyls "are told simply as informal narratives," and Smith finds it unusual that Parbū knew this one metrically (498). It is one of only two shown on the paṛ. These two probably represent the sāyl genre on the paṛ because they portray figures known to Pābūjī himself in exemplary petitions *related* to the story. The sāyl Parbū knew best is the "*sāyl* of the *khejaṛi* tree":

> Sonā, Pābūjī's sister, "was married to Sūro Devaṛo, ruler of Sirohī; she had a magnificent *khejaṛī* tree, grown from a seed Ḍhebo had given her. Its shade spread over twelve *kos*, its branches extended over thirteen kos. Once Jaisiṅgh Bhāṭī passed through Sirohī on his way home from a pilgrimage, and coveted the tree for its wood. The Devaṛos [people of Sirohī] refused to let him have it, but he nonetheless set his axe to the tree, which wept as he did so, and cut it down. Sonā, who had always wished to see Pābūjī and his men encamped beneath the tree, prayed to Pābūjī, and he and his companions mounted to pursue Bhāṭī. Ḍhēbo far outstripped the others, and challenged Bhāṭī; and in the ensuing battle he destroyed the entire Bhāṭī army, until only Jaisiṅgh himself was left alive." Pābūjī prevented Ḍhēbo from killing Jaisiṅgh, and told him only to cut off his ears and free him. "Then Pābūjī and his companions returned the tree to Sonā and brought it to life again; and to satisfy her wish they encamped for a while in its shade before returning to heaven." (499-500)

[69]Smith 1991, 505. Elsewhere, Smith says sāyls are episodes in which Pābūjī comes "either from a distance or after his ascent to heaven" (19) "to the aid of his earthly devotees" (498).

If *Pābūjī* rounds off the unfinished business of the *Rāmāyaṇa*, this sāyl rounds off the unfinished business of *Pābūjī*. Jaisiṅgh Bhāṭī is the Jaisalmer king who enabled Jindrāv Khīcī to slay Pābūjī. As far as we know, he still has Deval's cows. Again, he represents the high Rajput culture that survives the rustication of Koḷū after Pābūjī's death. His defeat and subordination to Pābūjī represents an aspiration of Pābūjī's worshipers for high Rajput recognition.

Jaisiṅgh Bhāṭī thus covets and cuts down an extraordinary weeping khejaṛī that belongs to Pābūjī's sister Sonā, which she grew from a seed she got from Ḍhēbo. Presumably (yet who knows in a world of sāyls?) Ḍhēbo gave it to her before he died, but it certainly recalls his pronouncement that once he had garlanded the khejaṛī with his entrails, it would henceforth have reddish pods—from which, of course, come seeds—to recall his heroism. Pābūjī and his warriors must somehow retrieve the tree or wood from Bhāṭī to return it to Sonā. Then they revive it so that they can fulfill her petition, which was not that he retrieve the khejaṛī, but that she be able to see Pābūjī and his men encamped beneath its vast shade.

The sight of Pābūjī and his men at ease beneath the śamī seems to be an image of afterlife completion and perfection that is denied the hero during his fractured real life. Other kingdoms' capitals—Phulvantī's Ūmarkoṭ, Khīcī's Jāyal, now Sonā's Sirohī, and Bhāṭī's Jaisalmer—have khejaṛi trees outside them, while capitals of sultans do not.[70] As far as one can tell, Pābūjī's "great village fortress of Koḷū" in "the barren sand desert" (Smith 1991, 290, 406, 430) has no khejaṛī of its own. In effect, the sāyl of the khejaṛī provides Pābūjī with such a śamī. Sonā's petition has the effect of setting Pābūjī under a sort of heavenly śamī, to which he can descend from Rāma's paradise or from his own court-temple in Koḷū, to meet the needs, and even fight the battles, of his devotees. It is probably no coincidence that the scene of the khejaṛī tree petition is placed on the paṛ precisely at a point that would correspond to the northeast corner of a temple: directly outside Pābūjī's court, just below its lower left corner, as he faces (presumably east) toward his devotees.[71] With Pābūjī and his men beneath it, Sonā's khejaṛī is thus located

[70]There is no khejaṛī tree mentioned outside Pātan, the capital of the Muslim rulers Mirzā Khān (the cow-killer; Smith 1991, 289-93) and Lakkhū Pathān (whose garden Pābūjī destroys to get saffron for his wedding; 390-99). Located in Gujarat (map, Smith 1991, xiv), it probably conflates the two Muslim opponents into one kingdom (perhaps linking Pāṭan secondarily with Paṭhāṇ), since "true saffron" would grow only in Kashmir (Yule and Burnell [1886] 1986, 780). There is also no khejaṛī on the way to Laṅkā in *Pābūjī* (cf. Hiltebeitel 1991a, 431-32: there is in the Rām Līlā, though it is only outside Ayodhyā).

[71]See plate 10 in Smith 1991. The facing direction is in any case not crucial, since the pattern works by axial rotation no matter which way a temple faces. The important point

in the same position that the old mendicant Brahman assigns to Jaffar and Farīd so that they can share otherworldly worship with the heroes of Palnāḍu.

Who then is Sonā? As Smith says, "Sonā plays no role in the epic narrative" (Smith 1991, 502, n. 2), by which, of course, he means in the parvāṛos. I have included her in Pābūjī's genealogical chart (table 2), but only from her appearance in sāyls and in Mūhato Naiṇasī's chronicle (see n. 9). These, however, make her quite prominent. She appears in the other two sāyl stories mentioned as known to Parbū. One is the second sāyl illustrated on the paṛ. Pābūjī's two sisters, Sonā and Pemā, once went bathing in a tank. Pemā left her necklace on the shore, and a crocodile swallowed it. She petitioned Pābūjī, who sent Ḍhēbo down from heaven. With his dagger, Ḍhēbo cut open all the creatures in the tank until he found and opened the crocodile, returned the necklace to Pemā, and revived all the creatures (Smith 1991, 500). Here Sonā is secondary, though both sisters are shown (499, scene 104).

More revealingly, Parbū knows a sāyl about Sonā that tells a variant of an episode that is part of the main "epical" narrative of the chronicler Naiṇasī, who recounts it as an incident in Pābūjī's *life*, thoroughly interwoven with stories equivalent to Parbū's parvāṛo episodes. But according to Parbū, the events "occurred after Pabūjī's ascent to heaven as a miraculous intervention on his part (*sāyl*)" (Smith 1991, 494, n. 26). Of Parbū's version, Smith tells us only that he "knows a story in which Pābūjī punishes Sonā's husband, Sūro Devaṛo, for beating her" (ibid). Naiṇasī's account gives this incident a rich background.

Sonā and her co-wife Vāghelī, both married to Sirohī (Sūro Devaṛo, king of Sirohī for Parbū), play *caupaṛ*, parcheesi.[72] Vāghelī's father Āno Vāghelo, an enemy of Pābūjī's Thorī (Dalit) companions and a figure of somewhat looming proportions,[73] had given Vāghelī "many ornaments," which she "made much of" and "praised them greatly."

---

is that the kṣetrapāla or other equivalent be at the deity's left hand (Hiltebeitel 1991a, 314). Cf. Biardeau 1981, 229, and Parpola in press, § 3.1.3; Hiltebeitel 1991a, 378, n. 51, on associations of the northeast with the Vedic term *aparājitā*, "invincible," which comes to be a name for the goddess personified in the śamī. The northeast also positions a temple's guardian deity (*kṣetrapāla* or *nirmalyadevatā*); see Hiltebeitel 1991a, 99-107, 142-59, 194, 351, 461-64. Such deities mark a temple's boundaries to neutralize sacrificial violence there.

[72]A family feud also arises in a caupar game in Harlan 1992, 148.

[73]In Nainasī, the seven Thorīs were Āno Vāghelo's servants; when famine struck, they killed an animal, and, challenged by Āno's son, killed the son. They fled, but Āno caught them and killed their father (as Smith notes, for Parbū, Āno doesn't kill their father; he *is* the father of two of them, Cādo and Ḍhēbo; Smith 1991, 493, n. 9). No one will hire the Thorīs for fear of Āno, until they come to Pābūjī (481-82). Later, when Pābūjī kills Āno, it convinces Mirzā Khān that Pābūjī is invincible (487-88).

Caught up in the game, the co-wives quarrel, and Vāghelī taunts Sonā: "Your brother eats in the company of Thorīs." Sirohī says to Sonā, "Why are you angry. She speaks the truth," to which Sonā replies, "you have no ministers like my brother's Thorīs." Enraged, Sirohī beats Sonā with three whip-lashes. Sonā writes to Pābūjī, who summons Cādo and his other Thorī companions to "ride against" Sirohi (Smith 1991, 483-84). On the way, Pābūjī and his nine companions, "all miracle-workers," kill Āno Vāghelo, whose "sway was great." Pābūjī then tells Sirohī he has come because he whipped his sister. They kill many Devaṛo warriors, but not Sirohī, since Sonā asks Pābūjī for the boon of nonwidowhood. He releases Sirohī and gives Sonā "the ornaments of Āno Vāghelo's wife" as a wedding gift. Sonā then tells Vāghelī that Pābūjī has killed her father to avenge the Thorīs, and "Vāghelī fell to her knees" (486-87).

Like much else in Naiṇasī, this story looks like chronicle-ized folk epic, perhaps based on an oral tradition before its episodes were divided into parvāṛos and sāyls.[74] In any case, it tells us two things about Sonā that are consistent with her portrayal in the sāyls of the khejaṛī and the crocodile. She is a champion of Pābūjī's Dalit companions: in one case she defends them to Sirohī, in the other she wants to see them with Pābūjī under the shade of her khejaṛi outside the Sirohī capital. And she is associated with jewels: in one case, with her sister Pemā's necklace, in the other with her co-wife Vāghelī's. Pābūjī's purpose in Naiṇasī's account is not only to restore his sister's honor after her whipping, but to elevate her above her rival by bringing her Vāghelī's *mother*'s ornaments, which are presumably even better than Vāghelī's own.

It is Sonā's connection with the śamī that brings these themes together, and no doubt supplies a major impulse behind much of what we find in her stories. Sonā means "gold." She is Pābūjī's only co-uterine sister, born, like him, from the "Saffron nymph" Kesarparī. It is probable that both ornaments and saffron are multiforms of gold in a metonymic chain that links episodes and images. Tracing backwards, Phulvantī gets her golden parrot; Pābūjī offers Ḍhēbo his last earthly opium in a golden bowl; and Ḍhēbo supplies Pābūjī with a "gold stick" to strike the toraṇ for his marriage to Phulvantī. That "gold stick" is, of course, an uprooted khejaṛī. In connecting Sonā with the khejaṛī, *Pābūjī* seems conversant with a widespread symbolism linking the śamī not only with fire but with gold.[75] Again, Biardeau has done the mapping.

[74]Qanungo 1969, 73-74 discusses it in the context of Rajput vendetta (*vair*) stories.

[75]I proposed a Tamil adaptation of this theme in the story of the self-replenishing "gold tree of Gingee." Although not identified as a śamī, it supplies the wealth for the building of the Gingee fort that Draupadī later descends to protect. Intriguing comparatively is the account of one Draupadī cult *pāratiyār* (*Mbh*-reciter) that the tree miraculously revived to full height

The connection is explained in a myth, indirectly connected with the *Rāmāyaṇa* through Rāma's ancestor Raghu, that Biardeau says is found widely in the Deccan. A young Brahman has to pay his guru a *dakṣiṇā* (guru's fee) of fourteen crores of gold coins, and asks king Raghu to supply it. Raghu is temporarily out of gold after a great *Viśvajit* sacrifice,[76] but he is too pious to leave a Brahman's request unmet. Fortunately, the "All-conquering" Viśvajit now guarantees victory over anyone he attacks. Remembering that Indra owes him "gifts," he prepares to attack Indroloka. Alarmed, Indra asks aid from Kubera, god of riches, and the latter showers goldpieces onto a śamī. Raghu collects what he needs for the young Brahman and lets his people loot the rest. The latter, ignorant of the source of this gold, believe it comes from the śamī.[77]

The story serves to explain the exchange of śamī leaves, identified as "gold," that takes place every year on the evening of Vijayādaśamī, after the śamīpūjā. This "popular *śamīpūjā*, the one celebrated by everyone, always retains the idea of combat. All the castes (but in principle only the men) assemble at the *śamī* tree. In the Deccan, where the *śamī* is rare, a bush is made of branches from a forest tree, the *āpaṭā* (*bauhinia tomentosa*), and there is a simulated scuffle to get hold of a branch. If there is a *śamī*, the people move around the tree jostling each other and casting *śamī* (or *āpaṭā*) leaves at the bottom. Then, in the houses, the women perform an *āratī* for the men and friends visit each other, exchanging *śamī* and *āpaṭā* leaves and saying 'it's gold'" (Biardeau 1984, 10). A particular instance outside Sholapur (Maharashtra) is instructive for the clear participation by Dalits. Mahār and Maṅg devotees of the goddess Ellamma, and especially Potrājs, personifiers of Pōta Rāju, come with long whiplike rope wicks that burn ashes at the end, which they hand out with blessings.[78] They gather at a large śamī for Vijayādaśamī in a park, where śamīpūja and sīmollanghana are performed. The tree, the only śamī around, is a point of civic pride, and during the śamīpūjā it is considered as the goddess herself: Vijayā, "Victory," or Aparājitā, "the Unvanquished." At evening, closing the festival, the tree's leaves of "gold" are exchanged along with wishes for a prosperous year.[79] The śamī's connection with gold is a multiform of its Vedic, and also popular, associations with fire: the Potrāj's burning wick being a case in point

---

in the time of Rāja Desing (Hiltebeitel 1988a, 64; see below chap. 12, § A).

[76]On dakṣinās in the Viśvajit sacrifice, see Hiltebeitel forthcoming. Again, oral epic folklore teems with Vedic surprises.

[77]Biardeau 1989a, 303; 1981, 223-24; 1984, 7-8.

[78]On Potrājs in relation to other forms of Pōta Rāju-Pōttu Rāja, see Hiltebeitel 1988a, 336 n. 3, 349, n. 21, 364-65, 379, 408-9; 1991a, 103, n. 37, 150, 472-73; 1985a, 174, 177-79, 189-95, all citing Biardeau, especially her 1981, 239-41 (= 1984, 19-22).

[79]Biardeau 1989a, 32; cf. 1981, 240-41; 1984, 21.

(Biardeau 1981; 1989a).

These popular forms of śamīpūjā not only explain the tree's connection with gold, and thus supply a metonymic explanation of Sonā's name, but clarify Sonā's story by telling of its function as an egalitarian rallying point for all castes, with distinctive roles for Dalit ritual specialists. In wishing to see all of Pābūjī's men beneath her vast śamī, Sonā provides just such an egalitarian ideal, one that benevolently complements Pābūjī's darker request that Deval mix the blood of his Rajput, Rebārī, and Nāyak Bhīl warriors. One is reminded that the jammi tree where Anapōtu Rāju meets his end dominates a grove where Bāluḍu and the other young multicaste heroes of Palnāḍu happily played tops before their falling out. Whereas Sonā's petition calls all the heroes back together to the śamī after their lives are over, the silent vow of Māncāla separates Anapōtu Rāju's brothers from him before they die, and leads to the violent interruption of the egalitarian multicaste meal that would have averted the war.

Yet if Sonā brings all Pābūjī's men together only in their afterlife, this is because the separations and fragmentations of Pābūjī's real life have made such a fulfillment something to long for. The "Hindu king" of Koḷū village has no real-life dealings with this co-uterine saffron-born "golden" sister, whose khejaṛī comes to stand outside his court and temple only after his heavenly ascent. Yet it is the relocation of this khejāṛi to the court of Pābūjī the god that retrospectively explains the dislocations in his life as a hero. As the Unvanquished goddess Aparājitā, the śamī functions as the goddess of the boundary, the protector of the frontier, and materializes a complementary aspect of the goddess who protects the lineage, who habitually resides in the palace or court of the capital.[80] Pābūjī's palace has a court for the lady Deval, but, during his lifetime, neither a goddess of the limit nor a sister's śamī to protect his frontier. As to what Deval might protect from their common court and temple, things are even more hopeless. The ascetic deity of the sand desert can have no lineage! Pābūjī loves his mare. He also loves she-camels and cows. But he ultimately cannot protect his borders, or Deval's cows. And though Deval loves Pābūjī, she cannot protect his lineage since he will remain an ascetic to the end.

[80]Biardeau 1989a, 299-300, 302, 306.

5 Opening *Ālhā*

Two corollary features are bolder in *Ālhā* than in any of our other regional martial epics: those concerning a heroic age, and affinities with a classical epic's chief heroine. *Ālhā*'s great battle between Delhi on one side and Kanauj and Mahobā on the other marks, with the fall of Mahobā, the point that brings the Kali yuga to a fourth of its completion.[1] A *Mahābhārata* heroic age is thus mapped onto a microheroic age of *Ālhā*. And Belā, *Ālhā*'s chief heroine, is provocatively identified with Draupadī. Putting these two features together, Schomer takes Belā's links with Draupadī as exemplary of the way that "interpenetration" of the two heroic ages is "present in most extra-textual commentary, repeatedly alluded to in an indirect way in the narrative itself, and often spelled out explicitly in the preliminary section of an oral performance." She says further it is "implicit in the Alha narrative as a whole, although it is only occasionally brought to the foreground" (1989, 144-45). This alternance between the tacit and explicit is important and well perceived.

There are many versions of *Ālhā*, but only one that is sufficiently accessible through translation and summary. The so-called "Farrukhabad *Ālhā*" or "Elliot *Ālhā*" was "reduced to writing" when Charles Elliot, District Collector of the Farrukhabad District in the United Provinces, assembled "some three or four minstrels" near Farrukhabad in the early 1860s "and employed one of them to compile a complete set of the entire cycle from their joint memories" (W&G 10, 58). First published in 1865 in a lithograph edition that was frequently reprinted through the remainder of the nineteenth century and apparently less often thereafter, it seems to have given way to more accessible printing press editions of different versions, though at least one of them claims to draw from it.[2]

[1]W&G 273. On W&G, see already chap. 1.

[2]See Elliot [1881] 1992, from which Philip Lutgendorf (1997) has kindly translated some passages for this book. Cf. Schomer 1989, 143, citing a 1970 Farrukhabad edition, stating that it has been "continually reprinted since" 1865. A similarly structured *Ālhakhanda*, composed and edited by Viśvambhara Ṅātha "Vācāla" ("the talkative") (1986, 2) in twenty-

In the mid-1870s William Waterfield translated portions of this text into an "English border ballad" style (10), and, after his death, the rest was summarized by the folklorist George A. Grierson. According to Schomer, the Elliot *Ālhā* reflects *Ālhā* tradition "as it had evolved by the late nineteenth century in the region around the city of Kanauj" (1989, 143). From what can be gleaned from other versions, arguments based on the Elliot *Ālhā* do not have equal force for all variants. Differences will be noted. But variants are no reason to devalue the Elliot *Ālhā*, or reject it as a valid text of reference.[3] Indeed, one can only marvel that it is so rich. The Kanauj area, along with "certain districts of Oudh, and in Bundelkhand," is one where oral *Ālhā* performance, "often sung to the accompaniment of drums, particularly in villages in the rainy season," is "most popular" (Dwivedi 1966, 23). My working hypothesis is that Kanauj (in the Ganges-Yamuna Doab) and Mahobā (in Bundelkhand), the two capitals, along with Delhi, of the three most important *Ālhā* kingdoms, define the two royal nubs of *Ālhā*'s "back-country" heartland—two contiguous areas, with the Yamuna between them, in which the story has its richest and deepest associations with the land, heroes, mythology, and the history of its primary locations;[4] and that versions found to the east and west of this heartland reflect flanking traditions that lose some of these associations while developing others.[5]

---

seven rather than twenty-three *laṛāī* or *laḍāī* ("battles," the term for "episodes" or "cantos"), draws from the text that "Eliyat Bahādur" commissioned Munśī Bholanātha Kāyastha to write, but offers improvements by separating out material condensed in the Elliot *Ālhā*, and adding some episodes, mainly marriages. Schomer names four other regionally distributed printed versions, mostly in fifty-two episodes, as "among the best known," but indicates that chapbook editions of single episodes are still more popular, reflecting the single-episode style of *Ālhā* performance. She also remarks that oral *Ālhā* "is never known as *Ālha-khand*," *khaṇḍ* ("section") having been introduced by Elliot on the model of the *Mahobā khaṇḍ* as a supposed section of the *Pṛthvīrāj-rāsau*, and ever since implying a book version (1984, 10, 15-16).

[3]Cf. Schomer 1989, 143-44, making the same point.

[4]For example, Baccha Singh, an *Ālhā* singer from Mahobā, invokes "the god of Kanauj" among other deities in beginning his performances.

[5]Recall chap. 2, § B at nn. 33-34. This approach, treating Kanauji and Bundelkhandi or Bundeli versions of *Ālhā* as reflecting a common core, will override Grierson's emphasis on a division of versions into "two classes, the Hindî (or Western) and the Biharî (or Eastern) recension," bracketing the "Kanaujî" Elliot *Ālhā* in the former, and Bundelkhandi and Bhojpuri versions in the latter. Grierson's sample from a Bhojpuri "eastern" variant shows major variations suggestive of a "flanking" tradition, as do variants I met in Agra to the west of the *Ālhā* "heartland." Grierson suggests that the "cycle" was "[p]robably . . . originally written in the Bundêl'khandî dialect of . . . Biharî" (1885a, 209). Jaiswal, differentiating Bundeli from Hindusthani, Braja, and Kanauji, finds written and oral versions of *Ālhā* to preserve the best specimens of Bundeli in what he calls the mixed Bundeli dialect of Banāphari (1962, 11).

Both Schomer (1989, 142, 149) and Lutgendorf (1979, 14-16) refer to traditions that *Ālhā* is "the *Mahābhārata* of the Kali yuga." Each questions whether its links with the *Mahābhārata* are original to its oral conception or represent "a later Sanskritization" (Schomer 1989, 143) resulting from "'external' interpretations by *paṇḍits*" (Lutgendorf 1979, 16). Schomer leans to the latter explanation (1989, 143 and n. 3), while Lutgendorf is noncommittal. The question is complicated. Grierson's Bhojpuri version (1885a; see n. 5) seems to handle *Mahābhārata* themes differently from the Elliot *Ālhā*, without the incarnational theme. But the text is too partial and brief to support conclusions. There is a less "*Mahābhārat*-ized" version of some of the epic's events in the medieval Hindi *Pṛthvīrāj-rāsau*,[6] what might be called an "over-*Mahābhārat*-ized" version in the Sanskrit *Bhaviṣya Purāṇa*, and in Jayānaka's *Pṛthvīrāja-vijaya* even a *Rāmāyaṇ*-ized kāvya on Pṛthvīrāja as an avatāra of Rāma, composed not long before Pṛthvīrāja's defeat and (apparent) death at the hands of Muhammad Ghori, also known as Shihāb al-Dīn, in 1193 (Pollock 1993, 274-77).

Do these texts influence oral *Ālhā*? Do Sanskrit epic and purāṇic themes in *Ālhā* "come from" the *Bhaviṣya Purāṇa*, as Schomer once suggests (1989, 143, n. 3)? Does *Ālhā* partially de-Sanskritize, de-"paṇḍitize," and demythologize the *Bhaviṣya*'s "over-*Mahābhārat*-ization"? Do chronicle-like *Rāsau* traditions (including the so-called *Parmāl-rāsau*, if it is separate from the *Pṛthvīrāj-rāsau*[7]), yield mythologized history of the type Smith imagines behind *Pābūjī*? These are necessary questions, but one must give up the expectation that their answers will lend themselves to theories designed to impose notions of development, influence, and causality on relations between written texts and oral traditions.

As with *Pābūjī*, one cannot assume that chronicle material connects with oral epic as a prior stage of its development, or that links with a

[6]Vaidya, recognizing numerous epical tropes, comments, "We have often said that the Rāsā (*rāsau*) is plainly modelled after the Mahābhārata" (1926, 337; see 334-38; cf. 1924, 18-21). Cf. Pritchett 1980, 57: "the *Mahabharata* of Hindi literature," translating a critic writing in Hindi, Dr. Syamsundardas.

[7]See R. B. Singh 1975, 245: it is debated whether the *Parmāl-rāsau*, a recent editor's name (Babu Shyam Sunder Das, *Paramāla Rāsau*, Introduction, p. 2) of the *Pṛthvīrāj-rāsau*'s *Mahobā Khaṇḍa*, was originally separate, as that editor, Schomer 1984, 15, and McGregor 1984, 22, maintain, or "authentically" part of the *Pṛthvīrāj-rāsau*. See also Dikshit 1977, 141-54; Tod [1829-32] 1972, I: 489-96. Schomer and McGregor say the text's "Mahoba viewpoint" suggests a separate provenance, McGregor adding that it was probably "compiled no earlier than the late 16th century" by a poet from Bundelkhand, whereas the oldest verses of the *Pṛthvīrāj-rāsau* probably existed by 1470 (1984, 18, 20). Cf. Pritchett 1980, 58, choosing to analyze a mid-length edited version of the *Pṛthvīrāj-rāsau*.

classical epic are extraneous loose ends. And, as with all our regional oral martial epics, it is not just a question of looking at the classical epics in Sanskrit to understand their "interpenetration" with oral epics, which is one of Schomer's constraints,[8] but of looking at folk traditions *of* the classical epics. But allowing that one cannot reconstruct either a written[9] or oral *Ālhā* prior to any of the texts in question, and that no solutions can be significant without contextualizing the available texts geographically, historically, and in relation to each other, I would emphasize the likelihood that links with the *Mahābhārata* are part of *Ālhā*'s primary process inspiration and earliest development as oral epic, and that along with *Ālhā*, the *Pṛthvīrāj-rāsau* and *Bhaviṣya Purāṇa* provide us with evidence that this inspiration was worked in different directions. Since I will focus mainly on the versions in the *Bhaviṣya Purāṇa* and Elliot *Ālhā*, the following table 4 will be a helpful referent for the discussion of correspondences between these two texts.

Table 4. Textual correspondences between the *Bhaviṣya Purāṇa*'s "*Ālhā* segment" and the Elliot *Ālhā*[10]

Bhaviṣya Purāṇa's *Ālhā* segment through its thirty-two adhyāyas	**Elliot *Ālhā* by "canto" in Waterfield and Grierson (1923)**
1 Pāṇḍavas, cursed by Śiva, appeal to Kṛṣṇa	
2 End of Pāṇḍavas; Śālivāhana encounters Īśamasīha	
3 Bhojarāja encounters Mahāmada	
4 Expansion of Agnivaṃśa; Kali appeals to Kṛṣṇa	
5 Births of Jayacandra and Pṛthivīrāja; their rivalry over taxes	
6 Pṛthivīrāja abducts Saṃyoginī	Canto 1, Wooing of King Prithī

[8]I count ten ways in which Schomer identifies "similarities and parallelisms between the two epics": 1. internecine wars of annihilation; 2. interpenetrating heroic ages; 3. overlapping geographies; 4. continuities in the classification of peoples; 5. self-destructions of the warrior class; 6. active roles for "cult deities . . . even though they are not central figures" (see chap. 2, § C above); 7. pentadic groups of heroes; 8. "relatively undifferentiated" character of the opposition; 9. parallels between the central heroines; and 10. the "most significant parallelism of all," the "incarnation scheme."

[9]Grierson rejects "the tradition of little value" that *Ālhā* "was composed by Jagnaik, sister's son of Parmāl" (W&G 10; cf. Dwivedi 1966, 23-24; Dikshit 1977, 151). I see no reason to suspect a written archetype.

[10]One may note that Śrīrāma Śarmā's edition of *BhvP* with Hindi commentary (1968) mutilates the purāṇa's account by editing out adhyāyas 8, 20-23, 25, 27, and 29-31.

7	1-27: Bhīṣmasiṃha gets mare Hariṇī; Parimala (Parmāl) recovers from snakebite and gets Jayacandra's assurance of an alliance	
	28-end: Nine-lākh chain	Canto 2, Nine-lākh chain
8	Nine-lākh chain continued	
9	Nine-lākh chain continued	
10	1-13: Kṛṣṇāṃśa (Ūdal), age nine, reads Śāstras; Parimala pays tax to Pṛthivīrāja but Lakṣaṇa refuses	
	14-34: Kṛṣṇāṃśa outwrestles Mahīpati's (Māhil's) son Abhaya	Canto 3, Mārō Feud, p. 72
	55-54: Birth of four magical horses from Hariṇī, which Parimala bestows on heroes	Canto 3, p. 69
	54-62: Young heroes meet Śāradā on deer hunt	Canto 3, pp. 69-70
11	1-7: Young heroes go to ocean and get boons from Śāradā	
	7-8: Malanā gives birth to Raṇajit	
	9-21: Kṛṣṇāṃśa goes to Urvīyā (Urai), where Mahīpati tries to capture him in an iron net	Canto 3, pp. 70-71
	22-25: Mahīpati goes to Delhi, convinces Pṛthivīrāja to attack Krsnāmśa in Mahāvatī (Mahobā)	
	26-56: Pṛthivīrāja is defeated	
	57-61: Balakhāni (Malkhān) builds Śirīṣākhya (Sirsā fort)	
12	War in Māhiṣmatī (Mārō)	Canto 3, pp. 74-143: Mārō Feud
13	1-13: Return to Mahāvatī; Mahīpati obtains Māhismatī; funerary rites at Gaya; death of Laksavrttī (Lākhā), who becomes an Apsaras	
	14-end: Āhlāda marries Svarnavatī (Sunwā)	Canto 4, Marriage of Ālhā and Sunwā
14	Birth of Indula (Indal); his trip to Indraloka to be suckled by Śācī	
15	Śāradā gives boons to heroes	Canto 22, p. 269
16	Balakhāni weds Gajamuktā (Gajmōtin)	Canto 5, Marriage of Malkhān and Gajmōtin
17	Brahmānanda (Brahmā) weds Velā (Belā)	Canto 6, Marriage of Brahmā and Belā
18	Krsnāmśa weds Puspavatī (Phulwā)	Canto 7, Marriage of Ūdal and Phulwā
19	Indula goes to Laṅkā seeking to wed Padminī	
20	Indula weds Padminī	
21	Sukhakhāni (Sulkhān) weds	

	Madanamañjarī	
22	1-25: Sports and previous lives of Krsnāmśa and Puspavatī	
	26-70: Krsnāmśa brings Candrāvalī (Candrā Bel) to Mahāvatī from Balīthaṭha	Canto 8, Return of Candrā Bel
23	Carrying off of Indula	Canto 9, Carrying off of Indal
24	1-36: Banishment of Āhlāda	Canto 10, Ālhā's Banishment
	37-73: Lakṣana's Digvijaya	Canto 12, The Gānjar War
	73-end: Pṛthivīrāja obtains the secret of how to kill Balakhāni and Sukhakhāni	
25	1-38: Lakṣaṇa weds Padminī	Canto 11, Marriage of Lākhan
	39-46: Death of Sukhakhāni	
	46-end: Death of Balakhāni, satī of Gajamuktā	Canto 13, Sirsā War (with satī of Gajmōtin)
26	Battle of Kīrtisāgara	Canto 14, Battle of Kīratsāgar
27	1-50: Return of Āhlāda	Canto 15, Return of Ālhā
	51-79: Battle of Vetravatī	Canto 16, Battle of the Betwā
28	Captivity of Kṛsnāṃśa	Canto 17, Carrying off of Ūdal
29	War with Chinese Buddhists	
30	Release of Laksana from prison in Delhi	
31	1-172: Brahmānanda's visit to Delhi; the wives of the Kauravāmśas	Canto 18, Home-bringing of Belā, I
		Canto 19, Home-bringing of Belā, II
	172-end: Velā's vengeance: she comes to fallen Brahmānanda, and takes him on all-India horseback-pilgrimage	Canto 20, Belā's vengeance, she comes to fallen Brahmā
32	1-15: Velā visits Mahāvatī, calls for war	Canto 20 continued, Belā comes to Mahobā
	16-72: Gathering of the armies at Kuruksetra	
	73-197: Eighteen-day war	
	198-206: Velā kills Tāraka (Tāhar)	Canto 20 continued, Belā kills Tāhar
		Canto 21, Battle of the Sandal Grove
		Canto 22, The Sandal Pillars
	207-9: Velā's satī	Canto 23, Belā Satī
	210-end: Death of Lakṣaṇa; Āhlāda goes to Plantain Forest; establishment of Kali; coming of Sahoddīna; death of Pṛthivīrāja	

A. Portions and Incarnations

That Belā's reincarnation of Draupadī is central to *Ālhā*'s interepic linkages becomes clear only as this epic unfolds. Among such correlations, reincarnations are only the most obvious. But since this is a point where the *Bhaviṣya Purāṇa*'s version of *Ālhā* is especially rich, let us chart our course by familiarizing ourselves with the main incarnations, listed in table 5, as they appear from our three main sources: (1) a "Kanauj" version, drawn from Schomer's list of incarnations that "emerge in the course of the [*Ālhā*] narrative" (1989, 148)—that is, mainly in the Elliot *Ālhā;* (2) a "Mahobā" version, recalled by the two lead singers of a prominent *Ālhā* troupe from Mahobā—Baccha Singh, titled Ālhā Samrāṭ ("Emperor of *Ālhā*") and Charan Singh, whose troupe's *Ālhā* performances are recorded on cassettes (Star Cassette Centre, Maudaha, Hamirpur District, Uttar Pradesh)—whom I interviewed in December 1995; and (3) those in the *Bhaviṣya Purāṇa*.

Table 5. *Ālhā* figures and the *Mahābhārata* characters they incarnate in three variants

Hero/Heroine	Kanauj	Mahobā	*Bhaviṣya Pur.*	Purāṇic Name
Belā	Draupadī	Draupadī	Draupadī	Velā
Brahmā	Arjuna	Arjuna	Arjuna	Brahmānanda
Ālhā	Yudhiṣṭhira	Yudhiṣṭhira	Balarāma	Āhlāda
Ūdal		Kṛṣṇa or Barbarīka	Kṛṣna	Udayasiṃha
Mīrā Tālhan	Bhīma	Kīcaka	Bhīma	Talana
Lākhan	Nakula	Nakula	Nakula	Lakṣaṇa
Malkhān	Sahadeva	Sahadeva	Yudhiṣṭhira	Balakhāni
Prithīrāj	Duryodhana	Duryodhana	Dhṛtarāṣṭra	Pṛthivīrāja
Tāhar	Karṇa	Karna	Karṇa	Tāraka
Chauṇrā	Droṇa		becomes Raktabīja	Cāmuṇḍa
Dhāndhū		Bhīma		
Māhil		Śakuni	Duryodhana	Mahīpati

Suffice it to say that whereas the Kanauj and Mahobā lists exhaust the incarnations in their respective sources, the full *Bhaviṣya Purāṇa* list would be much bigger. Let us also serve notice that table 5 opens onto some intriguing puzzles: the main one being that in the Elliot *Ālhā*, Ūdal incarnates no one. Schomer tries to compensate for this by listing a variant in which Ūdal incarnates Bhīma, and treating Bhīma's Elliot *Ālhā* incarnation in Mīrā Tālhan as the "alternate." She does not give her source for this adjustment of what is otherwise an Elliot *Ālhā* list, but possibly it comes from a "flanking" western Hindī variant, since I found it in Agra.[11] But Bhīma is only one piece of this puzzle, since, as table

[11]The informant, Kishan Sharma, a Brahman, insisted that the only *Mbh* figures to reincarnate themselves in *Ālhā* were the Pāṇḍavas.

5 suggests, his "movability" relates to that of Kṛṣṇa, whom I will discuss in the next section, leaving the intriguing figure of Barbarīka for chapter 12. Let us only repeat that nonuniformity does not signify triviality, and turn to the story.

It is a cliché of both colonial British and Hindu nationalist historiographies that Prithīrāj of Delhi—in Tod's ringing words, "the last of the Hindu emperors of India"[12]—draws the kings of Mahobā and Kanauj, Parmāl and Jaychand, respectively, into the pyrrhic war which, even though he wins it, leaves the fractious Rajputs decimated and North India open to Muslim imperial takeover at end of the twelfth century.[13] Although inscriptional and other evidence permits one to give credence to the historicity of the rivalries between these principals and a battle between them in 1182 that would correspond to their final battle in *Ālhā*, most other characters and events have no surer historical foothold than what is supplied by the bardic chronicle texts, which historians tend to regard as late and "fantastic."[14] This is the historians' judgment in particular on Ālhā, Ūdal, and numerous other figures who appear in both *Ālhā* and the chronicles, but who are without the barest traces in the solidifiable historical record. Here are some of the more salient incongruities between (a) the epical texts (*Rāsaus*, *Ālhā*) and grounded history; (b) between *Pṛthvīrāj-rāsau* and *Ālhā*; and (c) *between Parmāl-rāsau* and *Ālhā*:

(a) According to Majumdar, Pṛthivirāja was probably born between 1162-65, and is described as a minor as of 1177.[15] Yet according to *Ālhā*, he sired seven sons to fight his battles by 1182, and had a daughter

[12][1829-32, 1920] 1990, 114. Vaidya uses the phrase "last Hindu Emperor of India" twice (1924, i, 90), the second time italicizing "last"; Cf. Sherring 1872, 161; Dey [1899] 1927, 230: "the last Hindu king of Delhi"; Pritchett 1980, citing other critics writing similarly in Hindi about the *Pṛthivīrāj-rāsau*.

[13]Explanation of Muslim ascendancy by lack of "harmony among the kings of Hindustan" occurs already in a 1808 Bengali history by the Sanskritist Mrityunjay Vidyalankar, commissioned by the British; Chatterjee, viewing the "historiographic allegiances" of this author as "entirely precolonial," suggests that "comments on the disunity of Indian kings" might have been found "in Persian histories in circulation among the literati in late eighteenth-century Bengal" (1995a, 80, 82). Cf. Bose 1956, 193-95: the "cowardly" Parmāl whose "martial spirit was not up to the standard set by Rajput traditions" prevailed over "Alha and Udal, the two great patriots"; Munshi 1957, viii-xxix: "social stagnation and regional consciousness" replaced "Āryavarta Consciousness"; Majumdar 1957, 125-29: "the collapse of Hindu rule" was caused by internecine fights, false ideals of Ksatriya chivalry, ascendancy of regionalism over nationalism, and failure to produce patriots.

[14]Bose 1956, 192, who continues, "it is futile to treat them on a par with the actual story known from the evidence of inscriptions and Moslem accounts." Cf. 94-96, 195; Dikshit 141-49; Ray [1931-36] 1973, 2:719-29.

[15]Majumdar 1957, 104; 113; but cf. Vaidya 1926, 321.

Belā who reached twelve shortly before then. His chief ministers are named, but differ from his epical ones. Indeed, according to Vaidya, "Prithvīrāja was not in Delhi as the Rāsā [and other epical sources] represents but in Ajmer" (1926, 334-35). Muslim historians also describe an ignominious death for the Chandēl king Parmāl twenty years after his self-induced epical end, while inscriptions indicate that his son Trailokyavarman, unknown in the epical texts, was a king of mettle.[16]

(b) The *Pṛthvīrāj-rāsau* mentions three queens of Pṛthvīrāj, the youngest being Chamaṇḍ Rai's (Chauṉṟā's) younger sister. None is Agmā, mother of Belā and his seven sons, including Tāhar. *Ālhā*'s story of Belā's marriage to Brahmā is not mentioned in the *Rāsau*. Contrary to *Ālhā*, in which Chauṉṟā dies at the last battle with the Chandēls (1182), Chamaṇḍ Rai survives this to become Pṛthvīrāj's main general in his last battle with Shihāb al-Dīn (Muhammad Ghori) (1191-92), forcing the latter's capture in the initial battle before dying in a subsequent one.[17]

(c) *Parmāl-rāsau* tells that Parmāl was five when he acceded (c. 1165), which would make him "barely 17 at the time of the Cāhamana war, when we can hardly expect him to have a son capable of leading the army. That Brahmajit [Brahmā] is not represented as a minor is evident from the further statement that on his death fifty of his wives became *satī*" (Dikshit 1977, 149). Brahmā-Brahmajit has fifty wives rather than his one wife, Belā, in *Ālhā*. Yet we will find Brahmā a minor in *Ālhā* folklore of Agra (see chapter 14, § C). Wherever *Ālhā* figures appear in these other texts, their stories are thus already folk-epical in tone. The story that we now unfold is thus one that historians do not regard as factual.

Let us begin with the principal characters already mentioned, though not with the story's own beginning(s) (on which see § C). Despite Prithīrāj's efforts, his daughter Belā becomes betrothed to the Chandēl prince Brahmā of Mahobā. Brahmā is served by a group called the Banāphars, with whom he has been raised as a brother.[18] The Banāphars, numbering six in *Ālhā*, include three of the figures in table 5, and unlike the stable royal connections of Belā (Draupadī incarnate) and Brahmā (Arjuna incarnate), their incarnational identities are unstable from text to text. Of

[16]Ray (1931-36) 1973, 727-29; Bose 1956, 99-111; Dikshit 1977, 147-49. If, however, Pritchett is correct that "Prthviraj's age can be calculated as thirty-seven or thirty-eight at the time of his death" in the *Rāsau* (1980, 58), he was born eight to eleven years earlier than Majumdar estimates.

[17]Bose 1956, 190-91; Hoernle 1881, 4-5 n. 11, in Chand Bardai 1873-86; Tod [1829-32, 1920] 1990, 143-44.

[18]In the Ghâsî Râm Hindi version of *Ālhā*, the mothers of Brahmā and the Banāphars are sisters, which would presumably have the effect of accentuating the "brother" relationship further (Grierson 1885b, 255).

those already mentioned, Ālhā is the incarnation of Yudhiṣṭhira in *Ālhā* and of Balarāma in the *Bhaviṣya Purāṇa*; Ūdal is the incarnation of no one in the Elliot *Ālhā*, of Bhīma in an alternate oral version, and of Kṛṣṇa in the purāṇa; and Malkhān is the incarnation of Sahadeva in *Ālhā* and of Yudhiṣṭhira in the purāṇa. The other three Banāphars sort themselves out as shown in table 6:

Table 6. Lesser Banāphars

***Ālhā* name**	***BhvP* name**	***Ālhā* incarnation**	***Bhvp* incarnation**
Sulkhān	Sukhkhāni	no one	Dhṛṣṭadyumna
Ḍhēwā	Devasiṃha	no one	Sahadeva
Tōmar	no such hero	no one	

As we shall see, it is especially with the Banāphars that our narratives open onto folk *Mahābhārata*. Although their hybrid status is not much defined around Dalit/Brahman ambiguities, the Banāphars are *Ālhā*'s true heroes and, broadly speaking, its LSRSCs. Their full *Ālhā* number is six, but one hears virtually nothing of Sulkhān (who is more prominent as Sukhakhāni in *Bhaviṣya*[19]) and Tōmar (who is one of the purāṇa's few absentees). They appear in combinations with various other heroes that usually number five, seven, or twelve. Two groupings, however, define the underlying social continuum that structures their place in the poem. On the one hand, they are regarded as brothers of Brahmā, whose father, the Mahobā king Parmāl (who as Parimala in *Bhaviṣya* is the incarnation of Draupadī's father Drupada[20]), and mother, Queen Malhnā, raise them as sons (W&G 79, 125, 189, 216). In this case they form a group of seven, and the connection with Brahmā and Parmāl defines their primary Rajput-as-Kṣatriya connection.[21] On the other hand, they are linked with the Muslim Mīrā Tālhan, who, after a boundary dispute (57) with the Banāphars' fathers, became a "brother" to the four fathers (74), and then, when the four fathers were killed, an "uncle" to their sons (169). In these cases, the recurrent groupings number five.

The first group of five heroes to coalesce is the set of Mīrā Tālhan

[19]In *BhvP* 3.3.9.41-42, he is a portion (aṃśa) of Parsada, whom I take to be the same as Parṣata in 3.3.1.11-13, which refers to Dhṛṣṭadyumna. Parṣata in *Mbh* is usually Dhṛṣṭadyumna, but also a name for Drupada, whose portion goes to another *BhvP-Ālhā* hero, Parimala-Parmāl.

[20]An intriguing turnabout in the purāna's amśa scheme, on which see further chap. 8.

[21]This relation parallels Bāluḍu's with his multi-caste brothers in *Palnāḍu*, except that Anapōtu Rāju's counterpart is not one of the seven but the Brahman general Chauṉṟā.

and the four fathers. Let us note that *Ālhā* and *Bhaviṣya Purāṇa* give these heroes different titles. In *Ālhā*, Mīrā Tālhan is called the Saiyid of Banaras, and is thus accorded the mantle of a descendant of the Prophet, especially via Ḥusain. Meanwhile, Banāphar, according to Waterfield, is the title of a clan "still" found in Mahobā that claims descent from the *Ālhā*'s heroes.[22]

The *Bhaviṣya* uses neither of these terms, nor any equivalent. Rather, it introduces Tālana (Mīrā Tālhan), Deśarāja (Dasrāj), and Vatsarāja (Bachrāj), that is, the Saiyid and the two senior Banāphars, into Parimala's service under the much more high-toned and obviously Brahmanical title of *mantrins* or ministers.[23] But it leaves no doubt of their subaltern and parvenu status when it introduces them through the "hair-raising war" that precedes their friendship. Tālana is the son of the Mleccha Śatayatta, king of Varanasi (Vanarasa), named for being as tall as a palm tree. And Deśarāja and Vatsarāja are born to a beautiful Ābhīrī (Ahir or Cowherd) named Vratapā from the village of Vāksara, whose nine-year-long nine-Durgā-vow (Navadurgāvrata) secured a boon from the goddess Caṇḍikā of two sons like Rāma and Kṛṣṇa. "A king named Vasumant," whose name means "Rich" and is otherwise unknown, was struck by her beauty and married her, and their sons, Deśarāja and Vatsarāja, then conquered Magadha and became kings (4.22-30).

In the Elliot *Ālhā*, the border feud between the senior Banāphars and Mīrā Tālhan is settled by Parmāl's arbitration at Mahobā. Parmāl then appoints Mīrā Tālhan as the "commander of his army" or "captain of all his hosts of war," and as his "hereditary generals" he establishes the four senior Banāphars, who had previously been defenders of the gates of the city of Baksar (Sanskrit Vāksara, as above) in Bihar (W&G 15, 58, 64). These are not indifferent details, as we shall see in chapter 10. For now, however, I will only suggest that the border dispute between the Banāphar fathers and Mīrā Tālhan prior to the reconciliation that allows them to become the joint guardians of Mahobā, and of its goddess Śāradā, is analogous to the fight between Pōrmaṉṉaṉ and the Muslim Muttāl Rāvuttaṉ that allows them to become the joint guardians of Draupadī temples (Hiltebeitel 1988a, 113-16). The grounded connections between the goddess and city in the one case, and goddess temple (which is also

[22]W&G 12. Russell and Hira Lal [1916] 1993, 4:437 identify Banāphars as Yādavas, and thus of Lunar Dynasty origins, which may be pertinent to the connections of Ālhā, Ūdal, and Dhēwā with the Lunar Dynasty Pāndavas. Qanungo 1969, 102, mentions "descendants of Alha and Udan of the Banafar *got*" having "become Bengalis to all intents and purpose except in build and whiskers."

[23]*BhvP* 3.3.7.40. Henceforth, wherever the context is clear, references to the thirty-two adhyāyas of *BhvP* 3.3, the purāna's "*Ālhā* segment," will be cited by only adhyāya and verse. This verse would thus be cited as 7.40.

the Pāṇḍavas' palace) in the other, have similar introductory tales to explain them. Moreover, in each case, it is not just the goddess and the city or palace-temple that acquire such a combination of low status but high title claiming Muslim and Hindu guardians, but high status Kṣatriya kings of the lunar dynasty—the Pāṇḍavas and Parmāl—who obtain these heroes as guardians. Pōrmaṉṉaṉ, alias Pōttu Rāja, has of course the pan-south Indian royally elevating military title of Rāja. And the *rāvuttaṉ* of Muttāl Rāvuttaṉ means "cavalier, horseman, or trooper." Indeed, it most likely derives from either *rāja-dūta*, "King's messenger," or *rāja-putra*, Rajput, and connects Muttāl Rāvuttaṉ with a status title of Tamil Muslims who claim conversion by an eleventh-century saiyid (Hiltebeitel 1988a, 102).

This first group of five, consisting of the four senior Banāphars and the Saiyid, then anticipates other groupings in which the six Banāphar sons, replacing the four fathers, carry forward this alliance in new combinations. Thus, once the senior Banāphars have been killed, Mīrā Tālhan is the constant companion of their sons, training them to fight (W&G 74), and joining the four most prominent among them—Ālhā, Ūdal, Malkhān, and Ḍhēwā—on various escapades. In the most prominent, told in the Elliot *Ālhā*'s third chapter or "battle" (*laṛāī*) as "The Mārō Feud," the five disguise themselves as warrior-Jōgī-dancer-musicians to gain revenge for the killing of the two seniormost Banāphar fathers, Dasrāj (father of Ālhā and Ūdal) and Bachrāj (father of Malkhān) (75-143). Once they have fulfilled this preliminary and essentially initiatory mission, the subject of this chapter's section D, Mīrā and the young Banāphars return to become the guardians of Mahobā, and to form a group defined by many of the kind of low status traits we have met elsewhere.

The "low born" disesteem in which the Banāphars are held is mentioned repeatedly, usually by the treacherous Māhil, whenever they seek Rajput brides. Queen Malhnā's brother and the evil genius of the piece, Māhil incarnates no one in the Elliot *Ālhā*, Śakuni in the Bundelkhandi version known to Baccha Singh, and, under the name Mahīpati, Duryodhana in the *Bhaviṣya Purāṇa*.[24] Māhil's first attempt to thwart a Banāphar's courtship is that of the eldest, Ālhā. Māhil tells Ālhā's prospective father-in-law a story that the Banāphars' mothers were

[24]See table 4; in the Elliot *Ālhā* Duryodhana is incarnated in Pṛthvīrāj. In either case, one of the net effects of the reincarnated Duryodhana's efforts is thus to prevent the remarriage of the Pāṇḍavas and Draupadī-Belā. An association with the devious Śakuni is so transparent that it makes the purāṇa's Duryodhana-explanation, which I discuss in chap. 9, all the more striking by its rejection.

not Rajputs, but Ahirs or cowherds.[25] Says Māhil, Dasrāj and Bachrāj, of "Rajput blood," were in the woods chasing deer one day when by chance they saw Devī (or Dēbī) and Birmhā on a path to market to sell curds.

> There two wild bulls of the buffaloes fought,
> They barred that path unwide;
> A bull by the horns each maiden caught,
> And thrust him back aside.
> "The sons of these girls," stout Dasrāj cried,
> "Will be swordsmiths stark, God wot,"
>
> So Dasrāj took him Dēvī as bride,
> With Bachrāj was Birmhā's lot.[26]

Grierson, in the British mode of evaluating the legitimacy of Rajput and other royal genealogies, misses the folkloric significance of the Banāphars' low status. He suggests that their link with Ahirs has no evidential basis in *Ālhā*, and is no more than a "story . . . spread by their enemy Māhil" (W&G 60). In the purāṇa, when Mahīpati (Māhil) attempts the same intervention, he only says that Āhlāda (Ālhā) has come to be of low family (*kule hīnatvamāgataḥ*) because his mother is an Āryā Ābhīrī (*āryābhīrī*: an "Aryan" Ahir) (13.88-91). Here, however, the story is foundational, and is told not at this point in Āhlāda's courtship but in connection with the girls' own marriages. The two maidens are indeed Ābhīrīs, daughters of the Gopālaka king Dalavāhana, and accustomed to daily tethering of buffaloes. They seize the two buffaloes not on a forest path, but in front of many kings during a great Caṇḍikā *homa* performed by their father, when the assembled kings themselves find the buffaloes too much to handle. Dalavāhana, at the command of Durgā, then gives the older daughter Devakī (Devī) to Deśarāja (Dasrāj), and the younger daughter Brāhmī to Vatsarāja (Bachrāj) (9.1-4). It would seem that these buffaloes are intended for sacrifice to the goddess. Moreover, as we have seen, the purāṇa adds that it is not only the "Banāphars'" mothers who are Ahirs, but their paternal grandmother from Baksar, who entered the

[25]Ahirs are among the "older, pastoralist tradition" of peasants who used a Rajputizing idiom to express their values, but who were regarded as "'spurious' Rajputs" by those who stressed genealogical ascription over achievement (Kolff 1990, 73-74). On the early history of Ahir-Ābhīras up to a tenth-century Pratihāra inscription mentioning them as a menace to be removed in western India, see Thapar 1978b, 189 n. 100.

[26]W&G 82. I change the spelling of the second wife from Brahmā to Birmhā, an alternative, to avoid confusion with other Brahmās in this study. It is Brāhmī in *BhvP*.

family with a blessing of Caṇḍikā that came not from wrestling buffaloes but from her nine-year vow to the nine Durgās! Some of this checks out with the Elliot *Ālhā*, where the Gopālaka king Dalavahana is called Dalpat, king of Gwalior.[27] He is still the two girls' father, but merely gives them to Dasrāj and Bachrāj when Parmāl requests him to supply them with brides (W&G 65).

It is evident here, as it will be elsewhere, that the *Bhaviṣya Purāṇa* not only knows much the same folklore as the Elliot *Ālhā*, but that it can point us toward clarifications and the formation of hypotheses about *Ālhā* more widely. In brief, in the present instance, it would seem that whereas the purāṇa connects the story more with kings and the goddess, *Ālhā* places a momentary emphasis on the folkways of Ahirs. But the same major details, deployed at different points and to different ends, are at play in both texts.

B. Sons of Devakī

Clearly there is more to this Ābhīra connection. The *Bhaviṣya* names the oldest girl not just Devī but Devakī, the name of Kṛṣṇa's mother. She is the mother of Ālhā and Ūdal, the two Banāphars through whom the Elliot *Ālhā* most intriguingly reenplots the *Mahābhārata*. Here we return to our puzzle. In anticipation of its completion, I will call Ālhā the Elliot *Ālhā*'s "hidden king" and Ūdal its "hidden avatāra," and propose that while the purāṇa ignores—perhaps even subverts—this hidden royal standing of Ālhā, making him an incarnation of Balarāma rather than Yudhiṣṭhira, it so fully understands Ūdal's hidden avatāra that it eliminates the mystery by proclaiming it. Let me insist that I formulated these terms, before becoming aware of the purāṇic version of the story or doing any *Ālhā* fieldwork, entirely from reading Waterfield and Grierson's Elliot *Ālhā*, in which Ālhā is not a king and Ūdal incarnates no one.

In Sanskrit, *Āhlāda* fittingly means "refreshing, reviving, gladdening" (from *ā-hlād*, "to refresh," etc.), and also "joy," as when, emerging from a period of madness, "Āhlāda obtained the higher *āhlāda* (*āhlādaś-cāhlādam paramāptavān*)" upon hearing that his son is not dead but alive (23.67). His portrayal in the purāṇa stands out as one of the significant differences between its *Mahābhārata* incarnation scheme and *Ālhā*'s. While the folk epic (not only in the Elliot *Ālhā* but in Mahobā and Agra versions) regards Ālhā as an incarnation of Yudhiṣṭhira, the *Bhaviṣya*

[27]Gwalior, also called Gopīgiri, is mentioned along with Narwar and Mathura among thirteenth-century states of "petty Hindu rulers" (Bose 1956, 111). *Gwala* means "milkman."

calls Āhlāda Rāmāṃśa, "portion of Rāma," and means by this not Rāma the king (Rāma Dāśaratha) of the *Rāmāyaṇa*, but Balarāma, elder brother of Kṛṣṇa—or, more precisely, half-brother: son of the same father but of a different mother, Rohiṇī. The *Bhaviṣya* thus retains the brother-relation of Balarāma and Kṛṣṇa as a double reincarnation. But in doing so, it contrasts with *Ālha* in two significant ways. As one might expect, it tips the reincarnational scheme toward conventions of Sanskritic bhakti (as we shall see it do elsewhere). And in leaving underdeveloped the implications of Ālhā's royalty (Balarāma is not a king), it allows us to appreciate all the more how *Ālhā*, as a regional martial oral epic, plays upon Ālhā's reincarnation of Yudhiṣṭhira as the "hidden king." Rather than mythologically doubling Ālhā's elder brother relation to Ūdal, *Ālhā* can speak of him cryptically as the "elder brother" of the Chandēl prince Brahmā, incarnation of Arjuna (W&G 198).

As to Ūdal, despite his being an incarnation of no one in the Elliot *Ālhā*, here are some of his Kṛṣṇa traits that leap off Waterfield and Grierson's pages: Ūdal is dark (1923, 99, 204, 207); as he is the youngest Banāphar, Malhnā regards him as the youngest of her seven sons;[28] offered kingship, he refuses it to remain Brahmā's guardian;[29] he uproots a post he is tied to;[30] he is put into a pit;[31] while disguised, he plays the flute (75, 88, 97) and dances like a peacock (84), all the while filling women with thoughts of love;[32] his future bride even compares him to Rāma and Kṛṣṇa (92), and says that to have him as her husband would make their bed like Viṣṇu's heaven (92); Mahobā without him is said in an invocation to be "empty, as a garden without a bird, a court without a sovereign, a night without the moon, a lake without a lotus, a tree without its leaves, or a wife without her husband" (253). This is the language of urban *viraha*, the bhakti language of a city's "love in separation," and not far from the sentiments of Ayodhyā at the departure of Rāma, or of Mathurā at the returns of Kṛṣṇa.[33] An *Ālhā* singer in Kanauj also describes Deval (Devī) and Birma (Birmhā) as "daughters of Vasudev"—presumably, at some level of convoluted allusion, the same epic-purāṇic Vasudeva who is Devakī's husband and the father of Kṛṣṇa (Schomer 1984, Excerpts, 1-2). Add Schomer's comment: "paralleling . . . the *Bhagavad Gita* . . . , just as a battle, or a

[28]W&G 125. Kṛṣṇa is the seventh son of Devakī.

[29]W&G 241. According to *Mbh* 1.79.7, descendants of Yadu (Kṛsna would be included) can have no share of kingship.

[30]W&G 213; cf. the child Kṛṣṇa's uprooting of the two trees in *HV* 51.16-32.

[31]W&G 218. The Kauravas try to trap Kṛṣṇa in a pit in Tamil *Mbh* traditions during his embassy to the Kaurava court; see Hiltebeitel 1988a, 311-12.

[32]W&G 82-83; cf. 209, 213-14: general themes of Kṛsna's youthful sports.

[33]*Rām* 2.30.13-19; 35.17-38; 42; *HV* 2.45; 55.53-85 (see Hiltebeitel 1989c, 96).

fresh phase of battle, is about to begin," it is "typically" Ūdal "who speaks, exhorting the warriors to fight without fear of dying" (1989, 152). Note how the allusions move back and forth between the childhood Kṛṣṇa and the epic Kṛṣṇa.

As we shall see, such affinities multiply. How are we to see the relation between this veiled rapport with Kṛṣṇa in the Elliot *Ālhā*, on the one hand, and the open identification with Kṛṣṇa in the *Bhaviṣya Purāṇa*? While Schomer makes a brief reference to this purāṇa's treatment of Ūdal "as an incarnation of Kṛṣṇa" (1989, 143, n. 3), her suggestion that the "notion of the Ālhā as a reenactment of the *Mahābhārata* may have come from this text" (ibid.) seems not to have been supported by any study of the purāṇa. The two texts' incarnation schemes are too different to posit a linear derivation. Both must rework prior oral sources. Nonetheless, the purāṇa's portrayal of Udayasiṃha (Ūdal) as a reincarnation of Kṛṣṇa is absolutely central to it. Usually the purāṇa's long "*Ālhā* segment" simply calls him Kṛṣṇāṃśā, "portion of Kṛṣṇa," and at several point calls itself "The Story of Kṛṣṇāṃśa" (*Kṛṣṇāṃśacarita* and variants).

C. Frame Stories and Divine Interventions

Yet the case of Ūdal in the Elliot *Ālhā* poses problems. We must begin to consider what I will argue is this *Ālhā*'s tacit treatment of this "portion of Kṛṣṇa." Let me pose the question as follows: What is a "*Mahābhārata* of the Kali Yuga" without Kṛṣṇa? Is there a wider *Mahābhārata* frame story? There are at least three *Ālhā* answers now in print, plus an oral one I reserve for chapter 14. Of the three, one features Kṛṣṇa, one Śiva, and one the goddess. The first two are frame stories, the latter part of the main story. All three are divine interventions. Only the last two are paralleled in the *Bhaviṣya Purāṇa*.

The first is found in *Ālhā* variants:[34] after the *Mahābhārata* war, the Pāṇḍavas, who had not yet had their fill of fighting, besought Kṛṣṇa to let them have more of it, and Kṛṣṇa granted this by decreeing that they would be reborn in the Kali yuga, but this time to be defeated. Kṛṣṇa thus determines things in *Ālhā* from afar, and does not need to reincarnate himself. In these versions, with Kṛṣṇa's role set apart, Ūdal can be the incarnation of Bhīma.[35] This story is without echoes in the *Bhaviṣya Purāṇa*.

[34]Schomer 1989, 148; Lutgendorf 1979, 14.

[35]Kishan Sharma of Agra, who, as noted above, knows Ūdal as an incarnation of Bhīma, answered negatively to my question of whether the incarnations resulted from a pronouncement of Kṛṣṇa. He explained the (for him) dubious stories of incarnation ("I have not seen it") as resulting from a perception during the heroes' time that they were so strong they must be incarnations of the Pāṇḍavas.

The "Elliot *Ālhā*" tells a different story: "Śiva, it is said, once came to visit the Pāṇḍavas and one of them, Nakula, accidently shot him with an arrow, whereupon he cursed Draupadī to be reborn as Belā and to be the cause of many battles" (Schomer 1989, 148). Here, the divine decree comes from Śiva, not Kṛṣṇa, and the immediate focus of the reincarnations is not the Pāṇḍavas but Draupadī. Rather than Kṛṣṇa decreeing incarnations of others from the distant past, the possibility is left for his hidden presence in the story. If so, it is not a presence through incarnation (as with Brahma Nāyuḍu in *Palnāḍu*, who after all incarnates Viṣṇu rather than Kṛṣṇa) but a presence through evocation, including the bhakti evocation of presence through absence.

In this instance, such a story *is* featured in the *Bhaviṣya Purāṇa* (3.3.1), where it is a prologue to its entire *Ālhā* segment. But note the differences. The new story comes after Śiva has enabled Aśvatthāman to kill Draupadī's children and her brother Dhṛṣṭadyumna in the night raid that ends the *Mahābhārata* war. The Pāṇḍavas, led by Bhīma, are enraged and attack Śiva, first with weapons, then with palms and fists. Śiva only curses them to be reborn in the Kali yuga to enjoy the results of their transgression. The Pāṇḍavas get Kṛṣṇa to try to intercede, but Śiva says his "curse" (*śāpa*) is irreversible, and decrees the incarnations (*aṃśas*) that most of the major heroes and Draupadī will take. Draupadī's reincarnation as Velā (Belā) is included, but it is Bhīma who is singled out: he will have to be born in the womb of a Mlecchā (in this text, a Muslim) because he is "guilty of bad speech" (*durvacanāddusṭo*; 1.24). The purāṇa has nothing good to say about Muslims, whereas *Ālhā* sometimes tilts its ambivalence toward the positive. But the truly striking difference now follows. Having heard Śiva's outburst, Hari (Kṛṣṇa) smiles and says, "By the avatar of my śakti (*mayā śaktyavatāreṇa*), the Pāṇḍavas will be protected . . . " (30). Kṛṣṇa has a master plan, as we shall see. As Udayasiṃha, he is the "Risen Lion," a name, known also in the Elliot *Ālhā*, which probably stands behind his battlefield boast that his mother bore him as a lion with a heart "shaggy with hair" (W&G 110). These may be evocations of Narasiṃha, the destructive Man-Lion avatar.

The third story, as told in the Elliot *Ālhā*, links Ālhā and Ūdal with Śāradā in a myth that contrasts them with Chauṉrā, incarnation of Droṇa. Chauṉrā, a Brahman general, leads Prithīrāj's army from a "one-tusker elephant," and keeps assuming lethal bridal disguises. As incarnation of Droṇa, one of the chief warrior-Brahmans of the *Mahābhārata*, it is not surprising that he, like Droṇa, is central to his epic's mythology of

Brahmanicide.[36] The penultimate canto of the Elliot *Ālhā* tells the following story behind the events that lead to the deaths of the main heroes.

Once, when Chaunṟā worshiped Śāradā for twelve years, she appeared and invited him to be the first "knight" to fill her drinking vessel—that is, her skull bowl—to the brim with blood (see plates 7 and 8). When Chaunṟā proved unable to fill the bowl in his services to Prithīrāj and the goddess at Delhi, Śāradā took him to Mahobā, and there distributed two rolls of betel to him, five to Ūdal, and the rest to Ālhā.[37] The next morning, Ālhā and Ūdal's mother Devī, knowing this, sent Ālhā to Śāradā's temple, where Ālhā severed his own head for Śāradā, filling her cup to the brim before she revived him and made him immortal. Next Devī sent Ūdal, who hoped for the same boon. But Śāradā said only one brother could receive this favor, and gave him the boon of being slain by Chaunṟā, since one who dies at a Brahman's hand attains Viṣṇu's heaven. Finally Chaunṟā came and tried to blackmail Śāradā, threatening to implicate her in Brahmanicide by disemboweling himself if she denied him immortality. But she was finished dispensing immortalities, and granted him instead the double boon of killing Ūdal and being slain by Ālhā (W&G 269). This then requires Ālhā to kill Chaunṟā by squeezing him to death "so that no drop of his blood may fall to the earth," since Śāradā had also (we are not told when) given Chaunṟā a familiar additional boon of *near*-immortality: "that if a drop of his blood should fall to the earth myriads of Chaunṟās would rise from the ground in its place" (272).

In the *Bhaviṣya Purāṇa*, the goddess gives the heroes boons on two occasions. When Kṛṣṇāṃśa is ten, the youths worship Jagadambikā (the "World Mother," as in *Pābūjī*) for a month at an oceanside forest, and she responds to their bhakti with the following boons: "To Āhlāda divinity (*suratvam*), to Balakhāni strength (*balatvam*), to Deva [Devasiṃha] knowledge of time (*kālajñatvam*), to the king [Brahmānanda] knowledge of Brahman, and to Kṛṣṇāṃśa innate yoga (*yogatvam*)."[38]

[36]Compare Anapōtu Rāju in *Palnādu*. Droṇa, father of Aśvatthāman, does not ride an elephant in *Mbh*, but he dies when the elephant Aśvatthāman is slain to provide Yudhiṣthira with the pretext for his famous sotto voce lie that "Aśvatthāman (the elephant) is dead" (cf. Hiltebeitel 1988a, 190-94, 427-29, 444-46).

[37]Here and elsewhere in *Ālhā*, the roll of betel (*bīrā*) represents a challenge for the champion who takes it up. For the same custom in *Pābūjī*, also with the goddess Deval called upon to set the terms, but with the *bīro* leaves "typically from *campo* or *pīpal* trees," see J. D. Smith 1991, 338-40.

[38]11.1-6; *yogatvam*, literally, "yoga-ness," but multivalent in meaning. I translate in a way whose contextual appropriateness will be made clear later. Hohenberger (1967, 36) translates "*den Stand eine Yogin*," "the condition of a yogin."

This episode is unknown in the Elliot *Ālhā*, although there is nothing incongruous about the boons. The second story, the subject of a short adhyāya (15) of its own, parallels the *Ālhā* story just recounted, but has a different setting. The incident occurs after the marriages of Āhlāda and Kṛṣṇāṃśa (Ālhā and Ūdal) and before that of Balakhāni (Malkhān).[39] The purāṇa makes Cāmuṇḍa (Chauṉṛā) Devakī's second son, born a year after Āhlāda. After the sack of Mahāvatī (Mahobā)[40] that results in the capture and death of her husband, while she is seven months pregnant with Kṛṣṇāṃśa, Devakī throws Cāmuṇḍa into the Yamuna River.[41] He is then rescued and raised by the Brahman Sāmanta, Pṛthivīrāja's *purohita* or court priest (9.19-20, 29-32). When Cāmuṇḍa reaches age twelve, having completed four years of reciting what I take to be the *Devī Māhātmyam*,[42] Śāradā appears to test not only him and his two "brothers," but his cousins and mother. Fond of her devotees (*svabhaktān-bhaktavatsalā*), Śāradā challenges each to fill her pot (*kuṇḍikā*), and then grants boons with the results shown in table 7. Only Āhlāda and Kṛṣṇāṃśa fill the pot, while the desireless (*niṣkāma*) Devasiṃha wins mokṣa for

Table 7. Śāradā's Boons

Hero/Heroine	Offering	Śāradā's Boon
Sukhakhāni	*madhu* flowers	to be beloved of the gods
Balakhāni	meats (*maṃśair*)	death of a hero
Cāmuṇda	blood-drops (*raktakaiḥ*)	to become Raktabīja
Devakī	*havya*s and *arcana*s	a lady (*devī*) for a long time in her own country*
Āhlāda	limbs	speech that comes true#
Kṛṣṇāṃśa	head	superior strength

**bhaved devī cirakālam svalokagā* (15.11)[43]
#*vavatprokta* (15.11)[44]

[39]Perhaps a flashback, it comes in the text after Kṛṣṇāṃśa has reached fourteen (3.3.14.1), yet occurrs when Cāmuṇḍa, at least two years Kṛṣṇāṃśa's senior, is twelve (15.4).
[40]When citing *BhvP* I will usually refer to this Chandēl capital as Mahobā.
[41]Devakī's reasons are obscure in the text. According to Hohenberger, he was the smallest or poorest (*geringster*) of the family (1967, 34-35).
[42]The term used is *tricaritra* (3.3.15.4), triple-biography, presumably referring to the triple-biography of the goddess in *DM*, which is referred to just two verses earlier by the name *Saptaśatīstotra* (15.2) as the text that his brothers blissfully enter into through meditation (15.2).
[43]I follow the suggestion of R. Venkataraman (personal communication, November 1995).
[44]Quick-witted speech; foretelling; what he says will happen—again following a suggestion of R. Venkataraman.

having offered nothing. All are pleased (15.12). Here it is not a question of how three heroes resolve their quest for immortality and their exits from the story, but of how Devakī and five heroes—four of them Banāphars in *Ālhā*, and the fifth Cāmuṇḍa—obtain the goddess's preliminary blessings. But here the three heroes are brothers: something the Elliot *Ālhā* gives no hint of, and that is definitely not the case in Chand Bardai's *Pṛthvīrāj-rāsau* or for Baccha Singh in Mahobā.[45] Indeed, it seems that instead of throwing Chauṉrā into the river, Devī thwarts his plans by sending her two favored sons to Śāradā's temple before Chauṉrā can get there. Yet Camuṇḍā's boon of "becoming Raktabīja," the "Blood Seed" demon of the *Devī Māhātmyam*, is precisely the second boon from Śāradā that we need to know about in order to understand why Ālhā must squeeze Chaũṉrā to death so that his blood-drops won't touch the ground.[46]

Meanwhile, the theme of Brahmanicide is much more forceful in the Elliot *Ālhā* than in the purāṇa. Not only does Chauṉrā attempt blackmail over this issue by threatening to disembowel himself rather than actually offering his drops of blood; rather than having him "become Raktabīja," the Elliot *Ālhā* echoes the *Mahābhārata*'s brahmanicide mythology by making Chauṉrā the reincarnation of Droṇa. In the Elliot *Ālhā* it is a question of the goddess's drinking bowl rather than a pot. *Ālhā* would seem here to have correlated the goddess's drinking bowl of blood—which we have met before in *Pābūjī* and the Draupadī (and Kūttāṇṭavar) cult *Mahābhārata*—with Chauṉrā's incarnation of Droṇa, who is named for the *droṇa* vessels used to gather the juices from the pounded soma plant (analogous to blood, but also the drink of

[45]Chand presents Chamaṇḍ Rai as the youngest of three Dahima Rajput brothers (an "extinct" clan since Chamand's time, from west of Agra, according to Tod and others), all serving Pṛthvīrāj. Chamaṇḍ Rai is "the same age as Prithiràj, and his most beloved friend" (Hoernle 1881, 4-5, n. 11, in Chand Bardai 1873-86; Tod [1829-32, 1920] 1990, 143-44). But according Viśvambhara Nāthā (1986, 2), around the time Prthvīrāj became king of Delhi, a Brahman named Indradatta, resident in Baksar, had two sons who performed tapas and gained fame: Sūryamani, the elder, and Cāmuṇḍa Rāya (also called Caudā). By Devī's grace Sūryamaṇi became king of Rewa and Cāmuṇḍa Rāya a general (*senāpati*) under the Tomara Anandapāla. When India was attacked by Muhammad Ghori, Cāmunda Rāya captured him many times, leading Prthvīrāj's contingents. Mahobā then falls *after* these battles with Muhammad Ghori. Baccha Singh's story is close to *BhvP*: Chauṉrā is born in a village near Delhi of Ksatriya parents Langri Rai and Śaśīvratā. The latter floated him down the Yamuna where he was discovered by a Brāhmaṇi and raised a Brahman.

[46]On Raktabīja, see my 1988a, 301, 363-64; on Brahmarāksasas in such an aspect, 169-82. In Draupadī cult dramas, Duhśāsana's death may be similarly portrayed: after squeezing him to death (Hiltebeitel 1988b, Part 2), Bhīma checks himself from drinking Duhśāsana's blood and, at Krsṇa's advice, offers it to Vāyu so that the Wind prevents it from touching the ground (1988a, 407-9).

"immortality") in Vedic Soma sacrifices.[47] In the Elliot *Ālhā*, Chauṉrā serves the goddess in the image of the same Raktabīja he "becomes" in the purāṇa: the demon "Blood Seed," whose capacity to fill Śāradā's blood bowl would seem to require the offering of his own infinitely regenerative blood by his own bloodless killing. As the goddess's victim, he is received as an offering both in the form of the vessel (droṇa) that the goddess holds, and in the blood drops of his multiple personality, which her vessel contains.

In the last element of his name, Chauṉrā is also a "king": the purāṇa's Cāmuṇḍa is "king Chāmuṇḍ" or Chāmuṇḍ Rai (= Chauṉrā) in the *Pṛthvīrāj-rāsau* (W&G 29). In sum, he appears to impersonate the violent warrior goddess (Cāmuṇḍā) in the mixed-caste and mixed-gender role of a Brahman-Kṣatriya "King."[48] These considerations may help us understand Cauṉrā's lethal bridal disguises.

Meanwhile, one of Ālhā's hidden royal traits is that he is, at least in the Elliot *Ālhā*, an immortal royal Brahmanicide. As such, his immortality is confirmed with a counterimage. When Prithīrāj sees Chauṉrā's fall, he hits Ālhā with an arrow. But milk flows from Ālhā's wound instead of blood (W&G 273). In all this, Ālhā rounds off his destiny with a crescendo of reminders that he is an incarnation of Yudhiṣṭhira, who alone among the Pāṇḍavas and Draupadī enters heaven with his earthly frame, even though he carries, like Ālhā for the killing of Chauṉrā, the sin of Brahmanicide for his lie in the killing of Droṇa. We shall consider these episodes more closely.

If we pry apart these frames and interventions in their *Ālhā* and purāṇic variants, we can see some of the features that distinguish them. In the stories of the goddess's blessings, her *Ālhā* blessings are the heroes' exits from the story. In the purāṇa, she blesses with traits to be implemented in the story ahead. In *Ālhā*, it is Ālhā who offers her his head; in the purāṇa it is Kṛṣṇāṃśa. In *Ālhā*, Chauṉrā evokes the contradictions in the epic figure of Droṇa; in the purāṇa he evokes the purāṇic figure of Raktabīja, and the *Devi Māhātmyam* on top of the *Mahābhārata*.

As to the frame stories, in *Ālhā*, Kṛṣṇa gives a boon that will go awry:

[47]Curiously, in *BhvP*, despite his having no connection with Droṇa, Cāmuṇḍa is slain when Āhlāda "churns" (*mamantha*) him (3.3.32.205): a verb linked with the soma as elixir of immortality in the churning of the ocean myth.

[48]In *BhvP*, Pṛthivīrāja offers Cāmunda Balakhāni's kingdom if he defeats him (3.3.24.74). Cāmuṇḍa's sibling relation to the heroes in the purāṇa is curious, reminding one of Kṛṣṇa and Balarāma's purāṇic "sister" Ekanaṃśā, whom Kamsa dashes to death on a stone only to see her rise into the sky as the destructive goddess who laughs and announces herself as his death. *BhvP* evokes this episode (and Cāmunda's name) at the birth of Velā, when, along with an earthquake and a rain of blood mixed with powdered bones, Cāmundā Devī makes a loud inauspicious laugh in the sky (17.8).

the Pāṇḍavas will suffer defeat; or Śiva curses them, and Draupadī in particular is cursed to be the cause of many battles. In the purāṇa, Śiva's curse is that Bhīma will become a Muslim. In one case, it is a matter of recurrence and balance in karmic and cosmic cycles; in the other an opportunity taken for "prophesy" about "future"—*bhaviṣya*—conflict with Muslims. In *Ālhā*, the gods' initiatives never go beyond their responses to the initiatives of the heroes. Whether they are working together or against each other, the text is silent. The divine plan is barely disclosed, and left a mystery. In the purāṇa, the initiatives are with the gods: Kṛṣṇa will intercede against Śiva's curse, and do so with the "avatar of his own Śakti." As will become clear, Kṛṣṇa's Śakti is the goddess: ultimately, Yoganidrā, the feminine personification of "Yogic Sleep," whom he incorporates by his "innate yoga" (yogatvam), and also, in the story's unfolding, such goddesses as Jagadambikā, Durgā, and especially Śāradā, who harmonize their actions with his, and, for that matter, with Śiva's, time after time.

D. The Mārō Feud

The initiatory mission by which the young Banāphars avenge their fathers and become guardians of Mahobā is the Elliot *Ālhā*'s third "battle/chapter" (laṛāī), "The Mārō Feud" (W&G 67-143). Its stage is set in the second laṛāī, called "The Nine-lākh Chain." When Kariyā, crown prince of Mārō, steals the nine-lākh chain from Mahobā as a gift for his sister Bijaisin, he kills Dasrāj and Bachrāj, by now Mahobā's guardians, in their sleep. Their widows are left pregnant: Devī (already mother of Ālhā) bearing Ūdal, and Birmhā (already mother of Malkhān) bearing Sulkhān. The killing allows the Mārō chiefs to settle a score against the Banāphar fathers, and when they steal the chain, they also make off with Dasrāj and Bachrāj's heads to fix on the gate of Mārō, plus various treasures from the Chandēl palace and the danseuse Lākhā (66). Learning about this twelve years later, the young Banāphars plot revenge.

Their expedition and its destination are intriguing. Noticing that the Mahobā forces must ford the Narmada river to reach Mārō (W&G 102), Waterfield saw this detail as perhaps a "clue" that its undetermined location "was close to the Narmadâ, and on the further side."[49] Jambay is "the Baghēl king" (W&G 78), which might suggest that he rules in Baghelkhand, the region that neighbors Bundelkhand to the east and whose major city is Rewa. But Mārō seems to lie on the Narmada to the southwest of Bundelkhand. The *Bhaviṣya Purāṇa*, which knows Mārō as Māhiṣmatī, has the same story, except that the Mahobā forces construct

[49]Quoted in Grierson 1885a, 256, n. 13.

a bridge over the Narmadā to reach it (3.3.12.56). When Balakhāni (Malkhān) razes the city's palaces, the people run off to hide their wealth in Vindhya mountain caves (58), and, further along in the same story, the Māhiṣmatī princess obtains Rākṣasī magic to use against the five heroes (*pañcavirān*) from a magician-guru named Ailavilin whose hut is in a great forest on the Vindhya heights (93-108).

Māhiṣmatī can mean "City of the Buffalo," and is in Sanskrit mythology the city on the Narmada ruled by the Asura Kārtavīrya Arjuna and conquered by Paraśurāma (Bhārgava Rāma). In this epic-purāṇic context, it is a stronghold of the Haihaya-Yādavas, a segment of the Lunar Dynasty or Candravaṃśa, ruled by Kārtavīrya Arjuna, who either himself or through his sons provokes the slaughter of the Kṣatriyas twenty-one times over by Paraśurāma (see chap. 13). But in the referential area of *Ālhā*, it also figures in the Chauhān-Cāhamāna Rajput legend of origins, which tells that the "first seat of the government of 'Anhal, the first created Cauhan,' was Māhiṣmatī on the Narbada, from which city the power of the twenty-four *Śākhās* [branches] of the tribe spread throughout the length and breadth of India" (Ray [1931-36, 1973, 1052). One may thus consider the possibility of a mythical link between Māhiṣmatī and the Chauhān Pṛthivīrāj, although the latter is usually said to belong to the Fire Dynasty or Agnivaṃśa rather than the Lunar Dynasty. But the Baghēls themselves also claim to be Agnivaṃśa Rajputs as a branch of the Chalukyas or Solankhis, and to have migrated eastward from Gujarat (Sherring 1872, 156-57). One might thus suspect mythic links between Jambay and Pṛthivīrāj, the Chandēls' two enemies, and their two *Ālhā* kingdoms, Mārō and Delhi.[50] It is not, however, unusual for places and "dynasties" to have varied lineage affiliations (Chattopadhyaya 1994). On the Chandēl side, it may also be pertinent that the reign of Parmāl's grandfather Madanavarman "saw the restoration of Candella power" extending south to the Narmada (Bose 1956, 90). Since the young Banāphars serve the Chandēls, we can probably assume that resonances such as these underlie the representation of Mārō-Māhiṣmatī as a dangerous boundary "Baghēl" kingdom—location uncertain—in the Narmada-Vindhya area.[51]

[50]In *BhvP*, after Māhismatī is defeated, Prthivīrāja actually convinces Balakhāni that he and his brothers should be happy with Māhismatī's wealth, and give the Māhismatī kingdom to him (3.3.13.5-6).

[51]Kane [1930-62] 1975, 4:706, says Māhismatī on the Narmada is one of those places "about the exact location of which scholars have differed." Baccha Singh, who travels widely researching *Ālhā* locations, says the *Narmadā Purāṇa* (which I have not seen) indicates that Mārō is the mountain fort of Maṇḍū, a sixteenth-century Afghan stronghold (Kolff 1990, 40) in western Madhya Pradesh. There he found Jambay's throne still extant, seven gates, and the appropriate trans-Narmada location. Cf. Schomer 1984, 4. Maheshwar

Once Ūdal learns how his father and uncle died, his mother Devī asks Mīrā Tālhan to teach him to fight. Ūdal-Kṛṣṇāṃśa is now twelve (W&G 1923, 72; *BhvP* 3.3.12.1). Ḍhēwā, wise astrologer among the young Banāphars, takes his "war-art book," turns "his Vedas o'er," and advises that they assume the guise of Jōgīs—according to Grierson's note, "wandering devotees and jugglers" (W&G 74-75). They dye their clothes red, quilt them with folds and jewels, and take up diamond-studded hats, gold bangles, pearl earrings, weapons, and musical instruments, as shown in table 8:

Table 8. The "Banāphars'" Jōgī-musician disguises upon entering Mārō-Māhiṣmatī[52]

Hero	In *Ālhā*	In *Bhaviṣya Purāṇa*
Dhēwā	tambourine	*maddu* drum
Ālhā	drum	*ḍamaru* drum
Mīrā Tālhan	lyre	*vinā*
Malkhān	lute	bell metal gong (*kāmsya*)
Ūdal	flute	dancer (*nartaka*)

Singing of Rāma and of Pārvatī's wedding, they test their disguises on their mother. When she sees she has been fooled, as she does also in the *Bhaviṣya Purāṇa* (12.33-34), she says her litter will precede them to Mārō. Ūdal secures the aid of Parmāl's "Kshatrī" cavalry, elephant warriors, and gun troops by gifting them, and Parmāl gives the heroes five magical horses.[53] Calling on Kālī, Śiva, and Śāradā, they march to Mārō, camp in an acacia wood, boil deer meat, and hear their bards sing "their legends" and paṇḍits sing the Vedas (W&G 75-80).

on the north bank of the Narmada has also "been identified as Mahishmati, the ancient capital of King Kartiviryarjun" (Bradnock 1995, 386). Grierson cites V. A. Smith that "Mâṛô is now called Bijaipur, south of Mirzâpur, and still has Jambâ's ruined fort"; a "Bihar tradition" also "identifies it with Mâr'war, no doubt wrongly" (1885a, 256, n. 13). Kishan Sharma in Agra calls Mārō "Kalinga" (ordinarily Orissa, but see chap. 10, § D), and makes Kalinga's daughter Machalā (unmentioned in the Elliot *Ālhā*) a second wife of Ālhā (she is known as Machh'lâvatî in a "Western recension" variant summarized in Grierson 1885b, 128, but has a different father). Note how a eastern "flanking" versions tend to place Mārō west of the *Ālhā* heartland, and western "flanking" ones to its east.

[52] W&G 1923, 75 (cf. 82; 88: Ūdal on flute, Ālhā on lyre); *BhvP* 3.3.12.31-32.

[53] In *BhvP*, the mantrin heroes lead the army's divisions: Tālana the whole army, Devasiṃha its chariots, Āhlāda its elephants, Balakhāni its horses (3.3.12.27-28): three of the four divisions of a classical Sanskrit epic army, of which foot-soldiers—equivalent to *Ālhā*'s gun-bearers—would be the fourth. *BhvP* mentions no gun-bearers, *Ālhā* no chariots. Cf. Narayana Rao, Shulman, and Subrahmanyam 1992, 226-36, on guns in sixteenth- and seventeenth-century south Indian sources.

After ten days and nights in the camp, Ḍhēwā checks his star book again and advises that they renew their disguises. They put Rāma's mark on their forehead, ashes on their bodies, get their mother's blessing, and depart as Jōgī-pilgrims for Jambay's fort, announcing themselves as Bairāgīs (renunciants) seeking alms (W&G 80-81). As we shall see in chapter 10, their disguise combines traits of several mendicant orders, but especially of Gorakhpanthī or Gorakhnāthī Nāth ascetics. Here we may begin to question the relationship between such ascetics and the heroes of regional martial oral epics, and also appreciate that Kṛṣṇāṃśa's "innate yoga" relates to a continuum between his ascetic, warrior, and musician activities. Says the flute-playing Kṛṣṇāṃśa to queen Malanā on one of his disguised returns to Mahobā, "We are yogins, O queen, skilled in every battle" (26.57). When Devasiṃha (Ḍhēwā) applies his astrological knowledge to divine when to don the yogi-musician disguises upon entering a kingdom, he once refers to them as *sainyayoga*, "the yoga of the army" (23.38).

Introduced to Jambay, the Jōgīs sing and Ūdal dances, entrancing everyone. When Ūdal says it is time to move on, the porter asks them to stay the full four months of rains. But Ūdal says no, they are on their way from Bengal to Hinglāj. They are probably traveling west between the Śākta destinations of Kamākhyā in "Bengal" (more accurately, Assam) and Hing Lāj in Baluchistan,[54] and it is intriguing that Ḍhēwā consults the stars en route. As they go through the streets, women become infatuated, especially those at a well where Rūpā, Queen Kushlā's maid, pauses long to watch before going to tell Kushlā of the dark Jōgīs with eyes like gazelles who dance like peafowl and look like they "come from Paradise." Once invited inside Jambay's hall, Ūdal sings, plays flute, and tells Kushlā they were sold by their widowed mother to a Jōgī band. Kushlā sends for her son Kariyā and daughter Bijaisin to see, and also asks the Jōgīs to stay during the rains. Malkhān answers with the oft-repeated, "Waters that flow and Jōgīs that go, What power can make them stay?"[55] Although she offers them thrones and brides, they refuse and rise to leave. Kushlā bids them wait for alms, and returns with "three lives'" worth of gold and pearls on golden platters. Playing the fool, Ūdal strews the pearls on the palace floor, pretending he thinks they are fruits, and making this the pretext to demand the nine-lākh chain instead, which Kushlā says she will give him if he dances for her.[56]

[54]On which more in chap. 10.

[55]Cf. the recurrent refrain in Gold 1992: "A seated yogi's a stake in the ground, but a yogi once up is a fistful of wind."

[56]W&G 82-90. *BhvP* has no scene of Kṛsnāṃśa playing the fool and strewing pearls. But

Kushlā calls for Bijaisin, expecting this will be "the joy of her life" (we would think for now the chain *is* Bijaisin's, since Kariyā got it for *her*). Bijaisin comes bearing her betel case and gives five leaves to Ūdal, who is smitten, as is she. Kushlā is "troubled and angered," thinking Ūdal is no Jōgī but a lustful prince who has seen her daughter's face. But they trick her out of killing the Jōgīs, and Bijaisin admits her attraction. The women of Mārō say the Jōgīs are like Rāma and Kṛṣṇa and give them gold and silver.[57] And Kushlā gives over the nine-lākh chain. When the Jōgīs part, Bijaisin goes to a lattice, catches Ūdal's hand, and takes him to her bower and jewelled couch. She says she knows his guile, that he is Ūdal and has come for her from Mahobā. She threatens to tell Kariyā. Ūdal dissembles, but she recalls that they met and flirted at a marriage, and tells him she waters a fig tree and does weekly fasts to make him her husband. He finally admits his identity and affections, but says they will not marry until Mārō is bathed in blood. He asks her to tell Mārō's secrets if she loves him, and she tells him various things to avoid, and that victory will come if the Banāphars plant their guns in the acacia grove. She invites him to her maiden's bed, but he says no, it would break his Rājpūti or Rajput code (W&G 90-94).

Ūdal tells Malkhān and Ālhā that Bijaisin knows him and has given him Mārō's secrets for the promise of marrying her. But the brothers say there can be no marriage with the enemy, and approach Jambay's Iron Fort.[58] At Jambay's invitation they dance and sing, and, claiming that they have heard of Lākhā, ask to see her dance. Jambay sends for her, and as she dances near them, Ūdal secretly tosses her the chain. Lākhā recognizes them and hides it in her blouse. The Jōgīs head toward their camp, but as Lākhā dances toward the door, a breeze exposes the chain to Jambay, who tells Kariyā (who wears long boots) to retrieve it. Instead of going to Lākhā, however, who is allowed to proceed, Kariyā goes to his mother Kushlā and demands the chain from her (it is not clear why he doesn't ask Lākhā). Kushlā feigns that it is broken and being threaded, but he demands it no matter what. Kushlā then has to admit that she gave it to the Jōgīs (W&G 95-100). The nine-lākh chain, though it is not

---

from Gold 1992, one can infer that it is a Rajasthani oral epic convention to offer a platter of diamonds, rubies (149, 174, 208, 259), and pearls (201) to itinerant yogis, who are presumably expected to reject them—although they also may strew them on the floor (204).

[57]Here one may wonder whether the Elliot *Ālhā* knows the alternate tradition, found in *BhvP*, linking Ālhā with Rāma-Balarāma.

[58]In *BhvP*, Jambuka (Jambay) has no such fort at Mahismatī (Mārō). Rather, it is Marudhanva (Bisēn in *Ālhā*) that has more than one iron fort (*lohadurgesu*; 3.3.16.64; cf. 20), among them, as we shall see, a "village-shaped iron fort" (*lohadurgam . . . grāmarūpam*) occupied by Cāṇḍalas or Dalits that figures in the torture of Balakhāni (Malkhān) in his courtship of Gajamuktikā (Gajmōtin).

actually unstrung here, is thus first contrasted with a strew of unstrung pearls, and is then said to have been unstrung as part of the series of deceptions.[59]

From here, the Banāphars lead the Mahobā forces in a series of routs that result in the killing of Kushlā's and Jambay's four sons, Kariyā the last to go (W&G 100-24). When Jambay tells Kushlā of their loss, Bijaisin overhears. Promising to "bind" the "Mahōbā thief" Ūdal, she sends spells from her bower to silence his companions, and turns him into a ram, whom she delivers to Jambay. Ḍhēwā divines this from his star-book, and goes with Malkhān, the two of them again disguised as Jōgī-musicians, to Bijaisin's "master," a hut-dwelling "warlock," who now keeps the ram (Ūdal) as Bijaisin's "slave." They demand the ram, and the warlock gives it along with the spell to turn Ūdal back into a man. Malkhān kills him anyway before they return to Ālhā.[60] Then they attack the Iron Fort, which stands until Ūdal devises the trick of piling up acacia wood "thorn boughs" with powder below them to double the blaze and melt the wall's lead. Presumably this is Ūdal's cryptic reading of Bijaisin's signal that victory would come from planting guns in the acacia grove. Once Jambay is flushed from his fort, he takes to the field and Ālhā defeats him after a fight on elephants.[61] The heroes plunder and burn Mārō, and call for Kushlā. Devī gets Ūdal's promise that he won't harm women, and Ūdal demands Dasrāj's turban and crest, Lākhā, the nine-lākh chain, and a litter for Bijaisin so he may wed her. Avenging Dasrāj's death, they crush Jambay in a mill-press and place his head beside Dasrāj's, which laughs. Both skulls ask to be taken to Kāśī: Jambay, since he has no sons left of his own to perform his funerary rites there.

Now Ūdal calls for Bijaisin's litter and a paṇḍit to perform their wedding. But Ālhā, no doubt recalling the ram episode, says no, she will kill Ūdal in his sleep when she thinks of her father and brothers. Ālhā orders Ūdal to strike her, but Ūdal refuses. Then Malkhān cleaves her, calling on Mahādeva. As she dies, Bijaisin foretells Malkhān's death; and while Ūdal is lost in love, she tells him she will be reborn as Phulwā and

[59]In *BhvP*, after they bewilder the queen (= Kushlā) with song and dance, Kṛṣṇāṃśa dazzles Vijayaiṣiṇī (Bijaisin). She gets his promise to marry her in exchange for telling how to defeat her kinsmen (there is no bower scene, and her disclosure is not mentioned). See chap. 6, § C on the *BhvP*'s handling of the nine-lākh chain.

[60]In *BhvP*, Vijayaīṣiṇī (Bijaisin) uses her Rākṣasī *māyā* to turn the brothers over to her father, but there is nothing about turning Kṛṣṇāṃśa into a ram. Devasiṃha sees that it was done with the help of her guru Ailavilin, a former Daitya living in the Vindhya Mountains, and, leaving Āhlāda behind, the other four (including Kṛṣṇāṃśa) go to kill the magician (3.3.12.93-107). For a variant involving a ram in Nāth folklore, see White 1996, 261.

[61]This fight, which features Ālhā in a royal role, is not paralleled in *BhvP*.

predicts how they will meet to marry.[62]

Even beyond what I have been able to indicate (primarily in footnotes), it is clear that the *Bhaviṣya Purāṇa* and Elliot *Ālhā* draw on the same oral epic. In *Ālhā*, for example, Jambay's allies Ranga and Banga are Pathān leaders slain by Ūdal and Ḍhēwā (118-23); in *BhvP* Jambuka's allies Raṃkaṇa and Vaṃkaṇa are Mleccha leaders slain by Tālana (12.86-88). Moreover, in telling this part of the story, the purāṇa introduces some new incarnations, deepening its mythological groundplan and the questions it raises for us about *Ālhā*.

Of these, the most fully developed concerns Bijaisin, who, under the name Vijayaiṣiṇī, is an incarnation of Rādhā, or, more precisely, "she who is to be known as the Vraja-dwelling Rādhāyā in full part."[63] Her first sight of Kṛṣṇāṃśa among the wandering yogi-musicians is as momentous as Phulvantī's first glimpse of Pābūjī: "Having seen Puruṣottama with his dark-limbed beautiful form, fallen under his power, she was bewildered, eager for the goal of sexual union."[64] Kṛṣṇāṃśa meets little resistance when he uses his "smooth voice" (*ślakṣṇayā girā*) to exchange the promise of marriage for the secret of her father's defeat (39-41).

But it is when the predictions of her reincarnation come true, and Kṛṣṇāṃśa comes to win her hand, that the purāṇa, in what is otherwise a fairly parallel account to the Elliot *Ālhā*'s seventh canto on "The Marriage of Ūdal," develops these associations most richly. As with Ūdal in *Ālhā*, Kṛṣṇāṃśa goes to Mayūranagarī in the Indus country (Narwar-Kabul in *Ālhā*) to restore Parimala's depleted supply of horses (21.2-5; W&G 200). There Puṣpā, a Śūdra garland-maker's daughter, sees the sixteen-year old Kṛṣṇāṃśa "looking like a god, radiant like a sapphire jewel," and tells him that she gathers flowers to equal the weight of the beautiful princess Puṣpavatī (Phulwā), who has a row of virtues like

[62]W&G 127-41. In *BhvP*, Devakī, sword in hand, grinds Jambuka's bones, bathes, and weeps. They do not take Jambuka's head to Kāśī. When the queen and Vijayaisiṇī are called there, the queen dies, and Vijayaisinī takes a sword, cuts Balakhani's shoulder, slashes the other heroes, and bewilders Krsnāmśa. After she has slain a hundred heroes, Balakhāni tears off her head (!) and throws it on the funeral pyre. A heavenly voice then announces that a woman is not to be killed; its fruit will be in Balakhāni's death after marriage. The words about not killing a woman and the results of having done so thus come after the killing, and from a heavenly voice rather than from Devakī and Vijayaiṣinī (3.3.12.125-37).

[63]12.94: *pūrnā tu sa kalā jñeyā rādhāyā vrajavāsinī*; *pūrnā kalā*, "full part," may distinguish her from those described as amśas, "portions, fractions." Thanks to R. Venkataraman for this observation. The distinction is similar to that between avatāra and *pūrnāvatāra*.

[64]12.38: *dṛṣtvā sā sundaraṃ rūpam śyāmāmgam purusottamam/ mumoha vaśamāpannā maithunārtham samudyatā*."

Rādhā (*rādheva saguṇāvalī*; 21.10-13).[65] When she tells what it will take for Kṛṣṇāṃśa to win this bride, her words leave him "overwhelmed with memory/love" (*smarapīḍitaḥ*; 21.23).

Having been awakened from this bewilderment "with verses originated in Sāṃkhya" (!) by his astrologer-brother, "the time-knowing Devasiṃha,"[66] Kṛṣṇāṃśa remembers to buy the horses and return with them to Mahobā (21.24-25). But once he is there, "afflicted by Kāmadeva" and unable to get Puṣpā's words or Puṣpavatī's beauty out of his mind, he lauds the World Mother (Jagadambikā) by invoking her main epithets from the *Devī Māhātmyam*,[67] and she comes to him as Śāradā with instruction in his sleep (26-32). What follows, back in Mayūranagarī, is thus Śāradā's plan.

Kṛṣṇāṃśa sends Puṣpā to Puṣpavatī to captivate her with a beautiful necklace he has brought for her. When Puṣpavatī asks who it comes from, Puṣpā tells her it comes from "my sister named Kṛṣṇā, very beautiful and bewildering every world, who comes from Mahobā." Who wouldn't be curious, if not a little suspicious? Puṣpavatī says, "Show her to me quickly," and doesn't conceal that her thoughts have turned to suitors and the dangers they risk from her father and her brother Makaranda.[68] When Kṛṣṇāṃśa hears of this exchange, he pierces his nose, dresses as a woman, mounts a litter, and goes with Puṣpā to the palace. Here the purāṇa plays with late purāṇic conventions of Kṛṣṇalīlā. Having seen the mind-delighting Kṛṣṇā, Puṣpavatī says to Puṣpā, "Listen to my word, friend. Looking very much like this beautiful woman, I see a man like this every night making love to me in my dreams."[69] Kṛṣṇā/Kṛṣṇāṃśa tells Puṣpavatī (s)he is Udayasiṃha's "playful friend" (*lalitā sakhī*), and that the necklace (s)he has given her comes from him, from Kṛṣṇāṃśa, who is enfeebled (*mlānatvamāgatam*) by separation from the woman he dreams of. Daily he has the necklace fashioned (*racitam*)

[65]On the widely found north Indian folkloric theme of the girl whose weight is measured in flowers, see Hansen 1992, 9-10.

[66]In *BhvP*, Devasiṃha incarnates Sahadeva. Named by astrologers (3.3.8.32) and time-knowing (*kālajñaḥ* [11.6 and 28; 23.22], *kāladarśī* [13.104], *trikālajñaḥ* [19.12]) in the purāṇa, Devasimha probably draws this identity from the notion of Sahadeva as astrologer found also in Tamil (including Draupadī cult) *Mbh* folklore (Hiltebeitel 1988a, 321; 1991a, 49, 284, 418). The Elliot *Ālhā* knows Dhēwā as the Banāphars' astrologer (W&G 75, 80, 104, 129, 151), but does not give him a prior epic incarnation.

[67]Devamāyā, Mahāmāyā, Bewilderer of Madhu and Kaiṭabha, Slayer of Mahiṣāsura, Burner of Dhūmralocana, Destroyer of Caṇḍa and Muṇḍa, Drinker of the blood of Raktabīja, Destroyer of Niśumbha and Śumbha, etc.

[68]Makaranda, the juice of flowers, honey; a species of jasmine or mango (Monier-Williams [1989] 1964, 771), is a fitting brother for Puṣpāvatī, "she who has flowers."

[69]21.52: *yādṛśīyam śubha nārī tādṛśaḥ puruṣo mayā/ svapnānte pratyaham dṛṣṭo ramamāno mayā saha.*

with flowers for his worship of the goddess (21.53-57). Having heard this, Puṣpavatī tells Puṣpā she will be delighted to marry this man she is hearing of, and sends her visitors off with that message to Kṛṣṇāṃśa.

But before they can get out the door the inversions turn to farce. Makaranda is an incarnation of Mount Govardhana (21.63), who has presumably been incarnated to serve and attend his sister, the reembodiment of Rādhā, just as that mountain overlooked the terrain of Rādhā's former pastimes. Makaranda finds a chance to revive Govardhana's love for Kṛṣṇa too, or at least for this feminized "portion," "Kṛṣṇā." Seeing "the heart-stealing radiant face, dark as a blue lotus, with pleasing eyes," he says, "Listen to my words, dear one. Come quickly to my house. Be my wife now." The best "Kṛṣṇā" can do is remind Makaranda he is a fire-born prince and deserves a better mate than a Śūdrī keeping a firm vow of celibacy. It doesn't work. Makaranda seizes "her" by force, which compels "her" to send him off afflicted by a pain in his heart. When the lovesick Makaranda comes to Puṣpā, he hears that this sakhi of Kṛṣṇāṃśa has left for Mahobā, and that he can now expect Kṛṣṇāṃśa *him*self to come with an army (61-72)—to seek his sister's hand.

The Elliot *Ālhā* tells of Ūdal sending a necklace, piercing his nose, dressing as a woman, and going with the flower-girl to meet Phulwā. But there the similarities end, as the focus turns to Ahir folkways (his muscles, says Ūdal, come from chasing buffaloes—like his mother!—and watering gardens), to matters of rājpūti (he refuses to sit below Phulwā on the bed), and on to a long night of getting to know each other by playing dice and cards.[70] The purāṇic version thus tells us some interesting things about the nine-lākh chain. It also plays on Rādhā-Kṛṣṇa themes, and evokes rapports between Kṛṣṇa and Kṛṣṇā-Draupadī:[71] sexual humiliation in the in-laws' court, and intimations of a passion for jewels—matters to consider further in chapter 6.

The purāṇa, however, also makes *Mahābhārata* allusions at the very source of this story. Kāliya (Kariyā), oldest of the Māhiṣmatī princes, is the reincarnation of Jarāsandha (12.123). He seems to split Jarāsandha's mythology with his father, king Jambuka (Jambay). The latter, incarnation of a demon named Śṛgāla, "Jackal" (124), is a "slave of Śiva" (*śivakiṃkara*; 17) who uses Śiva's boons to capture the five heroes for a sacrifice he intends to offer to Śiva (*śaivaṃ yajñam*; 108-11), just as Jarāsandha intends to offer the sacrifice of a hundred kings to Śiva.[72]

[70]W&G 1923. 200-1; cf. Gold 1992, 99 n. 66: "'Playing parcheesi' appears in many Rajasthani stories and songs as a euphemism for sexual intercourse."

[71]The purāṇa clearly knows Draupadī as Krsnā: "As Kṛṣṇā was, so was she, moving with beauty by her qualities," says the text of Velā (Draupadī incarnate) at her birth (3.3.17.17).

[72]I am unable to identify Śṛgāla or Jambuka's other sons with *Mbh* figures. The same goes

We must thus consider the possibility that the *Mahābhārata*'s Jarāsandha story has oral epic repercussions. For we find the following pattern not only in *Ālhā*, but *Palnāḍu* and the Draupadī Cult *Mahābhārata*. In each, an incarnation of Viṣṇu joins the youthful heroes in donning disguises which he himself prompts (in the *Mahābhārata*, that of *snātaka* Brahmans), that enable the entry of an inviolable fort to eliminate its king—a king who not only stands in the way of the youthful heroes' ascendancy, but figures as a Śaivite backer of the heroes' opposition, and thus as a double opponent of Viṣṇu's incarnation.

Moreover, when we compare the folk epics themselves, the consistencies thicken. The mission to retrieve the nine-lākh chain from Mārō, and more particularly from Jambay's "Iron Fort," Lōhāgarh, holds numerous reminders of the plot to obtain Pōrmaṉṉaṉ's pūjā items (= weapons) from his "iron fort" within the seven-ringed "city" of Śivānandapuri.[73] In each case, the goddess requires or guides the expedition, and the "hidden avatāra" carries it out. In *Ālhā*, Śāradā works in conjunction with Devī. Śāradā "sets the events of the Alha in motion" by taking the form of a doe and "luring" Ūdal "into a garden. There it comes about that he hears of his father's murder" from his mother (Schomer 1989, 146). This prompts Ūdal to enable Devī to complete the twelve-year vow she has made to wear her wedding bracelets until Jambay's death.[74] In the Draupadī cult, the expedition is undertaken to safeguard the goddess Draupadī's vow not to rebind her hair until Duryodhana's death. As Kṛṣṇa determines the disguises that he, Bhīma, and Arjuna take to enter Śivānandapuri's iron fort, so Ūdal determines the disguises that allow him and his companions to enter Lōhāgarh. Kṛṣṇa and Ūdal have learned the secrets of how to destroy the two iron forts: in one case (in one variant) by Bhīma's leaning his mace against it, in the other by melting the fort's iron with a fire made from the "thorn boughs" of the "acacia grove" (W&G 132). Kṛṣṇa wants five pūjā items; Ūdal wants the nine-lākh chain and four other trophies: Lākhā, an elephant, a horse—all three of which were captured from Mahobā with the necklace—and fifth, as recompense for Dasrāj and Bachrāj's heads, the head of Jambay.[75] Ūdal's last charge is to bring his father Dasrāj's head from Mārō to Kāśī, or Banaras (129), reminding us that Kṛṣṇa also gets Pōrmaṉṉaṉ to sever his own father's

---

for the *veśyā* Laksavartī/Lākhā, who goes to Badarikā hermitage after completing her mission and becomes an Apsaras (3.3.13.13).

[73]Hiltebeitel 1988a, 339-40. One cannot tell whether Jambay's Iron Fort is the same as his "seven storied tower" (W&G 87).

[74]W&G 66-74. In the purāna (3.3.10.54-62), Śāradā as a doe leads Krsnāmśa into the garden of Mahīpati (Māhil); there, in slaying other deer, Krṣṇāṃśa incenses Mahīpati; but this is not the occasion of his learning of their fathers' deaths.

[75]W&G 66, 113, 138: once in Mārō, Ūdal also demands Bijaisin as his bride.

head, bring it to the Pāṇḍavas, and hold it outside Draupadī's temples in the manner of Bhairava as the guardian of Kāśī-Banaras (Hiltebeitel 1988a, 374-75, 445-46). Finally there is Bijaisin, whose Sanskrit name Vijayaiṣiṇī, "She who desires victory," shows an affinity with Vijayāmpāḷ, "Goddess Victory" or "Lady Victory," whom Arjuna impersonates when he cross-dresses to seduce Pōrmaṉṉaṉ. In concealing an identity with Durgā-Vijayā, goddess of Victory, each aids the avatar by revealing or obtaining the secret means of the fort's destruction.[76]

Considering that the story of Pōrmaṉṉaṉ's fort finds a precise multiform in *Palnāḍu*—with both narratives setting major conditions for the great battles to come—it would seem that we have probatory evidence for the migration of a key piece of interregional oral epic *Mahābhārata*-related folklore. As in the *Mahābhārata*'s *Jarāsandha vadha*, these border feuds are initiatory scenes that establish the heroes, whether they are kings themselves or servants of kings (as in *Ālhā* and *Palnāḍu*). Each episode occurs before the heroes must rectify the rupture that soon occurs, through the violation of a heroine, between the kingdom and the goddess—a violation of Draupadī, one of her incarnations, or a heroine "linked" with her. At this point in *Ālhā*, Belā has not even entered the scene. But Devī and Belā, like Draupadī, are connected with the goddess (and several other heroines, including Bijaisin) by that elegant metonym: the nine-lākh chain.

[76]Cf. Kṛṣṇa's role in securing the secrets of fort-entry from Kālī in the *Āravalli Cūravalli Katai*, a Draupadī cult variant of the Pōrmāṉṉaṉ cycle (Hiltebeitel 1991a, 406-29). There seems to be a variant describing Jarāsandha's fort in Sāralā Dāsa's Oriya *Mbh* (see Swain 1993, 181). See also Dumézil 1971, 132, on the possibility that the connection of the Śiśupāla-Jarāsandha cycle with the Rājasūya conserves older Indo-European themes (cf. Hiltebeitel 1975, 76).

6 The Nine-Lākh Chain

Heroines make interesting use of jewels in Indian oral epics, as we have seen with Māncāla and Phulvantī. It is the same in the Sanskrit epics, where the chief heroines take what seem to be cartloads of jewels into the forest. As noted in connection with Lakṣmaṇa's "ankle verse," while Sītā is being aerially abducted by Rāvaṇa, she drops her jewels in the hope that they will help Rāma find her, and she keeps a special crest-jewel as the last token of their union (Hiltebeitel 1980-81). Draupadī travels with a whole retinue, and a charioteer has the task of collecting her maids, clothes, and ornaments (*vibhūṣaṇam*)[1] when the Pāṇḍavas break camp (*Mbh* 3.24.4). Whatever Draupadī does with these jewels, *Ālhā* folklore seems not to have forgotten them.

A. Treasures

Many of *Ālhā*'s kingdoms have magical treasures, most of which figure in this epic's courtship stories when the heroes win their brides by overcoming the obstacles those treasures present. First, Jambay of Mārō has the impenetrable Iron Fort that contains Bijaisin: Ūdal's true love, and, through her reincarnation as Phulwā, his future bride (W&G 94-95, 127-34). But the pattern unfolds in the next four cantos that tell the Elliot *Ālhā*'s main marriage stories. Naipāli, king of Naināgarh, resists Ālhā's courtship of his daughter Sunwā with the "drum of life" that can revive slain warriors (W&G 163-71). Bisēn's king Gajrāj opposes Malkhān's courtship of Gajmōtin with his fire-breathing horse and a sorceress who turns armies to stone (192-94). To win Phulwā from Narwar, Ūdal must overcome her father Narpat's enchanted wooden horse, an arrow that never misses, and a javelin that always kills (W&G 202). And in Brahmā's courtship of Belā, Prithīrāj menaces the groom's party by his

[1]A collective singular (James Fitzgerald, personal communication, November 1996). Earlier, Draupadī's "superb wealth" dispirits the Kauravas' wives (2.52.36); later in the forest, Arjuna brings more "jewels of solar radiance" as gifts to Draupadī from Indra (3.161.26).

"chest a good yard wide and his eyes flaming like torches" (198; cf. 215, 254), and also has an unerring magic arrow for later battles (215, 264)—"gifts" if not treasures, the last two of which seem to correspond to his "angry glare" (*vakra dṛṣṭi*) and ability to aim the bow by sound alone (*śabdvan*), his defining traits in totally different stories in the *Pṛthvīrāj-rāsau* (Pritchett 1980, 61, 67-73). In each case, it is a question of lower status heroes (three Banāphars and a Chandēl) forcing marriage on higher status kings. Reversing the norm by which a bride "marries up," the fathers are forced to marry their daughters "down." Their resistance to doing so is bolstered by a dowry code in which "giving away a woman was, for the royal clans, tantamount to capitulating a territory" (Jain 1975, 254, n. 6). Prithīrāj is the only father among these who continues to oppose the completion of his daughter's marriage, and much follows from that. The four marriage cantos (4 to 7), narrated in the same sequence with the same or similar treasures in the *Bhaviṣya Purāṇa*,[2] mark the transition from the initiatory Mārō Feud to the events that draw Mahobā into the conflict between Delhi and Kanauj and the eventual war of the three kingdoms.[3]

It is, nonetheless, the treasures of Mahobā that are at the heart of the story, and are poignant where others are menacing. For whereas the others are there to pose challenges, with the loss of Mahobā's treasures comes the end of an age. In *Ālhā*, although not in the purāṇa, Parmāl has the Philosopher's Stone that turns iron and steel to gold.[4] In both texts, he also has five flying horses. So long as he retains these (mainly for his son Brahmā and the Banāphars), Prithīrāj cannot conquer Mahobā.[5] And

[2]In adhyāyas 13 (Āhlāda encounters the "drum of life" called *ḍakkāmṛta*, which Hohenberger [1967, 38] misidentifies as the "Unsterblichkeitstrank," the drink of immortality); 16 (Balakhāni encounters the fiery horse among four treasures of king Gajasena of Marudhanva, the others being his "fiery colored" two sons and daughter Gajamuktā/Gajamuktikā [Gajmōtin] herself; but no sorceress); 17 (Brahmānanda, encountering no treasures); and 21 (Kṛṣnāṃśa encounters a stone horse rather than a wooden one). The intervening material includes (20) Sukhakhāni's marriage to Madanamañjarī, daughter of the Varuna-worshiping Lahara of Laharī, who can produce inundations. The Elliot *Ālhā* has no marriage of Sulkhān.

[3]This includes the later marriage of Lākhan (Lakṣaṇa), prince and champion of Kanauj, to Kusumā (Padminī) of Bundī (Bindugaḍha). Though it has some of the features of the Banāphar marriage stories (the men of Bundī have menacing magic), its emphasis, as in the marriages of Prithīrāj and Brahmā, is more on high royal themes: the wife's descent from four *cakravartī* kings in *Ālhā* (W&G 217-19); a *svayaṃvara* in the purāṇa (25.1-38).

[4]W&G 115, 168, 243. *Paras patar*, "the stone (*patar*) which transforms into gold (*paras*)." A legend of the origin of the Chandēls, told according to Bose (1956, 1) by the bard Chand, author of the *Pṛthvīrāj-rāsau*, is that this stone was given to the first Chandēl by Candra, the Moon (ibid., 1-3; Dixit 1992, 61-62).

[5]W&G 215. Specifics on the five horses are elusive. Brahmā, Ūdal, and Malkhān each have one of the five; the fourth is ridden sometimes by Ālhā and his son Indal; and the fifth

for most of the story, Mahobā also has the nine-lākh chain. Bearing these treasures in mind, we may begin our introduction to Belā, incarnation of Draupadī.

B. Belā Demands Draupadī's Jewels

When Belā reaches twelve, her father sends her brother Tāhar out with the customary challenge-invitation to all the Rājas to come seek her hand by fighting. But Prithīrāj instructs Tāhar not to go to Mahobā lest the "low" Banāphars seek her. Prithīrāj's conditions are, however, too severe for any rāja to risk the courtship. Finally, Malkhān forces Tāhar to consider betrothing Belā to Brahmā. Ūdal and Ālhā then secure the wedding by upstaging all the Rajputs.

First, in Mahobā, Tāhar challenges Brahmā to withdraw a spear he has driven through seven underground iron plates, but Ūdal pulls it up "like a radish" (W&G 197). Then in Delhi, Ālhā proxies for both Brahmā and Parmāl. At the ceremonial exchange of presents between the two fathers-in-law (*samdhōrā*), Prithīrāj says his family custom calls for Parmāl to fix a betel leaf on Prithīrāj's chest. Parmāl flees at the sight of Prithī's yard-wide girth and fiery eyes. But "since an elder brother is the same as a father," Ālhā applies some curd to the massive chest, fixes the betel to it and embraces Prithīrāj, all in Parmāl's stead (128). Note the implication. If Ālhā stands in for Brahmā as "elder brother," he should also be the one marrying Belā! This implication is deepened at the offering of presents to the bride. As Philip Lutgendorf graciously summarizes and translates, when the Mahobā herald Rupnā Bārī, a Dalit, "brings a box of jewels to Belā in Delhi, the princess opens the box and looks at them, and flies into a rage." She gives Rupnā a message to take back to the bridegroom's camp:

> "You've brought jewelry of the Kali yuga, in coming to marry me, Chandēl lord.
> Take this message back to the camp and tell it to Ālhā:
> 'Bring the jewelry from Hastināpura, then I'll circumambulate the fire with the Chandēl;
> the bracelets and scarves (necklaces?) of the Dvāpara age, bring those, oh Banāphar Lord.'"[6]

---

belonged to Dasrāj (60, 154). Ḍhēwā (79, 154) and Mīrā Tālhan also have their favorite steeds, the latter's a mare named "the lioness" (62, 79, 127, 154).

[6]Lutgendorf 1997, citing Elliot [1881] 1992, 225-26. The "bracelets and scarves (necklaces?)" are *curiyāṃ cunarī*; for the latter, Pathak (1967, 348) gives "cloths died by being tied in different places so that white spots remain on them." "Jewelry" is throughout the passage "the standard Hindi word" *gahne*. I keep W&G's spelling for Candel/Chandēl.

By "the jewelry from Hastināpura," Belā evidently means Draupadī's jewels, although it is curious that they would be in the former Kaurava capital rather than the Pāṇḍava one of Indraprastha-Delhi.[7] It is also striking that she addresses her message to Ālhā rather than any of the Chandēls. It is thus Ālhā, not Brahmā, who obtains the jewels for her. Ālhā offers his head to Śāradā, "who stops him and goes to Indra lok; Indra summons Vāsuki and sends him to Pātāl lok to retrieve the jewels."[8] Rupnā then returns with the jewel box, and,

> Opening the box, Belā looked and her heart was greatly delighted.
> Laughing, Belā put on the jewelry. "Now my wish (*kāma*) is fulfilled."[9]

The purāṇa is barely interested in episodes that show the Banāphars upstaging the Mahobā Rajputs and matching those of Delhi. Of the three just mentioned, it includes only the last as part of its introduction of Velā. When her birth is accompanied by a terrible earthquake, a rain of blood mixed with powdered bone, and an inauspicious celestial laugh by Cāmuṇḍā Devī,[10] her father does his best to propitiate the Brahmans with gifts. But when Velā reaches twelve, she tells him, "Listen, O lord of the earth, whoever will bathe me in the hall with waterfalls of blood, he, the giver of the jewels of Draupadī, will be my husband."[11] Pṛthivīrāja has these words written on a golden leaf (*svarṇapatre*) and sends Tāraka out to find someone responsive to such conditions, offering the compensation (dowry?) of three lākhs of wealth and a one-lākh army. But Tāraka can find no willing king in Sindhudeśa (Sind) or Āryadeśa until he questions his maternal uncle Mahīpati, who recommends Brahmānanda (17.7-19). Here, Velā demands not only Draupadī's jewels but bloodshed, and states her conditions before her father sends Tāraka (Tāhar) to scour for suitors. When Brahmānanda comes to Delhi for the wedding, Pṛthivīrāja reiterates the demand for the jewels on Velā's behalf. But despite Velā's demand for waterfalls of blood, the scene is less bloody than in

[7]Delhi, her father's capital, is perhaps too near at hand, and Hāstinapura probably already an ancient site. Grierson summarizes, "Bēlā sees the pearls sent her by Parmāl and throws them away, crying that they are poor ornaments of modern times. She must have the jewels of the Dwāpara Yuga (or the age when she existed as Draupadī)" (W&G 198). "Modern times" is a gloss, and it is not clear how Grierson gets pearls.

[8]Lutgendorf 1997; cf. W&G 198.

[9]Lutgendorf 1997, translating from Elliot [1881] 1992, 227.

[10]See chap. 5, n. 48.

[11]*Maṇḍape raktadhārābhir yo māṃ saṃsnāpayiṣyati/ draupadyā bhūṣanam dātā sa me bhartā bhaviṣyati* (3.3.17.13). I translate *bhūṣanam* as a collective singular on the precedent of the *Mbh* passages (see n. 1 and below).

the Elliot *Ālhā*. Here it is not Āhlāda who gets the jewels with help from Śāradā, but his son Indula (Indal), incarnation of Indra's son Jayanta, who uses Indra's help to get them from Kubera, lord of riches. Nonetheless, Indula delivers them to his father, and it is still Āhlāda who gives them to Velā (17.36-39). Here, despite identifying Āhlāda as an incarnation of Balarāma rather than Yudhiṣṭhira, the purāṇa seems to retain *Ālhā*'s implication that Ālhā is a hidden king.

So Belā demands Draupadī's jewels. The *Mahābhārata* seems to tell us nothing more about them than what was mentioned at the beginning of this chapter. But a curious passage suggests some concepts behind them. Just after Draupadī's svayaṃvara, Dhṛtarāṣṭra misunderstands Vidura's news of the wedding. Thinking Duryodhana has won Draupadī rather than the Pāṇḍavas, Dhṛtarāṣṭra "then had his son Duryodhana told, 'Bring Draupadī's many jewels and bring Kṛṣṇā herself.'"[12] I believe that the blind and often greedy Dhṛtarāṣṭra is gleefully exulting in what he thinks is his new prize: he wants to "see" Draupadī *and* her jewels. As Shah indicates, "brides were given away properly bejewelled" (1995, 32), referring to the "abounding jewels" (*ratnair bahubhir*) that bedeck Draupadī as part of the display of wealth by which her father Drupada and the Pāñcālas have just prepared her for the arrival of the party of her five bridegrooms (1.190.6).

But one might also imagine that Dhṛtarāṣṭra is ordering that "jewels of Draupadī" be given *to* her by the Kauravas (the translators mistakenly think Dhṛtarāṣṭra has ordered the jewels "made" for Draupadī[13]). In this case, it would be implied that the groom's father or brothers should provide suitable jewels for the bride. The idea is odd, but not without a weak epic endorsement. Shah notes, "it was also enjoined in groom's family to welcome bride with gifts of various kinds" (1995, 32-33), citing an *Anuśāsana Parvan* line (13.46.3) where Bhīṣma recalls a saying of Prācetasa (apparently Dakṣa) that a bride should be adorned (*bhūṣayitavyā*) by fathers, brothers, fathers-in-law, and husband's brothers if they desire auspiciousness (*kalyāṇam*). Bhīṣma thus recommends a compromise between pure dowry, with its "gift of a virgin," and pure bride-price types of marriage.[14] But the key word is found only in some northern texts; instead of "adorned," the Critical Edition, and southern texts, reads

[12]*Mbh* 1.192.20. I thank James Fitzgerald (see n. 1) for clarifying that Draupadī and the jewels are serial subjects of *ānīyatām* in this verse. The plural for *bhūṣaṇam bahu* seems clearest here, although it could mean "big ornament."

[13]van Buitenen (1975, 380); Ganguli ([1984-96] 1870, 1:424).

[14]See Jamison 1996, 213-18 on the classical opposition between four maiden-"gift" types of marriage and Āsura marriage in which the bride is "priced"; 239-40 on jewels in the balance of marital exchange. Cf. Shah 1995, 34-35, 62-63, 80-81.

lālayitavyā: "she should be *cherished.*" A southern interpolation, however, taking Dhṛtarāṣṭra as giving Kaurava jewels *to* Draupadī, has him add that the ornaments are to be the best possessed among all his sons (1, 1946*). The variations might suggest that the welcoming father-in-law and the balanced marital exchange are better known in the south.

In any case, Draupadī does not demand any jewels from her in-laws, whether they be the Kauravas or the Pāṇḍavas. That is left to Belā, who demands Draupadī's jewels (again, no doubt those she brought with her from Pāñcāla) from her father-in-law Parmāl. In the purāṇa, she is making this demand of the incarnation of her own former father, since Parimala was Drupada in his previous life (32.12). It is thus not only "bridewealth" from the groom's father, but hiddenly a kind of resumed dowry. This may be one of the paurāṇika's satisfactions in Brahmanizing the story. But in *Ālhā*, Belā's demand is not only rather tempestuous and intriguingly "Dravidian," but very "low." She creates an Āsuric type of marriage in which the bride-price she wants is not demanded by or for her father but by herself and for herself. Add to this that like all of *Ālhā*'s Banāphar brides, she must be won by something further approaching a variety of Rākṣasa marriage, in which the suitor must fight the bride's own father and brothers to win her.[15]

The mixture of marriage types and the lowness of Belā's demand would seem to resonate with tribal traditions about Belā among Kols in Mirzapur District, Uttar Pradesh (Beck 1982, 24), and among "forest tribes" in the Vindhya-Kaimūr ranges (Crooke 1926, 162-63), who make Belā a sister of Rāja Lākhan. In these old songs (McGregor 1984, 13), the Kanauj prince Lākhan, the Banāphars' chief royal patron after Parmāl, is deified by the "jungle tribes" (ibid.). Cunningham supposes that the stories, and a pillar commemorating Lākhan from 1196, three years after Jaychand's death, point to Lākhan's leading "a prolonged struggle with the Muhammadans as the great leader of the Hindus" (1880, 129). Crooke mentions that "some say" he was "taken to Delhi, where he became a Musalmân" ([1896] 1968, 1:198). His "sister" Belā, prospers him with her blessings (Beck 1982, 24), and "now has a famous temple at Belaun on the banks of the Ganges in Bulandshahr" (Crooke [1896] 1968, 1:199). But her story is recognizably a variation on *Ālhā*:

> Once . . . Siva went to pay a visit to Hastinapura, and the bell of his bull Nandi disturbed the brothers Arjuna and Bhîma, who, thinking the

[15]The approximation of Rākṣasa marriage no doubt results from the stories being modeled on it as one of the types of marriage suitable only for Ksatriyas (see Jamison 1994; 1996, 218-35). As Grierson points out, the highly patterned combats do not correspond to actual Rajput customs (W&G 22-24).

god a wandering beggar, drove him out of the palace. Then he cursed the Râjput race that among them should be born two fatal women, who should work the ruin of their power. So the first was born Draupadî, who caused the war of the Mahâbhârata, and after her Belâ, to whom was due the unhappy warfare which paved the way to the Musalmân invasion. (ibid.)

This Belā's story and worship apparently tie in with the cult of a Bhangi sweeper hero named Jokhaiya, a Dalit who was slain in the war between Prithīrāj and Jaychand. At his shrine in Mainpuri District, "a sweeper, in consideration of a small fee, kills a pig and lets its blood fall on his altar."[16] One would like to know more about this "tribal"/Dalit *Ālhā*, and how it relates to other versions.[17] But its heroine's "low" appeal is of interest, for *Ālhā* also gives Belā low status characteristics. Already we know that her father fears she will marry a low Banāphar. And she demands Draupadī's jewels. A "peoples' princess," one could say that she undermines high Rajput pretensions, especially those of her father.

C. The Chain

Belā rejects Parmāl's meager pearls only in *Ālhā*, not in the purāṇa. This rejection has a curious resonance, since Malhnā, from the Elliot *Ālhā*'s beginning to near its end, is the main possessor of the nine-lakh chain. But more appropriately, instead of being the chain's possessor, Malhnā is its main handler, since she is Mahobā's chief queen: the position that would succeed to Belā. There is thus an equivalence between the two jewel treasures that Parmāl is *not* giving to Belā: those of Draupadī from the Dvāpara yuga, and the nine-lākh chain itself. This necklace is named for its value of nine hundred thousand rupees (W&G, 57; 62, n. 1). It appears in as many as eight episodes in the Elliot *Ālhā*, and five of those eight in the purāṇa. But one of these is uncertain.

Ālhā

1. Against King Jambay's will, Prince Kariyā of Mārō wants to go to Jājmāu Ghat on the Ganges, inside Kanauj territory, for the Dasarā holy fair. His sister Bijaisin asks what he will bring her, and he says a nine-lākh chain. At Jajmau, he learns from Māhil

Bhaviṣya Purāṇa

1. King Jambuka and Prince Kāliya of Mahismatī are invincible, thanks to a boon from Śiva. Kāliya gets Jambuka's permission to anoint himself and his armies at the Ganges. He asks his sister Vijayaisinī what she wants. She says, "A charming necklace

[16]Crooke 1926, 163; cf. [1896] 1968, 1:199-200.

[17]There is nothing further in the cited sources. Does this Belā even marry? Unlike *Pābūjī*, which has its own mechanisms (standardized texts, Dalit bards, the story of mixed blood in the goddess's bowl) for holding low-middle and low communities together, *Ālhā* seems to be more parcelled out.

that Māhil's sister Malhnā has such a chain. He attacks Mahobā to get it but is repulsed by the senior Banāphars Dasrāj and Bachrāj (W&G 61-64)	adorned with gems and pearls" (*graiveyakam hāram maṇimuktāvibhūsitam*; 8.8). After bathing, Kāliya looks for the necklace, first in Kānyakubja (Kanauj), but learns Kanauj is wealthless. Then he attacks Mahobā. Despite having Śiva's boon, he is repulsed by the senior "Banāphars" (8.1-26)
2. Malhnā insists that Parmāl reward Dasrāj and Bachrāj with brides from within the Chandēl land. King Dalpat of Gwalior volunteers his daughters Devī and Birmhā. Malhnā welcomes Devī to Mahobā by placing the nine-lākh chain around her neck, and also gives Birmhā a necklace. Parmāl then gives the new Banāphar families a village where they bear and raise their sons (W&G 65). It is after this episode that we learn the brides are buffalo-slinging Ahirs (see above).	2. Deśarāja and Vatsarāja obtain their Abhīrī brides on their own from king Dalavāhana of Gwalior, and a dowry that includes the dancer (*veśyā*) Lakṣāvṛttī, the two brides' friend. Once the brides reach Mahobā, Malanā gives Devakī a necklace (*graiveyakam*) and Brāhmī costly dresses and ornaments (*ṣoḍaśaśṛngāram tathā dvādaśabhūṣanam*: perhaps sixteen fine dresses and twelve jewels?). Parimala then gives them a village (9.1-9) where they bear their sons.
3. At least a year later, after the births of the senior Banāphars' older sons, Kariyā kills the senior Banāphars, detroys their village, plunders Mahobā, and heists the nine-lākh chain and other treasures, including the danseuse Lākhā (W&G 66).	3. At least three years later, Jambuka himself burns and sacks Mahobā, kills Deśarāja and Vatsarāja, and makes off with the necklace adorned with gems and jewels (*graiveyakam . . . hāram maniratna-vibhūsitam*; 9.27), and also other treasures, including Laksaratī (sic) (9.21-29).
4. With help from Lākhā and the young Banāphars' Jōgī disguises, Ūdal recovers the nine-lākh chain (which has become Bijaisin's and is handled by Queen Kushlā). They then avenge their fathers in the Mārō feud (W&G 73-177).	4. With help from Lakṣavartī (sic) and yogin disguises, Kṛsnāṃśa bewilders the queen and charms Vijayaisiṇī into handing over "the necklace dear to Deśarāja worth nine lākhs" (12.42). The young "Banāphars" then avenge their fathers by razing Mahismatī (12.35-124).

5. Malhnā places the nine-lākh chain on the neck of Ālhā's wife Sunwā in joy at her bridal homecoming (W&G 191).

6. Ūdal weaves a fourfold chain mixed with pearls in the garland he sends to Phulwā (Bijaisin reborn) (W&G 200).	6. Kṛṣṇāṃśa charms Puspavatī (Vijayaisiṇī reborn) with a lovely necklace he has concealed (*gunṭhitam*) and taken (*gṛhitvā*) from Mahobā, where it is daily decorated for worshiping the goddess. It was originally "fashioned (*racitam*) by Tvaṣṭr" (21.36-54).

7. When Prithīrāj attacks Mahobā at the battle of Kīratsāgar, he demands the nine-lākh chain from Malhnā, the five flying horses from Parmāl, their daughter Candrābal (already married according to the purāṇa) for

Tāhar, and two forts. When Chauṇṟā reaches Malhnā's litter and demands the chain, Malhnā calls on Ūdal, who comes, again in Jōgī guise, and rescues her (W&G 239-40).

8. With Brahmā dying of wounds, Belā, making her tragic bridal homecoming under Ālhā's guard, is received by Sunwā, then by Devī, who gives her the nine-lākh chain, and by Malhnā (W&G 265-66).

Note that in the purāṇa, a necklace is only once (in item 4 above) explicitly described as "the necklace dear to Deśarāja worth nine lākhs" (*deśarājapriyhāraṃ navalakṣasya mūlyakam* = Hindi *naulākhahār*). But it is clearly the same necklace through the purāṇa's first four episodes, and thus, I suspect, implicitly also in number 6, when Kṛṣṇāṃśa brings a necklace from Mahobā to court Puṣpavatī-Phulwā.

Looking over all eight *Ālhā* episodes, one sees that the nine-lākh chain is "lacked" by *Ālhā*'s three most prominent kingdoms outside Mahobā: by Mārō, Kanauj (at least in the purāṇa), and Delhi. Mārō and Delhi contend for it, while Kanauj is Mahobā's ally. A vied-for symbol of Mahobā's royalty and the "goods of life," it is linked especially with Queen Malhnā, who, along with Devī, places it over the necks of brides when they are welcomed to Mahobā.[18] Similarly, Kushlā, queen of Mārō, bestows it on Lākhā, who is loyal to Mahobā. No woman ever keeps it, much less possesses it. Rather, if I am right in including the sixth episode in the chain's history, it belongs to the goddess of Mahobā, Śāradā and is used to worship her—a point that seems to have been understood by Kipling.[19] Frequently identified with Durgā, Śāradā is also a queen, and thus the real queen of Mahobā.[20] The nine-lākh chain seems not to be strung permanently, but to be daily fashioned and refashioned, especially—if it is what Ūdal takes to court Phulwā—when combined with flowers (21.36, 54). Yet there is no set description of its

[18]It is not placed over Gajmōtin, Malkhān's wife, but her name means "large pearl" (W&G 236, n. 3): indeed, "elephantine pearl."

[19]Kipling, who would have had opportunity to know of Waterfield's 1875-76 translation of "The Nine-Lākh Chain or the Mārō Feud," titles his co-authored novel *Naulahka* after a "nine-lakh" necklace of "diamonds the size of hens' eggs, yokes of pearls, coils of sapphires the girth of a man's wrist, and emeralds until you can't rest—and they hang all that around the neck of an idol, or keep it stored in a temple . . ." (Kipling and Balestier [1891] 1905, 21). Kipling then named his new house in Brattleboro, Vermont, "Naulakha," correcting the novel's spelling, which was probably Balestier's. I find no one who has traced Kipling's experience of what one biographer calls "the Hindu (sic) word for nine 'lakhs' of rupees . . . and the name . . . applied in India to a fabulous jewel" (Carrington 1955, 140).

[20]Śāradā is "the patron goddess of Mahōbā" (W&G 35, 67-68, and 68, n. 1, 78 and n. 6). She has a shrine in the Mahobā Caṇḍikā temple, Candikā also being frequently mentioned in *BhvP*'s *Ālhā* sequence.

components. Strung and unstrung, it fits the situation where it is envisioned, or compared to, a strew of pearls.[21] Or according to Krishna Chaurasia and Zahir Singh, *Ālhā* scholars from Mahobā, it is made of gold and diamonds. Treated as the complement to Prithīrāj's nine-lākh golden earrings, similarly named for their value (W&G 263), one might also suppose that it is made of gold. In any case, the rivalries for it begin when the Mārō prince seeks it for his sister Bijaisin-Vijayaiṣiṇī, "She who is Desirous of Victory," when he goes to a fair at the Ganges.

D. Belā's Wedding

Once Belā receives Draupadī's buried treasure, the Banāphars join Brahmā's wedding party and guard him through the seven circuits around the wedding post. Prithīrāj's sons and allies make repeated attempts to kill him: standard fare at *Ālhā* weddings.[22]

In telling of Belā's wedding and homecoming (*gaunā*), the Elliot *Ālhā* seems to draw again on folklore that resonates with the *Mahābhārata*'s second book, which contains the killings of Jarāsandha and Śiśupāla, the Rājasūya sacrifice, and the dice match. The Rājasūya is of interest here for two things. First, it establishes its performer as an emperor, which is what is at stake when Kṛṣṇa tells Yudhiṣṭhira he cannot complete it without eliminating Jarāsandha of Magadha as imperial rival.[23] *Ālhā* begins with a story that betokens the imperial rivalry between Delhi and Kanauj: the "Wooing of King Prithī" or the "Rape of Sanjōgin,"[24] in which Prithīrāj abducts Jaychand's daughter Sanjōgin from her wedding ceremony. It then goes on to tell how Mahobā is subsumed in that rivalry, while the rivals themselves are then subsumed in the imperial sweep of the Ghurid Muslim Shihāb al-Dīn. Second, the *Mahābhārata* Rājasūya is concerned with establishing rank among Kṣatriyas (Thapar 1992, 145, 159, n. 34): from God and the emperor, as it were, on down. As Schomer indicates, issues of rank among Kṣatriyas are generally less prominent in the *Mahābhārata* than among Rajputs in *Ālhā* (1989, 149-50). So it would seem that *Ālhā*'s Rājasūya allusions build upon the episode's somewhat unusual focus on this theme—especially as it relates to Kṛṣṇa, whom Śiśupāla berates as a mere cowherd (*Mbh* 2.38.6; 41.17).

Presumably it is an issue that would interest *Ālhā* audiences sensitive to the mixed-caste Kṣatriya-Ahir identity of the Banāphars, and of Ūdal

[21]*Palnāḍu* is similarly elusive about Māncāla's necklace, which is golden, made of tulasi, of pearls, and actually strewn on the floor.

[22]See above nn. 3 and 15.

[23]See further Hiltebeitel in press-g on the highlighting of empire in the *Mbh*'s Rājasūya episode.

[24]So W&G 41, the latter title being Grierson's fancy as a parallel with Troy.

in particular. Like Kṛṣṇa, Ūdal (and the rest of the Banāphars) is susceptible to "mean caste" slurs and slights because of his combined Kṣatriya (Rajput) and cowherd (Ahir) background. Moreover, the obstreperous Śiśupāla is king of Cedi, the area that becomes the land of the Chandēls, and known from the fourteenth century on as Bundelkhand,[25] the *Ālhā* heartland. In this overlay of regional royal folklores, whenever Māhil slurs the Banāphars for their Ahir blood, he echoes the words of Śiśupāla.

When Brahmā is finally invited into the women's apartments to eat the wedding breakfast, Ūdal "insists on accompanying him as 'best man.'"[26] When they are seated, Chaunṟā, who has dressed himself as a woman, stabs Ūdal in the side. Belā rushes forth, "cuts her little finger, puts her blood into the wound, and heals it at once" (W&G 199). This incident—which has no parallel in the purāṇa—is paralleled in the Draupadī cult *Mahābhārata*'s reworking of the killing of Śiśupāla at the Rājasūya. After Kṛṣṇa has wounded his finger hurling his discus to end Śiśupāla's unpardonable tirade by beheading him, Draupadī, as Kṛṣṇa's "younger sister," rushes forth to stanch the blood with the end-piece of her sari (Hiltebeitel 1988a, 226-27). Wadley (1976, 158) has found this same *Mahābhārata*-derived folktale in Hindi-speaking north India connected with the ceremony of *rakhibandhana*, in which sisters tie a protective thread around their brothers' wrists. In that context, the story highlights the theme of sisterly ties of affection. Draupadī and Kṛṣṇa's sister-brother relation, which lies behind the story's connection with *rakhi*-tying, is thus north Indian *Mahābhārata* folklore as well.

In the Sanskrit *Mahābhārata*, the Rājasūya episode also hinges on Kṛṣṇa's status as "best man," but in another sense. The scene begins when Nārada sees all the Kṣatriyas present for the Rājasūya. Realizing that Kṛṣṇa is about to bring them to their doom, he understands that Kṛṣṇa is "Hari Nārāyaṇa, the lord who is to be praised with sacrifices (*hariṃ nārāyaṇaṃ jñātvā yajñairīḍyaṃ tamīśvaram*)" (2.33.20). When Śiśupāla fails to recognize what Nārada has seen, he berates Bhīṣma, who does understand, for naming Kṛṣṇa to receive the highest honor among all present, and further belittles Kṛṣṇa himself by calling him a Cowherd. The result is that Śiśupāla becomes the Rājasūya's victim: Kṛṣṇa beheads him, and then miraculously draws Śiśupāla's luminous spirit (*tejas*) into his own body so that it "entered the Best of Men (*viveśa . . . puruṣottamam*)" (2.42.24). The episode saves this term *puruṣottama*, "best of

[25]Dey [1899] 1927, 48, 226; Thapar 1978a, 340.

[26]Ūdal also insists on coming with Lākhan as "Best Man" (*sahbōlā*) at his wedding (W&G 218).

men" or "supreme Puruṣa," for this climax.[27] As we have seen, it is also used for Kṛṣṇāṃśa in the *Bhaviṣya Purāṇa* when Vijayaiṣiṇī is first struck by his dark beauty.

Ālhā thus seems to retain the "best man," cowherd, and brother-sister themes in its Belā-Ūdal vignette, but also to have inverted the manner in which the virgin heroine shows her solicitation. Belā stanches Ūdal's bleeding using blood from the tip of her own finger to heal his side. Considering that she never has sexual relations with her husband Brahmā, and thus never joins blood with him in that sense, this mixing of blood has a powerful impact. Since Ūdal and Sunwā (Ālhā's wife) refer to each other as "brother" and "sister" (W&G, 164, 185-87), a "brother-sister" relation must extend to Ūdal and Belā, since Brahmā, as we have seen, is likewise a "brother" to the Banāphars. As with Kṛṣṇa and Draupadī in the Draupadī cult, this relationship carries hidden ties between them.

Even after these trials, however, the Mahobā party does not get to take Belā home, since Prithīrāj reveals at the last moment that "it is the custom of his house never to send the bride to her husband's home immediately after the wedding, but that he will let her go in a year."[28] Prithīrāj has no intention to keep this promise, and its breach leads to the final war. Here one may note Grierson's shortsightedness in saying that the subject of *Ālhā*'s first canto on Prithīrāj's abduction of Sanjōgin "has no direct connection with the rest of the Ālhā cycle" (W&G 39). It is Prithīrāj's ability to steal his bride at the beginning of *Ālhā* from a then-"higher" imperial king that is prelude to his own imperial prevention of a lower prince from stealing his own daughter as a bride: an obsession that preoccupies Prithīrāj to the story's end.

E. Belā's Homebringing

When it comes time for Belā's homebringing, Parmāl calls for volunteers and offers a role of betel (a bīrā) to be taken up by the champion who will undertake this challenge. Ūdal lifts the betel, but Māhil—perpetual agent-provocateur in the Mahobā camp—tells Brahmā that Ūdal's "mean caste will give rise to difficulties, and spurs him to

[27]Earlier in the *Sabhā Parvan*, the term Puruṣottama has another precise usage: in plotting the death of Jarāsandha, Kṛṣṇa tells that one of Jarāsandha's allies is king Vāsudeva of Pundra who also claims the title of Purusottama, though falsely (2.13.17-18). When Kṛṣna releases the kings Jarāsandha has held captive, it is Kṛṣna whom they praise as Purusottama (22.33). Viewed in sequence, this deepens the usages of this "best man" theme.

[28]W&G 199; similarly *BhvP* 3.3.17.63-64, in which, rather than it being a matter of custom, Pṛthivīrāja, humiliated by the "Banāphars" in bridal jousts, says, "Velā is only twelve. This girl is not bearing separation from her father and mother. Therefore, leaving her here, go home happy. When she may be united with her husband, then you may again wish for her."

snatch the bīrā" from Ūdal (W&G 259). Brahmā, whose hotheadedness and lack of judgment can be surprising, does this, and both Ūdal and Ālhā feel disgraced and withdraw from the campaign for Belā. Here again one may remember the folkloric handling of the killing of Śiśupāla at the Rājasūya. The honor which Kṛṣṇa receives as "Best of Men," and which Śiśupāla so hotly contests, is also a kind of champion's portion. Draupadī cult dramas portray it not as a benediction with water—as in the Vedic ritual recalled in the *Mahābhārata*—but a role of betel.[29]

The upshot is that Brahmā must lead his march to Delhi accompanied only by the treacherous Māhil, and with no Banāphars to guard him.[30] His mother Malhnā sees the peril, and tries to get Lākhan to protect him. But Ūdal and Mīrā Tālhan persuade Lākhan to withdraw: an important moment, since Lākhan, incarnation of the Pāṇḍava Nakula, now joins ranks with the Banāphars, and in effect compensates for the loss of Malkhān, who is now no more. One thus sees Brahmā set out this one and only time as an independent hero attended by his betrayer. His inevitable doom thus accentuates the importance of the absent Banāphar guard.

When Brahmā reaches Delhi, he is a stern match for Prithīrāj's champions, killing three heroes, two of them Prithīrāj's sons (and thus Belā's brothers). Māhil then tells Prithīrāj "that a hero like Brahmā can be defeated only by fraud."[31] He proposes that Tāhar be brought to Brahmā in a litter, dressed as a woman and pretending to be Belā. Tāhar refuses: it would violate his Rajput code. But the Brahman Chaunṛā, we recall, has no such compunctions. He "dresses himself like a woman, arms himself with a poisoned dagger, and sets out on a gorgeous litter," Tāhar in attendance. When they reach the Mahobā camp, Tāhar embraces Brahmā and tells him Prithīrāj wishes to contend no more, and has sent him his daughter. The false Belā then "descends from the litter and strikes Brahmā in the heart with his dagger" (W&G 260).

The purāṇa tells this story too (31.161). But its closing war scenes are pitched in a different direction, which I will discuss in chapter 8. For now, it is only important to recognize that what follows in this chapter is *Ālhā*, not purāṇa.

When news reaches Delhi of Brahmā's "apparent death," Belā "isolates herself in her own apartments." At Mahobā, however, the news is that Brahmā can live only a day or two. Amid great lamentation, Ālhā and Ūdal "meditate revenge" (W&G 260). Here the motivations and

[29]See van Buitenen 1975, 22; Hiltebeitel 1988a, 226.

[30]*BhvP* 3.3.31.11-20 has much the same story, but without the betel leaf episode.

[31]Lutgendorf 1997 comments that Elliot [1881] 1992, 561, uses no word for "fraud" here; "that is Grierson's addition," though "obviously, trickery is involved."

underlying identities of Belā and the Banāphars—the virgin heroine-goddess and her LSRSCs—finally converge and clarify themselves. Belā, writing to Ūdal, "charges him with being at heart a woman," rebukes him for staying at ease at Mahobā and "sending Brahmā to his death," and implores him to "unite her with her husband" (261). This suggests that she already intends to become a satī. Having received the letter, Ūdal and Lākhan get Ālhā's permission and concoct a revealing subterfuge—and since Ūdal is throughout a master of disguises, the plan is surely his. They dress their troops in black uniforms, with black flags, and when they reach Delhi, tell Chauṉṟā, who comes to ask who they are, "that they have come to seek employment under Belā." Chauṉṟā, believing them,[32] convinces Prithīrāj to hire them at an exorbitant fee for eight days "to guard Belā's apartments," since Prithīrāj "has great fears of an attack" from Ūdal. Moreover, he should then "use them to sack Mahōbā" (261)! As elsewhere, one has a group of five: Ūdal and Ḏhēwā, Mīrā Tālhan, Lākhan, and another Kanauj champion—otherwise little heard of—named Dhanuā Tēlī. Ālhā remains for now in Mahobā. Belā, "imprisoned" (W&G 262) in her apartment—her "sealed shrine," if I may transport Shulman's term (1980, 192-211) to the north—thus has her LSRSCs right where they should be. Under their black guises, they have become the guardians of Belā's enclosure, poised to lead her forth.

The manner in which Belā and her guards make contact is intriguing. Ūdal and Lākhan play dice. As Lutgendorf translates,

> The die were first thrown by Lākhan, taking the name of Rāmcandra. "If Belā is true (*sāṃcī*), let the dice fall in my favor."[33]

Lutgendorf comments, "*Sāṃcī* obviously comes from *satya* (*sac* is the standard modern Hindi form). My sense of the meaning is the obvious one: it means if she is chaste, a virgin. It is evidently a challenge; he knows that she will overhear him. It is a means to establish contact with her, since he is in disguise and surrounded by enemies" (1997, 2). There is also a likely allusion here to the *Mahābhārata*, and once again to its second book. When Belā overhears, she sends a servant girl to find out who is "taking her name in vain" (W&G 262). Her "truth" and "chastity"—and, if we invoke the Draupadī cult *Mahābhārata*, her virginity—are, like Draupadī's, at stake in a dice match. Belā takes some convincing that it is Ūdal outside, "waiting to take her away on the home-bringing." But she at last sends for him. He tells her that Brahmā

[32]The Brahman-advisor-general has a Pōta Rāju-like stupidity here.

[33]Lutgendorf 1997, translating from Elliot [1881] 1992, 569. Cf. W&G 262: "If Bēlā is true I win."

is soon to die, and explains that he, Ūdal, is not to blame for Brahmā's having come for her alone, since Brahmā had snatched the betel from him.

Belā then tells of her seven births, only the last two of which have been human. From the first, when she and Brahmā were fish, to the last, the same pair reincarnated, and "in all these births she has had the same fate, never to be really united with her beloved."[34] Lutgendorf, however, comments, "The paraphrase 'never to be really united with her beloved' does not reflect the actual wording of the highly formulaic passage" (1997, 3). Having "puzzled" over it with his assistant, Mrs. Bhatnagar, Lutgendorf translates,

> "In my first birth I was a she-fish, and the Chandēl lord became a he-fish.
> Our *tapasyā* became broken (*khaṃḍita*), neither I nor the king was satisfied (*aghāy*).
> In my second birth I was a she-snake and the Chandēl lord became a he-snake.
> Our *tapasyā* was broken and neither I nor the king was satisfied."

In this "repeated pattern, . . . the first line describes an incarnation, and the second tells what went wrong that caused it to be incomplete. In both cases above, the latter line begins with a phrase meaning '(my? our?) *tapasyā* became broken (interrupted?).' The second half of the line may mean 'neither I nor the king was satiated.' That is my guess." Lutgendorf wonders whether *tapasyā* could "here refer to ardor in the erotic sense?" (1997, 3). I suspect that it does have that resonance, but that it has the usual prior sense of "penance" or "austerity," with erotic ardor as the outcome that is left un-"satisfied" because the *tapasyā* is repeatedly "broken." Belā does not repeat these terms for her last two births as a human:

> "The sixth birth was as Draupadī; I took avatar at Hastinapur.
> The Kauravas were my enemies, and five men were called my husbands.
> In my seventh birth I was Belā; I took avatar in Delhi.
> My father became my enemy and got my husband murdered."[35]

[34]W&G 262; cf. the seven births of the virginal Sri Lankan Pattiṉi (Parker 1909, 634; Obeyesekere 1984, 83, 127). The chaste yet sexy fish figures not only in the Draupadī cult, but in a pan-Indian *Mbh* folklore as the target Arjuna must pierce at Draupadī's svayaṃvara (1988a, 195-211). The original birth as a pair of fish might presage this theme.

[35]Lutgendorf 1997, 3, translating from Elliot [1881] 1992, 572-73.

But it is clear that marital dissatisfaction describes the last birth and is probably also implied in the sixth.[36] We shall see in chapter 14 that Baccha Singh knows a different version of Draupadī and Belā's successive "dissatisfactions." We shall also appreciate the power of Belā's identification, in the Elliot *Ālhā*, of her father as her last enemy.

Ūdal now tells Belā that he and her other guardians will be able to bear her away. Lākhan and Mīrā Tālhan come in, and Belā "tells them that when she was Draupadī, Mīrā was then Bhīmasēna and Lākhan was Nakula." She thus has the power to recall and reveal epic identities, to make *Mahābhārata* connections.[37] Ūdal then sheds his guise, goes to Prithīrāj to tell him he has come to bring Belā "home" to Mahobā, and demands her dowry. Prithīrāj throws down his precious golden earrings—worth nine lākhs like the nine-lākh chain—thinking Ūdal will bend over for them, exposing his neck. But Ūdal stays on his horse, picks up the earrings with his spear, and rides off.

Meanwhile, "Bēlā gets into her litter and starts off under the protection of Lākhan and Mīrā." She stops to collect her jewelry and bid farewell to her mother Agmā. Agmā implores her to stay and marry someone else, but Belā replies that she will not marry any Muslim "Mughul." *Ālhā* introduces this anachronism many times over, the Mughals making their entry into India several centuries after the time of Prithīrāj. But in this instance it may be a significant anachronism, since in the course of *Ālhā*'s textual history the Mughals come to be the true imperial successors of Prithīrāj, and Belā—with all her associations with the goddess of the land—prefers satī to accommodation to them.[38] Belā then says,

> "Think (don't think?) Belā has become a widow, (for) there (will be) widows in every house in Delhi.
> In three months and seventeen days, a river of blood will flow in Delhi.
> You won't be able to seek out a single *suhāgin* (auspicious unwidowed woman), a thunderbolt will fall on Delhi.
> My seven sisters-in-law, by Gangā, will become widows."[39]

[36]Belā seems to hint that even as Draupadī, she never consummated her marriage. Such a complaint could reflect her polyandry in the classical epic, which might be said to prevent her marital satisfaction with Arjuna. But given the folk context, Belā would seem to recall another life as a virgin, like the Draupadī of the Draupadī cult.

[37]Cf. Draupadī's clairvoyance (Hiltebeitel 1988a, 303-8) and determination of what is *Pāratam* or "*Mbh*" (1991a, 420) in Draupadī cult folklore.

[38]"Mughul" may connote not only "imperial" but "Sunnī" here, since Mīrā Tālhan, a Shī'ite, if not indeed an Ismā'īlī (see chap. 10), is among those to spring Belā from her father's imprisonment.

[39]Lutgendorf 1997, 4, translating from Elliot [1881] 1992, 577, and commenting, "She

It is like the prophesy Draupadī makes about the Kaurava women after her disrobing.[40]

Now begins the amazing march of Belā's litter on her bridal "home"-coming. Once she completes this tour, which I discuss in section I, she has only to meet Brahmā's dying wish: that she become a satī. She calls for Ūdal to get wood for her pyre from her father Prithīrāj's sandalwood grove. The Mahobā and Kanauj forces cut the grove down and bring the wood after routing the Delhi army, but Belā says it is damp; she now requires dry sandalwood from the twelve pillars in her father's audience-chamber. Ūdal is reluctant: it will mean certain death for all. But she threatens curses and says a satī's time is short. Of the seven days allowed her, three "have passed, and only four remain." Ūdal "must therefore hasten" (W&G 268). After several battles the pillars are brought to the camp where Brahmā's body lies. Belā instructs Ūdal to build the pyre. "She puts on all her ornaments, dresses herself in her bridal array, and ascends" (W&G 271).

Prithīrāj and his forces now arrive to protest that only a Mahobā Chandēl Rajput of Parmāl and Brahmā's clan can light the pyre, not any low Banāphar. But Ūdal is determined to follow Belā's command. Grave fighting resumes. Many die, including Mīrā Tālhan. As the Elliot *Ālhā* describes it, amid the tumult, "(no one) could set fire to the pyre, (so) Belā loosened her hair. A flame then flew from that hair and instantly ignited the great pyre."[41] Grierson's summary continues: "The pyre at once bursts into a blaze, so that with the corpse she is consumed" (W&G 271). Battle continues while the pyre burns, and after nearly all the great heroes beside Ālhā, his son Indal, Māhil, and Prithīrāj have died, the widows of the Mahobā heroes come to consume themselves in it (271-73).

Clearly, the Draupadī incarnated in Belā is more like the Draupadī of Draupadī cult folk traditions than the Draupadī of any classical *Mahābhārata*. Belā's homecoming is seldom orally performed because it is "inauspicious to hear"; there are stories of patrons coming to grief because of sponsoring it (Schomer 1984, 12-13). In this it is like the Terukkūttu drama on Draupadī's disrobing (Hiltebeitel 1988a, 228-29).

---

seems to swear by the goddess Gangā in the last line . . . ; in effect saying, 'May Gangā make it so that they may become widows.'" Cf. chap. 14, § A on Gangā's role in removing the Kaurava widows to heaven in the *Mbh*. Cf. W&G 262.

[40]See chap. 14, § A; also Hiltebeitel 1981, 188, citing *Mbh* 2.71.18-20, and, for the same prediction in Draupadī cult folklore, Hiltebeitel 1988a, 306.

[41]Lutgendorf 1997, 4, translating Elliot [1881] 1992, 639. Lutgendorf observes, "In the midst of the long description of the battle, a mere two lines cut away, as it were, to the scene. . . . Then it is back to the battle, to a dialogue between Lākhan and Pṛthīrāj." Cf. W&G 271.

We have noted Belā's virginity, her low status and Muslim guardian, her healing of Ūdal, her multiple lives with Arjuna. We must understand, it seems, that she also becomes a satī in Draupadī's jewels, and lights her pyre with a fire latent from Draupadī's hair.

F. Dasarā

Ālhā performance is said to be entertainment rather than ritual.[42] But the Elliot *Ālhā* has a rather explicit ritual subplot that has escaped notice. It draws on much the same Navarātrī-Dasarā complex as other regional oral martial epics and the Draupadī cult *Mahābhārata*. In *Ālhā*, however, Dasarā allusions are not indirect but direct, and to Dasarā itself rather than through the folklore of one of its primary components (e.g., the śamī). The evoked Dasarā is not, however, a regularized Brahmanical form of this royal festival. Like our other oral epics, *Ālhā* draws on folk transformations. While the Elliot *Ālhā* mentions royal Dasarās, it is only in folkloric variations on aspects of Dasarā subrites that one can trace the ritual's narrative unfoldings. Intriguingly, the *Ālhā* kings who perform or concern themselves with Dasarā, and with its subrites, are not those of Delhi and Kanauj, who, as we have seen, tap into imperial Rājasūya mythologies, but the lesser regional kings of Mahobā and Mārō.

After the imperial prologue confronting Delhi and Kanauj, the "story proper of the [*Ālhā*] cycle begins" (W&G 57) not only with the "Mārō Feud," but with the events of a Dasarā. The story continues to be tied in with Dasarā themes to its very end. The Dasarā in question is, according to Grierson, a fall Dasarā: "The great feast in October at the close of the rains, when kings go forth to battle and the exploits of Rāma are celebrated" (W&G 61, n. 1). On such a day, Kariyā, prince of Mārō, goes to bathe in the Ganges at the Jājmāu Ghāṭ, and promises Bijaisin-Vijayaiṣiṇī, "She who is desirous of victory," to bring her back a nine-lākh chain (51, 61-62). There he learns that he must attack Mahobā to get it. It is not, however, precisely Mahobā that he attacks. After Malhnā had given the nine-lākh chain to Devī, Devī had insisted on settling in "a home of their own" (W&G 65). As Lutgendorf translates,

> At one *kos* from Mahobā, a town was established for them.
> It was given the name Dasahara purvā, and there the Banāphar lords lived.[43]

Or as Waterfield rather freely rhymes,

[42]Blackburn 1989; Schomer 1989.
[43]Lutgendorf 1997, 4, translating Elliot [1881] 1992, 26.

So a hamlet a mile from Mahōbā wall
They gave the Banāphars to dwell
And Dasrāpur to this day they call
Where Ālhā's birth befell. (W&G 65).

Purvā, as Lutgendorf notes, "is given in *Bhargava*'s dictionary as 'a small village, a hamlet.'"[44] Dasahara purvā or Dasrāpur—with further variants Das'harpurwa, Daspurwā (W&G 58, 65), and said at Mahobā to have formerly been called Dasarapurwa, but now Dasrapur[45]—can hardly be anything than Dasarā-pur, "Dasarā-ville." The purāṇa knows it by various names, all beginning with *daśa*, "ten," with "the village called Daśāhārā" among them.[46] Today the spot is no more than a hollow below and a hill above, with a few cut stones partially showing above ground, a tank (the Madan Sāgar) and well nearby, and assurances that more remains have been found underground in the hill.[47] It is here that Kariyā kills the Banāphar fathers, burning the "hamlet" down (66).

Let us note that this name does not occur either in the western "Ghāsī Rām" *Ālhā* summarized by Grierson (1885b, 255, 258), in which the Banāphar fathers settle in Jhijhāvat Fort and their sons then have separate forts, or in the *Pṛthvīrāj-rāsau*, where their fort is the far grander one of Kalanjara.[48] The import of the name Dasrāpur in the Elliot *Ālhā*, where it is introduced as the birthplace of Ālhā, the hidden king, would thus seem to be transparent. I take the Banāphars' birth at Dasrāpur, with Ālhā first and Ūdal last, to indicate that they are not only Mahobā's guardians, but reside in a place that defines its royal power. From this base they set out to avenge the Dasarā-linked killing of their fathers and the theft of the nine-lākh chain—linked from the start with Mahobā's goddess Śāradā, and thus with Dasarā itself[49]—by making the sack of

[44]Lutgendorf 1997, 4; Pathak 1967, 694 s.v. *puravā*.

[45]According to Zahir Singh, retired principle of a college, and Krishna Chaurasia, Secretary of the Bundelkhand Development Council, two elderly gentlemen who conduct research on *Ālhā*, including *BhvP*.

[46]*Daśahārākhyanagaram* (19.55); cf. Daśapura (9.9); Daśagrāma (14.13); Daśagrāmapuram (14.18).

[47]Grierson seems to describe the same spot, but unless all has changed it is hard to believe he actually saw it: "where the ruins of [the Banāphars'] pleasure house are still to be seen towering on one of the hills above the beautiful Madan Sāgar Lake" (W&G 12).

[48]Dikshit 1977, 145, 148, 157. Kalanjara/Kalinjara is referred to as the Chandēls' "military capital," along with Mahobā as its "political capital" and Khajuraho as its "religious capital" (e.g., Bose 1956, 11). Zahir Singh of Mahobā used the same terms.

[49]According to the *Dharmasindhu*, a late eighteenth-century ritual manual (Biardeau 1989, 302), the "Unvanquished" goddess Aparājitā (i.e., Durgā) should be envisioned by the king as "wearing a beautiful necklace and a resplendent golden girdle" (*hārena tu vicitrena bhāsvatkanakamekhalā*) when worshiped during the royal śamīpūjā as embodied in the śamī

Mārō a kind of counter-Dasarā. Ūdal promises to accomplish this revenge, which occurs after a year-like twelve-year cycle that allows the boys to mature, in just nine days (W&G 72, 110)—a likely allusion to the nine days and nights (Navarātri) that would precede Dasarā's victorious tenth.

One thus has a double reference to Dasarā—one mainly temporal, the other mainly geographic—to open the story, with the two episodes linked by themes of revenge and rivalry over the precious chain. They reflect a narrative conception of Dasarā as a dangerous rite to perform. Kariyā is warned by Jambay that his Dasarā-journey to Jājmāu Ghāṭ is filled with peril, since Jājmāu belongs to Jaychand of Kanauj, who might imprison Kariyā because of Mārō's unpaid tribute. And Dasrāpur is burned down. The fact that the young Banāphars and Mīrā Tālhan remain twelve years at Dasrāpur after its restoration, before gaining revenge and retrieving the necklace, is a further indication that Dasarā holds the symbolism of extended "yearly" cycles of combat and revenge.[50] It is tempting to think that the name Jājmāu Ghāṭ, a site across the Yamuna from Kanpur, might mean the Yajamāna's or Sacrificer's Ghāṭ: a location situating the story's opposition between rival sacrificers.

The Elliot *Ālhā*'s treatment of Dasarā thus has much in common with the way the *Mahābhārata* brings out the latent violence in its Rājasūya and Aśvamedha sacrifices.[51] As the successor to these two most prominent Vedic royal sacrifices, Dasarā seems to carry forward elements of both,[52] centering worship on the goddess rather than on Vedic deities, and replacing the horse with the buffalo.[53] *Ālhā* defines a relation

---

(Kāśīnātha Upādhyāya 1968, 196). Cf. Kane [1930-62] 1975, 5,1: 190; Kinsley 1986, 107).

[50]Grierson indicates nothing in his summary of the western Ghāsī Rām variant (1885b, 256) that the bath occurs at Dasarā. In this account, not only is Kariyā there, but Parmāl, whose camp Kariyā raids in an initial unsuccessful attempt to get the nine-lākh chain. See also W&G 212: Ālhā tells Ūdal he should not bathe at Bithūr, another spot on the Ganges, during a Dasarā festival, because "he is sure to pick a fight with some Rāja there"—and sure enough, he does, this being where Ālhā's son Indal is abducted, upon which not only many battles follow, but a rupture between Ālhā and Ūdal. *BhvP* 3.3.23.4 knows this spot as Barhiṣmatī Sthāna, but mentions nothing about Dasarā.

[51]On the Rājasūya, see van Buitenen 1975, 3-30; Gehrts 1975, especially 166 on the rite's dangerous potential; Hiltebeitel 1977. On the Aśvamedha, see Biardeau and Péterfalvi 1986, 119-20, 128-31, 148, 166-67, 200, 215-16, 227, 239, 247, 262-63, 328-334, and Hiltebeitel 1988a, 395-96 and n. 4; 1991a, 94-95, 371-87.

[52]See Hiltebeitel 1985a, 171, 188-92; 1988a, 132-33. In what may be a carryover from the Rājasūya, in which a subrite calls for the king to shoot an arrow in the direction of a "relative" in the symbolic role of rival or enemy (Heesterman 1957, 129-32, 138-39; 1985, 119), the śamīpūja may call for the king to shoot an arrow at an effigy of his enemy (Hiltebeitel 1991a, 94-96, 152-53, 430-32).

[53]The canto on the Banāphars' revenge against Mārō opens with an invocation to the lion-riding, flesh-tearing Durgā, slayer of Mahisāsura, and overthrower of the earth's tyrants

between Rājasūya and Dasarā as royal rituals fused in its folklore, but pitched toward "little kingdoms" rather than the imperial rivals of Delhi and Kanauj. What concerns these little kingdoms are features of Dasarā specific to its tenth day: Vijayādaśamī, "Victory's tenth," Vijayā ("Victory") being Durgā and, as observed, a telling element in the name Bijaisin.

Beyond the Mārō Feud, *Ālhā*'s Dasarā subplot revolves around two episodes that launch the story's final battle: a boundary war that opens the final defense of Mahobā; and a ceremony connected with Navarātri and Vijayādaśamī, the sowing of sprouts.

G. The Death of Malkhān

Once the Banāphars have grown to marriageable age, they have at some point taken up two residences. Ālhā and Ūdal remain at Dasrāpur, while Malkhān and Sulkhān live at the frontier fort of Sirsā, where Malkhān comes into full view.

Malkhān performs the one truly shocking killing, the only violation of the Rajput code, that any Banāphar commits: the killing of Bijaisin.[54] As noted, he does this at Ālhā's command. Calling on Mahādeva (perhaps in connection with this "low" slaughterer's role), Malkhān cleaves Bijaisin's shoulder. When Bijaisin dies, predicting her reincarnation as Phulwā, she curses Malkhān to a death we must now consider:

> But, cruel Malkhān, woe to thee,
>   Thy brother's wife hast slain:
> So shalt thou die with no brother by,
>   Unhelped in an open plain. (W&G 140).

We have here once again the "curse of a maiden." Uttered in anger for preventing a virgin heroine's union with her husband, it is reminiscent of Māncāla's curse in *Palnāḍu*, and of Deval's, on behalf of Phulvantī, in *Pābūjī*. Like Bijaisin reborn as Phulwā, Phulvantī is maimed (in her former life as Śūrpaṇakhā rather than her current one) and then returned under a "flower"-name (in this life rather than the next) to marry the avataric hero, who in each case leaves the maiming to his henchman-brother. Indeed, Phulwā and Phulvantī have virtually the same name.

Bijaisin's curse requires Malkhān to die unaided, a "lone hero" on the

---

(W&G 68).

[54]Schomer 1989, 153. Malkhān also kills the "hermit" who holds Ūdal captive when Bijaisin turns him into a ram, but this is after Ūdal has identified the hermit as a "warlock" (W&G 133). He is especially sensitive to the Rajput code (see, e.g., 85).

"open plain." The question is inevitable: How much is he like Cāmpukā, Anapōtu Rāju, and Ḍhēbo? There is no discernible sexual tension between him and Bijaisin, no evocation of the mythology of the goddess and the buffalo. But there are other surprises.

When Tāhar goes to find Belā a suitor, he follows Prithīrāj's orders to avoid Mahobā. But "Tāhar meets Malkhān out hunting" (W&G 197). In the purāṇa, four of the heroes are defined by their hunting quarries. On the hunt that leads Kṛṣṇāṃśa to chase the golden deer that finally reveals herself to be Śāradā, Brahmānanda slays deer, Āhlāda tigers, Devasiṃha lions, and Balakhāni (Malkhān) boars (10.53-54). As with Cāmpukā, a boar quarry probably typifies meanness of rank.[55]

His hunt interrupted, having intercepted Tāhar, Malkhān proposes Brahmā as Belā's husband. He takes Tāhar and Chauṛrā prisoners at Sirsā, leaves them with Sulkhān, and heads toward Mahobā, where he "forces" Parmāl and (with Devī's cooperation) Malhnā "to give an unwilling consent" to the betrothal (W&G 197). Since he will die before Belā's "homecoming," this will be Malkhān's only direct involvement in her story, other than some further collaboration with Ūdal in arranging her marriage (197-98). He will thus never be one of her actual Banāphar guard.

If Malkhān is never to guard Belā, however, he is, among the Banāphars, the primary guardian of Mahobā. His role at Sirsā is an extension of the Banāphars' primary guardian role at Dasrāpur. Sirsā is an identifiable fort—Sirsagadh, on the river Pahuj—and Malkhān's defense of it is mentioned in the *Parmāl-rāsau*.[56] The purāṇa, calling it Śiriṣākhyapuram, tells that Balakhāni built it to accommodate the four castes, offending Pṛthivīrāja in doing so by cutting down a śirīṣa (*acacia sirissa*) forest.[57] Similarly, the Elliot *Ālhā* says it was built by Malkhān "in a forest wild" at a "strategic point, where a number of roads met, between Delhi and Mahōbā" (W&G 222). Malkhān speaks of himself as a "vassal" at this boundary location not only of Parmāl but of Prithīrāj (222, 227). Whatever one makes of this alleged fealty to Delhi, Malkhān defends only Mahobā in the Elliot *Ālhā*.

It is the treacherous Māhil who tells Prithīrāj that Malkhān has built Sirsā fort to bar the way to Mahobā, and moreover, that Mahobā cannot

[55]Low ritual status connected with hunting pertains also to Śiva as *mṛgavyādha*, slayer of Prajāpati-Brahmā in the form of a deer, and as a boar hunter (*kirāta*) during Arjuna's tapas.

[56]See Dikshit 1977, 144; W&G 223; Tod [1829] 1972, I: 489. Grierson notes: "It is now a village . . . in the Lahāra Pargana of the state of Gwalior. Legends of the battle still exist in the locality" (W&G 222, n. 1).

[57]11.57-60; 24.79-80. Cf. Kolff 1990, 62 on Jahangir's alleged practice against Rajputs of eliminating "powerful zamīndārs" by surrounding their villages, cutting down "the dense forests which were used by them as hide-outs," and then killing them "to the last man."

be taken so long as Parmāl has the five flying horses. Prithīrāj writes to Parmāl demanding them. Parmāl weakly commands Ālhā and Ūdal to come from Dasrāpur, reads them the letter when they arrive, and orders them to relinquish their mounts. They refuse, and Parmāl answers their insubordination by banishing them from Mahobā with a terrible triple curse—to be discussed in chapter 10—which insults Ālhā and Ūdal beyond their tolerance. They leave Dasrāpur and Mahobā amid great lamentation and go into exile at Kanauj with their mother, wives, Ḍhēwā, Indal, Ālhā's elephant Pachsāwad, and Mīrā Tālhan. On the way they refuse Malkhān's offer to live with him at Sirsā, leaving him there as Mahobā's "only defender" (W&G 215-16). One notes that Parmāl has not asked Malkhān for his horse, the mare Kabutrī, who is regularly listed as the sole mare among the five horses. Kabutrī plays her necessary part in what follows.

Prithīrāj gives Chauṉrā the honor of attacking Sirsā (W&G 225). Malkhān begins well, drags Chauṉrā from the howdah of his "one-tusker" elephant, binds him, takes him to his tent, dresses him as a girl, and sends him back to Prithīrāj with a letter describing him as a Chandēl bride fit for Prithīrāj's son, presumably Tāhar. Again Malkhān "forces" the issue of an impossible marriage, this time involving his opposite number: Delhi's Brahman-general-as-bride, the same Chauṉrā who will later slay Brahmā by pretending to be Belā. Malkhān thus prevents the marriage of Ūdal and Bijaisin, forces the fateful betrothal of Brahmā and Belā, and satirizes a mock union of Chauṉrā and Tāhar. The opposition of Chauṉrā, the high ritual status (Brahman) general of Delhi, and Malkhān, the low ritual status (Banāphar) general of Mahobā, supplies the narrative with ritually charged themes and motivations that remind us of Cāmpukā and Anapōtu Rāju.

The Delhi forces are initially repulsed. But Māhil tricks Malkhān's mother Birmhā into revealing that Malkhān is invulnerable in all but one spot on his body: a lotus mark on the sole of his foot.[58] Advised by Māhil, Prithīrāj orders the digging of two hundred pits, one hundred as decoys and the other hundred covered over, and concealing short spears driven into the ground and set upright below.[59] Malkhān is then chal-

[58]W&G 229. In *BhvP*, Śirīṣākhyapuram is defended by both Sukhakhāni, killed first with Pṛthivīrāja's Rudra weapon, and Balakhāni (3.3.25.39-61). After Sukhakhāni defeats Cāmunda and the two brothers send him back to Pṛthivīrāja dressed as a woman, Pṛthivīrāja sends female Brahmaṇīs as messengers to learn from Brāhmī how to kill Sukhakhāni, not Balakhāni (3.3.24.92-106).

[59]I draw on Lutgendorf 1997, 5, who translates and describes Elliot [1881] 1992, 432-33, 437. The spears are *sāṃgis*; there are two hundred rather than just one hundred pits (as in W&G); and the covering is not specified, although W&G describe it as a "roof of grass." According to Baccha Singh, there are hundreds of bayonets and spears (*barachīs*).

lenged to defend the land Prithirāj has "seized" (W&G 230-31). After the inevitable flourish of courageous defiance by both horse and rider, Malkhān meets his end:

> O'er every trench did Kabutrī pass,
> Nor lance nor pike did fear,
> But she marked not the treacherous roof of grass,
> And she fell on a hidden spear. (235).

As the horse falls, a "cruel blade" pierces the lotus mark on Malkhān's sole, killing him (235). His wife Gajmōtin vows to become satī, and predicts the widowing of the women of Delhi and the burning of the city. She joins her husband on the pyre at a crossroads on a spot known as Pachpēṛā, "five trees," after the trees that "wave o'er" their "lonely" cremation site (237). The trees are unnamed, but they remind us of the five (or fewer) trees at the site of Anapōtu Rāju's death as a "lone hero" by the jammi.[60]

According to Bacchā Singh, Malkhān emerges from the pit to be beheaded and fight on as a *ruṇḍ*, a headless and limbless trunk, with such power that he kills four thousand more soldiers and Prithīrāj's elephant.[61] Finally, Prithīrāj's minister Gop Chand announces that Malkhān is protected by Bhairõ (Bhairava), and advises Prithīrāj to have his warriors turn back, put their swords and shields away, and recite Bhairõ-mantras. This pacifies Malkhān's Bhairõ-power, and he dies. There is no Pachpēṛā, but there is a *satī-cabūtarā* (platform-shrine) where Gajmōtin became satī, and its mud cures wounds from iron.

Malkhān thus supplies the same "functions" in *Ālhā* that his counterparts do in *Elder brothers*, *Palnāḍu*, and *Pābūjī*. Each moves his story along through the same skeletal sequences: intervention by an LSRSC, a virgin's curse, impalement, and satī. It is not only a question of fleshing out these skeletal functions with themes of caste, sexuality, ritual, and mythic allusion, but of precise recurring details. Like one or more of his counterparts, Malkhān is *the* primary guardian, but from the furthest boundary; he sounds the war drum;[62] he hunts boar; he is a

[60]In *BhvP* 3.3.25.39-61, Pṛthivīrāja offers his kingdom to Balakhāni if he leaps twelve pits with his mare Kapota (like Kabutrī, "Pigeon"), but he conceals a thirteenth pit with earth and grasses. The horse falls in and Balakhāni's lotus-marked foot is split. He climbs out and continues to fight until Cāmunda beheads him. Gajamuktā then rather lyrically becomes satī (59) at a spot marked by neither trees nor crossroad.

[61]The dismembered Abhimanyu similarly grinds three Kaurava battalions like a grinding pestle in the Terukkūttu (Hiltebeitel 1988a, 402-3).

[62]During the combats that precede Ālhā's wedding to Sunwā, Ūdal momentarily secures the "drum of life" for the Banāphars from Sunwā's father, and calls on Malkhān to sound it and

boor with heroines. Yet unlike these other LSRSCs, Malkhān's death by impalement involves no śamī.

Nonetheless, although it must seem like reaching for a dangerous bough, both the acacia and the śirīṣa, which figure prominently in Malkhān's story, are thorny trees like the śamī, which the early seventeenth-century *Nirṇayasindhu* describes as having "reddish thorns" (*lohitakaṇṭakā*) when it is invoked for the śamī-pūja.[63] The acacia, according to Grierson, is "the Babul or gum-arabic tree" (W&G 79, n. 2); as noted, an acacia grove figures repeatedly in the Mārō episode, providing, at Ūdal's inspiration from Bijaisin, the "thorn boughs" that blaze along with guns to "melt" Jambay's Iron Fort. Risky as it is, this branch must tempt us once again.

Malkhān has alternate prior Pāṇḍava identities. *Ālhā* traditions usually make him Sahadeva's incarnation,[64] probably evoking Sahadeva's affinities with fire and Malkhān's juniority and lowness relative to Ālhā and Ūdal.[65] Yet it is not *Ālhā* but the *Bhaviṣya Purāṇa* that accentuates Balakhāni's (Malkhān's) lowness by association with Dalits, and connects him most deeply with fire. To win the fiery-complexioned Gajamuktā-Gajmōtin as his bride, he must overcome a variety of fiery obstacles that the purāṇa multiplies. Gajasena, Gajamuktā's father, is a "servant of Agni" (*agnisevaka*; 16.28) who has obtained his fiery blessings from Agni after a twelve-year penance (1-5). He first pretends to accept Gajamuktā's choice of Balakhāni, but then imprisons him and orders him beaten by Cāṇḍālas, Dalits.[66]

When Āhlāda and the other heroes come to Balakhāni's rescue, Gajasena's fire-power reduces their army to ashes (16.40-51), and they are only able to revive it with advice from the goddess that Āhlāda's son Indula ride the submarine mare, whose showers appease the fire[67] and

---

"marshal the host" (W&G 165-67).

[63]See chap. 4, n. 63 with citations.

[64]This identification is not made in W&G, but is mentioned by both Schomer 1989, 148, and Lutgendorf 1979, 15. For variations, see chap. 5, § A.

[65]On Sahadeva and fire, see Wikander 1957, 73 (Sahadeva sent to fetch fire [*Mbh* 2.61.6]), 89-95 (Sahadeva's contest with king Nīla, who also, under Agni's protection, has mastery of fire [2.28.11-37]). Sahadeva is youngest and thus "lowest" of the Pāṇḍavas, and, like Malkhān, has a lower status mother than his "brothers." Note that Baccha Singh complements Malkhān's connection with Sahadeva by a blessing of Bhairō, a low and wrathful-fiery form of Śiva.

[66]3.3.16.19-20. Cāṇḍālas also bring Kṛṣṇāṃśa and Puṣpavatī to him at Śirīṣākhya after Āhlāda, suspecting Kṛṣṇāṃśa of killing his son Indula, orders the Cāṇḍālas to beat Kṛṣṇāṃśa and kill him (23.19-28; cf. W&G 213: "executioners" receive the order to kill Ūdal, but do not take him to Sirsā). As noted above, Mahismatī has no iron fort in the purāṇa. Likewise, Gajrāj's kingdom of Bisēn has none in the Elliot *Ālhā*.

[67]*Śamībhūte* (var. -*bhrte*) *tadā vahnau* (16.56); *śamībhūte hi pāvakaḥ* (57). I follow Śarma

whose saliva revives the army (52-57). Finally, the heroes, again tricked and captured, must force their way out of Gajasena's "village-shaped iron fort (*lohadurgām . . . grāmarūpam*)" (63-64), residence of the above-mentioned Cāṇḍalas, before they can obtain Gajasena's consent for the wedding. The story line is similar in the Elliot *Ālhā*, but with the following differences: Malkhān is beaten, but not by Dalits; Ālhā's army is turned to stone, not burnt to ash; Indal (Indula) gets the drink of immortality from Śāradā to revive the army; and the iron fort belongs to Jambay of Mārō, not Gajrāj/Gajasena (W&G 193-94).

Yet even though the purāṇa deepens Balakhāni's fire connections, it makes him an incarnation not of Sahadeva but Yudhiṣṭhira. Śiva curses Yudhiṣṭhira to be born as Balakhāni and to be king of Śirīṣākhya (1.23), and after his final appearance as a *piśāca* or ghost, Balakhāni goes in this form on a chariot to the heavenly vault (*nākam*) and dissolves (*layaṃ gataḥ*) into Yudhiṣṭhira (26.47-50).[68] Otherwise, all references to Balakhāni's prior life as Yudhiṣṭhira recall the latter's personification and incarnation of dharma/Dharma. Balakhāni is Dharmāṃśa (16.7 and 10) and Dharmajāṃśa (9.17; 26.47), and also *dharmātmā* (20.42). In the ghost passage, Kṛṣṇāṃśa, grieving over Balakhāni's death as "a portion of the one born of Dharma," says he, Kṛṣṇāṃśa-Ūdal, has come to earth on Balakhāni's account, and demands sight (darshan) of Balakhāni quickly lest he die too, whereupon Balakhāni and Gajamuktā flit into view and tell their tragic story.

What kind of Dharma or dharma is it that the purāṇa imparts through Yudhiṣṭhira to Balakhāni? The god Dharma-Dharmarāja figures in the purāṇa's *Ālhā*-story. Worshiped by Puṣpavatī's brother Makaranda, Dharma reveals the black magic that the Bāhlīka princess Citrarekhā obtains from Yama's servant Citragupta.[69] It enables Citrarekhā to abduct Indula and turn him into her love-slave as a parrot by day and a man at night.[70] Dharma supplies Makaranda and the heroes with yantras to overcome her magic in the Bāhlīka kingdom (23.31-39, 46, 63), which typifies non-Ārya encroachment on the northwest with its army of "Mlecchas of ghastly (*paiśāca*) dharma" (87) that belongs to Citrarekhā's father, the Tomara King Abhinandana. Balakhāni leads the expedition into

---

1968, 2:43-44 in taking *śamī* in these verses as implying pacification of fire rather than any reference to the samī tree. Thanks to B. Hebbar for help in reading Śarma's Hindi translation.

[68]Cf. W&G 1923, 239: a ghost, but with no such destination.

[69]Citragupta records for Yama everyone's good and bad deeds. Citrarekhā may be the same as Chitra Rekha, a sorceress in Himachal Pradesh who figures in the story of Bāṇāsura (Justa 1993, 63; cf. Hiltebeitel 1991a, 187-207).

[70]Cf. the parallel story, with no role for Citragupta or Dharmarāja, in W&G 212-14; see also Gold 1992, 238, 266, 278.

this Paiśāca realm, encountering further magic (80-149), and eventually becomes a Paiśāca himself. Clearly, this is the same Dharma that the *Mahābhārata* knows behind, and prior to, the births of Vidura and Yudhiṣṭhira: a Dharma invoked through black magic, as in Yudhiṣṭhira's birth; a Dharma who punishes by anal impalement, behind Vidura's birth; and a Dharma linked with Yama whose yantras counteract the black magic of Yama's servant Citragupta.[71] It would thus appear that whereas the *Mahābhārata* softens the cruelty of this prior Dharma in the persons of Vidura and Yudhiṣṭhira, the paurāṇika revives it behind the destiny of the latter's incarnation, Balakhāni, recalling it to explain Malkhān's unique fatality of death by impalement.

H. Sprouts

Malkhān's story allows an interpretation of its preliminary boundary fights and images of fire and impalement by reference to Dasarā, but would not call for this interpretation by itself. Its sequel, involving a ritual often associated with Dasarā, provides one of the reasons why such an interpretation is offered.

In connection with Dasarā and some other goddess festivals, sprouting ceremonies can hold implications of combat. For Dasarā, the sowing is done at the beginning of the nine-day period of Navarātrī, and the sprouts are dispersed at the end. A form known as "Nine Grains" is common at Draupadī festivals,[72] and a latent violence has been noted in the Draupadī cult myth that tells how the seedlings are a source of contention between the Kauravas and Pāṇḍavas.[73]

Such seedling rituals are widely associated with Dasarā in north and central India. Among Gurkhās in Nepal, barley sprouts that grow through the nine days and nights of Navarātrī are uprooted on Dasarā "tenth" and distributed by Brahmans in small bunches "to their followers" (Crooke 1914, 457). At Jaipur, at the conclusion Navarātrī, sorghum seedlings are "uprooted and then carried in a procession to be thrown in the water" (Biardeau 1984, 9). Kols in central India—some of whom, we have seen, worship Belā—keep to the same calendar for their version of this popular ceremony, which they combine with possession by the goddess Shardamai (Śāradā), tongue or cheek-piercings, and animal sacrifices to her.[74]

Uprooting followed by either dispersal or distribution is a common end

[71]On Dharma and black magic (*abhicāra*) in the *Mbh*, and the episodes referred to here (including *Mbh* 1.101, on Aṇīmāṇḍavya or "Māṇḍavya-of-the-Stake" as the victim of Dharma's cruel punishment behind the birth of Vidura), see Hiltebeitel forthcoming.

[72]Hiltebeitel 1988a, 301-9; 1991a, 53-78.

[73]Hiltebeitel 1988a, 309; cf. 1991a, 75-77.

[74]Griffiths 1946, 169-70; cf. Babb 1975, 132-41.

to such ceremonies, each with variations and associated meanings. Another is for people to scuffle to obtain the seedlings to bury in their fields. Especially pertinent is the "popular śamīpūjā" in Maharashtra, noted in connection with Sonā's śamī tree on the borders of *Pābūjī*. There, people scuffle for the śamī and/or āpaṭā tree's "gold" leaves *mixed with uprooted sprouts of sorghum*, and then distribute the "gold" at home.[75] Seedlings, like golden leaves, are metonyms for the goddess and metaphors of her fertility and resplendence. In such practices, the dispersal of the sprouts and "gold" is clearly linked not just with the end of Navarātrī, but incorporated into a "popular" conception of the "goods of life," the "prosperity," that Vijayādaśamī distributes.

In north central and western India, the basic rite is called *Jawara*, named for the large millet (*jawar*, *javārā*: *Sorghum vulgare*) sprouted. In central India, Jawara is performed twice annually: in the spring month of Chaitra (March-April) in conjunction with Rāma's birthday, and in the fall month of Kunvar (September-October) in conjunction with Navarātrī and Dasarā, with the chief goddess sometimes being Śāradā. The winter crop is planted after Dasarā, and the vitality of the seedlings can be taken as an augur of its failure or success. Since sorghum "is not grown to a great extent in Central India, it is more usual to find that wheat rather than *jawar* is used."[76]

Sorghum, just noted in Dasarā rituals in Rajasthan and Maharashtra, looks to have been made the subject of a narrative turn on seedling rituals in *Palnāḍū*. "Very white" sorghum seeds are first mistaken for pearls and strung as such on necklaces. Their ripe plants are then fought over and uprooted, and the "vegetative pearls" distributed by each man to his family (Roghair 1982, 166-68)—like "gold" in the "popular śamīpūjā." The play of such conceptions at the popular level may remind us that the "two Dasarās" that open *Ālhā* involve conflict and combat over a nine-lākh chain.[77] As we have seen, it is not clear whether it is a pearl, diamond, or golden necklace, or, more likely, a combination. In belonging to Śāradā, it would seem to symbolize both. More than this, in the Elliot *Ālhā*, the Delhi forces demand the nine-lākh chain in the very midst of Mahobā's seedling ceremony at the Battle of Kīratsāgar.[78] As in *Palnāḍu*, seedlings and necklaces are strung together.

[75]Biardeau 1984, 10; cf. Babb 1975, 156.

[76]Griffiths 1946, 169-70; cf. Babb 1975, 132-34, 140.

[77]*Ālhā* speaks of two Dasarās, the autumn one that has been our main focus here, and one in Jēṭh (Jyeṣtha, May-June) which celebrates the birth of the Ganges (W&G 256, n. 1). The Ganges bath on spring Dasarā day, said to purify one "from ten sorts of sins" (idem), is the setting for the *Ālhā* story of the "carrying off of Indal" (212-14).

[78]As mentioned above in § C, in the seventh appearance of the nine-lākh chain in the Elliot *Ālhā*.

The Elliot *Ālhā* sets its seedling ritual in a festival called Bhujariā, which provokes the Battle of Kīratsāgar. The large Kīratsāgar (Sanskrit Kīrtisāgara) lake was constructed by the Chandēl king Kīrtivarman (1060-c. 1100),[79] and Mahobā tradition locates a grave of "Meer Tala Saiyad" (see plate 9) on "the northern hill top" nearby (despite Mīrā Tālhan's dying at the final battlefield in the Elliot *Ālhā*).[80] As Grierson describes the festival, "A *bhujariā* is a small leaf basket in which are sown wheat, barley, &c. The grain springs up and in about ten days forms a little garden (like the 'Gardens of Adonis' in the West). On the full moon of Sāwan [July-August], the women of Mahobā carry these *bhujariās* in procession to the Kīratsāgar [Lake], into which they throw them" (W&G 238). At Mahobā, Ālhā performances now occur at fairs (*melā*) during this ceremony. The ritual's and fair's preferred name is *Kajaliyān* (plural), although *Bhujariyān/Bhujariā* is also a readily known equivalent.[81] The ceremony at Mahobā is a form of Jawara that is detached from Dasarā, but still must be interpreted in relation to it. Variations of the rite in Chhattisgarh (eastern Madhya Pradesh), where it is called Bhojalī, make this evident.

In the rural area around Raipur, the ceremony is linked directly with Navarātrī, and married women predominate; in Phuljhar, the nine nights of sprouting simulate Navaratrī but occur in Bhādon (August-September), and unmarried girls predominate.[82] In Raipur, Bhojalī is primarily a goddess festival associated with sowing jawar as part of "both" the spring and fall Navarātrīs (Flueckiger 1983, 31-32). Married women and unmarried girls both participate, and men sow the seeds. Married women lead the singing, and songs reflect their participation by accentuating sexual and agricultural maturation and fertility. Girls bring soil from the fields to be placed in the baskets for the sowing, carry the baskets to the tank,

[79]Adopting Bose's chronology (1956, 197).

[80]The Muslim hero actually has two adjacent grave sites on this hilltop. There is also an open-air stone pavilion called Ālhā Baiṭhak, "Ālhā's Seat," on the lake's southeastern bank; see Dixit 1992, 66, 69. Yet Kishan Sharma of Agra tells that Mīrā Tālhan (or Talhān, as he calls him) and his brother Daula's mausoleums are in Alwar, and are frequented today by many pilgrims. He says Tālhan and Daula led one of five invasions by Muslim conquerors (including Mahmud of Ghazna and Muhammad Ghori) from the northwest; Tālhan and Daula settled in Mahobā, and first allied with Parmāl against king Kalinga (a.k.a. Jambay of Mārō; see chap. 5, n. 51).

[81]*Bhujariyan ko laḍāī* is the title of Bacchā Singh's five *Ālhā* cassettes on this episode (Star Cassette Centre: Maudaha, Hamirpur District). See Schomer 1984, mentioning that *Ālhā* fairs at this time also occur elsewhere; Dixit 1992, 63-64, on a Mahobā-Bundelkhandī version of the story; and W&G 238, giving "festival of Sanīnō" as another variant. *BhvP*'s version of the episode calls the festival a Vāmana Mahotsava, and says that it is done with barley and rice (26.3). Kols call it *Khajleniya* (Griffiths 1946, 170).

[82]See Flueckiger 1983, 28-40, and Hiltebeitel 1991a, 72-73, for an earlier summary.

and form ritual friendships there with the exchange of seedlings. In Phuljhar, however, Bhojalī is for unmarried girls only, and only rarely combined with goddess festivals (34). The girls sow the seeds, sing the songs themselves, and the ritual friendships formed through the seedling exchange are accentuated rather than fertility (35). Yet in both areas, on "the last of the nine days, the seedlings are carried in procession by unmarried participants to the village pond and immersed"; "the soil is washed off from their roots"; the seedlings "are distributed as *prasād*" and exchanged "to formalize a ritual friendship" (28). The goddess personified in the sprouts also has royal associations.[83]

Many of these details illuminate the *Ālhā* Bhujariā as a detached piece of Navarātrī-Dasarā ritual-as-folklore. After the sack of Sirsā, Prithīrāj attacks Mahobā at the onset of Bhujariā. Only a short time before the Sirsā war and the Bhujariā, queen Malhnā had secured Ūdal's help in bringing her daughter Candrābal (Sanskrit Candrāvalī; Chandrā Bel in W&G) back from Candrabāl's husband's house to Mahobā to join in this women's ceremony (W&G 203-11). Due, however, to Prithīrāj's attack, Mahobā is surrounded and its gates closed, so no one can carry the bhujariās to the lake on the full moon night. Malhnā beseeches the goddess (Devī) to summon Ūdal "for help" (238). Devī comes to the exiled Ūdal in his sleep and directs him to Mahobā. Heeding her, Ūdal ignores Ālhā, who tells him not to go, and leaves with Ḍhēwā, Lākhan, and Mīrā Tālhan, again all disguised as Jōgīs. First they go to the ruins of Sirsā and learn all that happened there from a bird-catcher and Malkhān and Gajmōtin's ghosts. Then they enter Mahobā, and Ūdal—still the Jōgī—promises to help with the festival and "be a brother to Chandrābal." Māhil overhears, and tells Prithīrāj to expel the Jōgī troops from their forest camp. The Jōgīs "refuse to march" until the period of the waxing moon is over. Prithīrāj then tells Malhnā he will lift the siege if he receives the five flying horses (not registering that one of them has just died with Malkhān), the two Chandēl forts of Khajuraho and Gwalior, the nine-lākh chain, and Candrābal as Tāhar's bride.[84]

[83]At Raipur songs tell that she comes from "the house of the king"; in Phuljhar (a former small kingdom and later *zamīndāri* or landed estate, whose old fort's ruins still stand) she comes from that kingdom itself (Flueckiger 1983, 28, 30-31).

[84]W&G 231. According to Krishna Chaurasia and Zahir Singh, Prithīrāj demands Kalanjara and Khajuraho, the philosopher's stone, and Candrāvalī (already married) *and her daughter* for Tāhar. In Dixit's Bundelkhandi account (1992, 64), he demands the nine lākh-chain, Candrāvalī, Kalanjara Fort, and the philosopher's stone. This version is close to *BhvP* in making Pṛthivīrāja's encampment outside Mahobā the occasion for Mahīpati-Māhil to provoke hostilities by tricking Parimala to attack the Delhi army at night (3.3.26.1-10). But Pṛthivīrāja is not on his way back from the Deccan (Dixit 64); rather, Mahīpati has urged him to come directly from Delhi to see the sprouting festival. Other accounts (including

It is never clear from Waterfield and Grierson's text how Candrābal, long married when she returns to Mahobā for Bhujariā, is repeatedly sought for Tāhar (W&G 240, 243). Grierson just notes the "contradiction."[85] Zahir Singh and Krishna Chaurasia explained that "in those days," a marriage was only as good as the ability to defend the wife from capture.[86] The purāṇa tells us Candrāvalī is long forgotten by her parents before Malanā sends for her to join in a Holikā festival,[87] and that her marriage is an unhappy one: her husband Kāmasena beats her.[88] Nonetheless, she is devoted to him, and spots the cupidity of Cāmuṇḍa (Chauṉrā), disguised as a Brahman named Devīdatta overwhelmed with lust at seeing her "decked in every jewel," as a threat to her marital chastity (35-39, 59). One should not miss the parallelism and opposition between the marriage obstacles that entangle the two pairs of brothers and sisters from Mahobā (Brahmā and Candrābal) and Delhi (Tāhar and Belā), and the implication that had their marriages been handled differently, all might have been well. In the one case, Prithīrāj prevents the union of Belā and Brahmā, Draupadī and Arjuna incarnate. In the other, he seeks to impose an inappropriate union between Tāhar (Karṇa incarnate) and Candrābal.[89] Perhaps Candrābal's ambiguous status is analogous to the alternating married and unmarried roles for women one finds in Bhojalī ceremonies.

Malhnā refuses Prithīrāj's demands. But Brahmā is useless in defending his sister, and says they should rely on the Jōgīs. Within Mahobā, the only defense comes from Māhil's son Abhai (Malhnā's

---

Pṛthvīrāj-rāsau) agree that Pṛthivīrāja opened hostilities after Parmāl killed some of his soldiers while Pṛthivīrāja was passing through Mahobā, but give different occasions that are not connected with the sprout-festival (Dikshit 1977, 144; Bose 1956, 93-94).

[85]W&G 1923, 29, 239, n. 2. Dixit 1992, 63-64 has her as Parmal's "princess"-daughter, and seems to conflate *Ālhā* and *Pṛthvīrāj-rāsau* by giving her the brothers Bramajit (from the former) and Samarjit (from the latter). He mentions that Tāhar and Chauṉrā help Ūdal bring her back to Mahobā for her "Chauthi," and that Prithīrāj then demands her in revenge for the killing of his soldiers but does not clarify her marital status.

[86]Jamison 1994 raises interesting points in this connection about the "legalities" of "Rākṣasa" marriage and scenes of "reabduction."

[87]The purāṇa parcels out the Bhujariyā into two rituals: Vāmana Mahotsava for the actual ceremony, and Holī for Candrāvalī's return to Mahobā.

[88]22.26-51. She has also married into a kingdom of Yādava lineage, with its capital at Balīṭhāṭha (26-32). This evidently gives her an affinity with the Banāphars through their Ābhīrī (= Yādava?) mothers, not to mention with the Yādava Kṛṣṇa. Parimala seems to have married his daughter "down" in the very fashion that other kings resist in opposing their daughters' marriages to the Banāphars. Yet, if the text makes him out more egalitarian or, more likely, less able to oppose such a marriage militarily, it also portrays the marriage itself as violent.

[89]Candrābal's tensions with Tāhar recalls Draupadī's incompatibility with Karṇa, which has so many resonances (Hiltebeitel 1980a; 1988a, 235 and n. 21, 288-89, 315-16).

nephew, who unlike his father is loyal to Mahobā) and Brahmā's younger brother Ranjit. Malhnā, who carries her own "gunpowder and flint and steel" (a superb anachronistic reminder of the latent violence of this rite, and the toughness of this queen), then has all the fourteen hundred women of Mahobā set off in procession, Candrābal in the middle and Malhnā leading, each in a litter with her bhujariā, each dressed in green (like the sprouts) and each carrying poison powder and a poison-dipped knife, swearing not to "fall alive into the enemies' hands or to be carried off to Delhi" (W&G 239). Abhai and Ranjit fight bravely but are soon killed trying to protect the procession:[90] a likely reflex of the link between heroes who die young and the doomed but beautiful seedlings.[91] Small platform-shrines or *chabūtrās*, still tended by women, are said to mark the sites of their deaths near the Kīratsāgar.[92]

At last Brahmā enters the fighting, and when he is surrounded, Ūdal and the other "Jōgīs" finally come to the field. Chauṉrā now reaches Malhnā's litter and demands the nine-lākh chain. She refuses, cries out for Ūdal, "if he is anywhere on earth or in heaven" (!), and Ūdal, still disguised, comes to the rescue. Chauṉrā takes flight. But Tāhar captures Candrābal's litter—a foreshadowing of the fight over Belā's litter—and leads her off to "Pachpēṛā, where the four roads join" (W&G 240). This Pachpēṛā, "Five Trees," is certainly different from the one outside far-away Sirsā that marks the spot of Malkhān's cremation and Gajmōtin's satī. It is thus instructive to see how the Elliot *Ālhā* brings together, through what are apparently three Pachpēṛās, the ritual interlinkages of the Iron Fort, impalement, satī, and bhujariā.[93]

Lākhan defeats Tāhar at this Kīratsāgar Pachpēṛā and rescues Candrābal and her bhujariā. Then an all-out attack forces Prithīrāj to retreat to the Kīratsāgar's south bank, while the litters and the women come with Ūdal to the north side. Candrābal seems to have an honorary role of being the first to throw her bhujariā into the water. But it floats to the other side where Prithīrāj, at Māhil's suggestion, orders Chauṉrā to take it up. Candrābal cries that "if the enemy gets it," the festival "will be ruined." So Ūdal goes to retrieve it, and after he brings it back, she steps "up to him to fasten the plants in his turban": a variation within the seedling rites of honoring the recipient, who is most commonly a brother,

[90]Their headless trunks fight on until Bhūrā Mughul waves a blue flag over them (240; cf. 50). Bhūrā Mughul is a "bad Muslim" (he slaughters cows on the altars of Devī; W&G 245) who becomes the eventual "last victim" of the "good Muslim" Mīrā Tālhan (271).

[91]Cf. Hiltebeitel 1991a, 65-66.

[92]Information from Zahir Singh and Krishna Chaurasia.

[93]Baccha Singh recalls only one Pachpēṛā, that at Mārō, in the middle of which was an akhāṛā or a wrestling place, with mango trees! Akhāṛās are connected with sites where *Ālhā* heroes are said to have wrestled: e.g., at Maihar in Banda District, Madhya Pradesh.

husband, or intended. Ūdal refuses to accept it, however, saying Lākhan is the "senior Jōgī."[94] Candrābal then gives Lākhan the first plant and Ūdal a second, signaling that Ūdal's protection of Mahobā is now contingent upon his subordination to Lākhan and Kanauj, while at the same time establishing Lākhan in a ritual bond with Candrābal that promises his protection of Mahobā. Having promised to be Candrābal's brother, Ūdal reciprocates by giving her a bracelet from his wrist (240-41). This exchange recalls the one between unmarried girls at Bhojalī, but transposes it to a "fictive" brother-sister relationship between Ūdal and Candrābal, a relationship like the one noticed earlier between Ūdal and Belā. Mahobā informants indicate that this ceremony, which completes Bhujariā, is precisely the north Indian rite of rakhibandhana, in which a sister ties a protective wristlet on her brother. Around Mahobā, *Ālhā*'s fusion of Bhujariā with rakhibandhana seems to have redefined the latter's timing: because the battle of Kīratsāgar delayed the Bhujariā by a day, it is done in Bundelkhand a day later than elsewhere.[95]

The exchange also unveils Ūdal's disguise, for it is when Ūdal the Jōgī gives Candrābal the bracelet that Malhnā and Candrābal recognize him, "and Prithīrāj, hopeless of success" until Ūdal returns to Kanauj, departs for Delhi. Parmāl then embraces Ūdal, weeps over him, and offers him "the philosopher's stone, and as guardian of Brahmā, the realm of Mahobā, if he will return and live there, instead of going back to Kanauj." But Ūdal recalls Parmāl's dreadful curses, and says that although he will come to help if needed, he will never return to live in Mahobā.[96]

This whole episode holds reminders of the contest over the *navadhānya* seedlings in the Draupadī cult drama *Turōpatai Kuṟavañci* (Hiltebeitel 1988a, 301-9): the disguises; the hidden threats of violence connected with the ceremony; the precariousness of the "married/virgin" heroine either entering the enemy camp to obtain the seeds (Draupadī) or

[94]Ūdal's Banāphar (i.e., Cowherd-Rajput) deference to the fully Rajput Lākhan, the Kanauj heir-apparent, replicates Kṛṣṇa's Yādava-Cowherd-Kṣatriya subordination to the "true" Kṣatriyas of the *Mbh*; see Hiltebeitel 1988a, 35, n. 6, 185-86, 220.

[95]According to Zahir Singh and Krishna Chaurasia, and also as worked into Dixit's account, when Prithīrāj's soldiers are killed in Parmāl's garden on the way back from the Deccan (a *Rāsau* story [see n. 84]), Prithīrāj vowed "he would take away the Mahobā princess, Chandravali, when she came to dispose of Kajarian at the Kirat Sagar in the month of Savan on the day of 'Purnima'" (Dixit 1992, 64). He attacked, but Ālhā (!) and Ūdal prevailed and killed his four sons. The Purṇimā was thus completed with rejoicings, with rakhibandhana, and disposing of Kajarian on the following day, the first day of Bhadon. Prithīrāj then attacked again, and Parmāl fled to the Kalanjara Fort (ibid.; cf. Crooke [1896] 1968, 2:293.

[96]W&G 241. Ūdal's refusal of "the realm" again recalls the Yādava theme of having "no share of kingship"; his refusal ever to return is also another scene of urban viraha bhakti.

demanded by the enemies who try to capture her seedlings (Candrābal); the rivalry over the seedlings (Kauravas and Pāṇḍavas; Delhi with its incarnate Kauravas and Mahobā plus Kanauj with their incarnate Pāṇḍavas); the interventions of Kṛṣṇa (who miraculously makes the burnt seeds grow) and Ūdal (who rescues Candrābal's seedlings from the water).

I. Belā's Tour

The Elliot *Ālhā*'s brings its Dasarā subplot to a close, after the "Battle at Kīratsāgar," with the return of Ālhā and Ūdal to defend Mahobā for the last time. Ālhā remains behind at Mahobā—more precisely at Dasrāpur (W&G 259)—while Ūdal sets out for Delhi in black disguise to form the Banāphar guard that springs Belā from her father's "prison." While her husband lies dying, the Banāphars attend her "homecoming."

First, Belā stops to worship the goddess and send a letter via the flower-girl Phulwā shaming Tāhar's manhood and challenging him to try to prevent Lākhan from taking her to Kanauj "in revenge for Sanjōgin (*vadlo līhaiṃ saṃjogini ko*)"—that is, Prithīrāj's abduction of Sanjōgin from Kanauj.[97] It is clear she is doing everything she can to gall her brother, since Kanauj is not her destination and Lākhan not a captor. Tāhar rides forth and Lākhan repulses him until Belā's litter reaches the Mahobā camp. There Ūdal rejoins her and gives her the nine-lākh earrings he has tricked from Prithīrāj for her dowry, which delights her. This seems to anticipate her receiving the nine-lākh chain, and it is intriguing that the total value of the two treasures, Belā's alone at the end, is eighteen lākhs: the *Mahābhārata*'s signature number as well as the maximum iconographic number of the goddess's weapon-bearing arms. As Belā's litter progresses, it is captured several times and each time regained as Belā's guardians fend off Prithīrāj, Chauṉrā, Tāhar—Duryodhana, Droṇa, and Karṇa incarnate (in the Elliot *Ālhā*)—and other attackers (W&G 263-65).

The passage is clearly agonistic: both sides vie for Belā and all that comes with her, just as they have vied over the nine-lākh chain and bhujariā, and as the Kauravas and Pāṇḍavas vie over Draupadī. The litter suggests a processional palanquin or "chariot," as in the procession of an icon. Even if there have never been hero cult or festival reenactments of *Ālhā*, as there are none, at least, today, one can hardly avoid the impression that the description is influenced by the imagery of processional rituals of both icons and royalty. Just as Draupadī's processional "chariot" is led from her temple by Pōttu Rāja through Tamil villages to a ritual battlefield identified as Kurukṣetra, Belā's litter is led by her

[97] W&G 263; Lutgendorf 1997, 5; Elliot [1881] 1992, 577.

Banāphar guard from her Delhi home to and through Mahobā to the site where Brahmā lies dying, which is not only a battlefield but the site where she will eventually become satī. The Elliot *Ālhā* makes her destination the final battlefield of the *Mahābhārata* of the Kali yuga.

Belā makes four stops on this tour. First, where Brahmā lies dying, she sees him for the first time since their betrothal, fans him with flowers and "utters a great cry of 'Awake, awake, my beloved'" (W&G 265). Brahmā regains consciousness. The passage has a formulaic and ritualized ring. Earlier, after Malkhān has been slain, before his widow Gajmōtin mounts his pyre to become satī, she utters virtually the same words:

> "Awake my husband, awake," she said,
> "Or wait till thy love shall come!"
> And still to every god they prayed,
> And still they beat the drum. (236)

In the purāṇa, when Velā approaches the unconscious and stupefied Brahmānanda at night, before the final war, he becomes "undead" in his little finger (*kaniṣṭhāmṛta-bhāvena*). After she tells him who she is and gives him water, she says, "O son of Malanā, I am Velā, daughter of the husband of the earth (*mahībhartuḥ*).[98] You are my resolute husband, slain by fraud and deceptions. Come alive, O lord of kings. Enjoy joys together with me."[99] Here the awakening clearly takes on the air of one of those last-moment revivals such as we saw in *Elder brothers*.[100] Once Brahmā regains consciousness, he calls Belā a traitor's daughter and orders her dismissed. But she convinces him she shares his cause, and he replies that "if anyone will bring him the head of Tāhar he will live again" (W&G 265). Belā promises to kill her own brother, Karṇa reincarnate.

When Belā returns to her litter, it is now under the "charge of Ālhā," who finally completes what remains of her Banāphar guard. Her next stop is Mahobā for her "homecoming." She is greeted by Sunwā, Devī, and Malhnā, and Devī gives her the nine-lākh chain (W&G 266). Then she persuades Ālhā to take her on a most curious outing. Following Lutgen-

[98]The name makes explicit the resonance of Pṛthivīrāja's name ("king of the earth") and his usual *BhvP* name Mahīpati ("lord [or husband] of the earth").

[99]31.172-77, closing with: *jīvanaṃ kuru rājendra bhunkṣva bhogānmayā saha*. Note that the *Mbh*'s postwar Aśvamedha centers on a revival of Arjuna, whom we find here reincarnated in Brahmā/Brahmānanda.

[100]Recall the Draupadī cult dying and rising rituals at Mēlaccēri-Gingee in which impersonators of the slain Young Pañcapāṇḍavas wiggle their toes, and variations on the death scene in the *Cilappatikāram* (Hiltebeitel 1988a, 336; 1991a, 339-80; in press-c). Gopi Chand's power of revival lies in his little finger (Kolff 1990, 78).

dorf's summary and translation, she has Ālhā conduct her to the Kīratsāgar lake and "asks to be shown Brahmā's villa there," where she would have been queen. Then they "get into a sandalwood boat which Ālhā rows, presumably to an island in the lake,[101] and approach the house"—to tour the empty palace, as Phulvantī also does at the end of *Pābūjī*.

> Belā entered the villa and saw the splendor on all sides.
> There was a *caupar* game set on a shelf so Belā took it down.
> "Come, O son of Dasrāj, you and I will play dice."
> Belā took on the form of Ratī and removed the veil from her breast.
> Ālhā, though inwardly agreeable (to her offer), hung his head downward (cast down his eyes, so as not to be tempted by the sight of her).
> She took the tenth (?)[102] form of a hag (*ḍayan*),[103] and (then he) said to Belā,
> "Belā, though you try to frighten me, I'm a Kṣatriya (*chatrī*) and not deceived.
> You are like my dharma-mother (*dharma ki mātā*)" (and Belā said?) "You are like my son, Banāphar Lord."
> "Remove that form, Belā, and assume (your) former form."
> (Belā said) "I am now convinced that there is no sin in your heart."
> Then Belā left the villa and came and sat in the boat.[104]

Once Belā returns to her litter, she is still under Ālhā's guard.

Given that in Grierson's summary there is only a reduced seduction scene and no caupar game,[105] Lutgendorf remarks, "It is (I assume) interesting to you that she uses the game of dice to try to tempt him, and also that she removes her *añcal* (Hindi for veil, end of sari), exposing her bosom, which seems a pretty outrageous thing for a Rajput princess to do" (1997, 6). Here the allusions to the *Mahābhārata* dice match are, I believe, unmistakable, and confirm that the prior allusion—Lākhan's

[101]As I recall, there is no island today in the Kīratsāgar.

[102]Lutgendorf 1997, 6, comments that the occurrence of *dasvāṃ*, "which seems to mean 'tenth,'" is of uncertain meaning here.

[103]Lutgendorf 1997, 6, cites McGregor 1993, 419, as tracing *ḍayan* to *ḍāin* and ultimately to Sanskrit *ḍākinī*. Grierson has "ogress" (W&G 266).

[104]Lutgendorf 1997, 6; Elliot [1881] 1992, 595-96. Cf. W&G 266, where Grierson cuts more than usual: perhaps, as Lutgendorf suggests, "due to Victorian scruples": at Brahmā's lakeside bungalow, Belā "tests" Ālhā, "first assuming a beautiful form, and attempting to seduce him, and then appearing as an ogress, and attempting to terrify him." Seeing that he is "unmoved by both apparitions" she learns that "she can trust him."

[105]See previous n. 104.

statement, "If Belā is true (*sāṃcī*), let the dice fall in my favor"—is this one's foreshadowing. Lākhan and Ālhā are the two implied kings among the Banāphars: the one as prince of Kanauj, the other as hidden king of Mahobā. And Belā is both a stake and a player. Like Draupadī after she is wagered, who puts herself in play by asking the question whether Yudhiṣṭhira could have truly wagered her if he wagered himself first,[106] Belā is put in play by Lākhan, and puts herself in play—even sexually—with Ālhā, inviting him to the game. In a Telugu folk *Mahābhārata*, it is Draupadī, rather than Yudhiṣṭhira, who plays dice with Duryodhana.[107] But *Ālhā* gives us the dice match everyone has been waiting for: the one between the Draupadī and Yudhiṣṭhira, reincarnated. The Elliot *Ālhā* retains, and at last seems to resolve, a fundamental *Mahābhārata* question that lies unsettled between Draupadī and Yudhiṣṭhira from the time of the dice match on: that of whether Yudhiṣṭhira gambled her away with any sin in his heart.[108]

Belā's alternate forms may remind one of Draupadī's folk evocations of Śrī and Kālī, and also of the Indo-European initiatory test of the would-be king who must kiss a hideous hag before she reveals herself to be a beautiful maiden and the "Sovereignty" he seeks (Hiltebeitel [1976] 1990, 175-91). Ālhā, of course, can pass this test only by its inversion, by averting his eyes and not kissing Belā, since his kingship is hidden. The sexual implications of this seduction scene are powerful, and it would seem that the Elliot *Ālhā* eliminates such overtones in Ālhā's relation to Belā only by putting them to this test. As to Belā's seductive lowering of her veil and baring of her breast, we have learned not to be surprised when she lowers high Rajput standards. The Terukkūttu drama "Dice Match and Disrobing" lowers and even reviles Draupadī around the same nexus of themes.[109]

Belā's third stopping place (without equivalent in the *Bhaviṣya Purāṇa*) is Sirsā fort, where Malkhān has died and Gajmōtin has become satī. As Gajmōtin had done before her, Belā now prophesies to Gajmōtin's ghost that the women of Mahobā and Delhi will soon be widows, and that she will soon become satī too.

Belā's fourth stop returns her to Brahmā (who is still alive despite the improbable length of her clearly symbolic journey). She reassures him she hasn't forgotten her brother's head, but first had to visit her mother-in-law at Mahobā: "Now I am going to Delhi to fetch it" (W&G 266).

[106]See Hiltebeitel forthcoming on the *Mbh*'s wagering.

[107]Rama Raju 1982; Hiltebeitel 1988a, 238.

[108]Cf. n. 104: in Grierson's paraphrase, whether she could trust him. On Draupadī's question, see also Hiltebeitel forthcoming.

[109]Hiltebeitel 1988a, 228-81; Frasca 1984, 351-400.

Belā dresses like Brahmā, armors herself, mounts Brahmā's horse, and sets off with the army, rejecting Ūdal's escort. Once again Belā reminds one of Māncāla, who dresses as a warrior and rides the fallen Bāluḍu's horse to fight his last battle.[110] But these similarities end here. As noted in chapter 3, Māncāla's foray seems curiously amorphous, rarely told, and largely unmotivated. Bāluḍu leaves her with no mission to behead an adversary in revenge;[111] and after she has fought, it seems she dies embracing Bāluḍu without it clear whether or not she becomes satī.[112] With all their other affinities, one must consider the possibility that Māncāla has been losing part of her story.

In any case, Belā goes forth to fight. As Brahmā had done, she goes without guard. But she does so intentionally: an image of the virgin-goddess-heroine who fights ultimately on her own. She stops at the Delhi border and sends a letter claiming that Brahmā has recovered from his wounds. In his name, she demands the remaining half of her dowry (this is unclear) and challenges Tāhar to bring it lest she burn Delhi to the ground. When they fight, her sleeve is torn, revealing her woman's bangles. Chaunṟā tries to warn Tāhar, but too late. She beheads her brother and brings his head to Brahmā, arousing him this last time with the words, "Awake, my lord, upon thy jewelled bed." Brahmā's revival at seeing his enemy's head is brief, and he dies "at peace" with a challenge to Belā to become satī. She begins a deep lament. Mahobā fills with weeping (W&G 266-67), and, as described above in section C, she lights her pyre with her hair.

It is thus during the march of Belā's litter, protected by her Banāphar guard, that she is first carried to Dasrāpur, then to Mahobā to receive the nine-lākh chain and put Ālhā to her test, and then, with Ālhā now her chief guard, to Sirsā, where she announces her satī and the widowhood of the women of Delhi. This tour, which looks like the festival procession of a goddess, ties together many of the Elliot *Ālhā*'s major themes. Above all, the nine-lākh chain ends up with Belā. Throughout, it seems to have combined its representation of gold and jewels as "prosperity" with the imagery of the "unvanquished" and "victorious" virgin. Belā's procession through Dasrāpur, Mahobā, and Sirsā thus provides one last reinforcement of the Dasarā-linked themes that unite these sites together into a royal complex. Indeed, just as Belā begins her homecoming under

[110]On Māncāla's war-ending ride, see the retelling of *Palnāḍu* in Chandra Sekhar 1961, 184. Each is disguised as her warrior husband. See Hansen 1992, 187-90 on Belā as a *vīrāṅganā* or woman warrior.

[111]She has, however, taken her own revenge on Anapōtu Rāja, resulting in his self-beheading before the battle.

[112]Or her death by fighting could be meant as another kind of satī death; see chap. 14.

the protection of Ūdal, she makes the last parts of her journey with Ālhā. The unvanquished virgin joins the hidden king.

None of this is found in the *Bhaviṣya Purāṇa*, where Āhlāda is an incarnation of Balarāma and the story is almost entirely different.[113] But other oral *Ālhā*s intensify the hidden kingship of Ālhā in ways that play upon his relations with Brahmā and Belā. In Agra, where the Chandēl lineage of Mahobā lacks centrality and can be virtually removed from the story, Kishan Sharma tells that when Parmāl dies soon after the senior Banāphars, and thus well *before* the final war, Ālhā is made regent of Mahobā because Brahmā is too young. As such, Ālhā occupies the Mahobā throne (*rājagaddī*), although he is not a Kṣatriya, and opposes all wars except the final one, which pits Prithīrāj not against Parmāl but against Malkhān. Indeed, in this account, the fight over Belā's homecoming is prior to the final war, and Belā's satī prior to Gajmōtin's![114] On the contrary, Baccha Singh tells that when Ālhā, at age thirteen, led the defense of Delhi against the "Mughals," Prithīrāj was so pleased that he offered him Belā to marry. But Ālhā declined, since he was subordinate to Brahmā, and, leaving Belā dissatisfied, told Prithīrāj that she should be given to Brahmā instead. In this light, we might suspect that there could be a less chaste reading of Belā's attempted seduction of Ālhā.

Belā's tour is on one level an inversion of Dasarā: a tour not of victory but defeat. As Ūdal says, hands joined and weeping, repeatedly invoking Belā's name as he approaches the pyre on which she has burned:

> "Why did you go and take birth in Delhi, you who caused the destruction of the lineage (*vaṃs kī hāni*).
> The lamp of Mahobā was extinguished, the Chandēl prince was slain."[115]

The *Bhaviṣya Purāṇa* describes the heroine similarly when Pṛthivīrāja predicts that if he doesn't receive the horses he demands from Parimala,

[113]*BhvP* omits the story of the sleeve and the last appeal that Brahmānanda revive. Velā's satī lacks most of the dramatic features it has in the Elliot *Ālhā* (the demand for sandalwood; putting on all her ornaments and dressing herself in bridal array; the lighting of the pyre with fire from her hair). The paurāṇika has Parimala command the lighting of the pyre, which meets the demand Prithīrāj makes in the Elliot *Ālhā* to keep a low Banāphar from doing so. See further chap. 8.

[114]For Kishan Sharma's narratives, see chap. 5, n. 51; above n. 80; and below chap. 14.

[115]Lutgendorf 1997, 7, translating Elliot [1881] 1992, 642 (I summarize Ūdal's approach from this translation, and take *vaṃs* in the singular—Lutgendorf translates "lineage(s)"—since the next line refers only to the Chandēls. Cf. W&G 272: "Born wast thou in Delhi to be the ruin of the clans."

"all the army-protectors will go to destruction by the fire of Velā" (*velāgninā*; 24.12). These descriptions echo the heavenly words that announce the birth of Draupadī: "Foremost among all women, Kṛṣṇā will lead the Kṣatra to destruction" (*Mbh* 1.155.44). As the "*Mahābhārata* of the Kali yuga" comes to a close, the heroes have failed to protect the goddess and the land. But they have also returned to protect the heroine who represents the goddess and the land, and who exhibits the goddess's powers of revival and revenge. Belā's march is thus not simply an inverted Dasarā tour of a lost and cherished kingdom. It is also an affirmation that although the mutually protective links between the goddess, the king, and the avatar are broken, they survive in hidden ways, and that even in defeat, something survives in the tellings.

Plate 1. Cāmpukā with drum and drumsticks at Vīramalai paṭukaḷam, where he is locally called Vīrapāhu

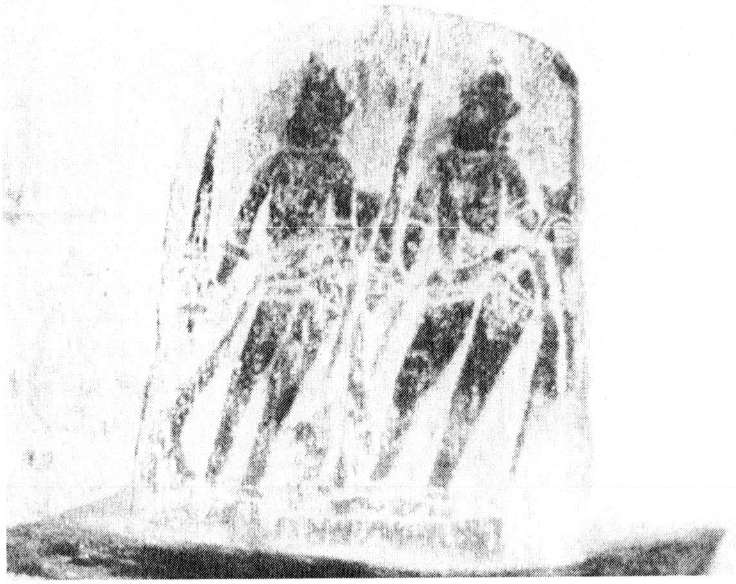

Plate 2. Two Muslim warriors, Jaffar and Farīd, at Temple of the Heroes, Kārempūḍi

Plate 3. Vīramalai paṭukaḷam from the back of Māyavār's shrine, facing the main temple. A tiny vaṉṉi maram sapling is planted behind the Māyavār shrine. The three shrines between Māyavār and the main temple mark the paṭukaḷam or dying ground of the major heroes.

Plate 4. Māyavār in his small Vīramalai paṭukaḷam shrine. Holding the bow and arrow which signal the end of the heroes' lives, he stands beside a vaṉṉi poised to shoot. A sacrificial post-stone to his right has perhaps a flower or cakra design on its top.

Plate 5. Po<u>nn</u>ar in his Vīramalai paṭukaḷam shrine, stabbing himself. Caṅkar is shown similarly in his shrine.

Plate 6. Weapons of the heroes of Palnāḍu at back wall of the Temple of the Heroes, Kārempūḍi. All are thickly coated with turmeric. The central huge broadsword is Kannama Dāsu's weapon. To its right is Brahma Nāyuḍu's weapon; to its left Bāluḍu's. Further to the left, upright from the floor, is a cross-grip sword of the kind found in many Draupadī temples.

Plate 7. Śāradā in her sanctum at the Bairāgarh Śāradā Devī temple

Plate 8. Colorful medallion on a branching votive spear (sang) at Bairāgarh (see also plates 16 and 17), showing Chauṉṟā, beheaded, filling Śāradā's bowl with his blood

Plate 9. One of two tombs for Mīrā Tālhan on the northern mountain overlooking the Kīratsāgar Lake at Mahobā. The lake extends into the background.

Plate 10. Tomb (kōri or gōr) near Kadali village of Rāja Desing's horse Pārācāri (foreground). On the other side of a tank a recently constructed masjid stands near the tombs of Mōvuttukkāraṉ and his horse Nīlavēṇi.

Plate 11. Well-maintained tomb of Mōvuttukkāraṉ (Mohabat Khan on the plaque) visited by young women and girls for immediate rewards

Plate 12. Satī platform of Rāṇiyammāḷ, wife of Rāja Desing, below the Gingee Fort. Steps in back of the platform lead down to the Ceṭṭikuḷam, a tank surrounded by crags and boulders.

Plate 13. Kalki on horseback with rider; or Desing's father Dhana Singh (Ta̱ciṅku), left, and uncle Tēraṇi Singh, right, as protectors of Gingee Fort. Mantaiveḷi or grazing ground, Gingee town below the fort.

Plate 14. Belā becomes satī. Elliot *Ālhā* illustration.

Plate 15. Memorial stone showing the Gingee king and his satī concubine at the Tī Pañcan̠ Kōvil; Mēlaccēri or "Old Gingee"

Plate 16. Belā's satī chabūtrā, Bairāgarh

Plate 17. Śāradā Devī Temple, Bairāgarh, with votive spears (sangs) outside entrance

Plate 18. Branching votive spear (sang) outside Bairāgarh Sāradā Devī Temple, showing the beheaded Chaunṟā filling Śāradā's bowl with his blood (as on plate 8) and, opposite to the right, a hand holding a bloody sword

7 The Story of Kṛṣṇāṃśa

The last two chapters have allowed us to appreciate that the *Bhaviṣya Purāṇa* frequently illuminates the Elliot *Ālhā* by a parallel version that must draw on a common regional martial oral epic folklore. We may now ask what kind of text the *Bhaviṣya*'s *Ālhā* segment is. I hypothesize that it is one that "over-*Mahābhārat*-izes" an oral *Ālhā* that it knows by Sanskritizing, Brahmanizing, and purāṇicizing it. It is a text that positions itself somewhere between oral *Ālha* and *Mahābhārata* by reenplotting into "*Ālhā*" the battle of Kurukṣetra.

Moreover, if we consider this reenplotment a kind of translation, we will be able to appreciate it as a kind of Rosetta stone that sharpens our ability to make intelligent moves back and forth over the divide between India's folk and classical epics, and to see that the divide itself has, in large part, been constructed by Western scholarship in ways that have allowed it to apply its own poorly adapted engineering solutions: oral tradition, great tradition, little tradition, myth and history, deification, oral formulaic verse, interpolation theory, legitimation theory, ideology, etc.[1] Going back to Ramanujan's three types of translation,[2] this example would be primarily indexical, but with a reverse situation from the one Ramanujan defines—a translation not from a purāṇic to a local-vernacular index, but from the local and vernacular to a purāṇic index. The purāṇas translate local material endlessly, but the purāṇa's *Ālhā* segment is unique, as far as I know, in being a translation of a regional folk epic into Sanskrit purāṇese.[3]

[1]Cf. Chatterjee 1995a, 169, on the maladaption of Europe-based analytical instruments to the "sheer vastness and intricacy" of Indian peasant history: "When those instruments now meet with the resistance of an intractably complex material, the fault surely is not of the Indian material but of the imported instruments."

[2]See chap. 2, § D.

[3]Cf. Shulman 1993, 67-84, on Śrīnātha's Brahmanized-purāṇicized "translation" of the Ciruttoṇṭar-Siriyāla story, comparable especially for transforming a harsh tale into a "vilāsic ontology" of divine play. But the story is not an epic; it already has a long literary history

Let us begin by asking what the *Bhaviṣya*'s *Ālhā* story has to say about itself intertextually, not only in relation to *Ālhā* and *Mahābhārata*, but in relation to other texts. We can then be more precise about its place on an *Ālhā-Mahābhārata* gradient.

A. What Kind of Text?

The paurāṇika places great weight on written texts, not only referring to many by name or allusion, but making Kṛṣṇāṃśa the best among the heroes at writing his name by age eight (9.49), and the most competent at reading sage philosophical inquiry (*paṭhitvānvīkṣikīṃ vidyām*) and dharmaśāstra by age nine (10.1-2). This provides Ūdal with a Brahmanical education, and distances the text from an oral tradition.

The text has a transparent name for itself: the *Kṛṣṇāṃśacarita* (or -*caritra*), "The story of Kṛṣṇāṃśa." The title refers to the *Ālhā* segment as a whole, and more narrowly to certain chapters (adhyāyas) which, in typical epic-purāṇic fashion, bring rewards to those who hear or read them. Usually, the auditors are just such hearers or readers.[4] But characters themselves may be said to follow the text: when the women follow the yogi-disguised Kṛṣṇāṃśa's advice and go with the barley and rice plants to the Kīrtisāgara lake, they "all went (according to) the auspicious *Kṛṣṇāṃśacaritam*" (26.2). And at one turning point, they marvel reflexively upon hearing that they are part of this awesome story themselves.

This comes when the "troubled (*apanna*)" Tāraka (Tāhar) reports to Pṛthivīrāja "about the highly amazing *Kṛṣṇāṃśacarita*" (24.2), which at this point defines a narrative that suggest to the speakers the impossibility of Delhi's quest for paramountcy so long as Kṛṣṇāṃśa and the "Banāphar" heroes remain allied with Parimala. Pṛthivīrāja's *mantrin* (minister) Candrabhaṭṭa then chimes in: "The all-doing goddess Vaiṣṇavī was praised by me, and at the end of three years the fear-removing boon-giver was pleased. An auspicious knowledge was given by her that makes for the scattering of weak intellect. I then, having become a possessor of knowledge about Kṛṣṇāṃśa, told this *caritra* of him that is destructive of sin." Accordingly, Candrabhaṭṭa recites "this auspicious speech-made

---

behind it; and it is in Telugu, not Sanskrit.

[4]When referred to by name, usually at the beginnings or ends of adhyāyas, the text is said to afford bliss (20.53) and to destroy the sins of the Kali yuga (22.70) or be destructive of Kali (23.140); it is seen through the strength of yoga (30.94), and, as known by Candrabhaṭṭa (bard Chand of the *Pṛthvīrāj-rāsau*) through his knowledge (*jñāna*) and devotion to the goddess Vaiṣṇavī, it destroys sin (24.2-6). The first four references, coming at the end of adhyāyas, are typical *phalaśrutis*. At 3.4.1.11, however, it is referred to as *Kṛṣṇasya caritam*, "The Story of Kṛṣṇa," which, just "heard," now leads the Ṛṣis to ask the bard to describe the lineages of Agnivaṃśa kings.

book (*grantha*), the glorification of the devotees of the goddess (*māhātmyaṃ devībhaktānām*), before the assembly (sabhā)." The schemer Mahīpati (Māhil) then confirms that Candrabhaṭṭa is in some manner telling the *Kṛṣṇāṃśacarita* itself, saying, "The story has described a youth named Udaya. . . ." Having heard it, Mahīpati then applies its lessons to recommend a double plan: use deceit to kill Balakhāni, and trick Parimala into believing that Brahmānanda can complete his marriage to Velā only if Pṛthivīrāja gets the four flying horses.[5]

Now Candrabhaṭṭa, whom the Elliot *Ālhā* doesn't mention, is none other than Chand Bardai, putative author of the *Pṛthvīrāj-rāsau*, in which he is a prominent figure as Pṛthivīrāja's bard.[6] Symmetrically, the putative author of *Ālhā*, Parimala's sister's son Jaganāyaka (in *Ālhā*, Jagnaik), also figures in the *Kṛṣṇāṃśacarita*, which introduces him through the same story that stands out as his only prominent episode in the Elliot *Ālhā*: his mission on behalf of Malhnā, after the battle of Kīratsāgar, to bring the Banāphars and Lākhan from Kanauj to defend Mahobā and prepare for the final battle with Prithīrāj.[7] The poets of the two traditional variants of the story thus both appear in the *Kṛṣṇāṃśacarita*. They are on opposite sides, something like Vyāsa and Sañjaya in the *Mahābhārata*: Chandrabhaṭṭa on the side of the incarnate Kauravas, Jaganāyaka on that of the incarnate Pāṇḍavas. But neither is a poet-author. Each is introduced toward the end of the text (in the episodes cited above), and each around a different point that the paurāṇika clearly regards as weighty. Through Candrabhaṭṭa, he evokes intertextual links between the literatures of Viṣṇu and the goddess. And through Jaganāyaka, he evokes connections between the lunar and solar dynasties. We must consider these matters, which have no parallel treatment in the Elliot *Ālhā*.

[5]24.3-13. Note that the paurāṇika seems to correct the demand to four rather than five horses, but *before* the death of Balakhāni's horse rather than after it.

[6]"It is important to remark, that the national faith of the Rajput never questions the power of their chief bard, whom they call Trikala, or cognizant of the past, the present, and the future. . . . Chand was the last whom they admitted to possess the supernatural vision" (Tod [1829-32] 1990, 721).

[7]*Ālhā* canto 15 (W&G 242-53), "The Return of Ālhā," is closely paralleled by 27.1-50: both include Jagnaik's fight with Chauṉrā, the theft and return of his horse, retrieval of his jewelled whip, and Lākhan's challenge before welcoming Jagnaik at Kanauj. The Elliot *Ālhā* introduces Jagnaik before this episode, but only in minor appearances, and without mentioning his reputation as the story's poet. The *Kṛṣṇāṃśacarita*, which knows him also as Jananāyaka (27.8-15) and Jagannāyaka (32.55, 103), and as an incarnation of Bhagadatta (Bhagadattāṃśa; 32.55), gives him a minor later role in the expedition to China (see below), and lets him survive the final battle, which he does not do in the Elliot *Ālhā*, though it is not said how he dies (W&G 31, 273). His name, Lord of the World (or Lord of the People, Jananāyaka), and his ambassador role suggest echoes of Kṛṣṇa.

One is reminded that Candrabhaṭṭa has obtained his auspicious knowledge of this "glorification of the devotees of the goddess," the *Kṛṣṇāṃśacarita*, by a three-year devotion to the goddess Vaiṣṇavī. As prewar hostilities mount, Pṛthivīrāja imprisons in Delhi his rival Lakṣaṇa (Lākhan), heir to the Kānyakubja (Kanauj) throne. Seeking to free Lakṣaṇa, Kṛṣṇāṃśa and company disguise themselves as yogi-musicians once again (with Kṛṣṇāṃśa again on flute) to fool Pṛthivīrāja by their līlā.[8] Candrabhaṭṭa, having seen through their disguises, tells Pṛthivīrāja, after the yogis have left, that, "by the grace of Devī" (*devīprasādatas*), he has "seen" the yogis' secret "play" (*krīḍam*); indeed, "I am seeing Kṛṣṇāṃśa by Yoganidrā, the sleep of yoga."[9] The theme of play (līlā) is recurrent.[10]

Yoganidrā is thus both a source of bardic inspiration and a form of the goddess closely related to Viṣṇu. The name Vaiṣṇavī has many resonances, but can generally be taken as a name for Durgā as Mahālakṣmī (Brown 1990, 135-38, 147). Indeed, we are told that Kṛṣṇāṃśa is not so much a "portion of Kṛṣṇa" as "the descent of Viṣṇu's śakti (*viṣṇor śaktyavatāraka*)" (11.1; 24.31), or an avatāra of Hari or Kṛṣṇa's śakti (1.30)—that is, in either case, an avatar of Vaiṣṇavī herself. Moreover, it is after the first such instance that the goddess grants him the boon of "innate yoga."[11] But the vision of Kṛṣṇāṃśa by means of Yoganidrā has other resonances. Yoganidrā is popular in the *Ālhā* area as an identity of the goddess Vindhyavāsinī, "She who dwells in the Vindhya mountains" that range south of the region (and include Mārō). Yoganidrā is further a form of Mahākālī taken by the great goddess in the *Devī Māhātmyam* as the first of her three caritas—her three transformations into the śaktis of Viṣṇu, Śiva, and Brahmā (the trimūrti).[12] In the latter text, Yoganidrā awakens Viṣṇu from *his* yogic sleep to kill the boon-seeking demons Madhu and Kaiṭabha. Had this pair of demons' request for immortality

[8]30.25-29. They sally forth as warrior yogis once again shortly after this, making their horses dance (60-61), but not explicitly as musicians.

[9]30.34-37. This episode is one of two devoted to the enhancement of Lakṣaṇa in the *Kṛṣṇāṃśacarita* that form its adhyāyas 29 and 30. Being without true counterparts in the Elliot *Ālhā*, they fall between its accounts of the "Carrying off of Ūdal" (Elliot *Ālhā* canto 17 = *BhvP* 28) and the "Home-Bringing of Belā" (cantos 18-19 = 31). I will discuss them in § E below.

[10]On līlā, see further 3.3.13.7: "When the powerful Kṛṣṇāṃśa was age thirteen, . . . a līlā of Hari was produced (*jātā harerlīlā*)"; 24.35: Kṛṣṇāṃśa and Āhlāda toy with two lotus-trampling (*kuvalayāpīḍa*) elephants "by their līlā"; 30.29: Pṛthivīrāja is "bewildered by the Kṛṣṇalīlā."

[11]*Yogatvam*; 11.6; see chap. 5 at n. 38.

[12]On Vindhyavāsinī-Yoganidrā, see Humes 1996, 49, who, however, is bent on selecting out, at the expense of *DM*, those aspects of this goddess's myths which highlight primordiality and independence as her only original aspects.

been rewarded, they would have killed Viṣṇu and destroyed the universe (*DM* 1.54-104). The goddess as Yoganidrā thus allows Candrabhaṭṭa to "see" that Kṛṣṇāṃśa's last musical flute-and-dance yoga is a divine līlā. Coming just before the *Kṛṣṇāṃśacarita*'s version of the final battle, one is reminded that Kṛṣṇa is also awakened from sleep when Arjuna and Duryodhana come to his bedside at Dvārakā to request the boon of his service at Kurukṣetra. That awakening of Kṛṣṇa, I have argued, also evokes epic versions of the awakening of Viṣṇu for his giving of boons to Madhu and Kaiṭabha.[13] In an intertextual spiral, epic evokes purāṇic myth, and purāṇic epic evokes the evocation.

The *Kṛṣṇāṃśacarita* is in fact laced with *Devī Māhātmyam* references. Raktabīja, the demon "Blood Seed" whom Kālī must defeat in that text, makes his appearance as Pṛthivīrāja's Brahman-general Cāmuṇḍa. The heroes sometimes invoke the goddess into the action by reciting the *Saptaśatīstotra* (another name for the *Devī Māhātmyam*) at the beginnings of episodes;[14] and, as we have seen, Kṛṣṇāṃṣa, by lauding the goddess with her most prominent *Devī Māhātmyam* epithets, gets her to awaken him from sleep with a plan to win the beautiful Puṣpavatī, Rādhā incarnate.[15]

In this regard, the references to Vaiṣṇavī, Yoganidrā, and the śakti of Viṣṇu's or Kṛṣṇa's avatāra are precise. Within the *Kṛṣṇāṃṣśacarita*, Māyādevī is credited with having created or fashioned (*vinirmitā*) Mahobā (Mahāvatī) (1.31). In the encompassing *Pratisarga Parvan* (the *Bhaviṣya Purāṇa*'s third book), we learn further that Mahobā is founded after the goddess favors a king named Rāṣṭrapāla, who had worshiped the Śakti Vaiṣṇavī as Śāradā.[16] This means that Mahobā is founded not only by the goddess worshiped in the *Devī Māhātmyam* as Vaiṣṇavī and Yoganidrā, but by the territorial goddess of Mahobā. Not only that, when Rāṣṭrapāla's second son Prajaya desires his own kingdom and worships Śāradā with tapas for twelve years, she appears to him, smiling and riding a horse, in the form of a flute-playing virgin (*kanyāmūrtimayī devī veṇuvādanatatparā*; 44), and leads him to the site on the bank of the Ganges where she fashions the city of Kānyakubja (Kanauj) for him (42-51). She thus establishes the two main allied kingdoms of *Ālhā*.[17] This

[13]On bhakti features of this scene, see Hiltebeitel [1976] 1990, 102-7; cf. also Brown's discussion (1990, 83-93) of variations of the Madhu-Kaiṭabha boon-granting myth from the *Mbh* through various purāṇas.

[14]E.g., 11.3, 15.1-3 (it is called both *Saptaśatī* and *Tricaritra*); 18.3-4. See chap. 5, n. 42.

[15]21.25-32 and chap. 5, § D.

[16]3.4.3.40-41. Rāṣṭrapāla is a Śukla (Caulukya) king, not a Chandēl, and is not a name connected with the latter dynasty.

[17]Cf. Schomer 1984, Excerpts, 1-2: in a recorded *Ālhā* song, the "patron goddess of Kanauj" is "Kshemkali."

flute-playing Vaiṣṇavī who is also Śāradā certainly evokes the flute-playing disguises of Kṛṣṇāṃśa, not to mention the flute-playing Kṛṣṇa.

Indeed, this combination suggests a fusion of "Kālī's sword and Kṛṣṇa's flute" reminiscent of the merger of the two in the Bengali songs of Rāmprasad (eighteenth century) and the life of Ramakrishna.[18] Such a connection might seem adventitious were it not that an additional *Pratisarga Parvan* passage reinforces the emphasis on Kṛṣṇa and Rādhā. The very first adhyāya that follows the *Kṛṣṇāṃśacarita* begins, "Homage to Śrī Gaṇeśa. Śrī Rādhā-Vallabha conquers" (3.4.1.1). And it continues, building from the end of the carita to the Ṛṣis' leading question about the lineages of the Agnivaṃśa kings (1-13), with the statement that toward the end of the time to be described, "there is an avatāra by a portion of Hari. He is surely the Śaktyavatāra of Rādhākṛṣṇa on earth."[19] Here—where the passage introduces events that will take place *after* the *Kṛṣṇāṃśacarita*—the reference must be to Caitanya, the incarnation, according to Gauḍiya Vaiṣṇavas, of Rādhā and Kṛṣṇa in one body. Within the *Kṛṣṇāṃśacarita*, "avatāra of Kṛṣṇa's śakti" refers to Kṛṣṇāṃśa, who is the incarnation of Kṛṣṇa just as his wife Puṣpavatī is the incarnation of Rādhā. Indeed, let us recall how the scene of Kṛṣṇāṃśa and Puṣpavatī's courtship plays on Kṛṣṇāṃśa-Kṛṣṇā's bisexuality. The pauraṇika thus casts Kṛṣṇāṃśa in the image of Caitanya.[20]

The play on Rādhā-Kṛṣṇa themes, the conjunction of identities between Kṛṣṇāṃśa and the goddess, and the recurrent emphasis on play itself, thus suggest that the *Kṛṣṇāṃśacarita* is composed in a milieu influenced by Gauḍiya Vaiṣṇavism, and in a conceptual world of late purāṇic bhakti. But how late? Later certainly than Arora's thirteenth-century estimate (1972, 19). Arora acknowledges that portions of the purāṇa were composed as late as the nineteenth century, and that this applies in particular to the *Pratisarga Parvan*, which includes not only the *Kṛṣṇāṃśacarita* but references to Calcutta, and which "ends with the arrival of the British in India and the rule of 'Victāvatī' (Queen Victoria)."[21] But he seems to assume some proximity between the text's "story of Ālhā and Ūdal (Besavāri version)" and the late-twelfth-century events it purports to

[18]Kripal 1995, 50-52, 83-85; Kinsley 1975.

[19]*Vikramākhyānakālāṃte 'vatāraḥ kalayā hareḥ/ sa ca śaktyavatāro hi rādhākṛṣṇasya bhūtale* (3.4.1.7).

[20]On Caitanya (Kṛṣṇacaitanya, Yajñāṃśa) in *BhvP* (3.4.19) as, among other things, a favorite ("Liebling") of Śāradā, equally a Śākta, Śaiva, and Vaiṣṇava, and "drunk with bhakti" (*bhaktimada*), see Hohenberger 1967, 79-81. Caitanya is the culminating figure in the paurāṇika's series of spiritual biographies. See further n. 22.

[21]The British hoisted the flag on the banks of the Hooghly to found Calcutta in 1690, and in 1717 it was still "known as a village" (Deb 1905, 9, 14). On Vikaṭāvatī (Victoria), see *BhvP* 3.4.22.75.

describe (1972, 4-5, 18-19). Since the *Kṛṣṇāṃśacarita* is clearly by a poet steeped in folklore from a central area of *Ālhā* tradition, it would appear, if the Besavāri version comes from around Kanpur, that this would be the first place to consider in looking for our author's native region.[22] But the text is certainly much later than the period it describes.

I propose on the basis of the *Kṛṣṇāṃśacarita*'s internal evidence that it can be no earlier than the north Indian atmosphere that produces Kṛṣṇa and Rām līlās, which can be traced back no earlier than the mid sixteenth century, but continue to be influential thereafter. Its inversions of Kṛṣṇa-Rādhā love-play are reminiscent of those in the *Brahmavaivarta Purāṇa*, which should probably be given a sixteenth-century date.[23] But on the basis of its place in the *Pratisarga Parvan*, one cannot ignore the attractions of a mid-nineteenth century date. For the moment, it is enough to note that the latter date is not far from the views of other scholars, who likewise offer no reasons to think that the *Kṛṣṇāṃśacarita* is earlier than, or originally independent of, the *Pratisarga Parvan*, which contains it as its third of its four *khaṇḍas*.[24] Following Bonazzoli, "We can suppose that the *Pratisarga Parvan*, more than any other, bore responsibility for the name *Bhaviṣya* being given to this purāṇa; more than all the other parvans it was meant to narrate future events and thereby more liable to receive new additions to keep the purāṇa up-to-date in different ages" (1979a, 27). I consider it most likely, however, that the whole of the

[22]I thank Romila Thapar for the following note: "The Baisvāri version of the *Ālhā* is a Hindi dialect version, recited largely in the Kanpur area (I think). It has remained part of the oral tradition for perhaps longer than the Braja and Bundelli versions, so some think that it is more authentic" (personal correspondence, November 4, 1995). Shaligram Shukla confirms the Kanpur-area geography for Besavāri (personal communication, April 1997). Cf. Hohenberger 1967, 7-8: the prominence of Mahobā in the work extends through family connections into all directions; Ujjain is the most frequently recalled site; but references to Caitanya and Puri (see n. 20) suggest Bengal or Orissa as the site of the last stages of composition. But the author seems to also know local Mahobā folklore. In any case, one may tentatively posit a Kanauj-Kanpur-Mahobā triangle for the central area of the author's *Ālhā*-familiarity.

[23]See Brown 1990, 222 (no earlier than fifteenth century); Dimmitt and van Buitenen 1978, 118-24, 127-30. One may suspect that such inversions show a tradition working inward on itself constructing "in-group" esoteric erotica in the face of out-group (Muslim) dominance.

[24]Portions of the parvan relating to Muhammad and the Bible (see chap. 9) are dated to a background of the Indian renaissance by Bonazzoli (1979a, 27-28, 36-39); to "as late as the 18th or even 19th century" by Diehl (1981, 75); and considered "a modern fabrication" by Kane (1930-62, 5, 2: 896-92). As to the parvan as a whole, Hohenberger suggests eighteenth century (1967, 6); R. N. Sharma considers it "practically a new work" with references to "British rule in India . . . Calcutta and Parliament . . . [that] betray its late date" (1984-85, 1: 3-4, repeating Hazra [1940] 1975, 169, verbatim without citation); Pargiter says "the Veṅkateśvara edition shows all the ancient matter utterly corrupted but the prophesies brought down to the nineteenth century" ([1913] 1962, xxviii).

parvan in its Venkateśvara Press edition (1897) is an update written earlier in the nineteenth century, and that where separate authorship is to be considered, it is more likely to be a case of editing in older material rather than interpolating new material. The question of a single authorship of a unified *Pratisarga Parvan* inclusive of the *Kṛṣṇāṃśacarita* is moot. I would only argue that the *Kṛṣṇāṃśacarita*'s structure of thirty-two adhyayas results from single authorship, and that the integration of older material in it is worth considering in only one instance.[25] From here on I will simply argue that the *Pratisarga Parvan*, with the *Kṛṣṇāṃśacarita* within it, is a conceptually congruous work, and I refer to a paurāṇika "author"—whether single or concerted—as a shorthand for the "author function" that lies behind it.

B. The Muslim Captivity of Ūdal

For the paurāṇika, then, *Ālhā* is a Kṛṣṇāṃśa līlā: one that is like "Draupadī cult līlās" in implicating not only the refined thematics of Braj but the dark thematics of the *Mahābhārata*.[26] But rather than being oriented toward ritual reenactment at local festivals like Rām Līlās, Kṛṣṇa Līlas, Pāṇḍav Līlās, Draupadī festivals, or, for that matter, *Ālhā* performances at local fairs, the *Kṛṣṇāṃśacarita* constructs its final battle as the centerpiece of a sweeping vision of the Kali yuga's disasters. This vision is ultimately a Vaiṣṇava theodicy of play. Here, the pauraṇika is explicit in two areas where the Elliot *Ālhā* is not: in the identity of Udayasiṃha-Ūdal as a "portion of Kṛṣṇa," which takes new twists at every turn; and in the nature of the disasters themselves.

As noted, whereas *Ālhā* can be ambivalent about Muslims, the *Kṛṣṇāṃśacarita* is not. The paurāṇika is most "wicked" in this regard in his version of "The Carrying off of Ūdal," *Ālhā*'s seventeenth canto and the last episode before the sequence that builds up to the final battle.[27] In *Ālhā*, at Sunwā's request, Ūdal sets out with a huge army to attend the

[25]The passage is in the last adhyāya: a portion in *triṣṭubhs* rather than *ślokas* (32.109-62) that could be by a different hand than the rest, and, if this were argued, is more likely an older embedded passage than an interpolated new one. Alternately, our main *Kṛṣṇāṃśacarita* author could have switched to triṣṭubhs for this battle scene to give the archaic feel of similar switches in the *Mbh*.

[26]Hiltebeitel 1995c; cf. 1988a, 183-90; forthcoming.

[27]W&G 256-58. Grierson appreciates an incongruity: "This Canto is wrongly placed, for Malkhān, who in Canto XIII was killed at Sirsā, appears here alive and well" (W&G 257). Possibly Malkhān's part is an oral slip, called forth by the mood of this being the Banāphars' last geste, rather than evidence (as Grierson takes it) that the episode is misplaced and unoriginal. The *Kṛṣṇāṃśacarita* retains the story's sequential place but "correctly" does not mention Balakhāni.

spring Dasarā at Biṭhūr.[28] There, Subhiā Birinī of Jhunnāgaṛh (natal home of Gajmōtin, Malkhān's wife), a Muslim gypsy (*naṭnī*) magician, turns Ūdal into a parrot, puts him in a cage, and takes him to the Jhārkhaṇḍ forest, the "hilly region between Birbhum . . . and Benares" in Chota Nagpur (Dey [1899] 1927, 81-82). Having turned him into a man for a game of caupar (dice, parcheesi), she interrupts the game at midnight to propose to him:

> "Marry me and just do what I tell you.
> Give up the name of Lord Nārāyaṇ, Ūdan, and say 'Ḳhudā, Ḳhudā.'"
> (Ūdal replies) "I will neither relinquish my *dharm* nor will I say 'Ḳhudā, Ḳhudā.'"[29]

When he refuses, she beats him, demanding that "he utter the Muslim cry of 'Allāhu Akbar.'" He still refuses (W&G 257).

Sunwā, a witness to all this, then uses her magic to become a female kite and come to Ūdal's rescue. As Grierson (W&G 257) puts it, she "commends his conduct in refusing to change his religion" (referring to his dharm, as above):

> "She beat you with a bamboo stave, why didn't you say the name 'Ḳhudā'?"
> Then Ūdani [Ūdal] said to Sunwā, "I tell you, sister-in-law,
> I hold to the way of Rajputs, and to the honor [*lāj*, lit. "shame"] of grasping a sword.
> How will I give up my dharm [and] Kṣatriyahood [*chatrīpan*] and become a Musalmān?
> I'll fall cut to pieces on the battlefield, but even then I won't let go of Rām's name."[30]

Since, however, Ūdal has been beaten by a woman, he refuses to let Sunwā bring him back to Mahobā and sends her instead to bring Ālhā and the army to defeat Subhiā in battle. The Banāphars (Malkhān, now slain, incongruously included) then fight an army of five hundred gypsies whom Subhiā creates with the "magic of Dacca."[31] Sunwā and Subhiā contend with spells, and then as female kites, until Subhiā's "spell of Bīr

[28]See chap. 6, n. 50.
[29]*Ḳhudā* is "the common Persian name of God": Lutgendorf 1997, 7-8, translating from Elliot [1881] 1992, 544.
[30]Lutgendorf 1997, 7-8, translating from Elliot [1881] 1992, 544.
[31]On Bengal as the land of black magic in north Indian folklore (something like Kerala in Tamil folklore), see Gold 1992, 63-66, 219-20, 265-66.

Mahamdī" loses effect. Sunwā then defeats Subhiā and tells Indal to kill her, but he refuses to kill a woman and instead cuts off her hair, ending her power (W&G 258).

This is not very ambivalent, to be sure, but let me propose that it portrays the Banāphars in one last battle before the denouement, acting on their own rather than on behalf of kings, and showing how they contend with and triumph over Islamic forces that work *at a popular or folk level corresponding to Ālhā's own level.* Indeed, the purāṇa's version of this episode also portrays the heroes in one last geste before the final war and its aftermath, in which politically motivated and historically known Islamic forces invade for real.

Yet whereas the heart of the *Ālhā* story is that Ūdal resists conversion, the *Kṛṣṇāṃśacarita*, to put it simply, envisions a Muslim captivity of God. Here Kṛṣṇāṃśa meets a seductive Mlecchā (again, Muslim) courtesan (*veśyā*) named Śobhā (or Śobhanā). She finds "the supremely delightful best of men (*paraṃ ramyaṃ . . . puruṣottamam*)" irresistible and wants to seduce him (28.6). This happens not at a Dasarā fair but in Vālmīki's "purifying lotus forest, the foremost iron bolt consisting of brahman (*brahmamayam lohakīlakamuttamam*) on the bank of the Gaṅgā" (3). This is none other than the Naimiṣa Forest, made once again, as it is not only in many purāṇas but in the *Mahābhārata*, a site for purāṇic recitation.[32] Before concerning himself with Śobhā, Kṛṣṇāṃśa gives a thousand cows to Brahmans and asks the learned Śāstris about the authors and "fruits" of each of the eighteen purāṇas. Dividing the latter into groups of six according to the three guṇas or qualities of primal matter, the sages tell him that the *Bhaviṣya* is among the lowest or darkest "tāmasic" purāṇas "devoted to the dharma of Śakti," and that, of all the purāṇas, the *Bhāgavata* is the best (28.9-15)—another reinforcement of the interplay between Śākta and Vaiṣṇava texts. Kṛṣṇāṃśa listens to the *Bhāgavata Śāstra* (sic) for seven days, and then gives more wealth to Brahmans and feeds a thousand of them.[33]

Śobhā, who seems not to have benefited from this edifying discourse, has become an almswoman (*bhikṣukī*) and set herself to meditating on "the heroic Mahāmada, the Paiśāca servant of Rudra" (28.20-21).

[32]See above chap. 4, n. 7, and *Mbh* 1.1.15: the Naimiṣa Forest Ṛṣis ask the bard Ugraśravas for the "ancient lore proclaimed (*proktam purāṇam*) by the supreme Ṛṣi Dvaipāyana [Vyāsa], which was revered (or "approved": *abhipūjitam*) by the gods and Brahman Ṛṣis when they heard it." See Bonazzoli 1981; Hiltebeitel in press-h and forthcoming.

[33]It is striking that the Bundela king Bir Singh Deo, ruler of Orccha from 1612-27 and notable for varied Brahmanical and purāṇicizing interests, "according to later legend, was well acquainted with the *dharmaśāstras* and once listened for seven days to recitations from the Mahapuranas" (Kolff 1990, 131 and *passim*). One could say that Kṛṣṇāṃśa and Bir Singh Deo (and similarly other Bundelas, 137) were "brought up" to the same standards.

Mahāmada ("the great drunk") is this text's name for Muhammad, and one wonders whether she is now a Muslim "gypsy" in the guise of a Buddhist nun. In any case, it is from worshiping Mahāmada that she draws magical powers (*māyā*) that enable her to transform Kṛṣṇāṃśa into a parrot, capture him in a cage, and take him home to Vāhlīka country to be her nightly lover and daily pet. As we have seen (chap. 6, § G), Āhlāda's son Indula gets similar treatment when he is captured by Citralekhā, whose father Abhinandana and his Tomara Kṣatriyas defend Vāhlīka with five lakhs of "Mlecchas of ghastly dharma" (*paiśāca-dharminaḥ*; 23.87-88). Now the Mlecchas are clearly Muslims;[34] Muhammad is the Paiśāca responsible for their dharma; and Vāhlīka, somewhat loosely located in the Punjab in classical epic sources, now extends into Balkh or Bactria.[35]

When Śobhā implores Kṛṣṇāṃśa to "protect me with the gift of pleasure," he lauds the World Mother (Jagadambikā) by reciting the *Rātrisūkta* (28.39), presumably the Ṛg Vedic "Hymn to Night,"[36] and responds with a long, discouraging speech on the virtues of monogamy (clearly not taking his cue from *Bhāgavata Purāṇa*). Spousal fidelity, he tells her, is the "Aryan way" (*āryavartman*), which he exemplifies further with the admonition, attributed to tradition (*smṛti*), that, "One should not speak Yāvanī speech even with the breaths gone from the throat (*na vaded yāvanīm bhāṣām prāṇaiḥ kaṃṭhagatairapi*); so even crushed by elephants, one should not go to a Jaina temple (*gajairāpīḍyamāno 'pi na gacchej jainamandiram*)" (53). Clearly the disasters of the Kali yuga are not limited to the magic of Mahāmada.[37]

Undaunted, Śobhā continues her tricks, but to no avail. And eventually, rather than availing herself of the "magic of Dacca," she goes to Madahīnapuram (Medina) to satisfy Mahāmada himself, who then comes, speaking Ārṣabha Bhāṣa ("bull talk"?), to the temple of Marusthaleśvara, Lord of the wilderness (i.e., Lord of the Rajasthan desert) to worship its Śivalingam.[38] The heroes and Svarṇavatī (Sunwā) must then contend not

[34]The Elliot *Ālhā*, at least in Grierson's summary, does not seem to highlight the religious identities among king Abhinandan's nine lākhs of soldiers (W&G 214).

[35]See Dey [1899] 1927, 19, 221; 1927, 113.

[36]*ṚV* 10.127; later, Āhlāda also worships Śāradā with the "Day Sūkta" (*Divāsūkta*; 31.93).

[37]Gahlot and Dhar 1989, 62-63, cite an overlapping Rajasthani "saying": "A Hindu had better be overtaken by a wild elephant than take refuge in a Jain temple, and he must not run across the shadow of it even to escape a tiger." Cf. the words attributed to Viṣṇu-Jagannātha spoken to Caitanya (called Yajñāṃśa) at Puri at *BhvP* 3.4.20.91: "By whom Yāvanī speech is spoken; by whom the Buddha is glanced at; when a great sin overtakes, I stay here, extinguishing guilt. When a man has glanced at me, in the Kali yuga he is purified." See Hohenberger 1967, 15, and above nn. 20 and 22 on Caitanya in *BhvP*.

[38]28.62-63. Once again Mahāmada is referred to as "the Paiśāca skilled in the intoxication

only with Śobhā and ten thousand gypsies (*naṭas*) attendant upon Śobhā's brother Sahura, but with Mahāmada himself—rather than "the spell of Bīr Mahamdī." "Devoted to meditation on Rudra," Mahāmada produces lions, monkeys, flies, serpents, vultures, and crows with his magic (*śambarī māyā*), but Svarṇavatī neutralizes them by invoking the goddess Kāmākṣī and creating far fiercer Tārkṣyas (Garuḍas) and Śarabhas (eight-legged monsters) (28.74-77). Finally, when the gypsy army is pulverized (*cūrṇitaḥ*) by Āhlāda, Śobhā becomes Svarṇavatī's slave (*dāsī*).[39]

Geographic, temporal, and textual horizons clearly widen from the oral epic to the purāṇa, which looks as if it has turned folk religion to fantasy. Nonetheless, but for Mahāmada's availability for a "late twelfth-century" visit to Rajasthan, which need not overly surprise us considering other things we will find in this text, the story fits squarely into the *Pratisarga Parvan*'s world history, which we may now begin to trace more attentively by returning to Jaganāyaka-Jagnaik, Parimala's sister's son.

C. Solar and Lunar Lines

As mentioned, Jaganāyaka, a complement to Candrabhaṭṭa (Chand Bardai) for his reputation as the *Ālhā*'s poet, provides the paurāṇika with a hidden link between the solar and lunar dynasties. As far as I can see, this link is not to be found outside his text. In the Elliot *Ālhā*, which seems to show no interest in Jagnaik's residence of Argal (W&G 244), Jagnaik refers to himself as "Jagnaik Chandēl" and "Jagnaik . . . of the Chandēl land" (247, 249). That is, he identifies himself matrilineally and as living matrilocally, and no longer in Argal.[40] With its old Kora fort, Argal, "on the Rhind river, in the Kora *pargannah*, in the district of Fathpûr" is the "principal seat" of the Gautam Rajputs (Sherring 1872, 202-4), to which vaṃśa, according to the *Kṛṣṇāṃśacarita*, Jagnaik belongs (27.2, 38; 32.55, 103). But in the purāṇa, the Gotamas or Gautamas are from Kacchapa or Kacchadeśa on the Indus River, and Jaganāyaka is the son not only of Parimalā (Parmāl's sister) but of Kamalāpati, a Sūryavaṃśin king of that realm.[41] The term *sūryavaṃśa/-in* is used three times in the passage that introduces Jaganāyaka. Yet when he undertakes

---

of māyā who was stationed there" (62). Hohenberger 1967, 49, reads Ārṣabha Bhāṣā as a form of speech.

[39]28.78-79. This is the second instances where Svarṇavatī becomes a female hawk, both occurring in Vāhlika-Balkh (cf. chap. 4, n. 57).

[40]It is not, however, made clear that Argal is Jagnaik's paternal residence. In the *Ālhā* edited by Chaudh'rî Ghâsî Râm, another "western" version in Hindi, Jagnaik (called Jâgin) is given the fort of Jag'nêrî by Parmāl (Grierson 1885b, 255), which could parallel the story cited below in the *BhvP*.

[41]According to Sherring, however, the Gautams are not solar but lunar (1872, 204)!

Malanā's mission to bring Āhlāda and Kṛṣṇāṃśa back from Kanauj to Mahobā, he no longer resides in Kacchadeśa. Having once failed to defend what was by then *his* kingdom against a tax-collecting siege by Pṛthivīrāja, he abandoned it and took refuge with his clan (*kula*) in Mahobā with Parimala, who gave him an unnamed "auspicious village." He is still, however, referred to as "that foremost Sūryavaṃśin" when he sets off for Kanauj (27.1-19).

Given our author's interest in connecting the two lineages, it is striking how shallow he makes them. The Sūryavaṃśins of Kacchadeśa on the Indus are clearly far from the Ayodhyā-Mithilā center of solar line descent, and are traced through only two generations (27.1-13).[42] And the Candravaṃśins of Mahobā, though well within the range of the more "segmented" extensions of the lunar dynasty, have a depth of only three generations.[43] Moreover, Pradyota and Udyota, the two fathers who are referred to as "Kṣatriyas born in the Candravaṃśa" (5.13), begin not with Mahobā as their own land but as "mantrins" of Jayacandra in Kanauj, who makes their sons into leaders of his army—Parimala of his cavalry, Bhiṣmaka of his elephants—before *giving* them Mahobā as his vassals after securing their military services for his rivalry with Pṛthivīrāja.[44] I assume Pradyota and Udyota are brothers, but this is not made clear. Table 9 gives the Kṛṣṇāṃśacarita's full information on these two lineages, and leaves a strong impression that the doubled names of the children of Pradyota are hints at an authorial design. For the moment, it will suffice to say that the paurāṇika looks no further into Chandēl history than oral *Ālhā*, which knows Parmāl as a Chandēl (W&G 60), indeed as the last Chandēl, but offers nothing (at least in the Waterfield and Grierson translation) about his ancestors.

[42]Their peripherality is like that of the Candravaṃśīya Kaikayas (32.29-33), both of them presumably "subclans" reflecting not real segmentation of any original solar and lunar dynasties, but a process of absorption of locally emergent lineages into Rajput networks at a point when their vassal or independent status allowed them to claim solar or lunar origins for their lineage or dynasty (cf. Chattopadhyay 1994).

[43]See Thapar 1978a, 301-2, 342; 1984, 46-48, 69; 1991, 16-17, on lunar dynasty segmentation.

[44]5.13-28. Also surprising, Māhil (Mahīpati) has ruled Mahobā to this point; displaced, he founds a new city at Urvīyā (Urai) (5.22-24). This also foreshortens the history of the displacements of the Parihāra-Pratihāras (Māhil-Māhipati's line) by the Chandēls, thought to have taken place in the mid eighth century (W&G 14). Mahobā informants Zahir Singh and Krishna Chaurasia also say that Parmāl "snatched Mahobā from Māhil, and thus Māhil caused trouble for Parmāl." The purānic author and these informants may thus know an *Ālhā* tradition that views Māhil, and possibly some earlier generations of his Parihāra line, as having ruled Mahobā prior to Parmāl, perhaps interrupting the Chandēl "dynasty," which historians may have reconstructed with some "tendency to 'dynasticize'" (Chattopadhyaya 1994, 161; Henige 1975, 576). Cf. Schomer 1984, 6-7.

Table 9. Solar (27.1-3) and Lunar (5.13-28) dynasties in the *Bhaviṣya Purāṇa*'s *Kṛṣṇāṃśacarita*

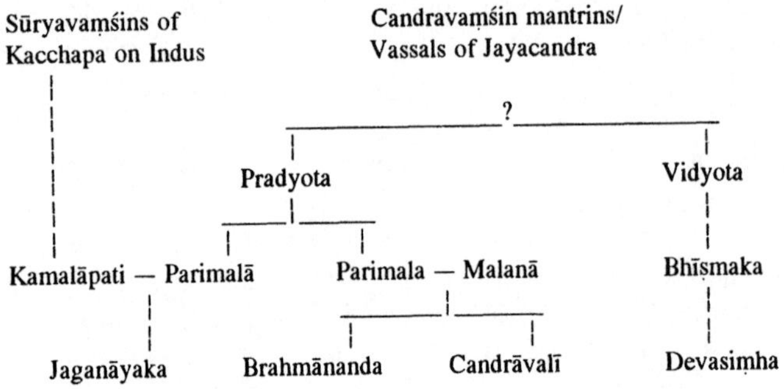

Now the first striking thing about Jaganāyaka's ambassadorial mission is that, as a Sūryavaṃśin, he puts himself at the service of his Candravaṃśa matriline. For whereas the Sūryavaṃśa comes into the story only peripherally, the Candravaṃśa, despite its lack of generational depth, is central. As the *Kṛṣṇāṃśacarita* frequently reminds us, Parimala is a scion of the lunar dynasty and is *the* Candravaṃśin. The author develops this theme adroitly, highlighting it in four episodes that would look like history were they not spun whole cloth out of *Ālhā* mythology. In the first, Pṛthivīrāja, claiming sway over all of Bhārata (India) and the right to tax all kings, even those "who have gone over to the side of Jayacandra," brings his army to Mahobā and threatens to destroy the city with his "terrible Rudra-weaponed armies" unless he receives a one-sixth tax from the "Candrakula progenitor" (*candrakulodbhava*).[45] Parimala pays the heavy sum, which does not prevent Pṛthivīrāja from plundering "his former enemy" (10.2-9). Pṛthivīrāja then goes to Kanauj and claims power (*daṇḍam*) over Jayacandra, whom he had tried to tax earlier,[46] but Lakṣaṇa (Lākhan) puts Pṛthivīrāja's forces to flight with his Vaiṣṇava-weapon (10-14). One appreciates by now that Pṛthivīrāja is ruthless in his taxation policies, and that these have been particularly grievous to kings of *both* the solar and lunar lineages, as well as to the more powerful Jayacandra. Moreover, the only defense the kings of these lines have

[45]Although one could say that in these episodes, and the digvijaya Lakṣaṇa undertakes for Jayacandra, the narrative depicts wars for the collection of "tribute," I translate by "tax" because I take the author to model his accounts on his understanding of an imperial system. On the distinction and the transition from tribute to tax in Mughal India, see Richards 1993, 83-87.

[46]The first attempt being at 5.34-35; see below.

against his "raudra" power will come not from themselves, but from two "vaiṣṇava" heroes, Lakṣaṇa and Kṛṣṇāṃśa. Of all this, the Elliot *Ālhā*, which does not seem to evidence much concern with the politics of taxation, tells only that Prithīrāj and Lākhan have Raudra and Vaiṣṇava weapons.[47]

When Pṛthivīrāja's makes his tax-collecting raid of Mahobā, Kṛṣṇāṃśa is only nine, the point in his young life at which we glimpsed him reading philosophy and dharmaśāstra (10.1-2). Within two years, Śāradā has appeared as a doe, led him into the forest, and given him her promise that she will rescue him whenever he remembers her (10.50). Shortly thereafter, she has also, as Jagadambikā, given him the delusive power of *yogatvam*, "innate yoga," as a boon (11.6). He has received his horse Bindula from Parimala (10.50); and he has twice taunted Mahīpati (Māhil) at the latter's capital of Urvīyā (Urai), outwrestling his son Abhaya (10.14-34) and returning to cause further havoc (11.9-21). Much of this is paralleled in the Elliot *Ālhā*,[48] but what follows is not. As Mahīpati (as I will call him from now on when he is in his purāṇic persona) rides to Delhi to provoke Pṛthivīrāja to attack Mahobā again, the eleven-year-old Kṛṣṇāṃśa is "infatuated for war (*yuddhadurmade*)" (22), and is this time able to lead Parimala's young "ministers" in repulsing the Delhi attack, even though Pṛthivīrāja brings "three thousand *śataghni*s [weapons known as "thousand-slayers"] against the Candravaṃśin's two thousand" (11.35). It is this battle that the paurāṇika sets as prelude to his next adhyāya's story of the young "Banāphars'" expedition to Māhiṣmatī-Mārō to avenge their fathers and recover the nine-lākh chain, which begins, as we have seen, with Ūdal-Kṛṣṇāṃśa having reached age twelve (12.1).

Candravaṃśa concerns go unspecified for some time. But they are implicit in the impasse that arises from Brahmānanda's unconsummated marriage to Velā (adhyāya 17), which leaves the lunar line's heir without his queen.[49] They return to the fore in the battle over the sprouts at Kīrtisāgara. Again, Mahīpati is in the thick of the intrigue. First he incites Pṛthivīrāja, "ever fond of strife," to camp outside Mahobā during the festival in a *śirīṣa* thicket. Then, "bowing to the Candravaṃśin king,"

[47]Yet see Schomer 1984, Excerpts, 3-4: in an oral *Ālhā* song recorded at Kanauj, Lākhan repeatedly taunts Chauṉrā as Prithīrāj's "darling tax-collector."

[48]The wrestling match with Māhil's son Abhay, bestowal of the horses, deer-hunt encounter with Śāradā, havoc in W&G 69-72 (see table 4).

[49]The only exception comes in another episode not found in the Elliot *Ālhā*: the attempt by the Pāñcāladeśa king to arrange his daughter's marriage to Devasiṃha, considering him "the best of Candravaṃśins" (20.28-31). Since Devasiṃha's celibacy prevents this, Parimala proposes Sukhakhāni as alternative groom, and the latter is accepted over Mahīpati's protests (see below).

he deceitfully tells Parimala that Pṛthivīrāja has come "for the sake of war," and that once he has worshiped the divine Śivalingam, "he will seize by force your daughter Candrāvalī and son Brahmānanda." Like the reader, Parimala has been prepared by Pṛthivīrāja's prior tactics to consider this plausible. "Swayed by fate," he heeds Mahīpati's (doubly) treacherous advice to attack Pṛthivīrāja's sleeping soldiers at night, and kills "five thousand sleeping Kṣatriya heroes." Pṛthivīrāja considers this "the utmost hostility" (*vairiṇam paramam*) and declares "big war (*mahadyuddham*)."[50]

As battle rages, Malanā invokes Śāradā, who wakens Kṛṣṇāṃśa, "O son, your mother the Earth is oppressed by Mahīrāja [the king of the Earth] (*putra te jananī bhūmir mahīrājena pīḍitā*). He will quickly meet destruction. Therefore, lift yourself up (*samuddhara*)" (26.15). These words remind us once again that Kṛṣṇāṃśa's "innate yoga" connects him with Yoganidrā, who awakens Viṣṇu from his yogic sleep. They also echo Viṣṇu's relief of the Earth's burden in several avatara myths, especially as Kṛṣṇa in the *Mahābhārata*. And so we are drawn into a purāṇic version of the relief of Mahobā in which the city, kingdom, queen Malanā, goddess Śāradā, and Devakī merge in the image of the Earth as Kṛṣṇāṃśa's aggrieved mother.

This account of the "Battle of Kīrtisāgara" differs from the Elliot *Ālhā*'s version in further ways. When Mahīpati perceives that it is Kṛṣṇāṃśa and company disguised as rescuing yogis, he deceives "the Candravaṃśin" (26.64) once again by telling Parimala they are enemies come to seize Malanā and Candrāvalī. This provokes a battle of mistaken identities that culminates in a duel between Brahmānanda and Kṛṣṇāṃśa, and produces the epic-purāṇic cliché that they are not only portions of Arjuna and Kṛṣṇa, but of Nara and Nārāyaṇa (76). But the culmination of the episode comes when Pṛthivīrāja's seven "Kaurava-portion" (*kauravāṃśa*) sons (counting Tāraka, the portion of Karṇa) attempt to keep the Mahobā women from carrying their rice and barley sprouts to the lake. After three of these Kauravaṃśas have been killed (90-95), Pṛthivīrāja, "miserable with grief over his sons, made a terrible resolution (*saṃkalpam kṛtavān ghoram*) whose hearing was borne over the entire earth: 'As the delightful Śirīṣākhyapuram was made empty by me, so too all Mahobā with Brahmānanda and the rest, all the Candravaṃsins will be destroyed by my arrows.'"[51]

With this resolution ringing in the world's ears, Pṛthivīrāja retreats to

[50]26.1-10. As observed (chap. 6, nn. 84 and 95), although this incident is not found in the Elliot *Ālhā*, it has similarities to other variants, including that of the *Pṛthvīrāj-rāsau*.

[51]*Śirīṣākhyapuraṃ ramyaṃ yathā śūnyaṃ mayā kṛtam/ tathā mahāvatī sarvā brahmānandādibhis saha/ kṣayam yāsyanti madbānaiḥ sarve te candravaṃśinaḥ* (26.103).

Delhi (26.105), and the distressed Malanā calls on Jaganāyaka to bring not only Kṛṣṇāṃśa this time, but Āhlāda too, from Kanauj (27.1-7). Jaganāyaka at first says that Āhlāda won't come because of Parimala's grievous insults over the horses. But Jaganāyaka agrees to go after hearing Malanā's passionate cry of encrypted bhakti, "Oh great-armed Rāmāṃśa, beautiful child Kṛṣṇāṃśa (*vatsa kṛṣṇāṃśa sundara*), where are you two gone together with Devakī, having abandoned me of impoverished share (*mandabhāginīm*)?" (6). When he finally reaches Kanauj, the Sūryavaṃśin makes his case plain to Lakṣaṇa: "O Mahārāja, summoned by the Candravaṃśin, I have come to you, O one who protects those who have surrendered; with his Raudra weapons, the powerful Mahīrāja, delighted with Mahīpati, will destroy the Candravaṃśin and his clan (kula). Therefore, together with your forces and united with Āhlāda and the rest, go, go now, Mahārāja, and restore the dead to life (*mṛtān-ujjīvayādhunā*)" (34-36). Jayacandra at first refuses to release the heroes, but agrees to discharge them on the pretext that they will accompany Lakṣaṇa on a "conquest of the regions" (digvijaya; 44).

This will now be the third "digvijaya" in four adhyāyas, all of them alluding to imperial politics by this ritualized form of conquest that is the epic equivalent of a subrite of the Rājasūya (van Buitenen 1975, 18-19). Just previously, without any apparent permission from Jayacandra, Kṛṣṇāṃśa, Devasiṃha, and Lakṣaṇa had made a "pretext" of launching a digvijaya to come to Mahobā's rescue at the Kīrtisāgara (26.19). And both expeditions are preceded by a "real digvijaya" in which Lakṣaṇa, accompanied by Kṛṣṇāṃśa and other "Banāphars," undertakes an expedition that rivals those of Pṛthivīrāja in collecting taxes.[52] This initial digvijaya is clearly the *Kṛṣṇāṃśacarita*'s counterpart to the Elliot *Ālhā*'s episode of "The Gānjar War" (canto 12). It occurs in the same place in the cycle, and each involves a military expedition endorsed by Jayacandra to tax kingdoms that lie primarily to the east and southeast,[53] thus making no direct challenge to Delhi's tax base in the west and northwest.

[52]24.37-73; for the details, see Hohenberger 1967, 45-46.

[53]See table 4. Grierson notes, "The meaning of [Gānjar] is obscure. The poem certainly uses it as the name of a tract of country, practically equivalent to all of India east of Gōrakhpur" (W&G 220, n. 1). Sherring describes a fascinating localization of this episode concerning Rāmkot, the "Fort of Rām" at Ayodhyā: Raja Samthar of Rāmkot "threw off his allegiance to Kanouj, and refused to pay the annual tribute. On this, Raja Jai Chand gave Alā and Udal the grant of all the Ganjar country; and they attacked and destroyed Râmkot, leaving it the shapeless mass of ruins we now find it." There are treasures there, but they bring ruin on their finders (1872, 219). Neither Rāmkot nor a king Samthar are among the Gānjar conquests in the Elliot *Ālhā* or the digvijaya conquests of Lakṣaṇa in the purāṇa. On Rāmkot as the central site of Rāmjanmabhūmī, the sacred land of Rāma's birth, and its discovery by Vikramāditya, see van der Veer 1989, 18-20.

This is a logical and typical orientation of Kanauj kings.[54] But whereas the purāṇic Lakṣaṇa leads the expedition under the high-toned title of a Vedic-sounding digvijaya, the Elliot *Ālhā*'s Lākhan stays home in Kanauj, and leaves the Gānjar fighting to the leadership of Ūdal. I will return to Lakṣaṇa's digvijaya. Suffice it to note for now that the paurāṇika embarks on a major upgrading of Lakṣaṇa's status and accountability, and deepens the story's implications for imperial history.

And so, against the background of this enhanced portrayal of Pṛthivirāja's aggrandizements, Mahīpati's machinations, Parimala's rash credulity, and Lakṣaṇa's potential for imperial succession, the war-opening battles of Śirīṣākhya and Kīrtisāgara—which follow immediately upon "Lakṣaṇa's Digvijaya"/"The Gānjar War"—move us toward a final war in which Parimala, who doesn't even come to the final war in the Elliot *Ālhā*, leads the "Candravaṃśa side (*pakṣa . . . candravaṃśinaḥ*)" as king of the "lunar line" (*śaśivaṃśin*; 32.59-61) against an enemy who has sworn the end of his line, city, and kingdom.

D. The Agnivaṃśa

Whatever may be the Sūryavaṃśa affinities of the Gautamas of Kacchadeśa, the paurāṇika is clearly aware—though he never uses their dynastic name—of Chandēl claims to Candravaṃśa descent, which first appear (rather curiously) in inscriptions during the reign of Paramardi (Parmāl) attributing lunar birth to the dynasty's ninth-century founder (Bose 1956, 1-3), and are recalled, as was mentioned, in the Elliot *Ālhā*. Indeed, the author has gone to great lengths to work out a pattern of recurrence between the trauma of the lunar dynasty in the *Mahābhārata* and the lunar dynasty's elimination in the *Kṛṣṇāṃśacarita*. I will say more about the solar and lunar lines, for they are important in epic and purāṇic texts. What is presently suggestive is that their shallow generational depth in the *Kṛṣṇāṃśacarita* is *not* typical of portrayals of the lunar and solar dynasties in other epic and purāṇic texts. One may thus detect that they are not what really interests the bhāviṣya paurāṇika. The solar and lunar lines are window dressing for his real concern, which is the Agnivaṃśa: the fire lineage, the royal lines that trace a third line of descent from Agni, god of fire.

Here we must let two speakers complete what they were saying in passages that I cut short. First, when Śiva curses the Pāṇḍavas and Draupadī to be reborn, and Kṛṣṇa counters by promising that he will help them, this is what the smiling (*vihasya*) Kṛṣṇa says in full: "By the avatar of my śakti (*mayā śaktyavatāreṇa*) the Pāṇḍavas will be protected. The

[54]Tripathi [1937] 1989, 100-6, 197-201, 229-34, 248-50, 309-10.

delightful city of Mahobā is created by Māyādevī. My portion, known as Udayasiṃha, will be born there as the son of Deśarāja, born in the womb of Devakī. A portion of my majesty (*mama dhāmāṃśa*) will be born as my guru (i.e., elder brother) Āhlāda. Having slain all the kings born into the Fire-lineage (Agnivaṃśa), I will establish Kali (*sthāpayiṣyāmi vai kalim*)" (1.30-34).

Second, let us allow Candrabhaṭṭa to complete what he has to tell Pṛthivīrāja when the "sleep of yoga" allows him to at last "see" behind Kṛṣṇāṃśa's musical flute-and-dance disguise, just before the final war: "At that time the skillful mantrin Candrabhaṭṭa, skilled in all the meanings of the śāstras, a worshiper of Vaiṣṇavī Śakti, approached Mahīrāja and said, 'Listen. I see this secret play (*rahaḥ krīḍā*) by the grace of Devī. Udaya Kṛṣṇāṃśa came to the refulgent Brahmā (*pūrṇa-brahmāṇam*). Inwardly pleased (*prasannātma*), he said, "Listen, you who are the personification of goodness (*sattva*). I now go to Delhi for the destruction of the Agnivaṃśa. Having slain the portions of the Kauravas, having established Kali on earth (*sthāpayitvā kaliṃ bhuvi*), having reached your side again, I do this secret play." Having thus spoken, riding Bindula, the hero stood beside you. By Yoganidrā I thus see Kṛṣṇāṃśa, O king (*ityahaṃ dṛṣṭavānbhūpa kṛṣṇāṃśaṃ yoganidrayā*)'" (30.33-37).

These passages allow us to appreciate how the rapport between Viṣṇu and the goddess is intertwined with the rapport between the solar and lunar dynasties. In each case there is a third party: in one Śiva, in the other—hardly fortuitously—the Agnivaṃśa.[55] The resolution to efface the lunar vaṃśa by the arch Agnivaṃśin and Rudra worshiper Pṛthivīrāja is but a byproduct of Kṛṣṇa's deeper design—or play—of effacing the Agnivaṃśa, ostensibly to mitigate the curse of Śiva and protect the portions of the Pāṇḍavas. When Pṛthivīrāja makes his vow to destroy the Candravaṃśa, Kṛṣṇāṃśa has all along intended to destroy the Agnivaṃśa, to which Pṛthivīrāja belongs.

Let us recall that *Ālhā*, as a "*Mahābhārata* of the Kali yuga," takes place a quarter of the way into the Kali yuga. In parallel, the *Kṛṣṇāṃśacarita*, distancing itself from the epic-purāṇic convention that the Kali yuga begins with the aftermath of the *Mahābhārata* war, identifies the real "establishment of Kali"—of the demon of the Kali yuga—as occurring through its "*Ālhā*'s" second "battle of Kurukṣetra" (see chap. 8). This real "establishment of Kali" links the coming of the "Mlecchas" with a judgment upon the Agnivaṃśa.

But what is the Agnivaṃśa? Why this terrible judgment? Surely it is not just a sectarian countering of Śiva or a second shielding of the Pāṇḍavas.

[55] Śiva figures prominently in the *Pṛthvīrāj-rāsau*'s version of the Agnivaṃśa origin myth (R. B. Singh 1975, 221).

An answer begins to emerge if we consider how the primary *Mahābhārata* adversaries incarnate into three of the prominent Rajput lineages that figure in the story: the lunar Chandēls, and the fire-lineage Chauhāns and Parihāras. The first thing to note are the shifts in lineage (vaṃśa) and incarnation (aṃśa) from one text to the other as shown in table 10.

Table 10. Aṃśa and vaṃśa realignments from the *Mahābhārata* to the *Kṛṣṇāṃśacarita*

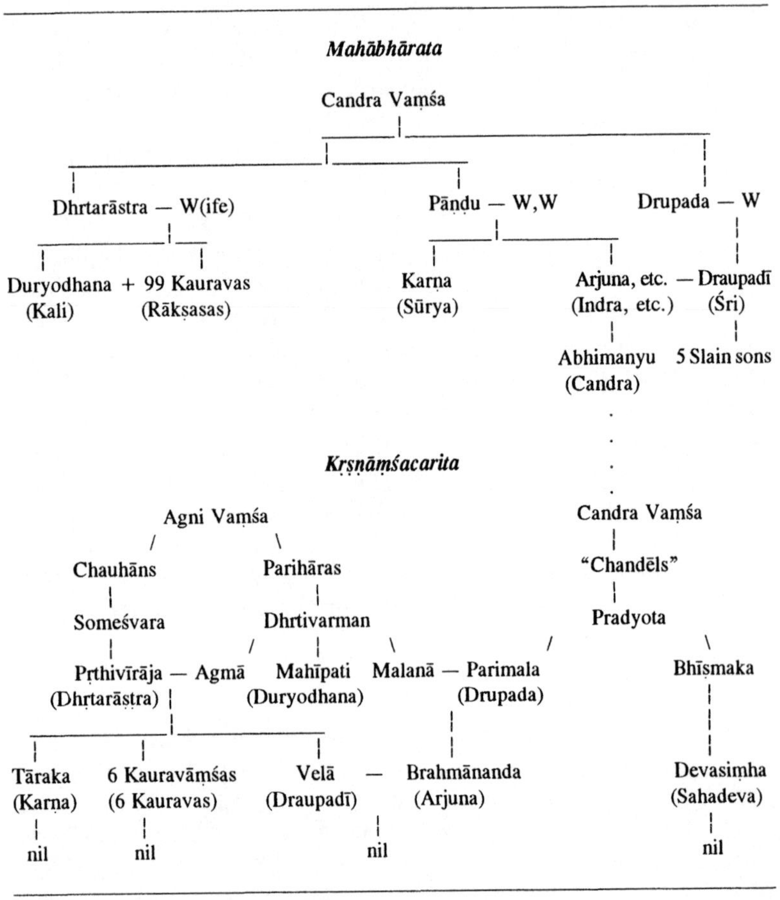

Whereas the "portions" of the Pāṇḍavas will either be born into the Chandēl lunar line or ultimately join its cause,[56] the portions of Dhṛtarāṣṭra and certain Kauravas—as lunar as the Pāṇḍavas in the *Mahābhārata*—are born into the Agnivaṃśa as either Parihāras or

[56]As with Yudhiṣthira as Balakhāni, Bhīma as Tālana, and Nakula as Lakṣaṇa.

Chauhāns, and ultimately join in common cause against the Chandēls. That is about it for simple statements.

As one can see, Karṇa and Draupadī also shift from the lunar to the fire line.[57] And while Arjuna (reborn as Brahmānanda) becomes the son of Draupadī's *Mahābhārata* father Drupada (reincarnated as Parimala), Draupadī (reborn as Velā) becomes the daughter of Arjuna's paternal uncle Dhṛtarāṣṭra (reincarnated as Pṛthivīrāja). This reincarnational pattern supplies the paternal components of a cross-cousin marriage, but of a fantastic sort in which it is not one's children who cross-marry but one's selves.[58] It is also obvious that the *Mahābhārata* theme of lineage continuity and regeneration, figuring Abhimanyu as the dynastic moon (Candra or Soma) that renews itself through his son Parikṣit after the war, is precisely what is absent in the desolation that ends the *Kṛṣṇāṃśacarita*.[59] Unlike Kṛṣṇa, who gives his sister Subhadrā to become Abhimanyu's mother, Kṛṣṇāṃśa has no sister through whom to bless a world renewal. His mission to destroy the Agnivaṃśa does not appear to entail saving a Candravaṃśa remnant. The lunar dynasty appears to be regenerated neither by its Pāṇḍava "portions" through its putative offshoot, the Chandēls, nor rerouted by its Kaurava "portions" through an Agnivaṃśa detour.

Yet the full extent of the *Kṛṣṇāṃśacarita*'s judgment on the Agnivaṃśa cannot come into view until we realize that its final battle embroils not only the Chauhāns and Parihāras, but two other major Agnivaṃśa lineages, the Paramāras and Caulukyas, along with numerous lesser lines. The Paramāra presence is minimal, and is embodied in a king named Gaṅgāsiṃha, maternal uncle of Lakṣaṇa (5.8-9), who rules at Kalpakṣetra (Kalpi) in the Gaṅgā-Yamunā Doab, the area known as Antarvedi, the "middle altar."[60] His kinship ties and location make him a logical Mahobā-Kanauj loyalist, and that is the side he joins and dies fighting for in the *Kṛṣṇāṃśacarita*'s final battle (32.183-85). But the Caulukya

[57]The Pāñcālas are descendants of Pūru, and a branch of the lunar dynasty (see Thapar 1978a, chart facing p. 376).

[58]For this pattern to have a *Mbh* foundation, Draupadī would have to be the daughter of Drupada and a (nonexistent) sister of Pāṇḍu and Dhṛtarāstra. Perhaps the pattern is a north Indian fantasization of the closeness of a cross-cousin type of marriage into a design that allows for the remarriage of spouses through consecutive lives. Since the pattern does not hold for *Ālhā*, where Prithīrāj is the incarnation of Duryodhana, I would doubt that it is influenced by Dravidian kinship patterns residual in north India. Cf. Trautmann 1981, 320-36, on such possibilities in the *Mbh* and early Buddhist literature.

[59]On Abhimanyu's incarnation of Soma-Candra and the revival of the Candravaṃśa, see Hiltebeitel [1976] 1990, 336-53; 1988a, 431.

[60]4.3-4; 27.49-50. Further along in the *Pratisarga Parvan* (3.4.1.11-46), we learn that his father Kalpasiṃha moved a Paramāra branch from Mālyavatī to Kalpaksetra, naming the city Kalāpa, and that Gaṅgāsimha died childless at Kurukṣetra (Hohenberger 1967, 20).

presence is major. For according to this text, King Jayacandra of Kanauj and his nephew Lakṣaṇa are Śuklavaṃśins, that is, Caulukyas, despite historical evidence that Jayacandra was a Gāhaḍavāla (Gaharwar).[61] Moreover, it is not only the *Kṛṣṇāṃśacarita* that changes Jayacandra's lineage, but the Elliot *Ālhā*. And remarkably, the *Ālhā* makes him neither a Gāhaḍavāla nor a Caulukya, but a Rāṭhoṛ.[62] Clearly the Gāhaḍavālas, whose "modern representatives" in Uttar Pradesh make lunar dynasty claims for themselves through Yayāti (Tripathi 1964, 296-97), but about whom inscriptions say no more than that their dynasty was founded "after the lines of the protectors of the earth born in the solar race had gone to heaven" (ibid., 300), left something of a folkloric vacuum that was filled in these two different ways.[63]

The important point, however, is that in the *Kṛṣṇāṃśacarita*, both Pṛthivīrāja and Jayacandra are Agnivaṃśins. Both the *Kṛṣṇāṃśacarita* and *Ālhā* open with the imperial rivalry between these two kings, but only the purāṇa makes it one between Agnivaṃśins. Moreover, whereas *Ālhā* actually opens with Prithīrāj's abduction of Jaychand's daughter Sanjōgin, the purāṇa gives its version of this story a prior "historical" setting. Here we learn that Jayacandra and Pṛthivīrāja have already opposed each other as bitter rivals for empire and the license to tax.[64] This has kindled a "terrible enmity (*ghoraṃ vairam*)"; each ruling "half the kingdom of Āryadeśa, . . . an enmity was born between them that was the destruction of the Agnivaṃśa (*agnivaṃśapranāśanam*)" (5.36-38). These words emphatically end the adhyāya that serves as prologue to the purāṇa's "translation" of *Ālhā* proper, which begins with the next chapter's story of Saṃyoginī's (Sanjōgin's) abduction.

E. Defending Folk Hinduism

Since it is a folkloric vacuum that the paurāṇika fills by making Gāhaḍavālas into Śuklavaṃśin-Caulukyas, it is thus safe to say that he has

[61]Tripathi 1964: the Gāhaḍavālas brought stability to Kanauj from about 1080 to the death of Jayacandra in 1193, beginning in the chaotic conditions that followed the attacks which weakened the Pratihāras, who had been a prior force in Kanauj since the early ninth century (219-91).

[62]"The tradition that Jaychand was a Rāṭhōr is incorrect. He was really a Gahaṛwar, but throughout the cycle he is called a Rāṭhōr" (W&G 39, n. 1). Tripathi 1964, 296-300, seems persuasive in dismissing arguments that the Gāhaḍavālas *were* Rāṭhōṛs (Rāṣṭrakūtas); the latter might have retained associations with Kanauj from prior raids of the area and opposition to its earlier rulers (ibid., 214, 219; cf. Thapar 1978a, 170-71).

[63]See Tripathi 1964, 292-97, on the chaotic conditions of their emergence and the obscurity of their origins.

[64]In *Pṛthvirāj-rāsau*, the abduction takes place in the midst of Jaychand's Rājasūya (Dwivedi 1966, 20-21).

filled it with what he considers to be Agnivaṃśa folklore. And here, although he usually appears to rely on oral *Ālhā*, he seems to have imported a theme from the *Pṛthvīrāj-rāsau*, in which Chand Bardāī (Candrabhaṭṭa) himself provides what may be the earliest version of the story that the ancestors of the four Agnikula Kṣatriya clans—the Chauhāns, Paramāras, Parihāras, and Caulukyas—emerged from a firepit (*agnikuṇḍa*) during a sacrifice performed at Mount Abu.[65]

As Agnivaṃśins, Jayacandra and his nephew Lakṣaṇa are essential to the purāṇic author's Agnivaṃśa subplot. This we see from two adhyāyas that break into the sequence of *Ālhā* episodes between "The Carrying off of Ūdal" and "The Home-Bringing of Belā." In introducing these two episodes at this juncture (see table 4), the *Kṛṣṇāṃśacarita* opens a considerable window on a transition that was discussed earlier. This is the passage, in Elliot *Ālhā* terms, from the Banāphars' last hurrah as guardians against the penetrations of Muslim magical folk religion to the events that embroil them, beginning with Belā's homecoming, in the final war. Following from the purāṇa's version of the Muslim captivity of Ūdal-Kṛṣṇāṃśa, we might expect it to continue widening our historical and geographical horizons. And so it does. We now begin to hear more and more about what might be called "outlandish" peoples and places: that is, those on, and beyond, the boundaries of Āryadeśa.

As adhyāya 29 opens, the Ṛṣis ask the bard Lomaharṣana about a girl named Kinnarī—as if she had just been mentioned, which she hasn't.[66] The bard responds: Born in the Caitraratha country, she is the granddaughter of the heavenly courtesan Mañjughoṣā and the sage (*muni*) Śuka, and daughter of their son Muni, who married a daughter of Kubera whom he won after twelve years of tapas to Śiva. Kinnarī did tapas on a snowy peak (or Mount Himatunga), and Rudra, granting Muni's request that she be given a growing kingdom, gave her in marriage to Makaranda, brother of Kṛṣṇāṃśa's wife Puṣpavatī. Rudra set a limit: after thirty years, the kingdom, Guruṇḍa on the snowy peak, would be destroyed (29.1-14). Meanwhile, another mountain kingdom, Netrapāla, is under attack (29.15ff.), with its city of Netrasiṃhagaḍha on Mount Navatunga "on the border of Kashmir" (13.21). Here rules king Netrasiṃha, who, as noted in chapter 6, once had the "drum of life" to revive slain warriors and fend off his daughter Svarṇavatī's suitors, until the drum was destroyed when she was wooed by Āhlāda. A pattern emerges. Mountain kingdoms associated with the natal families of Āhlāda and

[65]On this myth and its datings, with the paurāṇika's clearly one of the later variants, see chap. 13.

[66]Lomaharsaṇa is father of the bard Ugraśravas's who recites the *Mbh* to the Rṣis of the Naimiṣa Forest in the epic's outer frame; see chap. 4, n. 7.

Kṛṣṇāṃśa's wives are threatened.

But now a surprise.[67] Netrapāla is besieged by a Buddhist (*bauddha*) king called Nyunapati, "Lord of the Defective,"[68] or Bauddhasiṃha, "Buddhist Lion." The Buddhists, all magicians and worshipers of Lokamānya (*bauddhā māyāvinas sarve lokamānyaprapūjakāḥ*; 29.20), come mainly from China (*cīnadeśa*, 26), but also draw forces from Jāpaka and Śyāma, which would seem to be nothing but Japan and Siam.[69] Netrapāla is defended by Netrasiṃha's three sons (Svarṇavatī's brothers), and eight heroes: Kṛṣṇāṃśa, Devasiṃha, Indula, Tālana, Jaganāyaka, Maṇḍalīka (Āhlāda),[70] Dhānyapāla (a.k.a. Dhyānapāla), and Lallasiṃha. The last two, "portions" respectively of Yuyutsu and Kuntibhoja of the *Mahābhārata*, are permitted to come by Lakṣaṇa, their patron at Kanauj, and are mentioned here for the first time (21-24). After over a month's siege, the Bauddhas are repulsed and retreat to China. But there they make a battlefield (*yuddhabhūmi*), regroup and collect more Chinese, Śyāma, and Jāpaka forces. The Bauddhas and Āryas now fight a fortnight-long war, "increasing the world of Yama with seven hundred thousand Bauddhas and two hundred thousand warriors of Āryadeśa" (32-33). The Buddhists first deploy a *kalayantra* to make a wooden army: wooden foot soldiers; wooden warriors riding wooden horses, elephants, buffaloes, hogs (*kola*), lions, ganders, cuckoos, herons, jackals, and vultures (33-37). When Indula incinerates them with a fire-weapon, the Buddhists create energized iron horsemen, and then an iron lion. Before

[67]Only pieces of the following story have Elliot *Ālhā* parallels: A wooden horse belongs to Narpat, father of Ūdal's wife Phulwā, which Makrand rides until Devī finally destroys it with a kick (W&G 201-2); Makaranda rides a stone horse in the purāṇa (21.20-21). Sunwā's brothers are killed by Sātan, Rāja of Paṭṭi (unidentified by Grierson: W&G 221), in the "The Gānjar War" in which many kings are besieged for tribute. Sātan claims he had defeated Jaychand and not paid him tribute for twelve years.

[68]The name is certainly curious for a Buddhist, and philosophically suggestive: see Monier-Williams [1899] 1964, 573: less, diminished, defective, deficient, deprived, inferior, vulva.

[69]Though first mentioned as *śyāmajāpakadeśagāḥ* (29.19), which could be taken as "those from the country of the dark prayer-mutterers" or "dunkulfarbige, buddhistische Zauberer" (Hohenberger 1967, 50), it becomes likely that the Śyāmas and Jāpakas are distinct from the Chinese when they supplement the ten-lākh army of Cīnadeśa with a lākh each of Śyāmadeśa and Jāpaka forces (29.28); curiously the latter are never mentioned as having a *deśa*. On the Chinese as Mlecchas in classical sources (*Mbh*, *Manu*, *Matsya Purāṇa*), see Thapar 1978a, 174 and 190, n. 16.

[70]Āhlāda is present later in the episode (see below), and Maṇḍalīka rides an elephant (29.22), which is typical of Āhlāda. As meaning "provincial governor," Āhlāda could have this title at Kanauj where, as Lakṣaṇa says, it is borne by many feudatories (10.12). It is also used for Pṛthivīrāja's eldest brother as a Delhi courtier (32.146, 150). Schomer has also found "Mandalik" as a name for Yudhiṣṭhira as he is incarnate in Ālhā, used at a point when Prithīrāj looks down on Ālhā even though he is an incarnation of "Mandalik" (1984, Excerpts, 3 and 5).

they are destroyed, the iron conjurations kill two of Svarṇavatī's brothers. When Indula sees his maternal uncles slain, he pulverizes the kalayantra, binds Bauddhasiṃha, and brings him to Kṛṣṇāṃśa. The Āryas plunder the city before releasing Bauddhasiṃha in his own fort. There, he "gladly" gives his daughter Padmajā to Indula and heaps of wealth to Āhlāda. Finally, in what seems to be the point of the story, "An oath (*śapathaḥ*) was made there by all the hosts of Buddhists: 'We will not go to Āryadeśa for the sake of any kingdom (*āryadeśaṃ na yāsyāmaḥ kadācid-rāṣṭrahetave*)'" (52). This India-China nonaggression pact seems little-known to twentieth-century historians and politicians. The heroes then return to Netrapāla on the mountain borders of Kashmir, which are clearly meant to define a point not only on a Hindu-Buddhist divide, but an international boundary. As one can see, it is also, as in the story that precedes it—in which Balkh is made a boundary with Islam—a boundary at which the heroes, without participation by any of the story's imperial kings, guard Āryadeśa and Indian folk religion, by which it would be pointless to argue that the author means anything but folk Hinduism, against another religion's dark magicians.

The paurāṇika thus gives the "Banāphars" a second last hurrah before the denouement, which he now plunges into in the next adhyāya (30). This plunge also begins distinctively, as we may recall, with another episode not paralleled in the Elliot *Ālhā*: Kṛṣṇāṃśa's līlā as a yogi-musician in which he undertakes to release Lakṣaṇa from Pṛthivīrāja's prison in Delhi. This episode will allow some of the "Banāphars" a third last hurrah.

As is now clear, the author returns here not only to his continuing elevation of Lakṣaṇa over Jayacandra in the imperial politics of Kanauj, but to his enhancement of the main "Agnivaṃśa" conflict between Kanauj and Delhi. Picking up on Pṛthivīrāja's increasing rivalry with Lakṣaṇa, adhyāya 30 builds from Lakṣaṇa's marital situation. Padmākara, brother of Lakṣaṇa's wife Padminī, had arranged Padminī's svayaṃvara. But, already an ally of Pṛthivīrāja, Padmakāra had opposed her choice of Lakṣaṇa and fought him after hearing from Mahīpati that his sister was marrying a man who keeps company with sons of an Ābhīrī (25.1-38)—that is, with "Banāphars."[71] Now, while Lakṣaṇa's "Banāphar" companions are far off in China, Lakṣaṇa's father-in-law Kāmapāla Śāradānandana, king of Bindugaḍha, persuades Jayacandra to send Lakṣaṇa to Bindugaḍha on what they both seem to know is a collision course with Pṛthivīrāja (30.1-6).

[71]In the Elliot *Ālhā*'s Canto 11, Lakṣana's wife is Kusum Dē or Kusumā, which, like Padminī, means "lotus/flower." Her kingdom, Bundi, her brothers, and their whole story are quite different (W&G 217-19). Lākhan has a varied folklore, as indicated in chap. 6, § A.

Knowing that Lakṣaṇa is on his way, Padmākara invites Pṛthivīrāja to join him in fighting Lakṣaṇa, but Lakṣaṇa's forces triumph (30.7-9). It is then that Pṛthivīrāja hatches his plot with Padmākara to poison "my great enemy (*me mahāñchatrus*)" Lakṣaṇa, bind him, and hand him over to be imprisoned in Delhi (11). Padmākara complies, but Padminī worships the goddess Caṇḍikā, who comes to Lakṣaṇa in his sleep and tells him to mutter the tantric mantra "*Hriṃ Phaṭ Gheghe*," which removes all obstacles (13-15).

At this point, the eight heroes return from China and disperse. Finding Lakṣaṇa absent from Kanauj, Tālana, Dhānyapāla, Lallasiṃha, and Kṛṣṇāṃśa reassemble and begin to search for him in yogi-musician disguises. They dance their way into the home of Padmākara. Women swoon seeing Kṛṣṇāṃśa play flute, but Padminī recognizes him and asks the "lord yogin" how her husband, captured by Pṛthivīrāja, can be freed (30.16-25). Kṛṣṇāṃśa comforts her, and the heroes go disguised to Delhi, where, as we have seen, they fool Pṛthivīrāja, but not Candrabhaṭṭa, and do not find Lakṣaṇa (16-37).

Now fearful of Kṛṣṇāṃśa, Pṛthivīrāja sends a thousand Agnivaṃśa heroes to remove Lakṣaṇa from Delhi and take him to Bindugaḍha. Their leader Bhagadanta returns with Padmākara's assurance that his sister Padminī will make Lakṣaṇa, her husband, vanish with her secret knowledge (*vidyā*). The "Banāphars" mount a great search party of "twelve lakhs of Kṣatriyas badly crazed for battle" (30.32). First besieging Delhi, they only intimidate Pṛthivīrāja into showing them his house and swearing on Mahādeva that Lakṣaṇa is not there. Nor do they find Lakṣaṇa at Bindugaḍha (where king Kāmapāla misleads them) or Kanauj (where they inform Jayacandra of his nephew's disappearance; 38-54).

Svarṇavatī now swings into action with her new "servant" Śobhā, who, we are reminded, is skilled in Mleccha magic. They go to Jayacandra, who can tell them nothing. Śobhā announces that she will bring Lakṣaṇa and Padminī back by calling, once again, on "Mahāmada, the Paiśāca servant of Rudra" (30.55-60). The heroes set off with the two women magicians and search everywhere, "in home after home, among people after people," and from country to country, until they reach Bāhlīka, Śobhā's "own country of the Mleccha dwellers." There Śobhā sings and dances for the forest lord Markaṭeśvara, Lord of Apes. Worshiped by Mlecchas, he is invincible, but unable to help them find Lakṣaṇa. This leaves Śobhā without hope (61-69).

Svarṇavatī then worships Caṇḍikā during the springtime (Caitra) Navarātra, and on the ninth night the World Mother (Jagadambikā) tells her the previous life of Padminī. She was married to Maṇideva, who was slain by Bhīma in the *Mahābhārata*'s Yakṣa wars.[72] She prayed to Śiva for reunion with her husband, and after a hundred years Śiva responded: In the Kali yuga, nearly twelve hundred years into the Vikrama era,[73] Padminī will first marry a portion of Nakula—i.e., Lakṣaṇa—and enjoy great happiness with him. Having abandoned her body, she will then rejoin Maṇideva on Kailāsa, and the goddess Śāradā will make Maṇideva the protector of Mahobā (30.70-78). It is a strange interlude, even for Yakṣīs. Jagadambikā then tells Svarṇavatī where to find Padminī in the abode of Guhyakas on Mount Kailāsa. Padminī is sick with compassion at the news of her husband's capture. She heads to Bindugaḍha, and sends Svarṇavatī back to Mahobā with a letter telling Kṛṣṇaṃśa to rescue Lakṣaṇa from her brother.[74] But when Kṛṣṇāṃśa arrives at Bindugaḍha with a big army, he finds that Padminī is now helping her father and brother by giving them a "letter" (?*-patram*) that enables them to disappear and kill Kṛṣṇāṃśa's hosts invisibly. Kṛṣṇāṃśa then meditates on the goddess, obtains a divine eye, meets this challenge, binds the father and son, and rescues Lakṣaṇa. At last he brings Lakṣaṇa and Padminī, who finally seems to have ended her ambivalence, to the rejoicing Jayacandra. And as the Kanauj king gifts Brahmans, the bhaviṣya paurаṇika concludes his preambles: "Thus the auspicious *Kṛṣṇacaritam*. . . , seen by the strength of yoga (*yogabalena*)" (79-94).

Padminī's connection with Maṇideva is intriguing, since he seems to be a multiform of Maniya Deva or Devī, the guardian god(dess) of Mahobā. But this deity is hard to figure. Maniya Deo, a "granite tutelary deity of the Chandel Rajput kings,"[75] seems to have both female and male identities. The Elliot *Ālhā* has her definitely as a goddess, Maniyā Devī (W&G 33, 124, 170). Grierson annotates her as the "tutelary goddess of Mahōbā" (113). Smith and Black add that "Maniyá Deo is the tutelary goddess of the Chandels," and trace the connection to the Chandēl's "aboriginal" association with Maniyá Garh, their ancient fort on the river Ken (1879, 286). Noting that she may correspond to an image found in the ruins of this fort of a female with sword in hand, Mitra adds that Maniyā Deo or Devī is mentioned "in the bardic account of Cānd . . . as the goddess of the Candellas [Chandēls] to whom they

[72]A reference to *Mbh* 3.157-58, where the slain Yakṣa in question must be Maṇimat.

[73]30.75: *kalau vikramakāle hi śatadvadaśake 'ntike* (cf. 2.6-8). One should not miss the historical precision: with the Vikrama age beginning ca. 58 B.C., we are indeed in the twelfth century.

[74]This is a bit confusing, since it would seem she could give the letter directly to Kṛṣṇāṃśa, who is there with Svarṇavatī. It seems that the letter must be read by Parimala. Bindugaḍha seems to be south of Mahobā, so the latter would thus perhaps not be out of the way from Kailāsa.

[75]Dixit 1992, 71; cf. Bose 1956, 4.

appealed in times of danger" ([1958] 1977, 185). Yet Schomer takes "Maniya Dev" in oral *Ālhā* from Kanauj as the "patron god of Mahōba" (1984, Excerpts, 1-2). And in a composite of two oral accounts gathered by Crooke in and around Mahobā, the deity is originally a Brahman paṇḍit. Having predicted a full moon rather than a new moon, the Brahman goes home in distress, where his virgin daughter prays to Candra to "justify her father's words." Candra does so by impregnating her with a son who will found the Candella lunar line, but the father expels her to the jungle. The child is born and the two are brought home by a "Banāfar Rajput." Shamed by his daughter's "affair," the father "turned himself into a stone, and as his name was Mani Ram, he is now worshiped as Maniya Deva." Without mentioning Maniya Deva or this outcome, the *Parmāl-rāsau* (or *Mahobā Khaṇḍa* of the *Pṛthivīrāja Rāso*) has a related story: the father is a Brahman chaplain of a Gāhaḍavāla king of Kāśī, whose widowed (rather than virgin) sixteen-year-old daughter Hemavatī ("possessing gold") is impregnated by Candra, the Moon, when he sees her bathing on a hot summer night. Later, he gives her son, the first Chandēl (Nannuka-Candravarman), the philosopher's stone at age sixteen, which the son uses to amass gold to found his kingdom at Mahobā and support an expansionist army. Candra also directs him to perform a sacrifice at Khajuraho to erase his mother's shame.[76]

The paurāṇika, who probably knows some such local Mahobā folk traditions about this deity, but seems bent on improving them, clarifies the linkage in his account of the lineages of the Agnivaṃśa Kṣatriyas, which immediately follows the *Kṛṣṇāṃśacarita*. There he describes Mahobā not only as built by Śāradā, but "protected by Maṇideva (*maṇidevena rakṣitām*)" (3.4.3.40-41). He has thus given the deity an appropriate Sanskritized male Yakṣa identity from the *Mahābhārat*a. Or perhaps that too is part of the folk tradition he knows. Padminī's prior relation with Maṇideva thus makes her a link, through her two husbands, between Mahobā and Kanauj. In this she is like Śāradā herself, who, in the same sequence that mentions Maṇideva, founds both cities (4.3.39-51). The reunion of Padminī with Maṇideva after she has lived out her "epic" lifetime with Lakṣaṇa also occurs at the same time that the folk tradition has Maniya Deva (male) turning his back on Mahobā. According to informants at his temple, this occurs at the end of *Ālhā* when the philosopher's stone is thrown—by Malhnā, in the Elliot *Ālhā* (W&G 273)—into the Kīratsāgar. So is the god represented in the temple, where

[76]See Mitra [1958] 1977, 21-26; Dixit 1992, 61-62; Bose 1956, 2-4; R. B. Singh 1975, 245-57; Asopa 1976, 208-10; Wright 1873, 33. Bose and Singh support Vincent Smith's dubious view that the image (a slab covered with minium like so many in north India) looks to be originally Gond.

one sees only his back.

What is striking in all three of these last hurrahs, two of which are not found in the Elliot *Ālhā*, is that the Sanskritizing author projects the folk epic heroes and heroines as defenders of folk Hinduism against intrusions of Muslim and Buddhist folk religion. But is that really his purpose? The paurāṇika does not appear to relish such continuities in the folk tradition. Rather, he seems to sever them by consigning folk gods and heroes to a past defined by higher purposes, such as the establishment of international boundaries. By defending these boundaries, the folk heroes defend Āryadeśa. Ultimately they are defenders of Sanskritic Hinduism, not folk Hinduism. But, as the next chapter will show, it is not spatially but temporally—in the higher, divinely ordained continuities of purāṇic history—that the purpose of redesigning *Ālhā* becomes clear. It is with high historical purpose that the paurāṇika takes up the "unfinished business" of the *Mahābhārata*.

8 Kurukṣetra II

Once one is past its "historical" prologue, the *Kṛṣṇāṃśacarita* either runs in close parallel to the Elliot *Ālhā*, or shows such purāṇic additions as we have noted. But once the final war unfolds, the two stories touch at only a few points, most of which are now noted: (1) Brahmānanda sets out for Delhi with no "Banāphar" companions, only Mahīpati, to bring Velā to Mahobā; (2) Mahīpati counsels the fraud whereby Cāmuṇḍa, dressed as Velā, stabs Brahmānanda with Tāraka close by; (3) Velā comes and refreshes Brahmānanda; (4) Cāmuṇḍa beheads Kṛṣṇāṃśa (fifteenth day of battle in the purāṇa); (5) Āhlāda squeezes Cāmuṇḍa to death (sixteenth day); (6) Brahmānanda tells Velā to disguises herself as himself so as to kill Tāraka (sixteenth day); (7) riding Brahmānanda's horse, Velā decapitates Tāraka, who mistakes her for Brahmānanda (sixteenth day); (8) Velā becomes satī, as do other widows (sixteenth day); (9) Pṛthivīrāja kills Lakṣaṇa (seventeenth day); (10) Āhlāda goes to the forest of immortals (eighteenth day).

Even where the two stories remain parallel, there are important differences, especially regarding Belā's tour with Brahmā and the death of Lākhan. In the Elliot *Ālhā*, Belā makes only one tour: her homecoming, which folds her meetings with Brahmā into early and later moments while battle attends both her departure from Delhi and return to kill her brother. Her movements all occur between Delhi and Mahobā, and the final battle takes place somewhere between them. In the purāṇa, Velā makes two tours. First, with what is clearly the greater authorial emphasis, she takes the dying Brahmānanda on a pan-Indian horseback pilgrimage from Kapila in the east[1] to Setubandha in the south to

[1]Since other directional sites are well known (Setubandha is Rameshwaram in Tamilnadu), and since elsewhere the paurāṇika refers to Kapila or Kapilasthāna as a tīrtha defining an eastward limit (3.2.23.7; 3.2.10; 3.4.6), this eastern site's location is probably Kapilāśrama, the Rsi Kapila's hermitage on Sāgara Island near the mouth of the Ganges (see Dey [1899] 1927, 90). But given the paurāṇika's interest in the upper Narmadā area, it might also be Kapilā, the "portion of the river Narbada [Narmada] near its source," which, after "running

Dvārakā in the west to Badarī and mount Gandhamadana in the north before he tells her on Gandhamadana he wants her to kill Tāraka. When she convinces him to stay alive, she brings him back to north central India and deposits him at "dear Kurukṣetra (*priyam kurukṣetram*)," promising him she will return to him and go to Delhi to kill Tāraka after she first goes to Mahobā (31.179-86; 32.5). At this point, the eighteen-day war is yet to happen. Her second tour, in terms of *Ālhā* her homecoming to Mahobā, is only to impart news of Brahmānanda's tragedy and rally the Mahobā champions (32.1-6). Brahmānanda must thus survive not only this preposterous horseback pilgrimage and Velā's trip to Mahobā but fifteen days of battle before he "abandons stupefaction" once again to remind Velā he wants her to kill Tāraka (32.198-99).

The paurāṇika thus robs Velā of the initiative of figuring out how to kill Tāraka, but gives her—Draupadī incarnate—the initiative of making "dear Kurukṣetra" the place where the war will occur by having her deposit Brahmānanda there. He has thus contrived to have the final battle of the *Mahābhārata* of the Kali yuga take place not only in eighteen days, but *at* Kurukṣetra. Kurukṣetra, however, is not between Delhi and Mahobā. For the Mahobā forces to satisfy the paurāṇika's wish to have the battle there, they have to go well beyond Delhi to the northwest to accommodate him.

The paurāṇika also saves Lakṣaṇa's combat with Pṛthivīrāja for the war's last killing to round off the imperial rivalry he has heightened between them. In the Elliot *Ālhā*, Lākhan dies before Ūdal (W&G 272), while in "tribal" *Ālhā* he seems to live on (chap. 6, § A). Given that only items 4 through 10 occur in the *Kṛṣṇāṃśacarita*'s version of the final war, one may say that the paurāṇika compresses everything about the war that interests him from oral *Ālhā* into the its last four days. He thus leaves the first fourteen to play with.

A. Divine Plan, Master Plan

Kurukṣetra II is a strange affair. Pṛthivīrāja has been foiled in his attempt to eliminate his "great enemy" Lakṣaṇa on its eve. Having vowed the destruction of the Candravaṃśa, he will thus have to achieve it with the "Agnivaṃśa" divided. This, as we can infer from Candrabhaṭṭa's

---

for about two miles falls over the descent of about seventy feet into what is known as the Kapiladhârâ"—the river's first fall from the Amarakaṇṭaka mountain in eastern Madhya Pradesh (ibid. 90, 240; cf. Bhardwaj 1973, 49 and n. 26). Unlikely are Hardwar, "where Kapila Maharshi did penance" (Ragam 1963, 251), and Kapilavasthu where the Buddha was born in Nepal.

vision by the grace of Yoganidrā, must be part of Kṛṣṇāṃśa's divine plan. Moreover, Kurukṣetra is itself the site of a translation of the end of *Ālhā* into an eighteen-day war that ends the lunar dynasty—this much, straight from the *Mahābhārata*. Rather than a Dasarā subplot, the *Kṛṣṇāṃśacarita* overlays a Kurukṣetra supraplot on *Ālhā*—whatever *Ālhā* its author knew.

It is, however, not just *Mahābhārata* correlations—the aṃśas, the vaṃśas, the site, the duration, and perhaps a few coincidences—that interest this paurāṇika about what we might now call Kurukṣetra II. What consumes him is the Agnivaṃśa, evidently a non-*Mahābhārata* subject.[2] Kurukṣetra II is the site of his unfolding of what I have called a master plan on this very subject, one that he intertwines with an Agnivaṃśa frame story. I distinguish the Delhi-Kanauj rivalry as prologue from the frame itself, which will be discussed in section B of this chapter and in chapter 9. As we shall see, the paurāṇika *interprets* the Delhi-Kanauj rivalry *within this frame* as an intra-Agnivaṃśa feud. But first the plan.

As just outlined, Brahmānanda's trip to Delhi with Mahīpati (Māhil) to bring Velā "home" is one of the few points in common between the closing episodes of the Elliot *Ālhā* and the *Kṛṣṇāṃśacarita*. But things are different from the start. The war-opening adhyāya creates a few *Mahābhārata* echoes. After meditating on the goddess Śivā, Candrabhaṭṭa, "equal to Candra (*candratulyam*)," tells Pṛthivīrāja how to dispose of his anxieties about Kṛṣṇāṃśa: "Born at Mahobā as a portion of Jiṣṇu [Arjuna], Brahmānanda, Kṛṣṇāṃśa's best friend (*sakhaḥ śreṣṭhaḥ*), is always disposed to that dear one. When that son of Malanā [Malhnā] dies, then all the divine aṃśas will return to their destinations."[3] This reverses matters in the *Mahābhārata*, where it is Kṛṣṇa's death—as Vyāsa tells Arjuna—that signals the "great departure" of the Pāṇḍavas (16.9.25-36). Mahīpati and Pṛthivīrāja seize upon this news to concoct a plot to get to Brahmānanda through Malanā. Deceived by her brother's treachery, Malanā vouchsafes her son's departure under the illusion that Mahīpati will provide him safe escort to and back from Delhi. "Bewildered by divine māyā" (*mohitā devamāyayā*) and swearing on the reliability of her brother (*bandhu*), she overrides Parimala's protests that "Mahīpati is very cunning, and has arisen for my destruction" (31.16-17). Mahīpati, arch-Agnivaṃśin and incarnation of Duryodhana, is thus more at the center of things than ever, able to draw his sister into a scheme that is not his

[2]The *Mbh* does refer to Kirātas, mountaineer warrior-hunters (it is one of the same whom Śiva impersonates to wrestle with Arjuna in the *Kairātaparvan*), as "fire-born" (*agniyonija*; 7.87.30); so too is Draupadī's brother Dhṛṣṭadyumna born from fire. But there is no evidence of a vaṃśa or a vaṃśa myth.

[3]31.1-6, closing: *tadā te sarvadevāṃśā gamiṣyanti yato gatāḥ*.

alone, but part of a divine māyā that, as Candrabhaṭṭa has earlier seen, is spun not only by the goddess but by Kṛṣṇāṃśa.

Malanā is not Mahīpati's only sister. As in *Ālhā*, Agamā (Agmā), a second, is married to Pṛthivīrāja. Agamā is thus also Brahmānanda's mother's sister. When Brahmānanda arrives in Delhi, he finds this maternal aunt and her seven daughters-in-law where they have come at evening to the royal temple. The daughters-in-law are the wives (or, in three cases, widows since the battle of Kīrtisāgara) of Pṛthivīrāja and Agamā's seven sons. Each of the seven is an incarnate Kaurava.[4] The Elliot *Ālhā* tells us about the seven sons, and even about the deaths of three of them at the battle of Kīratsāgar. But it does not know them as Kauravāṃśas, and says nothing of their wives.[5]

The women, close kin that they are, greet Brahmānanda warmly. But his conversation with the Kauravāṃśa wives and widows turns sour. The four wives, wishing him a happy marriage but to leave their husbands unharmed, say this "arrow-made word": "Listen attentively. Your wife Velā, possessing the form of strife, is Kālī herself (*tava patnī svayaṃ kālī velā kalaharūpiṇī*). Destroy our husbands and we will be very miserable" (31.25).[6] Brahmānanda does not respond directly, but addresses the three widows. In a "speech versed in śruti and smṛti," he taunts them with the decline of satī practice from yuga to yuga—a rebuke at their having survived their husbands. Not only that, he invites them as women of the Kali yuga, the worst of times in which "there is no satī vow" and widows "enjoy another man," to "enjoy taintless happiness together with me" (27-32)! Impervious to the reproach, the widows shamelessly put on their best jewels and try to embrace him. Brahmānanda steps up the insults: "The husbands who were slain by my brother are freed/relieved from you (*yuṣmabhiḥ patayo muktā ye ca madbandhunā hatāḥ*)! So I won't take you" (31.35-36).[7] Having heard this "terrible word combined with laughter," the wives (*yoṣitaḥ*: presumably all seven) tell Pṛthivīrāja that the "cunning husband of Velā" destroys their dharma, and should be punished. Pṛthivīrāja then summons Brahmānanda, tells him he comes from "the lowest of royal clans (*bhūpakulādhamaḥ*)," and orders him imprisoned. Hearing this "terrible word," Brahmānanda removes his

[4]Counting Tāraka among the Kaurvāṃśas as a portion of Karna, as the text does (17.3-4).

[5]Except for Tāhar as an incarnation of Karṇa, the Kauravāṃśa identity of Pṛthivīrāja's other six sons was unknown to my Mahobā informants Zahir Singh, Krishna Caurasia, Baccha Singh, and others in his troupe.

[6]In the Elliot *Ālhā*, Brahmā kills three of Prithīrāj's sons on this trip to Delhi (W&G 260).

[7]The kinsman in question is Brahmānanda's brother Ranajit (Ranjit); in the purāna, a dark-limbed portion of the *Mbh*'s Sātyaki (11.8), who slew the three Kauravāṃśas and was then slain himself by Tāraka-Karnāmśa (26.90-100). See chap. 6, n. 90, on Ranjit's death in the Elliot *Ālhā*.

sword and rushes at Pṛthivīrāja, who finds protection from Cāmuṇḍa (36-41).

We meet many scenes of escalating "terrible words." Of this one, let us ask three questions. One, which allows no good (i.e., simple) answer, is whether, given the craziness of his reaction, Brahmānanda has any interest at all in really marrying Velā, this incarnate Kālī who at age twelve demanded a husband who could win her amid waterfalls of blood. His response is far worse than the wives' first arrowy words seem to deserve, softened as they are by good wishes and appeals for peace. If Velā is to be an incarnation of strife, Brahmānanda is her over-willing accessory.

A second question—Why does the paurāṇika "invent" this story?—may have several answers. One, textually convoluted but perhaps beginning to answer our first question, is that Brahmānanda's response provides an opportunity to exalt satī in anticipation of Velā's satī, which becomes a great reversal of the Kali yuga's decadence.[8] Such an exaltation, however, seems to tap into a persistent strain of essentializing distrust about the unsavory lust of widows: not only in the purāṇa, which makes such craving explicit among the three Kauravaṃśa widows, but also in the Elliot *Ālhā*, which leaves open such a shadow-side reading of the widowed Belā's attempt to seduce Ālhā. Not only does Belā test Ālhā to learn whether there is any sin in his heart; so does the dying Brahmā challenge Belā to become a satī to learn whether there is, by implication, any sin in hers.

But another answer to our second question is more straightforward: the paurāṇika's "invention" allows him to ask what is also our third question through the mouths of the listening Ṛṣis: "Of these women, how did their marriages come about? Tell us truly at length (*tattvaṃ no brūhi vistarāt*)" (42). The Ṛṣis give the author plenty of leeway. He will take a hundred and fifteen verses (31.158-32.10) before returning to the tragic end of Velā and Brahmānanda.

It would seem that the whole story is a set-up to make the Ṛṣis curious about the forwardness and degeneracy of the seven Kauravāṃśas' wives. They hear a fascinating vignette about each one. But they also receive information that will help them to understand the war that lies immediately ahead. This information is set forth in table 11.

In the first six cases, each Kauravāṃśa marries the youngest sister of ten brothers, themselves also Kauravāṃśas. The first three women become sexually active—"spoiled" in the conventional idiom—before marriage. Tāraka's future wife is ravaged by a Daitya, and the next two

[8] Both Ālhā and Ūdal commend satī in the *Pṛthvīrāj-rāsau*; see Tod [1829-32, 1920] 1990, 722-23.

Table 11. Wives of Pṛthivīrāja's Kauravāṃśa sons; the women's fathers; fathers' lineages; fathers' kingdoms; fathers' alliance at Kurukṣetra II; day of fathers' deaths there; the wives' prior suitors (rivals for their hands or obstructions to their marriages); number of the wives' Kauravāṃśa brothers; their Kauravāṃśa husbands' names; Kauravas whose aṃśas their husbands incarnate; places of their husbands' deaths

Wife	Suitor-opponent	Her father	Brothers	Lineage	Husband	Kingdom	Aṃśa of	Allied with	Slain at	Day slain
Mādireksanā	Daitya	Māyāvarman	10	Parihāra	Tāraka	Anga	Karna	Pṛthivīrāja	Kuruksetra	3
Prabhāvatī	Yakṣa	Mūlavarman	10	Śukla	Nṛhara	Gurjara	Duḥśāsana	Parimala	Kīrtisāgara	12
Madanāvatī	Gandharva	Kaikaya	10	Candra	Saradana	Kashmir	Uddarṣa	Parimala	Kīrtisāgara	13
Suvelā	Nāga	Nāgavarman	10	Nāga	Mardana	Puṇḍra	Durmukha	Pṛthivīrāja	Kīrtisāgara	4
Kāntimatā	Rākṣasa	Madrakeśa	10	Tomara	Sūryavarman	Madra	Vikarṇa	Pṛthivīrāja	Delhi	4
Vidyunmālā	Paiśāca	Pūrnāmala	10	Śārdūlīya	Bhīma	Magadha	Vivimsati	Pṛthivīrāja	Delhi	12
Kinnarī	x	Maṅkaṇa	8	Kinnara	Varddhana	Rome	Citrabana	Pṛthivīrāja	Delhi	*

* Maṅkana fights on the fifth day but becomes invisible and does not die (he also has a non-Kauravāmśa brother who fights on this day).
x No such story

have liaisons with a Yakṣa and Gandharva. The tone for these three is set by the first, Mādirekṣaṇā, who lives up to the ruder potential of her name —"she of liquory-eyes"—by catching the Daitya's fancy with an "eye that rolled drunkenly (*madāghūrṇitalocanam*)" (31.46-47). The fourth, Suvelā, is not sullied before marriage, but, as a lower counterpart to her namesake Velā—who demands that her suitor must provide her with Draupadī's jewels, which must come from heaven—she demands a snake ornament (*nāgabhūṣaṇam*, 102) that must come from outwitting a serpent king of Nāgaloka. Coming from a Nāga dynasty herself, she has an underworld Nāga to guard the jewel of her virginity. Wives two, three, and four become the debauched widows taunted by Brahmānanda. The fifth, seized by a Rākṣasa (a relative of Vibhīṣaṇa, who is warned to learn a lesson from his older brother Rāvaṇa and stop stealing women[9]), is again a case of defilement, but shortly after marriage rather than before it. And the sixth, Vidyunmālā, "Lightning-wreath," inspires another attempt at postmarital abduction, this one by a Paiśāca-Mleccha-cow-

[9]Rāksasa marriage being evidently no longer in fashion.

slaughterer: that is, a Muslim. This illicit union is thwarted, but only temporarily, as we shall see. Whatever the troubles, the fathers always think of Pṛthivīrāja as having the right sons for their daughters. Each time Pṛthivīrāja, who never questions the women's dubious characters, must also ask the "Banāphars" to rescue the suitors or husbands—that is, to rescue his own inept sons—and help work things out so that the marriages can either occur or be saved. He must then always reward the "Banāphar" heroes with great wealth: the last thing he wants to do, since they are always his enemies.

Finally, the seventh wife breaks some of the pattern, which suggests it has built up to the sixth. She is a virgin from Rome (apparently non-vestal) named Kinnarī ("What-woman?"), and is given by Kubera to the seventh Kauravāṃśa with no "Banāphar" intervention.[10] In her case, it is her origins rather than her lovers (or other rivals to her would-be Kauravāṃśa husband) that is outlandish.

With only seventy-five Kauravāṃśas accounted for so far,[11] we should expect more. But it seems we only reach ninety-eight, adding the sixteen reborn as the Viṣvaksena-clan brothers of Madanamañjarī (who marries the "Banāphar" Sukhakhāni), and the seven reborn as the Tomara brothers of Citrarekhā (one of the wives of Āhlāda's son Indula).

As this small sample already shows, aside from Pṛthivīrāja's seven Kauravāṃśa sons, other Kauravāṃśas have sisters who marry into both sides. The following table shows the connections of women marrying into the Mahobā faction. The first four are the wives of the four leading "Banāphar" heroes; the next three are the outlandish wives of Āhlāda's son Indula; and the last two are the wives of the "Banāphars'" two royal patron-companions. One can note that the author shows no interest in providing a wife for Tālana, the Muslim incarnation of Bhīma, despite the fact that as Mīrā Tālhan, he has nine sons and eighteen grandsons in the Elliot *Ālhā*.

[10] 31.43-157. Her father is the Kiṃnara ("What-man") Maṅkaṇa, "the lord of Rūpadeśa on the further shore from Cīnadeśa (China) and known by the wise as Rūmadeśa (Rome)," where "good-looking (fair-faced? *priyadarśana*) men of the Kiṃnara jāti dwell" (32.44).

[11] Now counting Mahīpati as the portion of Duryodhana, who is one of the hundred in the Mbh, but not counting Tāraka as the portion of Karna, who is not one of the hundred Kaurava sons of Dhṛtarāṣṭra. This total also includes the eight born in Rome as "What-men?" or Kinnaras: sons of Maṃkaṇa and brothers of Kinnarī, who marries the seventh Kauravāṃśa Vardhana. *BhvP* 3.3.32.44-47 lists these eight and says they had the same names in their former births. Seven—Virāvin, Pramāthin, Dīrgharomaka, Dīrghabāhu, Mahābāhu, Vyūdhorā, and Kanakadhvaja—are recognizable names of sons of Dhṛtarāṣṭra, or clear modifications thereof, leaving only the eighth, Prathama, unaccounted for. The passage follows others listing Kauravāṃśa sons arriving with their fathers at Kurukṣetra, but it does not explicitly identify the Roman sons as Kauravāṃśas.

Table 12. Wives of the Mahobā faction; their fathers' lineages, kingdoms, alliances, and days slain; epic-purāṇic heroines whom the wives incarnate; their husbands; whom the husbands incarnate; where and when the husbands are slain

Wife	Her father	Lineage	Kingdom	Alliance	Day slain
Amṃśa of	Husband	Amṃśa of	Slain at	Day slain	
A. Wives of the leading "Banāphar" heroes					
Svarṇavatī	Netrasiṃha	Śārdūlīya	Netrapāla	Mahobā	2
Revatī	Āhlāda	Balarāma	Unslain	immortal	
Puṣpavatī	Mayūradhvaja	Viṣvaksena	Sindhu	Mahobā	1
Rādhā	Kṛṣṇāṃśa	Kṛṣṇa	Kuruksetra	15	
Gajamuktā	Gajasena	Śārdūlīya	Marudhanva	Delhi	2
no one	Balakhāni	Yudhisthira	Śirīsākhya	prewar	
Madanamañjarī	Lahara	Bisena*	Lahari	Delhi	1
no one	Sukhakhāni	Dhṛstadyumna	Śirīsākhya	prewar	
B. Wives of Indula					
Citrarekhā	Abhinandana	Tomara	Bāhlīka	Delhi	#
no one	Indula	Jayanta	Kuruksetra	5	
Padminī	Āryasiṃha	Rākṣasa	Laṅkā	none	0
no one	Indula	Jayanta	same	5	
Padmajā	Bauddhasiṃha	none	Cīnadeśa	none	0
no one	Indula	Jayanta	same	5	
C. Wives of Kanauj and Mahobā princes					
Padminī	Śāradānandana	Visvaksena	Bindugaḍh	none	0
Manideva's wife	Laksana	Nakula	Kurukṣetra	17	
Velā	Pṛthivīrāja	Chauhān	Delhi	Self	postwar
Draupadī	Brahmānanda	Arjuna	Kurukṣetra	16	

* Bisena vaṃśa at 20.2, or Viṣvaksena at 32.16

Abhinandana comes to the war with his eight sons, but there is no mention of their fighting or deaths.

Mythologically, whereas Kauravāṃśa wives are defined by outlandish liaisons or origins, and none are incarnations of epic-purāṇic figures, wives of the Mahobā faction—even the far-flung brides of Indula—are not tainted before or during marriage. Of the four who have prior identities, three (Svarṇavatī, Puṣpavatī, and Velā) remarry the husband of their last lives (a conventional sign of *pativratā* or marital chastity), while the fourth (Padminī) has the same husband (Maṇideva) before and after her marriage to Lakṣaṇa.

As to the Kauravāṃśas whose sisters marry into one or the other of the two factions, one finds the surprise that twenty Kauravāṃśas, the sons of Mūlavarman and Kaikaya,[12] appear to fight on the side of Parimala,

[12]Taking *saputra* as "with sons" rather than "with son," which is how each is described at

presuming that sons always fight on the same sides as their fathers. They are thus pitted against Pṛthivīrāja, the incarnation of Dhṛtarāṣṭra, and Mahīpati, the incarnation of Duryodhana, not to mention most of the other Kauravāṃśas. The author has not interested himself in the Kauravāṃśas' heroics or deaths. He is content to have them make variegated camps "on the bank of the Gangā,"[13] bathe, and depart for the battlefield (32.14-15). Then, after listing them by name as they arrive, he forgets all about them, except for the three remaining sons of Pṛthivīrāja, who die *after* the war, and, of course, Tāraka, who dies on the sixteenth day. Candrabhaṭṭa's insight that Kṛṣṇāṃśa will "slay the portions of the Kauravas" as part of his destruction of the Agnivaṃśa (30.36) seems to tell us all we need to know.

But as we have seen, there is more to the Agnivaṃśa than just Chauhāns and Kauravāṃśas. Of the five marriages made by Pṛthivīrāja's Kauravāṃśa sons that are not outlandish, four are into Agnivaṃśa lineages, while the fifth is with the Kashmir-Kaikaya branch of the Candravaṃśa.[14] And of the five "Banāphar" marriages that are not outlandish, all are into Agnivaṃśa lineages. This is because, even though the paurāṇika seems to have fabricated most if not all of the branch-relations himself, he regards Tomaras ("who have never been included with the 'Agnikula'"[15]) as a branch of Chauhāns, Gurjaras as a Śukla-Caulukya kingdom (even though scholars speak more conventionally of the Gurjara-Pratihāras), Śārdūlīyas as a branch of Parihāra-Pratihāras, and Viṣvaksenas as a branch of Śukla-Caulukyas.[16] This of course means that, at least from the paurāṇika's perspective, Agnivaṃśa and Candravaṃśa kings from all over north India are rushing to Kurukṣetra to meet their deaths: as the *Mahābhārata* would put it, like moths to a flame. In particular, the arriving kings are especially those whose

the point of siding with Parimala (32.57-58). Both have just arrived at Kuruksetra with all ten of their Kauravāṃśa sons, each one named (32.26-33).

[13]The Ganges is quite a distance east of Kurukṣetra, which is west of the Yamuna. The presence of all the Kauravāṃśas on the bank of the Ganges is contrasted with those following Parimala, who camp at Syamantapañcaka near the dying Brahmānanda (32.11-13) —the site of Bhārgava Rāma's numerous destructions of the Kṣatriyas.

[14]Thus ten of the Kauravāṃśas, those born into the Nāgavaṃśa, are not Agnivaṃśins. Despite the fiery poison which the Nāga king exudes to defend the jewel demanded by Suvelā (31.114-16), Nāgas have a different descent.

[15]Baden-Powell 1899, 549; cf. 551-52.

[16]On Viṣvaksenas as Śukla-Caulukyas, Śārdūlīyas as Parihāras, and Tomaras as a Capahāni-Chauhāns in *BhvP*, see Hohenberger 1967, 20-23. On Gurjara-Pratihāras, and their primary claim to Sūryavaṃśa descent, see Thapar 1978a, 188, n. 100; 189, nn. 103 and 104, and, countering the argument that Pratihāras are Gurjaras, R. B. Singh 1975, 108-11. Unlike the *BhvP*'s Śuklas, Cālukyas of Vengi, Bādāmi and Kalyāni all claim solar rather than fire descent (Thapar 1978a, 189, n. 103).

daughters have married partisans of the senior Delhi and Mahobā branches of these lines, which have fatefully intermarried through Velā and Brahmānanda.[17]

Looking at it from the standpoint of these kings, if we define "side" as centered on loyalty to the two principle kings in each party—the Chandēl Parimala and "Caulukya" Jayacandra on the Mahobā side (M); the Chauhān Pṛthivīrāja and the Parihāra Mahīpati on the Delhi side (D)—we obtain the information about the ten daughter-giving kings shown in table 13.

Table 13. Agnivaṃśa and Candravaṃśa kings whose daughters marry Kauravāṃśas or "Banāphars": their Daughters; Kingdoms; Lineages; Sides taken at Kurukṣetra II; Candravaṃśa or Agnivaṃśa lineage alliances (LA) with the Delhi (D) or Mahobā (M) sides; and marriage alliances (MA) with either side through the daughter (and equivalents in Elliot *Ālhā*)

King	Daughter	Kingdom	Lineage	Side	LA	MA
A.						
Māyavarman	Mādireksanā	Anga	Parihāra	D	D	D
Mūlavarman	Prabhāvatī	Gurjara	Śukla	M	M	D
Kaikaya	Madanāvatī	Kashmir	Candra	M	M	D
Madrakeśa	Kāntimatā	Madra	Tomara	D	D	D
Pūrṇāmala (? Pūran)	Vidyunmālā	Magadha (Patna)	Śārdūlīya	D	D	D
B.						
Netrasiṃha (Naipāli)	Svarṇavatī (Sunwā)	Netrapāla (Naināgarh)	Śārdūlīya (Baghēl)	M	D	M
Mayūradhvaja (Narpat)	Puṣpavatī (Phulwā)	Sindhu (Narwar)	Viṣvaksena	M	M	M
Gajasena (Gajrāj)	Gajamuktā (Gajmōtin)	Marudhanva	Śārdūlīya (Bisēn)	D	D	M
Abhinandana (Abhinandan)	Citrarekhā (Chittar-rēkhā)	Bāhlīka (Balkh-Bukhārā)	Tomara	D	D	M
Lahara	Madanamañjarī	Lahari	Viṣvaksena	D	M	M

A. Kings whose daughters marry Kauravāṃśas
B. Kings whose daughters marry "Banāphars"

Three of the four main Agnivaṃśa lineages have branches on both sides: the Chauhāns (including Tomaras), Parihāras (including Śārdūlīyas), and Śukla-"Caulukyas" (including Viṣvaksenas). This is reminiscent of the *Mahābhārata*, where, for instance, Kurus and Yādavas

[17]Note that Laksana's intra-Śukla (Caulukya) marriage is with a family that suffers no mentioned casualties at Kuruksetra II.

split. In four cases, the kings' lineage alliance is consonant with their marriage alliance and side taken: three of them are allied with Delhi (the DDDs: Anga, Madra, and Magadha), one with Mahobā (the MMM: Sindhu or Sind). But in six cases, these affiliations are in conflict. It is uncommon to fight against agnates. In eight out of the ten cases, the lineage alliance is the same as the side chosen. One of the two exceptions is Netrasiṃha, a Śārdūlīya (from a Parihāra branch) who sides with Parimala rather than with the Parihāra Mahīpati. The other is Lahara, a Viṣvaksena (from a Caulukya branch) who sides with Pṛthivīrāja rather than with the "Caulukya" Jayacandra. Let it be noted, however, that where it comes to the clans of the two primary adversaries, no Candravaṃśin fights against Parimala, and no Chauhāns (e.g., Tomaras) fight against Pṛthivīrāja.

It is also more common to fight against affines than agnates. Of the ten, five fight against the side their daughters have married into. In four of these cases, lineage alliances take precedence over marriage alliances. Mūlavarman and Kaikaya, the two kings who override their daughters' marriage alliances with Delhi to fight for Parimala, have lineage ties, respectively, to Kanauj as Śuklavaṃśins ("Caulukyas"), and to Mahobā as Candravaṃśins (Chandēls). And Gajasena of Marudhanva and Abhinandana of Bāhlīka have the same reason for the reverse preference for Pṛthivīrāja: the former is a Śārdūlīya-Parihāra with a tie to Mahīpati, and the Tomaras, as mentioned, are considered to be a branch of the Chauhāns. Netrasiṃha is the only king whose alliance favors his daughter's marital in-laws over his own lineage ties. And Lahara is the only king to break both his lineage ties and his daughter's marriage ties, siding with Pṛthivīrāja to do so. I can only guess that this results from the pull of his having sixteen Kauravāṃśa sons (32.16-18).

Now of these ten kings, only five can be found in the Elliot *Ālhā*. Four of the five are fathers of "Banāphar" brides, and the other a father of one of the "Kauravāṃśa" brides—with the quotation marks to remind us that the purāṇa does not recognize the heroes as Banāphars, and the oral epic does not consider Prithīrāj's seven sons to be Kauravāṃśas.[18] In the latter case, there is no reason to doubt that king Pūran of Paṭnā is king Pūrṇāmala of Magadha. But *Ālhā* gives no indication that Pūran of Paṭnā has a daughter named Vidyunmālā who might have married one of the seven Delhi princes; and, although it makes Pūran an adversary of Jaychand and an ally of Prithīrāj, it does not even mention him among the

[18]There is also a Mannā Gūjar who could be the same as Mūlavarman of Gurjara, but if this were argued, one would have to explain why he is a Mahobā champion at Banāphar marriage scenes (including those of Brahmā and Lākhan) rather than an ally of Prithivīrāj (W&G 33). In any case, Mannā Gūjar has no daughter and no son-in-law in Delhi.

kings who come to the final battle.[19] As for the four fathers of "Banāphar" brides mentioned in *Ālhā*, we have seen that they are famous in both texts for the magical treasures or powers they deploy to discourage their daughters' suitors. Indeed, in the *Kṛṣṇāṃśacarita*, these treasures and powers are the complements, as narrative devices, to the obstacles Pṛthivīrāja faces in securing wives for his Kauravāṃśa sons. In the one case, incarnations of the Pāṇḍavas and their *Mahābhārata* allies overcome outlandish adversaries to complete the marriages that overeager kings have arranged for their ignoble daughters with the incarnate Kaurava sons of Pṛthivīrāja. In the other, the same heroes fight reluctant kings to win their noble daughters as brides for themselves. But whereas the *Kṛṣṇāṃśacarita* knows both types of stories, the Elliot *Ālhā* knows only the latter, and of these, only four of the five in question. It does not, as we have seen, include the marriage of Sulkhān-Sukhakhāni to Madanamañjarī, and it also makes no mention of Madanamañjari's father Lahara.

This whole schema of pitting Agnivaṃśa lineages against each other, first with Pṛthivīrāja and Jayacandra (and Mahīpati in the middle), and then with the kings who intermarry their daughters into the two factions, is thus a *Kṛṣṇāṃśacarita* creation. Indeed, let us recall that there is one more Agnivaṃśin present at Kurukṣetra II: the Paramāra king Gangāsiṃha, from the fourth original Agnivaṃśa line. He rules at Kalpakṣetra and fights for Parimala and dies on the fourteenth day. He too is unknown to the Elliot *Ālhā*. More than this, even when the Elliot *Ālhā* knows the kings in question, they are never described as Agnivaṃśins. Among the senior branch kings, we have already seen that Jayacandra—really a Gāhaḍavāla, but called a Rāṭhoṛ in *Ālhā*—has his Agnivaṃśa "Caulukya" identity pressed upon him. And among the daughter-marrying kings of the junior branches, one hardly hears of their vaṃśa connections at all, much less that they are Agnivaṃśins.[20]

But now we come to a disclosure that the *Kṛṣṇāṃśacarita* has saved for the end of its tale. The holocaust of the Agnivaṃśa is fed not only by the rivalry of Delhi and Kanauj, and by the supporting cast of the ten

[19]Pūran is one of the kings conquered by Ūdal for Jaychand in "The Gānjar War" (W&G 221), and fights on Prithīrāj's side against Kanauj and Mahobā in "The Battle of the Bētwā" (254). The purāna does not parallel these involvements. In Lakṣaṇa's *digvijaya*, which corresponds roughly to the Gānjar War, tax is exacted from Magadha, but its king is Vijayakārin (24.41), not Pūrṇāmala; and Pūrṇāmala makes no appearance at the (somewhat briefly recounted) battle of the Vetravatī (= Bētwā).

[20]Sunwā's father Naipāli of Naināgaṛh's identity as a Baghēl is the only exception. Though they do not appear to do so in *Ālhā*, Baghēls claim to be Agnivaṃśa Rajputs as a branch of Caulukyas or Solankhis, and to have migrated eastward from Gujarat (see chap. 5, § D and Sherring 1872, 156-57).

kings who intermarry their daughters, but by thousands of "little kings." Their first mention occurs after notice is given of the arrival at Kurukṣetra, in clear order of precedence, of all the kings and heroes. Pṛthivīrāja and Parimala (32.9-13), the Kauravāṃśas and the kings who intermarry their daughters (14-50), Lakṣaṇa, Tālana, lesser kings and what may be provincial governors,[21] and the remaining "Banāphars" (Āhlāda, Kṛṣṇāṃśa, and Indula) and Jaganāyaka (54-55) are each described as they arrive by their vaṃśa and/or aṃśa. Last—unnamed, unpedigreed, and undifferentiated—"little kings (*kṣudrabhūpāśca*) augmented by thousands came one by one to Kurukṣetra, the high place (*paraṃ sthānam*), agitated with intoxication (*madavihvalāḥ*)" (32.56). The adjective *kṣudra* connotes not only "little," but "low, base, or cruel," as in *kṣudradevatā*, the "little divinities" who receive inferior offerings, including blood sacrifice. As the two sides draw up to face each other, additional lesser kings arrive to swell the ranks of Pṛthivīrāja, so that as the eighteen-day war begins, he is surrounded by a thousand little kings (*kṣudrabhūmipāḥ*) augmented by a thousand armies, and is able to lead two thousand kings to war (71-73). One is thus given the impression that most of the "little kings" side with Pṛthivīrāja.

Once battle begins, the first thirteen days are orchestrated around the somewhat perfunctory deaths of the kings who intermarry their daughters. They fight and kill each other.[22] But the fourteenth day is special. When Lakṣaṇa kills Pṛthivīrāja's nephew Bhagadatta (174), it signals a "festival of battle (*yuddhamahotsava*)" (178) in which the few lesser kings who are named—including Gangāsiṃha (183), the pedigreed Paramāra Agnivaṃśin who has not married off his daughter—annihilate each other and their ranks: "Then three thousand kings, augmented by thousands, one by one, little kings against little kings, three thousand came together. All were slain by one another, having made frightful war."[23] The fourteenth day's battle in the *Mahābhārata*, described in the *Jayadrathavadha* and *Ghaṭotkacavadha* subparvans of the *Droṇa Parvan*, is likewise its text's vastest canvas for depicting the deaths of lesser kings. Arjuna slays countless kings and their supporters to complete his vow to kill Jayadratha on that day; the Kauravas kill many in trying to defend

[21]32.51-53. The Yādava rulers Vīrasena and Kāmasena (Candrāvalī's husband); Lakṣaṇa's Kanauj retainers Dhānyapāla and Lallasimha who may be among the "maṇḍalīkas" he mentions as numerous in his kingdom (3.3.10.12; cf. chap 7, n. 70).

[22]See tables 11 and 12, showing that their deaths occur on days 1-4 and 12-13, with day 5 marked for the disappearance of the Roman-Kinnara king Maṅkaṇa and Indula (32.130-42). Days 6-11 feature elephant fights and mostly inconclusive duels, with the exception being the death of Dhundhukāra, Pṛthivīrāja's oldest brother (143-62).

[23]32.184c-85: *triśatāni tato bhūpāḥ sahasrādhyāḥ pṛthakpṛthak// kṣudrabhūpāḥ kṣudrabhūpāṃs triśatāni samāyuyuḥ/ anyonyena hatāḥ sarve kṛtvā yuddham bhayānakam.*

Jayadratha; and the battle rages into the night for the killing of Ghaṭotkaca. Indeed, it is on this day that Jayadratha's father "Old Kṣatra" (Vṛddhakṣatra) dies: an emblem of the "old Kṣatriya order" that dies with him, as the "little kings" of the Agnivaṃśa die with the old order of the Agnivaṃśa Rajputs.[24]

Finally, after Kurukṣetra II is over—recall that the chief events of days fifteen through eighteen were summarized at the beginning of this chapter—Kali bows to the immortal Āhlāda, acknowledges him as Yogeśvara, and continues: "In the Kali yuga, coming all alone, by you the burden of the earth has been lifted (*bhuvo bhārastvayā hṛtaḥ*). Having slain all five thousand little kings severally (*hatvā tān pañcasāhasrān kṣudrabhūpān anekaśaḥ*), the Pāvakīya (Fire-lineage) kings, endowed with tapas and strength, you remained in the midst of yoga when so many were killed. . . . Tell me what boon your heart desires" (32.223-25).

Until this last adhyāya, the *Kṛṣṇāṃśacarita* has kept silent about the little kings. But if they have not been explicitly mentioned, we have had hints of their presence. One was Pṛthivīrāja's warning that if Parimala does not yield the four flying horses, "all the army lords will go to destruction by the fire of Velā."[25] Velā, Kālī incarnate to her sisters-in-law, is also a fire at the heart of the Agnivaṃśa. Kings big and little are consumed in her fire: like the "entire warrior class (*kṣatra*)" that is destined for destruction, according to a heavenly announcement, at the birth of Draupadī. As the conversation between Kali and Āhlāda suggests, the little kings are at the heart of Kurukṣetra II as the *mass-victims* of its "festival of battle." The phrase *yuddhamahotsava* echoes *Devī Māhātmyam* 2.55, where it is used to describe the battle between Durgā and Mahiṣāsura. The echo is another sign that as Kurukṣetra II concludes the mission of the aṃśas of Kṛṣṇa and Balarāma, it redefines oral *Ālhā* folklore through the goddess's Sanskrit textuality.

We also see here at last some of the things that the paurāṇika has done with Āhlāda's incarnation of Balarāma. As Balarāma's incarnation, Āhlāda is referred to as Śeṣāṃśa, "portion of Śeṣa" (23.133). In this he is like Balarāma himself, who is an incarnation of the world serpent Śeṣa, the "Remainder," also known as Ananta, the "Endless," who provides the serpent-couch upon which Viṣṇu awakens to regenerate the triple world after each occasional dissolution (*pralaya*), or night of Brahmā. The paurāṇika's translation would seem to connect Āhlāda's immortality, unique among the destinies of the story's aṃśas, with Ananta's infinity, and his lifting of the earth's burden with the world serpent's upholding of the earth. Āhlāda would also seem to have been invested with

[24]See Biardeau 1978, 169; Hiltebeitel 1988a, 404-5, 416, and forthcoming.

[25]24.12: *no cedvelāgninā sarve kṣayam yāsyanti sainyapāḥ.*

Balarāma's aspect of Saṃkarṣaṇa, the *vyūha* or aspect of Viṣṇu that replicates the destructive power of Rudra-Śiva. To have lifted the burden of the earth, the hidden king has become a destroyer.

B. The Establishment of Kali and the Last of the Little Kings

When he praises Āhlāda for relieving the burden of the earth, Kali is at the point of achieving what I have called his second establishment. In the *Pratisarga Parvan*, the Kali yuga does not begin (as in most purāṇas and in some *Mahābhārata* passages) with the end of the *Mahābhārata* war. Rather, as we shall see, it begins with the Flood. But there is also a sense that the Kali yuga *truly* begins with the end of the *Kṛṣṇāṃśacarita* as the result of Kṛṣṇa's promise at the beginning of this text, in his answer to Śiva at the end of the *Mahābhārata* war, that he will "establish" Kali by the destruction of the Agnivaṃśa. Kṛṣṇa will truly establish Kali in the Kali yuga through the "Banāphars," who include "portions" of the Pāṇḍavas, and Kṛṣṇāṃśa, the "śakti of his own avatāra," and he will do this "for the increase of the Kalidharma (or, the dharma of Kali)."[26]

In making his promise using causatives of the verb *sthā*, "to establish," with the name of the yuga—*sthāpayiṣyāmi vai kalim* (1.34); *sthāpayitvā kalim bhuvi* (30.36)—Kṛṣṇa echoes his own famous statement in *Bhagavad Gītā* 4.7-8 that, as Lord of yoga, he saves the world by his repeated avatars. But here, rather than working "for the establishment of dharma from yuga to yuga,"[27] he establishes the yuga by enabling adharma, of which Kali is the exemplar. But of course, "subtle" as such matters are—*sūkṣmo dharmaḥ*, "subtle dharma," is a repeated *Mahābhārata* refrain—adharma is the Kali yuga's true dharma. Just as he restores dharma (mixed with adharma) through the Pāṇḍavas, so he increases adharma (mixed with dharma) through their aṃśas. Yet in either case, he enables an "establishment of Kali."

The *Kṛṣṇāṃśacarita* plays out this second establishment of Kali through an Agnivaṃśa frame story that brings us back not only to the līlā of Kṛṣṇāṃśa and the Delhi-Kanauj rivalry of the text's prologue, but the thin presence of the Paramāras as the fourth of the chief Agnivaṃśa lineages. As we shall see, the Paramāras provide a thread that runs through the *Kṛṣṇāṃśacarita* between the past and future reaches of its Agnivaṃśa frame. Glimpsing for a moment this glorious past as it frames events prior to the *Kṛṣṇāṃśacarita*, the dwindled Paramāra line is named after Pramara, the first Paramāra, born from a fire pit on Mount Abu

[26] 2.3: *janiṣyante tadaṃśā vai kalidharma-vivṛddhaye*.
[27] *BhG* 4.8: *dharmasaṃsthāpanārthāya sambhavāmi yuge yuge*.

(3.1.6.45-7.4). Of Pramara's three greatest descendants, all mentioned when the Paramāras are counted among the Agnivaṃśa lineages in the *Pratisarga Parvan*'s fourth *khaṇḍa* (3.4.1.22-32), only the third seems to have actually been a Paramāra, and the earlier two, originally unrelated and probably fictional, connected with the third retrospectively. The first, number six or seven from Pramara, is the illustrious emperor Vikramāditya;[28] the second, the almost equally famous emperor Śālivāhana; and the third Bhojarāja. I will discuss the *Pratisarga Parvan*'s treatment of these kings in chapter 9. For now, what matters is that once the *Kṛṣṇāṃśacarita* moves on from its prologue, in which Śiva's curse and Kṛṣṇa's intercession set "*Ālhā*" destinies for the *Mahābhārata*'s heroes and heroines, it begins to draw this frame into its "Agnivaṃśa" rivalries by picking up Gangāsiṃha as a descendant of these grand Paramāras (3.2-3).

Gangāsiṃha rules virtuously (*dharmatas*) at Kalpakṣetra in the Antarvedi or Doab as a vassal of Jayacandra (4.1-4). He is not the only virtuous Agnivaṃśin, and that is how the thinned-down Paramāra thread is now woven into the Agnivaṃśa tapestry. While Gangāsiṃha begins his rule at Kalpakṣetra, the Tomara king Anangapāla of Indraprastha, who will be the grandfather of both Pṛthivīrāja and Jayacandra through his two daughters (5.1-12), is expanding the sway of the Chauhāns. In this way, as "many other kings became lords of villages and kingdoms (*grāmarāṣṭrapāḥ*), the Agnivaṃśa expanded its power (*agnivaṃśasya vistaro babhūva balavattaraḥ*): in Kapilasthāna to the east, in Vāhīka (Bāhlīka) to the west, in Cīnadeśa (China) to the north, in Setubandha (in Tamilnadu) to the south. Sixty lākhs of kings, powerful lords of villages, performers of Agnihotras, desiring the welfare of cows and Brahmans, became skilled in doing dharma like (the kings of the) Dvāpara (yuga). Time turned everywhere as it was known in the Dvāpara. In every house was wealth, among all people dharma, in every village a god, in every country sacrifice. On all sides the Mlecchas held the law of the Āryas."[29] Although we do not hear them called little kings, we realize now, from knowing the outcome of the *Kṛṣṇāṃśacarita*, that these six million rulers of kingdoms and villages are precisely the little Agnivaṃśa kings who will be decimated at Kurukṣetra II. Moreover, their legion extends to Vāhīka and China, from which, it now appears, intrusions of Mahāmada and the Buddhist king Nyūnapati-Bauddhasiṃha's are only further signs of the lack of distinction between Āryas and Mlecchas in

[28]According to Sherring 1872, 48, however, Paramāras (Ponwars) of Ghazipur District trace eighty-six generations from Raja Bikramadat (Vikramāditya).

[29]4.6-10, closing: *grāmegrāme sthito devo deśedeśe sthito makhaḥ/āryadharmakarā mlecchā babhuvuḥ sarvatomukhāḥ.*

this Agnivaṃśa expanse.[30]

Having seen the Mlecchas devoted to Ārya dharma, the terrible (*ghora*) Kali goes with the terror-striking Mlecchas (*mlecchayā saha bhīrukaḥ*) to the Blue Mountain (Nīlādri) and seeks refuge in Hari. Seeing the eternal Rādhā and Kṛṣṇa in Vṛndavana after twelve years of meditation, Kali lauds Hari and makes an appeal: "'My sons known as Mlecchas have taken on the character of Āryadharma. My fourfold home—dice, wine, gold, and laughter among women—is destroyed by the Agnivaṃśa Kṣatriyas.[31] Having abandoned my body, family (kula), and kingdom, having meditated on your feet and arms, O Janārdana, I stand in your refuge.' Having heard this, Lord Kṛṣṇa spoke, laughing aloud, 'Oh Kali, for your protection I will take birth in Mahobā. When my aṃśa reaches the earth, it will destroy this great power; it will establish the Mlecchavaṃśa kings on earth (*mlecchavaṃśasya bhūpālān sthāpayiṣyati bhūtale*).' Having thus spoken, Bhagavān disappeared. Then Kali, together with the Mlecchas, obtained supreme joy" (4.11-21). Kṛṣṇāṃśa's destruction of the Candravaṃśa and the Agnivaṃśa is thus not only a second "establishment of Kali," but an "establishment of the Mlecchavaṃśa." On the face of it, the Agnivaṃśa must be destroyed because its virtuous rule and vast spread to both foreign lands and little kingdoms have erased the boundaries between Āryas and Mlecchas. The dharma of Mlecchas, after all, is not to be Ārya but Mleccha.

Kṛṣṇāṃśa's promise to Kali leads also to a pact with the Asura Bali. We return to the story of Vidyunmālā, daughter of king Pūrṇāmala of Magadha and wife of the sixth Kauravāṃśa, where we left her at the beginning of this chapter: awaiting capture by a Muslim. When Bhīma, the sixth son of Pṛthivīrāja, brings this beautiful bride back to Delhi, "the great lord (*mahīpatiḥ*) Sahoda, stationed in Paiśāca country with ten thousand Mlecchas, rose up for Vidyunmālā's sake. At the command of Bali, he reached that auspicious place, Kurukṣetra. Having broken images of the gods, he mixed tīrtha-water with cow blood."[32] Sahoda sends a messenger to Pṛthivīrāja with a challenge to fight for Vidyunmālā. The "virtuous" Pṛthivīrāja, considering himself under the yoke of Cauryadeśa (the Land of Thieves?), goes to Kurukṣetra with an army of three hundred thousand. He fights a terrible war with Sahoda, and then with Bali too, who comes at night with a host of Daityas from the underworld, Pātāla, to destroy and devour (*bhakṣayitvā*) the Delhi army. Smitten with

[30] On the importance and problematics of "distinction" between classes of beings in the *Mbh*, see Hiltebeitel forthcoming.

[31] 4.16c-17: *matputrāśca smrtā mlecchā āryyadharmatvamāgatāh// caturgehaṃ ca me svāmin dyūtam madyaṃ suvarnakam/ strī hāsyaṃ cāgnivaṃśaiśca ksatriyaiśca vināśitam.*

[32] 31.140-41, closing: *bhittvā mūrtīh surāṇām goraktaistīrthajalam krtam.*

fear, Pṛthivīrāja calls on Śāradā for refuge, and the five "Banāphars," called here "high-powered gods" (*devāḥ*), arrive in a moment.[33] They slay thousands of Daityas and gratify Bali with their swords, leading him to offer them a boon. They reply, "These Daityas, let them not come with you to Āryadeśa. Having obtained Mlecchadeśa forever, devour those who go by the Mlecchadharma."[34] These "terrible, disagreeable words" do not please Bali. He tries to get them softened by praising Kṛṣṇāṃśa, who then dictates the terms of another international treaty: "So long as I am dwelling on earth, that long may you dwell at home. Having come to earth after that, do as is fit" (31.152). Hearing this, Sahoda returns to Paiśāca country; Bali goes back to Rasātala; and Pṛthivīrāja, relieved at the outcome, rewards the "Banāphars" for the sixth and last time in connection with the marriages of his seven sons (142-54).

Sahoda and Bali do not forget this treaty. On the morning of the eighteenth day of Kurukṣetra II, Kali comes to collect the "fruit" of his efforts. He praises Āhlāda, telling him he is truly named for bringing joy. In return for this, and for lifting the burden of the earth through the destruction of the five thousand little kings, Kali offers Āhlāda a boon (32.222-26). Āhlāda then asks the "god" (*deva*) Kali that his fame (*kīrti*) will be spread among people; and, saying he will do Kali's "unequaled work," he makes what seems an odd request: "Mahīrāja [Pṛthivīrāja] is filled with Śivabhakti and is a soul of virtue (*dharmātmā*). His eyes, which are blue in color, should purify me. Blue is always dear to you (*tava priyaḥ*); so too is it dear to me—giving misery (*duḥkha*) to the gods, O god, and increasing the joy of the Daityas" (227-29). Saying this, Āhlāda duels with Pṛthivīrāja, each fighting on their elephants, and when the elephants kill each other and go to heaven, he chases the fleeing king and seizes him by the hair. Then "the great blue given by Kali was put into his (presumably Āhlāda's) eyes."[35] From then on Śiva withdraws his protection from the "impure though still dear king

[33]The two heroic sons of Deśa (Āhlāda and Kṛṣṇāṃśa), of Vatsa (Balakhāni and Sukhakhāni), and Devasiṃha are each accounted for (31.148). This war is thus "dated" before the death of Balakhāni.

[34]31.150: *āryadeśaṃ ca te daityā nāgacchantu tvayā saha/ mlecchadeśam sadā prāpya bhakṣadhvaṃ mlecchadharmagān.*

[35]32.243cd: *kalidattaṃ mahānīlaṃ netrayos tena tatkṛtam.* In making what sense I can of this confusing but important passage, I have drawn on the Hindi translation of *BhvP* by Śarma (1968, 2:156-58), kindly translated for me by Balaji Hebbar. Śarma, however, takes what is "dear" to Kali and Āhlāda as their own eyes, with the result that Āhlāda asks Kali for blue eyes that are not only like Pṛthivīrāja's, but like Kali's. Śarma bafflingly then has the "great blue given by Kali" finally put "into the eyes of Mahīrāja." The Sanskrit, however, may just be saying that blue is dear to Kali and Āhlāda as a dark color of the Kali yuga (cf. Hiltebeitel [1976] 1990, 62-63).

(*aśuddhaṃ nṛpatiṃ priyam*)," and goes to Kailāsa. And Āhlāda, escorted by Kali, departs this world for the Plantain Forest (*kadalīvanam*) on Mount Gandhamadana to dedicate himself to yoga and remain immortal (230-36).

Seeing him so engaged, Kali, filled with gladness, leaves Āhlāda. He goes to Bali, and then comes with him and a host of Daityas to Gaura Deśa (probably Ghor/Ghur in Afghanastan, and not Bengal) to tell Sahoda (now called Sahoḍḍīna): "Go with your forces, protected by me at night. Having slain Pṛthivīrāja, seize Vidyunmālā" (239). It does not seem to be an impetuous passion. Sixteen years later,[36] Sahoḍḍīna conquers Pṛthivīrāja's (remaining) sons at Kurukṣetra. Summoning Mahīpati, he challenges Mahobā and plunders its wealth, but goes home after he is unable, despite efforts, to obtain a "lingam" in the Kīrtisāgara (32.240-42)—probably the philosophers' stone, which in the Elliot *Ālhā*, at least, was thrown there by Malhnā to remain forever after the desolation of Mahobā (W&G 273). Jayacandra, out of grief for his "son" (i.e., his nephew Lakṣaṇa), stops eating, becomes an ascetic (*yati*), and goes to heaven after a terrible battle with Sahoḍḍīna (243-44). And after several battles with Sahoḍḍīna, Pṛthivīrāja is captured, but dies unbound, slain at his own command by Candrabhaṭṭa with a luminous arrow, whereupon Candrabhaṭṭa burns in fire.[37]

Although the paurāṇika's version differs, and may indeed be old, he seems to allude to the *Pṛthvīrāj-rāsau*'s story that when Pṛthvīrāj was captured by Shihāb al-Dīn/Shihabuddin (whom we have been hearing of as Sahoda-Sahoḍḍīna, and who is also known as Muhammad Ghori or Muhammad of Ghor) and taken to Ghazna in Afghanistan, he was blinded in prison and eventually able, with Chand's clever help, to kill his captor with his talent of shooting at a target through hearing alone.[38] But if so, the paurāṇika's strange encapsulation has another focus. It seems that Pṛthivīrāja's blue eyes were "given by Kali," and that, with Kali's boon, Āhlāda is purified by the last look those eyes give before Śiva withdraws from the king's protection—perhaps foreshadowing Pṛthivīrāja's eventual blinding. In any event, the story that Shihāb al-Dīn lusted for Vidyunmālā, a daughter-in-law of Pṛthivīrāja, seems to be unknown outside the *Bhaviṣya Purāṇa*. Moreover, it is highly intriguing that while Chand Bardai claims Rajput credit for the assassination of Shihāb al-Dīn, the Ismā'īlīs claimed credit for it as well. In such accounts, after Shihāb al-

[36]Most sources place the final battle with Prthivīrāj, which comes still later, only eleven years after "Kuruksetra II."

[37]12.245-46. Through all this, the text is obscure and allusive, and not much clarified by Śarma 1968, 2:158-59.

[38]Pritchett 1980, 67-73. Cf. Vaidya 1926, 338; D. Sharma 1940, 741-42.

Dīn forced the submission of the Nizārī Ismā'īlīs of Quhistān in Persia and massacred those in Sind, the Nizārīs "claimed responsibility for the act."[39] Most interesting is one source which says that the "killers were half of them circumcised and half uncircumcised," by which "it has been suggested that the Ismâ'îlîs got together on the job with a certain Indian tribe which was also accused, having recently been subdued by him" (Hodgson 1955, 213). Nizārī missions into India through Sind during the Alamūt period (1090-1256) are at the heart of doubled Muslim-Hindu narratives that we shall explore further in chapters 10 and 11.

C. Duryodhana's Return

Thus Kali achieves his "establishment" through his Mleccha "sons," the Mlecchavaṃśa. Pṛthivīrāja achieves the destruction of the Candravaṃśa. And Kṛṣṇāṃśa achieves the destruction of the Agnivaṃśa. Or so it seems. For we cannot be sure of everything in this Kṛṣṇāṃśalīlā. Something has been left open. Mahīpati is still alive. As we have seen, he is the aṃśa of Duryodhana. And Duryodhana, in the *Mahābhārata*, is the aṃśa of Kali.

If we look back over the career of Mahīpati, of this incarnation of an incarnation of Kali, it is not hard to detect that he has worked hand-in-hand with most of these "higher" purāṇic designs: especially those of Kali himself. Mahīpati's scheming can be suspected to be motivated historically by the displacement of the Parihāras not only from Mahobā but Kanauj. He also always upholds the principle of caste hierarchy and the purity of Kṣatriya lines. Although he deceives Pṛthivīrāja as readily, if not as often, as he does Parimala, he has married his two sisters to them. He has thus married them to two of the three highest kings possible (Jayacandra being the third), but he clearly resents his subordination to the lunar Chandēls, whom he has taught Pṛthivīrāja to regard as "the lowest of royal clans" (*bhūpakulādhamaḥ*) because of their affiliation with the "Banāphars." Having opposed all marriages "down" by Agnivaṃśin kings to the low "Banāphars" themselves, he must indeed question Malanā's marriage to Parimala, and perhaps even Agamā's marriage to Pṛthivīrāja, since the latter is ultimately only an Agnivaṃśin who is forced to marry his own Kauravāṃśa sons to the most outlandish and degrading women imaginable, and his daughter "down" to a Chandēl.

Disdaining the Candravaṃśins and the intermarrying Agnivaṃśins, Mahīpati nonetheless allies himself with Pṛthivīrāja. Now in the *Kṛṣṇāṃśacarita*, Pṛthivīrāja is the incarnation of Dhṛtarāṣṭra, the *Mahābhārata*'s blind king and father of Duryodhana, whom Mahīpati

[39] Daftary 1990, 404; cf. Kassam 1995, 62.

himself incarnates. As Duryodhana plays on the blindness of Dhṛtarāṣṭra in the *Mahābhārata*, so Mahīpati plays on that of Pṛthivīrāja, who becomes literally blind in the end of the story.[40] Like Duryodhana, Mahīpati is thus a great leveler, undermining the hierarchical principles he supposedly stands for.

It is thus altogether fitting that Mahīpati ends up "established" as a vassal of Mleccha kings ruling *from Mahobā*. In the wider terms of the *Pratisarga Parvan*'s world history of north India, Mahīpati and the Parihāras are the Agnivaṃśa's only true survivors. Once the *Kṛṣṇāṃśa-carita* is over, the *Pratisarga Parvan*'s fourth khaṇḍa begins by tracing each of the four Agnivaṃśa lines from its origins to its end at Kurukṣetra II, and on into the medieval "future" of its "remnants."[41] The first four adhyāyas of khaṇḍa four end with a wind-up on each of the Agnivaṃśa lineages. For the Paramāras, once Gangāsiṃha dies childless at Kurukṣetra, caste-mixing becomes widespread among Paramāra women, and their Kṣatriya remnants (*śeṣās kṣatriyās*) all act like Vaiśyas and are equal to Mlecchas.[42] For the Chauhāns, once Pṛthivīrāja falls to Shihāb al-Dīn (now spelled Sahoddīna), the wives of the fallen Rājanyas carry on mixed-caste unions with Piśācas and Mlecchas, and produce offspring who are neither Āryas nor Mlecchas, but Jaṭṭas (no doubt Jats) and Mehanas (probably Meos)—although "here and there remnants are born as Capahāni (Chauhān) Kṣatriyas."[43] For the "Caulukya"-Śuklas, not

[40]See above at n. 38.

[41]As the bard (*sūta*) puts it in launching his account, "Listen at length to the account of the kings of the Agnivaṃśa (*agnivaṃśanṛpānām ca caritraṃ śṛṇu vistarāt*)" (3.4.1.13).

[42]3.4.1.45-46. Cf. Vaidya 1924, 116: Paramāras "have left very few representatives at the present day"; with "minor chiefs only," some branches "have now become Mahomedans."

[43]3.4.2.26-28, closing: *kvacitkvacicca ye śeṣāḥ kṣatriyāś capahānijāḥ*. Curiously, after saying such offspring were neither Ārya nor Mleccha, *BhvP* 3.4.2.28 tells that Jattas are known as Ārya and Mehanas as Mleccha. Meos (Meds, Meṛs, Mewatis) of Mewat in eastern Rajasthan and Bharatpur, from their earliest-known twelfth-century history, are linked, often adversarially, with Jats, and maintained a "dialogic" Hindu-Muslim identity up to Partition (Mayaram 1997, 27-30, 255-60; cf. chap. 1, n. 2). Early ethnographers called them Mairs (Tod [1829-32] 1972, 1:538-43: mountaineer "marauders," some in the north having become Muslims), or Meds and Meṛs, as described along with the Jats among the "Panjāb Rājputs" by Baden-Powell (1899, 533-40). Straddling a "so-called [Hindu-Muslim] faultline" (Mayaram 1997, 47), they have a history and folklore of resisting state regimes, whether Mughal, British imperial, Hindu, or Sikh, and now face both hinduizing and islamizing "religious nationalisms" (32 and *passim*). In recent folklore, their lawyer-spokesman Yasin Khan depicts a Rajput identity for their clans (one "*agnīvamś*"-Chauhān; others lunar from the Pāṇḍavas, solar from Rāma, Yaduvaṃśa from Kṛṣna, and one "small"; 131), despite opposition from the Alwar king, who views them as Śūdra and Dalit (Chamar), and not originally from India (126-36, 146). The king, Maharaja Jai Singh of Alwar (1882-1937), actually espoused a high Rajput nationalist rhetoric, Rām rājya state ritualism, and ties with Arya Samaj and Sanatan Dharma campaigns to "reconvert" Muslims

only do Jayacandra and Lakṣaṇa die sonless, but "all their chief Kṣatriya warriors were destroyed at Kurukṣetra"; henceforth "little-king remnants arose through caste-mixing" and were "corrupted" by Mlecchas.[44]

But for the Parihāras, when "all the Kṣatriyas were slain at Kurukṣetra, Mahīpati became the king of Mahobā. He then ruled the kingdom with Shihāb al-Dīn (Sahoddīna) for twenty years. Those who were partisans of the portion of Duryodhana died at Kurukṣetra."[45] Not only that, a descendant of the Parihāras' Śārdūlīya branch, Ghoravarman, rules in Kalanjara, formerly the great fort of the Chandēls, where he establishes a kingdom that continues by the grace of Mahāmāyā.[46] The Agnivaṃśa is thus doomed, with these major Parihāra and minor Chauhān exceptions, to merge into a great mixed-caste mass of Vaiśyas, Mlecchas, and little kings, the latter unpedigreed but for the name. Through the collusion of Kṛṣṇāṃśa, Āhlāda, Kali, Bali, Mahīpati, and the Mlecchas, they can no longer resist the establishment of Kali, now that their predecessors, the five thousand little Agnivaṃśa kings of Kurukṣetra II, have been annihilated.[47]

In terms of the *Kṛṣṇāṃśacarita*'s working of *Ālhā*'s folk *Mahābhārata* back into "true" Sanskritic idioms, this purāṇic complex would seem to center on a precise indexical translation. Mahīpati, incarnation of an incarnation of Kali, is both a remnant of the Candravaṃśa and a remnant of the Agnivaṃśa. Kṛṣṇāṃśa's mission to destroy the Agnivaṃśa *has* entailed saving a Candravaṃśa remnant after all: not via any of the Pāṇḍava "portions" who sided with the Chandēls, but via the king of the Kauravas, rerouted through an Agnivaṃśa detour by his reincarnation in Mahīpati, who survives Kurukṣetra II for a brief rule from Mahobā at the call of Shihāb al-Dīn. This would seem to be one more meaning of the "establishment of Kali": a collusion not only of Kali and Bali, but of a portion of Kali through a portion of Duryodhana. How fitting that Duryodhana, Kali incarnate, should share in the "establishment of Kali,"

---

and "purify" them, along with Dalits (54-71). Recall that Kishan Sharma places Mīrā Tālhan's tomb in Alwar, and links his "invasion" of India with those of Mahmud of Ghazna and Shihāb al-Dīn (chap. 6, n. 80).

[44]3.78-79: *sarve te ksatriyā mukhyāḥ kuruksetre layam gatah . . . śesāstu kṣudrabhūpālā varnsaṃkarasambhavāḥ . . . dūsitāḥ*.

[45]4.35-36: *kurukṣetre mṛtim prāptāh suyodhanakalāmśakāḥ*.

[46]4.37-39; for further details, see Hohenberger 1967, 19-23.

[47]The paurāṇika taps into traditions about Rajput lineages that are also reported by Sherring: various clans tracing their reduced history and migrations through changed conditions resulting from the conflicts between Prithīrāj, Jaychand, Parmāl, and Shihāb al-Dīn; Paramāras, Chauhāns, and other clans becoming degraded, or having many among them convert to Islam (1872, 148-49, on Paramāras; 160-62, on Chauhāns; 125-211, on numerous references to clan histories linked with Pṛthvīrāj and Jaychand). Cf. Wright 1873, 34-37, on manuscripts recounting Chandēl migrations after these events.

9 Time-Routes through the Kṛṣṇāṃśacarita

The *Bhaviṣya Purāṇa*, or "Purāṇa of the Future," is above all about time. The term *pratisarga*, referring to "secondary or continuous creation," defines one of the five traditional topics of a purāṇa.[1] It bears this meaning in the title of the *Bhaviṣya*'s third book, the *Pratisarga Parvan*. Bonazzoli, as cited in chapter 7, is no doubt right that this parvan best defines the purāṇa's futurist agenda, and that it has been subject to repeated updating, although I will question his view of how this took place with regard to the present text.

The *Kṛṣṇāṃśacarita*, embedded in the *Pratisarga Parvan*'s Agnivaṃśa frame story, tells of the destruction of the Agni and Candra vaṃśas by focusing primarily on three lineages and kingdoms: the Delhi Chauhāns, the "Caulukyas" of Kanauj, and the Mahobā Chandēls. The paurāṇika, however, provides two threads from this "*Ālhā*" back out to his past-as-prologue futurology. One, noticed at the end of the last chapter, is the Parihāra thread into the "future" through the rule of Mahīpati and Ghoravarman at Mahobā and Kalanjara. The other, noticed earlier, is the Paramāra thread back into the past through Gangāsiṃha. The Paramāras end up as the thinnest strand within the *Kṛṣṇāṃśacarita*: the first Agnivaṃśa lineage to dissolve into the mass of little kings on their decimation day, the fourteenth of Kurukṣetra II, with Gangāsiṃha's death. But within the frame, they begin as the thickest strand of the original Agnivaṃśa Kṣatriyas when they pass through the reigns of the great Vikramāditya, Śālivāhana, and Bhojarāja.

As observed in chapter 8, not only is the line of Paramāra descent between these three emperors fictive; the first two are probably figures of historicized myth. Following Sircar, who has made the most convincing study, Vikramāditya is probably based on Candragupta II

[1]The five are: primary creation (*sarga*); secondary creation; reigns of Manus (*manvantaras*); genealogy (*vaṃśa*) of gods and sages; and genealogical lists (*vaṃśānucarita*) of solar, lunar, and other kings, which in most purāṇas carry "all the known lineages and dynasties up to the mid-first millennium A.D" (Thapar 1992, 152).

Vikramāditya (376-413 A.D.), called Śakāri (Foe of the Śakas).[2] Candragupta II's triumphs over the Śakas were probably transposed back upon a fictional Vikramāditya, who is credited with founding an era in 58 or 57 B.C. that may have Scytho-Parthian origins in eastern Iran. Śālivāhana, linked with the Śaka era that seems actually to mark the beginning of Kuṣāṇa rule in 78 A.D., is probably a personification of the Śātavāhanas (based in Paithan on the Godavari river near Aurangabad in Maharashtra, but with origins in Andhra and north Kanara). He seems to draw his profile especially from the first dynast Simuka-Śātavāhana (mid-first century B.C.) and Gautamīputra Śātakarṇi (ca. 106-30 A.D.) who defeated a branch of Śakas.[3] The Paramāras then promote the Vikramāditya legend and era, and Bhoja Paramāra (1000/1018-55) in particular, who finds Vikramāditya's lost throne and listens to miraculous stories about him, enters the Vikramāditya legend as the Mleccha-halting Paramāra whose imperial claims are enhanced by the association.

The thread of empire that runs through these figures, and the links between empire and era that connects the mythology of the first two,[4] are sure reasons for rejecting the attempts by Edgerton and others to hold out for the historically possible: that a real but unattested Vikramāditya "might" have been a "local king of Mālava" who "founded the era of 58-57 B.C." (1926, lxiv, lxvi). As Sircar shows, Indian usages regarding eras are built over time upon the consensus of "successors and subordinates" within imperial traditions (1969, 159). It is unimaginable that a little king without known successors could have started an era.[5]

But the Agnivaṃśa frame is nestled into a still wider frame. The great

[2]Sircar 1969, *passim* and especially 18, 81-83, 89-91, 108-19, 161-67. Cf. Edgerton 1926, xxvi, lii, lviii-lxvi; Basham 1967, 74, 495; Rajan 1995, xv-xvi, xxix-xxx, and 235, n. 2; O'Brien 1996, 8-9.

[3]Pre-Paramāra Malwa connections are in each case provided: the Śātavāhanas by extending their Śaka-conquests and rule into Malwa; Candragupta II by conquering and annexing west Malwa and Ujjain from the Śakas (Sircar 1969, 65-71, 101-3).

[4]In some sources Vikramāditya and his era represent north India and Sanskrit, Śālivāhana and his era south India and Prakrit; in some the two become foes, in others they are even identified (Sircar 1969, 109-12, 118, 167, n. 36). Each becomes a "national hero of Indian folklore" (120, 167, n. 36). Cf. 158-59, 163-65 on the link between era and empire, including usage of the Vikram era by the imperial Pratihāras. The Paramāras also flourished under Bhoja (Basham 1967, 74).

[5]O'Brien's study (1996) is interesting in this regard. The Bhāṭṭika era of Jaisalmer kings of Rajasthan, dating from 624-25 A.D., begins as that of a "little kingdom," apparently tied into a popular (*laukika*) era marked by hundred-year cycles, and possibly dated to correspond to the Hijra of Muhammad, which marks the beginning of the Islamic era. The Bhāṭī clan does, however, trace a continuous descent (and appears prominently, as we have seen, in *Pābūjī*), and by the fourteenth century the era is subordinated to the Vikram era. Cf. also Hoernle 1909.

early "Paramāras" and, with them, the *Kṛṣṇāṃśacarita*, figure in only a quarter of this larger frame: the fourth that concerns the Kali yuga. The full outer frame pulls together all four yugas and is composed of a more complex set of strands that considerably enlarges the career of Kali himself: even into times that precede his yuga.[6] Combining the purāṇic conventions of genealogical lists (*vaṃśānucarita*) and yuga chronology, the *Pratisarga Parvan* opens onto a distinctive vision of the Kali yuga, and of the yugas that precede it.

A. How Do We Get to Where We Are?

The *Pratisarga Parvan* opens this vision in its first *khaṇḍa*, tracing the primal history of the solar line's Sūryavaṃśa-Ikṣvāku kings through the Satya (or Kṛta) yuga (3.1.1). For the Treta yuga, it continues this line through sixty-five Raghuvaṃśa kings, including Rāma, who were "all devoted to the worship of Devī" (3.1.2.1-38b), and introduces the founding of the lunar Candravaṃśa. Tracing this line from Candra to Saṃvaraṇa, it highlighs its segmentation through Yayāti's five sons: the Pauravas from Puru, Yādavas from Yadu, and Mlecchas from the other "three [who] attained Mlecchahood."[7] This is the first appearance of Mlecchas in this yuga-chronology (3.1.2.38c-72).[8] The Dvāpara yuga account then briefly locates the Yaduvaṃśa in Madhurā (Mathura) and the Mlecchavaṃśa in Marudeśa (Rajasthan) (3.4-5), but concentrates on the Paurava segment of the lunar line, following it through Kuru (after whom it becomes also the Kaurava line) to the main *Mahābhārata* generations, and on down to Śatānīka, the Pāṇḍavas' twenty-third descendant (3.1.3.1-94), who hears the beginning (first book) of the *Bhaviṣya Purāṇa*. From here on, although the list goes on, it describes what Śatānīka would hear about the "future," even though much of it (including the *Kṛṣṇāṃśacarita* and most of the *Pratisarga Parvan*) is told in the past tense.[9] The purāṇa's bard is from the beginning Lomaharṣaṇa, father of the *Mahābhārata*'s bard Ugraśravas. And his chief Ṛṣi-interlocutor in the *Pratisarga Parvan* is Śaunaka, the "master of the house" of the Nai-

[6]As does "Nala and Damayantī" (see Hiltebeitel forthcoming).

[7]3.1.2.48: *trayo mlecchatvamāgatāḥ*. On the three sons who originate Mleccha lines (Mlecchas, Bhojas, and Yavanas) in the *Mbh*, however, see Dumézil 1973, 18-19, 47-48.

[8]Alternately, *Viṣnu Purāṇa* 4.3.40-49 traces the Mlecchas' (Śakas, Yavanas, etc.) desertion (*parityāga*) of Vedic rites to pronouncements by Vasiṣṭha during the originary time of king Sagara. Several purāṇas amplify this scheme (Wilson [1840] 1972, 299-300).

[9]See Hohenberger 1967, 1-3, 11; *BhvP* 1.1 opens the purāna with the Ṛsis visiting king Śatānīka, who questions Vyāsa about *dharmaśāstra* and is referred to Vyāsa's pupil Sumanta; 3.1.3.93 mentions Śatānīka in the lunar genealogy; 3.4.6.1-42 describes how the future is known through a yogic journey (see below).

meṣeya Ṛṣis who listen to Ugraśravas in the *Mahābhārata*'s outer frame. Having heard *Mahābhārata* as purāṇa from the son, Śaunaka—twenty-three generations later—now hears purāṇa from the father.[10]

Now we learn that the Dvāpara age ends not with the *Mahābhārata*, but continues through some momentous novelties. The first comes when Śatānīka's great grandson, Kṣemaka, is killed by Mlecchas, and his son Pradyota performs a "sacrifice of Mlecchas (*mlecchayajña*)" in revenge (3.1.3.95-97). "How was this brilliant (*vicakṣaṇa*) sacrifice performed?" asks Śaunaka.[11] Lomaharṣaṇa answers: "Once, in Hāstinapura, Pradyota was caught up in the middle of a story (*āsthitaḥ sa kathāmadhye*)!" As in the *Mahābhārata* and *Rāmāyaṇa*, Naimiṣa Forest is once again where stories turn.[12] Nārada arrives and tells Pradyota, "Your father, slain by Mlecchas, has gone to Yamaloka. By the efficacy of a *mlecchayajña*, he will go to heaven." Eyes aflame, Pradyota summons Veda-knowing Brahmans to Kurukṣetra to offer up the Mlecchas. One might call this Kurukṣetra 1-A, since it comes after the *Mahābhārata* but is still in the Dvāpara yuga. Fashioning a vast four-cornered sacrificial pit (*yajña-kuṇḍa*), the Brahmans deploy Vedic mantra, and the Mlecchas—who include Hārahūṇas (Huns), Guruṇḍas, Śakas, Yavanas, Pallavas, Romajas (Hair-Born People? Romans?), Kharasaṃbhavas (Donkey-Born People), Dvīpasthitas (Island Dwellers), Cīnas (Chinese), and Sāgaramadhyagas (Ocean Farers)—are burnt to ash. The episode resembles and probably builds upon elements of two *Mahābhārata* sacrifices: Janamejaya's snake sacrifice, which pulls serpents worldwide into a firepit to avenge the biting of Janamejaya's father Parikṣit; and Yudhiṣṭhira's Rājasūya, which provokes the destruction of Kṣatriyas in the *Mahābhārata* war, and which Nārada prompts Yudhiṣṭhira to perform so as to transfer the latter's father Pāṇḍu to heaven. Pradyota gives the Brahmans their honoraria, his father Kṣemaka goes to heaven, and he himself comes to be known through the rest of his ten-thousand-year reign as Mlecchahantṛ, Mleccha-killer (3.1.4.1-10). Clearly, the Barbarian horizons will remain much the same in the *Kṛṣṇāṃśacarita*; but now we begin to see the type of history from which they unfold.

It is then during the shorter two-thousand-year reign of Pradyota's son Vedavat that the "Mleccha Kali," who, as we know, has yet to "establish" himself and his Mleccha following, eulogizes Viṣṇu and

[10]On Naimisa Forest, see chap. 4, n. 7; on the Naimiseya Rsis of the *Mbh*'s outer frame asking to hear Ugraśravas recite purāna, see chap. 7, n. 32.

[11]For *vicaksana*, I try to render both is meanings of "splendid" and "clever." Clearly Śaunaka approves.

[12]On Naimiṣa Forest conventions related to time and collapsing narrative frames, see chap. 4, n. 7, Hiltebeitel in press-h and forthcoming.

laments the destruction of his lineage. Viṣṇu delights him with the promise that the Mlecchavaṃśa will once again increase through a man named Ādama (*ādamo nāma puruṣah*) and his wife Havyavatī; they will originate from the mud or clay of Viṣṇu (*viṣṇukardamatas*; 3.1.4.11-19). Vedavat's son dies childless, leaving kings to rise from all four castes. And as the Dvāpara yuga winds down to its last eight thousand-plus years, Ādama and Havyavatī—the former named for his restraint of the senses (*indriyāṇi damitvā*) and devotion to meditation on the ātman (3.1.4.29)—find themselves in an Indianized Garden of Eden:

> A delightful great forest was made by the Lord, four *krośa*s in extent, in the eastern portion of the city of Pradāna. Having gone to the base of the tree of sin with the intention of seeing the wife, Kali approached quickly, having taken the form of a serpent. Tricked by that deceiver, the command of Viṣṇu was broken. The husband, having eaten that delightful fruit given according to the prevalent custom, food of air was made for the two with leaves of the fig (*udumbara*) tree. The daughters and sons born to them all then became Mlecchas.[13]

For the moment, let us just mention the most endearing detail. Ādama seems to eat the fruit *first*, for that must be what is meant by "given according to the prevalent custom" (*lokamārgapradam*). Despite her being the mother of Mlecchas, Eve has the makings of a good Indian wife, feeding her husband before herself. She is deceived by the serpent, but certainly no first sinner, and neither she, her husband, the author, nor the Lord is bothered about anyone's nakedness.

Thence follows the descent from Ādama and Havyavatī to the three sons of Nyūha/Noah (3.1.4.35-5.5). In his main story (4.45-5.5), Nyūha is a Mleccha Muni devoted to Viṣṇu. Elsewhere in the *Pratisarga Parvan*, he is also a Yavana or Greek (3.4.3.10); and, most important for our purposes, the last king before the onset of the Kali yuga.[14] Viṣṇu tells him in a dream to prepare for a world-dissolution (*pralaya*) in seven days by building a ship. Of biblical proportions,[15] this ark allows

[13]3.1.4.30-33: *pradānanagarasyaiva pūrvabhāge mahāvanam/ īśvareṇa kṛtaṃ ramyam catuhkrośāyatamsmrtam//pāpavṛksatale gatvāpatnīdarśanatatparaḥ/kalistatrāgatastūrṇam sarparūpam hi tatkrtam// vamcitā tena dhūrtena visnvājñā bhamgatāṃ gatā/ khāditvā tatphalam ramyaṃ lokamārgapradam patih// udumbarasya patraiśca tābhyām vāyvaśanam krtam/ sutāh putrās tato jātāḥ sarve mlecchā babhūvire.*

[14]3.2.5.10-11: *kalerāgamanam*; Hohenberger 1967, 12. The passage in the Nag Publishers edition has *kaleragamamanam* in the second usage, a seeming misprint leaving a metric irregularity. The passage occurs in the *Pratisarga Parvan*'s version of one of the tales of Vikramāditya and the genie (*vetāla*). Cf. Rajan 1995, 59-60, where Nyūha is not mentioned.

[15]Three hundred *hasta*s long, fifty wide, and thirty high (3.1.4.50; cf. *Gen*. 6:15).

Nyūha, his relatives, eighty-eight thousand Munis, and "all living beings" (*sarvajīva*) to survive the "rolled up" (*sāṃvartaka*) clouds of the Indian pralaya, which produce a biblical forty-day rain that inundates all of Bharatavarṣa.[16] The floating Munis revere Viṣṇu's Māyā—that is, the goddess—under names that resonate with the *Kṛṣṇāṃśacarita*: "Homage to Mahākālī, to Devakī. Homage to Mahālakṣmī, to the mother of Viṣṇu, to Rādhādevī. Homage to Revatī, Puṣpavatī, and Svarṇavatī. Homage to Kāmākṣī and the mother named Māyā. . . . O Bhairavī, protect us, your servants, from fear." Pleased, the goddess "makes the water peaceful."

In a year the earth is dry, and Nyūha lands on the slopes of two Himalayan peaks named Ārāc and Śiṣirā.[17] Dwelling there, the Mleccha (Nyūha) bewilders Viṣṇu, presumably by offering or praise, and pleases him. His Mleccha vaṃśa thus increases.[18] Also, for the increase of Kali himself and the "discord" he embodies, Viṣṇu turns his back on Vedic speech and makes Mleccha speech for Nyūha, who now, speaking "backwardly" or "against the hair" (*vilomam*), changes his three sons' good Sanskrit names Sīma, Śama, and Bhāva (3.1.4.44) to Sima, Hāma, and Yakūta (3.1.5.4-5), in which one can better recognize Shem, Ham, and Japheth.

From here on, as the Kali yuga gets underway, Nyūha's biblically identifiable descendants fill kingdoms named after them until the goddess Sarasvatī utters a curse: their Mleccha speech will increase in the Kali yuga, but it will be the very lowest (*mahādhamāḥ*) of all languages; meanwhile, the sound of Sanskrit (*saṃskṛtasyaiva vāṇī*) should be heeded in Bharatavarṣa (3.1.5.5-21). Mlecchas cover all the earth except Bharatavarṣa, up to the Sarasvatī River's auspicious bank. Sarasvatī, who hates Śūdras, Ābhīras, and Niṣādas for their encroachments even in the *Mahābhārata*,[19] thus makes it clear by her curse that she now defines her scruples no longer primarily by caste but by language, culture,[20] and, given all the emphasis on primordial descent, by something

[16]The condensation does not allow us to know whether "all *jīvas*" come in pairs. Other than the eighty-eight thousand Munis, Nyūha and his kin, those who remained were all destroyed (3.1.4.54)—that is, presumably all other *humans*.

[17]3.1.4.59: *himādrestaṭabhūmayah*, "slopes of the snowy peaks," seems to suggest that *ārācca śiṣinā nāma* be taken as two slopes (cf. Hohenberger 1967, 12) rather than one "peak 'Ārācca' (Ararat?)" (Bonazzoli 1979a, 34).

[18]"Then the Mleccha made Viṣṇu bewildered (*mleccho viṣṇumohaṃ tadākarot*)" (3.1.5.2); it does not say how, but Hohenberger supposes it is through an offering (1967, 12), as in *Gen.* 8:20-9:1, where Noah's offering is followed by God's blessing, "Be ye fruitful and multiply."

[19]Śūdras and Abhīras at 9.36.1-2, Nisādas at 3.130.4.

[20]See below on circumcision, beards, and beef eating as elements of the "Mlecchadharma" (*BhvP* 3.3.3.23-27).

approximating race. Yet one can probably also divine the principle by which so many improvements in biblical history are made in the names of the goddess—perhaps even including the exoneration of Eve.

The goddess has now to contend with the impact of a new barbarian teacher: Mūśa/Moses, the "Ācārya of the Mlecchas," who fills the world with his doctrines.[21] While god-praising Vedic speech is being destroyed, four Mleccha languages (of four hundred thousand languages total) take root in Bhāratavarṣa itself: Vrajabhāṣā, Mahārāṣṭrī, Yāvanī, and Gurundikā. The last, which the text derives from the "mutilation" (*ruṇḍa*) of "cows" (*go*),[22] may, following Hoffmann, derive its name from *Muruṇḍa*, originally connoting a Śaka people in India speaking an Iranian language; as *Guruṇḍa*, it would then have been applied over the centuries to Buddhists, Christians, and ultimately the British, from whom the paurāṇika selects "Sunday, February, and sixty" as three exemplary "Guruṇḍikā" words.[23]

Once the Mlecchas launch the Kali yuga by expanding their domains and languages and spreading the teachings of Moses, they are resisted by the Ṛṣi Kāśyapa, who undertakes a kind of Vedic missionary trip to Egypt. This expedition results in Mlecchas being brought into "India" for the first time: more specifically, into Brahmāvarta, the holy land between the Sarasvatī and Dṛṣadvatī near Kurukṣetra. Kāśyapa's sojourn in Egypt is still part of a biblical sequence, since, as Hohenberger observes (1967, 13-14), when the paurāṇika refers to Egypt as Miśra,[24] it stands for Mizraim of *Genesis* 10:6. The immigrants are either those whom Kāśyapa has converted to twiceborns and returned with himself, having made them "disciples";[25] or they are ten thousand (males by implication) whom his son Kaṇva has subdued by the power of Sanskrit speech.[26]

Upon accompanying Kaṇva back to the Punjab, the ten thousand do five years of tapas to Sarasvatī, who seems to upgrade them from Mlecchas by turning all their wives (not counted in the original number)

[21]*Mlecchācāryaśca mūśākhyas tanmataih pūritam jagat*; 3.1.5.30. The doctrines are not specified.

[22]3.4.22.70, as cited by Halbfass 1988, 194 and 515, n. 109.

[23]*Sande, pharvarī*, and *siksati* (3.1.5.37 and preceding); cf. Hoffman 1967, vii-xii. "Sunday" and "sixty" (with all the sixty-year jubilees in the Bible) could allude to a Christian preaching context. Hoffmann discusses "Gurundikā" and the vocabularies selected for the other three languages, confirming Vrajabhāsā as a form of old Hindi from around Mathura; Maharāstrī as a Prakrit; and tracing Yavanī to words of Iranian (rather than Greek) descent.

[24]3.1.5.9; cf. 6.12; 3.4.3.12; 21.15.

[25]3.4.3.11-14; cf. 6.1-16.

[26]It is intriguing that the conversion of Mlecchas should take place between the Sarasvatī and Drsadvatī, holy to Vedic Vrātyas. See Hiltebeitel forthcoming on Vrātya echoes in the *Mbh*'s sattra sacrifices, especially those performed in the Naimisa Forest and on the Sarasvatī; see also above chap. 4, n. 15.

and eight thousand of the men into Śūdras, plus two thousand of the men into Vaiśyas. One might wonder whether the author imagines a kind of inverse Exodus, with the majority of Mlecchas being led out of Egypt, but into the alternate "servitude" of becoming Śūdras. In any case, one of the Vaiśyas named Ācāryapṛthu does twelve years of tapas and wins Kaṇva's blessing to found the city of Rājaputra (Rājaputrapuram), perhaps Rajasthan (see below), or Rajgir in Bihar. There his wife Rājanyā has a son named Māgadha, to whom Kaṇva then gives the village of Māgadha, to the east (3.4.21.3-20). Alternately, under the name Āryapṛthu, he rules eight thousand Śūdras (who have perhaps migrated with him) in the land of Rājyaputra (*rājyaputradeśa*), here more likely Rajasthan, before his son Māgadha is consecrated, presumably at Māgadha.[27] One may note that the paurāṇika seems to "rajputize" this phase of history by the names he selects. Another son of Kāśyapa, Prāptavat, then divides Āryadeśa into nine kingdoms. It is intriguing that these stories of the conversion and rajputization of Mlecchas should all be connected with Kāśyapa, after whom Multan (Mūlasthāna) in Sind takes the alternate name of Kāśyapapura (Dey 1927, 96). It is in Arab Sind "sometime between A.D. 800 and 1000" that the *Devala-smṛti* is written as the first Sanskrit text to define various penitential rituals of *śuddhi* ("repurification") whereby individuals "polluted by association with mlecchas . . . could be readmitted to the Hindu caste system."[28]

From here on, however, it is Magadha (Māgadha) that comes into view, as it usually does in purāṇic genealogies, as the rising power of the Kali yuga: a land ruled by a lineage of nineteen listed but unpedigreed kings—descendants of Mleccha converts, Śūdras, and Vaiśyas.[29] While Magadha's power grows, Viṣṇu is born as a prince descended from Kāśyapa named Gautama (i.e., the Buddha). After perfecting the Bauddhadharma or Buddhist religion (*bauddhadharmaṃ ca saṃskṛtya*),

[27]3.1.6.17-18. These connections may recall the synchronism and rivalry between the Pradyotas of Avantī-Ujjain in Malwa (ca. 546-396) and the Haryankas (ca. 546-414), first of whom was the Buddha's contemporary Bimbasara, founder of Rājagṛha in Magadha (ca. 546-414 B.C.); see Sircar 1969, 26-36, 44-45. In the *Rām*, Rājagṛha is also the Kekaya capital on the upper Vitasta river southeast of Takṣaśilā (Schwartzberg 1992, 13 and 15).

[28]MacLean 1989, 78. It was the nineteenth-century rediscovery of this text, for which Sindī Muslims are both Mlecchas and Caṇḍālas, that "gave the modern *śuddhi* movement (aimed primarily at Muslims [and advanced by the Arya Samaj]) its classical referent for reconversion" (Maclean 1989, 79, 82; brackets mine). Kāśyapa's conversion of the Egyptians to "twiceborns" also looks like an anticipation or playback of this history. Cf. the views of Asopa 1976, 7-10 cited in chap. 14.

[29]3.1.6.20-35. See Pargiter [1913] 1962, x-ii; Thapar 1978a, 273, 352; 1984, 47, 70-71, 87-88, 113-14, 138-41; 160-64; 1991, 3, on Magadha in purāṇic lineages and in the formation of the monarchical metropolitan state; Sircar 1969, 51, 54, 66-68, on the "lowness" of Nandas, Mauryas, and Śātavāhanas.

he goes to Paṭṭaṇa (Patna, in Magadha country). This marks the passage of a fourth of the Kali yuga by the destruction of Vedadharma. Maurya kings of Magadha are then traced down to Aśoka (3.1.6.36-44). *Ālhā* claims the same one-fourth fraction for its *Mahābhārata* of the Kali yuga.

Hohenberger (1967, 5, 11-13) and Bonazzoli (1979a, 27-28, 33-39) are surely right to see the biblical features of this sequence as well worked from primarily Christian sources into a purāṇic frame or structure, and to discount Aufrecht's contention that it is a literary hoax perpetrated by an unscrupulous employee on the gullible owner of the Venkaṭeśvara Press, whom Aufrecht otherwise credits with good service to the distribution of purāṇas (1903, 276, 284). This press published its first printed edition of the *Bhaviṣya Purāṇa* in 1897. But if it is not a hoax, one can still not rule out parody. Pargiter, who sees the incorporation of *Genesis* material as a "pious fraud" and an "interpolation," nonetheless adds that being "able to point to such prophetic accounts in the literature would have been a valuable weapon . . . in the hands of the brahmans against adversaries of other creeds" ([1913] 1962, xviii, n. 1). Contextualizing such a view, Bonazzoli argues that a passage describing Jesus as Īśamasīha, Jesus/"Lord"-the-Messiah (3.3.2.21-32), is composed "by some clever *paṇḍit*" against the background of the nineteenth-century "Indian Renaissance" (1979a, 35-39): an argument, I will urge, that should be strengthened and extended beyond this one passage. Since both the *Genesis-Exodus* sequence and the Jesus passage are part of a *Pratisarga Parvan* "history" of the Mlecchas that also embraces the Buddha, Jesus, Muhammad, the Mughals, and the British in Calcutta, the whole train would seem to be an answer to Muslims as well as Christians. Moreover, the Jesus-passage carries this Mleccha history directly into the *Kṛṣṇāṃśacarita*, where its appearance in its second adhyāya sets it in a diptych beside a portrait of Muhammad in the third adhyāya. These consecutive adhyāyas come between adhyāya 1, which tells of Śiva's curse of the *Mahābhārata* heroes to be reborn in "*Ālhā*," and adhyāyas 4-6, which introduce the following: Kṛṣṇa's promise to Kali to establish the Mlecchavaṃśa; the actual incarnations starting with Bhīma's as the Mleccha Tālana or Mīrā Tālhan (4.28-29); and the destruction of the Agnivaṃśa as prologued through the imperial "Agnivaṃśa" rivalry between Delhi and Kanauj.[30]

The diptych thus places Jesus and Muhammad at the center of those *Kṛṣṇāṃśacarita* events that bring the *Pratisarga Parvan*'s wider Mleccha history into focus as it ties in with continuities from *Mahābhārata* to "*Ālhā*." The two portraits are a study in contrasts.

[30]See chap. 5, table 4.

The Jesus passage is set amid events that follow the reign of Vikramāditya, who had established the four corners of Bhāratavarṣa at the Indus in the west, Setubandha (Rameshwaram) in the south, Badarīsthana (Badrinath) in the north, and Kapila in the east, with eighteen kingdoms therein.[31] A hundred years after Vikramāditya, within the eighteen kingdoms, "various tongues were established and many dharmas advanced (*nānābhāṣāḥ sthitās tatra bahudharma-pravartakāḥ*)" (2.14)—presumably not only the Buddhist and other "heterodox" dharmas, but Mleccha teachings gathering strength from outside. "Having heard of the destruction of the dharma," hosts of Śakas and others now entered Āryadeśa by crossing the Indus and the Himalayas. They plundered the Āryas, seized their wives, and returned to their own countries (15-17).

Śālivāhana, Vikramāditya's grandson (*pautras*), then conquered the Śakas and other barbarian kings, seized their treasuries, made them submit to his royal staff (*daṇḍa*), defined the boundary of propriety (*maryyādā*) to distinguish Āryas from Mlecchas, and established the Indus as the geographical border between Sindhusthāna (Sind) as the "furthest of the Ārya kingdoms," and Mlecchasthāna, the land of Mlecchas, beyond the Indus. Sind, whose islamization begins as early as 711, thus becomes pivotal to this story, as it is to the story of Ismā'īlī missions in India.[32]

Having accomplished all this, Śālivāhana, now as supreme ruler over the Śakas, once came to a snowy mount (or Mount Himatunga), and there, in the middle of the land of the Hūṇas (Huns), he "saw an auspicious man (*puruṣa*) standing on a peak, yellowish-white-limbed (*gaurāṃgam*) and dressed in white (*śvetavastrakam*)," who joyfully announced himself; "Know me as the son of the Lord, born of a virgin womb, a proclaimer of the Mlecchadharma, whose highest goal is the vow of truth."[33] Asked further about his dharma, the son of the Lord replies that he has appeared because "truth has been destroyed in the borderless land of the Mlecchas," and that, as Īśāmasī, causing fear among the Dasyus, he has reached the status of Masīha (*masīhatvam upāgataḥ*). His dharma: by purifying the mind and body through murmured prayer (*japam*), one murmurs the taintless supreme (*japate nirmalaṃ paraṃ*), so

[31]3.3.2.9-13; cf. 3.2.23.7.

[32]MacLean 1989; Khan 1997a; Kassam 1995.

[33]2.22-24: *giristham purusam śubham . . . gaurāṃgaṃ śvetavastrakam// . . . īśaputram ca māṃ viddhi kumārīgarbhasaṃbhavam// mlecchadharmasya vaktāram satyavrataparāyanam.* This Jesus passage is also translated by Bonazzoli (1979a, 32-34), summarized with translated verses by Hohenberger (1967, 17-18), and discussed with translated verses by Diehl (1981). I do not note all my differences in translation. Śālivāhāna's encounter with the Huns, who invade India in the fifth and sixth century, must either be an intended anticipation or an unintended anachronism.

that, "by the rule of truthful speech, by mental oneness, by meditation, one may worship the Lord (Īśam) who is established in the maṇḍala of the sun," the immovable Lord in the Sun who "draws" all moving beings. "By so doing, the *masīhā*, ever purified and beneficent, goes to dissolution, having received the form of the Lord in the heart."[34]

Although the term *masīhā* is feminine, it seems that the paurāṇika also uses it in an Islamic sense, since Arabic *al-Masīḥ* can denote not only the son of God, but refer to "a spirit from Allah," and mean "purified" or "filled with blessing."[35] As if in derivation from this presumed spiritual quality, the son of the Lord finally gives his name as Īśamasīha (2.18-31). Śālivāhana bows "to him who was worshiped by Mlecchas," makes him stay in the terrible Mlecchasthāna, goes home to perform a horse sacrifice, and ascends to heaven (32-34).

As the Jesus passage is set in the aftermath of the reign of Vikramāditya, so the Muhammad passage is set in the aftermath of Śālivāhana. Through the five-hundred-year rule of the latter's "Paramāra" successors, the boundary of propriety (maryyādā) is lowered until the reign of the tenth, Bhojarāja: the "real" Paramāra Bhoja. Having seen this moral boundary destroyed, he undertakes an imperial digvijaya. Joined by the great Sanskrit poet Kālidāsa[36] and other Brahmans, he approaches the banks of the Indus with his army, conquers various kings, obtains their treasuries, and submits them to his royal scepter (daṇḍa). At this time a Mleccha named Mahāmada comes in the company of a teacher and a division of disciples (3.1-5). Hohenberger is surely right that Mahāmada must stand for Muhammad (1967, 18, n. 2): as elsewhere in the *Kṛṣṇāṃśacarita*, it would seem that the Prophet is conflated with Islamic invaders, perhaps in this case with Mahmud of Ghazna.

Bhojarāja worships Śiva in Marusthala (the Marwar area of Rajasthan), and Śiva, after purifying him, sends him to Mahākāleśvarasthala, which the god describes as follows: a land corrupted by Mlecchas called Vāhīkas, where Āryadharma counts for nothing; there a great magician

[34]2.26-31b, closing: *kṛtyena . . . masīhā vilayamgatā/ īśamūrtihradi prāptā nityaśuddhā śivamkarī*. Īśa is translated here as "Lord," as in Sanskrit; but it is also Hindi and Bengali, via Arabic, for "Jesus."

[35]Gibb and Kramers 1953, 173, 361. I do not follow Bonazzoli's view that "the śloka identifies *Masīhā* with impermanence" (1979a, 37; cf. 33). But Diehl's comment that Īśamasī (2.26) is "by some interpreted as a goddess" (1981, 74: he does not say by whom) is intriguing given the feminine of *masīhā* (2.30), and the tendency noticed above to introduce the goddess into biblical stories. Cf. Bonazzoli 1980, 221-23, 231 on the "tantric flavor" of *BhvP* 2.1.9.54-56, a passage referring to "devī in the form of a lingam."

[36]The paurāṇika seems to have brought Kālidāsa from the court of Vikramāditya, where he is already an anachronism (Sircar 1969, 122-23), to that of Bhoja where he is even more of one.

(*mahāmāyin*) named Mahāmada has come, whose highest goal is the work of Paiśācas (3.6-13). At the bank of the Indus, Mahāmada tells Bhojarāja, "Your god, O king, has come into my servitude. He would eat my leavings. Just watch!" In his harshness, Bhojarāja has an inclination toward Mlecchadharma. But Kālidāsa, recognizing his bewilderment, turns furiously against Mahāmada, and announces that he will slay this "ill-behaved Vāhīka lowest of men." Having murmured (*japtvā*) and offered ten thousand silent prayers, he turns Mahāmada to ash. Yet "having become ash, the magician (*māyāvī*) attained the state of Mleccha divinity (*mlecchadevatvam-āgataḥ*)" (20). His disciples take up their guru's ashes and return to Vāhīka country, approaching it in a non-intoxicated state (*madahīnatvamāgatam*, 21). There they found the city of Madahīna, "Without intoxication," i.e., Medina, which is "like a tīrtha to them"; but they dwell there "having intoxication as their highest goal (*madatatparāḥ*)" (21-22).

One night, using magic, Mahāmada then takes on a Paiśāca body to tell Bhojarāja that, although Āryadharma is the best of all dharmas, his doctrine (*matā*), "by the command of the lord (*īśājñayā*)," will make the Paiśācas' dharma harsh: they will circumcise, wear beards but not topknots, eat cows, and use a pestle (*musala*) rather than *kuśa* grass for their sacrament (*saṃskāra*). The latter implies that the name "Muslim" is derived from their being "born possessing a pestle (*musalavanto hi jātayo*)" (3.23-27). Having thus spoken, the god (deva) departs, and Bhojarāja comes home. He establishes the heaven-bestowing sound of Sanskrit among the three varṇas, and Prakrit among Śūdras; and during his fifty-year rule, the boundary of propriety resembles that of the gods. Āryavarta becomes a world of merit (*puṇyabhūmi*) between the Himalayas and Vindhyas; there Ārya varṇas are instituted, while caste mixture is entrenched beyond the Vindhyas (28-31)—that is, in south India!

The third adhyāya brings closure on this diptych in its last verse: The Mleccha realms are divided between the "Musala-possessors" on the far bank of the Indus, and followers of the "religions (*dharmmāḥ*) of Īśāmasīha"—note the plural—in the barbaric Tuṣa country and in various islands (3.32). No doubt the Christian "religions" are Catholic and Protestant, and Great Britain one or more of the islands. That it is a diptych can hardly be doubted. In this case we can even argue, along with Bonazzoli, that "the author of the two adhyāyas is most probably the same" (1979a, 35): a point that I would extend, allowing for the authorial redaction of variants, to most if not all of the *Kṛṣṇāṃśacarita*, and the earlier Mleccha history from Adam and Eve to the sojourn in Egypt.[37]

[37]With a "methodological approach" committed to arguing for "the process of inserting new topics" (1979a, 27), i.e., interpolation, Bonazzoli offers no thought on the two adhyāyas'

The Jesus and Muhammad passages show a common concern with the emergence of multiple tongues and dharmas; with etymology; with appearances by both Jesus and Muhammad on the borders of India; with boundaries of both propriety and land; with kings who restore the boundaries, but with diminishing returns from Vikramāditya through Śālivāhana to Bhoja. From the first to the last, Āryadeśa has shrunk from all India to north India, the latter being the constricted world of the heroes of *Ālhā*, whose story immediately follows. Contrasts are further evident between Jesus and Muhammad. Each attains a kind of divine "status": Jesus that of Masīha, Muhammad that of Mleccha divinity. Jesus teaches japam as a means to the highest realization; Muhammad is burnt to ash by japam. Jesus's dharma is essentially Upaniṣadic, and consonant with Veda;[38] Muhammad's dharma is demonic (paiśāca), and a caricature of Islam by way of non-Vedic customs.

Our author is doing comparative religions. On each side, however, it would seem to be not just a case of appropriation and parody, but of playful yet deliberate misunderstanding and distortion. This is obvious in the case of Islam and Muhammad, but equally so for Christians and Jesus. Although biblical Mlecchas are low in their speech and teachings, Jesus is not alone among them in having elevated Upaniṣadic insights. So too Hanūka (Enoch) "had Viṣṇu-bhakti as his highest goal, making fruit offerings, and always conquering (in the conviction) 'That art thou indeed (*tat tvaṃ hi asi*).'"[39] This of course depletes the biblical figures of any spiritual originality: a stance consonant with the Hindu Renaissance's Vedāntic elevation of the "spiritual East" to the source of all religious unity, the source from which other religions' (and even Hinduism's) differences can be "tolerated." Muslim (and also Buddhist) Mlecchas lack

---

context in the *Kṛṣṇāṃśacarita* or the *Pratisarga Parvan*.

[38]The māsihā goes to dissolution in the heart in the purified image of the Lord; the Lord is worshiped in the mandala of the sun. I do not agree with Diehl (1981, 74-75) that these descriptions are residues of Iranian sun worship (in the *BhvP* these are mainly in the first book). Some key passages are *BĀUp.* 2.3.3: distinguishing the *brahman* that is formed, mortal and unmoving from brahman that is unformed, immortal, and moving, the latter's "essence is the person (puruṣa) in the maṇḍala of the sun"; *Maitrī Up.* 6.1: this "golden puruṣa (*hiranmayaḥ puruṣah*) who is within the sun (*āditye*)" is also "within the lotus of the heart"; *ChUp.* 1.6.7: "the golden person who is seen in the sun has a golden beard and golden hair; all is golden to the tips of the fingernails"; *Katha Up.* 2.2.11 on the sun's purity; and various texts (e.g., *ChUp.* 8.6.5) on passage through the sun on the itinerary of liberation. Jesus is a "yellowish-white-limbed puruṣa" (*gaura* can mean golden, his skin being distinguished from the pure-white *śveta* of his clothes). The *Chatra Prakāś* repeatedly describes Rajputs slain in battle as ascending to the mansions of bliss in warlike dress through the solar orb (Pogson [1828] 1971, 39, 45, 52, 68, 76).

[39]3.1.4.39—following Hohenberger 1967, 12, taking '*hi*' as a metrical necessity. So too Ādama, as cited above.

Upaniṣadic refinements.

Moreover, resonances between the stories relating biblical and Muslim traditions and the *Kṛṣṇāṃśacarita*'s "*Ālhā*" suggest that the *Pratisarga Parvan* is a relatively congruent work. The "command" (*ājñā*) of Viṣṇu in paradise recalls the "divine command" (*īśājñā*) by which Mahāmada corrupts the Mlecchas (3.24) and the command (*ājñā*) of Śiva that determines the reincarnations of *Mahābhārata* heroes. The term for "deceiver" (*dhūrta*) describes not only Mahāmada (3.18) and Kali as the serpent in paradise (3.1.4.32), but the "rogue-deceiver" Mahīpati (20.34; 22.42), who, by incarnating Duryodhana, inherits (as it were) a portion of Kali that Duryodhana himself incarnated.

Historically, as Hohenberger observes, the *Pratisarga Parvan* also knows Mughal (*mukula*) history from about 1400 with its account of Timūr-Tamburlaine—called Timiralinga, "Dark Linga" or "Linga of Darkness" (3.4.6.44-57)—through the great Indian emperors to the plundering of Delhi in 1739 by the Persian Nādir Shāh (called the Daitya Nādara) during the Mughal rule of Muhammad Shāh (3.4.22.1-58). Thus 1739 could mark a terminus a quo for the text's history of the Mughals. If so, the same terminus would apply to its *Genesis-Exodus* sequence in its first khaṇḍa, its Jesus-Muhammad diptych in its third (the *Kṛṣṇāṃśacarita*), and the history of the Agnivaṃśa kings at the beginning of the fourth, since all these segments tie conceptually together.

Hohenberger suggests 1739 as a date "around" which the *Genesis-Exodus* sequence would already have had prior Indian tellings in response to the Syrian Bible of the Thomas Christians and Bible translations into various Indian tongues (1967, 7, 23-25). Recalling that "Sunday" is an example of "Guruṇḍa" speech, it is even possible that the *Pratisarga Parvan* answers not to vernacular Bible translations or the Syrian Bible, but to the English Bible. In any case, it surely knows details that condense from a biblical text, or from an oral tradition that has kept specific biblical details in mind. From the story of Adam and Eve, it knows man's birth from mud or clay, the east of Eden (Pradāna, "giving" or "gift," seems to be chosen for its homophony with "Paradise" and "Eden" rather than for any etymology), the divine command (with no explanation), and the fig leaves (to eat air rather than hide nakedness).[40] From the story of Noah, it knows the proportions of the ark. From the story of Jesus, it knows the virgin birth, perhaps the sermon on the mount, and, even if it is not biblical, the title "son of God."

Nonetheless, virtually *all* the biblical names seem to be of Arabic

[40]This matter is obscure to me.

rather than English derivation.[41] It appears that the paurāṇika knows the stories from some closeness to biblical sources, but prefers names familiar from Muslim usage.[42] Moreover, along with points that could be drawn from either Islamic or biblical sources (Adam's creation from mud; Jesus's virgin birth), there are at least three that could echo Muslim traditions: (1) the name Īsamasīha, as above; (2) a Hadith describing a dream in which Muhammad "saw at the Ka'ba a very handsome brown-complexioned man with beautiful locks, dripping with water, who walked supported by two men; to his question who this was the reply was given: al-Masīḥ" (Gibb and Kramers 1953, 361)—could the Ka'ba be transformed into the site for a sermon on a snowy mount? (3) Ahmadiyya traditions of Jesus' sojourn in Kashmir, possibly reflected in his revelation on the snowy peak—if, as Bonazzoli (1979a, 37-39) and Diehl (1981, 76-77) suppose, Hūṇadeśa (2.22) refers to Kashmir.[43] Given such considerations, it is probably best to assume that the paurāṇika and his Sanskrit-reading audience would have shared not only some awareness of Bible stories, but a knowledge of Islamic names and some familiarity with Islamic lore. Such Islamic names are well attested in nineteenth-century Bengali (Chatterjee 1995a, 87, 191-94).

Since references to Queen Victoria's Calcutta provide a mid- to even late-nineteenth-century terminus ad quem for other *Pratisarga Parvan* passages, I would suggest that this century-and-a-half-long window is not only a period in which to envision the composition of these obviously "late" segments, but of the *Genesis-Exodus* sequence and the *Kṛṣṇāṃśa-carita*—with its Jesus and Muhammad passages—as well. Clearly we are beginning to narrow this window. For the moment, let us register that a purāṇic project of this kind would not have been undertaken in isolation. For one thing, it is a kind of inverse hierohistory that connects the founding stories of the "western Mleccha" traditions not with the creation of the universe and the guiding hand of God in history, but with the great revivals Barbarism that go by the names of Buddhism, Christianity, and Islam. The threading into one such history of the seven mlecchācāryas whose stories it emphasizes—Adam, Enoch, Noah, Moses, Buddha,

[41]See Gibb and Kramers 1953 on Ādam (13-14); Hawwā (138), from which Havyavatī is more easily derived than from Eve; Nūh (450-51); Mūsā (414-15); 'Īsā (173-75) and al-Masīh (361). Yāfith (637-38) is no closer to Yākūta than Japheth.

[42]Cf. Bonazzoli 1979a, 34-35, who says both that "the source of all these [biblical] passages seems to be the Bible either read or heard," and that, for the Jesus passage, the "source seems to be both Christian and Muslim."

[43]I do not, however, agree that the "play on the words '*acala-cala*" of *ślokas* 29-30, although common in Sanskrit Literature," could be "an attempt to interpret 'Christ' as a kind of 'wanderer'" (Bonazzoli 1979a, 37). Bonazzoli ignores straightforward explanations by way of the Upaniṣads and *BhG* 18.61, as noted in the latter case by Diehl (1981, 74-75).

Jesus, and Muhammad—bears a five-sevenths resemblance to the sequence of prophet-"enunciators" (*nāṭiqs*) who mark the seven eras of Ismā'īlī heirohistory—Ādam, Nūḥ (Noah), Ibrāhīm (Abraham), Mūsā (Moses). 'Īsā (Jesus), and Muhammad, to be followed by the messianic Imām (the Mahdī, Rightily Guided One, or Qā'im, Riser).[44] Even if one cannot safely posit a direct Ismā'īlī or Shī'ite inspiration, the paurāṇika refashions an appropriated heirohistory *like* theirs that spirals downward into the depths of the Kali yuga, only to subsume and redeem it as a divine līla—without, let us note, a messiah. Moreover, if we are right about the nineteenth century as the period of composition, it is one that was preceded by over a century of attempts by European writers "to explain" Indian mythology within "the limits set by Genesis" (Mukherjee 1987, 10), and corresponds to the time in which William Jones was not only to link his discovery of the spread of Indo-European languages with the Tower of Babel, but to write *The History of the Life of Nader Shah* (1773) "for the sake of exposing 'the most infamously wicked' and of 'displaying the charms of liberty' by 'showing the odiousness of tyranny and oppression.'"[45] Who "owns" these "stories of old" (purāṇas) is thus as serious a question as how one tells them—in relation to other stories of religion, empire, eras, and invasion.[46] From our paurāṇika's perspective, the Bible is quite justifiably a Mleccha purāṇa.

B. The Buddhists and the Agnivaṃśa

Yet as we have seen, this pauraṇīka is no less interested in outlandish western Mlecchas who challenge the borders from outside than he is in those Mlecchas who begin, at least, by coming as immigrants from Egypt under the sponsorship of the great Ṛṣi Kāśyapa: the fifth-column Buddhists. It is in response to the rise of Buddhism in connection with Magadha imperial power that we get the *Pratisarga Parvan*'s account of the origin of the Agnikula Kṣatriyas. A Brahman named Kānyakubja arranges a sacrifice to Brahmā on Mount Arbuda (Mount Abu in Raja-

[44]Daftary 1990, 139-40, 219, 394, 564; there are also variants (see 105). The place of Kāśyapa in this heirohistory could be taken as an eighth such preceptor. The omission of Abraham might raise intriguing questions.

[45]Quoted from Jones's Preface by Mukherjee (1987, 38), though as Mukherjee shows (38-40), Jones resisted making Nādir Shah an "oriental despot." See ibid., 85-97, especially 93 on fitting "Creation, the Deluge and migrations" into the Genesis framework. It was also the period in which Voltaire could say, "there is no mention of Adam or Noah, or any of our sacred history in the ancient books of the Hindus" (Mukherjee 1987, 7, citing Voltaire, *Fragments sur l'Inde*, pp. 47-47)—a statement that the purāna and Jones might be said to "correct" with their novel antiquities.

[46]See Hiltebeitel 1994 on Jain treatments of Hindu purānic themes, and in press-g. Cf. Bhabha 1994a, 102-22, on strategies of receiving the English Bible.

sthan), and by means of Vedic mantra, four Kṣatriyas originate: the Sāmavedin Pramara, ancestor of the Paramāras, who lived in the Avanta city Ambāvatī (that is, Ujjain); the triple-vedin Śukla, ancestor of the Caulukyas, who went toward Ānarta and lived in Dvārakā; the Yajurvedin Capahāni, ancestor of the Chauhāns, who went to Ajamera (Ajmer) in the land of Rājyaputra (which is more clearly Rajputana-Rajasthan here than in the Ācāryapṛthu-Āryapṛthu story); and the Atharvevedin Parihāraka, ancestor of the Parihāras, who lived in Kalanjara. We shall look at the myth of Agnikula origins more closely in chapter 13, but no variant is more Brahmanical than this one: all Buddhists were destroyed, four hundred thousand struck by heavenly weapons.[47] Agnivaṃśa kings also destroy Buddhists at Bodh Gaya (3.4.21.23-35).

Problems with Buddhists persist into the *Kṛṣṇāṃśacarita* itself, where Agnivaṃśin heroes join the "Banāphars" in their anti-Buddhist China expedition.[48] But the important point is that the Agnivaṃśa Kṣatriyas are *created* to oppose them. As far as I know, a connection between the rise of the Agnikula and the suppression of Buddhism is historically unverifiable.[49] But that has not discouraged the inference and the generation of myths, including scholarly ones. Thus Crooke could say that the Agnikula origin myth "describes how, by a solemn act of purification or initiation, under the superintendence of one of the ancient Vedic Rishis or inspired saints, the 'fire-born' septs were created to help the Brāhmans in repressing Buddhism, Jainism, or other heresies, and in establishing the ancient traditional Hindu social policy, the temporary downfall of which, under the stress of foreign invasions, is carefully concealed in the Hindu sacred literature."[50] Similarly, the Muslim ideologue Abul Fazl, who recounts the ancestry of Akbar in strains reminiscent of a purāṇa[51] and chronicles

[47]3.1.6.45-7.4, especially 6.48: *sarve bauddhā vināśitāḥ/ caturlakṣāḥ smṛtā bauddhāḥ divyaśastraiḥ prahāritāḥ*. Note that the Parihāras are in Kalanjara, preceding the Chandēls in this pivotal fort, as pre-Chandēl history would expect.

[48]See chap. 9, § D. Recall also the cautionary words of Caitanya at Puri (chap. 7, n. 37).

[49]R. B. Singh 1975, 33, 158, insists there is no record of opposition to Buddhists in the history of the Agnikula clans. Stressing Hindu-Buddhist harmony, he suggests the legend may be a sixteenth-century back-reading from encounters with Muslims.

[50]Crooke in Tod [1829-32, 1920] 1990,1:xxxiii; Crooke refers to other texts than the *Pratisarga Parvan*, which does not conceal such matters. Regarding Crooke's notions of purification or initiation as supposititious, Asopa distinguishes "theories" that the Agnikula Kṣatriyas were born to help the Brahmans against Buddhists (1976, 28, 87, 90) from ones that they were former Buddhists whom the fire-birth purified (ibid., 26, 37-38). Crooke thinks the myth (and others like it) conceals the successes of Buddhism and other heterodoxies Asopa that it conceals the Agnikula Rajputs having originally been Brahmans (29-31, 39, 94, 98). On concealment theories regarding the Agnikula, see further chap. 13.

[51]See Richards 1993, 45-47 on Abul Fazl's *Akbar-Nama* and *Ain-i-Akbari*, which, I would suggest, appear to be purānic in much the same flavor as the *Pratisarga Parvan*. See further

Akbar's (and thus his own) familiarity with Rajputs (a band of whom eventually slew him from ambush),[52] gives a straightforward account of Agnikula opposition to Buddhists:

> To consume his passions, an ascetic named Mahābāha kindled the first flame in a fire temple, and was surrounded by other penitents. "About this time the Buddhists began to take alarm and appealed to the temporal sovereign, asserting that in this fire-temple many living things were consumed in flaming fire, and that it was advisable that the Brahmanical rites should be set aside." When the king followed their advice, the ascetics, "resolved on redress, sought by prayer a deliverer, who should overthrow Buddhism and restore their own faith. The Supreme Justice brought forth from this fire-temple, now long grown cold, a human form, resplendent with divine majesty and bearing in its hand a flashing sword." This champion of the Brahmans, named Dhanji, obtained the throne, renewed brahmanical observances, and became the ancestor of the Paramāras. (R. B. Singh 1975, 223-25)

As we shall see, the Paramāras are the first Agnivaṃśa clan to claim their ancestor's birth from fire. One should probably not make much of the distinction between their ancestor's being born from fire, and from a "fire-temple, now long grown cold" (R. B. Singh 1975, 224). Certainly Abul Fazl's version of this myth—"apparently based on some current tradition of the sixteenth century" (ibid.)—would have come from Hindu (Rajput and/or Brahman) sources.

Quite possibly, the origin myth of the Agnivaṃśa Rajputs may have absorbed themes from the history of Hūṇa invaders, who, by 500 A.D., had established powerful kingdoms in western India under Toramāṇa and his son Mihirakula. The latter was remembered by the seventh-century Chinese Buddhist pilgrim Hsüan Tsang as "a fierce persecutor of Buddhism,"[53] and by the fifteenth century, Hūṇas could be listed among Rajput *jagīrdārs*.[54] The myth also seems to reflect a "resurgence of Brahmanical Hinduism . . . in north India at the expense of Buddhism and Jainism," one that took place between the late eighth through twelfth

---

ibid., 26, 129.

[52]He was killed by the Bundela Rajput chief Bir Singh Deo under orders from Akbar's son Jahangir.

[53]Basham 1967, 68; adding: "The invasions of the Hūṇas destroyed and dispersed the older martial tribes of Rājasthān and their places were taken by newcomers, either acclimatized invaders or indigenous tribes from the hills, from whom most of the Rajput clans of the Middle Ages were descended" (69)—a sort of compromise, recognizing the "older martial tribes." Cf. Thapar 1978a, 170; 1992, 73.

[54]See Thapar 1978a, 190, n. 108, and 172, 177; Bose 1956, 3; D. Sharma 1959.

centuries with the population and royal courts becoming generally Vaiṣṇava, Śaiva, or Śākta.[55] Yet at the key crossroads of Sind, the predominant Buddhists (the Sammitīyas or Pudgalavādins) of lower Sind and the Indus trade routes *did* quite uniformly collaborate with eighth-century Arab invaders, separating themselves (and their merchant interests) from "Hindus" (avant la lettre), who followed the unsuccessful resistance of the Brahman king Dāhir (whose wife instigated a mass widow-burning after his death). While the results of Buddhist collaboration in Sind were short-lived, the history of Hinduism there continued in multiple forms, first with Brahman-led resistance continuing in upper Sind around Multān, and by the mid-ninth century yielding the earliest indications of Ismā'īlī-Hindu "syncretism."[56] To look ahead to the next chapter, one may suspect that the centrality of Multān for Ismā'īlī missions from Persia in the subsequent Alamūt period (1090-1256) draws not only on the earlier history of Alids and Fāṭimid Ismā'īlīs in upper Sind, but on determinations of both Nizārīs and hinterland Rajputs in that area and beyond to turn common peripheralities into resistant political alliances[57] while their Pīrs and Jōgīs forged interchangeable religions visions.

In any event, it is at the source of the mix of Mleccha (including Muslim) invasions and the rise of Buddhism that the *Pratisarga Parvan* places the origin of the Agnivaṃśa Kṣatriyas, and it is into this mix that it introduces the great "Paramāra" Vikramāditya.

C. Vikramāditya's Era

It cannot be an object of this study to explore the mythology or oft-doubted historicity of Vikramāditya.[58] For our purposes, however, he is a pivotal figure, and four points must be made in relation to the complex that surrounds him. These concern (1) his portrayal in the *Pratisarga Parvan*, (2) his relation to the other Agnivaṃśa lineages; (3) his "era"; and (4) his foothold in the *Kṛṣṇāṃśacarita*, which has to do with the Naimiṣa Forest.

1. The *Pratisarga Parvan* does not link Vikramāditya directly with the destruction of Buddhists, although it situates him historically after the death of Aśoka, by which it defines their ascendancy. It does, however, connect him with Mleccha history through the figure of Kali. Kali

[55]I quote from McGregor 1984, 4, 6, who speaks only of the period from 1000-1200 A.D. But the trend precedes this, and also has south Indian antecedents.
[56]MacLean 1989, 13, n. 43, 50-82, 131-37.
[57]Cf. Maclean 1989, 127-50; Kassam 1995, 47-67.
[58]See especially Sircar 1969, 94-168; Edgerton 1926, lviii-ciii; Pandey 1995, 372-78; Gold 1992, 61; above at nn. 2-5.

worships the Sun, and after five years Sūrya gives him a man named Śaka, who receives from Kali the city of Taittira in what the paurāṇika calls "Taittiri country" (*taittirideśa*). Śaka brings bands of Dasyu herdsmen (*gopān dasyagaṇān*) from that region under his power, and makes repeated efforts to destroy Āryadeśa (3.4.1.17-20). The Śakas have already appeared toward the end of the Dvāpara yuga to be sacrificed by Kṣemaka and regenerated through "Adam and Eve" with the help of Kali. And in the *Kṛṣṇāṃśacarita*, Vikramāditya's "grandson" Śālivāhana conquers "the hard-to-attack Śakas born in the Cīna-Taittiri region" (2.18) just before his encounter with Jesus in Hūṇadeśa. Taittiri also becomes associated with the Mughuls (Mukula) through the depredations of Tamburlaine, who will come from Taittiri, raid Delhi, mock Hindu gods, burn books, ridicule Viṣṇu's presence in *śālagrāma* stones, and return to Taittiri to build his fort with steps to the throne made of śālagrāmas brought back on camels (3.4.6.44-56). Taittiri in these passages derives from "Tartary," as Dey has perceived, citing the *Pratisarga Parvan* as his only source.[59] As with "Sunday, February, and sixty," it seems that the paurāṇika has Sanskritized an English (or Guruṇḍika) usage.

It is in this long-range history of conflicts with Buddhists, Muslims, and the British that we may probably understand Śiva's interest in sending Vikramāditya to earth as an ideal "Hindu" emperor to counter rival emperors of these other two faiths. Śiva establishes a lion throne decorated with thirty-two designs for Vikramāditya at Ujjain, and Pārvatī creates a Vaitāla (genie) to protect him and instruct him by riddles with the famous stories of "The King and the Corpse."[60] After hearing these stories, Vikramāditya performs a horse sacrifice that is celebrated by all the gods but Candra, who claims, no doubt significantly in relation to the disappearance of Candravaṃśa kings, that he cannot tarry on earth in the Kali yuga. The horse's wandering defines the aforementioned boundaries of Vikramāditya's empire at Kapilasthāna (east), Setubandhana (south), the Indus (west), and Badarīvana (north). After a thorn-free rule, he goes to heaven (3.2.23.3-16), leaving, as noted earlier, eighteen kingdoms within these clearly ideal imperial boundaries.

We have met these boundaries at the end of the *Kṛṣṇāṃśacarita*. These four corners of India are the same destinations that Velā and the dying Brahmānanda visit as pilgrims on horseback. Considering that they are defined by Vikramāditya's imperial Aśvamedha, it looks as if the

[59]Dey [1889] 1927, 200; 1927, 9-10, 118.

[60]3.1.7.18-2.22.37; Hohenberger says these twenty-two *vaitāla* stories agree "extensively with those of the *Vetālapañcaviṃśati*" (1967, 4). They are ignored by Edgerton 1926 and Rajan 1995.

paurāṇika makes Velā's vast subcontinental tour analogous to a failed Aśvamedha, just as the Elliot *Ālhā* represents her more regional north Indian tour as a failed Dasarā. Moreover, these boundaries partially overlap with those to which Pṛthivīrāja's grandfather, the Tomara king Anangapāla, extends the sway of the Agnivaṃśa.[61] While the eastern and southern boundaries remain the same, there are two significant extensions. It is the Agnivaṃśa's inappropriate western expansion of "India" to Vāhīka (beyond the Indus, where "Hindus" come to be confused with Muslims) and its northern expansion to China (beyond Badarī in upper Uttar Pradesh, where they come to be confused with Buddhists) that provides the pretext for Kali, toward the beginning of the *Kṛṣṇāṃśacarita* (4.6-7), to obtain Kṛṣṇa's promise to destroy the Agnivaṃśa.

2. Vikramāditya not only conquers the world for the "Paramāras" but unites the four Agnivaṃśa lineages by taking brides from the other three: a Chauhān princess Vīrā (3.4.2.8), a Caulukya princess Nijā (4.3.24), and a Parihāra princess Bhogavatī (4.4.10). The giving of daughters to Vikramāditya reconnects the four lines and signals his imperial preeminence among them.

3. The primary era used for recording the passage of years and calculating Indian history is the Vikrama era, beginning 58-57 B.C., which is named after Vikramāditya, supposedly to celebrate his victory after driving the Śakas from Ujjain.[62] It would seem, as I have already suggested, to retrospectively project a founding "Hindu" imperial history back from the period of the imperial Guptas into one when India first encountered imperial designs primarily from outsiders like Darius, Alexander the Great, Seleucus Nicator, and Kaniṣka, and non-Hindu insiders like Aśoka.[63] In this, the Vikramāditya legend is like the *Mahābhārata* and *Rāmāyaṇa*, which also project such an image into even deeper pasts. It would also appear that this turn of a new era is one of the factors, along with the biblical legends, that results in a reimagining of the conventional chronology of the yugas, and of the usual place that the purāṇas accord to the *Mahābhārata* among them. Along with Nyūha's ark, the "era" of Vikramāditya has precedence over the conventional yuga chronology in marking the temporal transitions that lead to

[61]See chap. 8, § B.

[62]Basham 1967, 495, who, arguing that "the legend is surely false," considers it a four-hundred-year backward projection of the expulsion of the Śakas by Candra Gupta II, who took the title Vikramāditya. See also ibid., 66.

[63]See Sircar 1969, 49-58, 71-76. Cf. n. 5 above on a parallelism between Muslim time-reckoning from the Hijra and the Bhāṭṭika and popular eras used by Jaisalmer kings of Rajasthan.

Kurukṣetra II in the *Pratisarga Parvan*'s world history. It serves as a kind of second golden age between the two heroic ages of the *Mahābhārata* and the *Kṛṣṇāṃśacarita*'s "*Ālhā*."

4. This brings us to Vikramāditya's foothold within the *Kṛṣṇāṃśacarita*. It comes in connection with Lakṣaṇa's digvijaya, the *carita*'s counterpart to "The Gānjar War."[64] To recap the purāṇa's account, Mahīpati (Māhil), miserable at the "Banāphars'" successes, comes to Delhi. There he hears Candrabhaṭṭa (Chand Bardai) tell that he has gained insight from the goddess Vaiṣṇavī into that "glorification of the devotees of the goddess" called the *Kṛṣṇāṃśacarita*. Mahīpati recognizes Udayasiṃha (Ūdal) in the telling, and convinces Pṛthivīrāja to demand the four horses from Parimala (Parmāl). The "Banāphars" refuse and go into exile at Śītalāsthāna, outside Kanauj, where they worship Ambikā. Jayacandra (Jaychand), heeding Parimala, refuses to employ them, and Lakṣaṇa (Lākhan) goes to fight them. But when he shoots an arrow with a Viṣṇu-mantra and sees it hit Kṛṣṇāṃśa's (Ūdal's) heart with no effect, he bows and stammers, "Know me a Vaiṣṇava, Lord. . . . I know you as the descent of the śakti of Kṛṣṇa." When Jayacandra hears of this, he sends two lotus-trampling (*kuvalayāpīḍau*) elephants against Āhlāda (Ālhā) and Kṛṣṇāṃśa to test them,[65] which the brothers kill as a līlā. Seeing this, Jayacandra gives them the "village of Rājagṛha" (3.3.24.1-36).

The passage inducts us deeply not only into the text's theology, but its geopolitics, since Rājagṛha. "the king's home," is presumably the old Magadha capital of that name (or at least its echo), and a far sight from Śītalāsthāna, a "place of Śītalā," goddess of smallpox. One may suspect that the "Banāphars'" presence there already signals trouble to the Magadha king Vijayakārin. It is then some months later that Jayacandra sends Lakṣaṇa on his digvijaya accompanied by the "Banāphars." As noted, it is mainly a tax collecting mission: in the purāṇa, to the east and southeast, beginning with Vārāṇasī and Magadha itself (24.37-51); in the Elliot *Ālhā*, to a vast tract east of Gorakhpur. Toward the end, the purāṇa gets interesting.

> The intoxicated heroes went to Vīrasiṃhapuram and made the city weep that was situated like a snowy peak,[66] protected by the yogin named Gorakha because the people were his devotees. The king's

[64]See chap. 7 at n. 53, and chap. 5, table 4.

[65]He has evidently heard the *HV* or one of its successor texts, in which Kuvalayāpīḍa is the elephant of Krsna's wicked uncle Kaṃsa.

[66]This could be the same "Hīmatunga" on which Jesus appears to Śālivāhana, but considering that it does not seem to be in Kashmir or Hūnadeśa, it is better to consider both as "snowy peaks."

> younger brother Pravīra and the army made terrible war with the army of Lakṣaṇa. Having slain a thousand heroes in a day, reaching home at evening, the powerful hero (Pravīra) worshiped that yogin. Inwardly pleased by the pūjā, (Gorakha) brought the king's army back to life. Having given them the strength of elephants, he resumed his yoga. A half-month of battle went by. Then those zestless ones (the "Banāphars") said to Devasiṃha, "How is victory to be ours, O king. Tell our object straightaway." Having heard, he said, "Listen to my word, Kṛṣṇāṃśa. Having conquered the yogin Gorakha by dancing, again make war. Surely you will then obtain victory." Thus addressed, Kṛṣṇāṃśa and the rest, having put on yogi disguises and established the army protected by Lakṣaṇa in battle, went, as morning approached, to the temple (*mandiram*) of that yogin. Kṛṣṇāṃśa was a dancer skilled in playing flute, Devasiṃha played the mṛdanga drum, and Tālana bore a vīṇā. Then Āhlāda, carrying the bell metal gong, sang the eternal *Gītā* (*jagau gītām sanātanīm*). Gorakha, possessor of every yoga, knowing their purpose in his heart, told them, "Choose a boon." Having heard, they said, "We bow to you. If you give a boon, great soul, give the science of revival (*saṃjīvani vidyā*) to Āhlāda." Having meditated in his heart, of calmed intellect, he said to them, "The science of revival will be yours for a year. After that, being fruitless, it will come back to me. From today, O hero, this universe (*jagat*) is abandoned by me. Where the disciple Bhartṛhari is, having gone there, I rest." So speaking the yogin disappeared. They went to the battlefront. Having conquered Pravīrasiṃha and Vīrasiṃha, having slain their host and plundered their home, having made the king a slave, Lakṣaṇa went forth gladly. (24.42-67)

Leaving Vīrasiṃhapura, the "Banāphars" complete their tax collecting in Kośala, and then go to the Naimiṣa Forest. There they give gifts to Brahmans, and Lakṣaṇa sponsors a "great festival" at the time of Holikā. Having bathed at all the tīrthas, the heroes return to Kanauj (68-72). *Ālhā* seems to tell a variant of this episode. As noted, it makes Gorakhpur, "City of Gorakhnāth," the western end of the Banāphars' Gānjar campaign.[67] There they conquer Rāja Hir Singh, who could be the same as Vīrasiṃha.[68] Ālhā does not meet Gorakhnāth in the Gānjar War, or go to Naimiṣa Forest after it. But he is Gorakhnāth's "disciple" in oral *Ālhā* traditions of Mahobā. We now see that he is also Gorakhnāth's

[67]See chap. 7 at nn. 53-54. On Gorakhpur as a center of the Gorakhnāthīs, see Briggs [1938], 1989, especially 86-90.

[68]But there is also a Sūraj of Gorakhpur who is imprisoned during the Gānjar campaign by Ūdal (W&G 221).

disciple in the *Kṛṣṇāṃśacarita*, where he obtains the "science of revival" (though only for a month) from Gorakhnāth for singing the "eternal *Gītā*." As we have noted, the Banāphars' Jōgī-musician disguises seem to be primarily those of Gorakhnāthī yogis.

The paurāṇika thus draws from varied *Ālhā* traditions linking Gorakhnāth with Ālhā, and singles out this scene and setting for his version of their special connection. But this is not all. In the same sequence, when the "Banāphars" close their mission at Naimiṣa Forest, the narrator intrudes: "Then we, the Munis, and the king were all established in samādhi, when Lakṣaṇa reached the Naimiṣa Forest" (24.71). The king in question is presumably Śatānīka, the Pāṇḍavas' descendant and chief auditor of the purāṇa.

This sequence thus draws together what seem to be the features of a set piece, which includes the stock setting of Naimiṣa Forest. This forest has come to be identified with Nimsar near Misrikh. Although the Elliot *Ālhā* does not have Ālhā go there, it mentions "Nimsar-Misrik" in a canto-invocation as a place where seven virgins once prayed for husbands: Gaurī won Śiva, Sītā got Rāma, Mandodarī won Rāvaṇa, Rādhā won Kṛṣṇa, Kusum Dē won Lākhan, Phulwā got Ūdal, and Gajmōtin won Malkhān (their marriage being the subject of the canto; W&G 192). As in the purāṇas and epics, it is a place where stories from different times are tied together as they flow into the Kali yuga. As a canto invocation, this *Ālhā* passage has an uncertain relation to the narrative; there do not seem to be actual stories about the visits of these *Ālhā* heroines' to Nimsar. What is striking by contrast in the *Kṛṣṇāṃśacarita* is that Naimiṣa Forest becomes an important location in the story.

There we have found ourselves once before at the beginning of Kṛṣṇāṃśa's encounter with the libidinous Muslim witch, Śobhanā.[69] Having gone with Puṣpavatī to this "purifying lotus forest served by the muni Vālmīki, the foremost iron bolt consisting of brahman on the bank of the Gangā" (28.3), Kṛṣṇāṃśa has distracted himself from Śobhanā's wiles by hearing about the eighteen purāṇas, and has learned that the *Bhāgavata* is the best (28.1-16). Here we see who has been there before him: "When the world reached the Kali yuga, a king named Vikrama [Vikramāditya], having come to earth from Kailāsa, convoked (*samāhvayat*) the Munis together. Then all those Munis, dwelling in Naimiṣa Forest, brought the bard [presumably Lomaharṣaṇa] in order for them to hear it [the *Bhāgavata*]. The eighteen upapurāṇas were also declared by the bard. Having thus heard this word, Kṛṣṇāṃśa, devoted to dharma,

[69]See chap. 7, § B.

having heard the foremost *Bhāgavata Śāstra* in seven days, gave gifts of golden cows to the twiceborn, and fed a thousand Brahmans devoted to Veda" (16-19).

So the real set-piece is the combination of Vikramāditya, Gorakhnāth, Bhartṛhari,[70] Lomaharṣaṇa, Śaunaka and the other Naimiṣeya Brahmans, and their purāṇic convocation or "colloquium" in the Naimiṣa Forest. This forest seems to be "always there" as the place in which *Mahābhārata* and purāṇa poets, and indeed Vālmīki too,[71] compose their storied wisdom. Indeed, why be surprised that the great Sanskrit poet Kālidāsa, usually associated with the court of Candragupta II (ca. 376-415 A.D.), shows up over six centuries later in the company of Bhojarāja deploying japam to turn Mahāmada to ash. Such is the power of poets, who can equally deploy the mantra of revival or the murmur of destruction, and turn time inside-out. Even if Kālidāsa does not make it to Naimiṣa Forest, he shares company with those who travel the imperial time-bands of "Vikramāditya."

For the *Pratisarga Parvan*'s history of the Agnivaṃśa, Vikramāditya is the temporal anchor for these figures. His golden age not only marks the high point of this dynasty; it is he who convokes the bards and Ṛṣis at Naimiṣa Forest to repeat and rehear the purāṇas *within* the Kali yuga. This colloquium called by Vikramāditya for the recitation of all the purāṇas and upapurāṇas is mentioned not only in the *Kṛṣṇāṃśacarita* but at another point in the wider *Pratisarga Parvan*, this time with the added information that it is for the hearing of eighty-eight thousand Munis (3.4.1.3-8). No doubt they are the same eighty-eight thousand who floated over the flood with Nyūha. One may further suppose that they have remained at Naimiṣa Forest, unnumbered, to meet Kṛṣṇāṃśa before his Muslim captivity, and to greet the "Banāphars" after their encounter with Gorakhnāth. These colloquia carry the purāṇic genre forward from the end of the *Mahābhārata* and the beginning of the Kali yuga on *into* the Kali yuga. In the *Bhaviṣya Purāṇa* particularly, the genre ties together "futures" and "pasts," from the golden age of Vikramāditya to "*Ālhā*" and the romances of the Gorakhnāthī Nāth Jōgīs.

Let us appreciate, however, that as the paurāṇika translates such north Indian folk epic and romance into purāṇa, he is encountering oral epics that have a corresponding convention of their own: that of the "Plantain Forest" (*kajaḷī van*) of the Nāth immortals.[72] Under the variant *Kanjarī*

[70]On links between these first three in Rajasthani folklore, see Gold (1992, 60-63) on Bhartrhari as Gorakhnāthī yogin, poet, and renunciant elder brother of Vikramāditya.
[71]See chap. 4, n. 7.
[72]See White 1996, 234-40, 476-77 on other north Indian (mainly romantic) oral epics drawing on these themes; also Gold 1992, 145, n. 17.

Ban, the "'Forest of Lampblack', the same as the Land of Darkness," and with tantric and alchemical associations, the Elliot *Ālhā* knows it as the place where Ālhā "is still waiting for the time of his reappearance," having gone there as an immortal after the last battle of *Ālhā*.[73] Like the Naimiṣa Forest as the home of twinkling celestial Ṛṣis, the Plantain Forest or Forest of Lampblack, where Gorakhnāth is the "Sovereign Guru" (Gold 1992, 158), is where "fourteen hundred invisible disciples are gathered, doing tapas, and . . . fourteen hundred visible disciples are doing tapas."[74] Yogis "camp" there with their *dhūnis* or hearths (316) and their "fire burns with saffron" (237). Indeed, the bhaviṣya pauraṇika is probably aware of this oral epic convention, and equally aware that it overlaps with a Sanskrit epic convention of the *Mahābhārata*. The paurāṇika situates the *Kadalī Vanam* or Plantain Forest on Mount Gandhamadana (3.3.32.236), where Bhīma, in the epic, meets the immortal Hanumān (*Mbh* 3.146.63 and 64; cf. 44) and learns that the path beyond this forest is a divine pathway travelled only by Siddhas and inaccessible to mortals (146.79; 147.40-41). There, says Hanumān, he listens to Apasaras and Gandharvas delight (*ramayanti*) him with songs of Rāma (39)! Just as it is where Hanumān resides as an immortal long after the *Rāmāyaṇa* to greet his brother Bhīma, it is the final destination of Āhlāda, to which he goes after Kurukṣetra II to depart this world, dedicate himself to yoga, and remain an immortal too.[75] Neither the Elliot *Ālhā* (at least as it is represented by Waterfield and Grierson) nor the *Kṛṣṇāṃśacarita* mentions Guru Gorakhnāth in connection with this forest, but the purāṇa, as we have seen, makes Āhlāda Gorakhnāth's disciple, and no doubt both texts know the forest's Nāth connections. Moreover, Baccha Singh tells a variant where the connection would be explicit, were it not that instead of a forest, Ālhā's final destination is a mountain cave. According to Baccha Singh, Gorakhnāth kept his hearth (dhūnī) in a cave on Gorakha Mountain near Mahobā, where it is still; Ālhā received Gorakhnāth's darshan and worshiped him regularly there. When Ālhā left this world, it was to join his guru there.

This double representation of Ālhā's afterworld as cave and forest

[73]W&G 273 and n. 3. Cf. Gold 1992, 145, n. 17; White 1996, 238: (1) *kadalī van*, a place associated with sensuality linked with the plantain trunk as a metaphor for women's thighs, and also "a grove of yogic realization and immortality"; (2) *kajalī van*, "'forest of black mercuric sulfide," of the mineral hierophany of the sexual essences of Śiva and the goddess, which does in fact constitute an elixir of immortality"; (3) *kajarī van*, "identified with Zulmāt, the name of the land of death and darkness (kaj[j]alī also means 'lampblack') to which Iskandar (Alexander the Great) traveled, according to Muslim legend."

[74]Gold 1992, 237. The description is formulaic; cf. 194; 246.

[75]See chap. 8, § B.

reminds us that both images can evoke the night sky.[76] Elsewhere, as noted earlier, I argue that the *Mahābhārata* develops two literary conventions concerning the Naimiṣa Forest as an image of the night sky of "twinkling" stars: the convention of the colloquium or symposium of celestial Ṛṣis, and the convention of time-collapsing narrative frames.[77] The *Bhaviṣya Purāṇa* works from, but also alters, these conventions. In the *Kṛṣṇāṃśacarita*, the second adhyāya opens at Naimiṣa Forest to mark the transition from the end of the *Mahābhārata* to the time of Vikramāditya. Once the purāṇa's Sūta finishes describing the last days of the Pāṇḍavas and tells us that their aṃśas will be reborn for "an increase of Kalidharma," Vyāsa, "settled at Cakratīrtha"—which is at Nimsar (Ragam 1963, 263)—tells the Munis to leave him while he, "under the sway of Yoganidrā," enters into "meditation beyond the three guṇas." The Munis, remaining at Naimiṣa, also enter a yogic state, and after twelve hundred years, they arise and bathe. It is the time of Vikramāditya (3.3.2.1-8), and they are present to hear the Sūta resume with an account of the aftermath of Vikramāditya's reign: from Śālivāhana's encounter with Jesus to Bhojarāja and Kālidāsa's encounter with Mahāmada, and on to "*Ālhā*."

Then, in the immediate aftermath of the *Kṛṣṇāṃśacarita*, the Ṛṣis remain at Naimiṣa Forest to hear the history of the Agnivaṃśa kings, beginning with the story of the "four born from fire" (3.4.1.1-12). Still in Naimiṣa, when they ask the Sūta to speak about kings who rule after the *Kṛṣṇāṃśacarita*, the bard begins with "the Paiśāca Kutukkoddīna" in Delhi (Qutb-ud-din, Shihāb al-Dīn's general, and successor as founder of the so-called Slave Dynasty): his battles, and the deteriorating conditions that follow him during a hundred years of Mleccha rule. This prompts the bard to urge the Ṛṣis to accompany him quickly to an auspicious mountain city called Viśālā. "In misery, they leave Naimiṣa (*duḥkhāt saṃtyajya naimiṣam*)," and at Viśālā, they all meditate on the all-knowing Hari. After years in samādhi, they ascend to the "home of Brahmā," or Satyaloka (3.4.6.1-10, 34). Vyāsa now says he has told about the "whole future heard by the exercise of yoga," and asks what else his audience

[76]Cf. Crooke ([1896] 1986, 283), who describes Ālhā's appearances on Mahiyâr Hill in the context of "a whole cycle of fairy legend centring round the belief that some of the heroes of old live in caves surrounded by their faithful followers, and will rise some day to win back their kingdom." Compare also the correspondence between the Guttikoṇda Cave and the milk sea as paradisal images in *Palnāḍu* and *Elder brothers* (chap. 3, 7), and *Mbh* 1, 189: A trail of golden lotuses formed from the tears of the goddess Śrī leads Indra from Naimiṣa Forest on the Ganges up the river to its source, where he is commanded by Śiva to a Himalayan cave to meet four other Indras doomed to take birth with him as the five Pāṇḍavas. See also Gold 1992, 58.

[77]See chap. 4, n. 7; Hiltebeitel in press-h and forthcoming.

wishes to hear. Manu, paying homage to Vyāsa as, among other things, "the witness (*sākṣiṇe*)," asks him to dispel his ignorance about the highest Brahman. Vyāsa then unfolds an unusual purāṇic cosmogony, with an account of the kalpas (the great temporal units that make up the days, years, and life Brahmā). It identifies Viṣṇu-Nārāyaṇa as the "living self" (*jīvātmā*) of sixteen parts and the "self of time" (*kālātmā*), and in effect maps the kalpas onto the body of Śiva, the more encompassing self of eighteen parts who is the "pacifier of living souls" (*jīvaśaṃkaraḥ*) (11-27). Whereas units of time pertain to saguṇa Brahman, the supreme Brahman is above time and born from the imperishable. The *padam* or "foot" of that supreme Brahman, "whose undecaying nature is a subtle light," is obtainable by ten years of samādhi, which the Ṛṣis have just completed. So they now experience the "denseness (*ghanakam*) of Saccidānanda," and in what would pass as an instant on earth (*bhūrlokātkṣanamātrakam*), they experience a hundred thousand earthly years (28-35). But opening their eyes on the second day, they see further deterioration of human life on earth: people living like cattle, caste-mixture, Mlecchas as heretics, heretics of many jātis, and propounders of many paths (*pāṣaṃdā bahujātīyā nānāmārgapradarśakāḥ*). Having seen all this "in the presence of Romaharṣaṇa" (i.e., Lomaharṣaṇa), the Ṛṣis pay him homage, and Vyāsa tells them to listen to him as he emerges from "the eternal Yoganidrā" to tell the "story of the kalpas," beginning with the depredations of Timirilinga ("Dark Phallus") or Tamburlaine (36-57) which lead on to the Mughal empire.

Lomaharṣaṇa (or Romaharṣaṇa)—in either case, "He who makes hair stand on end" with his horripilating tales—thus carries on the bardic mission reflected not only in his name, but that of his son Ugraśravas—"He who is terrifying to hear"—who recites the *Mahābhārata* to the celestial Ṛṣis. Lomaharṣaṇa does this with comings and goings at Naimiṣa Forest, which thus provides the location for the *Bhaviṣya Purāṇa*'s outer frame, just as Ugraśravas' arrival at Naimiṣa Forest to recite the *Mahābhārata* defines the outer frame of the *Mahābhārata*. In the latter, this outer Naimiṣa Forest frame both encompasses and occasionally surfaces within the inner frame of Vaiśampāyana's telling of the *Mahābhārata* at Janamejaya's snake sacrifice. Similarly, the *Bhaviṣya Purāṇa*'s outer Naimiṣa Forest frame both encompasses and occasionally surfaces within the inner frame of the *Pratisarga Parvan*'s refashioning of the yugas around the *Kṛṣṇāṃśacarita* as a second battle of Kurukṣetra anchored in the era of Vikramāditya. As we have seen, this inner frame of the yugas, from before and through Vikramāditya to beyond the *Kṛṣṇāṃścarita*, is threaded by a story of the origins and spread of the Mlecchas and the Agnivaṃśa.

With these reorientations, other conventions have also changed. Time-travel becomes explicit, as does the link between narrative and yoga, which is inspired by the grace of Yoganidrā, the Sleep of Yoga: a form of the goddess identified not only with Jagadambikā, but with Śāradā and Vindhyavāsinī of the *Ālhā* heartland. As a source of bardic insight, the "sleep of yoga" is not only the near-*samādhi* state of Viṣṇu, but the goddess herself in the form by which she awakens Kṛṣṇāṃśa to carry out, like Viṣṇu and Kṛṣṇa before him, his storied acts. Having been the Twinkling Forest of the Veda and the Momentous Forest of the *Mahābhārata*, Naimiṣa Forest is now the place where "triple-time-knowing" bards move in and out of the "sleep of yoga" by the goddess's grace.[78] Bonazzoli, historicizing rather than recognizing literary conventions, takes the setting of the Naimiṣa Forest as suggesting the absorption of ancient stories into the temporal stream of the Kali yuga through an "enthusiastic movement" of missionary Ṛṣis (1981, 49, 52-61). I would rather say that an epic narrative convention has been drawn into a purāṇic stream of yogic consciousness, the current of Yoganidrā.

Moreover, when the *Kṛṣṇāṃśacarita*'s second adhyāya opens with Vyāsa entering Yoganidrā to transport the Munis (and the readers) from the last days of the Pāṇḍavas to the time of Vikramāditya, he does so not only while staying in Naimiṣa Forest, but, as we have seen, at a specific place there: he is "settled at Cakratīrtha." Here we realize that purāṇic conventions of the Naimiṣa Forest might be worth a further study of their own. Cakratīrtha, "Tīrtha of the Wheel," is unmentioned in the *Mahābhārata*. But it comes in the purāṇas to be identified as a site within Naimiṣa Forest once the latter is associated with Nimsar on the Gomatī River.[79] The association is the pretext for introducing a new etymology that traces Naimiṣa not from *nimiṣa*, the twinkling of an eye or moment, but *nemi*, the rim or felly of a wheel.[80] As such, it is a spot beside the Gomatī where the Wheel of Dharma (*dharmacakra*) broke or rent (*Brahmāṇḍa Pur.* 1.2.8-9). Tagare summarizes the myth: Cakratīrtha is where Brahmā, seeking to insure a sacred place for the sages' sacrifices, "created mentally a wheel which went on running till it reached the vicinity of the Gomatī river near which its felly broke down" (1983, 8, n. 2). I believe this is a mistaken reading, implying that the wheel stops running where it "breaks down." As the *Brahmāṇḍa Purāṇa* tells the story,

[78]Like Chand Bardai (see chap. 7, n. 5), Lomaharsana is *trikālajña*, triple-time-knowing, at *BhvP*. 3.1.4.1 where Śaunaka invites him to tell the story of Pradyota's *mlecchayajña*. On the Momentous Forest (*nimesa* and *nimisa* both also meaning "moment"), see Hiltebeitel in press-h and forthcoming.

[79]See Hiltebeitel in press-h and forthcoming for discussion of the indeterminacy and mobility of prepurānic locations of Naimisa Forest.

[80]See Tagare 1980, 1:70-71, and 1983, 1:8, for discussion and citations.

> When they were seen by Svayambhu (Brahmā), the distinguished Munis, desirous of dharma and striving to reach a land of merit, questioned him. Wishing them well, the lord Vibhu (the widely existing one) said, "Well-naved, radiant with divine form, having seven divisions, praiseworthy, this incomparable wheel is turning. Alert, restrained, if you follow it to what you ask about, you will reach where it is broken (split). When this wheel goes where the felly is broken (shattered. scattered), it is to be considered a land of merit." Having thus addressed all the Ṛṣis, he became invisible.[81]

The setting, a purāṇic sattra of the thousand-year variety performed by Brahmā and the gods out of the desire to create the universe (1.2.5), is of a type known from *Pañcaviṃśa Brāhmaṇa* 25.27 (Caland [1931] 1982, 642-43). But now it is performed by a cast of characters that fills out offices mentioned in various sattras described in the *Mahābhārata*:[82]

> Brahmā himself became the master of the penance-house.[83] Iḍā (deified food as feminine) took on the position of wife.[84] The intelligent Mṛtyu (Death) of great splendor performed as śamitṛ in this sattra of the great-souled ones.[85] The gods (*vibudhāḥ*) stayed there for a thousand years. Where the whirling rim (*nemi*) of the dharmacakra broke (or rent) is known by that act as Naimiṣa, honored by Munis. . . . There at Naimiṣa the speakers of Brahman thought of a mountain (*menire śailam*). Since they were born at Naimiṣa, they are renowned as Naimiṣīyas.[86]

I believe we have here an instance of archaeoastronimical knowledge

[81]1.1.155b-59b: *yathā dṛṣṭaḥ svayaṃbhuvā/ pṛṣṭavanto viśiṣṭās te munayo dharmakāṅkṣiṇaḥ// deśaṃ puṇyam abhīpsato vibhunā tadhitaiṣinā/ sunābhaṃ divyarūpābhaṃ saptāṅgaṃ śubhaśaṃsanam// ānaupamyam idam cakraṃ varttamānam ataṃdritāḥ/ pṛṣṭato yāta niyatās tataḥ prāpsyatha pāṭitam// gacchatas tasya cakrasya yatra nemir viśīryate/ puṇyah sa deśo maṃtavyaḥ pratyuvāca tadā prabhuh// uktvā caivaṃ rsīn sarvān adṛśyatvam upāgamat.*
[82]See Hiltebeitel in press-h and forthcoming.
[83]*Tapogṛhapati*; Brahmā, like Śaunaka in the *Mbh*, is thus the "master of the house" (*gṛhapati*) as one in which the sattrins undertake tapas (as do the sattrins at the beginning of the *Mbh*). No wonder Śaunaka and the Naimiṣeya Ṛṣis can appear to Ugraśravas as "brahman itself" or "Brahmā himself" (1.1.12).
[84]As observed by Jamison (1996, 31), sattrins had wives. So, presumably, did those who hear the *Mbh* in the Naimiṣa Forest (see Hiltebeitel forthcoming).
[85]Mrtyu thus has the same position—that of *śamitr*—as Yama in the Naimisa Forest sattra of he gods that leads to the birth of the Pāṇḍavas (see above, n. 76).
[86]*Brahmāṇda Pur*. 1.2.6-8 and 13: especially 8: *bhramato dharmacakrasya yatra nemir aśīryata/ karmanā tena vikhyātaṃ naimisam munipūjitam*; and 13: *tatra te menire śailaṃ naimise brahmavādinaḥ/ naimiṣaṃ jajnire yasmān naimisīyās tataḥ smṛtāḥ*.

communicated by what Sullivan calls "the technical language of myth."[87] The Naimiṣīyas, now born in Naimiṣa Forest, desirous of dharma, heed Brahmā's instruction to alertly follow the whirling course of the dharmacakra till it breaks the plane of the earth. That point will be a "land of merit." What is important to realize is that the Ṛṣis begin from a celestial vantage point and follow their information down to earth. They also "thought of a mountain"—one thinks, of course, of Meru—to define and measure celestial movement against yet-to-emerge earthly orientations. Naimiṣa Forest thus remains in the stars, but now defined by a "Wheel of Dharma" which "breaks" at Naimiṣa Forest on the Gomatī. This would likely be where this perpetually turning cosmic wheel—the plane of the ecliptic—is "broken" ("rent, split, or shattered") by the celestial equator: a point where the celestial and earthly Naimiṣa Forests intersect.

What is intriguing in the *Bhaviṣya Purāṇa* is that it connects this site with movement in time. When the *Pratisarga Parvan* associates Cakratīrtha with yogic movements that transport the Naimiṣa Forest sages to the reign of Vikramāditya, it defines the beginning of an imperial era by Vikramāditya's convocation of eighty-eight thousand Ṛṣis—the same number who mark the transition to the Kali yuga on Nyūha's ark. Not surprisingly, the paurāṇika has Vikramāditya sponsor his era-launching colloquium so that the Ṛṣis hear purāṇas and upapurāṇas. In listening, they hear the *Bhaviṣya* itself, in which "*Ālhā*" and its second battle of Kurukṣetra are included as prophesy. In this way, the paurāṇika fashions history—including Mughal history—by writing it into the stars, and overwriting the era of Vikramāditya upon it.

D. Purāṇic Nationalism

In bringing us to Naimiṣa Forest, the paurāṇika thus brings us to what is for him the yogic end zone of epic-intertextuality. It is not just a matter of *Ālhā*, *Mahābhārata*, and *Bhaviṣya Purāṇa*, but of *Rāmāyaṇa*, and of

[87]See Sullivan 1966, 9, 165-69, 223-38, and *passim*. On the points which follow, see for comparison 234: mountains as "structural elements determinant of the four corners of the 'celestial earth,' namely the relationship of the helical rise of stars to given solar dates, the parameters of a world-age" (cf. 36-37, 66-67); 21-46, 143, 242-48: the beginning and end of eras as linked with myths referring to the precession of the equinoxes and the intersection of the ecliptic and the celestial equator; 251; 72-74, 93, 109: "inclination" of the "celestial earth" as metaphor for the obliquity of the ecliptic plane; 31: the importance of considering specific stars as the "point of view" from which cosmological myths are told. It is important to recognize that while one must sift through much that is unlikely in Santillana and Dechend's *Hamlet's Mill* (1969), they are right as to *how* some myths refer technically to stars, and that we cannot understand them without recognizing that we understand less about this technical language than those who told them. Cf. Kloetzli 1985.

north Indian oral romantic and "historical" epic traditions about Gorakhnāth and Vikramāditya. For this chapter, however, it is enough to conclude with some observations on the nature of our two main texts.

Insofar as they might relate to each other, it would be wrong to regard the Elliot *Ālhā*, or probably any oral *Alha*, as indebted to the *Bhaviṣya Purāṇa*'s *Ālhā* translation. If this surprising text has had influence anywhere, it is not likely to have been in "popular" or "folk" circles.[88] Rather, I would propose that both the *Kṛṣṇāṃśacarita* and the Elliot *Ālhā* be regarded as texts aimed at totally different audiences, produced quite close to each other in time.

Indeed, one may say that as texts they are antithetical. The *Kṛṣṇāṃśacarita* "appropriates" oral *Ālhā* to work it into a Brahmanical world history and geography that accounts not only for the triumph of Mlecchadom as a part of a divine plan, or divine līlā, but also the dissolution of all three Kṣatriya vaṃśas, the Solar, Lunar, and Agni lines. The divine plan is in fact the paurāṇika author's plan. The author has taken over the story. The purāṇa clearly dismisses any possibility that there might be true Kṣatriyas left to reckon with, and even more vigorously celebrates the demise of the "little kings." Oral *Ālhā*s keep the stories of such "little kings" alive.

As to the time of their composition, I have argued that the *Kṛṣṇāṃśacarita* is of a piece with a *Pratisarga Parvan* that is no earlier than the mid eighteenth century, written in time to demonize the 1739 invasion of Nadir Shah in the vein we have been tracing. The Elliot *Ālhā* is from the late 1860s. But they are probably closer than that. Chatterjee describes a Bengali history of the kingdoms of Delhi and Bengal, the *Rājābali*, written in 1808 by Mrityunjay Vidyalankar, a Brahman who taught Sanskrit at Fort William College in Calcutta.[89] Says Chatterjee, Mrityunjay "did not have to undertake any fresh 'research' into the subject; he was only writing down an account that was in circulation at the time among Brahman literati and their landowning patrons" (1995a, 77-78). Once again, "the defeat of Prithiviraj Chauhan at the hands of Shihabuddin/Muhammad Ghuri takes the form off a Puranic tale" (80). The "mythic" features that motivate Pṛthivīrāja's fall (cannibalism and

[88]Mahobā informants Zahir Singh and Krishna Chaurasia, with their research interests, know of and have access to the *BhvP*'s *Ālhā*-segment, and regard it, in the absence of Jagnaik's supposed original, as the closest thing to an "original." Although familiar with some incarnational details, including Krsṇa as Kṛṣnāmśa, and regarding them as authentic *Ālhā* variants, they were not conversant with the tenor of the text. Awareness such as theirs may filter back into popular traditions, but not likely with any major effects.

[89]It was commissioned for young East India Company officials to study the vernacular, and used by Ward ([1822] 1970, 44) for his "history" through the yugas (18-50). Cf. Guha 1997, 177-83, especially 183 on its "contest between histocial time and Puranic time."

patricide) are different from those that do so in the *Kṛṣṇāṃśacarita*, but the two histories clearly come from the same conceptual world. In each, there is a reclamation of yugas as imperial history by reference to Yudhiṣṭhira, Vikramāditya, and Śālivāhana.[90] Both tell of Vedic sacrifices performed to fix "India's" boundaries against invaders, and that in each case they fail, resulting in the penetration of "India" by those outside of caste. Mrityunjay tells of the end of the "Kṣatriya jāti" (parallel to the Solar and Lunar dynasties in the *Bhaviṣya Purāṇa*), followed by the rise of the "Rājput jāti" of the Nandas (recalling the rajputizing names used by the purāṇa in the founding of Magadha), then the "Nāstika" Buddhists by whom "the Vaidika religion was almost eradicated," then on to the "empire of the Hindu kings," which ends with the fall of Pṛthivīrāja and the "Chohān Rājput jāti" (equivalent to the Agnivaṃśa), and on to the "empire of the Musalaman."[91] Each text depicts the rise and fall of empires and dynasties as a result of "the play of divine will" (81) rather than a struggle for power, or patterns of accident, treachery, and revenge that typify nationalist historiography by the 1870s (88-91, 102-6).

But there are also differences, and these would seem to suggest that the *Pratisarga Parvan* and the *Kṛṣṇāṃśacarita* are later than Mrityunjay's *Rājābali*. One is the *Pratisarga Parvan*'s uneasy accommodation to Christianity: something that does not seem to enter the *Rājābali*, but becomes regular fare in nationalist historiography and reform Hinduism by the 1860s (Chatterjee 1995a, 92-93). Second, Mrityunjay tells his story without "Banāphars" to defend popular Hinduism against the incursions of popular Buddhism and popular Islam. The "appropriation of the popular" as "the timeless truth of the national culture" is likewise, according to Chatterjee (72-73), primarily a development of the second half of the nineteenth century. How else are we to understand our paurāṇika author's exaltation of folk heroes at the expense of folk culture? Finally, unlike Mrityunjay, the purāṇic author engages in a debate about the authenticity and survival of Rajputs, presenting the flip side of the prominent nationalist historiographical view that true Rajputs never compromised and "remain free to this day" (105-6).

How far can we be from the 1860s and '70s with this paurāṇika

[90]Vikramāditya, with his "rediscovery of Ayodhyā" nine hundred thousand (nine lākhs!) years after Rāma, and his supposed construction of the Rāma temple that Babar would later destroy, also enters what Pandey calls "Hindu history" with the Rāmjanmabhūmi controversy (1995, 373-78).

[91]Chatterjee 1995a, 79-81. The nineteenth-century use of biblical myth and genealogy to downgrade Rajputs was a tactic not only of the British and the Brahmans, but of the Dalit reformer Balaram—a positional complementarity that should not be the "complete mystery" that it is to Chatterjee (ibid., 193, 258, n. 45).

author? He may only anticipate these trends, but I suspect he reflects their emergence, and that Bonazzoli is correct that he writes against the background of the Indian Renaissance—and further, I suspect, near the transition from colonial to imperial rule.[92] We have only found more to substantiate Bonazzoli's argument.[93] Moreover, I see this background applying not only to the biblical sequence, but to the *Pratisarga Parvan* more or less as a whole. Chatterjee says the *Rājābali* "is not a nationalist history because its protagonists are gods and kings, not peoples. The bonds of 'nationness' have not yet been imagined that would justify the identification of the historian with the consciousness of a solidarity that is supposed to act itself out in history" (784). Our paurāṇika would seem to be transitional in this regard. Whereas others would later claim the purāṇas as a protonationalist resource, he actually writes purāṇa with a certain kind of national agenda.[94] It is still gods and kings, but there are also the "little kings" whose history is suppressed, national boundaries that should be honored, and Brahman sages who will always survive. I would call it a case of purāṇic nationalism.

[92]Halbfass 1988, 194, observes the similarity in "xenology" ("attitudes toward, and conceptions of, foreigners" [507 n. 2]) and "familiarity with the British" between the *BhvP*'s biblical sequence and the *Sarvadevavilāsa*, "written in Madras around 1800," which associates the "seizure of power by the 'low,' 'vile' (*nīca*) foreigners," described "as 'pale-faced' (*śvetamukha*) or 'Huns' (*hūṇa*)," with the reign of Rāvaṇa. Cf. 173 on the period around 1800 (with a statement that rather too strongly polarizes European and Indian currents of the period).

[93]Bonazzoli's only substantiations are, rather mysteriously, the somewhat doubtful allusions to Ahmadiyya notions of Jesus's visit to Kashmir (1979a, 37-39), and a statement—about as far from the mark as it could be, I think—that the Jesus passage "should perhaps be interpreted as an attempt of some Hindus to assimilate in their tradition all the values of their conquerors" (39).

[94]The paurāṇika also seems to use nineteenth-century terms for other nations (Japan, Siam; see chap. 7, n. 69) and historically identified geographical regions such as Taittiri for "Tartary," as noted above. Dey, who recognizes the latter identification, exemplifies the use of purāṇa as nationalist resource with his fantastic reconstructions of Central Asian names behind Rasātala and other purāṇic underworlds and their inhabitants ([1899] 1927, 167-68, 172-73; 1927). In recovering the "old nomenclature" behind such cosmological terms, Dey saw himself correcting the "ridiculous interpretations . . . put on them during the dark age of the Kali-yuga, one of the symptoms that generally precede the downfall of a nation" (1927, 144). Cf. Rocher 1986, 13, n. 24. Contrast the point made by Hansen, that "*Ālhā* tales, although based on a feudal setup, may have helped disseminate a new strand of nationalism, insofar as they proposed armed combat as the appropriate means of righting society's wrongs" (1992, 133). The same story had both "purāṇic" and "activist" (ibid.) nationalist potentials.

10 Their Name Is Legion

Not so long ago I suggested that the Draupadī cult's nearest counterpart seemed to be the Pāṇḍav Līlās of Garhwal, and that further study of this Garhwal cult was likely to open onto "astonishing parallels and significant variations . . . in the ways these two cults mythologize and ritualize the epic: one in the high mountains of India's far north, the other in the lowlands of the deep south, and with nothing to link them geographically or historically but Hinduism" (1988a, 132). Parallels and variations aside, it is the "nothing but Hinduism" that I wish to reconsider. It was meant as a sign of unease with those who had begun to argue that Hinduism was to be put in quotes as an invention of the British. This is not to say that the British and other colonialists did not invent a useful Hinduism centered, among other things, on Brahmanical concepts of caste and life-stage. But the Hinduism thus invented was one that virtually omitted the epics, which had also invented a much older (in-all-but-the-name) Hinduism worked around these same concepts. This earlier Hinduism *was* centered on the "epic" mode of the Kṣatriya, a mode that the British were motivated to both disinvent and reinvent in their own image, more or less simultaneously.

Kipling, writing in 1886, typically belittles the "two national epics"—the *Mahābhārata* and *Rāmāyaṇa*—in their first English translations (Pinney 1986, 177-78). Yet around the time of his assessment, Ravi Varma finds them a storehouse of images by which to enthuse large audiences not only as poster art for their homes but at museums and royal courts across India. Varma invented the sari as the national epic dress for women (Venniyoor 1982, 27), while at the same time he researched and painted the regional outfits of the contemporary, especially rural, women, whom Kipling expected to remember the two epics only as "love ditties." When the Gaekwad of Baroda commissioned fourteen Ravi Varma pictures in 1888, they were to "convey the drama of the two great texts of the Hindu religion, the *Ramayana* and the *Mahabharata*; they should evoke the beatitudes of *Satyam*, *Śivam*, *Sundram*, the True, the Good and the Beautiful, and should proclaim to all the world the splendour of

India's heritage" (ibid.). The echoes of Plato are striking.

Kipling's views complemented the rhetorical climate of competing turn-of-the-century interests remarked on by Metcalf: "The British conceived that India's buildings provided the best, if not the only, book from which long periods of its history could 'satisfactorily be read'"; "By 1900, then, alike in ethnography, archaeology, and architecture, the British had, or so they thought, ordered, and so mastered, at once India's past and its present" (1995, 151, 159). A dismissal of India's "national epics" is logical in this view, which, as is well known, held that India was a land without history whose history had to be reclaimed. The British could control museums, monuments, and ethnography as an exemplary record of the past, but India's Sanskrit epics could only elude them. The only pathbreaking British work on the epics remains Monier-Williams' *Indian epic poetry* (1863), which quickly yielded to work done by Indians, Germans, French, Americans, Dutch, Scandinavians, Russians, etc. At most, along with the purāṇas, the epics could interest British historians like V. A. Smith and Pargiter who took it as their task to extricate and sanction material that bore on royal genealogies of ancient Kṣatriya kings and contemporary princes. No matter that most of this was invented as well; the British were determined to reinvent it as their own kind of history. As we have seen in the case of Waterfield, Grierson, and Sewell, they took more interest in oral epics than in classical ones, but with mainly the same concerns.[1] Metcalf also remarks on how the "Sepoy Mutiny" was "cast in heroic form to create a 'mythic' triumph" and "monuments associated with the events of 1857 were organized in a sacral way" (1995, 156).

Scholars persist in either ignoring or deconstructing the Kṣatriya, often with good reasons, but with no sense of the pre-nineteenth-century history of the discourse, or of the parallel deconstructive discourse, probably from the nineteenth century, in the *Bhaviṣya Purāṇa*.[2] My goal is to examine these histories to reconsider what there is besides, and along

[1]See also Temple 1884-1900; Burnell 1894, 1895, 1896; and chap. 4 on J. D. Smith's treatment of *Pābūjī*.

[2]See Hiltebeitel 1995c and in press-g, which extends the above discussion; also Biardeau 1989b; Pollock 1993, 1994. The net effect of reading pertinent essays in Dalmia and von Stietencron 1995 on this question is to observe that discourse on the Kṣatriya is highly fragmented. Thapar 1992, 60-88, who does so much with royal genealogies and recognizes *Rām* and *Mbh* "in origin as epics, civilisational symbols" (74), fails to see them as central to classical Indian religious "imagined communities," which she defines around the "religious sect" (77). The irony is that "Rāmrājya" is precisely the "imagined community" that she wants to deconstruct. But granted that there was no "monolithic" Hinduism to encounter Islam (78-79), and that the "need to create the idea of a single Hindu *community* appears to have been a concern of more recent times" (84, my italics).

with, Hinduism, that links the Draupadī cult and Pāṇḍav Līlās. In this and the remaining chapters, I wish to relate the notion of an "underground" pan-Indian folk *Mahābhārata*, which I once suggested as a way of thinking about what might relate the Draupadī cult and the Pāṇḍav Līlās (1991b, 421), to historical contexts.[3] One guide in this pursuit is an astute remark by D. D. Kosambi: "Don't be misled by the Indian *kshatriya* caste, which was oftener than not a brahmanical fiction. . . ."[4] "Oftener than not"! With this challenge to rethink Brahmanical constructions of the Kṣatriya, we have something to illumine the *Bhaviṣya Purāṇa*'s dismissal of any possibility that there might be true Kṣatriyas left, and its celebration of the demise of the "little kings." It is now also plain that it is not only Hinduism that animates this "underground *Mahābhārata*," but a certain Islam.

A. Rajputs and Afghans

One cannot avoid the impression, or indeed the hypothesis, that it is precisely the little kings of oral *Ālhā*, those whom *Ālhā* is not only about, but who would have celebrated its "little kingdom" ideal at fairs, festivals, and major village and family events, whom the *Bhaviṣya paurāṇika* is attempting to discount, dispossess, discredit, and, at least symbolically, abolish. The purāṇa's *Pratisarga Parvan*, which accommodates the British, the Bible, and especially Jesus in surprisingly positive ways—especially in contrast to Muslims and Buddhists—would seem to have complemented and accommodated itself to the British mid-to late-eighteenth century design of "war[ring] down intermediary chieftains and magnates in order to deal with village elites," whom the British then sought to "peasantize" from the early nineteenth century through the insurgency of 1857.[5] Little kings must be neutralized because they are

[3]My argument will differ from one anticipated by Zoller, who writes: "I am now convinced that Paṇduan [an oral epic version of *Mbh* from the western Garhwal-Himalayas] is an expression of a (once) powerful South Asian oral Mahābhārata tradition, a tradition existing parallel to the written Sanskrit tradition(s), but quite independent from the latter in many ways. And I think it possible that this parallel tradition may one day turn out to be more than an underground Mahābhārata, as you once called it, when more extant oral traditions will have been scrutinized. Don't you think it possible, that the modern oral traditions may contain—despite more or less intensive interactions with the Sanskrit texts—relics of a state prior to its writing down?" (personal communication, December 1996). See Zoller 1993. I for now do not think that such strains antecede the type of goddess worshiped by the Pallavas, southern Calukyas, and Rajputs, or, if it is further back, the origins of Navarātrī and Dasarā.

[4]Kosambi, letter to Pierre Vidal-Naquet, dated 4.7.1964, as quoted in Thapar 1992, 106.

[5]C. A. Bayly 1990, 107 (quote), 23-28, 67-68, 138-50, 174, 189-94, 205; Roy 1994, 136-95, especially 139; 235-47; Stokes 1978, 42-43, 68, 120-204.

anti-imperial, whatever the empire. Perhaps one can hear a sympathetic echo of the paurāṇika's obliteration of the Agnivaṃśa in the closing comments by F. O. Mayne, Collector and Magistrate of Banda in Bundelkhand, in his *Narrative of events* on the "popular rebellion" there during the insurgency:

> Talwars [swords] and matchlocks were scarce in Bundelkhand, but armed with spears and scythes, and iron-bound lathies, and extemporary axes, formed of chopping knives fastened on sticks, they imagined to be warriors, chose their own kings, and defied all comers. Never was revolution more rapid—never more complete.[6]

As Roy says, "Seldom do we have such a graphic testimony of the people's political consciousness crystallized into an alternate order" (1994, 225). Although Mayne says of those who "mustered to attack Banda before the British left it" that "[t]heir caste was not specified but none of them were thakurs or Rajputs" (ibid.), we may wonder whether he too has obliterated the Rajputs from his account, denying them recognition when they join ranks with the "turbulent," "plundering," and undifferentiated masses that the British served up in their own version of the apocalypse of the little kings.[7]

Meanwhile, the Elliot *Ālhā*, a work of minstrels from Kanauj who sang it popularly in the 1860s, with the popular rebellion still continuing through that decade in nearby Bundelkhand, does not overly concern itself with boundaries between religions, and indeed has only positive things to say about the close relationship between the Banāphars and their Muslim ally, Mīrā Tālhan, the Saiyid of Banaras. Whereas the purāṇa ties its history straight into the British period, the Elliot *Ālhā* omits all reference to the British. Likewise, as if by compensation, this *Ālhā* makes frequent reference to Mughals and Mughal-period weaponry such as cannons and guns. Such firearms have no mention in the purāṇa, and one suspects that this "Mughal complex" serves to highlight the Rajput chivalry that opposes it, for the heroes use mainly swords. Moreover, when Belā prefers satī to remarrying a "Mughul," the disparaging usage may also

[6]Quoted in Roy 1994, 225, from F. O. Mayne, *Narrative of events attending the outbreak of disturbances and the restoration of authority in the district of Banda*, 1857-58, cited without further bibliographical information (Roy 3, 274).

[7]Bundela Rajputs did sometimes face popular opposition to their own plundering, as is registered in the *Chatra Prakāś* (Pogson 1828, 71, 79, 81 [sometimes spelled *Chhatra Prakāś*]), a poem by the bard Lal (or Gorelal) celebrating the anti-imperial careers of Champat Rai (d. 1662) and his son Chatrasal (d. 1731). But in the circumstances of 1857, one may doubt Mayne's observation; see generally Baker 1993, 95-101, on Bundela and Baghel Rajputs' participation.

connote "imperial" and "Sunnī," since Mīrā Tālhan, a Shī'ite, if not, as we shall see, an Ismā'īlī, is among those who spring Belā from her father's imprisonment.[8] Each text thus has its own style of archaism, which is balanced by a complementary style of contemporizing anachronism. They also differ in the ways they join history to the aṃśa and vaṃśa conventions of epic and purāṇic pasts. In *Ālhā*, reincarnations take place from the *Mahābhārata* with a sense of divine mystery, and respect for the karmic autonomy of each heroine and hero. There is no purāṇic scheme to derive the entire action from the work of gods pulling strings. If *Ālhā* has a prophetic plan for its hidden king and avatar, it is a cryptic one. It provides no explanation of the perceived evils of the Kali yuga as a divine līlā, an explanation that amounts, in Pierre Bourdieu's terms, to a theodicy of privilege. When it speaks of vaṃśas, as when all the "Kshatrīs" are summoned for battle at Ālhā's marriage, it is not to condemn but to rejoice.

> Call the Baghēl, call the Chandēl,/ Every Thākur, Janwār, Pamār,// Sūrajbansī, Chandarbansī,/ Rāghubansī and Rājkumār;// The men of Hārā and Būndī call,/ Bais, Sōmbansī and Gahilwār,// Rāthōrs, Guhlōts, and Saksēnās, all/ Whose portion are swords and the battle scar.// Summon the Tōmars of Tumar fort,/ Mainpurī Chauhāns and chiefs of Mārwār,// Nikumbh and Gaur, the Bhadāwar power,/ Jādav and crafty Parihār.// Each royal clan of Rājasthān,/ Thirty and six on the roll they are;// Habshī savage who feeds on man,/ and fierce Durrānī who comes from far. (W&G 159)

This roll nods to the Rajasthan-based "western Rajput" standard of thirty-six clans. But it mentions clans not found in western Rajput sources, and adds Abyssinians (Habshi) and Afghan Durranis.[9] If anything, it downplays the Agnivaṃśa, making no reference to it, leaving the Caulukyas unmentioned, and referring to the Paramāras only by their Bundelkhand offshoot, the Pamārs. The clans whose eradication is announced in the purāṇa were clearly very much alive in the social imagination of nineteenth-century *Ālhā* performers and audiences, as they are today.

It would seem that if an "underground" pan-Indian *Mahābhārata* is to

[8]See chap. 6 at n. 38.

[9]On Habshi, see Richards 1993, 32, 112. Durrani is the name for an "off-shoot" of the Abdali tribe of Afghans (G. Singh 1959, 1); this roll might not have included them before the impact of Ahmad Shah Durrani's career of leading nine Durrani invasions into northern India from 1747-1770 (40-323). See Tod's five lists of thirty-six ([1829-32, 1920] 1990, facing p. 90), none of which mention Thākur, Janwār, Rājkumār, or Saksēnā, or localize clans to specific forts. The best guide I know of to the Rajput clans of *Ālhā* (though also omitting those just mentioned) is Sherring 1872, 117-243.

be historically contextualized, we must look to the earlier history of such groups. I will now argue that we must look primarily at Rajputs and Afghans to understand the background in which *Ālhā* travels and possibly cross-fertilizes other oral martial epics as well.[10] But what do I mean by Rajputs and Afghans of this kind? And under what conditions would they be linked with the recurrence of oral martial epics in different parts of India? "In the middle ages," says Qanungo, "'Rajput' ordinarily meant a trooper in the service of a chief or a free-lance captain, and sometimes was applied in applause even to a brigand of desperate courage" (1969, 99). From this perspective, *rājpūt*, although meaning "son of a king," at first denoted "various individuals who achieved such statuses as 'horse-soldier', 'trooper' or 'headman of a village', and then pretended to be connected with the family of some king" (Kolff 1990, 71-72). Such military adventurers, Kolff finds, have their roots in a pastoralist pre-Mughal world that, from the sixteenth century onwards, was increasingly delegitimized by the new Rajput Great Tradition" (82), which claimed genealogically ascribed rather than martially achieved status.[11] This "oldest layer of Rajputhood as an open status group of warrior ascetics in search of patronage and marriage" (84) developed patterns of "seasonal vagabondage" by the husband in which his asceticism was less concerned with otherworldly renunciatory ideals than with "the ability to ascetically fight one's way back home" to his hard-won and precariously held wives and estate (75, 82).

Rajput soldiery of this kind takes form in the thirteenth to fifteenth centuries, a period notable to Kolff for two things: "a greater number of such pastoralist bands than previously succeeded in achieving, and passing on to their heirs, some measure of landed status" (71); and oral regional martial epics like *Ālhā*, *Pābūjī*, *Devnārāyaṇ*,[12] and *Palnāḍu* underwent

[10]Cf. McGregor 1984, 14, on "dissemination" of "Dholā-māru" "furthered by the movement of Rajput families and communities across the Ganges plain in Muslim service, or in search of new territories, in the medieval centuries."

[11]See on achieved status Kolff 1990, 121-24, 132-33; 1995, 257-61, 290. Although I single out certain groups, it is important to register Kolff's point that the military service tradition of *naukarī* "came out in many statures and colours, and that, for all its shared culture of soldiering and its continuity at the local and 'folk' level, it manifested itself in a multitude of groupings, a variety of origins and identities" (119; cf. 142). Cf. Gordon 1994, 192-93, on the "likely origin" in "military service" of the term *Maratha* to designate Marathi-speaking units in the armies of the Deccan sultanates.

[12]Kolff 1990, 81-84. Kolff comments on the Rajasthani *Devnārāyaṇ* epic that it presents "a clash between pastoralism on the one hand and the claims of genealogical status and territorial rule on the other. *Jauhar* and *satī* are conspicuous elements in the story" (84; cf. Malik 1993; Blackburn et al. 1989, 216-18). Against a thirteenth-century background, the interventions of Viṣṇu and the goddess guarantee the survival of pastoralist Gujar traditions while bringing the last Chauhān king of Ajmer to his fall. The Banāphars' pastoralist (Ahir)

their formative developments. Such oral hero tales would seem to have circulated through the earliest form of what Kolff calls the "Hindustani military labor market."[13] Yet even earlier than this, from 1010 when Mahmud of Ghazna in his pro-Abbasid Sunnī fervor destroyed Hindu kingdoms and temples and sought to expunge the Ismā'īlīs of Multan, and especially soon thereafter, from 1051 to 1160, when Ismā'īlīs were able to regroup, Nizārī Ismā'īlīs Indianized their missions with already-destabilized Rajputs among their converts. This span, which Kassam calls the "seeding period" of the Satpanth and describes as the "crucible in which the social basis of an indigenous Ismā'īlī community was forged through intermarriages, political alliances, and a common cause requiring mutual trust and material support" with Rajputs and other Hindus, was begun with the recapture of lower Sind by the Ismā'īlī-influenced Sūmrah kings, noted for continuing some Hindu practices, and ended with renewed massacres of the Ismā'īlis in Multan by the Ghurids in 1160 and 1175—the latter under Shihāb al-Dīn, the eventual conqueror of Prithīrāj Chauhān.[14] As we shall see, one of the things forged in the continuation and aftermath of this period was an underground Ismā'īlī folk *Mahābhārata*.

Bundela Rajputs are among those who emerge on the scene in these times, arriving in Bundelkhand "as early as the thirteenth century" and more concentratedly in the fourteenth, when they displace and replace the defeated Chandēls.[15] They arrive allegedly as a branch of Gaharwars from Banaras, which, let us note, is the home, at the beginning of *Ālhā*, of the Saiyid of Banaras, Mīrā Tālhan, and his eighteen sons. While *Ālhā* is not primarily "their story," it is natural and I think safe to hypothesize that it was the Bundela variant of this early type of Rajput culture that provided the regional Rajput milieu in which the fall of the Mahobā Chandēls, Delhi Chauhāns, and "Rāṭhoṛs" of Kanauj was reimagined in the distinctive way that took shape as *Ālhā*. Moreover, if Jaiswal is right that "the best specimens of written Bundeli are extant in the bardic songs of Ālhā written, or preserved, largely in Banāphari," which he describes

---

links and opposition to the last Chauhān king of Delhi make obvious parallels. On "Ahirs and other Rajputising peasants and pastoralists," see Kolff 1990, 74.

[13]Alavi criticizes Kolff for "the simplicity and ease of sale and purchase which the word market seems to convey" (1995, 56, n. 1), but I do not think it oversimplifies matters in *Ālhā*, where heroes define loyalties by those who provide their salt. Especially strong recruiting was carried out among the armed peasantry of areas steeped in *Ālhā*, the "extremely popular song" that, according to Kolff, "more than any other epic, reflects the heroic service traditions of Hindustan" (1990, 170; cf. 119).

[14]Kassam 1995, 121 (quote), 47-48, 57-94, 120-21; Khan 1997b, 39-106. Recall the doubled Ismā'īlī and Rajput traditions of Shihāb al-Dīn's blinding (chap. 8 at n. 38).

[15]Kolff 1990, 121; cf. Luard 1907, 13-15.

as "a mixed form of dialect of Bundeli which derives its name from Banāphar, a Rajput tribe" (1962, 11), it seems likely that it would be singers in Banāphari who found audiences for the story of this clans' own heroes in this milieu.[16] Indeed, though it is a purely speculative point, it is possible that in making Bundelkhandi history their own, Banāphari and Bundela singers introduced the Banāphar heroes, Mīrā Tālhan, and Belā into the story. In any case, whether historical or not, the Banāphars and Mīrā Tālhan are early adventurer-servicemen of the kind Kolff describes; and while courtly Muslim and Brahmanical authors ignored them, Bundela folk culture put them at the center of the story.

Bundela state records from Orccha indicate that up to the mid-thirteenth century, Bundelas intermarried with Chauhāns, Parihāras, Rāṭhoṛs, Tonwaras, Baghēls, and other Rajput clans (Luard 1907, 13-14). But after establishing themselves in Bundelkhand by defeating the tribal Khangārs, they admit to intermarrying only with two clans in their own region: Dandheras, who claim to be a separated segment of Chauhāns;[17] and Pamārs or Panwars, allegedly a segmented branch of Paramāras displaced from Rajasthan, where they lost most of their lands and left only "a few branches" (Gahlot and Dhar 1989, 80). A British diagnosis was that the latter "have lost some of the characteristics of true Rajputs, through association with Jats and Bundelas" (Bingley [1870] 1979, 116). With these two groups, Bundelas formed a "three branch" division marking their status as inferior to the "thirty-six branch" division of "western Rajput" clans (Jain 1975, 262-63). Bundelas, not to mention Banāphars, thus begin their association with the *Ālhā* heartland as low status Rajputs, setting precedent for later developments under the Mughals that would deny them the ascribed status of western Rajputs and then make them the exemplary case of "spurious Rajputs" for the British. Moreover, while Bundelas claim to be Sūryavaṃśi (Solar Dynasty) Rajputs themselves,[18] their marriages are confined to two clans that claim dubious branch relations to two of the western Rajput clans—the Paramāras and Chauhāns—which, *in* Rajasthan, claim to be authentic Agnivaṃśins. This would seem to suggest a reason why *Ālhā*, unlike the *Pṛthvīrāj-rāsau* and *Kṛṣṇāṃśacarita*, would tell its version of the story by leveling out claims to high status made through the Agnivaṃśa. *Ālhā* audiences in Bundelkhand do not seem to have invested much in the Agnikula myth.

Yet it is not just Rajputs but Afghans who fill in this social picture. As

[16]This is not to discount the possibility that Kanauji and other dialectical *Ālhā*s might have developed simultaneously, but it is unlikely that they would have developed earlier.

[17]Luard 1907, 14-16; Kolff 1990, 121.

[18]Luard 1907, 11; Jain 1975, 247; confirmed by Baccha Singh.

to what we mean by "Afghans," we may begin by noting that the early rulers of the Delhi Sultanate who overthrew Prithīrāj Chauhān were primarily Turks, who were established in Afghanistan before they invaded India. Their armies "consisted of Turkish, Persian, and Afghan mercenaries, but for convenience' sake," says Thapar, they can be "referred to as Afghan armies, on the assumption that the majority of soldiers must have been Afghan" (1966, 237). Meanwhile, Prithīrāj's conqueror Shihāb al-Dīn (Muhammad Ghuri) and his dynasty at Ghor appear "to have been Afghans, though some believe they might have been Turki or Persian perhaps" (Khurana 1991-92, 40). Afghans thus enter the picture primarily as "troopers," like early Rajputs, in a situation where Turk and Afghan are not always clearly separable. I thus use the term "Afghan" and even "Paṭhān" primarily in this extendable cultural sense, which it takes on in South Asia, rather than with any precisionable ethnic requirement—even though at times one can be more ethnically precise. But also, as indicated in chapter 1, Afghan troopers, especially when they oppose imperial regimes in Delhi, are among the potential carriers of Ismā'īlī and other Shī'ī religious practices and ideas, especially insofar as such traditions may have been transmitted under the cover of Sufism and Shī'ism more widely.

Leaving aside the Afghan Lodi rulers (1451-1526), at this ground level, up to the time of the Afghan Sher Shah in the early sixteenth century, "Afghans and Rajputs were not really exclusive or even distinct ethnic groups at all," but rather denotations of "soldiers' identities" by which they could "register membership in the war-band they had decided to join" (Kolff 1990, 57-58). The two identities could also shift. Kolff shows that a good proportion of Sher Shah's army, "exclusively" Afghan according to his biographer, was composed of Rajput recruits (1990, 39, 58-67). With no way to attain purāṇic vaṃśa pedigrees of the type superannuated by the *Kṛṣṇāṃśacarita*, or the aristocratic titles bestowed by the Lodis and Mughals, such Rajputs and Afghans had to "achieve" their status rather than claim it as genealogically "ascribed."[19]

By the seventeenth century, as Subrahmanyam comments, Mughal expansion in the Deccan provided Bundela Rajputs, Afghans, and others not only opportunity to offer service, but "a means of seeking a new territorial base for themselves, and eventually for their own descendants." The eighteenth century then opened onto "a change in the scale of human circulation, in movements of pilgrims, elites, and militarized war-bands"

[19]Kolff 1990, 63; cf. 36-38 on the "insufficiency of genealogy" and the discrediting of the Afghan aristocracy's Lodi titles by Sher Sur Khan (Sher Shah), who succeeded the Lodis as an Afghan sultan in the early sixteenth century espousing a detribalized egalitarian Afghan unity under his sultan's law.

whose "magnification in scale" was "not merely an issue of numbers," but of its "wide, even sub-continental scale" (1995, 20, 9). Afghans from Rohilkhand, neighboring Bundelkhand to the north, would by the late eighteenth century be a population with pre-Mughal and Mughal-period traditions behind them as military adventurers, swords-for-hire who could fight their way home or keep home on the move.[20]

Muhammad Khan Bangash, eventual founder of the Rohilla Afghan state at Farrukhabad in 1713 began his career at about age twenty-one, in 1685, as one of a four- to five-thousand-strong Paṭhān (Afghan) warband led by Yasin Khan that would cross the Yamuna from its home in Mau (Shamsābad Pargana, on the Ganges) at the end of the rainy season in about October, hire out to one of the contending Bundela chiefs, and fight for about eight months before returning home by the next rains (Irvine 1878, 270). This warband, of which more will be said shortly, thus accommodated itself to the Bundela seasonal pattern, which marked its end-of-the-rainy-season expeditions by Dasarā.[21] Even after establishing himself as a "virtually independent" power, Muhammad Khan Bangash still "sided with various Bundelā chiefs at different times" while holding "high appointments under the Mughal emperors" and carrying out imperial campaigns into Bundelkhand between 1720 to 1729.[22] That *Ālhā*—and the Elliot *Ālhā* in particular, which is *from* Farrukhabad—should thrive in such a milieu is not surprising. *Pābūjī* also evokes a Rajput-Afghan interface when its hero cannot marry until he obtains saffron from the gardens of the Afghan Lakkhū Paṭhāṇ (J. D. Smith 1991, 399).

If such Rajputs and Afghans are exemplary achievers, their example is paralleled in *Ālhā*'s portrayal of the naukarī (military service) heroes who defend the higher Chandēl Rajputs of Mahobā in the throes of their submergence beneath the "imperial" moves of Prithvirāj and Shihāb al-Dīn.[23] Although as Saiyid of Banaras, Mīrā Tālhan has the title of a

[20]Sixteenth-century Mughals described Afghans and Rajputs as "two martial *qaums*" having "cordial relations" (Chandra 1994, 18). On Rajputs' "seasonal vagabondage" as "warrior-ascetics," see Kolff 1990, 75-84; on the "vagrant identity" of Afghans "ready to migrate with their women, children, tents, and flocks to whatever camp their chiefs would determine upon," 32-35, 159; on Bundelas' "two occupations of service and landholding" in "jungly home country" from which they were "difficult to dislodge," 120.

[21]On Dasarā at Orccha as "the season for the recommencement of wars and forays," with procession to a *maidān* near a gate "where the *chhonkar* or *shamī* tree" was worshiped, see Luard 1907, 39; at Panna and Ajaigarh, ibid. 179, 250.

[22]Luard 1907, 172; cf. Irvine 1878, 283-305; Gupta 1987, 65-88.

[23]On *naukarī* and *naukar*, see Kolff 1990, 20: "honorable service in the warband"; 196: "originally a Mongolian word meaning retainer, comrade, a soldier in the service of a Mongolian clan he did not belong to by birth, a free warrior," coming to denote "long-distance soldiering," an "honorable calling" with "strong ascetic overtones."

descendant of the Prophet that "by definition" could come "by birth only, in actual fact it could be acquired by effort or even by luck" (Kolff 1990, 18). It too could be "achieved."[24] And the Banāphar fathers, originally "guardians" of Baksar (Buxar), come into Parmāl's service in a role that seems to evoke Baksar's identity as a primary recruiting ground for "military labor," and suggest that the senior Banāphars themselves, and their sons after them, can be viewed as Baksariya *jama'dārs* or "jobber commanders," either in an early phase recalled by *Ālhā*, or as projected back into it from a later perspective.[25] In the *Kṛṣṇāṃśacarita*, Baksar is called Vāksara, and is further the home of the Ābhīra (Cowherd) wives of the "Banāphar" fathers (4.22-27), suggesting the mixed character of Baksar's military service pool.

Afghans and Rajputs of such types thus spread out into local, regional, imperial, colonial, and poligar (insurgent and otherwise) armies through the Mughal and British periods, including the Madras Army of the British East India Company[26]—though not so the Bengal army, whose recruitment policies were part of the reason for the continued dispersal of Afghans and Bundelas in the colonial period. In conditions of Mughal service, their loyalties were usually less lasting than their spirit of

[24]Of the "Muzaffarnager farmers who became the famous Sayyids of Barha," for whom the title meant "an inflection of social status or professional identity," the Mughal Jahangir wrote, "some people make remarks about their lineage, but their bravery is a convincing proof of their being Saiyids" (Kolff 1990, 58, 18). On Saiyids as Shahids (martyrs), see Crooke [1896] 1968, 201. Sikh and Sheikh are also used as terms of achieved status (ibid.).

[25]On jama'dārs ["jobber commanders"] involved in "military entrepreneurship" becoming distinct from *zamīndārs* involved in "land control," see Kolff 1990, 164-73, suggesting that the fall of the Jaunpur Sharqi Sultanate, with the "scattering of its army of 'innumerable zamindars'" in the 1480s, gave "Baksariya" the meaning "private soldier emancipated form *zamīndārī* patronage" (172). Baksar, a Brahman pilgrimage center on the Ganges, grew into a recruitment center under Sher Shah, who, from about 1511, built up his "exclusively" Afghan Army with this area's agrarian-based Rajputs to become king of Delhi (1540-45) after overthrowing the Mughal Humayun (38-63). A late seventeenth-century Mughal manuscript "sums up its infantry in the phrase 'Baksariyahs and Bundelahs'" (120). Baksar continued to serve as such a center for the East India Company until the late eighteenth century (59-64, 160, 171-79; Qanungo 1969, 101-2; Alavi 1995, 41, 51, 73).

[26]S. Bayly defines poligar, Tamil *pālaiyakkārar*, as "south Indian warrior chief" (1989, 465; cf. 48-52; Dirks 1979 and 1982 on these "little kings"). Eighteenth-century "nayaka and poligar armies" "drew most of their military men from their own kin and caste groups, but their forces also contained Rajputs and other north Indian and Deccani warriors, including many Muslims," among them Paṭhāns disaffected from the nawāb of Arcot, who fought for Hindu poligars in the mid to late eighteenth century (Bayly 1989, 61, 196). Rajputs also helped the British defend Coimbatore in 1800 while Rajputs and Marathas opposed them on the side of the poligar-led insurgents (Rajayyan 1971, 136-38, 151). Bundela soldiering in the south for Mughal, Golconda, and colonial powers (including the Dutch) continued from at least 1670 to the mid-nineteenth century (Kolff 1990, 151-58).

resistance, which they often shared with similarly disaffected groups.[27] Under British colonial and imperial rule, it was much the same. Pertinently, "Stephen Lushington, the celebrated Collector of Poligar Peshkash (tribute) who helped to defeat the last of the independent south Indian poligars, reported that in his day [1799-1800] the military spirit of these warrior chiefs was 'inflated by the Jargon of the Vagrant Mussalman Patans [Paṭhāns] or Rajahpoots, who frequently for a time engage in the service of the Principal Poligars, and while they promote their own purposes flatter the Poligar into belief in his Prowess little short of heroism.'"[28]

Alavi traces the polities and movements of Rajputs and Afghans in the late eighteenth and early nineteenth centuries in north India in relation to British patterns of military recruitment, especially for the Bengal army, and in connection with popular religion.[29] The Company—whose perspective Lushington exemplified—peripheralized "mercenary" soldiers such as Bundelas, Buksarias, and Afghans, whose similar military lifestyles and allegedly indiscriminate loyalties recruiters viewed with "repugnance."[30] Meanwhile, it promoted a sanskritized military of Brahmans and mainly Bihari Rajputs for the Bengal army. Alavi describes numerous ways in which Company policy not only avoided interference with these soldiers' religious practices, but actively encouraged the reshaping of such practices by attempting to "invent" a high caste status for the sepoys through "military diet and cantonment celebrations." In so doing, "the Company was promoting sanskritization of the military."[31]

Company recruiters "furthered their interests by manipulating local religious arenas and symbols for their own purposes, gaining credibility by circulating stories claiming the fulfillment of religious prophesies at the site of the popular religious fairs."[32] But in cantonments, the British

[27]See Richards 1993, 120, 193, 246-48; cf. 66, 80, 87 (along with Indian Muslims, Jats, and Gujars); 145-47, 208-13 (along with Marathas and Indian Muslims); 256-57, 293-94 (along with Sikhs and Jats). Cf. Mayaram 1997, 31-49.

[28]S. Bayly 1993, 466, quoting from Lushington 1916, 4, which is unavailable to me. Lushington was Collector of Ramnad (Rajayyan 1971, 199).

[29]Alavi criticizes Kolff's view regarding the Mughal period (1995, 12, 56, n. 1) but rather extends it for this later period (51).

[30]Alavi 1995, 73; on Afghans see also 194-216, especially 198-200 and 209 on convergences with Bundela and other Rajputs; on Bundela Rajputs, see also Roy 1994, 36-37. Along with one thousand five hundred Sepoys, the Rani of Jhansi drew her greatest support from "10,000 Bundelas and vilayaties" (i.e., "rebel" Rajputs and Afghans; 68).

[31]Alavi 1995, 75-76; cf. 79—and in recruiting Gurkha "tribals," a "Hinduization of the regiments" (266).

[32]Alavi 1995, 69: e.g., in Awadh in 1839, a prophesy of the return of Rāvaṇa's son Inderjit, who had his own advance recruiting agent to form his army, which attracted both Hindus and Muslims, as did recruiters in North Bihar who claimed they were forming "a Hindu

urged that popular religion give way to a regimented high caste ideal. From 1793, the Commander-in-Chief "gave sanction to the celebration of Indian festivals in the cantonment," thereby encouraging a merger of "the cantonment world and the religious world of the recruit." Sepoys were to welcome "participation of European officers in these festivities," and could use firearms at them so long as they were regulated (Alavi 1995, 79-80). Sanskritized festivals found favor: Holi, with Brahman dancing boys and Brahman musicians as entertainers (80-81); and especially Rām Līlā, for which the Company found "similar ends" in its cantonments to those which Cheyt Singh, son of a Brahman father and a Rajput mother, found slightly earlier (in the 1780s) in his newly founded kingdom of Banares.[33] Whereas the Rāja sought "to project the image of a Hindu army" and "create a Hindu symbol of legitimacy and achieve independence from the Nawab of Awadh," the Company patronized Rām Līlā "to create a Hindu symbol of legitimacy" (33, 81). Sepoys dressed up as Rāma's monkeys and used new military technology to blow up Rāvaṇa's mud forts, while the Company, by making them "celebrate Ramlila independent of the patronage of any priestly figure, created a superior status for them" (82). With his mud forts, Rāvaṇa begins to look like another little king.[34]

Alavi documents instances of sepoys' arrogant and casuistical disregard of local folk religion in the 1810s (1995, 87-89). Although the policy of high caste identity for the Bengal army showed signs of backfiring as early as the 1820s,[35] the Company continued it. The 1820s thus launched the period of the "regimental pandit and the regimental maulvi" (92). One might imagine the author of the *Kṛṣṇāṃśacarita* having an affinity with the former. While the Bengal army peripheralized "mercenary" warrior populations, he peripheralized their oral epic. His work could almost be a sepoy's *Ālhā* for Sanskrit-reading Brahmans of the Bengal army. But it is unlikely that Brahman sepoys would have read the *Kṛṣṇāṃśacarita*. The paurāṇika's real bogeys are Muslim Mlecchas and the Kṣatriya pretensions of Rajputs. For Rajputs themselves, whose status was more at stake in relation to the epics they celebrated at festivals than

---

army for the purpose of taking Mecca from the Muslims," which even enlisted "a small number of Muslims from eastern Awadh" (69-71).

[33]On the Brahmanical character of the Banaras Rām Līlā, in contrast to "Draupadī cult līlās," see Hiltebeitel 1995c.

[34]As he is in *Pābūjī*, and also to those who try to find him in central India (see chap. 4, n. 18). Note also Kolff's mention of a song attributed to Tulsidas which describes Rāma's "faithful ascetic warrior" Hanumān as "a great Rajput" (1990, 196-97).

[35]Alavi 1995, 75: a "decade of mutinies," since the Sepoys were now concerned with "the slightest infringement of the ritual rules instituted by the company to define their own status and identity" (90; cf. 226: 1800-19 as another "decade of mutinies").

it was for Brahmans, the Company, surely under Brahman influence, endorsed a high status Rām tradition rather than a lower status *Mahābhārata* tradition like *Ālhā* or Pāṇḍav Līlā.

In such a context, we would be justified in studying the Elliot *Ālhā*, as it would have taken form during this period up to 1868, as a counter-tradition not only to the *Kṛṣṇāṃśacarita*, which, as it were, "corrects" oral *Ālhās*, but to the development of religious practices and martial folklores in the Company army. If *Ālhā* singers of 1868 were not directly aware of the *Kṛṣṇāṃśacarita*, they would have been aware of Company sepoy traditions, since, as Roy documents, there are numerous instances of opposition between "rebellious" sepoys and Bundela Rajputs during the 1857 insurgency, despite their common opposition to the British.[36]

In any case, the British did not invent the cantonment pattern. The "long and arduous north Indian campaigns" of the Marathas, for instance, required "provisions, base for operations, and cantonments" for their "troops in the rainy season," whose "entanglements" in the north meant they could not spend the rains in Maharashtra and return north after Dasarā (Gupta 1987, 230). The cantonment during the rainy season, waiting for Dasarā away from home with one's mixed-caste and often intercommunal war-band, listening to martial *and* romantic tales told by itinerant Jōgīs, Bairāgīs, Gosains and Fakirs—this is one of the settings in which a Rajput-Afghan culture can be imagined, before British sanskritizations and regimentations, to have been a carrier and cross-fertilizer of *Mahābhārata*- and *Rāmāyaṇa*-linked oral epic traditions. *Ālhā* at home is performed "at night, primarily during the monsoon season," "before all-male audiences" by male professionals of two types: "Jogis (wandering mendicants) and Nats (acrobats)."[37] It is as if a military camp setting is recreated near home, with women *at* home in *parda*.[38] With warrior-Jōgīs in the warbands themselves, seasonably encamped armies would presumably not have had to miss their *Ālhā* when the rains found them on the road.

B. Rajputs and Afghans Looking South

Thinking about Rajput-Afghan culture has meant rethinking some of the findings of volumes one and two of *The Cult of Draupadī*. It also

[36]Roy 1994, 39, 137, 156-58, 161, 169, 242.

[37]Schomer 1984, 3; Blackburn et al. 1989, 197-98; Dwivedi 1966, 23. *Alhā* fairs at the Kīratsāgar in Mahobā and at Bairāgarh (see chap. 14) occur in the rainy season.

[38]Cf. Khan 1996, 55 and *passim*: Kāmad, low status Rajasthani minstrels with Muslim affiliations, have recently, in efforts to "rehinduize" (and "rerajputize") their tradition, taken to preventing their wives and daughters from continuing to perform as dancers with men, and excluding them from singing *bhajans* and even attending public performances.

enables us to think about diffusions of different kinds, including circulating diffusion, and diffusion in different directions. Not everything fits, but let us start with what does.

Many Draupadī temples are connected with cantonments and pāḷaiyams, the military camps or headquarters of poligar (*pāḷaiyakkārar*) chiefdoms.[39] The point was first made to me in 1975 by K. T. Pandurangi about the Kalassipalayam temple in Bangalore, which is affiliated with Vaṉṉiyars still living in its old cantonment area (Hiltebeitel 1988a, 39). Devanampattanam, home to both a Draupadī and a Kūttāṇṭavar temple, was the site of Fort St. David, purchased by the British East India Company from the Marathas of Gingee in 1690 and soon thereafter contested by Sarūp Singh, father of Rāja Desing, the subject of our next chapter (Srinivasachari 1943, 370). Nearby is Pakkiripāḷaiyam, "Camp of the Fakir,"[40] home to a Draupadī temple and my two chief Terukkūttu informants R. S. Natarajan and R. S. Mayakrishnan. Examples near Madras are two temples at Poonamallee (center of the East India Company army of the Madras Presidency) and one at nearby Ālantūr (Allundur), below Saint Thomas Mount, also a Company army base (Rajayyan 1971, 224). A bronze plaque at the Ālantūr temple entrance identifies it as the Śrī Ārṭilari Dharmarāja Kōyil, said to be named after a British colonel who founded it after a vision of Draupadī. Colonel Ārṭilari, apparently not blinded by this dangerous vision,[41] ordered the temple "built by the military," and then handed it over to its first Vaṉṉiyar trustees. As noted elsewhere (Hiltebeitel 1988a, 39), this colonel must be a personification of the *artillery* of Vaṉṉiyar (and other) sepoys, who probably built the temple themselves with Company encouragement. Current memory of the colonel's generosity probably recalls Company involvement of the type Alavi adduces in connection with its sponsorship of north Indian cantonment festivities.

Draupadī festivals in the Bangalore and Madras cantonments are homogeneous: a suggestive reduction to a ten- or twelve-day module highlighting features of Navarātrī-Dasarā, goat sacrifice, and sword-pressing (Hiltebeitel 1991a, 288, 296-97, 351-53). We may now suspect this module to result not only from partial Brahmanization and "urban and diaspora modifications" (288), but Company influence. Parallels and overlap between this module and distinctively south Indian ten-day Muharram cycles were probably also influenced not only by competition and syncretism, but, at least in cantonment towns and cities, by Company

[39]S. Bayly 1989, 465; see n. 26 above.

[40]I do not know the origins of this suggestive name.

[41]See Hiltebeitel 1988a, 88-99; 1992a, 511-13; Masilamani-Meyer 1997, 168-70 for further examples of blinding under such circumstances.

interaction. Both recall epochal battles and heroic deaths, especially of youthful heroes. Muharram, which mourns the martyrdom of Muhammad's grandson Ḥusayn and his small group of relatives and companions, is of course fundamentally a Shī'ite festival, though in India it is also conducted by those who "would identify themselves as Sunnīs,"[42] and in south India especially it is joined by Hindus.[43] Muharram "displays of self-mortification by ash-smeared Bhairagis (Saivite Sanyasis)" along with "faqirs in beads" coincide with Draupadī festival processions with penitents flagellated by whip-bearers personifying Pōttu Rāja, and notions that not only Pōttu Rāja but the (usually) Muslim Muttāl Rāvuttāṉ are commanders in the Pāṇḍavas' and Draupadī's army, itself ritually replicated in festival processions.[44] The "mystic weirdness of south India's Mohurram fire-pit rituals" could also speak as well for those of Draupadī.[45] But this only describes conditions in which a certain type of Draupadī festival and a certain type of Muharram would have taken shape by the late eighteenth and early nineteenth centuries—that is, by the time we get colonial observations upon them. Obviously, eighteenth-century connections of Draupadī temples with pāḷaiyam military camps and seventeenth-century connections with the nayaks of Gingee are older. But I suggest that at least from the late seventeenth century on, and with Rāja Desing marking a point of transition, these developments were affected by an Afghan-Rajput military culture that would at least by then have imparted its artifacts and idioms to Draupadī cult rituals and folklore.[46] But this impact cannot begin that late. As the earliest oral martial epics to give evidence of how Rajput-Afghan culture was regionally seeded in both north and south India, *Ālhā* and *Palnāḍu* recall processes that must

[42]Bayly 1989, 141-42; cf. Mayaram 1997, 258-60.

[43]"Colonial observers often commented on . . . the involvement of Hindu worshipers in Mohurram rites in localities such as Melapalayam, Salem, and Nellore" (S. Bayly 1989, 142)—i.e., pāḷaiyam and cantonment localities (Melapalaiyam is associated with the cult of Yusuf Khan [ibid., 200]). On the procession-destination for Muharram in Madras, established by the nawāb of Arcot Muhammad Ali Wallajah, ally of the British and eventual adversary of Yusuf Khan, see Bayly 1989, 182; a local Muharram in Kilpauk, with firewalking, is still linked with his tradition (Lee Weissman, personal communication). Cf. Hiltebeitel 1991a, 440, n. 3; 469, n. 65

[44]Quoting S. Bayly 1989, 141 (Bhairagi should be Bairagi or Bairāgī, from Sanskrit *vairāgī*); cf. Hiltebeitel 1988a 110, 114; 1991a, 170-82, 448-68, 488.

[45]Quote from S. Bayly 1989, 142. Cf. S. Bayly 1993, 470-71; Assayag 1995, 59-64 (the *pañjah* symbol of Muharram is associated with the Pāṇdavas and worshiped by Lingayats in Belgaum District, Karnataka); Hiltebeitel 1991a, 440, n. 3; 469, n. 65; 1992a, 519.

[46]Cf. S. Bayly 1993, 478, on facilitation of Muslim expansion into hinterland areas by the nayaks and poligars, and the culture of "power divinities" linked with blood sacrifice among "warrior groups . . . seeking to consolidate their rule over expanding *palaiyam* domains." Cf. S. Bayly 1989 12-14, 22-30, 48-55, 137-50, 211.

go back at least to the thirteenth to fourteenth centuries. Here are some more pieces of the puzzle.

Draupadī cult firewalkers wear yellow garments reminiscent of Rajput warriors, who wore saffron-dyed yellow "when about to sacrifice themselves in a desperate conflict, a sacrifice to their supposed ancestor Sūrya."[47] As Tod puts it, drawing on the *Pṛthvīrāj-rāsau*, "The brothers [Ālhā and Ūdal], ere they reached Mahobā, halted to put on the saffron robe, the sign of 'no quarter' with the rajput warrior."[48] In the image of warriors consecrated for battle (*dīkṣitas*), *kāppukkāraṉs* who don turmeric-dyed wristlets at Draupadī festivals often wear turmeric-dyed clothes while sleeping in seclusion away from their homes at the temple. They do not wake to a woman's face—other than Draupadī's, before whom they maintain their chaste commitment to her martial rituals (Hiltebeitel 1991a, 89, 141). We shall meet something similar with Rāja Desing and his Muslim (and as we shall see, Afghan) comrade-in-arms Mōvuttukkāraṉ, even down to the wristlet.

Meanwhile, women firewalkers are like satīs who ascend the pyre "in a robe dyed with turmeric."[49] In the Gingee area mythology that explains her post-war firewalk, Draupadi, like Belā, inspires a mass satī. It would now appear to be significant that it is only in the more "rajputized" Gingee area that we find this myth.[50] Such a mass satī is tantamount to a *jauhar*, the mass-burning of (mainly) Rajput women (and sometimes their children) on a pyre in anticipation of their husbands' deaths in battle[51]—which perforce becomes a mass satī if it is delayed

[47]Dymock 1890, 447; cited in Hiltebeitel 1991a, 443; cf. Weinberger-Thomas 1996, 34-35 and 223, n. 57; Harlan 1992, 184, n. 2, and in press, 10 (linking the last stand with a renunciation that protects the family the hero renounces); Gordon 1994, 187 (sallying forth wearing the saffron turban as a sign of being already dead to the world). As indicated above (n. 18), Bundelas are Sūryavaṃśa Rajputs.

[48]Tod [1829-32, 1920] 1990,1:719. Cf. Tod (1829-32) 1972, 2:375: "Five hundred Haras, 'the sons of one father,' put on the saffron robe, and rallied round their chief, determined to die with him" (which they do not).

[49]Dymock 1890, 446; cf. Roghair 1982, 355, as cited in Hiltebeitel 1991a, 445.

[50]Hiltebeitel 1988a, 441-42; 1991a, 406.

[51]See chap. 9, § B on such a rite instigated by a Brahman queen in eighth-century Sind. Cf. Kolff 1990: "the last ascetic sacrifice of Rajputs, when they kill their wives and children, and then sell their lives dearly on the field of battle" (xiii), supported by an ideology in which "the women of a man's household were the substance of his achievement [and] could have no existence independent of his life's adventure" (102). The 1673 burning of his three hundred and seventy wives and concubines, plus his children and grandchildren, by the last Thanjavur nayak before sallying forth with his till-then estranged son to a doomed last stand (Narayana Rao, Shulman, and Subrahmanyam 1992, 304-13) has surely this Rajput inflection.

until after the husbands have been slain.[52] To appreciate how a south Indian might imagine a firewalk-like jauhar, one can see Ravi Varma's painting "Johar" at the Citra Art Gallery in Trivandrum: fourteen women dressed in saris shaded yellow to orange, some with red trim; one toward the left raising her left arm as she and those ahead of her cover their heads with the ends of their saris, filing toward the right, where one stands above the rest pointing into a portal of flames, and the one before her leaps, hair loose and flying.[53] As S. Bayly says, "One custom which the poligars did share with the Rajputs was sati" (1989, 55). But it is not necessary to otherwise contrast the poligars' and other Tamil warrior populations' "Kshatriya ideal" with "the Persianate refinement of the north Indian Rajput courts" (ibid.). It was not the high Rajput tradition but a low one that had its south Indian "spread" and reception among "predator groups and with the immigration of 'Vaduga' [northern] warrior cultivators from Andhra and the Deccan" (ibid., 34).

These pieces certainly fit one part of our picture. Then there is the aforementioned Muttāl Rāvuttan̲, Draupadi's (usually) Muslim guardian. Although Tamil *rāvuttan̲* is taken to mean "trooper" or "horseman," and to denote a group of Muslims in the southern districts of Tamilnadu converted by missionaries, chief of whom is the ostensibly Shī'ī Sayyid Nathar Shāh (Hiltebeitel 1988a, 102), the hero Muttāl Rāvuttan̲ is both "rajputized" and "afghanized": at one temple, he may be "Muttāla Rāja," at another "Muhammad Khan" (ibid., 104). In certain texts, his name even reverts (I assume: theoretically it could be the other way around) from Muttāl Rāvuttan̲ to "Muttāl Rajput!" In a chapbook edition of the Terukkūttu folk drama that performs his story, he is called Muttāl Rājaputtiran̲ and is said to come from Nepal.[54] Alternately, as Muttālarājaputtiran̲, the same rajputized name is used in the *Śrī Tiraupatātēvi Mān̲miyam*. There, Draupadī describes Muttāl Rajput as her chief marshal and a "little king (*cir̲r̲arācan̲*)" from a "small country (*cir̲u tēcam*)" on the Tāmbaraparaṇi river near Tirunelveli in the deep south of Tamilnadu. She agrees to stay in Gingee so long as he and her

[52]See Harlan 1992, 184, n. 1, on Tod's account of the Padminī story; see Tod [1829-32] 1970, 1:212-16.

[53]The painting is unfortunately not reproduced in Venniyoor 1981.

[54]Sanmukam N.d., 37 (the author is from Cor̲apuram village, Villupuram Taluk, South Arcot), from the chapbook drama collection of S. Rajarathinam, Lecturer at the District Institute of Education and Training in Krishnagiri. I had earlier given up on finding this text (Hiltebeitel 1988a, 113, n. 15). The publisher, the defunct Śrī Vāṇi Vilācam Press of Cuddalore, gives the principal character this (re-)rajputized name in both the title and throughout the work, despite advertising the otherwise identical title with the name "*Muttālrāvuttan̲*" on the back of another drama (Municāmi Nāyakar and Vīrappa Pataiyākṣi N.d. [cited in ibid., 466]).

"chief minister" Pōttu Rāja will serve her as guardians (Hiltebeitel 1991a, 488). Were one to look for "the historical" M. R., one might choose between a little Tamil king who went north, a rajputized Gurkha, or a reconverted late eighteenth-century Rohilla Afghan who served in Nepal, such as Alavi describes (1995, 213).

One also finds matching pieces without background: lemons impaled or otherwise offered for north Indian satīs and south Indian fire-walkers;[55] the "cross-hilted dagger" used in Draupadī cult ritual that is also a Rajput weapon;[56] the name Pirutivirāja (= Pṛthivīrāja) used by the Mēlaccēri Draupadī temple's elderly chief trustee, Gopāla Goundar, to identify the king whom Draupadī temporarily blinds when he does not believe that her stone icon could have hair.[57] But for now I single out only one piece of unusual interest. Touring Bundelkhand, a south Indianist may be struck by the numerous red pennants high up in the outer branches of trees, marking the sites of Hindu temples. Southern Brahmanical temples do not, as far as I know, have flags in trees. Rather, they have flagstaffs (*dhvajastambhas* or *koṭi-k-kampams*) or "flag-trees" (*koṭimarams*) of a different sort: tall posts outside the entrance topped with triple-planed frames with bells on them pointed in toward the sanctum. These have no parallel at northern Brahmanical temples (Hiltebeitel 1991a, 91-92). Draupadī temples may have flagstaffs of this Brahmanical type, but a few also put pennants in trees: not regularly, but at a festival's beginning, "undetected" at night, as if to signal a military operation.[58] At the temple of the Palnad heroes, two banners are hung in trees, one for each of the two rival factions (Roghair 1982, 26). In both cases we seem to find south Indian hero cult adaptations of a north Indian practice transmitted by Rajputs, for whom flags in trees outside Hindu temples mark a space that may need to be *permanently* defended, by them.

Turning to the hero cults linked with *Palnāḍu* and *Elder brothers*, there is no need to reiterate ritual parallels.[59] Of moment is the

[55]Weinberger-Thomas 1996, 74-83; Hiltebeitel 1991a, 280, 448, 462. Many of these things are done more generally for south Indian village goddesses. But rituals for them, patronized by village and caste headmen in the image of little kings, would have felt the same influences.

[56]Tamil *alaku* or *kaṭṭāri* (Hiltebeitel 1991a, 454 with fig. 15); Hindi *kattāra* (Chand Bardai 1873-86, 1886 fascicule, plate 3). It is also among the weapons in the temple of the heroes of Palnāḍu (see plate 6).

[57]See above n. 41; Hiltebeitel 1988a, 99; 1991b, 420-21: On Prithīrāj Chauhān's blindness at the end of his life, see chap. 8, n. 38 and § C.

[58]Frasca 1984, 277; Hiltebeitel 1991a, 87-88.

[59]See especially Hiltebeitel 1991a, 223-24 (impregnation rituals), 166-69, 239, 316-17, 374 (patukaḷam variations), 355-66 (revival rites, with parallels in the story of Khan Sahib).

composition of the armies of two epics. In *Elder brothers*, Cāmpukā describes the army he raises for the campaign against the boar Kompaṉ: "there are a crore of Muslims, a crore of wrestlers, a crore of Marātta soldiers, a crore of silk weavers, and a crore of resident army men" (Beck 1992, 659). We would expect to find Afghans and Shī'as among the ten million Muslims, and perhaps Rajputs among the ten million Marathas. The resident army thus mixes with the "mercenaries."

Palnāḍu is still more revealing. As noted, the migration of the people of Palnāḍu is required by the Brahmans of their original north Indian home, who refuse to complete "the people's" Dasarā because their elders, and in particular king Alagu Rāju, "are guilty of murdering children, sages, and cows." Along with the jammi tree, they depart with a flagstaff (dhvajastambha) among the ritual artifacts stipulated by the Brahmans. On their way, they parade their flags and banners (Roghair 1982, 166). The people are initially defined by the four castes. But the penitents are really the elders and the people's army: ". . . there were 24,000 Gōsangi soldiers. Then there were Cikkuls, Cinguls, Arabs, Rohilas, Mughals, and Paṭāṇs. With clubmen, macemen, Ābēdārs and Śubedars, the army set forth."[60] Gōsangis are Mādiga Dalits (ibid., 188, n. 20); typically, they go first.[61] Rohilas (Rohillas) and Pāṭaṇs are Afghans. Roghair could not identify Cikkuls and Cinguls other than as "warlike peoples" who would "postdate the epic time," and who "may be added for their sound value" (ibid., n. 21). But surely they are Rajputs, who do not postdate this epic's time in any sense. The soundplay on the typical Rajput name *Singh* is simply modified by a Telugu *u* ending, as in Tamil and Telugu Tē*ciṅku*/De*siṅgu*. The anachronistic "Mughals" is also interesting, as it is in *Ālhā*. Here it works both ways. Not only are Mughals antedated into the epic; one can still rejoin the epic heroes from Mughal times. As we saw in chapter 3, it was in the "time of Aurangzīb" (one of taqīyya for Ismā'īlīs) that Jaffar and Farīd came to Kārempūḍi with their army and took living samādhi to "worship with" the Palnad heroes.

There are also other hints that "the people" include Rajputs becoming Telugus. *Ābēdār* is probably not "a creation to rhyme with Śūbēdar" (sūbahdār), but *havildar*.[62] Alagu Rāju, who leads this expedition with Brahma Nāyuḍu (Viṣṇu incarnate) as his minister, is a "shining scion of the lunar race" (Roghair 1982, 165): some kind of Chandarbansī or

[60]Roghair 1982, 161-62; cf. 267: the troops of one of the great Palnad heroes, Ala Rācamallu, also consist of "Cikkuls, Cinguls, Arabs, Rohilas, Mughals, Paṭāns, and others."

[61]Like Cāmpukā, in leading the vast army of the elder brothers.

[62]Roghair 1982, 188, n. 22 (quote). As the form *avultār* suggests, as used in the *Teciṅku Rājaṉ Katai* for one of the nawāb's Afghan retainers (Canmukacuntaram 1984, 156).

Sōmbansī Rajput; probably a Haihaya, as current informants claim.[63] Indeed, according to the Kārempūḍi Pīṭhādhipati, the people's kings are Haihaya Rajputs or Kṣatriyas. The sins they must atone for by their pilgrimage—"murdering children, sages, and cows" (162)—were committed seven generations earlier by none other than the Haihaya Kārtavīrya Arjuna, provoker of Paraśurāma.[64] And their homeland of Pālamācāpuri is in Jambanipuri or Jabalpur,[65] which Roghair was told is "the ancient Cēdi homeland of the Haihayas" that is "believed to have been in Cēdi in present-day Madhya Pradesh" (187, 94). Indeed, according to Babu, Brahma Nāyuḍu "migrated into Andhra Desa along with king Anugu Raju (sic) in consequence of the invasion of their realm in the north by Muhammad Ghori" (1996, 35), a story he said was in the epic songs (personal communication, January 1997). The events which bring closure on the world of *Ālhā* would thus be the impetus for the people's migration to Palnāḍu!

In any case, if, following Roghair, the Palnad people's northern homeland is "believed to have been in Cēdi," they have come from the classical epic country of Śiśupāla that in medieval times is overlapped by Bundelkhand. In folk epic contexts, we now see that Kārtavīrya Arjuna is credited with two capitals. In *Palnāḍu*, the rājas of Palnāḍu descend from him, and come from near Jabalpur. In *Ālhā*, the Chandēl and Banāphar heroes' first great opponents, the Baghēl kings and princes of Mārō, rule from a capital which some say is the former Afghan stronghold of Maṇḍū, others Māhiṣmatī, Kārtavīrya Arjuna's mythical stronghold. Jabalpur and Maṇḍū are both on the Narmada, and so is Māhiṣmatī in so far as it has been identified with Maheshwar. The Mārō rulers and the people of Palnāḍu thus begin to look "related," with varied Agnivaṃśa and Haihaya Candravaṃśa descent myths.[66] The Bundelkhand-Baghelkhand-Narmada basin area could thus be a primary terrain through which stories like these travelled, and a source from which they migrated to Palnāḍu.

But it is the women of Palnāḍu who supply the most vivid section of the puzzle. They leave Pālamācāpuri for Palnāḍu under a specific injunction of the Brahmans: "they wore indigo saris and indigo blouses" (161-

[63]Working from circumstantial inscriptional evidence, Roghair (1982, 71-80) and others have attempted to link Alagu Rāja with the Haihayas, a Yaduvaṃśa branch of the Somavaṃśa, who come to be tied in with the Western Cālukyas of Kalyān.

[64]In most versions of this classical myth, Kārtavīrya attempts to steal the cow of Jamadagni, and then kills Jamadagni, Paraśurāma's father (see chap. 13). Roghair mentions Kārtavīrya Arjuna in connection with the migration story, but not in connection with the faults that cause the penitential migration.

[65]Oral communication, January 1997.

[66]See chap. 5 at nn. 50 and 51.

62). Indigo is a polluting dye. Throwing an indigo veil over a woman about to become satī is a way to "dissipate the frenzy" of her *sat*: the "internal fire" that disposes her to "become satī." Other ways include throwing indigo-darkened water over her, getting her to drink indigo-mixed water, or placing an indigo-covered coconut on her pyre. Other than a Śūdrā, a married woman would never wear blue saris while her husband is alive. All this typifies the satī practice and ideology of north Indian Rajputs[67] and explains the indigo saris and blouses of the future women of Palnāḍu. Although the women migrate with their penitential husbands, they are virtual satīs. Symbolically widowed by their husbands' deadly sins, they are under a protracted condition of defilement that is comparable to Draupadī's vow of dishevelment. Indeed, both indigo and dishevelment carry overtones of menstrual pollution.[68] Aspersion with indigo-darkened water also dispels the frenzy of jhūjhars: warriors who continue to fight after they are beheaded. The parallel must be that a woman without her husband is like a warrior without his head. *Ālhā* has two such episodes. And since jhūjhārs often die fighting off cattle raiders, indigo-colored water is also offered to Pābūjī, who died on such a mission.[69] The people thus begin their migration from north India to Palnāḍu as a virtual Afghan-Rajput warband, differing from others only in that their journey is a penitential pilgrimage rather than a military campaign for some chieftain, and in that they bring their women with them as protracted satīs rather than leave them at home. They might remind one of Vrātyas.

In the nineteenth- and twentieth-century forms that we find regional martial oral epics, and probably for as much as six centuries before that, Afghans and Rajputs have thus made important contributions to transmitting them, and contributing to their related hero cults—not only in north India, but south. One may thus hypothesize that "underground" folk *Mahābhārata* and *Rāmāyaṇa* has been enriched by this mobile Afghan-Rajput culture, along with the combination of Rajputs and herders with Kṣatriya self-images that one finds repeatedly in these traditions, and in others more or less like them.[70]

[67]For these points and further exposition, see Weinberger-Thomas 1996, 34-42.

[68]Weinberger-Thomas 1996, 39-42: along with uses of indigo, one may dissipate a satī's sat by the touch of a menstruating woman or a Dalit. For Draupadī, see Hiltebeitel 1981, 1991a, 396-98.

[69]Weinberger-Thomas 1996, 43, and 225, nn. 84-85; Rose 1926, 91-92; W&G 50, 240 (here two jhūjhars: the young princes Abhai and Ranjit, who die at the Battle of Kīratsāgar; see chap. 6, n. 90). Cf. Srivastava 1997, 74.

[70]Flueckiger 1996 does not say who patronizes *panḍvānī* [folk *Mbh*] in Chhatisgarh, but Rajputs and Ahirs are probably among them (cf. 136-41 on the comparable *Candainī*). On Rajputs in Garhwali *Mbh* traditions, see Sax 1986; 1994; 1995a, 137-49; Zoller 1993, 205-

But now things become more complicated. There are pieces that don't fit. Marathas, for instance, are not Rajputs, and it was a cheap trick to pass one off for the other in the elder brothers' army. As Gordon has shown, Rajput and Maratha styles of soldiering differed significantly, as both did, as well, from the south Indian nayak style first developed under the Vijayanagar rulers (1994, 182-208). But at least by the seventeenth century, the situation in the south was more mixed and varied than Gordon mentions. The twins' hero cult and oral epic are rooted in the Trichy area, whose dominant royal culture through the late seventeenth and eighteenth centuries at Thanjavur was a highly Brahmanized Maratha one, and not, like Gingee's, one of Marathas followed by Afghans and Rajputs under far less Brahmanical influence. Elsewhere during this period Marathas and Rajputs had as complex a history of martial interactions as Rajputs and Afghans—with Maratha-Bundela relations entangled even up to the 1857 insurgency.[71]

More instructive than nonfitting pieces are places where the picture is incomplete. Pōta Rāju-Pōttu Rāja is an obvious case: the signpost of a Telugu-Nayak culture in the Palnad and Gingee (Draupadī) hero cults in connection with a unique ritual apparatus. Yet when it comes to his surfacing in oral epic, it has been suggested in chapter 5 that the myth of the destruction of his Sivanandi Fort may be a variant of a probably older *Ālhā* story: the destruction of the Iron Fort in the Mārō Feud episode, with the latter further echoing the *Mahābhārata*'s Jarāsandha episode.

But enough for now of Pōta Rāju. Granted that the picture can never be complete, it is time, in the remainder of this and the last three chapters, for a few case studies to seek some idea of what a more filled-out picture might look like. Let us, however, try to keep our balance on the prickly matter of north "versus" south. South Indian colleagues who have followed this project have returned to no area of unease more repeatedly than the sense that I am presenting some "master narrative"

---

35. For Rajasthani folk *Mbh*s, see Smith n.d. and Mayaram 1997, 41-42, 128-40, 255-57 on Rajput clans among the Meos. "Rajput"-herder alliances repeat themselves in *Pābūjī* (Rajputs and Rebārīs), *Ālhā* (Rajputs and Ahirs through the Banāphars), *Palnādu* (Velamas and Gollas), and the Draupadī cult (Vanniyars and Kōnārs).

[71]See especially the young Chatrasal's 1667 inspirational meeting with Śivāji, defining Chatrasal's anti-Mughal course in Bundelkhand (Gupta 1980, 21-23) and later events in his career (81-90); Dalpat Rao's participation in Mughal operations against the Marathas at Gingee from 1694-98 (Luard 1907, 96-98); Maratha expansion in Bundelkhand and deteriorating Maratha-Bundela relations up to the establishment of British paramountcy there (1731-1803: for different slants, Andhere 1984; Gupta 1987); and Maratha-Bundela cooperation (mainly) in 1857 (Roy 1994, 81-136). On Tod's Rajputs as "feudal" and "nationalizing" versus Marathas as "predatory" and "denationalizing," and as "two opposed groups where previously no absolute distinction had existed," see Peabody 1996, 208-14.

of a double north Indian colonization of the south: first, through the supposedly north Indian classical epics; second, through a rajputization of south Indian regional oral martial epics.[72] On the first point, I do not share the assumption that the *Mahābhārata* is north Indian.[73] On the second, I hope to show that the picture gets complicated just because things work both ways. Indeed, to anticipate chapters 12 and 13, I do not regard Rajputs of the type we are discussing as entirely north Indian.

C. The Egalitarian Warband

Rāja Desing refers to his lifelong Paṭhān friend Mōvuttukkāraṉ as a brother, albeit a younger brother (*tampi*), as we shall see. This has an egalitarian ring. Similarly, Mīrā Tālhan is a surrogate father to the Banāphars and the Chandēl prince Brahmā. According to the Elliot *Ālhā*, the Pāṇḍava brotherhood reincarnates itself into a Muslim (Bhīma in Mīrā Tālhan), two Banāphars (Yudhiṣṭhira in Ālhā, Sahadeva in Malkhān), and two Rajput princes (Arjuna in Brahmā, Nakula in Lākhan). Brothers in their last life, they "share salt" in this one, especially when traveling in their warrior-Jōgī-musician disguises. It would appear that it is just this type of compatibility, with its egalitarian implications, that impassions the paurāṇika author of the *Kṛṣṇāṃśacarita* to translate *Ālhā* into a countertale of erased geographical, linguistic, and moral boundaries (maryyādā), commingling of religions (dharmas), breakdown of caste hierarchy (though only in the sub-Brahman castes), and intercaste and interreligious miscegenation. In making history of this tale, he begins it with Śiva's curse that Bhīma must be reborn as a "Mleccha" because he has sinned, carries it forward through the collusion of the demon Kali and the supreme deity Viṣṇu, and brings it to a head when Kali's Mleccha princes (mainly Muslims) become indistinguishable from Kṣatriyas (i.e., Rajputs and especially Agnivaṃśins). What could have provoked such creativity?

The formation of the Farrukhabad nawābī, an eighteenth-century Afghan state (1713-71), may suggest some answers. As observed above, before he established his nawābī and led imperial expeditions against the Bundelas, Muhammad Khan Bangash was a Paṭhān soldier of fortune whose war band, adapting itself to the Bundela seasonal pattern linked with the fall festival of Dasarā, fought both for and against various Bundela chiefs. According to Alavi, he "integrated [his] Afghan ruling house with the Rajput society and economy which it had subordinated to

[72]The "master narrative" question was raised by S. D. Lourdu at the workshop of folk religion at St. Xavier's College in 1994.

[73]Suffice it to say that wherever it was composed, and the south cannot be ruled out, it is all-Indian in scope and must have had a rather rapid pan-Indian dissemination. See Hiltebeitel forthcoming, following some cues from Madeleine Biardeau.

its rule." His army was "multi-tiered." On top were "high pedigree" Afghans of his own Bangash "tribe," whom he had induced to migrate to Farrukhabad, and from whom "he selected 18 leaders, giving them the rank of Jamadar" (he also gave several his daughters). Next were Afghans recruited from Mughal armies, and below them, as the "rank and file," were "locally recruited Rajput peasants many of whom were converts to Islam." There was also a special group, often selected after conversion for duties in the police, elite corps, or the nawāb's private guard, of Brahman and Rajput "Hindu" boys, seven to thirteen. These "the Nawab's recruiting officers had orders to procure," whether by payment or default of payment, or by seizure after the suppression of troublesome villages (Alavi 1995, 195-96; 199-200). Irvine calls them *chelas*, "pupils or disciples," but notes that in Muhammad Khan Bangash's time they were "always known as *Tifl-i-Sirkár* (sons of the State)."

To "strengthen the fragile bonds which knitted together this heterogeneous group of soldiers," Muhammad Khan drew on Afghan, Rajput, and Mughal military customs, one of which was an "Afghan tribal custom, very popular in his army" (Alavi 1995, 196-97). The "Afghan" custom in question may have been drawn from his own Bangash tribe, many members of which had in the sixteenth century taken up the military cause of an Afghan-based movement called Roshaniyya, founded by the Punjab-born Pir-i-Roshan (1525-ca. 1580). Once that movement—apparently Ismā'īlī-inspired[74]—was suppressed as heretical under Akbar, the Roshaniyyas, with the Bangash still prominent among the tribes in mountain forts that continued to support them, carried out anti-Mughal political resistance until 1630, when the emperor Shah Jahan showed clemency to one of Pir-i-Roshan's descendants and allowed him "to retire to a place near Farrukhabad on the Ganges, where he died in 1647"—only sixty-six years before Muhammad Khan Bangash arrived to found his nawābī there. Irvine describes the community as reduced to "a state of poverty" but still actively holding a jagīr up to 1796, and still informative about their history in the 1870s (1878, 357-64).

One of Muhammad Khan Bangash's chelas—"Daler (or Dalel) Khán" (as Irvine calls him), or Duleel Khan to Pogson—is interesting in this connection. Irvine, as author of a "chronicle" on the Bangash nawābs, says that Duleel Khan (as I will call him) was "by birth a Bundela Thákur," or possibly a Jat (1878, 286). But in "oral traditions" from around Banda he was "called the son of Muhammad Khán Bangash," and "was given, they say, by his father to Rájah Chattrasál who adopted him" (365). According to Pogson's translation of the *Chatra Prakāś*, Chatrasal

[74]Suggesting Ismā'īlī inspiration, see Rose 1911-19, 3:335; Titus 1959, 110-12; Caroe 1964, 198-229 (quote 229; cf. Rose 1911-19, 3:337).

and *his* father Champat Rai, founder of the Bundela state at Panna in 1675, also maintained a "brother"-relation with Duleel Khan through two generations, which was effected with Champat Rai through an exchange of turbans ([1834] 1971, 48-51, 89-90)—a brotherhood that may have been "real" by Duleel Khan's birth, just as his Afghan identity would then have been "achieved." When, however, the Bundelas came to think that "Chattrasál had nursed [Dullel Khan] to be like a snake in their sleeves," they drew Chatrasal into battle with him, and Duleel Khan was killed. But Hindi poets then composed couplets (*dohas*) in his praise (355-57). "Dalel's chest was a yard wide" (367-68), like that of Prithīrāj. Both "Paṭháns and Bundelas, on account of his bravery, styled him 'Súrmán' (brave, bold), the mark of which is that a man's arms touch his knees when standing upright. Daler Khán had this pecularity" (286). So did Rāma (*Rām* 1.1.10). In their four-day final battle, "Muhammad's son jumped exultantly, his followers shouted 'Ali, 'Ali" (367). When entreated to turn back, he called on "the good name of the Bangash" and his "Paṭhán honor": "Rájah and Maharájah will flee at the sight of my bare sword. Said brave Dalel, boldly in the battlefield, call 'Ali, Ali' as Hindus call on Hanumán" (371). A tomb near Maudha named Dalel Shahíd celebrates him as a martyr by marking the spot where his left hand was severed (367). And a "tomb and *masjid* with a well still exist" near Hamirpur "where he received the cup of martyrdom" (367). There Bundelas honor him. Boys of twelve, brought there by their fathers, first take up their sword and shield after laying them on his tomb, and the parents pray their son will be as brave as Duleel Khan (286).

As chela and "son" of Muhammad Khan Bangash and adopted son of Chatrasal Bundela, Duleel Khan thus upholds a bireligious kinship, and, with the cry "'Ali, 'Ali," a folklore that clearly recalls him and his "father" Muhammad Khan Bangash as Shī'as, if not necessarily Roshan-iyyas or Ismā'īlīs. As we shall see, Chatrasal was also introduced to Ismā'īlī ideas through his guru Prāṇnāth. It is thus possible that the tiered hierarchy of Muhammad Khan Bangash's court reproduces something of a militarized version of the ranking system within the Ismā'īlī *da'wa* or mission, which itself corresponded to concepts of messianic hierarchy.[75] In any case, this hierarchial system was also regularly subverted by rituals of equality. At "a regular ceremony held" in the nawāb's "audience hall," Muhammad Khan Bangash

> always wore clothes of the commonest stuff. In his audience hall and in his house the only carpet consisted of rows of common mats, and

[75]Daftary 1990, 105-6, 244, 293-97, 394-95, 411-16; Kassam 1995, 57.

> on these the Paṭháns and chelas and all persons, high and low, had to be content to sit. . . . At meal times five to six hundred Paṭháns would sit down to the same trays. To each were given two unleavened cakes . . . with a cupful of meat, and a flat dish of *paláo*, or whatever else there was, all receiving an equal share. The same food was placed before the Nawáb. Paṭháns generally eat *paláo* of cow and buffalo flesh, and this the Nawáb liked.[76]

It is clear that the chelas were among those who sat on the common mats, but Irvine seems to imply that they did not—having converted Brahmans and Rajputs among them—join the six hundred Paṭhāns in eating cow and buffalo pulao. On the other hand, a chela like Duleel Khan could become an Afghan, and thus probably also a commensal Paṭhān. Irvine mentions that when nobles from Delhi visited the nawāb, they were "astonished" by these ceremonies, and "surprised at the contrast between the Nawab's great wealth and power and the simplicity of his personal habits."[77] They would also have shocked the author of the *Kṛṣṇāṃśacarita*, but without his giving them a positive turn. They do not seem to have provoked anything from the singers of the Elliot *Ālhā*, for whom the Farrukhabad area was home in the 1860s.

We do not have to posit these Farrukhabad meals as a direct provocation for the leveling egalitarianism attributed to Mlecchas in the *Kṛṣṇāṃśacarita*. There is no doubt a longer history of egalitarian traditions of Islam in India, and of Brahmanical perceptions of them, to supply our paurāṇika with sufficient provocation. Yet I suspect, given the prominence of *Ālhā* in the Farrukhabad area and his interests in both *Ālhā* and eighteenth-century history, that something of this experiment might have reached him. What is now worth recalling are the egalitarian meals in two of our regional oral marital epics: *Palnāḍu* and *Pābūjī*. Both epics project a harmonious intercaste ideal linked with some form of śamīpūjā, with the śamī as the egalitarian rallying point for all "castes" and not necessarily excluding Muslims.[78] This means that the meal is implicitly a communal Dasarā meal or (what could amount to the same thing) the opening of a war expedition. In *Palnāḍu*, the meal comes before the war. In *Pābūjī*, the key scenes come after the war, but are reflections on the

[76]Irvine 1878, 338. Cf. Alavi 1995, 196-97 and 199, n. 17, summarizing somewhat selectively; 212-13 on similar efforts later and elsewhere.

[77]Quoting first Irvine 1878, 338, then Alavi 1995, 197.

[78]At least in Āliśetti Gāleyya's oral version, Rohillas from Farrukhabad and other Muslims (Arabs, Mughals, Paṭhāns) are among the people of Palnāḍu as part of its original migrating army, and thus could be thought to have shared *Palnāḍu*'s fateful "intercaste meal"; but they are not mentioned among the diners, and we certainly cannot attribute these meals to Afghans.

beginnings and ends of all wars. In each case, something goes, or has gone, wrong.

In *Palnāḍu*, it is the "sweet" blood of the Brahman Anapōtu Rāju, shed under the jammi, and offered to Bāluḍu in his food, that makes everyone go crazy, interrupting the egalitarian multicaste meal that could have averted the war (see chap. 3). Yet this meal, known as *chāpa kūḍu* or "mat rice," has narrative complexities and variants that undermine the historicizing and, for some, I believe, wishful notion that Brahma Nāyuḍu was a radical social reformer on a scale somewhere between Basava and Rāmānuja.[79] According to the Kārempūḍi Pīṭhādhipati, Brahma Nāyuḍu taught that all castes were equal, and—as if anticipating Muhammad Khan Bangash—that they should eat sitting at the same mat. But he taught this as a "pretext" (the Pīṭhādhipati used the English word) to provoke Nāyakurālu, his female opposite number, who made the new institution the occasion to request twenty-four hours as "minister" of the rival Reḍḍi Rājas, during which time she further heightened the enmity between the two factions, building up to the cock fight and the exile of the heroes.[80] According to Hanumantha Rao, "Even members of his [Brahma Nāyuḍu's] own family, including his own son [presumably Bāluḍu] opposed his policies and upheld the social order based upon caste. . . . Further, the war is called *Kulamapōru*, which may mean battle for caste" (1973, 268). These "caste-ist" interests and motivations are not, however, apparent in Āliśeṭṭi Gāleyya's version or in the allusions to the epic story in the early fifteenth century *Krīḍābhirāmamu* (Roghair 1982, 81). But then neither are there any hints that Brahma Nāyuḍu urges radical social reform.

Babu also shows how Brahma Nāyuḍu's institution of chāpa kūḍu played itself out among Dalits. Brahma Nāyuḍu began by attempting to bring both Mālas and Gōsangis (Mādigas) into the intercaste meal, but this "failed." One day, in a prior skirmish between these two main Dalit factions, when Brahma Nāyuḍu called the Mādigas to battle, a messenger told him they "were attending a *Gaddapatu*" and "would come [only] after some time." Gaddapatu is the Mādiga practice of going to the forest

[79]See Hanumantha Rao 1973, 267-69, supposing that, "In converting people, he seems to have adopted methods of Ramanuja," among which, along with the plausible occurrence of the name "*dāsa* (slave)" affixed to names, Hanumantha Rao mentions encouraging "inter-dining (*cāpakūdu*) and inter-caste marriages," neither of which Rāmānuja countenanced (cf. ibid., 265). Interestingly, "Tradition would have us believe that he [Brahma Nāyudu] married girls from all four principal castes and adopted a *Pañcama*, Kannamadāsa as his son." Roghair accepts this perspective with minor reservations (1982, 78-79, 121), as does Babu 1996, 4, 31-32, 102-3, adopting Hanumantha Rao's term "Vīra Vaiṣṇavism" for Brahma Nāyuḍu's alleged movement. Clearly, however, Rāmānuja's Śrī Vaiṣṇavism influences the epic, *Palnāḍu*, if not Brahma Nāyuḍu himself.

[80]Oral communication, January 1997. For a different version, see Roghair 1982, 217-18.

when they spot vultures making rounds in the sky, hoping to obtain the meat of dead cattle. Brahma Nāyuḍu became angry upon hearing this and declared that henceforth Mādigas should maintain a distance of seven *paggams* or twenty-four yards from Mālas, and not be allowed entrance to the temples of Ankamma and the Heroes or to beat their *tappeta* (a tambourine-shaped drum covered only on one side) at the festivals since this "half drum" was "not liked by Ankamma." So at the battle of Kārempūḍi, the Mādigas twice "refused to fight." The explosive meal before the battle of Kārempūḍi was then the final chāpa kūḍu, and the Mādigas were absent.[81]

In *Pābūjī*, the "golden" Sonā's wish to see all of Pābūjī's men camp beneath her vast śamī tree reestablishes a luminous egalitarian ideal after it has been given a darker tinge by Pābūjī's last request, as he ascends to heaven: that Deval not separate the blood of his Rajput, Rebārī, and Nāyak Bhīl warriors.

What has gone wrong is that each of these meals is tinged with blood. In each case a multicaste brotherhood meal under a śamī spills over into bloodshed. But now we must see that what has gone wrong has done so only in appearance. The meals, linked with śamīpūja and evoking a communal Dasarā meal, must really be offered to the goddess. And the goddess demands not just food, nor even meat, but human blood. Nāyakurālu—whom Roghair describes, surely correctly, as "an avatar of Ankamma, the local Goddess" (1982, 136)—opposes the intercaste meal which Brahma Nāyuḍu institutes. But interactively, through their opposition, the two ministers only ratchet the action toward the final war. And when Akka Pinakka, another multiform of the goddess, serves up a leaf-cup of Brahman blood, it is the signal for the heroes of Palnāḍu to become an offering to Ankamma herself as the goddess of the Kārempūḍi battlefield. Similarly, when Deval is asked to mingle the blood, she is only asked to do above as she has done below: to join in her heavenly cup what she has mingled in the earth.[82] Palnad festival-goers actually celebrate a corresponding intercaste meal, but *after* the battle-enactments (Roghair 1982, 29). This implements the epic's ideal of what Roghair calls "a casteless brotherhood" bound together "by an heroic code" (195) in a ritual medium that neutralizes the story's bloodshed, just as the sāyl

[81]Babu 1996, 103-4, 139-41 (quotes), supplemented by an interview with the author January 1997 concerning the order of events. Cf. Roghair 1982, 349 and 363, n. 66, and Elmore 1915, 103-4, on the Mādigas' refusal to join the final battle. Babu added orally that Brahma Nāyuḍu's ruling now prevents Mādigas from attending the platform outside the Ankamma temple where Mālas recite *Palnāḍu*, but that with their own claims to superiority, Mādigas say the story is irrelevant and that they don't care.

[82]J. D. Smith (1989, 190) also compares the blood-mixing scene in *Pābūjī* with the shared meal in *Palnāḍu*, but does not relate them to the scene under Sonā's khejaṛī tree.

of the khejaṛi tree neutralizes the blood-letting of war in a post-war setting to show that those whose blood is now mixed in heaven can still remind us of peace on earth.

Rajputs and Afghans thus both had (or imparted) egalitarian ideals, which must be one of the reasons they so readily intermingled. Bundela Rajputs in particular have some special tendencies of this sort. Their participation in the "three branch" division noted in section A, which marks their status as inferior to the "thirty-six branch" division of "Western Rajput" clans, shows, unlike the latter, "no tendency for internal hierarchical segmentation" (Jain 1975, 262-63). The term *kuri*, implying a "sprout" or branching relationship, is used by Bundelas to designate the segmentation of both the eastern and western clan-clusters from one apical ancestor (244-46). Bundelas also forged regional ties of "pseudo-agnation" through a so-called "line of milk" or "milk brotherhood" with Ahirs, whose men formed their militias, and whose women provided their princes with wet-nurses (267-68). The *Chatra Prakāś* describes the Bundelas' endless string of battles against "Ufghans," most celebrated of whom was the aforemention Duleel Khan, in whom the Rajputs saw a son and brother.[83] Chatrasal's early warband of thirty warriors, reminiscent of the multicaste brothers in *Palnāḍu*, consisted of several Brahmans and Rajputs, a barber, a fisherman, and a Muslim.[84] Whether Afghans and Rajputs interdined, however, is a matter on which our oral epics and other sources are silent.

Yet hero cults repeat this impulse, as can be discerned in Khan's studies of the cult of Rāmdeo in Marwar (the Jodhpur area of west-central Rajasthan). As was mentioned in chapter 1, it is with the cult of Rāmdeo, also called Ramshāh Pīr, that we widen the question of Ismā'īlī influences. Rāmdeo's worshipers sometimes identify their sect as the Satpanth, but also have such other names as Mahāpanth and Nizārpanth or Nizārī Dharm, the last two being secret names.[85] Rāmdeo's paired names are illustrative of the sect's double register of Hindu and Ismā'īlī features. As

[83]See n. 7 on the *Chatra Prakāś*. Many such "Ufgahns" or Afghans were sent by the Mughals, others by Muhammad Khan Bangash, and some locally entrenched in Bundelkhand.

[84]Later joined by Gond tribesmen, Baniyas, a Chhipi (dyer), Ahir, and more Muslims (Gupta 1980, 25, n. 33, 28, 130; Kolff 1990, 151). But Bundelas also seized upon Rajput prerogatives to lord it over the "non-Aryan" Khangar populations they conquered (Jain 1975, 266-70).

[85]Khan 1996, 33; 1997b, 67-68. Similarly, Shāh Nizār is a name—the only one said to be secretively disclosed in the gināns of Shams Pīr—of the messianic Qā'im (Kassam 1995, 327), presumably keeping secret his identification with the Imāms of Alamūt, the Nizāri stronghold. Another name for the sect is Guptīs "(lit. secret)—a designation . . . for all Nizaris practicing *taqīyya* and hiding their real identity" (Khan 1997b, 41).

Khan remarks, his sectarian following is one of a small number of "'obscure' religious movements" among the "'forgotten branches' of Ismailism in Rajasthan," but also "found in neighboring areas, such as Gujarat, Madhya Pradesh and Punjab," that share a genre of messianic "prophetic songs," sung at night vigils, called "poems of the time to come" (*Āgam vāṇīs*). These songs are themselves folk variants of the ginā̄ns, the "songs of 'wisdom'" (from Sanskrit *jñāna*) of the early Satpanth or Khojā Pīrs. They are known from manuscripts going back to the eighteenth century, but the earliest are probably composed by at least the fourteenth century with some of them (notably including those attributed to Shams Pīr) having still prior oral transmission.[86]

While the *Āgam vāṇīs* have a secretive character, those who organize the Rāmdeo vigils at which they are sung include "ascetics of a religious mendicant order (*bhekh*)" called Kāmaḍs, who sing other songs about Rāmdeo more publicly (Khan 1993, 40; 1996, 33). Drawn mainly from Dalit communities, and especially the Meghwāl (or Meghval), and in some areas Bhīl tribals, Kāmaḍs are the usual priests at a network of cult centers or seats (*gaddī*) that link Rāmdeo with other figures. In her beautifully researched description of this network, Khan reconstructs fragments of oral epic, and a history traceable over three generations from the first half of the fourteenth to the early fifteenth century, behind this extraordinary "little king" Rajput missionary-hero.

Rāmdeo's grandfather is Raṇsī Tanwar, a Tomara (Tanwar) Rajput alleged to have lost the throne of Delhi to a Sunnī Sultan (Khan 1996, 38), and also a descendant of Arjuna and an ardent devotee of Kṛṣṇa (1993, 38-39). He and a Meghwāl Dalit named Khiwan are converted by a Nizārī missionary: the above-named Shams Pīr, also known to Rāmdeo's followers as Samas Rishi, who comes from Iran (presumably Alamūt). Historical reconstructions vary. According to Kassam, one can infer from the ginā̄ns attributed to Shams Pīr, and from other sources, that he worked as a missionary of the Ismā'īlī *da'wa* directed from Alamūt up to its fall to the Mongols in 1256, and indigenized his mission thereafter to close out what must have been a very long career (according to the genealogy preserved on his tomb, he was born in Ghazna in 1165 and was buried in Ucch in 1277).[87] Khan, drawing on stories connecting Shams Pīr with Raṇsī Tanwar and Khiwan in the Rāmdeo cycle, settles on the early fourteenth century as the time Shams comes to Multan, during which he would have kept concealment first from the Mongols until 1306, and from the anti-Shī'a policies of Allauddin Khilji, the Delhi sultan whose reign (1296-1316) established imperial sway as far south as

[86]Khan 1997a; 1997b, 45, 155-57; Shackle and Moir 1992, 15.
[87]Kassam 1995, 84 and 93; cf. 77, 90, 114-15; Nanji 1978, 63.

Madurai, and no doubt did much to sow seeds for common Hindu and Muslim forms of resistance to it (1997b, 69-75). Kassam's dating seems to make sense from the literary sources, leaving it likely that the links with the Rāmdeo tradition's folklore would have grown around the Pīr's developing hagiography.

Rāmdeo's followers further identify Shams Pīr/Samas Rishi as an indirect spiritual disciple of a probably Nāth-inspired guru named Gusāīnjī, who is also identified as the formless god ("*Alakh*, *Niranjan*, *Nirākār*, etc.") and the sect's primal guru (*ādi guru*). Shams preached primarily to Hindus (including obviously Rajputs) and Muslims; Gusāīnjī to Hindus and Dalits "who could not receive initiation from 'higher caste' gurus" (34, 41-43). Raṇsī Tanwar and Khiwan establish cult centers and become Pīrs through Shams Pīr's initiation; but they also become martyrs through his curse, and through the persecution of the unnamed Sunnī emperor of Delhi—possibly the just mentioned Alauddin Khilji—who orders them "cut with a magic saw consisting of a margosa leaf."[88] Raṇsī's lineage is one of "high-caste Rajputs," but at a small-scale (little king) local level. Narainā, the cult center Raṇsī founds as a missionary of Shams Pīr's teachings, is also considered his jāgīr: a precarious one, since most of his sons die trying to defend it against the Sunnī emperor. The two surviving sons, one of them Ajmal, Rāmdeo's father, flee to Marwar, abandoning Narainā to be administered for some time by Dalit Meghwāls, descendants of Khiwan.[89] Rāmdeo, who is considered along with Pābūjī as one of the five Pīrs of Rajasthani folk culture,[90] then inherits an area in Marwar which his father had cleared of Rākṣas, and establishes a "small kingdom there" that "was in fact a *jagīr* granted by the local [Rāṭhoṛ] ruler." But he settles nearby at Runichā-Rāmdeorā, his cult center, and the jagīr reverts to the Rāṭhoṛ.[91] Despite its fragmentation, it is another loser's epic of mobile "little Rajput" resistance to imperial power in Delhi, this time with the Muslim, Rajput, and Dalit partners all being Nizārīs.

The Nizārī connection has dimmed and been largely forgotten over

[88]As Khan has detected (1996, 38-39; 1997b, 72), the "saw of punishment" seems to have been a "specific torture" used by to punish Ismā'īlīs. Their bones become flowers (collected cremation bones are called flowers; Weinberger-Thomas 1996, 85), their blood becomes milk.

[89]Khan 1996, 38, 42. The present custodians are Rajputs, though not Tanwar-Tomaras.

[90]Joining Harbu, Gogā, and Mallināth or Mehā, although others may be included in very different lists, including Ghāzī Miyān, as mentioned below. At one temple a painting of the Five Pīrs complements one of the five Pāṇḍavas, apparently connecting the folk heroes with the classical heroes by a Nizārī "system of correspondences" rather than a Hindu pattern of reincarnations (Khan 1996, 48).

[91]Khan 1996, 34-35, 38-44; 1997b, 69-80.

time. Cult centers founded or administered by Dalits have attracted only Dalits. Only those founded by Rajputs open "little kingdom" umbrellas for multiple castes. Rāmdeo, "derisively nick-named *dhedhō kā dev* (the 'god of the pariahs')," now attracts all castes at his (Khan 1997b, 62), while at the Mīyālā center founded by his paternal uncle Dhanrāj Pīr, one finds among "traditional worshipers . . . not only Meghwāl and Regar but Mālī, Jain, Bhīl and a good number of Mer (Rāwat)" (1996, 43; cf. 1997b, 80-82, 117-18). The devotees are thus variously Dalit, low, and tribal, plus the religiously "dialogic" Muslim/Hindu Mers or Meos, and the Jains.[92] Since the 1920s, there have been attempts to "rehinduize" them all. But the forgotten Nizārī impulses are still traceable in ritual and myth. At Rāmdeo's cult center at Ruṇichā-Rāmdeorā, "as a whole, the configuration is that of a *kabristān* or Muslim cemetery, somewhat altered to meet the basic requirements of a Hindu temple," with both Hindu and Muslim features on the graves of Rāmdeo, his parents, sons, disciples, last descendant, and Dalit adoptive sister.[93] Temple and battlefield terrains that include shrines for Muslims remind one of the hero cults of *Ālhā*, *Palnāḍu*, and the Draupadī cult *Mahābhārata*. We shall find something similar in connection with the ballad of Rāja Desing.

Moreover, in the "poems of the time to come," "Hindu and Turks will drink from the same cup" (1997a, 418), and God—that is, Rāmdeo, understood as Kalki and the Nikalank (faultless) avatār, and bearing various Muslim messianic titles—will return to marry a Dalit girl named Meghṛī (or Meghṛī Rāṇī), symbolizing "the Megh or Meghval community . . . and, as such, all the oppressed people who will triumph and be redeemed at the end of the Kali Yuga" (1997a, 417). As anticipated by the pāval or *ghatpāṭ* ritual, which, under Nizārī influence, took root among little Rajput and Dalit communities of Rajasthan and Madhya Pradesh, and which consisted of a shared cup and tantric meal open to all castes including Dalits,[94] brotherhood (and also it seems sisterhood[95])

[92]Mayaram 1997, 64-71. See chap. 8, n. 43, on Mayaram's use of "dialogic" to discuss the Meos, to whom she also ascribes Shī'ī subcurrents (60, 256-60). Cf. Khan 1996, 37, 50-56, and 1997b, 159, 225-26, 269-70, offering fine critical discussion of rehinduization, incomplete conversion, syncretism, dissidence, folk spontaneity, deislamicization, sanskritization, etc., as interpretative strategies. Cf. Mayaram 1997, 45.

[93]Khan 1996, 44; 1997b, 62-63.

[94]*Pāval* (with several variants) is the sacred drink taken at the *ghatpāt* (lit. "pot-throne," the throne being a wooden plank) ceremony; see Khan 1994; 1997b, 53-54, 127-37, 143-44, 159, 179-80, 194-99, 210-16, 245-46; Nanji 1988, 66-67; Shackle and Moir 1992, 13; Kassam 1995, 105-12, 266-67, 320-70. Srivastava explains Rāmdeo's "popularity among lower castes . . . primarily by his mission of human equality" (1997, 65).

[95]Gināns attributed to Shams that describe the Nizārī origins of the ritual in the circular *garbī* dances affirm gender equality: "Man and woman are one and the same though their bodies are distinct; those on the path of religion (*dharma*) are equal"; "regard all others as

comes with the apocalypse.

Indeed, the theme is rich, and has been disseminated among other Dalit and low status populations.[96] A closely related sectarian group of similar history and profile—the Bishnoī—also sings "poems of the time to come" that call the bride Vasudhā Kunvārī, "the Virgin Earth." Khan traces this second name along with the bride's messianic story to the ginān s, which include songs with "war-like and eschatological themes" that we must look at more closely. The Nizārī inspiration itself also draws the folklore of the Shī'ī martyrdoms of Karbalā, which are recalled on the fifth or seventh day of Muharram. These center on the unconsummated wedding of Qasim, the young son of the earlier-slain Ḥasan, to Ḥusayn's daughter Fatemeh (or Sakīnah [Gaborieau 1975, 296]), in which all the parties, but especially the young bride and groom, accept that when the wedding music changes to the drums of war, the groom will march to his death. In Iran, there is a beautiful *ta'ziyeh* or passion play on this theme (Humayuni 1979). In north India and Nepal, such a story also becomes part of the martyrdom legend of Ghāzī Miyān, known too as Bālā Pīr (Youthful Pīr) but born as Sālār Mas'ūd. Son of the eleventh-century Mahmud of Ghazna's sister, he gets linked as well with the late twelfth-century Prithīrāj Chauhān (Elliot 1879, 251-53). Slain in 1033 as a youth of nineteen on a raiding expedition at Bahraich (a hundred kilometers northeast of Lucknow in eastern Uttar Pradesh), he has a tomb there by the thirteenth century where he comes to be worshiped, as he also does elsewhere from Bengal to Rajasthan (Schwerin 1981, 149). Now a warrior (*ghāzī*)-martyr with a new marriage story (Gaborieau 1975, 295), he is worshiped as one of the five Pīrs by *both* Hindus and Muslims (Schwerin 1981, 151-53). The fair at Bahraich that commemorates his death in battle, vastly attended in the nineteenth century (Elliot 1879, 252) as it still is today (Schwerin 1981, 149), is called "Nuptials (*Urs*) of Ghāzī Miyān," and recalls that the nineteen-year-old hero "had on his bridal clothes, and was about to be married, when he was martyred" (Elliot 1879, 252). In Nepal, his *urs* is celebrated, down to the change from wedding music to war music and the lamentation songs (*marsiyah*) that follow, by recalling him as *both* Ḥasan and Ḥusayn in a

[96]Khan 1997a, 413; 1996, 49, n. 73. Cf. 1997b, 143: the *Kāyam rāi* will marry a Mahar girl among the Berars of Madhya Pradesh; 149, in a Meghwal *bhajan* song of recognition: "Wake up, O Meghri, recognize your fiance"; 157-58, in the same song, Meghrī has already been chosen in the first yuga; 181; 119, a *vānī* song: "The wedding altar will be at Chittor, the bridegroom's party will establish its camp at Delhi," implying eternal empire. On Rāmdev or the last avatar as emperor, see Khan 1997b, 80, 148, 230, and 248 (similarly for last Sikh guru). Cf. Shackle and Moir 1992, 97-98, 176-77; and Khan 1996, 49, n. 73, with the verse, "In the four ages I have wandered in countless forms, but no marriage has taken place. Have the wedding performed, o my Master. Be gracious, o miraculous lord."

single unconsummated marriage with Ghāzī Miyān's own bride Bībī Joharā, "daughter of Sayyid" (Gaborieau 1975, 289-97). In north India, Ghāzī Miyān is especially popular among the "dialogic" Meos, some of whom claim he converted them to Islam (Schwerin 1981, 144, 152). His worship as one of the five Pīrs is also popular among "lower caste Hindus (Doms, Nats, Mirasis) and those converted from lower castes to Islam (Lal Begis, Julahas)" (154). Moreover, "[s]ome subcastes of the [Dalit] Doms identify Lal Beg with Ghazi Miyan" (155). Khan numbers the Lāl Begis among the "'lost branches' of the Ismailis" (1997b, 271), and notes that Lāl Beg is worshiped in Nizārī-inspired traditions by these same populations, known also as Chuhṛās, who overlap with Meghs and other Dalit groups of the former Northwest Provinces and Punjab (155-57). Hindu Bhangīs (sweepers) know him as "Lál Guru, which is the familiar name of the Rákshasa Aronákarat" (Elliot 1879, 32). Mainly known as Bālā Shāh (Youthful King), Lāl Beg is the disciple of Bālmīk (Vālmīki) and the messianic avatar. In an *Āgam vāṇī*-like song, he is the "true saint and prophet," "the male buffalo," and leader of an eschatological army he inspires among the living, and also resurrects, even from "the burnt dead."[97] The "vat" or the "pitcher and cup" come with him through the yugas. He is "Níkáhil" and 'Alī who "equipped his Duldul," and he holds "the bow from Multán" (Rose 1911-19, 1:182-83, 192, 199-205, especially 200-3). Yet we are not told whether, like so many of his counterparts just mentioned, he has a messianic bride.

Then too, one must reconsider elements of the Lausen epic of West Bengal, whose hero makes the sun rise in the west on a new moon night, has an army of Dalit Ḍom retainers whom Dharma resurrects from the dead, and whose cult includes a fermented rice wine jug distributed, like the ghaṭpāt, at new moon vigils.[98] In the "big" *Dasa avatāra* ginān of the Imāmshāhī branch of the Satpanth,[99] the last of the good or auspicious signs of the Nikalank avatar's "open" (i.e., nonsecret) arrival at the end of the Kali yuga is, "And the sun will rise in the west" (Khakee 1972, 182). One of Ṣadruddīn's gināns also identifies the "Lord of Alamut" as "Lord Ali in the West" and "glorious as a risen sun" (Shackle and Moir 1992, 87-89), while one of Sham Pīr's gināns tells

[97]The Shāh (see n. 85) burns the sinner's body to ashes, then sprinkles pāval to make one sit up (Khakee 1972, 440)—this, according to the "big" *Dasa avatāra* ginān of the Imāmshāhīs who split from the Nizārīs, but attributed to Imām Shāh and considered his elaboration (for the sect founded shortly after 1513 by his son) of earlier short *Dasa avatāra* gināns attributed to Shams Pīr and his grandson Ṣadruddīn (Khakee 1972, 5-6; Daftary 1990, 484). Though formerly important, due to islamizing reforms it is no longer used in Khojā services (ibid., 485).

[98]See Hiltebeitel 1991a, 302-8; cf. Khan 1997b, 198; Nanji 1988, 66.

[99]See above n. 97.

how the ghaṭpāt was secretively brought to Bengal by Bairāgīs (Kassam 1995, 303-4). Rose notes that Bairāgī Fakirs and Sādhus moved among the Ismā'īlī-influenced sweepers (Dalits) in Punjab (1911-19, 1: 204), and no doubt they didn't stop there.

We may thus begin to ask whether in some of our oral epics, themes of unconsummated mystic marriage, eschatological brotherhood, radical commensality, and the renewal of the virgin earth have drawn something from a Nizārī inspiration. But egalitarian images, however varied and harsh they may be in their outcomes and in relation to the realities that contradict them, are thematized mainly in connection with north Indian oral epics and hero cults, and with what look to be carryovers in *Palnāḍu* and *Desing*. At Draupadī festivals, vegetarian offerings may be made to all deities at certain times, including Pōttu Rāja and Muttāl Rāvuttaṉ. But usually, food and other offerings are differentiated. Blood sacrifices, liquor, and other impurities are offered only to Muttāl Rāvuttaṉ—out of Draupadī's line of sight, and also at nonfestival times—leaving Muttāl Rāvuttaṉ to eat such fare and get drunk alone (Hiltebeitel 1988a, 116-19). Nor is there any indication of the elder brothers' dining with Cāmpukā or their crore of Muslim soldiers.

D. Warrior-Ascetics and Wandering Minstrels

What inspired such images of brotherhood? No doubt more than just the camaraderie of warriors away from home. *Ālhā* tells us that the heroes themselves embodied certain spiritual disciplines in their travels. When the young Banāphars and Mīrā Tālhan break camp, check their starbook, and depart for Mārō, they don what come to be their habitual disguises as Jōgī-musicians: Rāma's mark on their forehead, ashes on their bodies, musical instruments in hand, they are Jōgī-pilgrims. Arriving, they announce themselves as Bairāgīs seeking alms (W&G 80-81, 84). As noted in chapter 5, they seem to be disguised primarily as Gorakhnāthī Nāth Jōgīs. They dye their clothes red (W&G 75); such Jōgīs wear yellow/red/ochre robes colored originally by Pārvatī's blood (Briggs [1938] 1989, 18, 207). Nāth lore also has king Bharthari's "army of consecrated warriors" "clad in red dyed clothes" (Kolff 1990, 79). Just as Mīrā Tālhan is one the Jōgī-musicians, some Gorakhnāthīs are Muslims (Briggs 1-2, n. 1, 5-6, 66, 71, etc.)—indeed, there is even a subdivision of Nāths called "Ismail Jogis" (White 1996, 505, n. 163). Their wanderers' refrain, "Waters that flow and Jōgīs that go, What power can make them stay?" (W&G 89, 98, 130) echoes such Jōgīs' accent on movement (Briggs 12). Hinglāj in Baluchistan, repeatedly mentioned as their destination on their way from Bengal (W&G 82-83, 89, 97), is the Vāmacāra (left-handed Tantric) shrine of Hinglāj Mātā, goddess of Dasnāmī Gosain, Nāth, and Gorakhnāthī Jōgī pilgrims, who is also worshiped by Muslims as Bībī (presumably Fāṭimah as Lady [*bībī*] Fāṭimah) or Nānī and by Dalit followers of Rāmdeo. Located in a remote and fantastic gorge, her temple—"a low mud edifice, containing a shapeless stone situated in a cavern"—is one of the fifty-two pīṭhas marking sites where the limbs of Satī fell, and houses Satī's cranial aperture or *brahmarandhra*.[100] Some Gorakhnāthīs are balladeers, "especially Bhartri Yogīs," who "play musical instruments . . . and sing cyclic songs, or ballads, including those of . . . Puran Bhagat, Rāja Rasālū, Hīr and Rāñjha, Gūgā Pīr"—that is, various oral epics—as also songs about Gor-akhnāthī Jōgīs, the goddess, and Gaṇeśa. Indeed, in the case of *Puran Bhagat* and *Gūgā* (also called Gūgā Pīr, a Rajput who became a Muslim, whom we met in *Pābūjī*), Gorakhnāth and his band figure prominently in the stories.[101] Fourteenth-century Gorakhnāthī balladeers produced a "vigorous popular literature" (McGregor 1984, 21) which was no doubt concurrent with, and influential upon, early *Ālhā*, whose title hero is one of Gorakhnāth's disciples.[102]

But it would be a mistake to overemphasize one ascetic order. The Banāphars and Mīrā Tālhan seem to be modelled on a generic type of militant-ascetic-minstrel who moves like, and sometimes among, the troops. Calling themselves Bairāgīs as well as Jōgīs, the *Ālhā* heroes' disguises are as much Vaiṣṇava as Śaiva. Bairāgīs normally wear white, but some wear ochre.[103] "Militant monastic orders" of "Bairāgī" Vaiṣṇavas and "Gosain" or "Sanyasi" (Sannyāsī) Śaivas have a history—which a Hindi monastic text, probably from the nineteenth century, traces back to a battle between them at Hardwar in 1254—of fighting each other over precedence, "policing," and "collection of pilgrim dues" at fairs and pilgrimage sites; and they are no doubt older than that.[104] Both groups have absorbed low caste members into their ranks, and high caste monks have generally resisted commensality with low caste ones—except,

[100]Quotes from Dey [1899] 1927, 75-76; cf. Briggs [1938] 1989, 15, 17, 34, 104-14, 169; Khan 1996, 31-32; 1997, 131, 154, 226; White 1996, 121-22 and 414, n. 237. Possibly the Jōgīs move east to west through the goddess's body, from her yoni (at Gauhati in Assam) to her cranial aperture. See Dey [1899] 1927, 76, and MacLean 1989, 14-15, on her Muslim names; Khan 1993, 43 on her connection with Rāmdeo.

[101]Gill 1986, 132-36, 141-44, 148-51; Lapoint 1978, 284-86; see Briggs [1938] 1989, 181, 183 on Gūgā becoming a Muslim.

[102]See chap. 9, § C.

[103]Ghurye 1964, 151, 163, 172; Gahlot and Dhar 1989, 48.

[104]Lorenzen 1978, 69-70; Orr 1940, 88. According to White 1991, 259, n. 74 (citing Joshi [1965], 188, 191, and plate 11), "A Śaivite military order (*akhāḍa*), variously named after Bhairava and Dattātreya, was founded in Ujjain in 1146." Cf. White 1996, 345: "the earliest religious group to take up arms after the Muslim conquest may have been the Nāth Siddhas."

at times, among Bairāgīs. When gathered like an army at the Kumbha Mela, they are "fed without distinction" (Ghurye 1964, 184); and when fighting, their "various groups shared a common mess."[105] Śaivite Dasnāmī orders, linked with Śankara's orthodox Brahmanical teachings, explain the influx by a story that they took the advice of Akbar's minister Birbal "to initiate large numbers of non-Brahmans into the sannyāsī order and arm them for the protection of Brahman sannyāsīs" against militant Muslim Fakirs.[106] But this is clearly an elite gloss on older fluidities not only between high and low caste members, but between the groups themselves, among whom should be mentioned not only the *Āgam vāṇī* singers of various sects, but the low status Muslim musicians called Dafālīs who across north India sing ballads of Ghāzī Miyān (Gaborieau 1975, 295). As Khan observes, Rajasthani Kāmaḍs or Kāmaḍiyās, like Nāths, are householder-ascetics worshiping Hinglāj Mātā; "conspicuous by their saffron clothes," they "maintain an ascetic hearth called *dhūṇi*, like the Nātha and the Gosāīn (although also some Vaishnava Rāmānandī ascetics follow the same custom)" (1996, 32-33). We shall also meet crossovers between Jōgīs and Fakirs. Indeed, the *Pṛthvīrāj-rāsau* provides a prototype instance. When the bard Chand Bardai goes to Ghazna to conspire with the blinded and captive Pṛthvīrāj to kill Shihāb al-Dīn by aiming an arrow from hearing the sound alone, Chand "dresses as a wandering ascetic, ash-smeared, with tangled hair. He has 'the strength of Saraswati, and the strength of his own throat, and the heart of a great hero.' Hindus take him for a deity, and Muslims for a saint" (Pritchett 1980, 67). As we have seen, fort-entry by mendicant minstrel disguise is a recurrent theme.

Among the somewhat loosely classified four Vaiṣṇava Bairāgī orders called the "four-sampradaya *khalsa*" are the Rāmānandīs, named after but probably not actually founded by a fourteenth- or fifteenth-century Brahman named Rāmānand. The only one of the four orders to worship Rām as the supreme form of Viṣṇu, they appear likeliest to have lent a layer to the *Ālhā* heroes' disguise.[107] Concealing their identity from King Jambay of Mārō, the Banāphars and Mīrā Tālhan wear Rāma's fore-

[105]Orr 1940, 89. Otherwise strict caste distinctions apply (Ghurye 1964, 171). Cf. Orr 1940, 89: "This relaxation of caste-rules extended only to actual combatants. The Bairagis were nominally vegetarians, but this rule was also largely disregarded. Free use was likewise made of hemp, opium, and other narcotics"; cf. Pinch 1996 on the influx model (26-29, 38, 104) and the commensality issue (58-59, 63, 66, 69, 76, 100) among Rāmānandīs.

[106]Farquhar 1925, 442; Lorenzen 1978, 69.

[107]See Burghart 1978b, 130; Lorenzen 1978, 69-70; and van der Veer 1989, 135-36 on the four branches. I follow Burghart's view that Rāmānand is fashioned as the sect's founder only in the seventeenth century (1984b, 134); cf. van der Veer 1989, xii, 86, and, more accepting of the sect's modern tradition, Pinch 1996, 48-66.

head mark, chant "Rāma" (W&G 82; 77), and raise their right hands for Rāma (96). Yet when Jambay is captured and the heroes set forth to plunder his treasury, abandoning their common cover the Banāphars shout Rāma's name in victory while Mīrā shouts the Shī'ī—and probably Nizārī—cry "Alī" (137), which we have just heard from Duleel Khan. In this vein, Orr mentions "a class of Muslim ascetics called Aligols" who "acquired their name from the habit of charging the enemy in a *gol* or mass, and invoking the aid of Alee in their onset."[108]

For Rāmānandīs, however, to have lent, or at least been evoked to represent, such a layer, they must have been a more fluid movement than they have become. Whereas late sixteenth- or early seventeenth-century hagiography claims Rāmānand had five Brahmans, a married Brahman couple, a Kṣatriya, a woman, a weaver (it is unmentioned that this weaver, Kabir, was a Muslim), a cobbler, a farmer, and a barber as his twelve chief disciples, genealogists of an early eighteenth-century reform regimentalized the order by purging the women, Śūdras, and Dalits from the list over the issue of who could have passed on initiation to the sect's thirty-six spiritual lineages. Henceforth, all lineages would be said to descend from Rāmānand's male Brahman disciples, except two: one from a Kṣatriya, and one from an uncertain "Ram Kabir" (Burghart 1978b, 130-31). Around this time, Rāmānandis seem to have regained prominence at Ayodhya from the Daśanāmī Gosains, having lost it there to these Śaivites shortly before.[109] A Rajput Rāmānandī named Bālānand achieved their regimentalization at a conference that not only pruned the list of Rāmānand's disciples, but reorganized the four orders so that they could defend themselves against the Gosains.

Since then, Rāmānandī Nāgās (the order's "naked" ascetic militants) have dominated the four orders in leading and giving their name to the Bairāgīs' Rāmdal, or "army of Rām."[110] The early nineteenth century found them prominent at Baksar (Pinch 32-33, 37-38), the noted recruitment center of "Hindustani military labor" and home of the Banāphar fathers. Early twentieth-century anti-elitist "radical" Rāmānandīs then purged Rāmānuja from the accounts as Rāmānand's predecessor, and other south Indian Śrī Vaiṣṇavas from the sect's lineage, and added to Rāmānand's "achievements" the reconversion of Muslims, whom he took on as disciples, "cleansing" them in the name an "egalitarian" vision.[111] Projecting "egalitarianism" onto premodern India, not to mention an

[108]Orr 1940, 94, with citations.

[109]Burghart 1978a, 126; van der Veer 1989, 142.

[110]Orr 1940, 88-89; van der Veer 1989, 137-41.

[111]Pinch 1996, 48, 71-73 (using the term "egalitarian" on 72); Burghart 1978b, 131-33; van der Veer 1989, 87.

order tied to Rāma and the hierarchical ideals of Rāmrājya (the once and future kingdom of Rām), is fraught with perils. I suggest that the term be used only, as in the last section, to describe an impracticable ideal held up in rhetoric, ritual, or myth—whether Hindu or Muslim, otherworldly or messianic.[112] But it seems that if we are to consider some such impulse among India's "militant monastic orders" that would be open to Muslims, modern Rāmānandīs are poor candidates to help us understand Mīrā Tālhan's Shī'ī cries and his Jōgī-Bairāgī disguise.[113]

Rather than turning to orders initiated (in both senses) by Brahmans, or even to Nāths, our best insights come from warrior-ascetic orders that link Muslims with low status Rajputs and Dalits. Of this unusual type, we are sufficiently informed of two examples.[114] One, the Praṇāmīs, originates at Jamnagar in Kutch (Gujarat) but soon takes root in the western Bundela capital of Panna after their second guru Prāṇnāth (1618-94)—a Thakur "Kṣatriya" from Jamnagar—affiliates them with Chatrasal Bundela in 1683.[115] The other, the above-mentioned sect that worships Rāmdeo in Rajasthan, hereafter called Nizārpanth, has within it an order, the Kāmaḍs, which also—as Kāmaḍiyāpanth (Khan 1997b, 67)—yields one of the sect's alternate names.

The two sects begin their lineages similarly. After a founding guru is

[112]Pinch is fair to conclude that modern radical Rāmānandīs' attempts "to foster a more egalitarian monastic spirit" were "largely successful" (148), but the concept drives too much of his argument without considering the same radicals' politicized treatment of Muslims in the realm of Rāmrājya (see 71-73, 109-10). Cf. n. 19 above on Sher Shah; Nanji 1978, 102, on the oath to accept egalitarian organizational principles among Nizārīs; and Khan 1997b, 270 contrasting "the egalitarian views of the Ismailis" with "the 'universal' ideology of the Arya Samaj." On Rāmrājya, see above, n. 2.

[113]See van der Veer 1989, 149-50: according to a legend linked with the advent of Rāmānandīs to Ayodhya, at Hanumān's hill there, Hanumān was worshipped "for centuries by yogis, Dashanamis and even Muslim *faqirs,*" until he inspired a dream to undo this by chasing away the Śaivites and Muslims. Shuja-ud-Daulah had stopped there to worship Hanumān with his Daśanāmi regiment.

[114]Barely for the Praṇāmīs, on whom see most usefully Growse 1879; Gupta 1980, 93-106; McGregor 1984, 141-42. Cf. Khan 1997b, 175-219, on the Bishnoi and other Rajasthani sects akin to Rāmdeo's. Note too that Nizārī Khojās are thought to have been converted Rajputs or Ksatriyas (42-43; Daftary 1990, 479). Dādupanthis also have some of these features (Gahlot and Dhar 1989, 53-55; Ghurye 1964, 197-200; Orr 1947, 199-208, 219-20; Khan 1993, 46-47). Cf. Chatterjee 1995a, 187-97, on the Balarāmī or Balāhāḍi sect and akhāṛā formed by the Hadi (Dalit) prophet Balarām (ca. 1780-1860), with rejection of Brahmanical and other esoteric forms, Nāth features, low-caste Muslim followers, a mix of Quranic and purānic myths and lineages, and the notion that while Hābel's (Abel's) line includes the four jātis of "Sheikh, Saiyad, Mughal, and Pathan," Kabel's (Cain's) includes lower status Muslims "and, believe it or not, Rajput" (193). Cf. chap. 9, n. 91.

[115]Growse 1879, 171; Gupta 1980, 93-95; McGregor 1984, 141-2, 205; cf. Pogson [1828] 1971, 96-102.

said to have grounded each in a form of Hindu worship,[116] a second provides links to Iran. Prāṇnāth visited the Iranian port of Bandar Abbas and also travelled in Arabia as well as Rajasthan (Gupta 1980, 96); Nizārpanthīs trace their lineage through Shams Pīr/Samas Rishi, who is from Iran himself. Both sects teach a formless god and discourage image worship.[117] Praṇāmīs have Vaiṣṇava ties, and no doubt encouraged the idea that Chatrasal was an avatar of Viṣṇu;[118] Nizārpanthīs "claim to be basically Vaiṣṇava."[119] Praṇāmīs "were a kind of *bairāgī* . . . and possibly came close to the phenomenon of the famous 'fighting ascetics' of North India";[120] "originally" the Kāmaḍiyā was probably by name "the man with the staff," as in the variant *Kambariyā* ("one having a *kampam*, staff"), and practiced standing "at the entrance of the shrine with a staff or club in his right hand" during local festivals (Khan 1996, 43). Both sects affiliate with low status Rajputs opposed to imperial rule from Delhi: Praṇāmīs with the powerful Bundela clan of Chatrasal; Nizārpanthīs, though not prominently martial, with their "favorite deity" Rāmdeo who, though "credited with miracles rather than heroic feats," is still a Rajput whose clan has a brief early history of martyrdoms and retreats from encounters with a Delhi sultan.[121]

Until recently, Praṇāmīs were "treated as outcastes"; Kāmaḍs, "since Independence, have been listed among 'scheduled castes'" (Khan 1996, 31). Prāṇnāth "according to some high caste Hindus is said to have been a Muslim prince" (Gupta 1980, 103); some low caste Kāmaḍs regard Shams Pīr "as a Hindu saint wandering in the guise of Muslim Fakir to

[116]Of Śiva, Śakti, and Rāma according to Kāmaḍ legends (Khan 1996, 31-32, 42); of Kṛṣṇa and the *Bhāgavata Purāṇa* in the case of the Praṇāmīs' first guru, Dev Chandra (1581-1655), a Kayastha and disciple of one Haridas Gosain (Gupta 1980, 93-95).

[117]Khan 1996, 32-33, 50; 1997b, 141-42; Gupta 1980, 99 and n. 20.

[118]Bundelas changed from Śaivas to Vaiṣṇavas in the mid sixteenth century, and the majority who stayed in the Madras Presidency through the nineteenth century remained so (Kolff 1990, 121, 133, 154). The *Chatra Prakāś* underlines its Vaiṣṇava orientation by identifying Chatrasal as an avatar (Pogson [1828] 1971, 15, 19, 55, 77, 85), by its worship of "Bal Govind" (18-19), and its references to the yoganidrā theme (7-8, 100).

[119]Khan 1996, 32; 1997b, 65, 70.

[120]Kolff 1990, 150-51. Prāṇnāth remained in Bundelkhand from 1683, after meeting Chatrasal, to his death in 1694 (Gupta 1980, 96-97). Kolff says he arrived at Chatrasal's Panna kingdom with one thousand, one hundred Bairāgīs, but in 1742 (151, n. 73, citing *Panna Gazetteer* 37). Although Prāṇnāth "is believed to have accompanied Chhatrasāla in his battles against Aurangzeb, the sect does not appear to have a Nāgā section" (Ghurye 1964, 196).

[121]Khan 1996, 31, 38, 42-44; 1997b, 74-81. On Delhi as "the *dar al-mulk* [seat of the empire] of the great sultans and the center of the circle of Islam," see Richards 193, 125. Kassam 1995, 66-67 and 166, on the 1206 uprising of a far-flung group of Ismā'īlīs in Delhi, and a ginān attributed to Shams Pīr in which the Shāh as Mahdī or Qā'im will capture Delhi Fort as part of his messianic conquest.

avoid persecution from Muhammadan rulers; others think he was rather a Muslim who had donned the robe of a Hindu yogi" (Khan 1996, 37). In each case Muslim and Hindu elements combine in worship and ritual: "a Panja (open palm) instead of a Kalash at the top" of the Prāṇnāth temple in Panna is cited by detractors as evidence that Prāṇnāth was a Muslim; at Nizārpanth centers, the Muslim features, mainly evident on graves, are now sometimes altered in the current "rehinduizing" mode, or have become sources of Hindu-Muslim "'communal' conflict."[122] Most striking are the death legends and funerary practices common to the two main cult centers: Prāṇnāth "met his death by burying himself alive in the ground. . . . Even now the Pranamis who die in Panna, are still buried, while all those who die elsewhere are cremated" (Gupta 1980, 103, n. 2). Rāmdeo took "living samādhi" (Khan 1995, 304) as did his paternal uncle Dhanrāj Pīr (1997b, 80); and while Kāmaḍs are said to do so as well (1996, 32), "a strange custom still prevails in the area surrounding Rāmdeorā: in order to follow Rāmdeo's example, the members of all the Hindu communities, from Brahmans to Harijans, bury their dead instead of cremating them" (44). At Panna, high caste Hindus mention such burials as further evidence that Prāṇnāth was a Muslim; at Rāmdeorā, the "unorthodox practice (traditionally associated with Muslims and low-caste Hindus)" is integrated into upper caste consciousness as a kind of ascetic samādhi.[123] I have mentioned "taking living samādhi" in connection with Jaffar and Farīd, the two Muslims "of Aurangzīb's time" who wanted to "worship with" the Palnad heroes.

But Kāmaḍs are also intriguing with regard to *Ālhā* and its heroes' musicality. Although Khan mentions briefly that Praṇāmīs, like Kāmaḍs, sing *Āgam vāṇīs* or "poems of the time to come" at night vigils (1997a, 401, 424, n. 4), available sources say nothing of their musical practices. But Kāmaḍs are known "as wandering minstrels or jugglers singing hymns in praise of Bābā Rāmdeo," accompanying themselves with a five-stringed folk instrument called *tandurā* or *chauturā* similar to the classical *tamburā* (Khan 1996, 29, 31). Gahlot and Dhar describe Kāmaḍ men and women moving "about the country side singing songs in praise of

[122]Gupta 1980, 103; Khan 1996, 33, 37, 39, 41, 43-44, 47; 1997b, 62-66.

[123]Khan 1996, 44. Khan notes that Nāths and Dasnāmi Gosains also have "the custom of 'taking living *samadhi*'; theoretically it means that they bury themselves alive in a state of deep meditation (*samadhi*), but practically, it refers" to burial rather than cremation (1995, 304); similarly, Gupta notes that the practice is "not unknown to other Vairagis and Gosains professing Hinduism as well" (1980, 103, n. 32). Where Muslim-Hindu interaction lies behind it, the practice almost certainly involves resurrection of the body. As mentioned earlier, Ismā'īlī-influenced Chuhrā Dalits in Punjab, for whom such resurrection is a tenet, have an *Āgam vāṇī*-like hymn that promises, "the burnt dead have been revived" to fight in the apocalyptic "war of Ganesh" (Rose 1911-19, 2:200, 205). See n. 97 above.

Ramdeo to the accompaniment of the stringed instrument, *Rawan Hatta* or *Tamboora*" (1989, 194), which must be the same as or similar to the *Rāvaṇhattho* played by bhopo singers of *Pābūjī*.

If Praṇāmīs and Nizārpanthīs each have versions of the *Āgam vāṇīs* or "poems of the time to come," they must also share at least the outlines of a common messianism. For the Praṇāmīs, Prāṇnāth—undoubtedly under Nizārī inspiration—espoused in the "best-known" of his fourteen works, the *Qiyāmat-nāmā* or "Book of the Resurrection," a vision in which "Jesus and Muhammad, both prophets of Islam," are "seen in the context of the day of judgment as forerunners of the *avatār* Kalki who will make 'east' and 'west' one" (McGregor 1984, 141). Growse's translation of this work makes it clear that Kalki is both the Qā'im and the Nikalank avatar, whom the text calls "Kalanki":

> Thus it is declared the glory of the Hindus, that the last of the Prophets shall be of them. And the Lord Christ, that great Prophet, was king of the poor Jews. . . . It is also stated in the Hindu books that the Budh Kalanki will assuredly come. When he has come, he will make all alike; east and west will both be under him. . . . Kalanki, it is said, will be on a horse—this everyone knows—and astrologers say that Vijayábhinand will make an end of the Kali Yug. Now the Gospel says that Christ is the head of all, and that He will come and do justice. The Jews say, that Moses is the greatest, and that all will be saved through him. All follow different customs and proclaim the greatness of their own master. Thus idly quarrelling they fix upon different names; but in the end all is the same, the supreme God.[124]

Kalanki will come on the "night of power," like the *Qur'ān* (179), though it does not indicate whether he will marry a Dalit girl at the end of the Kali yuga. But for Nizārpanthīs, who understand Rāmdeo not only as Kalki but the Nikalank avatar, the king of the resurrection (*Qā'im* or *Kāyam Rāi*), the real Imam, 'Alī, and the true emperor (*sacchā badshāh*), their *Āgam vāṇīs* tell that his marriage to Meghṛī Rāṇī is preceded by the eschatological conquest of the demon Kalinga, who personifies the Kali yuga. Under the name Śyām (a name for Kṛṣṇa) and "incarnated as the Nikalank king," Rāmdeo will ride a white horse and lead an army comprised "of Puranic heroes and gods (the Pāṇḍavas, Draupadī, Hariś-candra, Prahlād, Brahmā, Śeṣnāg, Hanumān, etc.), as well as figures

[124]Growse 1879, 178-79. Growse regards the text as "very curious, both from the advanced liberalism of its theological ideas and also from the uncouthness of the language, in which the construction of the sentences is purely Hindi, while the vocabulary is mainly supplied from Persian and Arabic sources" (171).

known by Muslim names: Isuf, Alladin, Dal Khoja and Makkardin, Fatima"—as Khan notes, including "at least" one Khojā.[125]

These themes all trace back to the Khojās and their gināns: in particular those attributed to Shams Pīr, who is pivotal not only for the Rāmdeo cult, but in the formation of the Satpanth. As Kassam argues, the gināns of Shams Pīr—and this is so whether or not the songs are precisely his (Khan 1997b, 45)—reflect upon the crucial transformation of Nizārī missions in India. Following upon the "seeding period" of alliances with Rajputs and other Hindus that ended with the first Ghurid massacre of Ismā'īlīs in Multan in 1160,[126] this transformative period included three momentous events for Ismā'īlīs in Sind: Ḥasan II's declaration of the *Qiyāmah* or Resurrection from a pulpit at Alamūt in 1162; the second Ghurid massacre of Ismā'īlīs in Multan by Shihāb al-Dīn in 1175; and the destruction of Alamūt in 1256. It is enough to say here that when Ḥasan II, the fourth lord of Alamūt and the first to declare himself Imām, announced the Qiyāmah, his declaration, to quote a fine passage from Kassam, "spiritualized an aspiration that for centuries had been materially sought. It created an opening, a window in the space of which religious forms were represented as fluid signs."[127] If Shams Pīr's dates as a missionary from Alamūt carry at least through the end of the long lifetime (1165-1277) ascribed to him on his tomb,[128] his gināns would reflect (or reflect back) on the spirit of the Qiyāmah, which was openly proclaimed from Alamūt under Ḥasan II and his successor Muhammad II up to 1212. This spirit, as Kassam says, "would have made" Shams Pīr's "innovative articulation of Satpanth both possible and permissible."[129]

Meanwhile, as Kassam further suggests, the songs in which Shams Pīr predicts that the Shāh[130] will come from Alamūt to win the apocalyptic battle could well have been inspired while Alamūt Fort still stood, although they could also recall that period, since the Qiyāmah's "realized eschatology" is, I believe, sufficient to explain the warfare themes. In arguing, however, that the messianic songs evoke some "high probability

[125]Khan 1997a, 416-18, with discussion of the *Āgam vānīs* of the similar Bishnoi and Jasnāthi movements, which add such details as the horse being Duldul, who after having been Muhammad's horse becomes the horse of 'Alī; cf. Khan 1997b, 204, 217-18, and 1996, 416-17 and 1997b, 80, 150, 230, on Rāmdeo as "true emperor."

[126]See at n. 14 above.

[127]Kassam 1995, 56-62 (61 quote); cf. Hodgson 1955, 148-84; Daftary 1990, 386-96, on these events and the Qiyāmah doctrine.

[128]See at n. 87 above.

[129]Kassam 1995, 115; "Satpanth tradition strictly maintains that the *gināns* were composed by Ismā'īlī *pīrs* who were *authorized* to do so by the *imām*" (90).

[130]The "King," as he usually calls 'Alī as Imām and Qā'im.

of gaining back the region" of Sind through the "promise of reinforcements from Alamūt" (1995, 114), Kassam sustains a forced historical reading. She seems to forget that the post-Qiyāmah period from 1212 to the destruction of Alamūt in 1256 was for Nizārīs one of religious accommodation to Sunnī regimes and retreat from impracticable politics. And she overlooks the wider debilitating conditions in India that link the massacres of Ismā'īlīs in Multan with the establishment of Sunnī rule in Delhi.[131] Though Shams Pīr's apocalyptic gināns sustain a tension between an historical present and the throes of the time to come, the battle scenes are clearly messianic. What enlivens this apocalypse is the innovative transformation, made possible by the Qiyāmah, of "religious forms" into "fluid signs"—which, as Kassam reminds us elsewhere—afforded "camouflage and sanctuary" in times of taqīyya after massacres and persecutions.[132] Like the more folkloric *Āgam vāṇis* of the Nizārpanthīs and other lost sects of the Ismā'īlīs, Shams Pīr's Khojā gināns sing of such fluidity in the Muslim-Hindu composition of the Shāh's eschatological army.[133] One song in particular, for us a proof text, must be cited in extenso:

> Yes sir! There the Swāmi Rājā mounts the horse Duldul.
> He grants the believer (*mu'min*) his heart's desire. . . .
> Yes sir! There a nightingale sings, and a hammock swings;
> The [army] rides before the wind. . . .
> Yes sir! There in Yodhā is the brave bowholder Bhīma;
> Fearless, all treasures are his.
> Yes sir! There three hundred and thirty bowmen climb;
> Arjuna's army is endless.
> Yes sir! There Sahadeva and Nakula are truly praiseworthy;
> They destroy the mountain with their weapons. . . .
> Yes Sir! There king Yudhiṣṭhira delivered ninety million;
> Twelve [million] attained the Lord (*Khudāvand*).[134]

[131]Kassam 1995, 99-100 [historicizing the story of Kalinga], 104-5 ["imminent help," "actual battle scenes," and "the impending arrival of the Shāh . . . who gives repeated assurances and pledges of military aid"], 114-15 [Alamūt as an "established power base" giving Ismā'īlīs "confidence" that they might regain power in Multan], 122 [the decades before the fall of Alamūt as "a time when the Nizārī Ismā'īlīs were still in power"].

[132]Kassam 1995, 71-72; quoted in chap. 1.

[133]Many features are paralleled and extended (as will be mentioned) in the presumably later "big" *Dasa avatāra* ginān (see above n. 97). Note that Khakee (1972, 41) says the latter "appears intellectually at an unphilosophical, unsophisticated, and folk-lorish level."

[134]This is the third of three verses which evoke the widely attested ginānic theme of souls saved through the four yugas: five crores by Prahlād, seven by Hariścandra, nine by Yudhiṣṭhira, and twelve by Pīr Sadruddīn.

Yes sir! There a countless million march in the Shāh's army;
Their endless limits cannot be fathomed.
Yes sir! There five hundred thousand came with Lord (*īśvar*) Gorakha;
They all came blowing trumpets.
Yes sir! There seventy-thousand mounted with Ḥusayn;
The entire world was shaken with rumbling noise.
Yes sir! There about nine hundred million and fifty-six
Of the castes of Medhā and Ḍamara found salvation.
Yes sir! There thirty-two million of the Kīnara caste ascended;
They all attained the shining Lord (*nara*). . . .
Yes sir! There former armies walk around the Shāh;
Six hundred and forty thousand attain union.
Yes sir! The Shāh advances four arm-lengths on his wooden slippers;
He slays the demon Kalinga.
Yes sir! There Queen Surjā[135] warns, "Listen Kālinga!
'Alī has come with a great army."
Yes sir! There comes 'Alī from the West to the East;
And Yodhā meets its end. . . .[136]
Yes sir! There the Shāh has now become manifest in his tenth form;
He is known by the name and form (*rūpa*) of 'Ālī. . . .
Yes sir! There before the world is the Shāh's sword Ḍhulfikār;
So brightly does the Light (tejas) of 'Alī shine forth.
Yes sir! There six thousand instruments will play for the Shāh;[137]
'Alī will come on to the field. . . .
Yes sir! There, Pīr Shams says,
"Listen, O Gathering of believers (*mu'min*)!
You will have a vision (*dīdār*) of the Shah."
Yes sir! There Pīr Shams, the Qalandar[138] of 'Alī says:
The sky will thunder with the Shāh's countless weapons!
The Sāheb of innumerable wanderers will mount his horse.
And nothing will be able to arrest his speed. (Kassam 1995, 240-43)

[135]Kalinga's queen, but converted to the Satpanth—according to the "big" *Dasa avatāra*, by Pīr Shams in the form of a parrot (Khakee 1972, 73-78).
[136]From here, several verses describe the Shāh taking on Viṣṇu's avatars, up to the tenth.
[137]Curiously, Kassam mentions that "*ginān* recitation is not (presently) accompanied by any musical instruments," but indicates that this is likely the result of recent islamization (1995, 4, 126, n. 12). In the *Dasa avatāra*, the Shāh's army has many musicians (including Yoginīs and Dattātreya beyond those mentioned here), and their instruments (drums, bells, vīnā) are in effect weapons (Khakee 1972, 234, 252-53, 252, 266-68, 322).
[138]"Wonder working . . . wild, ecstatic *ṣūfī*" (Kassam 1995, 82).

The Shāh is manifest in his luminosity as 'Alī,[139] of whom Shams's songs give vision (*dīdār*, and elsewhere *darśan*).[140] 'Alī Shāh mounts the riderless horse Duldul, the white mare of Muhammad, who "survived" Muhammad, "and according to Shī'ah tradition, was inherited by 'Alī" to be ridden in historical battles.[141] Now Duldul waits to be remounted by the apocalyptic 'Alī, in whom Shams Pīr sees the reality behind the tenth avatar Kalki, who will also ride a white horse.[142] Having sided with the Pāṇḍavas in the past, destroying the Kauravas by sending an army to what can only be Kurukṣetra,[143] 'Alī will now "come onto the field" with his army at Yodhā,[144] where the demon Kalinga dwells in his "crooked" Cīnab Fort (237)—probably another name for Multan.[145] 'Alī's spectral army of "countless millions" rides before the wind, uniting resurrected armies of the past: "former armies" that "walk around the Shāh"—including not only the Pāṇḍavas' vast hosts, but the companions of Ḥusayn from Karbalā, now increased ten

[139]"The Imāms are from Light; they are ever-present (*qā'im*) in the world" (Kassam 1995, 327). See further below.

[140]"O Brother, realize the true vision (*darśan*) of your Shāh Pīr!" "When the vision (*darśan*) of 'Alī Shāh is attained, the mind will frolic in joy" (Kassam 1995, 238, 247; on *dīdār*, cf. 190, 214, 223, 306, 358).

[141]Kassam 1995, 390; see n. 125 above. According to Khakee, Duldul is originally a mule, but in Satpanth texts a horse (1972, 44, 225; cf. 224-28, 232-33, 287 on Duldul's decoration and mounting).

[142]Shams Pīr's accounts of Viṣṇu's avatars drive toward his revelations concerning the ninth (involving Buddha in the *Mbh*; see below) and tenth. Referring to Kalki, Shams Pīr says, "Know the *avatār* of this fourth age is Nakalaṅka; know that he is a Muslim; . . . He has taken form (*avatār*) as the man Islām Shāh. . . . Shams revealed the Shāh's form, and they beheld the four-armed Swāmi. . . . They said, 'All our hopes have been fulfilled, for we saw Kṛṣna himself!'" (Kassam 1990, 192-93). This looks like an adroit allusion to Arjuna's relief at seeing the "familiar" four-armed Kṛṣna after seeing Kṛṣna's frightful apocalyptic nature as Time in *BhG* 11.46-50. Similarly, Shams's promise to those who convert, "you will enter Heaven's (*svarga*) gate, O believers, attain the divine vision (*dīdār*) and your sins will vanish" (112, cf. 368), could recall *BhG* 2.32: "As if by chance presented, the open gate of heaven (*svargadvāra*)—happy the warriors, Pārtha, who get such a war." *Svargadvāra* is used frequently in the *Mbh*.

[143]Shams does not mention the place (Kassam 1995, 175, 226), and neither does the "big" *Dasa avatāra*, but Khakee indicates that Kurukṣetra is the latter text's battlefield site (1972, 29).

[144]Yodhā may refer to "warriors," as with Khakee's translation of *jodhā* (1972, 203).

[145]Kassam 1995, 94-95, 113. Cīnab is perhaps Multan coded as Kalinga's fort, but not doomed, as is Yodhā (241-42), which is perhaps his kingdom. Another of Shams Pīr's ginān̄s foretells that at the end of the Kali yuga, after the Shāh captures Delhi, the Pāṇḍavas will join him in expelling the wicked from Multan (166; cf. 179, 202). In a fairly recent Gujarati biography of Shams Pīr, Cīnab is said to lie on his route from Ghazna to Kashmir (375). Kassam's history behind Cīnab is, however, forced (see n. 131). In the "big" *Dasa avatāra*, Cīnab has become China (*Cīna Māhā Cīna*), although also a fortified city (192) *in* Cīna Māhā Cīna that is once called Cīnab (333).

thousandfold (seventy thousand warriors rather than just seventy-two).[146] These are joined by legions of Dalits and others of low caste, for that is surely who is meant by Medhas (with the variant Meghas) and Ḍamaras: no doubt the religiously "dialogic" low status Rajput Meḍs, Meṛs, or Meos in this ginān;[147] Dalit Meghs or Meghwāls as the variant in others;[148] and probably Dalit Ḍoms.[149] Kassam, with her emphasis on kings and alliances, important as it is, often fails to notice Shams Pīr's promises to the oppressed,[150] which must lie behind his importance to Dalit followers of Rāmdeo, beginning with the Meghwāl Khiwan being storied as one of Shams's disciples. And amid it all comes Gorakha (Gorakhnāth) with five hundred thousand trumpet-blowing disciples. Indeed, when "My Shāh, . . . the man who is Nakalaṅkī, will mount," the "nine Nāths, the eighty-four Siddhas, [a]nd the different types of Jogīs . . . will all cry, Bravo! Bravo!" (253).[151]

As Khan observes, epic-purāṇic characters, mentioned widely in the

[146]Cf. Kassam 1995, 343-44: along with the Pāṇḍavas and Medhas, just mentioned, Husayn's followers will be present, "and Light (*nūr*) will shower upon them." Cf. Khakee 1972, 255: "seventeen thousand Husainis," whom Khakee takes as Syads (Saiyids). On Karbalā, see Daftary 1990, 49-50.

[147]See chap. 8, n. 43, and n. 92 above. Recall that in the ginān quoted above, it is specifically a question of "castes."

[148]Medha and Megha are clearly alternates in these variants (see especially Kassam 1995, 340 and 343), perhaps resulting from transmission among Khojās who interacted with different low castes and Dalits. Cf. 266, 349, 357-58: Medhas among those attaining "freedom and Divine vision [*dīdār*]." As Khakee observes, "'Megha' which usually means 'clouds' (in Gujarat also 'rain') also seems to be some kinds of beings, who were liberated" (1972, 55, n. 80).

[149]See Elliot 1879, 84-85, and Rose 1911-19,1:249-51 on Domra or Dúmṛá as a variant for Ḍom, and also for Chuhṛá(s). overlapping with Meghs and other Dalit groups of the Northwest Provinces and Punjab. "Dammars, a tribe of Jáṭs, . . . immigrants from Sind" (Rose 222), are a less likely possibility for Damaras, given that they go primarily by other names. As noted above, Chuhrás have Nizārī-influenced traditions about Lāl Beg.

[150]Kassam interprets Medha (forgetting Megha) only with reference to Sanskrit "Medhā: 'intelligence'" (389). Cf. Shackle and Moir 1992, 176: "The 'Meghs' (Sk. *megha-* 'cloud') are perhaps included through vague recollection of [Kālidāsa's poem] the *Meghadūta*." A ginān in which Satgur Nur goes to the "city of the Bhils" (125) prompts more such gymnastics by Shackle and Moir, even while recognizing that it "appears to suggest the tribal territory of the Bhils" (198). Of course, double meanings would be expected. For what Kassam brings out on low caste, see 1995, 168, 188, 241, 258 (God, the Shāh, created the sixteen castes, guiding "each and every soul to our path"), 293-94 and 400-1.

[151]Shams Pīr seems to refer to himself disguised as a Jōgī, though chastising that for a Jōgī "who practices discipline," it is no use "merely to don earrings" (Kassam 1995, 190-91; cf. 275)—clearly referring to Kānphata (Split-ear) Nāths. Likewise, in the "big" *Dasa avatāra*, Gorakhnāth and his Munīvars blow horns (Khakee 1972, 252), while the Shāh is further joined by the sixty-four Yoginīs (who offer to suck the demon army dry [322]) and Dattātreya (252; see n. 137 above).

gināns, are often code names for Nizārī Pīrs.[152] Of particular interest, found in both the gināns and *Āgam vāṇīs*, is Pīr Ṣadruddīn, known also as Sahadeva or "Sahadev Joshi" because his messianic poems are inspired by knowledge of astrology.[153] Said to have been a great grandson of Shams Pīr, Ṣadruddīn-Sahadeva is "supposed" to have invented "a 'system of equivalences' between Hindu and Muslim concepts and terminologies," although "some Ismaili sources point to a greater antiquity for these ideas" than his late fourteenth/early fifteenth century dates.[154] It is certainly interesting that it is an astrologer who identifies the equivalences, but perhaps he only formalized more fluid double registers such as we have been describing. His epic name echoes the astrological reputation of Sahadeva Pāṇḍava—mainly a creation of *Mahābhārata* folklores that is also frequently evoked in *Ālhā*'s portrayal the Banāphar Ḍhēwā.[155] Continuing Shams Pīr's depiction of the Shāh's eschatological army, Ṣadruddīn foretells that, between the dire Last Judgment upon the Qazis, Mullahs, and Maulanas[156] and the beheading of Kalinga,

> The Sayyids of India will attack, and the five Pandavas will join them. Mighty armies there will be struck with terror. (Shackle and Moir 1992, 117)

The "Sayyids of India" would refer to those "who claimed descent from the main *dāīs*" (the early Nizārī missionaries from Alamūt), stressing their Alid descent, although they too were "popularly called 'Pirs.'"[157] Let us ask again: How *are* we to understand Mīrā Tālhan, the Saiyid of Banaras?[158]

Indeed, one begins to see considerable overlap between these prophetic Nizārī-inspired poetries and *Ālhā*. The *Āgam vāṇīs* tell that the Nikalank

[152]Khan 1997b, 49, 227. Cf. Khan 1997a, 413-14; 1996, 46; 1997b, 48-50; Hollister 1953, 357; Nanji 1978, 113; Daftary 1990, 484-85.
[153]Khan 1997a, 414-17, 1997b, 48-49.
[154]Khan 1997b, 42-43; cf. 238; 1996, 45-46; Nanji 1978, 74; Daftary 1990, 479; Kassam 1995, 105.
[155]See chap. 5, n. 66, on Ḍhēwā and Sahadeva. Cf. Khan 1997b, 90: Nizārī Pīrs of the Alamūt period correlated the five Imāms of Alamūt with the five Pāṇḍavas and with the Shī'ite "five sacred bodies" or "Holy Five" of Muhammad, 'Alī, Hasan, Husayn, and Fātimah (sometimes also correlated with śakti; 50). See also Kassam 1995, 348.
[156]As Khan says, "representing the religious authorities of the Sunnis . . . ruling in Delhi" (1997a, 414).
[157]Khan 1997b, 43; Nanji 1978, 71, 90. See also n. 146 above.
[158]Curiously, with eighteen sons Mīrā is like the *dā'ī* (missionary) Pīr Hasan Kabiruddin, also "credited with a substantial number of ginans" (Shackle and Moir 1992, 7). The name Mīrā is also associated with two "obscure" ginān composers (174).

avatar's revelations will be "the fifth secret Veda,"[159] while *Ālhā* projects itself as "the Mahābhārata (itself a fifth Veda) of the Kali yuga." The *Āgam vāṇīs* tell that "Hindu and Turks will drink from the same cup,"[160] as is implicit in the pilgrim journeys and military adventures of the disguised Banāphars with Mīrā Tālhan. Kalinga is not only the name of the demon king of the Kali yuga whom the Nikalank avatar's army will behead (Khan 1997a, 414); it is also an alternate name for Mārō and for the king of Mārō, where the Banāphars undergo their initiatory episode of the nine-lākh chain. According to Kishan Sharma of Agra, Kalinga, king of Kalinga, is the father not only of Karinghā or Kariyā—names which now look to be variants on "Kalinga"—but of a daughter named Machalā, whom Ūdal forces Kalinga to marry to Ālhā. Ūdal then beheads Kalinga and retrieves his own father Jasrāj's head from the dome of the Kalinga palace.[161] Alternately, in the Elliot *Ālhā*, Karinghā-Kariyā sets everything in motion, killing the Banāphar fathers, razing Dasrāpur, and stealing the nine-lākh chain for his sister Bijaisin, who will be reborn as Phulwā to marry Ūdal. Then, when the Banāphars as Jōgīs penetrate Mārō's Iron Fort to retrieve the chain, Karinghā overrules his mother Kushlā, who seems to want to assist the Jōgīs. Rising to prevent their exit, he wears "long boots" that "creaked as on he strode" (W&G 99)—as if he were bringing to life the famous headless statue of the long-booted Kūṣāṇa emperor Kaniṣka in the Mathura Museum.[162] Finally slain by Malkhān, Karinghā-Kariyā's head is carried to Mahobā to bring satisfaction to Queen Malhnā (124-26). Indeed, it looks as if different versions know the persona and story of "Kalinga" in different fragments. In the *Bhaviṣya Purāṇa,* which "establishes" Kali as lord of the Kaliyuga, Karinghā-Kariyā is called Kaliya. As one of Kali's mid-yuga kings, he appears to hold "Kali" in his name. Moreover, he is the incarnation of Jarāsandha, in whom we have seen the classical *Mahābhārata*'s prototype of the king whose fort the avatar destroys.[163] Meanwhile, the ginān̄s hold the same elements in play. Just as Queen Kushlā can try to help the Jōgīs, Kalinga's wife

[159]Khan 1997a, 418. For the ginān̄s, cf. Kassam 201: "He himself is the Veda and the Qur'ān." But ultimately the Vedas and purāṇas are no use (364).

[160]As cited in § C. Again (see n. 156), the *Āgam vāṇīs* sustain more ambiguity than the ginān̄s, for as Khan notes, when Shams Pīr predicts that "Hindus and Muslims will eat together," he describes an "abnormality" or "calamity" of the Kali yuga (1997a, 418; cf. Kassam 1995, 261-62).

[161]Gyan Chaturvedi kindly sponsored an Agra performance of the related episode of Machalā's abduction, at which this narrative was elicited. Cf. chap. 5, n. 51.

[162]Basham 1967, plate 30a. See chap. 5, § D.

[163]See chap. 5, § D, at nn. 71-72.

Surjādevi is faithful to the Imām.[164] Although Cīnab, Kalinga's fort, remains obscure, Kalin-ga's head falls there,[165] and it is conquered, like Mārō (or Kalinga), by a group which its king fails to recognize that includes enigmatic forms of Kṛṣṇa, the Pāṇḍavas, and an important 'Alid Muslim—Ḥusayn rather than Mīrā Tālhan. In the ginans, the Pāṇḍavas and the Saiyids of India join ranks against this Kali yuga demon. In *Ālhā*, the Pāṇḍavas reincarnate in the Banāphars and Mīrā Tālhan to defeat not only him, but Prithīrāj, incarnation of Duryodhana, himself the incarnation of Kali.

Then there is Draupadī, much esteemed in Shams Pīr's ginans and reincarnated in *Ālhā* as the satī Belā. Shams centers her story on one scene: "Luckily, he came as Kṛṣṇa! He protected Draupadī with reams of cloth."[166] The *he* in question is of course the Shāh 'Alī, who also becomes the Buddha to save Draupadī and the Pāṇḍavas. These enigmas probably have something to do with Buddhist-Muslim accommodations in Sind. Taking the various passages from Pīr Shams's ginans together, the story is roughly consistent with the more elaborated version of the "big" *Dasa avatāra*.[167] Whereas the Kṛṣṇa avatar is the Shāh's eighth and focuses on Kṛṣṇa's childhood, his ninth is that of Buddha in which he comes to the Pāṇḍavas and is recognized by Draupadī when she is fixed in concentration; she then delivers him "into the hands of Yudhiṣṭhira," after which, while seated "in deep concentration (*dhyāna*)" himself, the

[164]See n. 135 above.

[165]In the "big" *Dasa avatāra*, "Cīna Māhā Cīna"/Cīnab is China. Kālīgo (as he is usually called) or Kārīgā (Khakee 1972, 184) "descends" into it at the end of the Dvāpara yuga and rules there through the whole Kali yuga, at the end of which his city "sinks" (one thinks of possible astronomical readings) when his head is thrown back there from "India" (*Jambudvīpa*) as a rusult of his losing battle with the Shāh (39, 352, 365-367).

[166]Kassam 1995, 216, translating *Pañcāvalī* (i.e., Pāñcālī) by "Draupadī" here. See similarly Khakee 1972, 29.

[167]Here Kṛṣṇa, the Shāh's eighth incarnation, directly becomes his ninth by becoming the Buddha after Krsna has killed Kamsa. As Buddha, he then kills Duryodhana, his battlefield being *Kulakhetra* rather than Kuruksetra (Khakee 1972, 342-43). Beyond what Khakee translates from the text, his introduction adds the more adversarial story that the Buddha speaks Farsī, and comes in deformed shape while the Pāṇḍavas are performing a yajña to expiate the killings at Kurukṣetra. He tells them that the Nabi (Prophet) is now the incarnaton of Brahmā, and that the Brahmans' teachings about idols, tīrthas, the Gangā, and worship of stones and trees are "now wrong." Bhīma, impressed by the Satpanth teachings, tells Yudhisṭhira. The Brahmans try to prevent from Yudhiṣṭhira from hearing the Buddha, but the Buddha instructs the Pāṇḍavas to kill a cow. Yudhiṣṭhira puts the cow's head on his own head, and his brothers put the cow's legs on theirs. When the people of "Hasnāpuri" see them walking like this through the streets doing japa (muttering prayers) to Buddha, their talk washes away the Pāṇḍavas' sins. The Brahmans then use the cow's intestines for sacred threads. Buddha then tells the Pāṇḍavas to go to Hemācala (for the equivalent of their ascent to heaven) because the Kali era is about to begin (30-34).

Buddha saves the Pāṇḍavas, destroys the Kauravas, kills Duryodhana, and brings the Pāṇḍavas mokṣa.[168] Since Draupadī is protected by the Shāh-Kṛṣṇa at her disrobing, it seems that she must recognize the Shāh as Buddha on another, as yet undeterminable, occasion. In any case, three verses found in two of Pīr Shams's gināns are most revealing:

For the sake of the True Religion (*sat dharma*),
  Draupadī endured suffering;
She did not surrender her chastity,
  and thus she acquired every happiness (*sukha*).

The *satī* did not forsake her purity,
  and her hero came to meet her;
She fixed her concentration [upon him]
  when the devil tried to disrobe her.

None is superior to Draupadī upon whom posterity
  may shower great praise;
But today whoever performs the ghaṭ ceremony,
  know that one to be a *satī*.[169]

The "hero" whom Draupadī recognizes in fixed concentration is apparently 'Alī as Kṛṣṇa, who then becomes the Buddha.[170] Similarly, Belā's hero, when it comes to rescuing her and lighting her pyre, is Ūdal, who is also hiddenly Kṛṣṇa. But most important, Shams celebrates Draupadī as the model satī (pure or virtuous woman) for those who perform the *ghaṭ* or *ghaṭpāṭ* ceremony. According to Khan, "Draupadī is portrayed in the ginān/Āgam vāṇīs as an avatar of Devī and virtuous woman of the yuga—as there is one in each yuga, to accompany the avatar of Vishnu."[171]

Let us note that these two gināns go on to mention that Medhas—that is, I believe, followers of low caste—are among the "deities," and presumably satīs, who join the ceremony.[172] For although the term satī, "chaste" or "pure," is used pointedly in Shams's gināns for other hero-

[168]Kassam 1995, 192-93, 226, 242, 266, 289, 340. He also gives an army to the Pāndavas' victory, and inspires "great faith (*dīn*)" in the five and Nārāyaṇa (175)!

[169]Kassam 1995, 266 and 289, quoting the former. In the latter, Draupadī "sacrificed all her happiness," with the difference "due to a mere vowel" (289, n. 2).

[170]See above, nn. 167 and 168, and also n. 142 on Kassam 1995, 192-93, a ginān presenting such shifts of planes and in epic idioms.

[171]Personal communication, December 12, 1997.

[172]See above at nn. 148-150. Ginān 53 (Kassam 1995, 266-67) ends on this note, while ginān 65 (289-90) continues with other matters. See similarly Khakee 1972, 217-23, 302.

ines,[173] it also apparently refers to both men and women as satī (as in the passage just cited),[174] and is used for all who participate in the circular *garbī* dance from which Shams originates the ghaṭpāṭ ceremony for the Satpanth and first imparts the pāval drink that culminates it.[175] As to the term "deities" (apparently *devas*, as in the "big" *Dasa avatāra*, which combines terms to speak of "all the divine sages [*sarave deva rikīsara*]" [221]), I believe it is used in the same fashion Khan suggests for the word *rikīsara/rīkhīsar* (from Sanskrit Ṛṣi), where it doubles for *mu'min*, the Muslim pious believer: it "was dictated by the desire of the missionaries to increase the standing of ordinary people and of those belonging to the depressed classes and to impart them with a kind of self-confidence so that they should be proud of following the new religion."[176] Shams sings that gods and demons both inhabit human bodies (Kassam 1995, 268, 290), and there is an equivalence in number between the thirty-three crores of gods who are always saved (173, 340, 343, 349, 357) and the souls saved through the four yugas: five crores by Prahlād, seven by Hariścandra, nine by Yudhiṣṭhira, and "twelve crore pious (satī)" by Ṣadruddīn.[177] In the same garbī songs, Shams refers to a still greater number—ninety-nine crore—of "Meghas" or "Medhas" among the many souls saved with the "spread of the Ratnayug."[178]

Now as Kassam has nicely seen, Shams Pīr's cycle of twenty-eight garbī songs, which closes the collection she translates, tells a "narrative about conversion" in which the Pīr, joining the dance and singing "songs

[173]For Queen Radīyā to whom the Lord as Śyāma gives divine nectar to revive her and her child (Kassam 1995, 176); for Emnābāī, a secret follower of Shams who lives with Hindu in-laws who regard her as defiling and passes Shams's test of carrying an unbaked pot full of water (185-87, 249-50, 400); and for the goddess Durgā-Bhavānī as Kanyā-kumvārī, "youthful virgin" (382). Cf. also the "big" *Dasa avatāra*'s portrayal of Queen Surjā as a satī in an inverse situation, killing her husband Kālīgo by the power of her satī's word (Khakee 1972, 345-51).

[174]See n. 95 above and Kassam 1995, 271, 291-92. Cf. Shackle and Moir 1992, 89, 95, 103-5, 174-77, on the theme of the Pīr as handmaiden and bride.

[175]See above, n. 94; Kassam 1995, e.g. 340; Shackle and Moir 1992, 13, 201.

[176]Khan 1997b, 58, n. 11. In the garbīs, Shams Pīr stresses confidence or "firm faith" (*viśvās*) (Kassam 1995, 324, 333, 369), and promises that the rīkhīsars will reign (322, 338, 364)—also a refrain in the "big" *Dasa avatāra*.

[177]Kassam 1995, 340, 343, in the garbīs; 234, 240 (see n. 131) in "warlike" ginans. Kassam misleadingly considers the garbīs' emphasis on saving souls a feature that distinguishes them from the other songs (110-11).

[178]Kassam 1995, 340 (Meghas) and 343 (Medhas); see also 349: Medhas and the rest are "among the gathering filled with saints (*awliyā*) who bear the Divine Light (*teja*)"—a gathering that recreates "primordial beginnings," and includes the Creator and the Holy Five (see n. 155) plus Adam as created from Light (*nūr*); 338-39: identifying himself as Brahmā, Shams also gave the troubled Ṛṣis pāval to drink at creation; 357: gods (*deva*), goddesses (*devī*), Yakṣas, and Medhas, Kinnars enter the True Path and attain salvation.

of wisdom," transforms the garbī dancers' Hindu consciousness about the nine nights of Navarātrī, plus the tenth night of Dasarā, into a Satpanth Ismā'īlī consciousness.[179] "Not ceasing to dance" through the full ten nights, yet gradually introducing "major change . . . without dramatic upheaval"[180] Shams, by the end, wins over not only five hundred dancing Hindu villagers and thirty-five of their thirty-six Veda-chanting and story-telling Brahmans, but, as the news spreads, "great kings" (363), the king, queen, and ministers of the city, the citizens and creatures of the city, and worshipers (*pūjārīs*), Jogīs, Sannyāsīs, and Bairāgīs (366). As both Khan and Kassam observe, in transforming Navarātrī and Dasarā from within, the garbī songs draw on popular folk expressions of that festival complex. For Khan, they show that the Ismā'īlī Pīrs "appreciated the importance" of the goddess cult and "understood that they could not simply uproot it, incompatible as it might have appeared within the Islamic tradition"; the "choice of a pot (*kalaś*, *ghaṭ*)" reflects its use in folk rituals to symbolize the goddess (Khan 1997b, 53-54). Kassam indicates that in Gujarat where "Garbī is a popular folkloric dance akin to . . . the rāsa" performed for Kṛṣṇa, it can refer to "an earthen pot with holes on the side" used to hold lamps "celebrating their deity's luminous presence" (1995, 106). Shams Pīr begins his songs in anger at Navarātrī's idolatrous worship of Durgā as Mātā Bhavānī (the fearsome Mother Bhavānī).[181] But once he instructs his new followers to drink pāval from the enthroned pot, which fills their hearts with divine light (nūr), it is ultimately the goddess's aniconic luminosity that he transforms into a vision (dīdār) of the luminous 'Alī.[182]

Supposing, however, that Shams Pīr's garbī songs reflect an "inward, spiritual, and quiescent" turn after the "Satpanth was forced underground" by the fall of Alamūt, Kassam interprets this new consciousness as a "subtle but significant reorientation" away from that of the more warlike gināns (1995, 104). But as I have indicated, although one can see the latter as reflecting the realized eschatology of the Qiyāmah period (1162-1212) as it would have been sustained for some time thereafter, I do not think the warlike ginānns are promises of military relief. And without that point of distinction from the garbī songs, I do not think one can hold that there is an "easy to miss" difference between them, since both reflect the same realized eschatology: one in mythic terms, the other

[179] Kassam 1995, 106-11 (quote 106), 320-70; cf. Khan 1997b, 53-54.

[180] See Khan 1997b, 54 (first quote); Kassam 1995, 108 (second quote), 359.

[181] Kassam 1995, 320-21; "O Careless Ones! Cast off [the goddess] Māta Bhavānī! Serve instead the manifestation (*avatār*) of 'Alī" (345).

[182] Durgā is constituted from divine light (*tejas*) in the *Devī Māhātmyā* (2.10-33). Cf. Kassam 1995, 106-7, with a different emphasis.

in ritual terms, but both equally warlike, and also equally camouflaging their imagery by the "undergrounding" poetics of taqīyya. For after all, what Shams Pīr begins with is a Hindu consciousness about Navarātrī and Dasarā, with its iconic worship of the warrior goddess; and what he ends with is a Satpanth Ismā'īlī consciousness of a kind of "inner jihād," with its vision of the luminous triumph of the conquering hidden Imām.

Yet the two religious languages remain in tension even in this final vision. Khan mentions that the holy water stored in the enthroned jar is referred to not only as pāval and *amī* or *amṛt* (*amṛta*, the drink of immortality in Sanskrit), but as *ghaṭ-gangā*,[183] in that the water pot representing Durgā "is supposed to contain water from the Ganga which is equated with divine ambrosia or *amṛt*" (1997b, 151, n. 7). Moreover, "milk seems to have been used during earlier rituals of the Nizaris."[184] What is inescapable in such "songs of wisdom" is that the vision opened by drinking the pāval is afforded by Gangā water that comes from the *heavenly* Ganges, the Milky Way. The light imagery is not a sign of new quiescence (Kassam 1995, 110) but a realization, in both Ismā'īlī and Hindu terms, of what is in the cup: not just liquid but liquid light—the celestial milky light of the heavenly river. In the garbī songs, one not only drinks this light but bathes in it, and is showered by it.[185] Let us not forget, the dancers dance at night.[186] In one of Shams's other gināns, when a blind mendicant satisfies Shams's demand, which others have refused, for someone to willingly offer his own flesh, the Shāh brings the "cupful of Light (*nūr*)," and when the blind mendicant drinks it, "lo! he witnessed the whole universe!" (207). Most decisively, on Shams Pīr's ninth night of Navarātrī,

> He danced with a purpose
> and imparted many teachings.
> He praised the Panjtan Pāk[187]
> who were born of Divine Light (*nūr*).
> From the Light (*nūr*) of the Panjtan Pāk,
> [Pole Star] Dhruva was created.

[183]1997b, 135, "the last term also being used by the Gujarati Nizarpanthis."

[184]Khan 1997b, 137, referring to a discussion on 71-72. Cf. Nanji 1988, 66; Shackle and Moir 1992, 75, 161: the ginās refer to five ingredients—milk, sugar, clarified butter, wheat flour, and water.

[185]Kassam 1995, 328, 330, 334, 343, 352; cf. 211, a non-garbī ginān in which the Shāh is a gardener who brings showers of light.

[186]A ginān verse by Sayyid Imam Shah makes such a setting explicit: "Keep awake during the last watches of the night and reflect, o brother believer. From heavens above the houris have come, bringing vessels of light" (Shackle and Moir 1992, 91 and 172).

[187]See n. 155 above: the Holy Five of the Shī'as, all of whom are now mentioned.

It took him 70,000 years to ascend,
and it will take him the same to descend.
Prophet (*nabī*) Muḥammed is the name of that star,
and 'Alī is [his] crown.
Around his beautiful neck flashes
the brilliant Light (*nūr*) of Fāṭimah.[188]
Bathed in Light (*teja*) between his two ears[189]
are the Imāms Ḥasan and Ḥusayn. . . . (Kassam 1995, 354)

Muhammad is Dhruva, the Pole Star, with the other four holy ones of the Panjtan Pāk adorning and concentrated within him. Around him all other stars—in epic and purāṇic terms, Ṛṣis—revolve. Yet Dhruva-Muhammad also ascends and descends. This is something more precise than an "interiorization of salvation as eternal life in a heavenly abode of bliss" (Kassam 1995, 111). Shams deploys Islamic and epic-purāṇic "technical languages" of astronomical myth.[190]

Not pursuing such points, Kassam does recognize the basic imagery: "An image is created of a heaven filled with divine light (*nūr*) where millions of enlightened souls congregate by the Ganges and where the 124,000 prophets are also gathered" (Kassam 1995, 111). Indeed, a ginān attributed to Ṣadruddīn invokes the Ganges as *gatiuṅ gaṅgā*, "the holy stream (Gangā) of the congregations" (Shackle and Moir 1992, 89 and 169). Yet Kassam does not mention that directly following the verse on the prophets, the very next one says, "Ḥusayn's followers will be present, and Light (*nūr*) will shower upon them" (1995, 344). As in the warlike ginān, Ḥusayn's army will be resurrected to join the Shāh's eschatological army. Here, with Ḥusayn's army made manifest to the garbī dancers, we realize that the ghaṭpāṭ is a double evocation of

[188]Making her the necklace of the Pole Star, Muhammad.
[189]I suggest this refers to the practice of concentration (*dhyāna*), as when Buddha destroys the Kauravas (see n. 168 above), or when Shams says, "Focus between the brows where the sun is ablaze, and take the universe in the hand" (Kassam 1995, 334). For a similar verse on the Holy Five attributed to Ṣadruddīn, see Shackle and Moir 1992, 109, 183.
[190]See chap. 9, n. 87. For eighth-century Persian Shī'a background to such "Ismaili gnosis," see Corbin 1983, 169: "For all eternity, *Five* Lights, of *five* colors, exist in the Sea of Whiteness (*Baḥr al-bayḍā*), the heavenly Palace of the Limit of Limits. These Lights are the 'members' (*jawāriḥ*) and the epiphanies of a single Person of Light (*shakṣ-e nūrānī*); in human form, on the plane of terrestrial humanity (*basharīya*), they appear as Muḥammad, Ali, Fātima, Hasan and Ḥusayn. . . . Beneath the Sea of Whiteness, nine domes . . . are arranged, each with its distinctive color. . . . [reaching down to the] microcosmic Earth which is the 'Earth of the Heart.'" Shams's description is not unlike that of Durgā formed of light in the *Devī Māhātmyā* (see n. 178). Note that in his cosmic roaming (see Kassam 1995, 320), at Meru, Shams "witnessed many wonders that were endless in number," and "bade the sun [to descend]" (350).

Navarātri-Dasarā and Muharram. Following Kassam's insightful analysis of rapports between Navarātrī-Dasarā and the Satpanth ghaṭpāṭ, and the story of Shams Pīr's transformation of the former into the latter, it would seem that Satpanth Ismā'īlīs made the *ghatpāṭ* a mystical equivalent, suitable for times of taqīyya, of both Dasarā and Muharram.

There is little information about South Asian Ismā'īlī practices concerning Muharram. Khan informs me that the Āghā Khān prohibited Muharram participation in the nineteenth century, while Seyyed Hossein Nasr indicates that such participation is nonetheless common.[191] But one source is decisive. During the recital of the special prayer that accompanies the ghaṭpāṭ among Nizārī Satpanthīs "in their *jama'at khanas* [congregation places] on Friday evenings and other special evenings . . . a clump of earth from Karbala, over which the *hāzar* Imam has recited some verses of the Qur'an, is dissolved. This is done on a special low table, in a white china pot containing clean water. It is then drunk by all the members of the community, who are present. This same water is also given to an Ismaili on his death bed."[192] The ghaṭpāṭ thus transforms Navarātrī while commemorating Karbalā. At night-long ghaṭpāṭ vigils—on star-filled moonless nights, in fact—when the cup is passed that illumines the presence of 'Alī, the vision (darśan, dīdār) of his messianic army is illumined by the dust of Karbalā.[193] In reverse, the saving of souls through the yugas, which Kassam considers a distinguishing feature of the garbīs, is found not only in them, but in the warlike gināns as well.[194] Indeed, the warlike/quiescent opposition simply does not hold.[195] In two successive garbīs, Shams sings, "This is the age (*yuga*) of the last battlefield; O my Brothers, be vigilant!" "no fifth age" follows (346, 347). It would appear that the aforementioned Ratnayug, the "age of jewels," is another name for the luminous cosmos of the apocalypse. Another garbī mentions that those whose minds are pure can witness the "pious gathering" of saved Medhas and Rīkhīsars, along with the

[191]Personal communications, December 1997.

[192]Khakee 1972, 408, indicating also that Imāmshāhīs do the ceremony with a tiny clump of earth from the tomb of Imām Shāh.

[193]It is worth noting that the religiously "dialogic" Meos (see chap. 8, n. 43), whose singers know both a Mewati folk *Mbh* and "a rare narrative called *Hasan Husain*" (see chap. 1, n. 3) along with stories about the martyrdom and dismemberment of 'Alī (Mayaram 1997, 258), celebrate both Dasarā and Muharram (46, 60).

[194]See n. 177. One might look further at the presumed lateness—Shackle and Moir even propose the late eighteenth century (1992, 200)—of the garbī songs. While they mention the names of later Imāms and Pīrs (Kassam 1997, 105), the criterion weakens when we realize that Shams's other gināns also mention the most prominent of them, Sadruddīn (169, 234).

[195]Cf. Khakee 1972, 79-84, 224, 238-40, 263: the saving of the five, seven, nine, and twelve crores of souls through each yuga is accompanied by battles, and all the souls thus saved join the Shāh's apocalyptic army, coming in a moment to join him on his chariot.

Pāṇḍavas and the usual purāṇic figures, "all present at the site of the Ganges"; "Pervading the gathering of the Ganges, they fill it night and day with Light."[196] The faithful who realize that they are Ṛṣis are no less the oppressed of the earth than they are stars above.

Finally, the cup of light will also be drunk in the eschatological marriage. Shams sings:

> Few understand the *ghaṭ* ceremony
> and the stature of the water-pot;
> The virgin of the universe [Viśva-kuṃvārī] will drink it
> and wed Śyāma, Lord of the three worlds.
>
> She is called Bībī Fāṭimah—
> know that she is the virgin of the universe;
> Pīr Shams says: the *ghaṭ* was established
> by the order (*farmān*) of the Shāh. (Kassam 1995, 265; cf. 268)

It will be the ultimate interreligious marriage, for Śyāma, once again, is Kṛṣṇa (that is, 'Alī as Kṛṣṇa), and Fāṭimah, Muhammad's daughter, is 'Alī's wife. Clearly Fāṭimah, like Draupadī, is a virtuous woman of the yuga—*this* yuga. As Khan shows, it is from this ginānic theme that the *Āgam vāṇīs* of the Rāmdeo cult derive their promise that the Nikālank avatar will consummate his long unfulfilled betrothal to a Dalit girl who represents the earth's oppressed and the earth itself.[197] Alternately, Ṣadruddīn sings, "Soon my righteous sovereign will appear, the mounted Tenth Lord. The Lord Ali will wed the maiden creation"; but on the model of Muhammad's marriages, "four happy brides" will "greet the Master of the Resurrection (*kāyam sāmi*)" at the apocalyptic ghaṭpāṭ (Shackle and Moir 1992, 89). There is also a Brahmanized variant in the *Kalki Purāṇa* in which Kalki marries two Kṣatriya princesses (Khan 1997a, 410-12). The purāṇic story would seem to bear much the same relation to the apocalypse of the *Āgam vāṇīs* that the *Bhaviṣya Purāṇa*'s *Kṛṣṇāṃśacarita* bears to oral *Ālhā*. As one would expect, the *Kalki Purāṇa* calls Kalki's chief antagonist Kali rather than Kalinga (411), reminding us that Kali takes on new roles in the *Pratisarga Parvan* as a

[196] Kassam 1995, 258. Recall that Shams makes the sun descend; see n. 185, and the stories mentioned by Kassam (79 and n. 24, 379). Recall that according to Alberuni, Hindu astronomers place Multan on the line that runs from Laṅkā to Meru (chap. 4, n. 5).

[197] See n. 96 above. Khan takes Viśva-kumvārī, "literally the Virgin Universe or the Virgin Earth . . . as a symbol of the converted community," or of "the mystic union of the Nizārī community with God" (1997a, 413). The theme recurs in the "big" Dasa avatāra (Khakee 1972, 405-6).

whole, and in the *Kṛṣṇāṃśacarita* in particular, to enhance his profile as the reigning demon of the Kali yuga. Remembering that Draupadī is the model satī for the ghāṭpāṭ, and that primary among the satīs whom she inspires are Dalit Medhas and Meghas, we must keep these varied identifications of the eschatological bride in mind in considering the low status Belā, and other Draupadīs we shall meet.

Although Shams Pīr's garbīs tell that he finally gets the Hindus to throw away their idols and sacred threads and to see the *Qur'ān* as the fourth and ultimate Veda, the transformation he works is one that carries to the very end a kind of religious bilingualism—in Kassam's terms, "a religious language mutually recognized by Hindus and Satpanth Ismā'īlīs alike" (1995, 110). Yet I believe it is not enough to say that the gināns "reveal a pedagogic method" by which the *dā'ī*s (missionaries) "were able to lead [the faithful] to the 'true path' (*satpanth*) consisting of nothing more than the fulfillment of their former beliefs."[198] They also left this space of "fluid signs" open to coexistence in a world where they could continue to value alliances with varying shades of comparably "open" Hindus: Dalits, villagers, kings and queens, and, as we have now seen, Bairāgīs, Sannyāsīs, and in particular Nāths. Khan observes that if the Nizārīs "absorbed a number of Nath elements, and still more, 'infiltrated' the Nath milieu (very much in the manner of spies penetrating foreign circles under a forged identity)," the Nāths, too, "when they had been approached by Ismaili missionaries . . . would have retained certain Nizari influences."[199] More than this, it would seem that Nizārīs and Nāths were primary among those who spun material from their own and other Muslim-Hindu interactions to weave a common cloth that they, and others they influenced, could deploy on either of two different narrative registers.[200] In the gināns and *Āgam vāṇī*s, Nizārīs and those they

[198]Mallison 1989, 94-95; cf. Khan 1996, 36.

[199]Khan 1997b, 223; cf. 46-51, 139-40, 220-34. As we have seen, Nāths, Jogīs, and Bairāgis not only join Shams but trumpet and applaud 'Alī's eschatological army (at n. 151 above).

[200]I emphasize a double register as something open to "conscious" narrative permutations on both sides, with future and past interchangeable, since both Hindus and Ismā'īlīs have cyclical heirohistories (on those of the Ismā'īlīs, see Daftary 105, 139-40, 219, 231-49, 291-98; Corbin 1957). Others have interpreted the gināns' correspondences differently: e.g., Nanji as "anagogic," "mystic in the broadest sense," and a product of "mythopoesis" (1978, 100, 114); Asani as retaining "models of proper behaviour" for the "new converts" (1991, 14); Shackle and Moir as "confused" "accretions added by later authors" (1992, 23); Kassam 1994 more suggestively as a [potentially mutual] relation of figure and ground. Khan (see n. 92) and Kassam (1995, 6-19) are surely right to stress politics and critique confusionistic models of syncretism, and Khan to emphasize the messianic. For valuable comparative parallels to the hermeneutics of taqīyya, multiple and dialogic messianisms, open secrecy, and "justice beyond the law," see Caputo (1997, 69-143) on Jacques Derrida.

influenced thematize a cosmic apocalypse of the future, which, as we have seen, also cycles itself through the past. *Ālhā*, sung by Nāth and other minstrels and permeated by their idioms, thematizes a regional apocalypse of the past, which also holds promise of a once and future return. As is now evident, each tradition constructs these stories out of the same traumatic historical period and its events, from Shihāb al-Dīn's massacre of Ismā'īlīs to Pṛthīrāj Chauhān's defeat of the Chandēls; and from Shihāb al-Dīn's defeat of Prithīrāj through the fall of Alamūt.

Ālhā thus forces us to problematize the wandering warrior-ascetic-minstrel because its heroes, one of them a Shī'ī Muslim, become Jōgī-Bairāgī-fighting-musicians and because their joint disguise has this double apocalyptic register. Only *Ālhā* reflects such clear imbrication of a Muslim co-inspiration. But it would be a mistake, even if the Islamic ties are thinner and less precise, and if they give shape only to specific characters or incidents rather than share in the design of a whole story, to think that the sectarian traditions that feed other regional martial oral epics are without similar impulses. If we hold the question of prophetic images in reserve and reiterate the principle that, no matter what order or sect a regional oral epic singles out, intersectarian and intercommunal warrior-ascetic-minstrel traditions stand behind it, other regional oral martial epics begin to march in tune.

In *Pābūjī*, which as one would expect is closest in this regard to *Ālhā*, two revealing episodes make it explicitly a matter of Gorakhnāthī Jōgīs. First, when the Rebārī herder Harmal resigns himself to the dangerous task of reconnoitering Laṅkā[201] for the she-camels that Pābūjī has promised Kelam (Pābūjī's brother's daughter) at her wedding, he announces his spy-disguise to his mother: "My mind is set on the ochre dress of the jogī" (J. D. Smith 1991, 343). No sooner does Harmal obtain his Jōgī paraphernalia in the market (including a pair of tongs from the ironsmith for his dhūṇī) and "put on the fine dress of holy men and *jogīs*," than "the battle-horn of Guru Gorakhnāth" sounds, announcing the arrival of a virtual army of Jōgīs led by Gorakhnāth himself.[202] Answering Gorakhnāth about his name, house, and home, Harmal says, "O Guru, O holy man, a wandering *jogī* has no house and home; I am a master-*jogī*, wandering in all directions, bathing at holy places. . . . the Sky released me and Mother Earth took me." After other formulaic exchanges, Gorakhnāth initiates Harmal and gives him the magic items

[201]On Laṅkā, "land of witches" "beyond the seven seas," see chap. 4, n. 18.

[202]As J. D. Smith says, Gorakhnāth's synchronism with Pābūjī, in both oral epic and Naiṇasī's chronicle, is not "serious history" but "an inflation of history occurring prior to Naiṇasī's time" (seventeenth century) that is paralleled in other Rajasthani folklore (1991, 74-75).

that will allow him to complete his Laṅkā mission. As with the Banāphars, Harmal's disguise has to fool his mother (though his wife sees through it) and his Rajput chieftain (Pābūjī, though the latter's minister Cādo sees through it) (343-52).

Next, such formulas recur when the twelve-year-old Rūpnāth is left as the last of Pābūjī's clan to avenge the Rāṭhoṛs against Jindrāv Khīcī. Once Rūpnāth completes his revenge, he tells his grandmother, "I myself have remained a disciple of Guru Gorakhnāth, and I need neither kingdom nor throne—I need nothing. Grandmother, give me your blessing; with your blessing my mind is set on the ochre dress of a *jogī*." He establishes his dhūṇī at a shrine he makes famous (Smith 1991, 464-77). His renunciation is perhaps gratuitous, since his clan's kingdom at Koḷū has been destroyed, like Mahobā. Rūpnāth combines the twelve-year-old's revenge of Ūdal with the final Jōgī-destination of Ālhā. Yet *Pābūjī* goes beyond *Ālhā* in imprinting a sectarian seal: when Harmal and Rūpnāth become Jōgīs, whether in the former's temporary disguise or the latter's permanent pledge, Gorakhnāth authenticates the initiation himself by performing the heroes' painful "split-ear" (Kānphaṭa) initiation (346, 467-68). This is something Ālhā and his companions seem to have missed. On the other hand, *Pābūjī*'s Jōgīs do not play music and sing. That is left to itinerant Cāraṇs, who sing praise-songs (chāvaḷīs) of King Karṇa and the Pāvār (Paramāra) hero Jagdīs, and narrative songs (parvāṛos) of Pābūjī in the middle of his story (e.g., 334-35).

Moving south, there is at first a striking difference. *Elder brothers* and *Palnāḍu* heroes never wander as ascetics, much less as warrior-ascetic-minstrels. Yet as we have seen in chapter 3, each epic knows the figure of Viṣṇu disguised as an almanac-bearing mendicant from Kāśī who comes to shape crucial scenes. In addition to carrying an almanac (like the Banāphar Ḍhēwā in his Jōgī disguise), the Telugu Viṣṇu, a Brahman, "wore ochre robes and carried a water pot, an ash pot, sacred grass, and a deerskin" (Roghair 1982, 336); the Tamil Viṣṇu, an ascetic of unnamed caste,[203] carries a right-spiralled conch and a "Gopāla's box" filled with Śiva's sacred ash (*vipūti*). As noted in chapter 3 (item 7), this stock south Indian oral epic figure combines Śaiva and Vaiṣṇava features. In *Palnāḍu*, he comes not only from Kāśī but heads toward Kāñci: from north to south, and from Śiva's city to one "more generally known as a Vaiṣṇavite city" (Roghair 1982, 244, 361).

Moreover, he is not entirely alone. Each epic incorporates a story whose main older Tamil and Telugu tellings have been beautifully treated by Shulman: that of the husband and wife whose dedication to feeding

[203]In his first appearance, "He looked like an ascetic (*taṉṉāci*), a penitent (*tavaci*), a wandering renouncer (*paratēci*), a Vaiṣṇavite mendicant (*tācaṉ*)" (Beck 1992, 104-5).

Śaiva ascetics brings them face to face with Śiva himself in ascetic disguise, who has come to share their love (in Cekkiḻār's twelfth-century Tamil *Periya Purāṇam*), or test them (in Telugu versions beginning with Somanātha's thirteenth-century *Basavapurāṇamu*), by demanding that they feed him their boy (1993, 18-86). With no need to repeat this famous "Ciṟuttoṇṭar-Siriyāla story" (named after the father), I note only how each folk epic incorporates a variant into its larger design and connects it with the almanac-bearing Viṣṇu.

Palnāḍu's version introduces the story of Bāluḍu's last fight and the death his father Brahma Nāyuḍu, Viṣṇu incarnate, has engineered for him. Taking leave for Kārempūḍi, Bāluḍu reveals to his mother that in a previous life (one of several illustrative of filicide) he was that very boy who was "served as a human meat curry."[204] The divine diner, Śiva, is of course a Jangam, one of those Vīraśaiva or Lingāyat saints whose militancy (despite Lingāyats having no militant orders as such), anti-iconic vehemence, Upaniṣadic monism, espousal of the moving over the stationary, opposition to Brahmanical ritualism, and literalizing of sacrificial violence are sufficiently known.[205] Roghair glosses Jangam as "minstrel priest" (1982, 374) and mentions Jangams along with the Piccaguṇṭlu and Māla and Mādiga Dalits as "non-Brahman singers" (34). Śiva's disguise has no direct connection with the almanac-bearing Viṣṇu other than through this epic's tendency, noted in chapter 3, to fuse Śaiva and Vaiṣṇava sectarian imagery. Thus, just as Viṣṇu goes from Kāśī to Kāñci, Śiva comes to Śivakāñci for this adventure (300); just as Viṣṇu carries a Śaivite ash-pot along with his almanac, the Jangam Śiva carries a Viṣṇuite conch along with his "bell, mendicant's pouch, and banner pole."[206] Indeed there is not much to differentiate this Jangam Śiva from the Vaiṣṇava (and, as we have seen, martial) "people of Palnāḍu," who carry images of Viṣṇu and Lakṣmī along with "conch, gong, mendicants' pouch, and banner pole" and sing "Hari Rām" (like a

[204]Roghair 1982, 297; Jangam singers note that Bāluḍu, a Vaiṣṇava, thus had a Śaiva incarnation (125).

[205]See Shulman 1993, 49, 66; Ramanujan 1973; Narayana Rao 1990; Weinberger-Thomas 1996, 29, on the "Pavilion of the heads of heroes" (*Vīraśiromanṭapa*) constructed by king Anavema Reddi of Kondavidu in 1378 at the Śrīśailam Mallikārjuna temple to accommodate head-offerings to Śiva.

[206]Roghair 1982, 299, 306. That mendicant Sannyāsis normally carry a conch (Nanjundayya and Iyer 1931, 4:580) does not prevent its primary association with Viṣṇu. On the conch-trumpet, Sullivan's insight into its underworldly and solstice-marking symbolism for the Incas (1996, 62-65, 284-85, fig. 3.13) deserves some comparative thinking for India. Cf. Hiltebeitel 1991a, 44-45, 52, 413-14 on the conch and the Pāṇḍavas' younger sister Caṅkovati-Caṅkotari ("Conch-belly"), wife of Pōrmannaṉ or Vīrapattiraṉ (29, n. 26, 45, n. 15, 107, 109, 418-23).

Rāmdal, or "army of Rām") on their penitential pilgrimage from their original northern home to Palnāḍu (161-62).

Moreover, in one of *Palnāḍu*'s most stunning adaptations, it is not a question of Śiva coming alone for this intimate meal, but among a crore of Jangams. Having fed such a number once, the mother apparently made it a practice and "would not serve less than a crore of Jangams." Deciding to test her devotion, Śiva uses illusion to diminish the crore by one, and makes all the other Jangams vanish. When the mother sends her husband out to find the last Jangam needed, he finds only Śiva: a "Jangam Preceptor" in the form of a filthy leper who can be cured only by eating a mother's first-born seven-year-old son (Roghair 1982, 298-301). I submit that the introduction of this crore of Jangams is a reflex of the story's narration in a regional martial epic.[207] It cannot be by accident that the "people of Palnāḍu," Afghans included, have so much in common with Jangams who descend like a virtual Rāmdal.[208] The crore of Jangams complicates the story considerably. When the leper joins the lack-crore with his demand, the ten million minus one "had no idea what was happening." The mother ends up cooking her son for the full crore, which makes it incongruous when Śiva makes his last demand that he not be left to eat by himself (302-5)! It is this demand, crucial to all other versions, that puts the parents to their last double test: Śiva's call to join him so he doesn't have to alone, and his demand that they summon the cooked boy to join them for the meal. This amazing grace inspires the parents' last ounce of incredulous devotion, which brings their boy back to life. In all other versions mentioned by Shulman, Śiva is the only ascetic present.[209]

In *Elder brothers*, it is again a matter of a woman dedicated to feeding hosts of ascetics.[210] But the episode, wholly detached from the Śaivite story, looks like a Vaiṣṇava revision.[211] When Tāmarai cannot conceive, Viṣṇu appears as the almanac-bearing mendicant and tells her

[207]For other changes, see Shulman 1993, 85-86. The leper probably comes from Śrīnātha's version (72), but not the crore of Jangams.

[208]Jangams singing *Basava Purāṇa* and Vaiṣṇava devotees are among "dancers, singers, and rope dancers" who attend a duel that follows a Dasarā (Roghair 1982, 283).

[209]Note that Śiva begins as a fierce Bhairava ascetic from the north in Cekkiḻār's oldest telling (Shulman 1993, 21-30). To this degree, the Śaiva Siddhānta poet thus doubly disowns him: Śiva is neither a Śaiva Siddhāntin nor a southerner. Similarly, in Śrīnātha's light-romance Brahmanical Telugu version, Śiva becomes a Bhairava again (76-78) while also remaining a Jangam (71). Śrīnātha defuses the situation by having Śiva clear Kāñci of ascetics of all kinds, including heretics and Kāpālikas (72).

[210]Both folk epic versions also concentrate on the wife's devotion rather than the husband's (cf. Shulman 1993, 85), who is something of a bumpkin.

[211]This episode doubles some themes found in a shorter earlier one (Beck 1992, 177-79).

four things she must do—the last, feeding a thousand devotees (*tācarkaḷ*)—before she sets off for Arjuna's ascetic pillar in Banaras, where her penance will bring her "two sons for the land and a daughter for the house" (Beck 1992, 268-77). When the time comes, she sends her husband Kuṉṉuṭaiyā to Srirangam to bring back a thousand mendicants. Before Kuṉṉuṭaiyā arrives, Viṣṇu makes every Srirangam mendicant vanish. Viṣṇu calls together boys grazing cows and goats, gives each a conch, gong, and Vaiṣṇava mark, and takes the form of an ascetic (*taṉṉāci*) himself with a right-spiralled conch, "Gopāla box," and begging bowl. Kuṉṉuṭaiyā is overjoyed to find these mendicants and takes them to Tāmarai; but when she lays out a thousand banana leaves, there is one mendicant too few. Kuṉṉuṭaiyā says it must be the "very old beggar" who is missing, and offers to eat that meal himself! But Tāmarai goes back to Srirangam, sees the old beggar disappear in a flash of light, recognizes him as Viṣṇu, carries him home, and seats "the great mendicant (*periyatācaṉ*)" in front of his food. He blows his conch "and the heavens shook," making everyone but Tāmarai swoon; then he strews sacred ash to dissipate the dizziness, eats "a little rice," and tells Tāmarai she is ready to go to Banaras (298-307). Instead of presaging the main hero's death, the episode leads to the twins' and their sister's birth. On the surface, it is a gently humorous Vaiṣṇava pastoral interlude with no echoes of child sacrifice, and no militancy on the part of the ascetics. *Elder brothers* does not tie in self-consciously with militant ascetics. But if it presents a softer gentler version of the Ciṟuttoṇṭar story, it is again defined by its oral epic connections.

According to Farquhar, although warrior-ascetic bands plundered down the west coast as far as Calicut in Kerala, "the enlisting of ascetics as soldiers never infected to any extent the monastic orders of South India."[212] Śaiva Siddhāntins, for whom Cekkiḻār first composed the Ciṟuttoṇṭar story, and Śrī Vaiṣṇavas, whose great pilgrimage center at Srirangam brings the *Elder brothers* variant into focus, are Tamil cases in point. In such surroundings, it is not surprising that Draupadī cult folklore follows the classical *Mahābhārata* in never having the Pāṇḍavas disguise themselves as anything more interestingly militant than Brahmans[213] and having Durvāsas and his horde of ascetics remain "twelve thousand Vedic Brahmans" (*vētappirāmaṇāḷ paṉṉīrāyiram*) when they descend upon the exiled Pāṇḍavas in the forest and get Draupadī to feed them from her inexhaustible pot.[214]

[212]Farquhar 1925, 441; cf. Ghurye 1964, 224-25.

[213]Hiltebeitel 1988a, 169-82; 1991a, 50-52, 128.

[214]See Muṇicuvāmi Upāttiyāyar n.d., 20-21; cf. Pukaḻenti Pulavar 1980, 5-17 (summarized in Arunachalam 1976, 100): Durvāsas comes with Kṛṣṇa; the food is supplied differently.

Tamilnadu does not seem to have been a scene of militant ascetics until the early nineteenth century, after the so-called Sannyāsī or Fakir rebellion in Bengal (1760s to 1800) was subdued by the British, and Sannyāsis and Fakirs, apparently with encouragement from the Marathas, the Nizam of Hyderabad, the sons of Tippu Sultan, and the remaining poligars, found still-turbulent situations to attract them to the south.[215] What is most fascinating are Tamil instances where pilgrims, Sannyāsīs, and Fakirs use their covers to gain entrance to British forts and cantonments in support of anti-British rebellion. Rajayyan tells of one such instance from the Poligar Wars that turns oral epic themes into (what may be) historical reality. In January 1801, about two hundred insurgents, seeking to free two brothers of Kattabomman (whom the British had hung) and others from imprisonment at Palayamkottai, "disguised themselves as pilgrims, going to the sacred temple of Tiruchendur. Clad in yellow robes, playing *kavadi*, chanting *manthrams*, blowing the conch shell, distributing holy ash," they circled the fort. Then they disappeared and reappeared as hawkers selling firewood, plantain leaves, and fruits at prohibitive prices, but also concealing weapons. The fort soldiers spurned the prices, but allowed the hawkers to sell to the prisoners on the pretext that the items would be used in ceremonies for those who had died in jail. Once contact was made, the breakout was effected with a waiting escape party, a few horses, and a war whoop (1971, 196-200). In 1806, Fakirs, Sannyāsīs, and Lingāyats gained access to cantonments all over south India to stir sepoys to rebellion by spreading macabre rumors and new apocalyptic teachings, delivering prophesies of British defeat, telling legends, singing laments, and, above all, posing as puppeteers to perform puppet shows on inflammatory themes. The Vellore Mutiny, set off prematurely on July 10, 1806, four days before a planned general insurrection, was the major failed outcome of their efforts.[216]

The story of the Tiruchendur pilgrims must give us pause, since it sounds so much like an echo of the Draupadī cult story of Pōttu Rāja-

[215]Chinnian 1982, 14-31; Lorenzen 1978, 72-75; Pinch 1996, 24-25.

[216]Chinnian 1982, 14-25. See Nanjundayya and Iyer 1931, 4:570-85, on "Sanyāsis": householder ascetics claiming Jangam origins, magicians and jugglers who "practice divination by professing to read the incidents of *Rāmāyana* and *Bhārata* from a palm-leaf book" (583). A 1711 letter from Rāja Desing's father Sarūp Singh to the British at Devanampatnam decries their mix of merchanting and pillaging, and says he "can only compare you to the Fuckeers of the country, who make a Trade of begging and are generally the greatest thieves imaginable" (Srinivasachari 1943, 376). On Fakirs in the Deccan, see Assayag 1995: their ritual instruments, with weapons like Pōttu Rāja's, symbolic decapitation like Aravān̲'s, and tests of fire (113-15); their music (118), "théâtralisme" (123-26), and syncretism with Lingāyats (152, n. 14).

Pōrmannan's fort. As part of Kṛṣṇa's plan to help the Pāṇḍavas enter Pōrmannan's city of Śivānandapuri, Bhīma, like a Tiruchendur pilgrim, disguises himself as a wood-seller and hawks wood outside the walls.[217] Perhaps we may propose that both stories are echoes, one historical and the other mythic, of a type of "fort-entry" story, now familiar, that has made for good telling all over India—no matter which events are real and which imagined; which religions, sects, or "nations" lie behind the oppositions; and whether the fort is in Tiruchendur, Magadha, Mārō, Cīnab, Kalinga, *or Śivānandapuri*.

What do the Pāṇḍavas want from Pōttu Rāja? They want him and his weapons: the militant-ascetic ones (whip, five-pronged trident, pennant, bow and arrow), the musical ones (*pampai* drum, *mallāri* drum, drumsticks, hourglass-shaped *uṭakkai* drum, bell, and *cilampu* or anklet-rattle), and the pūjā ones (turmeric, pūjā box, fire post, *karagam* pot). Of course, they are all, in a sense, militant-ascetic pūjā weapons.[218] He and these items are the prize the Pāṇḍavas must secure by entering *his* fort. Then, in reverse, it is Pōttu Rāja and these weapons that are the Pāṇḍavas' and the goddess Draupadī's indispensable advantages in gaining access elsewhere: to subdue Muttāl Rāvuttan so that he too becomes their battle-companion and Draupadī's servant; and to enter—with Pōttu Rāja and his "weapons" always leading their processions—another fort: the battlefield-fort of Kurukṣetra, so that Tiraupatiyamman can win the *Mahābhārata* war.[219]

Once again, *Palnāḍu* provides parallels that deepen our sense of what is going on. There, not only does Brahma Nāyuḍu, Viṣṇu incarnate, help the heroes enter Pōta Rāju's Śivanandi fort; when Pōta Rāju takes birth along with the battlefield-goddess Ankālamma from Pārvatī's sweat, it is to help Ankālamma and her hundred Śaktis enter still one more fort: the iron, brass, and bronze-walled fort of the Śaivite city of Kalyāṇ. Their object is to conquer this Lingāyat bastion for the goddess's worship. Pōta Rāju thus becomes her servant in terminating the Śaivite exclusivism of the Lingāyats there; henceforth, as this account sees it, the Lingāyats of Kalyāṇ, like Pōta Rāju, will perform animal sacrifice and worship not only Śiva, but the goddess.[220] The Andhra Pōta Rāju thus helps bring

[217]Hiltebeitel 1988a, 340. Cf. the Draupadī cult multiform on Kālī's "Wheel Fort" (ibid. 1991a, 406, 411-13).

[218]For this list, and discussion, see Hiltebeitel 1988a, 385-89.

[219]For these features, see Hiltebeitel 1988a, 113-14, 366-67; 1991a, 33, 399-438; 448-75.

[220]Roghair 1982, 194-200; note the measure of exclusivism: Kalyāṇ's kings "wear *lingas* on their bodies, and even the trees and mortars of the city bear *lingas*" (194); the Vaiṣṇava Nārada motivates the action (194), Viṣṇu is the goddess's "patron God" (196), and the sacrificial cry is "Gōvindā!" (197). Like a Tiruchendur pilgrim, Ankālamma goes about Kalyān in disguise hawking tamarind buds and fruit (196). Like 'Alī in entering Cīnab, Pōta

popular Vīraśaivism into the orbit of the goddess.

But Pōta Rāju does not become precisely a Lingāyat or a Jangam himself. The Tamil Pōttu Rāja, at least, seems to blur these lines. With his service to the goddess, his penitential and musical weapons, his blend of subtlety and stupidity, his mixed Rāja, Dalit, and Brahman traits, with long matted hair, a lingam and yoni on his head, his ancestry and name traced through a lineage of lingams, his own body "full of lingams,"[221] we now see that the irrepressible Pōttu Rāja-Pōrmaṉṉaṉ, who has been so much else besides, is the Draupadī cult's embodiment and caricature, mobile for all processions yet fixed like a stake with a severed head in his hand, of a goddess-worshiping Lingāyat-Vīraśaiva militant-ascetic-minstrel, who, with his battle-companion Muttāl Rāvuttaṉ, has joined the Pāṇḍava army.

Rāju aims to change people's religion.

[221]See Hiltebeitel 1991a, 487 (stupidity and subtlety); 1988a, 251, 382, and 257 (on matted hair); 1991a, 133-34, 252 (lingam and yoni on head); 1988a, 339 (lineage of lingams); 1988b, part 1 (body full of lingams). The Mylapore (Madras) Dharmarāja temple has a Lingāyat pūcāri (Hiltebeitel 1991a, 23). Gaṇāchāri is a high office among Lingāyats and Draupadī temple officiants, in the latter case linked with paraphernalia and traits of Pōttu Rāja (Hiltebeitel 1991a, 24-33; Thurston and Rangachari [1904] 1965, 4:271).

11 The Ballad of Rāja Desing

The seventeenth through nineteenth centuries were a period of dislocation for Afghans and Rajputs in the north, but things were more fluid in the south. From 1697 to 1916, Muslim and Rajput rule, nominal though it was from about 1750 on, alternated at Gingee, the heart of the Draupadī cult core area. In 1697, by appointment of the Mughal emperor Aurangzīb, Gingee became a *killēdāri* (a fort under command or governorship) of the nawābs of Arcot. They were not Afghans,[1] but Afghans and Rajputs had preceded them into the area, and formed the underpinnings of its martial culture.[2] In 1700, the emperor then assigned Gingee as jāgīr (titled land) to a Bundela Rajput from Bundelkhand, Sarūp Singh.[3] As Subrahmanyam observes, a fragmenting of *zamīndāris* (land-lord-held domains) in Bundelkhand by the late seventeenth century resulted in a "lack of home territories (*watans*)" for aggressive Bundelas to claim (1995, 20). The end of Aurangzīb's reign (1707) then marked a turning point for them: their "long absences . . . in wars in Afghanistan and the Deccan were detrimental to their role as owners of estates" (watans), while fighting such wars "was increasingly unprofitable."[4] The

[1]Sadatulla Khan—born Sayyad Khan and titled upon becoming nawāb and *faujdār* (military commander) of Arcot (Krishnaswamy Aiyangar 1930, 13)—was a Navaiyat, one of a "high-ranking" and "elite" group of "Shafi'i Muslims who are thought to have originated in the Basra region, and to have settled along the Konkan coast during the 13th century" before rising to "prominence as merchants and state officials" under the Bijapur sultans (S. Bayly 1993, 464-65) and serving Aurangzīb as "troopers" (Srinivasachari 1943, 364).

[2]Afghans plundered the area in 1666, as did the Marathas in 1678 (Hiltebeitel 1988a, 22).

[3]According to Nārāyaṇan̲ Piḷḷai's *Karnāṭaka Rājākkal Cavistāra Carittiram*, a Mackenzie manuscript written a century later (1802-3), Sarūp Singh was at this point "an officer in immediate attendance on the Raja of Bundelkhand," while another Rajput named Śivanāth Singh, in the service of the Jaipur rāja, preceded him in 1699 as *killedar* of Gingee, with Gingee as his jāgīr, having served in a contingent sent by the Jaipur rāja that fought for Aurangzīb in the siege of the Marathas at Gingee, which ended in 1697 (Krishnaswamy Aiyangar 1930, 12; Srinivasachari 1943, 353-55 [quote 354]; Dikshitar 1952).

[4]Kolff 1990, 144-45. Earlier, Bundelas had signed on for expeditions to the Deccan under other Mughals, beginning with Akbar (125-26, 137, 140-41, 147-48), and also under the Marathas (144). Then, "some of them settled in the South" (152).

late seventeenth and early eighteenth centuries occasioned what has been called a "jagir crisis": there were fewer and fewer productive lands to confer, and service in the Deccan was a means to try to get the last of what was left.[5] In such circumstances, Sarūp Singh's son, Rāja Desing (probably Tej Singh in Bundeli), made a stand for a home away from home,[6] and, by defying the nawāb, came, after a brief rule of only a few months (1713-14), to be the last of the Nayak, Maratha, and Bundela kings to rule or govern Gingee as one or another variety of Hindu.[7]

A. The Story and Its Settings

Subrahmanyam's recent diggings reveal several accounts of Rāja Desing's Bundela ancestry. One, plausible, traces his lineage back to Bir Singh Deo, most prominent of the Bundela kings of Orccha from 1605 to 1627; another, less likely but no less interesting, to Chatrasal Bundela (1662-1731), founder of the Panna kingdom in 1675 who, as we have seen, brought Praṇāmī teachings into his kingdom by affiliating with the guru Prāṇnāth in 1683.[8] After Desing, the nawābs retained Gingee Fort nominally until 1801, despite interludes of French capture from 1750-61, British control thereafter, and seizures of the fort by Hyder Ali and Tippu Sultan in 1780 and 1792.[9] But descendants of Desing claimed title to Gingee as a jāgīr as late as 1916 when Sûrabanâden Singh, seemingly the last such claimant, died impoverished at Mēlaccēri, on Gingee's outskirts, where Draupadī has her "original temple." A convert to Catholicism,

[5]See Richards 1993, 244-45, 254-56, 263, 267, 291-92.

[6]Cf. Subrahmanyam in press, 12: He "paid the price of his life for what he imagined to be his *qil adârî*, and perhaps even his *watan*." Cf. C. A. Bayly 1990, 24, on "the southern Afghans of Jinjee" and the Rohillas near Delhi among the "Afghan Sultanates" that attempted to retain power after the death of Aurangzīb in 1707.

[7]Subrahmanyam, whom I thank for making available his studies of Rāja Desing (1995 and in press), differs here, and suggests that I offer a "communalistic" reading. But although *Desing* has Vaiṣṇava features, it does not allow one to detach "Vaiṣṇavism" from "Hinduism"; it is not only Marathas who assert a sense of "Hindu-ness" in pre-colonial India, but Bundelas (as in Gorelāl's *Chatra Prakāś*, by a contemporary of Desing). Cf. Richards 1993, 210: Marathas considered Rajputs as "Hindu."

[8]See chap. 10 at n. 115. The more likely account comes from the Brahman-authored Persian biography of Desing's opponent, the nawāb of Arcot (Subrahmanyam 1995 and in press); the implausible Chatrasal connection (Chatrasal dies before Desing is sent to Gingee, whereas he actually outlives Desing by seventeen years) is made in a Marathi text, drawing on Maratha connections with Chatrasal, as Subrahmanyam observes. The Tamil ballad makes its hero the grandson of Cūraciṅkurāja<u>n</u> (Caṇmukacuntaram 1984, 35), a name unknown in Desing's other genealogies. It is not clear who is referred to as the "Raja of Bundelkhand" (which by the end of the seventeenth century had three main kingdoms) whom Sarūp Singh is said to have served. On Bir Singh Deo, see chaps. 7, n. 33; 9, n. 52.

[9]See Edwardes 1926, 3, on dates.

twenty years earlier at forty-five Sûrabanâden Singh had signed the parish record of his baptism as a "Kṣatriya" and "king of Jinji."[10] Today, according to Krishnan Singh, a Mēlaccēri resident and "Singh"/Bundela community pūcāri interviewed in January 1997, there are still fifteen Singh families in Mēlaccēri who claim descent from Rāja Desing.[11]

According to Krishnan Singh and others,[12] Rāja Desing would visit Mēlaccēri's Kālī temple and a Bhairava temple on Mēlaccēri Mountain to the village's west. The Bhairava temple is now all but inaccessible: the mountain path to it overrun with thorn trees since the government claimed the area a forestry preserve. It is, however, one of three Mēlaccēri temples where Krishnan Singh is pūcāri, and it is where Singh community people used to go for tonsure and ear-boring. Bhairava is their clan deity (*kulateyvam*). Rāja Desing could also reach a cave that opens near the Bhairava temple via a tunnel from the Gingee Fort. The tunnel (at least five kilometers from mountain to mountain) linking the King's Fort and the Bhairava temple can be added to the folklore about a cave within the King's Fort housing a gold-producing tree that grew anew to full height in Desing's time (and is still alive but inaccessible because the cave is filled with insects and bees), and tunnels linking the King's Fort with the Queen's Fort and the Singavaram Ranganātha temple.[13] This subterranean network recalls the mythology of otherworldly caves that we have noted at the ends of *Ālhā* and *Palnāḍu*.[14]

Krishnan Singh said there is no story of Rāja Desing ever worshiping at the Mēlaccēri Draupadī temple.[15] Although Desing is sometimes identified by Terukkūttu artists as a great patron of the dramas they perform at Draupadī festivals, statements to this effect have been rather vague, and sound more like prestige claims than recollections.[16] There are thus

[10]Hiltebeitel 1988a, 19-23, 29-30, 452-53. Mēlaccēri residents today say an unexcavated mound must be what remains of Heras's palace "in the middle" of the village (1926, 42).

[11]Krishnan Singh was unfamiliar with the designation "Bundela," but others in Gingee recognize it. In 1921, over ten thousand still identified themselves as Bundelas in the Madras census, having been more numerous earlier over districts stretching from Andhra to Tirunelveli. After that, incentives for such an identity—beginning with efforts by the British to discredit it (see Thurston and Rangachari [1904] 1965, 6:240-41)—seem to have diminished.

[12]Other Mēlaccēri residents consulted in the interview with Krishnan Singh, and corroborating this account, were J. Paracuraman, a tailor, and M. Rangaswamy.

[13]See Hiltebeitel 1988a, 64 and 53 (Gingee Mēlaccēri area map). Singavaram is about two miles northeast of the fort complex.

[14]See chap. 9, n. 76.

[15]Desing ignores Draupadī, yet one version of the story about the king who doubts that Draupadī's Mēlaccēri icon could have hair calls the king Desing (Hiltebeitel 1988a, 99-100).

[16]Rukmani 1995, 276: "Was Chenchi Raja [Desing] a north Indian Rajput king who came there and popularized the cult of Draupadī?"; Hiltebeitel 1988a, 100 (with personal commu-

no reliable direct links between Desing and the Draupadī cult. Nonetheless, "The Ballad of Rāja Desing" describes an Afghan-Rajput culture around Gingee that surely impacted on the cult during this seventeenth-through nineteenth-century period.

Not incidentally, the most comparable ballad from the early period of nawābī rule is the *Kāṉ Sāhipu Cantai*, about Yusuf Khan or Khan Sahib, hung by the British in 1764 as a "rebel commandant" after serving them and the nawāb for years. Yusuf Khan initially collects taxes for the nawāb; Desing refuses to pay them. But each ends up as the nawāb's foe by "behav[ing] as if he were an independent ruler."[17] Each rises briefly to rule a former Nayakate: one renewing Hindu rule in Gingee; the other governing Madurai as a Muslim patron of Mīnākṣī and Śiva (S. Bayly 1989, 199). Each dies when the nawāb (in Khan Sahib's case, allied with the British) defeats him. In ballad diction, each insults the nawāb as a Labbai seller of dried fish.[18] Khan Sahib was born a Vēḷāḷar Hindu, and his ballad portrays him as a great Mīnākṣī devotee, earning her favor even as a Muslim. As such, while he may have converted "for advancement in his soldier's career," he "gradually rose in rank as orderly, naik, havildar, [and] jamedar" to finally become subahdar of Madurai.[19] As a jama'dār, with Tēvar recruits, he provides a south Indian example of a "jobber commandant" who converts what may initially have been an "achieved Rajput" status into that of an "achieved Afghan."[20] It can be no accident that the "Labbai" insult of the nawāb is made in one ballad by a Rajput and the other by an Afghan. As we shall see, the nawāb is also perceived in *Desing* as an extension of Mughal and even British imperial cultures, which Rajputs and Afghans were resisting.

In terms of our classification of chapter 2, both ballads would be "historical" epics. So far, they have attracted study only as "historical

---

nication from Richard Frasca), 149. Frasca (1990, 58) and Perumal (1981, 102-3, 191) mention Terukkūttu dramas on Raja Desing. Cf. Hiltebeitel 1988a, 70.

[17]Vanamamalai 1969, 74, said of Yusuf Khan.

[18]Desing in Caṇmukacuntaram 1984, 101 (see below); Yusuf Khan at his death scene, translated in S. Bayly 1989, 205, with the note, "The term 'Labbai' with its connotations of dark skin and low-ranking Muslim convert status is clearly meant as a deadly insult." Cf. Bayly 1993, 455, 462-64. See Pandian 1978, 144-57: though it can connote Tamil rather than Urdu speakers, it can be viewed negatively or positively. Thurston and Rangachari [1904] 1965, 4:200 cite "Rāvuttan (a horse soldier)" as a Labbai caste title.

[19]S. Bayly 1989, 208-9; Arunachalam 1976, 143; Vēlālar according to S. Ravindran. Cf. S. Bayly 1989, 195, n. 17, on varied traditions of his birth. A havildar is an army officer subordinate to subahdar. In the British East India Company army, the latter, as governor of a province, was the highest native rank.

[20]He comes after his death to have a bifurcated cult at both Hindu and Muslim shrines (S. Bayly 1989, 196-203, 207-15).

ballads" and interest only for their blend of fact with fiction.[21] Otherwise, one receives only bare notices of *Desing*'s popularity. The nineteenth-century song collector Gover remarked that "sepoys of the British Army are fond of singing the exploits of a certain Raja of Gingee," but the poem is "quite modern" and "not worth translating" ([1871] 1959, 194). Its popularity has been until recently mentioned,[22] but is in little evidence today. Inquiries around Gingee found numerous acknowledgments of its declining popularity and mention of only four people who knew it, one of whom—Srinivasan of Marūr village, Gingee Taluk, Viluppuram District[23]—S. Ravindran and I tracked down with some difficulty on January 4, 1997. Srinivasan learned it from his father: "If there was a festival (*tiruviḻā*) or temple chariot (*tēr*) somewhere, we would sit in a corner at the festival and sing and people would give us money. But that was in those days." In the last twenty years, this was to be only the third time he performed it, the other two being at the Gingee taluk office in 1983 at a commemoration of Rāja Desing honoring the Bundela Singh community and at another politically sponsored occasion at Gingee Fort. No one asks for it in the villages. Srinivasan comes from the Pūvitaiyar community of cow-keeping beggars (*piccaikkārar*) found in Andhra and Tamilnadu who give oracles by the nods of their cows and beg by singing songs.[24] They have, in other words, some similarity to the Piccaguṇṭlu mentioned in chapter 3 in connection with *Palnāḍu*. Indeed, their names are Tamil and Telugu equivalents.

I see this *Katai* as enlightening in four ways that are important for this book: in its south Indian tenor, metaphors, and motivations, as sprung from the same soil as *Elder brothers*, *Palnāḍu*, and the Draupadī cult *Mahābhārata*; in certain themes and narrative tensions, as a cousin of *Ālhā*; in texture, as a product of Afghan-Rajput culture carried south; and in what is most haunting about it, a sense that it has some ghosts of Nāth folklore and Ismā'īlī-Praṇāmī messianism. These features will be inseparable. The indented account will follow the printed *Tēciṅkurājaṉ*

[21]Subrahmanyam 1995 and in press, and Shulman 1997, however, are markers of a major collaborative work in progress being done along with V. Narayana Rao on Rāja Desing. I thank these authors for letting me see and hear these studies while in progress.

[22]Maindron [1909] 1992, 87-107; Arunachalam 1976, 138-43.

[23]Roughly, the western half of the former South Arcot.

[24]They trace their begging to a visit to their Andhra home by Rāma, during whose forest wanderings they offered him the top or bottom of what they planted. Rāma picked the top, thinking it would be rice, but they planted groundnuts. Next year he picked the bottom and they planted rice. So he cursed them to live by begging (S. Ravindran, whom I thank for this and much other information on Pūvitaiyars). A few Pūvitaiyars in Jayamkoṇṭāṉ village five kilometers south of Gingee were said by others in July 1998 to know the ballad, but they indicated they know only snatches and told Ravindran and me to go find Srinivasan!

katai from the edition of Cu. Caṇmukacuntaram (1984),[25] but I will also relate Srinivasan's sung version and cite others.[26] I foreground the printed ballad because it maintains interesting narrative tensions by leaving questions unanswered; I bring in Srinivasan's version especially when it "resolves" such tensions by its more straightforward account. I see nothing to be gained by imagining either version as "prior" in the sense of having more or less primary process, or by supposing that Srinivasan's solutions are late or false.[27] There are other explanations than his of what the printed ballad leaves inconclusive. But it is just as easy to imagine that the printed Tamil ballad sustains narrative tension by unsettling the story as it is that this oral Tamil version settles it.

B. The Printed Ballad and an Oral Telling

> Far to the north on Mount Meru, many lākhs (hundreds of thousands) of Ṛṣis perform tapas to Karttā, filling the heavens with the sounds, "Śiva Śiva," "Hara Hara," and "Kōvintā."[28] Among them a Tulukkaṉ Fakir (*pakkiri*) performs a crore of austerities towards Karttā, towards Bhagavan. He knows mantra, tantra, and the great sciences. In this manner, all the Ṛṣis are there doing tapas. (23-25)

The frame story begins by supplying an interreligious universe. A Tulukkaṉ is a Muslim or Turk, but, in the phrase *Puttani Tuluker*, it is also used for Paṭhāns or Afghans (S. Bayly 1993, 463), so quite possibly the Fakir is an Afghan. Karttā, the "Maker," a somewhat neutral name for divinity here that is also used by Christians, attracts the tapas of both the Ṛṣis and the Fakir, both of whom also call on Karttā by Hindu names. It is thus implied that the Fakir is counted among the Ṛṣis.[29]

[25]Work on both the oral and written versions was done with the help of S. Ravindran, whose comments I often cite. We also examined a version, different at some points, edited by C. Karunāṉantacuvāmi (1875), a copy of which Ravindran located in the Adyar Theosophical Society Library, and the "large print" (*periya eḻuttu*) version attributed to the perennial author Pukaḻentippulavar (Pukaḻentippulavar n.d.), which Caṇmukacuntaram claims to have "corrected" (*tiruntip patippāka*; 1984, 4), in which variations are only slight.

[26]Most significantly, a twenty-five minute prose narration by Jayaraman, the pucari of the Gingee Māriyammaṉ temple, July 29, 1998.

[27]Shulman 1997, 3, who compares the Tamil ballad to a Telugu version, finds the prevalence of English loan words and "the rich lexical borrowings from Persian and Urdu" in both to suggest a late eighteenth- or early nineteenth-century date for them.

[28]This call to Govinda (Tamil *Kōvintā*), which occurs over and over in this ballad, is also prominent in the Draupadi cult and other south Indian oral epics and hero cult rituals; see citations in Hiltebeitel 1988a and 1991a; de Bruin 1994, Part 1, 108.

[29]I thank S. Ravindran on Karttā. On overlap between Fakirs and Jōgīs in Rajasthani folklore, see Gold 1992, 147; cf. chap. 10, § D above. Muttāl Rāvuttaṉ can be Pakkiri Cāmi ("Fakir Swamy") in Tirunelveli District. The Telugu version (see n. 27 above) has a pur-

> Pārācāri, a horse born in the world of the gods, losing direction,[30] comes grazing on those slopes. Seeing this horse looking like a crore of rising suns, shining like gold, the Tulukkan̲, who is from Koṅku Tēca,[31] runs toward it. The horse roars.[32] The Tulukkan̲ uses black ointment (*añcan̲am*) to determine the horse's strength.[33] Then he spreads a magic net to capture it, takes it to Delhi, and presents it to the lord of Delhi, the padshah or emperor.[34] The latter, seeing that no one can ride it, sends word to the fifty-six kings, whom we later learn are southern kings.[35] But the Fakir predicts their failure, explaining, "A child born from a divine boon (*teyva varattāl pir̲anta kuḻantai*), having come, can ride it. He who has come to relieve the burden of the earth (*pūmipāram tīrkka vantavan̲*) can ride the horse. A son born at the feet of the Lord (*tēvar aṭiyil pir̲anta piḷḷai*) can ride the horse" (29). The padshah accepts the horse as a gift, and rewards the Fakir with riches. But when Pārācāri is bound with iron, the horse's neighs shake the palace. (25-36)

Srinivasan has a different opening. There was an all-knowing Yogi (dare one say, Jōgī?). Once he entered a maṇḍapa to escape a rain, rolled the body-dirt from his tapas into two balls and made them into horses: one white (Pārācāri), one black (Nīlavēṇi). He gave them wings so their legs would never ache from walking. Realizing he couldn't manage them himself, he took them to the Delhi padshah, his friend. The padshah could not manage them either, so he announced that whoever rode

---

āṇic frame of Indra questioning Nārada. On all matters of Muslim-Hindu ambiguity which will interest us, it gives Indra straight Hindu answers that keep the two religions and their adherents totally distinct. Given, as Shulman observes, that the Tamil and Telugu printed versions are otherwise close, it seems the latter has "corrected" on these points.

[30]*Teyva lōkattil pir̲anta kutirai/ ticai tappi varukutu pār* (25): perhaps better, "missing direction," "erring in its sense of direction."

[31]Kongunad, in Tamilnadu.

[32]*Karccan̲i ceyttu*: i.e., like a lion (S. Ravindran); Desing is also like a lion, as noted below.

[33]The Fakir uses *mai* (= *añcan̲am*), a paste for black magic made from a primapara: *mai pottu pakkara* is "seeing with the *mai*" (S. Ravindran). Muttāl Rāvuttan̲ also has access to this type of black magic (Hiltebeitel 1988a, 107-9), which is a specialty of Kerala not far from the Fakir's Kongunad home (Thurston and Rangachari [1904] 1965, 6:38-39, 122-6).

[34]Padshah is Persian "for emperor or great king" (Richards 1993, 301). The printed ballad usually calls him *tillipaturai*, "lord of Delhi," and once *pātcā* or padshah (Can̲mukacuntram 1984, 79; Pukaḻentippulavar n.d., 28): that is, the Mughal emperor. Srinivasan favors *pātcā* throughout, and I will usually use "padshah" for both versions. Historically, for the start of the story this would be Aurangzīb, but by the end Aurangzīb should have three successors, with the last, Farrukhsiyar, demanding the tribute. The ballad, however, knows only one Delhi ruler. Srinivasan knew no personal name for the padshah in question.

[35]*Kan̲n̲ata tēcattār*; 70; see Subrahmanyam 1995, 50. On the fifty-six rājas as an idiom in southern folk epic, see also Roghair 1982, 148, 152, n. 13, 174, 235.

Pārācāri would get the horse and his daughter and need not pay tribute.

Tēraṇi Makārājaṉ, king of Gingee, is among the fifty-six kings summoned to Delhi. Taking leave of his full-wombed wife Rāmpāyi, he goes with his younger brother Taraṇi Singh.[36] The padshah challenges the fifty-six, offering riches and the horse to whoever rides it, but prison to whoever shirks it in fear. The fifty-six agree, but when the horse is led out it neighs like thunder. They fall down as if it had destroyed the universe (*aṇṭam iṭintu viḻuntāṟ pōla*), as if it had destroyed the fort (*kōṭṭai iṭintu viḻuntāṟpōl*; 43).[37] Only Tēraṇi Makārājaṉ remains standing, but he is speechless. They all prefer seven years in prison as the padshah's slaves (*aṭimai*) to the risk of riding the horse (36-45).

In Tēraṇi Makārājaṉ's absence, Desing is born at Gingee Fort. He fills his early years with princely pursuits, including horse-riding and hunting, with his friend Mōvuttukkāraṉ (Mohabat Khan in other sources). At five he keeps asking where his father is.[38] Rāmpāyi finally tells him of his father's imprisonment, and that Desing must wait two more years to see him. Not Desing; he wants to go to Delhi now. His mother refuses him permission and faints. While she is still swooning, Desing circles her three times, bows at her feet, and leaves with Mōvuttukkāraṉ. He prays to Ranganātha (Viṣṇu), calling himself "your child (*uṉ kuḻantai*; 53)." Ranganātha promises to protect him.[39] Desing and Mōvuttukkāraṉ leave for Delhi (45-54).

[36]Behind Tēraṇi Makārājaṉ is presumably Sarūp (Surūp, Corūp) Singh, Desing's historical father, of whom there are hints of a Mughal relation: British *Despatches* reports of 1711-1714 describe him as "a considerable prince and a Rajaput too. This Mughal's mother was of that family," and "as being related to the Mughal family . . . [which] might mean that he was related to one of the Rajput ladies in the harem of the Emperor" (Srinivasachari 1943, 406, 354). One Marathi account calls Desing's grandfather Sultan Singh, another gives an uncle that name (Subrahmanyam 1995 and in press). Srinivasan calls the father Rām Singh and the uncle Tēraṇi Singh: the only one of Rām Singh's four companions (who include Corūp Singh!) *not* to go to Delhi. Jayaraman calls the father Taṉciṅku (Dhana Singh, name of a "clansman" [*tāyāti*] in the printed ballad) and the uncle Tēraṇi Singh.

[37]The first line repeats the effect the horse's stamping has when it is first brought to Delhi fort, making them fall off their horses and the lord of Delhi fall off his elephant (31). The second line, not found there, is thus incremental: not only are the horse's sounds like the destruction of the universe in their effects; they are like the destruction of the fort! Note this parallelism and its echoes with "fort-destruction" or *kōṭṭai iṭittal* rituals (using the same verb to describe them) and myths in the Draupadī cult and other traditions (Hiltebeitel 1988a, 339-40, 353-61 [dramas and myths]; 1991a, 401-32 [rituals]).

[38]Srinivasan's version makes him seven at this point.

[39]A matter for further note: Ranganātha speaks to Desing here. Recall that Bundelas changed from Śaivas to Vaisṇavas in the mid-sixteenth century (see chap. 10, n. 118).

In ten days they reach Delhi, where they rove like lion cubs.[40] Desing is a child.[41] Appearing like a crore of rising suns, he stuns the Delhi court.[42] All rise to salute him, the padshah among them. When Desing announces his name and his challenge, Tēraṇi Makārājan̲, his father, and the padshah try to dissuade him.[43] Laughing, Desing chides his father: "You are imprisoned for being afraid of the horse, but I will ride it and take it away with me." Tēraṇi screams and falls. Desing goes to the stable. Pārācāri neighs like thunder, and all fifty-six kings collapse in shock. Desing tells Mōvuttukkāran̲ to release the horse. Calling "Kōvintā, Śrī Kṛṣṇa," Desing mounts and salutes the horse as it leaps. Telling his father not to worry about him since death eventually comes to all, he draws the reins and whips the horse into a ride through the skies. Looking on, even the gods are afraid. Hills and mountains shake. Pārācāri leaps to Sri Lanka and circles it four times. All living beings shiver. The horse flies for five days and nights, and then heads toward Devaloka (the heavens), thinking, "This child (*pālakan̲*) will kill me." Desing pulls it back to an earthly course, but the descent is treacherous. Seeing no city or country, he prays again to Viṣṇu, closing his eyes and lying on the horse. Viṣṇu appears, slaps Pārācāri, holds the reins, and scolds the horse for thinking of killing the child in the heavens. He orders Pārācāri to take Desing to Delhi and promises, "In a few days there will be a war. In the war I'll quickly[44] give you mokṣa along with the child" (54-68).

The fifty-six kings celebrate Desing's return. The padshah gives him many presents, including the horse Nīlavēṇi, whom Desing gives to Mōvuttukkāran̲, keeping Pārācāri.[45] The padshah then offers

[40]*Ciṅkak kuttipōla*; 55—punning on his name; cf. 78: he rules Gingee like a lion; 84; 123: he sits like a lion in his royal court; 154: he approaches the battlefield like a lion.

[41]*Pālakan̲, kul̲antai* (55). If he is five, Mōvuttukkāran̲, supposedly four years younger by the time they die, should be one!

[42]Rider (56) thus matches horse (25); recall also that Ūdal is Udayasimha, the "risen lion."

[43]This son-father pattern reflects the *yuva rāja-mansabdār* one operative in seventeenth-century Bundelkhand: the son, "crown prince and champion of the clan," "may raise his head in the jungles"; the father, holder of an imperial office (*mansab*) that demands "attendance" upon the emperor "with rival lords" (Kolff 1990, 126 and *passim*).

[44]*Calti* = *jaldi*: This Tamil Viṣṇu speaks Hindi; but then so does everyone else, including Desing (78, 89), prefer calti to Tamil equivalents. Similarly, the nawāb of Arcot's presumably Telugu minister Paṅkāru Nāyakkar prefers *salām* to *vaṇakkam*.

[45]The gift of a horse "represented the oath of martial fealty by a Rajput 'vassal' (jagir-dar), to his politically superior kinsman" (Jain 1975, 260)—the padshah then also gives his daughter. Nārāyaṇan̲ Pillai has Desing get his horse after his father dies, on the way from Bundelkhand to Gingee, from the Rāja of Bidanur or Bednūr, on the west of the Mysore plateau (Srinivasachari 1943, 421). Not heavenly, it is only a very spirited horse which he gets for his services to the Rāja (Krishnaswamy Aiyangar 1930, 8, 15).

Desing his daughter Rāṇiyammāḷ (or Rāṇipai); Desing can marry her when he wishes. Desing refuses, calls "Kōvintā Kōvintā," and asks leave; he has not seen Gingee in six months. The padshah then implores Tēraṇi Makārājan̲ to consent to his son's marriage. Tēraṇi says, "The boy is only five. When he is twenty he will marry your daughter." The padshah declares that Gingee's king will no longer owe tax, and frees the fifty-six kings. The Gingee party leaves (68-76).

Srinivasan's oral version clarifies: When the padshah offers his daughter, Desing refuses, saying "I am from a Rajput clan and you are a lowly (*kīlān̲a*) Muslim. So I cannot marry her. But I'll give her my sword and your daughter can garland it. That will make me her husband."[46] They plant the sword in the marriage pantal, and Rāṇiyammāḷ garlands it. Bride and groom do not even see each other.

Seven years of happy rule pass. Then Desing's father and mother die.[47] Desing's uncle Taraṇi Singh becomes regent. At eighteen, Desing marries Rāṇiyammāḷ in Delhi. His wedding and crowning take six months. But a curtain (*tirai*) keeps the bride and groom from seeing each other, both at the marriage and back in Gingee.[48] Neither may see the other's face. Desing rules Gingee like a lion cub. (76-78)

In Srinivasan's version, Rāṇiyammāḷ marries Desing's sword earlier and is kept separate from him in the Rāṇikkōṭṭai, the "Queen's Fort," or *rāṇimāḷikai*, "queen's palace," where she never sees him.[49]

[46]One finds other variations: Karuṇān̲antacuvāmī has the child Desing hug the padshah for offering his daughter; then his father insists on the wait (1875, 26). Nārāyaṇan̲ Piḷḷai puts Desing in Bundelkhand when his father dies; he comes *from there* to Gingee with his presumably Hindu wife (Srinivasachari 1943, 411). J. K. Habibur Rahman, a Gingee Muslim conversant with the story, says Desing's wife was not the padshah's daughter: "After Shah Jahan there were no intermarriages." Jayaraman (see n. 27) says the Rāṇi, named Intirāni (Indrānī), is daughter of a Hindu wife of the padshah and main stake of the "horse competition"; the padshah gives Gingee to Desing with her as "agreement" (*oppantam*). Cēṣātti-ri makes her the daughter of a general Bhīm Singh of the Delhi army (1994, 195).

[47]Another anachronism: his father went to heaven when Desing was eight (77), but he should be seven plus five, i.e., twelve.

[48]Cf. the fingernail extensions in *Elder brothers*, all means to keep spouses apart. In a Marathi version of Desing's story the word for curtain is *pardā* (Subrahmanyam 1995, 41). Curtains also denote secrecy in Pīr Shams's ginans (Kassam 170, 235, 274).

[49]Most likely, the oral ballad refers to the northernmost of the three interlinked mountain forts that comprise the total Gingee Fort (see Hiltebeitel 1988a, 53, map 3): the Krishnagiri or Rāṇikōṭṭai, paired with the Rājagiri or Rājakōṭṭai (where Desing resides). *Rāṇimāḷikai*, Srinivasan's term, corresponds to *irāṇi araṇman̲ai* in the printed ballad (Caṇmukacuntaram 1984, 140). The Queen's Fort as a place of marital separation is much like the residences of Māncāla in *Palnādu* and the twins' wives in *Elder brothers*.

Now the padshah asks his minister whether the fifty-six kings are all paying their taxes. One is delinquent, the nawāb of Arcot, Caitullā,[50] who has not paid for twelve years. The padshah sends a letter demanding payment in eight days lest the nawāb be jailed. The nawāb offers to pay, but his coffers are low. He requests twenty days and asks his accountant if all his tributaries (poligars) are paid up. The one holdout is at Gingee Fort, where Tēraṇi Rājaṉ and now Desing are twelve years in arrears. The nawāb orders his general Tōṉṟa Mallaṇṇaṉ[51] to collect, and sends a huge army with him. When Mallaṇṇaṉ passes Arani Fort, its ruler Veṅkaṭarāyar tells him that Desing, a devotee of Viṣṇu, will kill him unless he puts a Vaiṣṇava forehead mark (*nāmam*) on himself and his elephant (78-92).

Mallaṇṇaṉ camps along the Caṅkarāparaṇi River for three days, and sounds the *nakāru* drum the fourth morning. Desing is doing pūjā to Viṣṇu. His uncle Taraṇi Singh interrupts to say the nawāb's army has come and is sounding the drum. Desing laughs. He knows that Gingee has paid the nawāb no tax for twelve years. He tells his uncle to send messengers to the nawāb's army, which he will tear into strips. Meanwhile, he will finish his prayers (92-95).

Mallaṇṇaṉ puts on a nāmam of powdered limestone mixed with his own spittle (*eccil*), with the red line in the middle made of blood from stabbing his elephant.[52] In the court he salutes Desing, who says he is now twenty-two and has never before seen the nawāb's army "in my territory" (*eṉ cīmaiyil*; 99). Why has it come now; how does Mallaṇṇaṉ dare sound the drum before Gingee Fort? Mallaṇṇaṉ shivers, falls at Desing's feet, and says Desing is the only poligar in arrears with his taxes. Desing draws his sword but holds back as Mallaṇṇaṉ faints. Desing instructs Mallaṇṇaṉ to tell the nawāb that if he's a man, he should come and fight himself: "Must I pay tax to a Labbai who sells dried fish?"[53] Mallaṇṇaṉ shivers and falls like a corpse. Revived, he apologizes for having come. Desing says the forehead mark saved his life. But if the nawāb comes like that, he will kill him.

[50] *Cait* is presumably "Saiyid." The ballad keeps this title (see Subrahmanyam 1995, 13).

[51] The Todar Mall of more historical sources, appointed "Sheristadar of the Karnātak" under the nawāb of Arcot after the fall of the Marathas at Gingee in 1697, and sent to take Gingee Fort from Desing. Provoked by Desing's arrogance, he tried "not to make much of the 'characteristic stupidity of the *Bundela*'" (Srinivasachari 1943, 413]). Jayaraman makes Toṉṟa Mallaṉ (sic) the padshah's "servant" (*cuppāṇṭi*).

[52] He uses lime and brick powder in Jayaraman's account. Subrahmanyam 1995, 54, notes his impurity and hypocrisy, but that he is still a Vaisnava, later calling on Visnu.

[53] *Karuvātu vikkiṟa lappai* (101). Srinivasan and Jayaraman do not use the phrase. On Labbais, see above, n. 18.

Mallaṉṉaṉ flees to Arcot, reaching it the same day (95-104).[54]

The nawāb thinks Mallaṉṉaṉ returns with tribute and that all is well. But hearing Desing's challenge, he swears to destroy Gingee Fort (*iṭittup poṭuṟēṉ ceñcik kōṭṭaiyai nāṉ*) in two "hours."[55] A letter comes from Desing taunting him further with insinuations of femininity. The nawāb tells his minister Paṅkāru Nāyakkar[56] to summon the one hundred and seventy-two poligars to Arcot. When they arrive, he commands Paṅkāru to ready the army with eighty crores of guard rifles, enough bullets, sixty thousand cannon, tents of white and green, over fifty crores of cannonballs, twenty thousand elephants, fifty thousand camels, eighty thousand lances, a hundred and twenty thousand sepoys, and uniforms for all.[57] They march on Gingee, the nawāb calling on Allah. Desing is doing pūjā. His uncle interrupts to say that the nawāb surrounds the fort; Desing should pay the tax. Desing breaks his prayer, opens his eyes, and says, "You are sixty and lack intelligence. Don't disturb my pūjā. Wait a little and order my horse. I'll slice them like cucumbers, tear them into strips." The uncle retreats. Desing continues the pūjā (104-18).

Cupaṅki Turai of Tiruvannamalai now tells the nawāb, "Give me two 'hours' and I'll capture Gingee Fort. There are three thousand houses at Tēvaṉūr Pēṭṭai.[58] In a minute (*nimiṣa*) I'll capture it."[59] With three thousand horsemen he destroys the village's buildings, plunders its cattle and wealth, and brings the nawāb the spoils. The people of Tēvaṉūr seek Desing's protection, breaking his prayers. Realizing that the nawāb's forces have entered "my territory" (*eṉ*

[54]Srinivasan has Desing rage like a lion, offering the nawāb grain or gold, but as a gift, not as tribute, which he can collect on the battlefield. Jayaraman has Desing offer straw, sand and stones from the river, or his sword. Maindron [1909] 1992, 96-98, remarks on Desing's "mutisme" in not recalling that the emperor had excused him from taxes. The story does not recognize imperial successions after Aurangzīb's death, which might "explain" the renewed demand (Krishnaswamy Aiyangar 1930, 7, 12, 14-19). See above, n. 34.

[55]*Nāḻis* (106), also *nāḻikai* (194), each meaning forty-eight minutes, but for the sake of fluidity, henceforth "hours" in quotes.

[56]Paṅkāru Nāyuṭu, king of Kalahasti for Srinivasan; Bangāru Yāchamanāyaka of Venkatagiri (Krishnasamy Aiyangar 1930, 18), a kinsman of other Yachamanāyakas behind this story (ibid., 10-12), and probably a descendent of the early seventeenth-century "kingmaker" Yācama Nāyakar of Velugōṭi, who "consolidated his gains by carving himself a large slice of Senji territory" (Narayana Rao, Shulman, and Subrahmanyam 1992, 248-64, quote 253).

[57]*Cippāy*, "sepoy," used regularly, sometimes alternates rhythmically with *irāja*, "king," for Desing himself: "Rāja Desing . . . , soldier (sepoy) Desing." (138, 140, 150). Srinivasan, without details, describes the nawāb's army as having a thousand lākhs of troops.

[58]Tēvaṉūr (Devanur) is north of Gingee.

[59]Srinivasan's padshah receives Desing's challenge directly, and then orders the destruction of six villages near Gingee, among them Malaiyaṉūr but not Tēvaṉūr. Jayaraman has him give orders in Delhi to Toṉṟa Mallaṉ, who then camps at Tēvaṉūr.

> *cīmaiyil*), speaking of "our Tamil side's territory" (*namatu cīmaiyil tamiḻc ciṟai*) and the "Muslim side" (*tulukkaṉ ciṟai*; 121),[60] Desing says he will repay their loss by plundering Arcot, and returns to his pūjā. His clansman Taṉciṅku arrives, and Desing says, "If the Tulukkaṉ has entered the Ranganātha temple, I'll do the pūjā by cutting up the Tulukkaṉ." Taṉciṅku approves. Desing finds his three hundred friends and clansmen assembled in court. He says three hundred horsemen are enough to defeat the nawāb's eighty thousand, and hundred thousand sepoys.[61] He recalls his friend Mōvuttukkāraṉ in Vaḻutāvūr,[62] knowing that he is about to be married. (118-25)

In Srinivasan's version, Tēraṇi Singh, Desing's paternal uncle, tells Desing he should not fight the nawāb without his companion (*tuṇai*) and friend (*naṇpaṉ*) Mōvuttakkāraṉ: "If you send an *olai* (a letter on palm leaf) to him he'll be here. If you go to battle together you can win a glorious victory." Desing writes, "Dear Mōvuttakkāraṉ, I am going to fight the nawāb's troops. If you really have devotion (*pakti*) and trust (*vicuvācam*) toward me, the moment you see this olai you should join me at Gingee. Yours, so says Desing."

Desing now asks Tēraṇi who should carry the olai. "Son, Gingee's first guardian (*mutal kāval*) is Māyappakkiri. Call Māyappakkiri." Māyappakkiri sees Desing, removes his cap, does salaam, and kneels. "Swāmi Tēciṅkurāja, since my birth I have been the first guardian of Gingee Fort, and nobody has ever called me to the king's chamber. What is the reason?" Desing tells what he wants and offers "money and land; and if that is not enough, Māyappakkiri, I'll give you part of Gingee

[60]See Subrahmanyam 1995, 58; *Tamil Lexicon* 1982 (1926-39), 3:1465.

[61]Nārāyaṇaṉ Piḷḷai's account suggests that the three hundred clansmen-horsemen could be (or renew in number) the three hundred who come to Gingee with Desing's father (Krishnaswamy Aiyangar 1930, 12).

[62]Vaḻutāvūr (Valadavur) was one of the eight *parganahs* of Desing's (and first his father's) jāgīr (Krishnaswamy Aiyangar 1930, 12, 19), and had been raided by the British from Fort St. David in Devanampattinam in their conflict with Sarūp Singh (Desing's father) from 1710-12 (Srinivasachari 1943, 382, 386-87, 391-92, 409). As Mohabat Khan, Mōvuttukkāraṉ is spoken of by the British as captain of the forces at Vaḻatāvūr and an ally of Sarūp Singh by 1711 (Srinivasachari 1943, 382, 386-87, 391-92, 409), which, if Mōvuttukkāraṉ is to die at eighteen in 1714 according to the ballad, leaves him fifteen at the time. Srinivasachari is thus left to imagine two Mohabat Khans of Vaḻatāvūr (1943, 426). Only *Desing* and sources based on it mention the heroes' childhoods and, for that matter, Desing's upbringing in Gingee. My chief Terukkūttu informants R. S. Natarajan and R. S. Mayakrishnan, whose village of Pakkiripalayam is very near Vaḻatāvūr, say that within their lifetime there was still a ruined fort of Mōvuttukkāraṉ, but that it is now dismantled as an agricultural site. They know of no one who performs the story locally in either ballad or drama form, and no one who claims descent from Mōvuttukkāraṉ.

Fort; if that is not enough, the gold bangle I am wearing." Māyappakkiri laughs and says, "I am doing this because you are my friend and because I ate your salt." He wants no rewards, but knows the dangerous mission may cost his life. Shouting "Allah Rādhā"[63] and "Nagore Allah,"[64] exiting Gingee, he sees a thousand swords shining and devises a familiar ruse. He puts a nāmam on his forehead. Stabbing an elephant, he draws blood and applies it to the nāmam.[65] He dons an old cloth and a leather cap, takes a staff in hand, and comes like a beggar (*piccaikkāraṉ*), saluting the nawāb's troops. He tells Tōṉṟa Mallaṇṇaṉ, "I am a beggar. I beg to earn a living. For the past six months I have been with Rāja Desing. Today I heard that the nawāb has come. So I come to see the nawāb and ask for alms. Just leave me a little way to go through."

But Pañkāru Nāyuṭu, a clever man (*keṭṭikkāraṉ*), says, "I saw you yesterday at Gingee. Today you're dressed as a beggar, Māyappakkiri. Yesterday when I went to ask Rāja Desing for the tribute, you said you could let no one in without the king's permission. Aren't you the same Māyappakkiri?" "Sir (*aiyā*), am I Māyappakkiri? I am definitely not Māyappakkiri. I am only a beggar. Please leave me passage." Tōṉṟa Mallaṇṇaṉ says, "Where do we have the justice (*niyāyam*) to block a beggar? If the padshah learns of this he won't spare us. Poor man, let him go. Pañkāru Nāyuṭu suspects everyone." They make way. When Māyappakkiri reaches the other bank of the Cañkarāparaṇi, he removes his leather cap, laughs aloud, announces his identity and mission, and says Mōvuttakkāraṉ will be back to fight in a few hours. Pañkāru Nāyuṭu fires a cannon shot, tearing Māyappakkiri's right shoulder. But he reaches Vaḻutāvūr.

Drums are sounding. It is an auspicious time (*nalla ilakkiṉam*) for Mōvuttukkāraṉ's wedding. He is coming on an elephant. The Cuvāmiyar (Swami) is reading the Vedas. He gives Mōvuttukkāraṉ the tāli. Chanting "Allah Rādhā," Mōvuttakkāraṉ is about to tie it on his bride when the olai arrives. Shouting "Sanctuary, Gingee olai," Māyappakkiri enters the wedding pantal. Hearing this, Mōvuttukkāraṉ puts the tāli on a plate. He takes in his arms the dying Māyappakkiri, whose last words are that the olai will have to speak for itself.

Māyappakkiri, "the Illusionist Fakir," may or may not be the same as the Tulukkaṉ Fakir who finds the horse at the beginning of the printed ballad. If he is the same, he can move between such identities as a companion of Ṛṣis on Mount Meru and the first guardian of Gingee Fort. I do not think we should discount the possibility of such interchangeable roles.

[63] Rādhā, Kṛṣṇa's favorite among the Gopīs.

[64] Allah of Nagore, a major Muslim pilgrimage site on the Tamil coast above Nagapattinam.

[65] Thus he does this rather than Tōṉṟa Mallaṇṇaṉ; see above at n. 51.

Mōvuttukkāraṉ is at the wedding pantal, tying the turmeric wristlet (mañcaḷ kaṅkaṇam kaṭṭi). Calling "Allah Allah" and "Rāma Rāma," he goes to tie the tāli; but receiving Desing's message, he leaves the tāli behind and draws his sword. He requests a happy send-off to fight the nawāb, but his mother asks him to wait a day. He replies, "I want but two 'hours' to kill the nawāb, plunder Arcot, and crown the king of Gingee. Then I will return to tie the tāli, or I will die at the nawāb's hands.[66] I will not squander having been a child in your womb. Should I die, I will reach a good abode, and my name will remain in the world. Once a year on an auspicious day, perform the necessary ceremonies." His mother gives leave, but Nīlavēṇi stalls. He coaxes her,[67] promising sugar made with gold. At the Caṅkarāparaṇi, he sees the nawāb's camp. Rather than go around it, he fights through it to Gingee Fort. He meets Desing and asks permission to destroy the nawāb's army. Looking at his wedding clothes, Desing asks, "Did you tie the tāli or not? Why did you leave the wedding pantal?" Mōvuttukkāraṉ answers, "What are you saying, Rāja Desing? For a sepoy who holds a sword, what does he need a woman?"[68] He invites Desing to his wedding—in Arcot;[69] and asks leave to fight. (125-36)

Srinivasan follows the same skein, but has different unfoldings. Mōvuttukkāraṉ tells his mother, "I can have a thousand marriages just like this. I can have as many young women like this as I want. But I can never find a friend like Rāja Desing. I am leaving." His mother wants him to tie the tāli and then go, but he says if he dies, his wife would "lose her mañcaḷ and kuṅkumam (her auspicious yellow and red marriage adornments); let us not do that sin (pāvam)." She wants him to eat curd-rice, then buttermilk and rice, from her hand; he says he will get "blood-rice" in Gingee. "Nīlavēṇiyammā" cavorts in protest at the word "battle" (caṇṭai); he coaxes her not with golden sugar but a reminder that he has fed her wheat bread (kōṭumai roṭṭi) and arrack rather than grass and water. Fighting through the nawāb's troops, Mōvuttukkāraṉ kills lākhs

---

[66]Jayaraman makes this a moment of origins: "Mōvuttukkāraṉ said, 'I'll come back and tie the tāli.' He left, and the women of his household tied it. That's why in Muslim weddings the women of the groom's family tie the tāli, and not the groom himself."

[67]Unlike the printed ballad, Srinivasan's Nīlavēṇi ("Nīlavēṇiyammā, Nīlavēṇitāyē") and Pārācāri ("Pārācāritāyē") are both clearly mares. Jayaraman's Pārācāri is a "he" (avaṉ).

[68]Kaṭṭi piṭitta cippāy mārukkup/ peṇṭāṭṭi eṉṉaṭṭirku (136). Peṇṭāṭṭi, woman or wife.

[69]Since both heroes imagine crowning Desing in Arcot, this means that his wedding must follow the war. But it also suggests, since we know he will die, that the war will be his wedding: a reminder of Bāludu's "virgin battle" in Palnāḍu, and that the "elder brothers" and Desing are also virgin warriors.

with his pair of swinging ribboned blades (*cuḻalkatti*).[70] When Nīlavēṇi dodges four cannonballs from Paṅkāru Nāyuṭu and Tōṉra Mallaṇṇaṉ, who are hiding in a cave, Paṅkāru Nāyuṭu tells Mallaṇṇaṉ, "As long as he has the horse, we can do nothing to him," and they flee to Arcot.

Opening his eyes after Nīlavēṇi jumps the cannonballs, Mōvuttukkāraṉ says, "O Nīlavēṇi mother, do you see blood flowing in the river? It might be dangerous to be here any more. Let us go and see what the king wants." Desing thinks the approaching Mōvuttukkāraṉ is the nawāb, and says. "We should kill him before he sits on our throne." Seeing Desing's angry face, Mōvuttukkāraṉ salutes him and stands before him. Desing asks, "Who are you? What is your name? What is your native place?" Mōvuttukkāraṉ answers, "Lord (*cāmi*), you ask me who I am? I was in your service (*toṇṭu*). We studied together. We learned riding together. I am your friend Mōvuttukkāraṉ." Desing says this cannot be Mōvuttukkāraṉ: "I gave him a white dress and black horse. How did you get the red hat? Your horse is red. Your dress is red. Your cap and sword are also red." Mōvuttukkāraṉ says the red comes from the blood left from fighting through the nawāb's guard. He urges Desing to wash Nīlavēṇi in the river to know the truth. This removes Desing's doubts, and Desing offers Mōvuttukkāraṉ tāmpūlam on a golden plate and urges him to rest.

But when Mōvuttukkāraṉ removes his clothes, Desing asks, "Why is the kaṅkaṇam on your wrist? Why the forehead band (*paṭṭaiyam*)? Why all the gold on you? Why the silk clothes? And why the sacred thread (*pūnūl*)!"[71] Here, Desing does not know that Mōvuttukkāraṉ has left his wedding, or even that he is getting married; indeed, Desing's dear friend cannot have invited him. Mōvuttukkāraṉ says, "You have found out what I didn't want you to know. If you didn't find out, you would have started suspecting me. This Friday is my *mukūrttam* (the auspicious hour for a wedding) in Vaḻutāvūr. I was about to tie the tāli. The olai you wrote came. So I left. I put the tāli on the plate and left, and came running. Seeing your olai and being thrilled, I left the tāli on the plate and came here." Desing says, "What have you done, Mōvuttukkāraṉ? For my sake you have spoiled your whole life. Is it good? How could you ever bring yourself to leave the marriage pantal when the girl is sitting there? How could you bring yourself to come here dressed as a groom? Am I that important?" Mōvuttukkāraṉ replies, "Lord, don't say such things. If I

[70]According to S. Ravindran, ribbons of sharp-edged rolled steel fixed to a handle.

[71]S. Ravindran suggests that the singer would understand the headband as a practice of north Indian Ksatriyas. As to the sacred thread, recall that the marriage of this Muslim hero is being performed by a Cuvāmiyar reading the Vedas. On the wristlet, see the discussion in chap. 10, § B; with it, Mōvuttukkāraṉ, in terms of *Palnādu*, fights his "virgin battle" (see above, n. 69) as a "bridegroom of war."

want I can marry any number of times. But I'll never find anyone like you. Whether I live or die, you'll always be my life-breath (*uyir-mūccu*). Don't insult me again." That Mōvuttukkāraṉ has in this version concealed his wedding from Desing deepens the questions about the implied nature of their bond, which, like that of the heroes and their horses, overrides the bonds with wives and mothers. In the printed ballad, it is Desing's wife who tells him he is her "life-breath," as we shall see.

Desing makes one more attempt at deflection: "The war you have fought is already enough. There is limitless cash in the treasury. Take it all. Pile it on your horse. Go to Vaḻutāvūr. Finish your wedding and then come." Mōvuttukkāraṉ replies, "I should listen to this? I never take a step back that I have put forward. It is not an insult for the Rāja clan (*kulam*) to take a step back that you put forward, but it is certainly an insult for the Paṭhān (*Paṭṭāṉi*) clan.[72] Get up. Let us go to war." In the printed ballad, as soon to be noted, it is Desing who repeatedly utters the line about not retracing a step put forward. Here it is spoken by Mōvuttukkāraṉ in a line that identifies him as an Afghan or Paṭhān, and holds up the maxim as defining a Paṭhān practice that poses a challenge to Rajputs, and specifically to his Rajput companion Desing.

> Happy, Desing hugs Mōvuttukkāraṉ. They will go to war, but first Desing wants to take leave of his wife: "It is three years since I married. I will come having looked at the woman's face."[73] He repeats this to his uncle, who stops him: "What are you doing, child? You were born on a Friday. The queen was born on a Friday. Your horse was born on a Friday. This war is born on a Friday. If you stay today and go tomorrow you will win and return."[74] Desing laughs: "The nawāb has surrounded the fort. Will I do nothing while a Tulukkaṉ comes to the Ranga temple? I'll tear him to pieces. I'll cut his army. I was born in a royal family (*irāja kulattil*)[75] as one with

[72] *Muṉ vaittu kālai piṉ vaittāl uṉ rājakkulattiṟku avamāṉam alla āṉāl atu niccayamāka eṉ paṭṭāṉi kulattiṟku avamāṉam.* Srinivasan uses both *rājaputtira kulam* and *rājakkulam.* Let us register, however, that what is important is that Mōvuttukkāraṉ is *folklorically* a Pathān *for Śrinivasan,* not that this is historically correct, which is unverifiable.

[73] *Pencāti mukattaip pārttu vārēṉ* (137).

[74] In the most ambitious Marathi version, the context for recommending a one-day postponement is Navarātri and Dasarā: villagers tell Desing of the nawāb's arrival while Desing performs the āyudha pūjā on the ninth day, and Desing will not listen to his commanders' urgings to wait for the tenth—part of this version's more "aggressive 'Hindu' symbolism," according to Subrahmanyam 1995 and in press. This suggests it would be the goddess rather than Visnu who would withhold "victory," which the tenth-day Dasarā ceremonies would secure.

[75] Or "Rajput family," as in Srinivasan's usage (see above, n. 72).

honor (*rōṣak kāraṉāka*). One can die at six or a hundred or the day one is born. I'll never take back a step put forward." Tarani Singh says, "What are you saying, son. You are not listening. I raised you. I did not eat your rice, you ate mine. Our guru said you cannot see your wife for six months. It's now only three. You'll have to wait three more." Seeing Desing's anger, he suggests Desing talk to Rāṇiyammāḷ through a curtain. Desing agrees. A curtain is drawn in the queen's palace. Sent for quickly, Rāṇiyammāḷ makes herself up. Seeing the curtain angers her. She asks why it must separate them.[76] Desing says he seeks leave to fight the nawāb. Rāṇiyammāḷ says, "What are you saying, lord of my breath (*eṉ pirāṇa nātā*)? You can fight from inside our fort for five years. You must not go outside the fort." He replies, "What are you saying, jewel of my eye (*kaṇmaṇi*)? When is a woman ready for war? I now take leave." These terms of affection are deeply ironic. "Lord of my breath," used here fifteen times in refrain (144-45), has the sting that Desing's recklessness is to be Rāṇiyammāḷ's sure death warrant. She will use it again as she prepares to become satī (200). For Desing to call her "jewel of my eye" (idiomatically, "apple of my eye") has the sting that he has never seen her. She says, "You got married in a corner (*mūlaiyil*).[77] I never know any happiness or comfort. Don't go to war. If you leave without listening to me, you will not win. But if you come back scared after fighting, I will not open the fort's gates. I will mount cannon on the ramparts and fire them. But go and come comfortably (*cukamāy*), lord of my breath." Desing laughs and says, "Don't be angry with me. I now take leave. Take care of the fort." Rāṇiyammāḷ offers areca nut and betel.[78] Desing puts his hand inside the curtain for it. She pulls it inside. Seeing its beauty, she wonders at that of his face and asks what her sin might be that this is written on her head.[79] She touches his hand to her eyes and cries. Desing withdraws his hand and says he is parting. He goes to the fort and calls for his horse (137-46).

Desing promises Pārācāri sugar made of gold and a golden bridle, and says they are off to fight. Knowing Desing will die, Pārācāri

[76]The queen's surprise suggests that the six months is something new to her. Since Desing is soon reported to be twenty-two, he is well past twenty, which his father promised for his wedding. The guru's stipulation thus appears to be extra. On curtains, see n. 48.

[77]Presumably this refers to their curtained wedding.

[78]*Pākku veṟṟilai*, which is the same as *pānsupāri* (Srinivasachari 1943, 428) or *tāmpūlam*, which is offered in so many similar scenes, including the heroes' final departures in *Elder brothers*, *Palnādu*, *Karna mōtcam*, and *Ālhā*.

[79]*Eṉ talai eḻuttu eppaṭi irukkutō* (145), referring to "head fate" (*talai viti*), fate written on one's forehead, but also like the olai an oral reminder of the ultimacy of what is "written."

shivers and rolls on the ground. Desing reminds her[80] how much she cost and how well she has been treated; if they die, it will be at the same place, and together they will obtain mokṣa. Pārācāri regains her poise and Desing mounts. His three hundred horsemen mount and all go to the Ranganātha temple. Desing enters, offers pūjā, promises the god a gold crown if he wins, and asks signs of blessing. But Viṣṇu shows disfavor by inauspicious signs. Desing angers. He will not retrace a step put forward. He scolds Ranganātha: "It's not you who will live or die. You have only one birth" (153). But he leaves asking the god not to kill him unjustly (*aniyāyamāy*) and to accept him at his feet whether he lives or dies in battle. He comes out, mounts his horse, goes around the temple and toward the battlefield. (146-54)

Srinivasan has Desing visit Ranganātha much earlier in the day: after the nawāb's attack of villages north of Gingee and before Māyappakkiri's mission to Vaḻutāvūr, and thus well before Desing visits Rāṇiyammāḷ. Here the Delhi padshah accompanies the nawāb, and gives the order to pillage six villages. Once Desing promises the villagers restitution, he goes to his uncle Tēraṇi Singh for a blessing (*varam*). Tēraṇi says Desing should seek the blessing of "Ranganātha at Singavaram (Ciṅkāpuram); he is our talking god (*pēcum teyvar*). If he blesses you, you will surely win." Desing sets forth. At the temple, he chants, "Kōvintā, Gopāla." He does pūjā, saying, "We have come to Singavaram to ask Ranganātha's blessings. If he gives it well and good. If not we will destroy Singavaram." Offering flowers and garlands, he says, "Ranganātha Cāmi, the nawāb has come with a hundred thousand crores of troops. I have to fight them. Open your mouth and bless me. I'll go to war and return victorious." Ranganātha says, "Son, you were born on a Friday. Your father died on a Friday. Your sword was made on a Friday. If you wait today and go tomorrow, victory is yours." Facing east, Rangacāmi then turns west: an oddity, since Ranganātha, as viewed at the ancient Pallava-period Singavaram temple, lies face up sleeping on his back. In the printed ballad, this turning west is the last of Ranganātha's signs, and he operates at this point only by omens (*cakuṉaṅkaḷ*), not by speaking.

Angry, Desing says, "Let us destroy Singavaram." He raises his sword and is about to strike Ranganātha, who stays his hand and says, "Son, why are you angry. Did you dare to attack me because I asked you to wait a day and go tomorrow?" Desing says, "Lord, I grew up drinking tiger milk. I'll leave you alone because of your forehead mark, or because of the words 'Hari' on your forehead. Otherwise I'd have killed

[80]See above, n. 67: Srinivasan makes her a mare. I continue to follow this ascription in summarizing the printed ballad, which does not, however, clarify Pārācāri's gender.

you long ago. Can you give me your varam?" Ranganatha answers, "I say once again, Friday is a favorable day to the padshah but it is not favorable to our Singavaram. If you wait today and go tomorrow I myself will come on the tip of your sword and fight. I will stand at the battle-front and fight, and insure your victory. Wait today and go tomorrow." It seems by now that Friday is a problem because it is sacred to Muslims, from the padshah to Mōvuttukkāraṉ, whose wedding is auspicious on this day. Note that the warnings about Friday are made by the paternal uncle Taraṇi Singh in the printed ballad, not by Ranganātha.

Desing won't listen and only asks, "Can you give me the varam or not?" Ranganātha replies, "Desing, king of Gingee, whatever I say, you refuse to hear and insist on going to war. I'll grant your wish and give a varam according to your fate (*viti*)." Desing says, "This is more than enough, Lord Ranganātha. The blessing you give is enough. I will go to battle and come back." But Ranganātha now signals ill omens, still urging him to wait and win tomorrow. Desing replies, "It is I who should be afraid, Lord Ranganātha. Why are you afraid? I take only one birth. If I die on the battlefield it is merit (*puṇṇiyam*) for me. If I die on a spear-tip I attain mokṣa. Even if I die it is enough if in all four directions they speak of me as one who fought bravely. I take leave, Lord Ranganātha." It is a curious statement for a Hindu to say he has only one birth,[81] and Ranganātha will, as it were, correct Desing at the end of this version. In the printed ballad Desing chides Ranganātha as the one who has only one birth, and who thus fails to understand Desing's motives.

Back at Gingee Fort, Tēraṇi Singh asks whether Desing got the god's varam. Desing tells how Ranganātha first refused, and then gave it after Desing's threat. But without indicating the varam's precarious formulation, Desing says, "Let's not delay. Get up. We will go make war."

Still later, having determined with Mōvuttukkāraṉ to start fighting, Desing says, "Father Tēraṇi Singh, get up. Let the army go to war." Tēraṇi says, "I'm not stopping you. I asked you to go to Ranganātha, which you did. You wrote an olai to Mōvuttukkāraṉ and he's now here. But you have a wife. Go to her and receive tāmpūlam. It will be good if you do that." As Desing starts out, the Rāṇi is casting dice (*pakaṭai*) with her friends and the dice scatter. The maids say it is because her husband, the Gingee king, is coming. The Rāṇi says she is eight days since her period, and should still be in seclusion: "It doesn't augur well if he sees me now. Tie seven screens." Rather than complain about one screen, she orders seven. Desing stands beyond the curtains, says he is about to fight the nawāb's vast army, and asks her to say a good word and give him

[81]A point noted by S. Ravindran.

tāmpūlam. She says, "It's only eight days since my period. The pollution period (*tīṭṭu*) is not yet over. Since I was born the daughter of the Delhi padshah and you won the competition to marry me, I have not known anyone else but my maidservants. You have kept me in the queen's palace.[82] Now you come at the last moment and ask for tāmpūlam. Without the pollution period being over, how will I give you tāmpūlam? Be patient for a day and go tomorrow." Addressing the goddess of the Gingee Fort, she asks, "What shall I do, Kamalakkaṉṉi?" But finally she feeds him, but without the ironies or released affections of the written ballad. Desing says, "It is more than enough. I will go to war."

Desing returns to Gingee Fort. He tells Tēraṇi Singh, "Get up. Let us go to war and fight." They prepare carts (*vāṇṭi*), elephants, and horses, and load cannons on the carts. Desing comes to the stables. Pārācāri sees him and neighs. He says, "Mother Pārācāri, victory or defeat is ours. Don't fear." He puts on her silver reins and golden chains, and rides out of the fort like lightning.

> Hearing Pārācāri's approach, the nawāb's camp scatters. Paṅkāru Nāyakkar advises a ruse (*upāyam*): breach the Malaiyaṉūr and Tāḻāṉ-ūr lakes to flood the Caṅkarāparaṇi and break Desing's advance.[83] The nawāb agrees. Paṅkāru breaches the lakes. He sets nine guards at the gates to protect the nawāb in the middle of the camp.[84] Reaching the river, Desing tells his companions: "I do not have divine strength on my side, O jama'dārs. I am relying on the strength of my hand, O jama'dārs.[85] If you are one who eats milk-rice, go back to Gingee; if you are one who eats blood-rice, follow me. If you are one who doesn't waken in the face of womankind, follow me.[86] To win on the

[82]*Rāṇimālikai*; see n. 49 on this place of the Rāṇi's separation.

[83]Jayaraman makes this breaching a ruse to separate Desing from his forces, described as "all the people of Gingee": only the two heroes "jumped into the floods" because "they were murdering people" across the river. Nārāyaṇaṉ Piḷḷai says the river was in spate because it was the rainy season, and that Desing wouldn't wait a few hours for it to recede (1930, 19). An *end* of the rainy season could suggest Dasarā; cf. n. 74 above.

[84]Several are Hindu; one, the havildar Mōvuttukkāraṉ, has Desing's friend's name (156).

[85]*Eṉakkut teyvapalam illaiyatā/ camētāru mārē// eṉkai palam koṇṭu pōṟēṉatā/ camētāru mārē* (157). For *camētār*, Fabricius gives "(*Pers.*) Jemidar, a native military officer" ([1779, enlarged 1897] 1972, 348). As noted in chap. 10, both before the British and up to the 1857 insurgency, the term denoted "jobber commanders," especially Rajput and Rajput-turned-"Afghan" Baksariyas (Kolff 1990, 145-50, 164, 169-73). In colonial practice in the Madras Presidency, Rajputs were "recognized and registered as Bundelas, i.e., by the clan name of their jemadars" (152). Desing addresses his "jama'dārs" also as younger and older brothers (*aṇṇaṉ mārē tampi mārē*; Caṇmukacuntaram 1984, 177; cf. 157); all but Mōvuttuk-kāraṉ have Rajput names (159). Cf. § A and n. 11 above.

[86]*Peṇcāti mukattil viḻiyātavar* (157), literally. It could also be, "one who does not look

battlefield brings fame, to die quickly brings mokṣa." He sees water rushing. Taraṇi Singh says it is the work of the foreign bandit Paṅkāru Nāyakkar;[87] wait till it recedes. Desing laughs and plunges in the river. Most of his jama'dārs follow, but some turn back. (154-60)

The oral version, without mention of guards, jama'dārs, or oaths, likewise has the nawāb's "minister" Paṅkāru Nāyuṭu (sic) scheme to breach the two lakes,[88] and Desing spurn his uncle's advice to wait until the river recedes. The water runs up to Pārācāri's jaw and Nīlavēṇi's neck. Only Desing and Mōvuttukkāraṉ reach the other bank. The army is carried away by the flood. Tēraṇi Singh, stranded behind, calls, "It is not a good omen for the army to be washed out." Desing answers, "What does the army have to do if the two of us are there? Go back to the fort and defend it. We'll go to war and come back."

Mōvuttukkāraṉ kneels before Desing and asks permission to fight the "first battle" (*mutaṟ cantai, mutal yuttam*). Desing says they should fight side-by-side. Mōvuttukkāraṉ persists: "That will be fame (or "name": *pēr*) for you but not for me." He wants a quarter of an "hour" to demolish the foe. Desing happily "gives permission for the first battle." Mōvuttukkāraṉ jumps on Nīlavēṇi, spurring her with his left leg.[89] Nīlavēṇi leaps cannonballs opening the fray. Cupaṅki Turai orders three thousand horsemen to surround Mōvuttukkāraṉ, who breaks free and kills hundreds in each direction: north, west, east. Last, in the south, she lifts her forelegs onto the brow of Cupaṅki's elephant. Mōvuttukkāraṉ draws his sword and kills the mahout. Cupaṅki tries to flee, but Mōvuttukkāraṉ catches his right arm. Cupaṅki salutes with his left hand and pleads for his life. Mōvuttukkāraṉ lets him flee with one hand left. Mōvuttukkāraṉ searches for the nawāb, but Sheikh Muhammad of Timiri Fort intercepts him and spears him in the throat. He extracts the spear. About to behead Sheikh Muhammad, he heeds his plea and cuts off only his offending hand. He kills more sepoys. But being only a boy of eighteen, he tires and is put off by the stench of blood.[90] As he turns back toward

at/open his eyes to his wife's face/a woman's face."

[87]The Rajput calls the Telugu Nayak a "foreign bandit" (*cīmai kollakkāraṉ*), using a term (*cīmai*) that can imply "European" (S. Ravindran).

[88]In both versions Paṅkāru describes the lakes as deep enough to submerge a banyan (Tāḻāṉūr Lake) and a palm tree (Malaiyaṉūr Lake); see Caṇmukacuntaram 1985, 155.

[89]Srinivasan has this same line (S. Ravindran), but for Mōvuttukkāraṉ's departure from Vaḻatāvūr. Elsewhere it is more frequent for there to be shared terms and images, but different verses, often connected with or spoken by different figures (as noted).

[90]*Irattak kavalu* (173); Caṇmukacuntaram (1984, 207) explains *kavalu* by *vātai*, "stench."

Desing, Nīlavēṇi comes dancing Bharatnāṭyam.[91] But a soldier shoots Mōvuttukkāraṉ from ambush. A bullet pierces his forehead. He falls shouting, "Allah Allah, Hari Kōvintā," and reaches Vaikuṇṭha.[92] Nīlavēṇi circles, sniffs at him and weeps. The nawāb tells Paṅkāru Nāyakkar to capture Nīlavēṇi, but the horse fights back to Desing. Desing sees her and weeps: "My younger brother who grew up with me is dead. I have lost half my strength." He hugs Nīlavēṇi, who leads him to Mōvuttukkāraṉ. Desing kneels, holds the body on his lap, and weeps, "How could you leave me?" He swears to kill the nawāb, and orders a big pit dug. Nīlavēṇi kneels beside it. Desing kills her with one stroke and buries her with Mōvuttukkāraṉ. He orders a big mausoleum (*periya kōri*) built over the grave, shouts "Nārāyaṇā Kōvintā," and commands his jama'dārs to fight by the code: "Don't kill sepoys who run or hide, but kill those who face and fight you. Don't kill the poor or beggars." His jama'dārs agree. (160-78)

According to Srinivisan, Mōvuttukkāraṉ says, "Why should both of us fight together? What if both of us die? Please wait under this *ātti* tree.[93] I'll go first, fight, and if I'm tired, then you can join me. If we take turns and fight then we'll overcome the thousand crore army." Whatever his reason, Mōvuttukkāraṉ expresses what is true for all sidekicks: to be heroes, they must die alone.[94] The "first battle," either fought by or denied to an LSRSC, is a feature in all our oral martial epics.

Desing says, "If that is your wish, so be it." Other than fighting in each direction (but proceeding south-east-north-west), Mōvuttukkāraṉ meets fewer specific foes and different circumstances. He kills crores of troops, but is unable to find the heads of the nawāb or the padshah. He turns west, where only Paṅkāru Nāyuṭu, Tōṉṟa Mallaṇṇaṉ, the nawāb, and the padshah are left. Seeing him coming toward the river, Mallaṇṇaṉ takes up some sand from the riverbank, ties it up in his waistfold (*maṭi*), and climbs with it up into a *puṉṉai* tree on Mōvuttukkāraṉ's path. Tricking Mōvuttukkāraṉ into looking up as he passes beneath the tree, Mallaṇṇaṉ pours the sand in his eyes. Jumping down, he takes one of Mōvuttukkāraṉ's ribboned blades and slices him in two. Mōvuttukkāraṉ reaches not Vaikuṇṭha but Paraloka: heaven, literally, "the Otherworld."

Seeking to return Nīlavēṇi to the padshah (rather than the nawāb),

[91] *Parata nāṭṭiyam āti varukutul nīlavēnik kutirai* (173). It is perhaps fitting for a mare.
[92] The heaven of Visnu.
[93] The ātti tree (*bauhina racemosa*) is sacred as tree of birth and death in myths and rituals of Kūttāṇṭavar. See Hiltebeitel in press-a and below, chap. 12.
[94] Jayaraman has him fight first as Desing's "general" (*talaipati*). Nārāyaṇaṉ Pillai has the two fight together (Krishnaswamy Aiyangar 1930, 20).

Mallaṉṉaṉ (rather than Paṅkāru Nāyuṭu) grabs her reins. But Nīlavēṇi tramples him, swings him by the hair, hits him on the ground, takes off his head with her mouth, and brings it to Desing. Desing sees the riderless horse and calls, "Nīlavēṇi mother, where is your king on you? Where is my friend Mōvuttukkāraṉ?" Nīlavēṇi vomits (*kakki*) Mallaṉṉaṉ's head onto the ground. Desing sees the "treacherous" head and Nīlavēṇi's tears, and asks her to show him the calamity (*vipattu*). He rides behind her to the fallen Mōvuttukkāraṉ. There he says, "You left your marriage to be with your friend. Has your life left you? Will you die fighting? My companion, have you left me?" He holds his cheek against Mōvuttukkāraṉ's; face against face, he cries. He decides, "We'll arrange a pearl palanquin (*muttu pallākku*) on the horse and send his body to his mother's house." He brings a palanquin unlike any ever seen before.[95] He sets it on the horse and lays Mōvuttukkāraṉ on it. Patting her on the way, Desing says, "Nīlavēṇi mother, be careful. Take him to Vaḻutāvūr." He builds a mausoleum (*kōri*) where Mōvuttukkāraṉ was killed. Back in Vaḻutāvūr, Mōvuttukkāraṉ's father Abdul Khan and his mother Arkābu take their son's body and cremate it, following Hindu fashion.[96] Nīlavēṇi must also lose her life, since Desing tells Pārācāri she too has now lost her friend.

Desing now leaves for the battlefield. Pārācāri dances Bharatnāṭyam and dodges cannonballs. Daud Khan[97] gives a sign and thirty thousand horsemen surround Desing, who laughs and takes his sword in

[95] How this should be available when he is fighting alone is unclarified.

[96] Asked if there is a Muslim narrative centered on Mōvuttukkāraṉ, Habibur Rahman (see n. 46 above) xeroxed for me the Tamil Islamic Encyclopedia entry "Muhammat Kāṉ," which does speak to the question: Saiyid Khan migrated from Bombay to become zamīndār of Vaḻatāvūr. He befriended the Gingee king Corūp Singh, since they both spoke Marathi, and their sons became inseparable. When Muhammad Khan was about to marry, Desing was expected at the wedding. But the moment Muhammad Khan heard about the siege of Gingee he left. He split the nawāb's forces and met Desing, who said, "We shall fight together." Muhammad Khan replied, "When the general (*talaipati*) is here, why should you fight?" He cut through the enemy but after releasing Apaṅki (sic) Turai and killing (sic) Sheikh Muhammad of Timiri Fort, he went in search of the nawāb and was killed by a bullet from behind. Hearing this, Desing ran to his side. As he hugged him, his life too left his body (*Islāmiyak kalaikkalañciyam* 1980, 3:753). The padshah and Rāni are not mentioned.

[97] The text's Tāvuttukkāraṉ (179), later said to be from Chetput (186), is the Dowlat Khan of Nārāyaṇaṉ Piḷḷai's account (Krishnaswamy Aiyangar 1930, 20). Nārāyaṇaṉ Pillai gives the nawāb a different ally in Chetput named Salabhat Khan (ibid., 18). Srinivasan mentions a king of Chetput, but not by name. Kirusṇacāmippāvalar (1917, 17-22, 105-7) gives Daud Khan a much larger part: a half-brother of Desing with a Muslim mother, he is sold into slavery to an Arab merchant, serves him in Constantinople, comes back, allies with the nawāb, shoots Mōvuttukkāraṉ while lying among the corpses as if he were dead, and then tries to shoot Desing, who shoots him instead with a pistol that he keeps at his side.

both hands. Having the gods—the goddess of the heavenly voice (*ākāya vāṇi*), the goddess Earth, Candra, Sūrya, and Ranganātha—as witness (*cāṭci*), he shouts "Rāma Rāma" and "Deva"; he severs heads, or cuts foes to strips, or into eight pieces with one stroke. For three and a half "hours," his allies Jeya Rāmu, Kaṅkā Rāmu, and Taraṇi Singh[98] do the same. Pārācāri dodges more cannonballs and bullets. After fighting fifteen "hours," the nawāb's camp fears it won't survive a food and water shortage. Some flee. Daud Khan sends twenty thousand horse against Desing, who cuts them to strips, as he does with two thousand elephants carrying pestles in their trunks. He finds Daud Khan on an elephant, and Pārācāri lifts her forelegs onto the elephant's brow. Desing kills the mahout and seizes Daud Khan, who wants to run away. Refusing to spare him, Desing kills him (178-84).

The nawāb's sepoys flee. News of Daud Khan's death reaches the nawāb, who runs and hides. Desing kills fifty thousand soldiers and two thousand elephants. His hands tire, but sepoys who see him still run for their lives. He turns back toward Gingee with five horsemen, and reaches the Caṅkarāparaṇi, which now flows knee-high. He washes his sword, puts it in its scabbard, drinks three handfuls, and sits beneath a tree.[99] His clansman Taṉciṅku comes and asks why he returns. Desing says he has killed the nawāb, but Taṉciṅku corrects: "It was Daud Khan of Cēttuppaṭṭu[100] you killed, not the nawāb. He is hiding at the base of a hill; don't leave the job unfinished." Desing laughs and summons Pārācāri. But now Ranganātha stands in the way. Desing worships the god, who says, "Listen, child. You fight so much today. Stop. Resume tomorrow. I'll accompany you tomorrow, son (*makaṉē*)." Worshiping, Desing says, "You left me and I lost half my strength." But Desing will never take back a step put forward. The nawāb sends Mallaṇṇaṉ to offer peace. Desing refuses. It is too late: his friend Mōvuttukkāraṉ and the nawāb's friend Daud Khan are dead. "If I have the strength, let Arcot be mine." Mallaṇṇaṉ flees. The nawāb sends Veṅkaṭarāyaṉ with five hundred horse. They are routed; Veṅkaṭarāyaṉ is spared only because he shows Desing his Brahman's sacred thread. All one hundred and seventy-two Poligars fall. (184-92)

As in *Elder brothers*, *Karṇa mōṭcam*, *Ālhā*, and *Palnāḍu*, Viṣṇu (or his incarnation) withdraws his protection. Srinivasan does not give Ranganātha a last appeal to the hero. But note that Ranganātha does speak to

[98]Here, Desing has not ordered his uncle at the river to stay back and defend the fort.
[99]Unnamed; but note the ātti tree in the oral version mentioned above at n. 93.
[100]Chetput, about twenty miles northwest of Gingee just over the (former) South Arcot border into (former) North Arcot.

Desing in the printed ballad.[101] Srinivasan's Ranganātha has already spoken his ambiguous varam and saves his last words for the denouement, and not for Desing but the Rāṇi.

Srinivasan gives Desing a much wider terrain to seek his foes, and again loses specificities of the local battle. With no allies, Desing mounts Pārācāri and starts his journey (*payaṇam*). "Mother Pārācāri, you have lost your friend, and I have lost my friend. Only two of us are left. Let us go." He heads south to Dhanuṣkoṭi (near Rameshwaram, where Rāma crossed the sea to Laṅkā), then east, killing what foes are left in each direction. Heading north, he destroys Arcot city, the fort and all the palaces, and also destroys Delhi! Even after this, he cannot find the padshah, nawāb, or Paṅkāru Nāyuṭu. "Perhaps they are hiding at the border of Senji," he says, and heads toward Mattiyappēṭṭai.[102]

Finally Desing sees the nawāb on an elephant. Pārācāri raises her forelegs to its brow. Desing kills the mahout. The nawāb offers him nine times what he plundered, but Desing says it's too late: our two friends are dead; "If strength is in my hand, Arcot is mine. If strength is in your hand, Gingee is yours." As tribute, he offers not Gingee Fort but a spear. But another mahout tied in an enclosure (*toṭṭi*) under the elephant's belly cuts off Pārācāri's right hind leg. The horse falls with but three legs. Desing fights for three and a half "hours" on the disabled horse.[103] Again, on one hind leg, she raises her forelegs to the elephant's brow. "If it could stand for a 'moment's hour' the nawāb would die."[104] The concealed mahout cuts off the left hind leg. Seeing Pārācāri fall, Desing jumps off. Holding his sword in both hands, he kills her. Overcome with rage, he enters the nawāb's camp and chops sepoys like cucumbers. Finally, with no one left to fight,

[101]See also n. 39 above.

[102]The story's death sites have varied names, as we shall see. S. Ravindran suggests that Mattiyappēttai—a "middle (or center) outside a market town"—may be where the nawāb hides outside Gingee, which the Irattiṉa Nāyakar edition calls Naṭuvaṉapālaiyam, "the camp in the middle (*natu*) of the forest" (Pukaḻentippulavar n.d., 78, line 3; Canmukacuntaram drops this line [1984, 196]). Krishnan, interviewed in July 1998 and from the nearest village to the "camp" site, confirms the location but with another etymology: the nearby hill is where, "hiding behind a rock, they struck at the horse's legs." He says Mattiyappēṭṭai is a misconstrual of Pātiyappēṭṭai—from Arabic *Fath* (pronounced "Fateh") + *pēt*, "Place of Victory"—describing the area where a Muslim Mohabat Khan died (his inverse explanation), or where the nawāb achieved victory (Habibur Rahman's explanation).

[103]Nārāyaṇaṉ Piḷḷai has Desing fight on as a footman (Krishnaswamy Aiyangar 1930, 20).

[104]*Nimiṣa nāḻikai kutirai iruntāl/ navāppu pōyviṭuvāṉ* (194). A nimiṣa thus qualifies an "hour," as when Cupaṅki Turai wants to capture Gingee Fort in a "moment" of two "hours" (118). It seems we must imagine the horse struggling to stand on one leg for just the nick of time in which Desing's sword-flash would kill the nawāb.

he crosses his legs and sits, saying, "There is no one in front of me to take my life. Will I go back to Gingee Fort with my life? Quick, quick (*calti calti*), send the cakra, Ranganātha. There is no justice (*niyāyam*) in my living any longer, Ranganātha Cuvāmi!" He worships, saying, "Kōvintā Nārāyaṇā." Then, "loosening his sword, he throws it in the air; opening his chest, he lies down (*paṭuttaṉ*) on the ground."[105] The sword falls and impales his chest.[106] Calling on Viṣṇu three more times—as Kṛṣṇa, Rāma, and Ranga—he expires. The nawāb takes his body, weeps over it, and praises him for leaving the earthly world for the golden world.[107] He orders Paṅkāru Nāyakkar to make a mausoleum for Pārācāri and to prepare Desing's palanquin to bring his body to Gingee. (192-99)

In Srinivasan's song, the fight with the nawāb hinges on more trickery from Paṅkāru Nāyuṭu, who transforms the nawāb's elephant into a folkloric contraption. Hiding with the others at Mattiyappēṭṭai, Paṅkāru makes a big elephant out of mud (*maṇ*), and builds a hole (*toṭṭi*) into its belly.[108] Desing says, "Mother Pārācāri, Paṅkāru Nāyuṭu and the nawāb are our enemies. They have built an elephant, and Paṅkāru is hiding in it. Building a howdah (*ampāri*), the Arcot nawāb is in the howdah. That is a mud elephant (*maṇ yāṉai*), but you are a live horse. Raise up your front legs. If you raise your front legs and put them on the elephant, I'll be right behind you and kill him. Once I kill him, then it will be over. We can go back to Gingee." He presses Pārācāri forward. When she is about to place her forelegs up, Paṅkāru cuts off one hind leg, and Pārācāri falls to one side. As Desing looks with amazement at his fallen horse, the nawāb uses his goad (*aṅkucam*) and strikes him on his side. The Gingee rāja falls down. Seeing himself fallen, Desing draws up his

[105] *Kattiyaik kaḻaṟṟi ākāyam eṟintāṉ/ rājā tēciṅku// mārpai virittu maṇmēlē patuttaṉ/ rājā teciṅku* (197). His "lying down" makes this battlefield another paṭukaḷam: a recurrent Tamil term for a ritual battlefield (Hiltebeitel 1991a, 208-13, 320-38, 400-38).

[106] Recall the impalements in *Elder brothers* and *Palnādu*. Jayaraman has Desing toss up his sword of eight *tōlās* (only 3.2 pounds figured from Tamil Lexicon 1982 [1926-39], 4:2114) that has been his throughout. Nārāyaṇaṉ Pillai has a sepoy shoot Desing (Krishnaswamy Aiyangar 1930, 20). Kirusṇacāmippāvalar has him shoot himself while weeping over Mōvuttukkāraṉ (see n. 96 above) and seeing Cupaṅki Turai about to kill him (1917, 110).

[107] The *poṉ pūmi*, golden world or golden earth, is moksa, according to the editor Caṇmukacuntaram 1984, 207.

[108] *Vayiṟṟilē toṭṭi vaittu* (he put an enclosure in the belly) rather than *āṉai vayiṟṟil totti katti* (he tied an enclosure on the belly), as in Canmukacuntarm 1984, 194. Pukaḻentippulavar n.d. has *āṉaiyiṉ mēlē totti vaittu* (he put the enclosure on the elephant). For this *totti* ("trough, manger, crib, cistern, reservoir") one is left to imagine anything from a basket to a hole. Jayaraman makes it a hanging net (*valai*) under the elephant, tied over its back.

sash and winds it tightly around his wounds, tying everything up inside.[109] He stands up and looks. The nawāb jumps off the elephant and runs away. Desing cuts Paṅkāru Nāyuṭu into two pieces.[110] He decides not to spare the nawāb, wherever he goes. But thinking so, as he is about to climb onto his horse, he sees her wound. "Mother, the queen has told us to come back if we have a wound on the front but not if we have a wound on the back. Now you have a wound on the back. We should not go back to Gingee. That is our fate. As long as the four directions are there it is enough if we leave a lasting fame (*kīriti*). Even if we die it doesn't matter." Desing's resolution to die without returning to Gingee recalls the old Tamil warrior's practice of restoring honor by wilfully dying after a wound to the back. But Desing combines this with an extension of his own identity pronouns to Pārācāri, since it is only she who has such a wound.[111] In the printed ballad, Desing's non-return follows from his promise to Pārācāri that they will obtain mokṣa together and die at the same place (Caṇmukacuntaram 1984, 149). Now he cuts Pārācāri (killing her). He then holds the sword against his breast, throws it into the air, holds his chest open to it, and falls down cut in twain. No one knows at this point that he has fallen, so the nawāb and the padshah come to the site later. No one, that is, except Ranganātha.

> The palanquin is at the fort gate. Rāṇiyammāḷ learns the news and cries, "If he is wounded on his chest, bring him in. If he is wounded on his back, turn around." She sees the chest-wound and takes the body inside the fort. She leads the people of Gingee Fort in lamentation. She calls for them to dig a firepit (*akkiṉi kuḻiya veṭṭa*), and to pile sandalwood logs and kuṃkum logs.[112] She bathes, and puts flowers in her hair. She prays to Ranganātha, the goddess Earth, and the goddess of the heavenly voice. She walks around the firepit. She looks at Desing. When she has taken in enough of him,[113] she jumps into the fire with the king (*rājāvuṭaṉē tīyil kutittāḷ*). The divine

[109]Recall that Ḍhēbo and Bāludu fight on disemboweled after hanging their entrails on a tree (see chap. 4, n. 54).

[110]Paṅkāru Nāyuṭu does not survive, as Paṅkāru Nāyakkar does in the printed ballad.

[111]Jayaraman rationalizes the same connection. Desing reflects, "Two front legs but only one hind leg. And that too not the right but the left. What was the word the Rāṇi said? 'Come if you have a front-wound; if you have a back-wound don't return.' This wound will make her think I was running away. . . ." Cf. Subrahmanyam 1995, 61-62.

[112]I assume, logs dotted with marks of red kuṅkum powder.

[113]*Kaṅkaḷ kuḷira rājāvaip pārttāḷ*, literally, "She looks at the king to cool her eyes." The phrase is used for seeing someone or something beautiful, including a god in bhakti usage, and looking until one is satisfied (S. Ravindran). She does not look twice now for her first *and* last time at Desing's face: perhaps a romanticization by Maindron [1909] 1992, 106-7.

dundubhi drum sounds inside Gingee Fort. The heavenly flower-chariot (*puṣpaka vimāṉam*) comes for the king. Both climb into it together. The flower chariot comes to stand inside Gingee Fort. The king and queen attain Vaikuṇṭha. Rāja Desing reaches the feet of Lord Ranga.[114] (199-201)

Srinivasan says nothing of goddesses or the heavenly chariot. His ballad ends with Ranganātha taking over the scene. Knowing alone that Desing has died, the god comes fast (*vēkam*) to Gingee Fort. There he calls, "Rāṇiyammā!" She asks, "What is the reason for your coming, seeking the Queen's Fort (Rāṇikkōṭṭai) on foot?" Ranganātha says, "Has your husband who went to war come back?" She says, "No, Cāmi." He says, "He is waging a valiant battle in Mattiyappēṭṭai. Let us go there and try to stop him." "Let us go," says the Rāṇi. Ranganātha comes to Tēraṇi Singh. "Perhaps your son has returned from war," he says. Tēraṇi joins them. They reach the place where Desing has died. Looking at him, the Rāṇi cries, "Aiyō, lord of my breath (*pirāṇa pati*), are you dead? Has your life left you?" She hugs him cheek to cheek and lets her tears flow. "I was born as the daughter of the Delhi padshah, and you won me in a horse competition (*kutirai pōṭṭi*). You married me and brought me here. What comfort (*cukam*) have I enjoyed having married you? What benefit (*palam*)? Cāmi, have you left me? You who would call me '*Kaṇṇē*' ('[Apple of my] eye'), '*Peṇṇē*' ('Girl')? I have never seen your face. Now at the end I am seeing your face."

The padshah and the nawāb arrive. "You have logs of kuṅkum and sandal" (it is not clear who says this). The Rāṇi prepares a firepit (*akkiṉikuṇṭam*). In it they place Rāja Desing. The Rāṇi combs her hair and adorns herself. So Ranganātha asks her, "Do you want to become satī?"[115] "Yes, Cāmi, that is the explanation (*viyākkiyaṉam*).[116] Let this be a lesson to women like me. Let the world praise me, saying she became satī along with her husband. Give me permission. Leave me."

Ranganātha says, "Before you become satī let me tell you something. Having married your husband, you never saw anything of life, and it was no sin of yours.[117] So in this life you can become satī. In the next I'll

[114]Although Desing is still a bhakta of Ranganātha, Jayaraman provides the couple a Śaivite destination: "They piled kuṃkum and sandalwood logs and both went to Kailāsa." Nārāyaṉan Piḷḷai tells of no heavenly ascent (Krishnaswamy Aiyangar 1930, 21-22).

[115]I adopt the north Indian paraphrase because the Tamil, "Do you want to climb as a log/body with (*utaṉ kaṭṭai eri*)," seems to defy translation. It implies climbing "with the husband," without mentioning him, like Sanskrit *sahagamana*, "going with" (the husband).

[116]A strange choice of a highly Sanskritic word here, which normally means "annotation, commentary." S. Ravindran suggests also "promise" as a possible translation.

[117]Recall that in the printed ballad, Rāniyammāḷ asks at Desing's departure for battle what

make you be born as Yākajōti. I'll be born as Kaṇṇaṉ. I'll make your king to be born as the five Pūtams (Bhūtams) as kings. Then you will enjoy pleasure." "So be it, Cāmi," she says. "Your wish (*cittam*) is my fortune (*pākkiyam*)!" The Rāṇi combs her hair and dresses herself (repeated). She jumps into the firepit (*kutittāḷ akkiṉi kuṇṭattil*). There she dies with her king.

The padshah says, "When are we going to meet such a brave man? What if you had waited today and come tomorrow? We would not have been able to defeat you. We could only defeat you so. Let your name be praised by the world. Let the whole country say that you are a good man. And let the world say in praise that you became satī." Having thus addressed the Rāṇi—his own daughter!—the padshah goes back to Delhi. The nawāb returns to Arcot. Tēraṇi Singh reaches Gingee. Having cremated Desing, Ranganātha Perumāḷ says, "Only when an equally brave person rules over Gingee will I [again] be the talking Ranganātha (*pēcum raṅkanātar*). From today I'll become a stone statue and remain at Singavaram." So saying, Ranganātha goes to Singavaram and becomes a stone statue.

C. Rajput-Afghan Heroism Goes South

Let us then consider this story's south Indian hero cult tenor, its kinship with *Ālhā*, its transplantation south of Afghan-Rajput culture, and its possible ghosts of Nāth folklore and Ismā'īlī-Praṇāmī messianism.

As was noted in chapter 1, one way *Desing* differs from a regional oral martial epic is in its near total indifference to its region's own landed caste traditions. This applies as well to the Gingee region's nayak history. To the extent that a Paṅkāru Nāyuṭu or Paṅkāru Nāyakkar is involved in the story, he is on the side of the nawāb. As Gordon remarks, "the Mughals were utterly unable to 'plant' Rajput families to control populations" in the Deccan (1994, 205), and it seems that if that is what they tried to accomplish with Rāja Desing's father, these Rajputs had the intention neither to accommodate the emperor nor to assimilate with Tamils. Yet *Desing* gives its northern hero some southern checkpoints. The south Indian colorings of the ballad's metaphors and motivations are often distinctive. The following have been noted: the omnipresent call "Kōvintā"; extraordinary means to keep young heroes and their wives apart; virgin heroes primed for virgin battles; paṭukaḷam scenes of death by self-induced impalement; images and vows of "fort destruction" that echo in their phrasing other fort-destruction myths and rituals; and the "notorious" Viṣṇu, also known as Ranganātha, with his withdrawals of

sin might be written on her head (see n. 79 above).

protection.[118] Vividly paralleled in the cults and folklores of *Elder brothers*, *Palnāḍu*, and the Draupadī cult *Mahābhārata*, other than the troubled marriages, these features of *Desing* are unparalleled in *Ālhā*, though some of them do find counterparts—mostly less vivid—in *Pābūjī*.

As to *Ālhā* affinities, in one fundamental strain, *Ālhā* and *Desing* are telling "the same story." A prince from "Bundelkhand" (to use the region's current name)—Chandēl in one case, Bundela in the other—inopportunely weds the daughter of an imperial Delhi ruler. Untenable conditions keep the couple apart; their marriage can never be consummated. Both epics depict a situation where a Delhi ruler would "marry his daughter down" to a "Bundelkhandi" prince: a situation that is historically conceivable, while strained, in *Ālhā*, but inconceivable in *Desing*. Moreover, even though the printed ballad never quite says so, other ballad and related folk sources are clear that as daughter of the Mughal emperor, even if she has a Hindu mother or name,[119] the Rāṇi is a Muslim. Mughal emperors married Rajputs' daughters, but never married their daughters *to* Rajputs.[120] It is further inconceivable that Aurangzīb in particular would overlook the high-pedigree claims of other Rajputs to select a "spurious" Bundela Rajput for his daughter—not to mention a Bundela from Gingee, a tributary to one of his own tributaries.[121] A fractious tributary relation such as that between Delhi and Mahobā is thus transposed by way of Bundela Rajputs into an imagined one between Delhi and Gingee.

Moreover, the padshah's daughter becomes satī, and the Mughals opposed satī.[122] It is thus utterly amazing that in Srinivasan's version, the

[118]See above, nn. 28 ("Kōvintā"); 48 and 49 (extraordinary separations); 105 (patukaḷam impalement scenes); 37 (fort destructions); *passim* (virgin battles, Viṣnu's withdrawals).

[119]See above, n. 46. Srinivasan has her worship Kamalakkaṉṉi, goddess of the Gingee Fort (on whom see Hiltebeitel 1985a, 180-95; 1988a, 61-62, 70, 213-15); but, confirming that she is Muslim, he explained that in taking on Desing's family and personal deities, she makes Kamalakkaṉṉi her family deity (*kulateyvam*), since Kamalakkaṉṉi is the personal divinity (*iṣṭateyvam*) of Rāja Desing's mother! Had Desing worshiped Kamalakaṉṉi rather than Ranganātha, she could have been the story's counterpart to *Ālhā*'s Śāradā. For a different view of Rāṇiyammāḷ in this regard, see Subrahmanyam 1995 and in press.

[120]While in marrying daughters to Akbar, who initiated the practice, some Rajputs and their bards accepted him as a "Muslim Rajput" equivalent to Rāma, others like the Rana of Mewar saw such submission as disgraceful (see Richards 1993, 20-23; Ziegler 1978, 224, 231-35; Chandra 1994, 27-30, 74-75, 82). Cf. Gordon 1994, 190: unlike Rajputs, Marathas did not marry their daughters to leaders they served. Cf. also Khan 1997b, discussing a comparable folklore of a sultan's daughter marrying a Dalit; Beck 1978, 170-75, in which Poṉṉar, in *Elder brothers*, refuses the daughter of the Chola emperor, with disastrous results.

[121]Aurangzīb's later years (1681-1707) were marked by increasing conflicts with the high Rajput clans (Chandra 1994, 95-98).

[122]Akbar in particular (Chandra 1994, 32, 42, 44).

padshah should be present at the end to praise his own daughter's satī. Jayaraman darkens this scene. When Rāṇiyammāḷ (whom he also calls Intirāṇi) determines to become satī, "the padshah and the nawāb arrived, and the padshah said, 'Ammā, I am sorry.[123] I did not do it knowingly.' This woman (*inta ammā*) replied, 'There is no relationship (*panta pācam*) between you and me. If you had any love for me, would you have sent them here? Would you have made such a war if you had wanted your daughter to live?'" The same strains are present even in sources where the padshah remains in Delhi. Nārāyaṇan Piḷḷai tells that the Rāṇi "sent back word that the Nawab was her father"—the suitable surrogate—so that she could ask *his* permission to become satī, which he grants after finding her unshakable and pays the expenses (Srinivasachari 1943, 416). Kiruṣṇacāmippāvalar, rather than having the Rāṇi sever her paternal ties with her final words, has the nawāb fear her satī's power of retaliation. Seeing her about to jump into the firepit, he says, "I did not kill your husband. I am disturbed by the intensity of your *kaṟpu* (chastity). You should not be angry at me. You should continue to rule this town." She refuses to listen and jumps, whereafter, fearing her kaṟpu, he names the town of Rāṇippēṭṭai near Vellore after her (1917, 110-11). All of this is interesting for its bearing on satīs' relation to their fathers, which will be taken up in chapter 14. But what is striking for now are the reminders of *Ālhā*. In each case the satī's father is the Delhi emperor. Prithīrāj opposes Belā's satī; Srinivasan's padshah says nothing until his daughter's satī is finished, and then praises her or uneasily apologizes. Meanwhile, just as Ūdal, concealing an identity of Kṛṣṇa, oversees Belā's satī, the talking Ranganātha oversees the Rāṇi's.

In these two epics, however, the question of paramountcy hinges as much on horses as women. In *Ālhā*, the Banāphars have magical heavenly flying horses, which Prithīrāj demands for himself. In *Desing*, the padshah obtains a magical heavenly flying horse but must find a rider who can take it away. This opposition is suggestive. On one register, the horses would appear to be linked with Hindu symbolisms of sovereignty, in each case a divided sovereignty. In *Ālhā*, the magical horses are the means by which the heroes carry out their campaigns, which the *Kṛṣṇāṃśacarita* clarifies as imperial "conquests of the regions" (digvijayas). Even though the paramount emperor, Prithīrāj, doesn't possess the horses, they define the boundaries of his "India," the space that is his to conquer and rule, but which he cannot rule because he is an incarnation of Duryodhana (or Dhṛtarāṣṭra), and also because the horses belong to the Banāphar heroes. In *Desing*, with the emperor a Muslim, the printed

[123] *Maṉṉiccutu*: according to S. Ravindran, a very formal usage (apologies being awkward in Tamil) reserved for an unpardonable thing, a huge mistake or crime.

ballad suggests the same symbolism. The divine flying horse that loses direction on the slopes of Mount Meru would seem a fine allegory of the Aśvamedha horse under inverted conditions of Muslim rule. The Muslims have seized the lost horse—ungendered, but on appearance seemingly male. Captured by a Muslim Fakir and then held in Delhi, it menaces the court of the padshah, who must find a Hindu prince to free and ride it. It is destined by Viṣṇu to help Desing to "momentarily" recreate Gingee as a Hindu little kingdom, and then, in the same "moment," to obtain mokṣa with Desing and pave his way to heaven—or, more accurately, to pave the way for Desing and Rāṇiyammāḷ, once she, like Belā, has commanded sandalwood logs for her satī. Pārācāri dies a one-legged sacrificial horse, dismembered *alive* by the nawāb's henchmen before Desing literalizes the role of sacrificer by giving the coup de grace.

In Srinivasan's version, however, the typical Rajput relationship between rider and mare overrides such an Aśvamedha symbolism, for which the horse should be a stallion.[124] But even with this and a different frame story, Pārācāri's last ride with Desing restores an Aśvamedha-Rājasūya symbolism at the end. Seeking to find and kill not only the nawāb of Arcot but the Delhi padshah, Desing and Pārācāri undertake a vast "conquest of the regions": from Dhanuṣkoṭi in the south to the east, and then to Delhi in the north before returning (one assumes by a westward route, as with Mōvuttukkāra<u>n</u>'s last ride on Nīlavēṇi) for their last fight with the nawāb on the mud elephant. To "destroy" Delhi is of course to momentarily unseat the padshah. Both Desing and Mōvuttukkāra<u>n</u> make their final "conquests of the regions" in an inauspicious ritually inverse (*apradakṣiṇa*) direction, presumably portending the disasters to come. Their last rides define the "India" that they lose. It is much like the dying Brahmānanda's last pan-India "pilgrimage" ride with Velā in the *Kṛṣṇāṃśacarita*, which marks its four directions with the same southern destination,[125] but without the reverse directional symbolism.

There are also parallels in hero type—with the proviso that Desing, as sole Rajput hero, bears traits in one person that *Ālhā* distributes among several. Desing is like Brahmā in marrying the Delhi princess, and like Ālhā in embodying the kingly ideal. But he is also like Ūdal. As boys, Ūdal and Desing ask their mothers about their fathers' fates, and impetuously resolve, despite their youth, to set matters right. Ūdal is Udayasiṃha, the "risen lion"; Desing is "like a crore of risen suns" and a "youthful lion." Most important, as the Tulukka<u>n</u> fakir announces, Desing "has come to relieve the burden of the earth." Like Ūdal, and also

[124]As "sacrificed," these mares, like Malkhān's Kabutrī (chap. 6, § G), die horrible deaths, about which one could raise some questions.

[125]Setubandha, Dhanuskoti, and Rameshwaram are all sites at one pilgrimage destination.

like Chatrasal Bundela in Gorelal's *Chatra Prakāś*, Desing is a hidden avatar—so hidden that the secret is known only to a Tulukkaṉ Fakir and the Mughal emperor—and to anyone who hears the beginning of his story. As Srinivasan also explained, after finishing: "Ranganātha fixed all this to lessen the burden of the earth. The weight of the world was sinking it." If in the printed ballad the only goddesses Desing (and others) call to witness are the Earth goddess and the goddess of the heavenly voice, this is enough to evoke this same design, since it is the goddess Earth's burden Desing must relieve through his bond with Ranganātha.

As to the transplantation south of Rajput-Afghan culture, the clearest example is Mōvuttukkāraṉ's claim, in Srinivasan's oral version: "It is not an insult for the Rāja kulam to take a step back that you put forward, but it is certainly an insult for the Paṭhān kulam." Here the Rajput-Afghan ethos is recalled formulaically. Mōvuttukkāraṉ exemplifies the Paṭhān-Afghan component of this culture as it takes root in Gingee. It stands in opposition to the imperial Mughal culture of Arcot and Delhi, and indeed, in Srinivasan's telling, to the colonial on its way to imperial culture of the British. As Srinivasan sings it, when Mōvuttukkāraṉ rides to Desing's aid, he asks Nīlavēṇi, "Do you know who's standing guard there?" And in answer to his own question, he describes not only Tōṉṟa Mallaṇṇaṉ, Veṅkaṭarāyaṉ of Arani, the Kalahasti[126] king Paṅkāra Nāyuṭu, and the kings of Chetput, Tiruvannamalai, and Ettūr, but Veḷḷaikkāra Turai of Ceṉṉapaṭṭaṉam: that is, "the white-man sahib from Chennai (Madras)."

The ballad deepens the relationship between Desing and Mōvuttukkāraṉ by extending it from childhood to their reunion in heaven. In Desing's reference to Mōvuttukkāraṉ as a brother (albeit a younger one) there is the familiar egalitarian ring noted in chapter 10. But the bond requires Mōvuttukkāraṉ to accept a subordinate's role to a Hindu little king. Hindu-Muslim relations begin cosmically and in apparent harmony with the Fakir and the Ṛṣis on Mount Meru, center of the universe. But when they are brought down to earth, it is amid increasing conflicts: from Delhi, center of Mughal India, tensions escalate into a bitter rivalry between two "kingdoms," Arcot and Gingee, at the center of early eighteenth-century northern Tamilnadu—or, more precisely, of the portion of the Carnatic-Payanghat ("the region of the Carnatic below the Ghats") that comes, in part as a result of these events, to form the *subah* of Arcot. The Muslim and Hindu associations of Arcot and Gingee are never in doubt when Desing calls the nawāb a Labbai fish-seller, decries his defilement of the Ranganātha temple, and says, "If strength is in my hand, Arcot is mine. If strength is in your hand, Gingee is yours."

[126]Venkatagiri in the printed ballad.

This Muslim-Hindu opposition, however, must be politically and theologically distinguished from the Muslim-Hindu companionship between Desing and Mōvuttukkāraṉ. The opposition with the nawāb (and in Srinivasan's version, also directly with the padshah) is imperial, and is caricatured by politically expedient and even hypocritical evocations of Hindu-Muslim court life on the Mughal frontier: for example, Tōṉṟa Mallaṇṇaṉ's false and impure forehead mark. The nawāb calls only on Allah, and never in combination with a Hindu deity. On the contrary, the companionship with Mōvuttukkāraṉ is an intimate Rajput-Afghan bond that is nonetheless imagined as a total subordination—at least on earth—of the Paṭhān to Desing's little kingdom ideal. As the story's LSRSC, Mōvuttukkāraṉ leaves his wedding asking "but two 'hours'" to "crown the king of Gingee." He fights the "first battle" as a lone hero. In both Srinivasan's version and the printed ballad, he combines Muslim and Hindu names when he calls on God. He is the true way-paver to heaven for those who are to follow: Nīlavēṇi (but only in the printed ballad), Pārācāri, Desing, and the Muslim Rāṇiyammāḷ. On the other hand, like the nawāb who calls only on Allah, Desing calls only on Hindu deities, and dies ascending to Viṣṇu's feet. This religious doubling characteristic of the subordinate, but not of the Hindu little king, replicates the relation of Muttāl Rāvuttaṉ to Draupadī, the goddess as little kingdom queen, and of countless other shrines in the Deccan with a "Hindu centrality and Muslim excentration."[127] One also finds such subordination in Srinivasan's Māyappakkiri, who guards Desing's fort, runs his fateful message, and may have begun the printed ballad among the heavenly Ṛṣis.

Another sign of this culture's transplantation can be found in oaths and curses. When Desing addresses his jama'dārs before crossing the river, he says, "If you are one who eats milk-rice, go back to Gingee; if you are one who eats blood-rice, follow me. If you are one who doesn't waken in the face of womankind, follow me. To win on the battlefield brings fame, to die quickly brings mokṣa." This three-part formula bears analogy to Parmāl's triple curse in *Ālhā*, which, it will be recalled, condemns the Banāphars, if they remain in Mahobā, to have their food be cow's flesh, their water be cow's blood, and their wives in bed be like their mothers—to which the *Kṛṣṇāṃśacarita* adds a fourth: their hall will be like a brahmanicide.[128] In each case, the warrior band is bound together by either acceptance or rejection of a set of transformations that would color food with blood, sex with incest or avoidance, and death with either mokṣa or its impossibility (which would follow from Parmāl's curses that imply cow slaughter and brahmanicide). What better confir-

[127] Assayag 1995, 158; cf. Hiltebeitel 1988a, 122-25; Khan 1997b, 21.

[128] W&G 215; *BhvP* 3.3.24.16-19. See chap. 6, § G.

mation could one ask of Kolff's early Rajput who must "ascetically fight his way home" than Desing's exaltation of waking alone, or Mōvuttukkāran̲'s remark, "For a sepoy who holds a sword, what does he need a woman?"

These triple formulas are only loosely similar. But a document from the southern poligar wars at the turn of the eighteenth to nineteenth century strengthens the similarities. In the flush of recent successes, on June 16, 1801, the insurgent leader Marudu Pandyan, addressing all inhabitants of the peninsula of Jambudvīpa ("Iṇdia"), posted a "proclamation" in two places: one at the gateway of the palace of the nawāb of the Carnatic (no longer at Arcot) in Tiruchirapalli (Trichy); the other on the wall of the great Sriranga temple just outside that city. Rajayyan strains to find "nationalist" and "patriotic" motives in Marudu and the insurgents, who, he admits, "had no definite knowledge of the political developments" outside peninsular India, and who wished to see the nawāb restored to Arcot, the Marathas to Thanjavur, and the Nayaks to Madurai. But he is certainly right to emphasize Trichy and Srirangam as the tactically chosen political and spiritual centers respectively of an imagined solidarity (1971, 234-37). Once Marudu has finished his appeal to the deaf ears of the princes, who had already sided with the British, he turns to the people and the soldiers:

> It is therefore recommended that every man in his place and palayam fly to arms and unite together. . . . Therefore you Brahmans, Kshetriyas, Vysyas, Sudras and Musselmen, all who wear whiskers, whether civil or military, serving in the field or elsewhere, and you subedars, jamedars, havildars, nayaks and sepoys in the service of the low wretches [the British] and all capable of bearing arms, let them in the first place display their bravery as follows:
>
> Wherever you find any of the low wretches destroy them and continue to do so until they are extirpated. Whoever serves the low wretches will never enjoy eternal bliss after death, I know this. Consider and deliberate upon it. And he who does not subscribe to this may his whiskers be like the hair of my secret parts and his food be tasteless and without nourishment and may his wife and children belong to another and be considered as the offspring of the low wretches to whom he had prostituted her. (Rajayyan 1971, 236)

Eager to adjust his hero to "the light of modern concepts of liberalism" (235), Rajayyan is a little embarrassed: "It might appear strange that the rebels at times used unrefined language. But what is to be remembered is that they belonged to the ranks of the common people and that the words they used were in condemnation of the people who remained indifferent to the cause of rebellion or turned traitors" (1971, 236, n. 60). More realistically, Marudu Pandyan adopts an idiom not of the people but of the warband. Trying to rally a most heterogeneous band of fighters, including some on the other side, he summons them by a variant of a Rajput oath. Those whom he curses will have their food be tasteless, their wives be violated, and their deaths be unliberating—to which he adds, their whiskers will be like his pubic hair. In addressing "subedars, jamedars, havildars, nayaks and sepoys," Maradu commands the same idiom as Rāja Desing, but in a form closer to *Ālhā*. Some of the "palayam" (pāḷaiyam) soldiers he seeks to rally could have heard both.

Vivid evidence of some kind of transplantation is also found in parallel stories about confrontations between Bundela heroes on their horses and nawābs on their elephants. Irvine follows his "chronicle" of a year-long battle between Chatrasal Bundela and Muhammad Khan Bangash with a "more romantic" account from the "oral tradition":

> Muhammad Khán, armed to the teeth, was standing up to his full height in the howdah, the sides of which were some three feet high. Suddenly they see bearing down upon them two Bundela horsemen with spears in their hands, and as they come they avoid all encounter. When stopped by any of Muhammad Khán's men, they reply, "We have something to tell your Nawáb." At length they came close to Muhammad Khán's elephant. There they halted, and one of them got out a small bag from his waist-cloth and eat (sic) some tobacco. Then grasping his spear firmly in his hand, he shouted out "Bangash, keep a sharp look out, I am at you." He so impelled his horse, that it placed its two forefeet on the trunk of the Nawáb's elephant; he then made a thrust with his spear. The Nawáb avoided the blow, and shot an arrow at the man with such force, that he fell dead from his horse. The horse was killed by the elephant. The second horseman did as the first, and was killed in the same way. The Nawáb exclaimed to Mangal Khán Musenagari—"How brave must these Bundelas be." (Irvine 1878, 292)

Irvine dates this fighting to 1727 (288-89), thirteen years after Desing's death. It could thus be a folkloric transplant from Gingee back to Bundelkhand, though if this were the case, one would need to explain why it is told about two unnamed heroes, and why other details differ. One might indeed answer this by recalling that in their defense of Gingee, Desing is not the only one who tries this tactic. Mōvuttukkāraṉ successfully challenges Cupaṅki Turai in this way. Perhaps Irvine's source is recalling these two very heroes, each as Rajputs. But it is more likely that both stories reflect a home-grown Bundela-Afghan tradition that epitomizes a distinctive mode of heroism. The horse and rider make their ultimate challenge and face death with defiance against representatives of greater political power—most typically that of the Mughal empire. Yet almost in reverse, Duleel Khan, refusing the advice of his three hundred horsemen, rides straight toward the howdah of Chatrasal and is killed by a "ball in his chest" (286).

Finally, signs of the transplantation of Rajput-Afghan culture are also found in ritual specific to the Gingee area. At Mēlaccēri, there is the current tradition that Rāja Desing worshiped at a mountainside Bhairava temple nearby, where a few Singh/Bundela community members continue to perform their clan ceremonies. In current Bundelkhand folklore, Ālhā and Ūdal also worshiped at a Bhairava temple outside Mahobā, which I visited in December 1995. Bhairava in this aspect of a Singh/Bundela "family deity" is probably another north Indian transplant to the south.[129] Then there is the seeming fusion of Hindu and Muslim ritual that occurs in both the printed and oral ballads. Other than Mōvuttukkāra<u>n</u>'s calling on Allah along with Rāma or Rādhā at his wedding, there is nothing typically Islamic about it.[130] Nor, of course, is there anything Islamic about Rāṇiyammāḷ's satī. Yet *kōri*, from Urdu,[131] is both Desing's and the nawāb's term for the tombs they order for Mōvuttukkāra<u>n</u> and the two marvelous horses. These monuments can still be found at a battlefield site called Nīlāmpuṇṭi, near the hamlet of Kadali, about four miles north of Gingee on the Arani road. On the east side of a shaded tank is a Muslim tomb shrine (dargāh) for Mōvuttukkāra<u>n</u> and a tiered brick monument, eroding, for Nīlavēṇi (see plates 10 and 11). People, especially girls and young women, come to Mōvuttukkāra<u>n</u> on Fridays for immediate rewards (*kai mēlē palam*, literally "rewards or fruits on the hand"). Across the tank on the west side is a similar brick monument for Pārācāri, surrounded by what seems a miscellany of offering stones. And on a turn of the road in the nearby village, there is a neglected stone-sided earth-topped rectangular platform to mark the spot where Rāja Desing died. Until 1983, the platform was the base for a maṇḍapa housing Desing's sword, but when the maṇḍapa fell down that year, it was never rebuilt and the sword was stolen. "On Fridays, one can hear screams. One wouldn't walk here on Fridays."[132] Everything continues

[129]On Bhairava's association with the north, see also chap. 10, n. 204.

[130]Except secondarily in Jayaraman's version; see above, n. 66.

[131]From *gōr*, "Muhammadan tomb, mausoleum" (*Tamil Lexicon* 2, 1193).

[132]According to Noor, a local resident interviewed in January 1997. But cf. n. 102 above: Krishnan calls the area Pātiyappēttai, the tombs "samādhis," and says the village is named both Kadali and Nīlāmpunti. Cēsāttiri calls the tank the Moṭṭai Cetti Kulam (the Bald or Shaved-headed Chettiyar Tank), the dargāh a samādhi, and says Desing's platform (*mēṭai*) was "destroyed" (*a<u>l</u>inta*) (1994, 199 and plates following 136).

to turn on that memorable Friday which ends the life of both heroes and their horses, yet leaves the dashing Paṭhān who left his wedding pantal able to fulfill from the grave the immediate wishes of girls and young women. As to the Rāṇi, other traditions indicate that she became satī where Desing was cremated, below the Gingee Fort (see plate 12).[133]

And so we come to the ghosts. And fair to say, some will doubt them. First, if we recall our Nāth folklore, the "hamlet of Kadali" leaves a haunting echo. Krishnan, pointing at Kadali Hill from the Nīlāmpuṇṭi tank, says that is where, "hiding behind a rock, they struck at the horse's legs" (see n. 102). And Nārāyaṇan̲ Piḷḷai says that "Kadalimalai" is where Desing fell from being shot with a gun (see n. 106). There, the nawāb allowed his Bundela followers to "raise a new town" where they "built at the spot a temple to Desing," the monuments to Mōvuttukkāran̲ and Pārācāri, and also ones for "the other Muhammadans who fell" (Srinivasachari 1943, 416-17, 428). Nārāyaṇan̲ Piḷḷai's Kadalimalai is definitely *Kaṭali*malai (Dikshitar 1952, 52), as it is also Kaṭali in Cēṣāttiri's account (1994, 199) and in an alphabetical list of Tamilnadu villages (Kirāmankalin̲ 1972, 33). *Kaṭali* is the Indian bloodwood tree (*Lagerstroemia flos-reginae*), also known as *pūmarutu*. But local people know nothing of this tree, and two (Krishnan, Habibur Rahman) claim that Kaṭalimalai was originally *Kaḷari*malai, the "Battlefield Mountain": the place where the heroes met their end.[134] The name of the village thus derives from that of the mountain. In these circumstances, I venture an alternate etymology, despite the problems it raises. What if it were not originally *kaṭali* or *kaḷari* but *katali*, the plantain tree?[135] Katalimalai

[133] A flower garden was raised at the Chettikulam where Desing was cremated and a pipal and margosa (the conventional "marriage trees") were planted there (Srinivasachari 1943, 417). As plate 12 shows, no trees are beside this satī platform today.

[134] On kalari (in Kerala's martial arts, "military training ground") as semantically akin to kalam, patukalam, and kalappali, see Hiltebeitel 1988a, 321; 1991a, 170-71, 318; cf. nn. 105 and 118 above.

[135] Dental and retroflex "t's" are usually clearly differentiated in Tamil, and consistent in their equivalence to the corresponding "t/d" Sanskrit dentals and retroflexes. Yet as Indira Peterson suggests (personal communication, March 1997), a correspondence between Sanskrit *kadali* and Tamil *katali* is plausible on the analogy of Sanskrit *kadamba*/Tamil *kaṭampam, kaṭampu*: the cadamba tree which yields the *kaṭampa-van̲am*, the "ancient forest of *kaṭampu* trees" on which the city of "Madura, according to legends, was built" (*Tamil Lexicon* 2, 659). David Shulman cautions (personal communication, January 1997), however, that the latter is one tree rather than two, and it is likely that Sanskrit *kadamba* is of Dravidian derivation (see Turner 1966, 136). But Turner (ibid.) indicates that Sanskrit *kadalī*, "plantain," has an alternate *kaḍalī* of Austroasiatic derivation; and further uncertainty arises as to the Indo-Aryan form that might have been used—we have noted *kajalī* and *kanjarī* (see chap. 9 at n. 73); Turner cites also Marathi *karar[ī]*, "banana," which indeed brings us close to Tamil *kaḷari*. Cf. chap. 13, n. 84, for the usage *vedi* instead of *vedi*. In any case, such shifts are "not uncommon in colloquial Tamil" (S. Ravindran).

would then be the Plantain Mountain. The name Katalimalai for a new village of the heroic and immortal dead would be another fitting transposition of Rajput oral epic folklore, and a tribute to the Rajput-Afghan culture it celebrated, with not only a temple for Desing and a monument for his Paṭhān comrade, but memorials for the "other Muhammadans" who were their followers.[136] According to both Krishnan and the wife of Saiyad Bakar Sahib who live in "Kadali" today, there are tunnels from somewhere near the Nīlāmpuṇṭi tank: one to Gingee fort and one to Arcot. The Gingee folklore that links Rāja Desing with subterranean caves and an ever-renewable gold-producing tree thus has another extension. Could it also have another complement, and possibly its earliest inspiration, in the naming of the hill and village of Desing's death after the mountain forest of the Nāth immortals? This would put closure to his ballad with a folklore like that of other oral epics that equate caves and mountains with the otherworldly destinies of their heroes.[137]

As to Ismā'īlī ghosts, we have caught only glimpses, but I believe they are impressive. To begin with the Muslim figures, what is a Fakir doing with the heavenly Ṛṣis on Mount Meru? At the base of the Satpanth's system of correspondences for Ismā'īlī missions in India is the equation between *mu'min*, the general Arabic term for "pious believer," and *ṛṣi*, with the latter, under the form *rīkhīsar*, used to designate the Satpanth faithful.[138] Rather than being a term limited mainly to Brahmans, as it is in Sanskrit literatures, "Ṛṣi" was "applied to all the followers of the Nizari Ismaili sect, regardless of their rank and caste" (Khan 1997b, 135). Among followers of Rāmdeo, Meghwāl Dalits in particular consider themselves "the direct descendants of one Megh Rishi" (130), and Satgur Nur (also called Nur Muhammad), the first "archetypal" Pīr sent to the subcontinent from Alamūt, is also called Matang Ṛṣi, with the story that

[136]Cf. the Kabristan as cult center for Rāmdeo (chap. 10, § C). Kadali hamlet seems to have a mixed Hindu and Muslim population today with the latter, some say, having declined.

[137]See chap. 9, nn. 73 and 74, and above, nn. 13 and 14, and recall the frame-setting of *Desing* on Mount Meru. Mount Gandhamadana, site of the Plantain Forest in the *Kṛṣṇāṃśa-carita*, known also simply as "Himālaya" in the *Mbh* (3.157.1-10), is a vantage point from which the Pāṇḍavas can see the cosmological mountains Mandara and Meru (160.1-37) and be "within range" of the "great peak Himavat" from which they march with Draupadī toward Mount Meru on their ascent to heaven (17.2.1-2; see Hiltebeitel forthcoming). The "Plantain Forest" is already the alchemical paradise (with a "philosopher's stone") of the twelfth-century Telugu Lingāyat *vacana* poetess Mahādevīyakka (Ramanujan 1973, 133), and before that, the haunt of Hanumān, whom a song attributed to Tulsidas later recognizes as a model Rajput (see chaps. 9, following n. 74, and 10, n. 34). The Kajali Forest also figures along with Gorakhnāth in the *Guga* epic, whose Chauhān Rajput hero also rides a flying blue horse and encounters Prithīrāj Chauhān, who establishes the worship of Guga's flag (Lapoint 1978).

[138]Khan 1997b, 47; see chap. 10 at n. 176.

he came as a parrot; or alternately, in a Meghwāl story, Matang Ṛṣi was Satgur Nur's disciple, who preached to the Meghwāls, was an avatar of Śiva, Viṣṇu, and 'Alī, and "an incarnation of Kalki renamed *Nikalank avatār*" (100). Matanga Ṛṣi figures in the Sanskrit *Rāmāyaṇa*, subtly but implicitly, as the prototypical Dalit-Ṛṣi. Polluted by drops of buffalo blood, he and his necessarily Dalit-Ṛṣi disciples have left the earth so that Rāma can enter their ashram without suffering pollution from their contact, and have taken their place among the stars.[139] In contrast, Rāmdeo, who as Nikalank avatar came to earth to preach to Dalits, "is called *ṛṣi ro rāj*, the king of *ṛṣis*" (148).

Likewise, the Fakir descends from the realm of heavenly Ṛṣis around Mount Meru to earth, bringing the heavenly horse that has lost its way to his friend the Delhi padshah. His counterpart and perhaps extension in Srinivasan's oral version is Māyappakkiri, the "Illusionist Fakir" as first guardian of Gingee Fort: a marvelous figure who combines Muslim (leather cap) and Hindu (nāmam) traits into a Fakir-Bairāgī disguise.[140] Carrying from fort to fort the message that will unpack Srinivasan's version of the story's secrets, he uses this disguise toward martial ends, claiming the inviolability of the beggar to gain passage through an army. Māyappakkiri probably personifies an image of the Pūvitaiyars, the narrator Srinivasan's jāti, as beggars and raconteurs worked into their version of the story. As such, Pūvitaiyars like Srinivasan would also be Māyappakkiri's extension. And if Māyappakkiri is further an allomorph of the Fakir who starts out with the celestial Ṛṣis, the Pūvitaiyars may be said to carry forward his interreligious minstrel-ascetic tradition. In any case, in the printed ballad it is again the Fakir who holds the story's messianic secret, telling the padshah, "A child born from a divine boon, having come, can ride it. He who has come to relieve the burden of the earth can ride the horse." It can hardly be insignificant that the deepest secrets of *Desing* always travel with a vagabond Fakir who either dwells with the Ṛṣis or can pass as a Bairāgī. Similarly, Pīr Shams "witnessed many wonders that were endless in number" on Mount Meru—in his cosmic roaming, which also brought him and his secrets to Sind.[141]

Looking from Māyappakkiri to Mōvuttukkāraṉ, certain other things become intriguing. As has been noted, whereas the nawāb and Rāja Desing are religiously "communal," calling only on divine names used

[139]*Rām* 3.69-71; 4.11. This argument, which I plan to develop further, can be found preliminarily in Hiltebeitel 1980c, 201-11. Possibly Satgur Nur's story also borrows from Bāṇabhaṭṭa's *Kādambarī*, in which another Matanga's story is told by a narrator-parrot.
[140]A combination noted in chap. 10, § D. Cf. Assayag 1995, 147-52 for other southern examples.
[141]See chap. 10, n. 190.

normatively by Muslims and Hindus, these two speak the same Hindu-Muslim argot in their invocations. Mōvuttukkāraṉ is the most frequent voice of religious doubling. In the printed ballad he falls shouting, "Allah Allah, Hari Kōvintā," and attains Vaikuṇṭha; in Srinivasan's telling, he goes without a cry to Paraloka, which according to S. Ravindran is a name Tamil Christians use when reciting, "Our father who art in Paraloka." But most interesting is his wedding. The printed ballad has him say, "Allah Allah" and "Rāma Rāma" when about to tie the tāli;[142] in Srinivasan's song, he chants "Allah Rādhā" at this moment. Similarly, when Srinivasan's Māyappakkiri puts on a blood-smeared Vaiṣṇava forehead mark and leaves Gingee with Desing's message, a Fakir in the guise of a Bairāgī, he shouts, "Allah Rādhā" and "Nagore Allah." Māyappakkiri carries the message from Desing that brings Mōvuttukkāraṉ to leave his wedding not only unconsummated but incomplete.

Taken as a whole, the Hindu deities called on with Allah sound north Indian—especially Rādhā,[143] who is little known in the south. But why call "Allah Allah, Hari Kōvintā" at death and "Allah Allah, Rāma Rāma" or "Allah Rādhā" at a wedding? The naming of Allah with Hari Kōvintā probably connects with other instances where Viṣṇu-Kṛṣṇa is called on in salvific situations. As to "Allah Rāma" and "Allah Rādhā," it is the latter pairing, found only in Srinivasan's version, that should alert us. Indeed, the printed version may normalize and masculinize by "correcting" "Rādhā" to "Rāma" to leave Allah in a less compromising situation. "Allah Rādhā." Either this is doggerel or something profound. Habibur Rahman suggested that the invocation may play on the phrase *radhiya Allahu 'anha*, "May Allah's contentment be upon her (or him)," an honorific used after an especially saintly person's name.[144] But for Srinivasan, it is clearly "Rādhā Allah," which, as Habibur Rahman mused, is no problem, since if Allah has a hundred names he can have a thousand. In any case, *Desing* is a text that resembles the Satpanth ginān̄s and the *Āgam vāṇīs* of forgotten Ismā'īlī sects, and is also similar to *Ālhā*, in having distinct yet interpenetrating Hindu and Muslim planes of allusion. Here, Rādhā is coupled not with Kṛṣṇa but with Allah. Before Mōvuttuk-

[142]In Karunāṉantacuvāmi's edition, which has some differences in this scene, Mōvuttukkāraṉ says, "Allah Allah," "Rāma Rāma," and "Kōvintā Kōvintā" as he prepares to tie the tāli, at which point Desing's messengers come shouting "Rāmu Rāmurē Rāmu Rāmurē Mōvuttukkaraṉē" ("Rām Rām," the north Indian greeting) as they bring the letter that stops him before tying it (1875, 49).

[143]See W&G 192 and chap. 9, § C: in an invocation Rādhā is one of the seven virgins who pray at Nimsar-Misrik (Naimiṣa Forest) and obtain husbands, in her case Kṛṣṇa—even though she is not ordinarily a virgin when she unites with Kṛṣṇa, or ordinarily his wife.

[144]Conversation centered on Abu Sail 1998, 17, about the women of paradise, which uses the phrase five times. Thanks to Seyyed Hosein Nasr for translation and comment.

kāraṉ invites Desing to his "wedding in Arcot," becomes a "bridegroom of battle," and satisfies, after death, the wishes of young women and girls, he first approaches his wedding, to the tune of a Cuvāmiyar reciting the Vedas, with the words "Allah Rādhā" on his lips. In connection with this uncompleted wedding, this call would seem not only a reminder of a fractured Hindu-Muslim bond but a sign of messianic consummation. Mōvuttukkāraṉ's wedding is a secret from Desing: "You have found out what I didn't want you to know." Whatever Mōvuttukkāraṉ's reason for not telling Desing about his nuptials, it is as if Srinivasan's story now brings Desing into a mystery that the battle to come will make a messianic secret for both of them. It would seem that the Ismā'īlī gināns hold the key to this secret. As we have seen in chapter 10, Pīr Shams's gināns hold forth the image of the messianic wedding as one between Bībī Fātimah and Śyāma-Kṛṣṇa, who is also 'Alī. Although I know of no precedent for "Allah Rādhā," it would seem that it too evokes such an interreligious messianic wedding, but with the genders reversed—probably in keeping with the story, in which Mōvuttukkāraṉ is a Muslim groom.[145] In the gināns, the Pīrs describe themselves in the image of the messianic bride: "Throughout the ages I have waited in hope, but You have not wed me. Now I am in the prime of my youth, so preserve my honour, o Lord of the three worlds."[146] But they can also, though it seems more rarely,[147] focus on the messianic groom, as in a ginān of Pīr Shams: "Thousands of husbands sleep easy, but this groom is still a child" (Kassam 1995, 211). When Pīr Shams ties the kāṅkana "bracelet" on the wrists of devotees at the ghaṭpāṭ ceremony, which, as we have seen, is celebrated at the messianic wedding, it is with the promise that they will attain Vaikuṇṭha.[148] Before death in battle takes Mōvuttukkāraṉ to Vaikuṇṭha, the young groom mystifies Desing when he comes before him still wearing a turmeric-coated kaṅkaṇam on his wrist, a forehead band, and a sacred thread. All this happens on a Friday, the day and night for ghaṭpāṭ (Kassam 1995, 305, 369).

---

[145]According to Khan (1997b, 50), "in the theatre of Hindu mythology revised by the Nizari Pirs . . . Fatima was naturally identified with the great goddess (Śakti)."

[146]Shackle and Moir 1992, 97, in a ginān that sustains this theme; 169, commenting that the community is also sometimes portrayed "as an eager bride." Cf. chap. 10, n. 174.

[147]Shackle and Moir 1992, 169, say, "the Imam is quite often described in the gināns as a bridegroom," but the expectant focus in these cases is usually on the bride.

[148]See Kassam 1995, 297, with a note on kāṅkana, clearly the same term (from Sanskrit kaṅkana, "bracelet") as is used in Desing, as a bangle or bracelet that, like thread-tying, forms a bond between guru and disciple. Glass bracelets seem to have the same role in the cult of Ghāzī Miyān (Gaborieau 1975, 289, 292). Cf. n. 71 above. Throughout the gināns attributed to Pīr Shams, and also in the "big" Dasa avatāra, the Vaisnava Vaikuntha is the main Hindu term for paradise. Cf. Khan 1997b, 134.

Yet the ballad is not Mōvuttukkāraṉ's story. It only carries his story as a kind of double for Desing's story. And Mōvuttukkāraṉ's story carries no story, at least as we receive it, of his unfulfilled bride. She is not Meghṛī Rāṇī waiting for the apocalypse. Indeed, it is not even indicated whether she waits at the wedding pantal in Vaḻutāvūr to greet the unique pearl palanquin that brings back his body, which Desing sends with Nīlavēṇi—again, only in Srinivasan's version.[149] The riderless horse is of course primarily a Muslim image, familiar from Muhammad's white mare Duldul, who becomes the messianic mount of 'Alī.[150] It is also, along with footprints and the empty throne, another symbol of the Nikalank avatar (Khan 1997b, 128, 151, n. 2). Desing calls out, "Nīla-vēṇi mother, where is your king on you? Where is my dear friend Mōvuttukkāraṉ?" Active on her own, the black mare, fighting her way back to Desing, chews off and vomits the head of Mallaṉṉaṉ, Mōvuttukāraṉ's slayer (Srinivasan's version). Yet Desing's story also carries the story of the other horse: the celestial horse he alone can ride in Delhi. It is he who gets to ride the white horse, and in Srinivasan's version, the white mare that is like Duldul. If Desing dies fulfilling his promise to his horse,[151] it is perhaps because she is no ordinary horse. The story begins with two riderless horses, and when the avatar Desing rides the white one to lift the burden of the earth, it is he who looks like the Nikalank avatar—and like Muhammad and 'Alī. Indeed, it will not be too much to suggest that Desing is the "true emperor."[152] The padshah involuntarily rises to salute him, a five-year-old, when he enters the Delhi court to ride Pārācāri. Desing matches Pārācāri in being lion-like and like a rising sun. In *Desing*, and perhaps also in *Ālhā* where Ūdal is the Risen Lion, such descriptions are antiphonal to the Mughal imperial insignia: "the emblem of the lion and the rising sun (*sher-a-khurshed*)" (Beach,

[149]Cf. n. 96 above. Yet recall n. 66: Jayaraman has her receive a tāli after Mōvuttukkāraṉ has left.

[150]See chap. 10, § C (end); nn. 125 and 141 above; and Humayuni 1979, 13: The ta'ziyeh on the doomed marriage of Ḥasan's son Qasem and Ḥusayn's daughter Fatemeh begins when Fatemeh, at the 'Alid camp at Karbalā, sees the return of the riderless horse of her youthful brother Ali Akbar, and "lets out a wail that reaches the heavens." She refuses Ḥusayn's instruction to mount her martyred brother's horse for her wedding, and Ḥusayn supplies his own horse, which will be riderless the same day when it carries Qasem into battle (22)—and I assume again at Ḥusayn's martyrdom. In the Nepali story in which Ḥasan and Ḥusayn die the death of Ghāzī Miyān at Bahraich, their (single) horse returns from battle to tell that they have gone to heaven, whereupon Bībī Fāṭimah weeps along with the birds of the forest and the fish in the lakes (Gaborieau 1975, 293-94); see chap. 10, § C.

[151]See at n. 111 above.

[152]Cf. chap. 10, § D on Rāmdeo as the "true emperor" (*sacchā badshāh*). Note how Srinivasan's version repeatedly brings out Desing's contestation as one that ultimately opposes him to the padshah, not just the nawāb.

Koch, and Thackston 1997, 194). Desing rides Pārācāri to "destroy" Delhi before he ends his last battle; so too, according to Shams Pīr, the Shāh's messianic conquest will include his capture of Delhi Fort.[153] It is as if the ballad's double register fills out Desing's and the Rāṇi's story where it leaves Mōvuttukkāraṉ's and his fiancée's story incomplete—though that incompletion looks rich in deferred meaning.

Back on the ground at Gingee, certain icons leave a similar and perhaps related uncertainty: one that is compounded by the fact that they were differently identified in 1984 and 1998. Plate 13 shows these images from a photo I took in 1984, long before I had any thoughts about Ismā'īlīs. I reached the site of these stones while following the icons of the three goddesses worshiped at the Gingee Fort buffalo sacrifice: Kamalakkaṉṉi and Kāḷīyammaṉ, who jointly receive one buffalo near the granary outside the fort; and Māriyammaṉ, given a second one at a crossroads near a dargāh.[154] After the sacrifices, Kāḷi and Māriyammaṉ's karakam pots and Kamalakkaṉṉi's silver trident are brought to a grazing ground or *mantaiveḷi* to romp and "kiss" and enjoy reuniting for the first time since the last festival. There, beside their waiting processional chariot (tēr), I noticed the two stones, and then described them as follows:

> The chariot itself is set beside two well carved slabs of a general hero stone type, which stand upright on a concrete platform facing eastward toward a Nandi which lies at their feet. . . . Both slabs show "heroes" bearing long pole-like weapons,[155] which could be identified as swords or lances. But attendants of the chariot identified the weapon as a *cukkumāntaṭi*, and further identified the "hero" on each stone as Mahāviṣṇu in his Kalki *avatāra*. (Hiltebeitel 1985a, 187)

Preoccupied at the time with the name of the weapon, and dubious about the identification of the "hero" as Kalki (185-87), I failed to ask what are now some intriguing questions. But fourteen years later, no one could be found who knew much about these icons except Jayaraman, the Māriyammaṉ temple pūcāri, and he had an entirely different identification: "The

[153]See chap. 10, n. 121.

[154]Or so I was told in 1984. In 1998, Jayaraman, the current Māriyammaṉ temple pūcārī, said the second buffalo sacrificed at the dargāh is offered to appease the "Muslim spirits" (*tulukka teyvatai*), and that it is the bigger of the two. In 1984, when celebrants reached the dargāh, some got possessed. But when the buffalo was sacrificed, people were steered away from the dargāh to avoid bringing bloodshed to it. According to Ansar Shariff, in 1984 it was three generations old and visited by both Hindus and Muslims.

[155]More correctly, this applies only to the figure on the left. On the right stone, the weapon must be a curved sword. But both were identified as *cukkumāntati*s.

statues are of the "little kings" (*ci<u>rr</u>a rācan*) Dhana Singh (Ta<u>n</u>ciṅku) and Tēraṇi Singh, Desing's father and uncle. In about 1908 they were moved from inside the fort, where you can still see a similar one. They are the fathers (*takappa<u>n</u>*) of this city, so we worship them along with Kamalakka<u>nn</u>i. In those days they were on the edge of town. They served as a kind of guardian deity (*kāval teyvam*) for the whole city."[156] It is surprising that the father and uncle should be guardians rather than Desing himself. Perhaps Jayaraman is caught with a need to explain each stone separately. The similar one he mentions that is still inside the fort (in the fort museum) has the same outline of a rampant horse with two riders. Cēṣāttiri captions it "Rāja Desing on horse with Rāṇipai."[157]

In any case, the Kalki identification and the questions it raises cannot be dismissed. What is Kalki doing with a second figure? Who is it? What gender? On the left slab, whose total design is otherwise close to "Rāja Desing on horse with Rāṇipai," the figure behind "Kalki" (or "Dhana Singh") does not seem to be actually riding; rather, he (as it would appear) or she extends a disproportionately long arm to hold aloft a circular object (a shield?) above the weapon. On the right, however, the co-rider appears to be a woman. She has long hair, and a female attendant stands behind her holding what is probably an umbrella over her head. In conventional icons, Kalki does not ride with a companion, or, more particularly, with a woman.[158] The "Desing" in the fort could be its prototype, since he clearly rides with a woman (with breasts and stripes on the cloth covering her single visible leg). Yet Desing and Rāṇiyammāḷ never met in real life. If this stone depicts them, it must be a satī stone depicting a version of their heavenly ascent with Pārācāri. As to Dhana and Tēraṇi Singh, there is also no reason—even from Jayaraman—to think that either would have a female co-rider. In fact, none of the explanations is iconographically persuasive. We would seem to have a varied folk tradition that draws from the area's mix of Hindu and Muslim sources, so evident at the Gingee buffalo sacrifice itself.[159] But insofar as Kalki has been part of this mix, a residue of local Bundela-Praṇāmī

[156]Jayaraman gives not only a date but motivation: "In big temples at full moon the god rides a horse vāhana. So people saw this Tērani Singh riding on a horse and connected it with the full moon day that comes on the eighth day of the festival to Kamalakka<u>nn</u>i, when the tēr comes there" to the mantaiveli. The Nandi was also moved there from the fort for the pūjā that occurs when cattle are honored at the mantaiveli during Māṭṭu ("Bull") Poṅkal.

[157]*Rāṇipāyuta<u>n</u> kutiraiyi<u>n</u> mītu tēciṅkurāja<u>n</u>* (Cēsāttiri 1994, last plate before p. 169). Rāṇipaī is Rāṇiyammāl (see above after n. 45). Cēsāttiri offers no discussion. "Desing" carries a straight lance-like weapon, as on the left slab in plate 13, but holds it in the middle.

[158]See Gopinatha Rao 1971,1:223: in purānic prescriptions, Kalki should have four arms and ride a horse, and "may also be made to carry" a sword, arrow, cakra, and conch.

[159]See n. 153 above and Hiltebeitel 1988a, 57 and n. 10.

folklore would seem the best candidate to provide the male rider with a messianic bride—who could also be the satī Rāṇipai's avataric double.

In ballad versions of *Desing*, however, the Rāṇi's story has other consummations. In the printed ballad, she simply ascends with Desing to Vaikuṇṭha in the flower chariot after her satī. More interesting in Srinivasan's telling is what Ranganātha discloses in his last words to her as she is about to become satī. Ranganātha has a precedent in allotting himself a future life as Kaṇṇaṉ to join company with the reincarnated Rāṇi and Rāja Desing. Kaṇṇaṉ is of course the Tamil name of Kṛṣṇa. And as Srinivasan soon confirmed, once he had finished his narrative, Yākajōti, the Rāṇi's next-life identity, is Draupadī. And the five Pūtams—whom Rāja Desing will divide into—are the Pāṇḍavas. Here things get literally spectral, since Pūtam ordinarily means "ghost."[160] Indeed, Ranganātha gives a new life not only to Desing, but new lives to the Pāṇḍavas. For Desing, this abundantly overrides his claim, in the sung version, to have only one birth. S. Ravindran and I asked, How can this be if the *Mahābhārata* comes in time before the story of Rāja Desing? "The yugas repeat (*maṟupaṭi*)," said Srinivasan, who looked like he had answered this question before. Do other characters from the ballad reincarnate in the next *Mahābhārata*? "The nawāb will become Duryodhana," Srinivasan replied. "Mōvuttukkāraṉ?" I asked. No, Mōvuttukkāraṉ has no future.[161] But as we have seen, returns of the Pāṇḍavas and Draupadī along with Muslim heroes *are* sung of in the ginān̄s and *Āgam vāṇīs*. Desing and the Bundelas and Afghans of Gingee could have been familiar with such traditions, as could those who stayed on to tell their story.

Yākajōti, "Light of the sacrifice," is not a name for Draupadī I have met elsewhere. Although the emphasis on light might have bireligious possibilities, it probably recalls Draupadī's Tamil name Yākaceṉi, "She whose army is the sacrifice" (Hiltebeitel 1988a, 194, 338, 392) and her birth from (and other associations with) fire. We have already had

[160] The Pāṇḍavas are also identified with the five pūtams/bhūtams as "elements" in the *Mbh* (5.63.2; 12.38.37; 12.53.18). Cf. Hiltebeitel 1991a, 341-2 and 364-65, on varying usages, including five Bhūtams in Draupadī cult ritual as five bodies dying on the paṭukaḷam. Presumably the Pāṇḍavas are now "ghosts" between lives.

[161] Jayaraman turns to *Rāmāyaṇa* here: Mōvuttukkāraṉ's last thoughts are that he should die seeing Desing as the vulture Jaṭāyus died seeing Rāma. The new life/lives differ from the mokṣa that Ranganātha promises Desing in the printed ballad. Cf. de Bruin 1994, 242: in her translated version of the play *Karṇa mōṭcam*, Kṛṣṇa promises Karṇa a future birth, signaling that mokṣa can denote "liberation from the demonic aspects of [one's] character." Karṇa's is next born as Ciṟuttoṇṭar Nāyaṉar (de Bruin 1994, *Supplement*, 313). But this may be only a regional folkloric connection with this ever-popular butchered saint (though I have now heard it in Dharmapuri District [August 1998]). In *Palnādu*, Bāluḍu is Ciṟuttoṇṭar-Siriyāla reborn (Roghair 1982, 297; see chap. 10 at n. 204).

intimations of Draupadī in Srinivasan's narrative when the Rāṇi plays dice. As when Belā's "truth" is staked, and when Belā plays dice with Ālhā in the desolation of Mahobā, the allusions to Draupadī are vivid and unmistakable. Moreover, in the Rāṇi's case there is the sense that the allusion contains a hint of a relation between dicing and menstruation—a point to consider in chapter 14. For now, the Rāṇi learns that as a future Draupadī, she will have the pleasures she missed with Desing, and they will be multiplied, one takes it, fivefold. This too is a recycled theme, which goes back to the *Mahābhārata* story that Draupadī was an overanxious maiden in her previous life who got five husbands because she asked Śiva for a husband five times—a story enhanced in the southern recension of the *Mahābhārata*, and further in Draupadī cult folklore, which transforms the overanxious maiden into the oversexed Nāḷāyaṇi, who, after her husband Maudgalya ceases to satisfy her with his form of five lights, asks Śiva for five husbands to replace them.[162] In all these cases, including the Rāṇi's, there is the hint that to become Draupadī with the "fortune" of having five husbands involves some sexual overcompensation.[163] Ranganātha says the Rāṇi's deprivation in this life is through "no sin of her own." The sexual nonfulfillment in her marriage with Desing is accounted for by her "low" Muslim birth as the padshah's daughter, which is at least not a sin in and of itself.

Here, however, the Rāṇi's full story doubles with the incomplete story of Mōvuttukkāraṉ's fiancée. Both are Muslim women, and "lowly" by Srinivasan's telling. But only the Rāṇi will have her marriage consummated, and that by becoming satī like a Rajput wife and awaiting her fulfillment within the cyclic rounds of Hindu time. In leaving *both* Mōvuttukkāraṉ and his bride without futures, *Desing* may thus hinduize a messianic vision that remains only latent in their portrayal.

According to Srinivasan, there is no connection between Draupadī worship at Mēlaccēri (which he knows of), or elsewhere, and the story of Desing: "If the Rāṇi had not become satī, there would be no connection at all."[164] If this is so, Srinivasan's *Mahābhārata* sources must lie elsewhere. I have suggested that they lie in an "underground" oral *Mahābhārata* carrying traditions of Rajput-Afghan culture passed on from

[162]Perhaps her name "Light of the sacrifice" also evokes this story. See Hiltebeitel 1991a, 484-85; de Bruin 1994, 238, on the Tamil folklore; Scheuer 1982, 99-105, and Hiltebeitel forthcoming on the southern recension variant.

[163]This turn of the Rāṇi's *pākkiyam* (Sanskrit *bhāgyam*) reminds one of Draupadī's own "impoverished fortune" or "share" (*mandabhāgyam*), which describes her when she has lost her sons, father, and brothers (*Mbh* 10.10.26), and which she inherits from the weeping Śrī, whom Draupadī incarnates, in the myth of the former Indras (1.189.13). On the question of whether the Rāṇi has sinned, see above nn. 79 and 117.

[164]As we have seen, connections between Desing and Draupadī worship are unimpressive.

Bundelkhand with Praṇāmī-Ismā'īlī colorations. I would also insist that it is the Praṇāmī connection that is most decisive for this hypothesis, and for the primary process not only of *Desing*'s oral but its primary printed versions as well. Yet once we detach Srinivasan's coda from the Draupadī cult, we see that while the latter also draws on folk *Mahābhārata* traditions, there is much less in its "underground" that one might trace to the ginān̄s. Similarly, while *Alhā*'s folk *Mahābhārata* seems to echo frequently with that of the ginān̄s, the other oral martial epics discussed have less immediate echoes. Only *Desing*, the last to develop, gives a glimpse of certain *Ālhā*-like elements as they recrystallized in being transported one more time. *Desing* tells of unconsummated marriage on a double plane, both Hindu and Muslim. Only here is a Muslim hero the subject of such a story, yet with the difference that unlike the Hindu grooms, he doesn't actually tie the tāli. His incomplete marriage is forever pending, like that of his northern counterpart Ghāzī Miyān. Indeed, aside from Ghāzī Miyān's being the primary rather than a secondary figure in his story, he might be Mōvuttukkāra̱ṉ's prototype. On the contrary, Desing and Rāṇiyammāḷ, Brahmā and Belā, Pābūjī and Phulvantī, Bāluḍu and Māncāla, the elder brothers and their wives, and the folkloric virginal Draupadī and the Pāṇḍavas are central and, as such, Hindu little royalty who are fully married, but in marriages that remain unconsummated while they are alive.

Yet their lives also differ from those in the Sanskrit epics that frame them. Taken as a package, it looks as if they too have been affected by the combination of influences just mentioned. The Sanskrit epics do not dwell on Dalit heroes, unconsummated marriages,[165] virginal wives, palaces for their detainment, flying horses, bridegrooms of war,[166] egalitarian meals, messianic concealment, riderless horses, resurrected armies,[167] otherworldly brotherhood, messianic marriages, stories on two religious planes, or, of course, Muslims—in particular, those marrying Hindus and fighting beside them in this world and the next.[168]

[165]One could hardly count Ambā here, whose betrothal in the *Mbh*, after it is interrupted by Bhīsma, has nothing left to consummate but bitterness against Bhīsma. As to Lakṣmana and Urmilā, the folk tradition seems to invent the theme (see chap. 4, sequence 2).

[166]See above, nn. 69, 71, and 150 on Ḥasan's son Qasem (the latter also on Ghāzī Miyān).

[167]Beside Husayn's and the Pāṇḍavas' armies (see chap. 10 at nn. 146 and 193) and Lausen's Ḍom army (chap. 10 at n. 98), see Daftary 1990, 60, 62, 65-66, 559-65, on the resurrection of an army, or of a leader (Imām, Mahdī) and partisans, as linked with the concepts of *raj'a*, "return," *ghayba*, "absence" or occultation, and *dawr*, "cycles." See also chaps. 3, n. 67, and 10, n. 123. In Sanskrit literature, the model for the resurrection of an army is Śukra's revivals of armies *of the demons*.

[168]Khan 1997b, 253, suggests that the suppressed military ideal of the Nizārīs, found in the ginān̄s with their eschatological armies, resurfaces with the Sikhs. I would add that it also

If we ask finally what holds most if not all of these strains together at their inspirational source, one would have to think of the Shī'ī theme of the martyr's mystical marriage with God. In what Schimmel calls "the most touching poem in honor of the martyrs of Kerbela in the Sindhi language" (1979, 213), Shah Abdul Latif's *Sur Kedaro* provides a model for the marsiyah laments of Muharram. Not only is the "hardship of martyrdom" a wedding:

> In their martyrdom was all the coquetry of Love;
> Some intoxicated people may understand the mystery of the case of Kerbela.[169]

Bhakti, karma, satī, and jāti could take this mystery in different directions. But I believe that from the moment it became a bireligious theme in Sind, with all the rest that widens it out into visions of heroic pasts and futures, it has remained dialogic. Mōvuttukkāraṉ, Mīrā Tālhan, Jaffar and Farīd, and Muttāl Rāvuttaṉ would seem to provide glimpses of how a Shī'ī and in some cases specifically Ismā'īlī messianism comes to lie latent in some regional oral martial epics that are primarily about Hindu little kings and queens. Yet the singers of such tales have taken as their primary option the hinduizing one of narrating apocalypses of the past that recycle some of the unfinished business of the Indian epics. So far, only Srinivasan's *Desing* gives us a *Mahābhārata*, if not exactly an apocalypse, of the future.

---

resurfaces in regional oral martial epics and *Desing*.

[169]Schimmel 1979, 221; cf. 215 for a closer translation.

12 Barbarīka, Aravāṉ, Kūttāṇṭavar: Furthering the Case of the Severed Head

From the late twelfth through the fourteenth centuries, Nāths, Bairāgīs, Jogīs, and Satpanth Ismā'īlīs, as we have now seen, minted underground *Mahābhāratas* with interregional and interreligious currency. But they were not just talking between themselves. There were others for whom the *Mahābhārata* was already important: and, safe to say, not just the Sanskrit *Mahābhārata* (which was by this time regionalized in different recensions[1]), but regionally grounded folk *Mahābhāratas*. The Ismā'īlī case is especially interesting, for Pīr Shams and other early ginān composers would not have made so much of the *Mahābhārata* were it not already important to the communities they addressed in Sind. These included—even before the Nāths, Bairāgīs, and Jogīs, who show up only at the end of Shams's garbī dance—villagers, Brahmans, and little hinterland Rajput kings and queens who were fond of Navarātri and Dasarā. From this point, leaving our Ismā'īlī hypothesis behind, we must raise the question of what kind of prior folk *Mahābhāratas* and, for that matter, *Rāmāyaṇas*,[2] such hinterland populations, centered in their Rajputs,

[1]The Poona Critical Edition of the *Mbh* begins its work with regional manuscripts going back to this period and implying, of course, much earlier recensional history.

[2]Although I focus mainly on folk *Mbh*, the same little-rajputization process is seen in some folk *Rām*. Along with *Pābūjī*, I note two indications: "Nundodaree [i.e., Mandodarī], the chief wife of Ravanu [Rāvaṇa] . . . after the death of her husband, went to Ramu [Rāma] weeping. Ramu, not knowing who she was, gave her this blessing, that she should never become a widow. Finding his mistake, (having just killed her husband,) he ordered Hunooman continually to throw wood into the fire, according to a proverb among the Hindoos, that as long as the body of the husband is burning, a woman is not called a widow. To this day, therefore, Hunooman keeps laying logs on the fire; and every time a Hindoo puts his fingers in his ears and hears a sound, he says he hears the bones of Ravunu burning"; "Ram Chunder, in order to ascertain whether Seeta was innocent or polluted, in consequence of having been detained by Rawun, put her into a furnace. . . . Thus was her innocence established; and burning of the Holee [the fires of the Spring Holi festival], as it is termed, has been established in commemoration of that fiery ordeal" (Pogson [1828] 1971, 4, 71). These examples, drawn it seems from familiarity with Bundela folklore, suggest satī folklores. Satpanth ginans also transform folk *Rām* themes (Kassam 1995, 174, 192; Shackle and Moir 1992, 193), but with no such intensity as *Mbh* ones. In the "big"

would have maintained and developed. Before and beyond twelfth- to fifteenth-century remintings, and the beginnings in that period of regional oral martial epics disseminated into little hinterland Rajput kingdoms by the diffusion of military labor and militant Jogīs and Fakirs, we can discern in earlier medieval times a period when folk *Mahābhāratas* were already centering themselves on little kingdom traditions preoccupied with land and the goddess. We begin by picking up a well-known problem.

A. Reopening the Case

In Draupadī cult myth and ritual, discussion of severed heads often carries one back and forth from Pōttu Rāja to Aravāṉ. A head pops up in Pōttu Rāja's hand in the Gingee core area of the Tamil Draupadī cult. But in Telugu settings (outside the Draupadī cult's extension into southern Andhra) this occurs only where Pōta Rāju is taken as a double for Bhairava.[3] Somewhere along this boundary, we near the end of tracing things in this book only from north to south. The fusing of the severed head into Pōttu Rāja's mythology in the Draupadī cult's Gingee area is a sign, along with Aravāṉ's severed head, that, having reached Tamilnadu, we must begin to turn around and start looking from south to north.

In its wider ramifications, the case of the severed head has tested our best sleuths.[4] Narrowed down to certain recurrences, however, it brings forth evidence of folk *Mahābhārata* elements from pre-twelfth-century sources. These elements, at least as of now, can be called pan-Indian. But the case is baffling. The problem is that every time matters seem to be solved, there's another severed head. The case can be narrowed to minimally two victims with "the same story," a crime that has taken place at least twice in exactly the same circumstances of time and place, and a chief suspect who seems to have gotten away every time with the

---

Dasa avatāra, the Shāh's seventh avatar is Rāma, but only Hanumān joins the Shāh's army, as his standard bearer (Khakee 1972, 262, 322, 357-60). Presumably Rāma is exempt for having been the Shāh himself, and thus not subject to being liberated, while Hanumān can join the army of liberated souls (see chap. 10, n. 195).

[3]See Sewell 1882, xv, xxi, xxiii, on Bhairava with head in hand; Roghair 1982, 146, n. 34, 195, on Pōta Rāju as Bhairava. Draupadī's cult in Andhra seems to transition the head-holding to Pōta Rāju (Hiltebeitel 1991a, 105-7), whereas south of the Gingee core area, Draupadī temples tend to have Vīrapattiraṉ (Vīrabhadra) instead of Pōttu Rāja, with the head held now that of Dakṣa (Hiltebeitel 1991a, 110-16, 314-16, 400-29). On Pōttu Rāja holding a severed head, see Hiltebeitel 1978; 1988a, 333-93; 1991a, 109-10, 320-38.

[4]See especially Heesterman's 1967 article by this title, now a chapter in his 1985 (45-58). Cf. Rose 1926; Vogel 1930-32; Shulman 1980, 127-29, 347; O'Flaherty 1980; Witzel 1987; S. Bayly 1989, 53-55 and *passim*; Heesterman 1993, 43-44; Shulman 1993; Zoller 1993. For my efforts, see n. 18 below.

same old alibis.[5] Victim: Aravāṉ, also known as Kūttāṇṭavar, if you hear the story in Tamilnadu (and where the Draupadī cult extends into southern Andhra); Barbarīka, if you hear it further into Andhra, or in Bundelkhand, Himachal Pradesh, Rajasthan (and western Uttar Pradesh), or Garhwal (northern Uttar Pradesh). Time: beginning of the *Mahābhārata* war. Place: Kurukṣetra. Chief suspect: Kṛṣṇa. Same old story: under consideration. Indeed, as we shall see, it is also the same story in Orissa, but with another victim; and with still another victim of nearly the same plot at Kurukṣetra itself.

Finding the far-flung folklore of Barbarīka has been an unfolding story in itself. It appears that none of the fieldworkers (myself included) were looking for Barbarīka when his story popped up. My trail—one of chance finds all around, whether in articles, encounters, or generous personal communications from colleagues—has led from Andhra[6] to Rajasthan thanks to Domique-Sila Khan,[7] back to Andhra thanks to P. Nagaraj,[8] then to Mahobā,[9] to Garhwal thanks to William Sax,[10] to Himachal Pradesh,[11] and finally back again to Andhra thanks to M. V. Krishnayya.[12] Krishnayya had never heard of Barbarīk until I gave a preliminary account of this chapter's findings at a folklore conference in Hyderabad on "Ritual and Narrative" in August 1997. Soon thereafter, he "accidently" saw a short notice in "Eenadu," the prominent Telugu daily (November 9, 1997), about a ceremony for Barbarīk performed by Marwari business families of Visakhapatnam, and followed it up by getting the local Marwaris' version of the story from a knowledgeable member of that community named Chandmal Agarwal (Krishnayya 1997). He was then "stunned" to find a printed version of Barbarīk's story in the Telugu folk genre of *burrakatha*.[13] Along with generously translating it, he

[5]Cf. Shulman 1993, 18-86: With basically the same problem of divinely prompted filicide, Śiva's Telugu devotees do not let him off with the same "old tricks" he used on his Tamil ones. Here it is a matter of self-conscious theological and intertextual transformations.

[6]Via Subba Rao 1976:272-73, cited in Hiltebeitel 1988a, 317; 1991a, 302, with need of this further discussion.

[7]Via generous personal communications of 3/17/93, 6/6/93, 8/8/93, 10/2/93, 12/21/97.

[8]Of the Centre for Folk Culture Studies, University of Hyderabad, met in Mysore (January 1995) and Hyderabad (August 1997).

[9]In my own fieldwork, December 1995, as below.

[10]Via a generous E-mail of March 1996.

[11]B. R. Sharma 1993 and H. R. Justa 1993. I follow Sharma (37), who says Barbarīk is the original identity of the victim in Himachal Pradesh, which Justa does not mention.

[12]Via letters (Krishnayya 1997, 1998) and follow-up E-mail (1/2/98, 2/23/98). I only modify these sources to standardize the spellings "Barbarīk" and "Babrīk" as proximate regional ones for "Barbarīka" (as he would be called in Sanskrit).

[13]See Brahmanandam 1992. Krishnayya found this title—*The Burrakatha of Vīra-Barbarīka known as Madhava vijayam*—in a list assembled by Daniel Negers, who has completed a

comments, "That means Barbareek's story is part of narrative entertainment traditions of Telugu people like other stories and ballads" (1998).

In fact, I chose to open my findings on this case at Hyderabad to see if I could learn more about Barbarīk in Andhra from other conferees who knew the state. The results, both from Nagaraj and Krishnayya, have not only helped fill out the dossier but lend weight to my suspicion of Rajput connections for the Telugu stories. Changing little from the Hyderabad presentation, and leaving loose ends as they were, I insert Krishnayya's reports near the end, since they answer to gaps and tighten some circles. I thus hope to share something of my delight in gaining some fresh clarity so near the end of this project. Yet with new clarity comes new leads, and a recognition that even with mounting evidence, it is not likely that the case will ever be closed. But that cannot be said of this book.

B. Tracking Barbarīka

Beginning with my own stroke of good fortune, I (AH) started a December 8, 1995, interview in Mahobā with my usual opening question about incarnations, with Gyan Chaturvedi (GC) of the Department of Political Science, St. John's College, Agra, as translator. The respondents were *Ālhā* singers Baccha Singh (BS) and Charan Singh (CS):

> AH—Can you tell me about *Ālhā* heroes who are incarnations of heroes from the *Mahābhārata*?
>
> BS—*Mahābhārat* is in the Dvāpara age. And in the *Mahābhārat* the Kaurav and the Pāṇḍav are the two sides, two dynasties (*vaṃś*). From the Kaurav dynasty we have Prithivīrāj and from the Pāṇḍav dynasty we have Ālhā-Ūdal. Ālhā had the blessing of Gorakhnāth. So Ālhā was the avatar of Dharam (Dharma, Yudhiṣṭhira), and Ūdal was from the part (*aṃś*) of Kṛṣṇa.[14] Balrao, Babrahon [Babhruvāhana], Babrīk—one name, by the blessings (*varadān*: boons) of Kṛṣṇa Bhagavan. And Malkhān is the avatār of Sahadev. Lakhān is Nakul. Chacha Sayyid, Tāla Sayyid is the avatar of Kīcak. Brahmā is the avatar of Arjun. Duryodhan is the avatar in Prithivīrāj. Bhīm is the avatar in Dandhu. Prithivīrāj is in the Kaurav dynasty. So in this way they are avatars.
>
> AH—So who is Babrīk; whose avatar is he?
>
> BS—Babrīk belonged to the *Mahābhārat* age.

---

dissertation on this genre. In *burrakatha* performance, "the main narrator stands, with others to his side playing minor instruments, one of them a joker" (Krishnayya 1998).

[14] *Krsnake amś sè Ūdal*—"a part of Kṛṣṇa becomes Ūdal." GC suggests "divine element" for *amś*.

CS (intervening)—Said to be Ūdal's (*Ūdal ke batai jate hain*).

BS (continuing)—With Kṛṣṇa's blessing [all] these blessings take place.

GC—But Ālhā had the boon [or blessing] of Gorakhnāth. He was born in Mahobā.[15]

AH—Can you explain the story of Babrīk?

GC—He doesn't know that story. Can you explain it?

CS—Do it properly (*kaide sè*)!

BS (after a thoughtful pause)—This Babrīk was born of Nāg Kanyā (Serpent Maiden), the daughter of a Nāg. She remained as a Nāg; and when she came close to him [Bhīmsen, Bhīma], she became a maiden (*kanyā*). He [Babrīk] was born of Bhīmsen. This maiden fell in love with Bhīmsen. And from her this son was born of Bhīmsen and Nāg Kanyā.

CS—Yes, yes (*hain, hain*).

AH—So is there a meaning to the name Babrīk?

BS—It is a name. . . . Yes, yes, there is a meaning to it. When Bhīmsen was born, the paṇḍits had researched as to what kind of man he will be. He would be like this. He would be like that. He would be powerful. He may be bad. So after this research was done he was floated in the water. Meanwhile, this Nāg Kanyā had a boon, "You shall receive your husband as a corpse (*tumkō murda-pati prāpt hogā*)." Bhīmsen was floating in the river, and she (Nāg Kanyā) had gone for a bath in the river. She saw Bhīmsen floating downriver. So she worshiped Śiv, and Śiv gave the boon that the dead husband would come alive. Because of this Śivapūjā, Bhīmsen comes alive.

GC—Therefore, what is the reason for the name Babrīk?

BS—Names are given.

GC—It doesn't have a particular meaning. He says, "It's a name."

AH—What is the time this momentary death happens in Bhīma's life?

BS—It is when Bhīmsen is born.

AH—Ah. So do they then get married, and have Babrīk as their child.

BS—Ah. So they had this child called Babrīk who was very strong. He was so strong that there was no one in the army of either the Kaurav or Pāṇḍav who could fight with him. So both armies gathered face to face, and there is going to be a war. And Babrīk decided he would fight on the side of the losing army. So the war was about to start, and Kṛṣṇa thought, "Victory is going to be that of Arjun.

[15]Returning to this question, we learned that Ālhā has a special boon from Gorakhnāth but is included among those blessed by Kṛṣṇa.

Therefore Babrīk will fight on the side of the Kauravs." So Kṛṣṇa Bhagavan assumed the form of a Brahman and asked for the head of Babrīk. So Babrīk cut off his head with his own hand and gave it as gift (*dān*) to Kṛṣṇa, who had assumed the form of a Brahman. *Chāl kiya* (It's a *chāl*, a violation of moral order, deceit)!

CS—Chāl kiya!

GC—Chāl kiya!

BS [again]—Chāl kiya! [All agree.].[16] So the severed head of Babrīk said to Kṛṣṇa, "Place my head on top of a mountain where I can watch the war between the Kauravs and Pāṇḍavs and observe the war." So the point came when the Kauravs started losing. The head of Babrīk laughed, because the thought occurred to him, "If I were not in this condition I would have fought on the side of the Kauravs against Arjun and defeated the Pāṇḍavs." Now by this mere laughter, the chariot of Arjun was pushed backward by many steps. Such was the bravery of Babrīk. Arjun was surprised at this episode and asked Kṛṣṇa what happened. So Kṛṣṇa picked up the severed head that was at the top of the mountain and placed it at the foot of the mountain. One more chāl! So the war came to an end. And Arjun was victorious. So after he was victorious, Kṛṣṇa said, "Now, I will explain it to you."[17] He takes all of them to the severed head of Babrīk and says, "See, he is so brave that if I had not taken his severed head, there is no one in the entire army who could have taken him." So Kṛṣṇa said to Babrīk, "Now you ask for the boon that you want." Babrīk answered, "I have been deprived from fighting the war. I have not received the satisfaction of using my sword-arm." So Kṛṣṇa said, "Go (*jao*)! And in the time of tomorrow (*kal-kāl*, the future) you shall have an avatar called Ūdal (*jaye tumhāra kal-kāl maiṇ Ūdal kè nām se avatār hogā*)."

There's a story no one would have told you! These research institute people of Bundelkhand, they could not have told you. I have taken this *Ālhā* story out of the purāṇas.

CS—It is not taken from *Mahābhārat*. It is distinct from *Mahābhārat*.

BS—I have taken it out of the purāṇas. No one will tell this.

CS—The *Ālhā* story is distinct from *Mahābhārat*.

[16]Cf. J. D. Smith 1990, 13; 1991, 97-98, translating Rajasthani *chal-* as "dupe," but noting that the *Pābūjī* bard Parbū Bhopo "was explicit" that, in the song he sings about the world mother in the hollow śamī, the "meaning . . . was 'exterminate.'" Like various Rajasthani folk heroines and goddesses (including Deval, Sītā, and Draupadī), she "dupes" and "destroys" adversaries on two sides.

[17]I.e., how they won, and what made Arjun's chariot go backward.

BS—But I have made comparisons (*milake*) with *Mahābhārat*. The war in *Mahābhārat*, which had involved seven army divisions, it involved only three in *Ālhā*.

AH—Is there anything special about Babrīk's hair?

BS—Yes. The hair of Babrīk was like a snake (*babrīk ke bāl nāg-saman thè*).

AH—Does Kṛṣṇa have any avatar?

GC—Does Kṛṣṇa come into *Ālhā* as avatar?

BS—Yes, yes (*Jī, jī*). The aṃś of Kṛṣṇa becomes Maniya Devatā. Maniya Devatā is the aṃś of Kṛṣṇa. "But," says Babrīk, "just as you are assisting Arjun in the Dvāpara age, so you [must] come with me when I take the avatar." Kṛṣṇa says, "Go. Maniya Dev has my aṃś. He shall protect you."

To what extent *is* this the same old story: the one heard in Tamilnadu about Aravāṉ (especially in the Draupadī cult) or Kūttāṇṭavar (the same hero, *mutatis mutandis*, in his own Kūttāṇṭavar cult)?[18] To a very basic extent: It is the same old story because it tells that, for the Pāṇḍavas to win the war, one of their sons (or grandsons) must offer his head. The youth, who must demonstrate the greatest courage and fortitude, is a Kṣatriya only on his Pāṇḍava father's (or grandfather's) side. On his mother's side, there is usually a lower, non-Kṣatriya component: from a Nāgī in the versions told so far; alternately from a Rākṣasī. Somehow his prowess becomes monstrous and endangers the course which Kṛṣṇa has set for the Pāṇḍavas' victory. Kṛṣṇa foresees the danger, devises devious means to avert it, secures the head, and grants boons as recompense. Whatever one refines further from this boiler plate, one can safely reason that all variants spring from a common *Bauopfer*-type conception, reflected in both north and south Indian folk *Mahābhārata*s, that victory requires the Pāṇḍavas to offer a son of low-to-monstrous status not only to obtain victory, but to avoid offering themselves or Kṛṣṇa. Moreover, once one looks at other variants of this story, one sees that even where the names and narratives differ, the stories connect through telling details.

Comparison may begin with the different parents. Aravāṉ is the son of Arjuna and a Serpent Maiden named Ulūpī. Barbarīka's stories can be provisionally divided by the differing accounts of his parents. In Bundelkhand and Garhwal, and with a variant that we shall note in Orissa, he is the son of Bhīma and an unnamed Serpent Maiden. In Rajasthan and Andhra, he is sired by Ghaṭotkaca: that is, his father is the son of Bhīma and the Rākṣasī Hiḍimbā. Khan's correspondence on Rajasthan does not

[18]See Hiltebeitel 1988a, 317-32; 1991a, 283-319, primarily on the Draupadī cult; and 1995b, in press-a, and in press-b, primarily on the Kūttāntavar cult.

indicate his mother. In Andhra, accounts differ. Chandmal Agarwal's Marwari tale calls her Ahilyavati, while the burrakatha calls her Maurvī. Ghaṭotkaca meets Maurvī as a result of Kṛṣṇa's conflicts with Narakāsura, king of Prāgjyotiṣpuram.[19] But according to Nagaraj, who could not recall the wife's name, Ghaṭotkāca meets her in Duryodhana's kingdom when he helps his brother Abhimanyu win *his* bride Śaśirekhā by preventing her marriage to Duryodhana's son Lakṣaṇakumāra. Sources on Himachal Pradesh make Barbarīk a Yakṣa, and are not forthcoming about either of his parents.

The Bundelkhand story of conception after revival of his father's floating corpse is unknown from other variants. Perhaps a tantric theme, it reminds one of a more general capacity of Serpent Maidens to revive the dead. Ulūpī uses this capacity (with no help from Śiva) to revive Arjuna. Years after the battle of Kurukṣetra where her son Aravāṇ (Irāvat in Sanskrit) has died, she reanimates Arjuna after he is slain by Babhruvāhana, one of the other sons Arjuna sired beside Aravāṇ during his youthful pan-Indian tour of sexual self-discovery. Baccha Singh's remark that Babrahon [Babhruvāhana] and Babrīk are "one name" suggests their stories have fused.[20] Unlike folk-*Mahābhārata* traditions shared by Aravāṇ and Barbarīka, the Babhruvāhana story is known from the Sanskrit epic (14.78-82), and thus gives that textual background to the theme that the Pāṇḍavas engender sons who endanger them and have the capacity to upstage and kill them. Babhruvāhana, a classical patricide (Goldman 1978, 329-33), fights Arjuna over the Aśvamedha horse which Arjuna follows and protects on behalf of Yudhiṣṭhira. The patricidal theme may relate to cycles of revenge. A Garhwali *Mahābhārata* folklore built on the practice of Himalayan ball games, where the ball is equivalent to a captured head, provides an analog, although without reference to Babrīl [Barbarīka]. The Pāṇḍavas and Kauravas contend for the ball, which represents the trophy-head that either side stands to lose; and the Pāṇḍavas win (Zoller 1993, 216-19). The myth has its counterparts in local Garhwali Rajput stories of the recovery of a clan-ancestral father's (rather than a son's) head (214-15, 227-28, 232): a theme we have noted in the "Mārō Feud" episode at the opening of *Ālhā*.

Babhruvāhana opposes not only Arjuna but Arjuna's protection of Yudhiṣṭhira's Aśvamedha horse, which also makes Babhruvāhana a classi-

<hr>

[19]China, in the narrative (Krishnayya 1998, translating Brahmanandam 1992, 10), but in classical Sanskrit texts, identified as Assam. For the story, see below.
[20]The two names may also alternate in Andhra. M. V. Krishnayya has found that among Gollas and Jalari fishermen living close to each other and sharing stories and cultural events, including festivals, the Golla storytellers know a variant of Barbarīk's story in which he is called not Barbarīk but Babhruvāhana (personal communication, 1/2/98).

cal anti-imperialist. This brings us to Barbarīka's determination to bring victory to the losing side. Sax's Garhwal variant also has Babrīl declare this intention. Aravān̠ agrees to sacrifice himself for the Kauravas and has to be won back by Kṛṣṇa's scheming to do so for the Pāṇḍavas. But unlike Barbarīka, Aravān̠ has no preference for losers.

When the Garhwali Babrīl chooses to fight for the losers, there is an informative setting. Here the story unfolds around the God- or "fate"-defying paradox of Babrīl's determination. After Kṛṣṇa, Arjuna, and Babrīl have gone out and chosen the battlefield (*yuddh-bhūmi*: i.e., Kurukṣetra),[21] Babrīl tells Kṛṣṇa: "I will fight on the side of the losers, and cause the winners to lose." Here fighting for the losers would change the winners. Kṛṣṇa can tell he is being challenged, but his response is now more measured. To test Babrīl, and perhaps his own ability to protect the Pāṇḍavas, he takes five leaves from a tree in the name of the Pāṇḍavas and places them under his foot. Then he tells Babrīl to shoot all the tree's leaves. The arrow pierces every leaf on the tree, soars into the sky, and swerves down to pierce Kṛṣṇa's foot and the leaves beneath it.

It is much the same story in Himachal Pradesh where Barbarīk is "said to have come in the form of Kamru Nag in Mandi District."[22] Before the war, Kṛṣṇa and Arjuna are walking beside Kurukṣetra and come across Kamru Nag, a mighty Yakṣa, heading toward the battlefield with his host. Kṛṣṇa asks his purpose. Kamru Nag says he has heard about the war and descended from the skies to win glory and "tip the scales" of battle: "I can kill the whole army with a single arrow just as my master Lord Shiva burnt the three cities with a single arrow." Kṛṣṇa puts him to the test of piercing every leaf in a tree, and the arrow goes through them all plus "a few leaves" Kṛṣṇa hides in his hands. Kṛṣṇa then disguises himself as a Brahman and asks for Kamru Nag's head. Kamru Nag grants this, but wants to see the war from "a lofty hill tree." Kṛṣṇa beheads him and puts his head in the tree where Kamru Nag now has a temple on a thick-forested hill where he likes there to be no noise (Justa 1993, 61-62).

This variant, where the victim takes on a local identity, leads us to another victim whose story I summarized in volume 1 of *The cult of Draupadī*, reducing the parallel to a clause: "Having seen Bhuriśravas' invincibility as an archer. . ." (1988a, 317). As Cunningham reports from his 1878-79 Kurukṣetra tour, one finds there a "large village" called Bhor or Bhoré "on a mound just half-way between Thanesar and Pehoa." The village is named after the Kaurava warrior Bhuriśravas, as is a tank

[21] In his involvement in "finding the battlefield," Barbarīka's role is reminiscent of Balarāma's in the *Mahābhārata* and Aravān̠'s in the Draupadī cult of spatially defining the battlefield; see Hiltebeitel 1991a, 309-19 and forthcoming.

[22] B. R. Sharma 1993, 37; see above, n. 11.

where Arjuna slew him. In a story Cunningham "received on the spot," Arjuna's treachery stays close to the story line of the Sanskrit epic: after Bhuriśravas has abandoned his weapons and is seated, Arjuna severs his two arms (rather than only the right: *Mbh* 7.118.17) before Bhuriśravas is beheaded (in the *Mahābhārata* by Sātyaki [118.31-36]). But now we learn that Bhuriśravas has fallen afoul of the same plot as Barbarīk.

> Arjun struck off both his arms with an arrow. It is said that an eagle (*gidh*, or vulture) flew away with one of the arms to the west where Shujâh Bâdshâh afterwards reigned. On this arm was an armlet with the Koh-i-nûr diamond, which was afterward taken by Ranjit Singh, and is now with Queen Victoria.[23]
>
> When Bhurishrava first came to Kurukshetra he intended to have joined the Kauravas. He was met by Krishna, who asked him, "Why have you come here with only three arrows?" He replied that three arrows were sufficient to annihilate the whole army, and that with one arrow he could pierce every single leaf of a tree. Krishna pointed out a tree to be shot at, and at the same time concealed one of the leaves of the tree under his foot. The arrow was shot, and all the leaves of the tree were found to have been pierced as well as the leaf under Krishna's foot, although the foot itself was not hurt. Krishna thought that it would be very unlucky for the Pandavas to have so powerful an archer against them. So he assumed the form of a Brahman and asked Bhurishrava to give him his head. The archer consented, but with the condition that his head should be placed on the pinnacle of Krishna's chariot, so that he might behold the fight which he had come purposely to see. His head was cut off and placed on the pinnacle of the chariot, and the Pandavas were at once victorious. (1970, 99)

One would like to know when Kṛṣṇa takes the disguise, who severs the head, who puts the head on the pinnacle of his chariot, why it is Kṛṣṇa's chariot and not Arjuna's, and how this sequence works. I assume that the leaf-shooting and disguise occur again shortly before the war, the arm- and head-severing within it, and the war-watch from that point to its end.

But the trail is not yet cold. In Orissa it begins to look like a serial crime. In the Oriya *Mahābhārata* by the (probably) fifteenth century "ploughman" Sāralādāsa, filled with "dreamlike narrative sequence(s)" expressing "protest" from a folklore of "the left," Kṛṣṇa's "astonishing

[23]Shujâh Bâdshâh is presumably Shuja-ud-daula, nawāb of Awadh from 1754-75; see Barnett 1980, 42-95, notably on the battle of Baksar, Shuja's Rajput soldiers and Abyssinian officers, and his statebuilding "between empires"; Ranjit Singh established a Sikh kingdom in the Punjab in 1799 and ruled it as Maharaja from 1801-39.

cruelty" is epitomized in another dejà vu:[24]

> Belala Sena, the son of Bhima and the snake goddess, Belavali (Vasuki's daughter) . . . [could] have put paid to the Mahabharata war in one second by demolishing the Kauravas with a single shot from his bow: so incredibly skilful was he. But Krsna wished to enjoy the sports of war for the full eighteen days. He, therefore, first of all tested Belala's skill [with the leaf test?] to verify that it was indeed as great as reputed. Then, finding that it was so, he flatteringly extracted from Belala a promise to accede to whatever request he might make. When Belala unhesitatingly agreed, Krsna promptly asked for the gift of his head.
>
> Belala assented on one condition. Thinking [that it would be a request for the head's return], the wily Krsna immediately preempted this . . . ; under no circumstances would Belala regain his head. This blunt statement affronted Belala, for it was unheard of for Kshatriyas to desire the return of a gift, once given. All he desired was the grant of divine eyes, so that with his head on a column he might watch the eighteen-day war. (Boulton 1976, 11)

Boulton links the episode with others of "symbolic" history (1976, 22), but gives no background on the victim. He comments that Kṛṣṇa plays "the role of sacrificial priest" with Belala as a "fit offering" for being "noble, pure and innocent," "dignified," and "calm and detached, because of the promise of coming divinity" (15). Within our casebook, however, Belala's story has one unique twist. It provides the only instance before us where the victim-hero would have fought *against* the Kauravas and *for* the Pāṇḍavas. This leaves Kṛṣṇa with no more motivation than his own stark wish to enjoy a full eighteen days of war-sports.

Sāralādāsa seems to cast a wide folkloric *and literary* net.[25] The Kamru Nag and Bhuriśravas stories, on the other hand, seem to localize the stock story and alter several features. Bhuriśravas at least is not youthful, not a Pāṇḍava scion, and evidently not a *pre*war battlefield sacrifice. Two traits probably promote him to replacement: his dismemberment, doubled by the second arm; and his identification with the

[24]Quoting Boulton 1976, 11, 13, 23-24: Kṛṣṇa's body will not burn after he dies because it "is too deeply stained with sin" (17)—above all from his dalliances with the Gopīs, which are linked with the *Gītāgovinda* and the Brahmanical "right" (24). Sāralādāsa is a "ploughman" (5); a Śūdra poet from near Cuttack of the fifteenth century (Mohanty 1990, 267; Patnaik 1993, 170); thirteenth century (Mishra 1995, 144).

[25]Boulton 1976, 1-6; Patnaik 1993; Swain 1993. On Belavali, cf. the "Nāga" Suvelā, wife of the fourth "Kauravāṃśa," who demands a snake ornament for her betrothal (chap. 8, § A). For once we get a name for Bhīma's Nāgī wife.

sacrificial stake, which he bears as his flagstaff emblem (*yūpaketu*; 7.118.16). His variant triangulates with the Garhwal, Himachal Pradesh, and Mahobā "Barbarīka" stories: as in Garhwal and Himachal Pradesh but not Mahobā, there is the shooting of the leaves down to the foot or hand; as in Himachal Pradesh and Mahobā but not Garhwal, Kṛṣṇa demands the head while disguised as a Brahman.

When Kṛṣṇa is not disguised as a Brahman but entirely himself, as in Garhwal and Orissa, there is less scope for deception. But the Garhwal story does tell us more than the Mahobā story about the deliberations leading to the sacrifice. Knowing that he cannot protect the Pāṇḍavas without eliminating Babrīl, Kṛṣṇa goes to Yudhiṣṭhira and tells him they have now chosen the battlefield, but since the battlefield demands "the sacrifice of a thirty-two lakṣaṇa warrior," Yudhiṣṭhira must select a victim from among the three who have chosen it: Kṛṣṇa himself, Arjuna, and Babrīl. Babrīl saves Yudhiṣṭhira the anguish. He says that slaying either of the others is unimaginable, and tells Kṛṣṇa: "You cut off my head and hang it up, because I must see the *Mahābhārata* war." Kṛṣṇa says, "OK, I will enliven your head, and you cut it off yourself. And you [familiar form] will see the war." Here we find themes familiar from the Tamil Aravāṉ story: only a thirty-two lakṣaṇa warrior will do for the prewar sacrifice;[26] Kṛṣṇa, Arjuna, and either Aravāṉ or Babrīl are the only choices; the hero rules out the other two and selects himself.

But other features of Aravāṉ's sacrifice are absent from these Barbarīka stories. There is nothing apparent about the goddess. In Mahobā, Babrīk offers his head as "gift" (*dān*), not "sacrifice" (*bali*); and he offers it to Kṛṣṇa in the guise of a Brahman, not to Kālī. In Garhwal, Kṛṣṇa tells Yudhiṣṭhira the sacrifice demands the victim's "blood, his bali." Again, Babrīl seems to offer it to Kṛṣṇa, whom he calls Ishwar and Bhagwan, and says, "You cut off my head!" This would seem to rule out, or at least minimize, any connection with Dasarā such as is evoked in Aravāṉ stories.[27] But the goddess may not be far from these accounts. In Himachal Pradesh it seems again to be just an exchange of boons, but ultimately the blood from the battlefield goes to Draupadī as Kālī (Justa 1993, 62). In Rajasthan, where Barbarīk's main shrine is at a village named Kāṭ Śyām near Jaipur, his head is in some places worshipped during the fall festival to the goddess (Navarātri or Durgā Pūjā), and immersed in a tank or well on Vijayādaśamī, the "tenth" day that celebrates her Dasarā victory.[28] In Andhra, as we shall see, Barbarīk has even closer ties with the goddess.

[26]On this feature, see Hiltebeitel 1988a, 306, n. 33; 1995b, 465 and n. 10; in press-b.
[27]Hiltebeitel 1988a, 321-22; 1991a, 284-85, 314-16.
[28]Khan, personal communication (see n. 7).

Unlike Aravāṉ, who secures boons from Kṛṣṇa before he performs his battlefield sacrifice and is never a talking head before the war starts, in Mahobā Babrīk speaks immediately after he has severed his head to demand that it be placed on a mountain so that he can watch the war. In Himachal Pradesh it is a fair exchange. In Garhwal, Babrīl does not have to ask. Kṛṣṇa mercifully promises to enliven his head and put it on a mountain.[29] Once it is severed, Bhīma deposits it on a peak, and Kṛṣṇa keeps the life-breath (*prāṇ-vāyu*) within it for the war's eighteen days. Barbarīka's mountain top vantage point is found also in Himachal Pradesh and Andhra, and is different from the viewing position of Aravāṉ's head, which, if mentioned, is usually the top of a post (as with Bhuriśravas and Belala Sena) or the lap of Kālī.[30] In Mahobā, however, Babrīk does not stay on the peak for all eighteen days. Rather, when the Kauravas start losing, he laughs and Arjuna's chariot is forced backward. Kṛṣṇa saves his explanation for the end of the war, and in the meantime, removes the head from the mountain top to its base. This second "deception" must still allow Babrīk to see the war, but not panoptically. It must also neutralize the fierce power of his laughter. Here we have an intriguing tie-in with a Kūttāṇṭavar cult theme. Kūttāṇṭavar temples are often paired: one on a mountain outside a village, one in the village. Kūttāṇṭavar is always fiercest on the mountain, which is where his *cāmiyāṭi*s (possessed worshipers) get possessed at the beginning of his festivals before descending to the village temple, where his head then watches the eighteen-day festival that is equivalent to the war. Even in villages like Kūvākkam[31] with no mountain in sight, one may hear that the festival begins when "Cāmi comes down from the mountain," and ends when he returns to it. "Cāmi climbing down" (*cāmi iraṅkiyaccu*) is a trope for the god's possession of a person, while his "climbing the mountain" connotes coming out of possession, as in the phrase *cāmi malaiyēriyiruccu*, "Cāmi has climbed the mountain," which is said when a deity leaves someone he has possessed, leaves him to his natural self, so that in leaving, Cāmi goes back to the mountain alone: to his divine place (Hiltebeitel in press-a). As with Babrīk, there is something overpowering about Kūttāṇṭavar that could destroy the divinely ordered progress of the eighteen-day war, or the festival that enacts it, were he not brought down from the mountain to

[29]On the Garhwali theme of enlivening the head, and even making it rise to the top of the cosmic tree during the Kaurava-Pāṇḍava ball game, see Zoller 1993, 212-29, on the concept of *mīr*, a force associated with the local goddess of a village-settling clan (rather than with Kṛṣṇa).

[30]On these variations, see Hiltebeitel 1991a, 318-19, and ibid., 258 (plate 14), 294, 375 on Kālī's lap. Cf. Zoller 1993, 211 (head on pole).

[31]In Ulundurpet Taluk, South Arcot, Tamilnadu: site of Kūttāṇṭavar's most publicized festival, which attracts transsexuals called Alis (Hiltebeitel 1995b and in press-a and b).

regularize possession within the festival by his sacrifice at the village temple, and were he not returned to the mountain at the festival's end.[32]

Kūttāṇṭavar and also Draupadī cult stories share with Baccha Singh's Mahobā story a postwar visit to the severed head. At Mahobā, when the war is over Kṛṣṇa tells Arjuna he will explain what forced Arjuna's chariot backward, and takes Arjuna to Babrīk. Babrīk makes no utterance here, but Kṛṣṇa tells Arjuna that his chariot was driven backward by one who, had he not been beheaded, would have killed him. Draupadī and Kūttāṇṭavar cult informants tell that after the war, the Pāṇḍavas and Draupadī wrangle over which of them won the war, and Kṛṣṇa says they should ask Aravāṉ, who saw the whole thing. It is now that Aravāṉ becomes a talking head, and says that all his eyes saw was the work of Kṛṣṇa's discus cutting heads and his conch holding them, or else that he saw the conch blowing, the cakra beheading, and Kālī's skull-bowl (*kapāla*) holding the blood.[33] In Himachal Pradesh we find a northern variant that is closer to this Tamil outcome than the Mahobā version. After the war, Arjuna and Bhīma have "a heated discussion" over which of them produced the victory, and Kṛṣṇa directs them to ask the "prophetic head installed on a tree-top." Kamru Nag said, "In the midst of hundreds and thousands of puny warriors shooting their arrows and wielding their maces, sounding their kettle-drums, I saw the great Mahakali Khapra and Sudershan Chakra gigantic, shining forth everywhere in the war. This war was won for you by Lord Krishna and Mahakali, Krishna's Sudershan Chakra and Dropadi's Khappar" (Justa 1993, 62). Again, it is Kṛṣṇa's cakra (discus) and Draupadī's *khappar* (begging bowl, skull-bowl), which is also Kālī's khappar. These stories are beginning to speak for themselves.

In each case the visit resolves a question with an answer that shows Kṛṣṇa holding all the cards. But in the Mahobā story, Kṛṣṇa invites Babrīk to choose a boon *now*, and Babrīk replies that he wants the satisfaction of using his sword-arm, since he was deprived of fighting in the war. This is really the second boon he has obtained, and the two are clearly interchangeable with two of the three boons acquired by Aravāṉ, who obtains a succession of increasingly contradictory boons that accumulate through the development of his story: to stay alive so that he can die a hero on the eighth day of battle, thus keeping his Sanskrit exit from the story; to be allowed to watch the entire eighteen-day war with his severed head; and to marry before his sacrifice to secure him the ancestral rites denied to anyone who dies a bachelor. While Aravāṉ gets to watch the

[32]One finds something analogous at a few Draupadī temples where it is probably an adoption from the Kūttāntavar cult. I plan further study of the relation between the two cults.

[33]See chap. 10, n. 206, on the conch.

war from a post or Kālī's lap, Babrīk gets to see it from a mountain top. And while Aravāṉ, despite his battlefield sacrifice, gets to have his body reconstituted so that he can fight on the eighth day of battle, Babrīk gets to satisfy his sword-arm in his next life. None of these Barbarīkas, however, gets an equivalent to Aravāṉ's third boon, which is especially distinctive of Aravāṉ's identity as Kūttāṇṭavar: a bride who will marry him despite his impending death.[34]

One could go on trying to square the circle. In Sanskrit, *barbarīka*—from *barbara*, "barbarian"—means "curly hair or a particular mode of wearing the hair" (Monier-Williams [1899] 1964, 722). Nagaraj says that in Andhra, where Barbarīk is Ghaṭotkaca's son, he has so much head-hair that to all those below the mountain, its spread looks vast as a cloud.[35] In Rajasthan, according to a Hindi book on his main shrine at Kāṭ Śyām near Jaipur, "Barbarīk, as Ghaṭotkaca's son, had at his birth the hair naturally disheveled and standing on end, that is why he was given the name 'barbarīka.'"[36] To find that Barbarīka has extraordinary hair in Andhra and Rajasthan, where he is the grandson of a Rākṣasī and son of the wild Ghaṭotkaca, might not be surprising. But to learn that "the hair of Babrīk is like a snake" in Mahobā, where he is the son of Bhīma and a Serpent Maiden, is fascinating, considering that snakes lack hair. Yet Aravāṉ's body is reconstituted for his eighth-day fight by snakes that stiffen to form his flesh. Are they also "like hair that stands on end"?[37]

The question that opened the Mahobā interview with Baccha Singh and Charan Singh could have yielded nothing more interesting than that, from at least one perspective, Ūdal is an aṃś of Kṛṣṇa, and that Bhīma takes incarnation in Dandhu (see chap. 5, § A). Instead it brought up a treasure—thanks to Baccha Singh, a treasure hunter himself.[38] Yet what a multifaceted gem it is. First of all, Baccha Singh went beyond my question to mention a hero whom he included in his list of aṃśas and avatars, but did not identify as one: "Balrao, Babrahon [Babhruvāhana],

[34]On Aravāṉ's three boons, see Hiltebeitel 1995b, 451-53 on their order of appearance in his textual history (first boon ca. ninth century, second ca. fourteenth century, and third only in folk traditions) and in press-a on their relation to his "three deaths," and the likelihood that the marriage boon derives from the Kūttāṇṭavar cult, not the Draupadī cult.

[35]Subba Rao 1976, 272-73 mentions nothing of this.

[36]*bal nahi svarne ke karan uske lambe aur khare bal the[?/ tho?]/ isliye ghatotkach ne apne putr ka nam "barbarīk"* (Khan, personal communication, 8/8/93).

[37]See Hiltebeitel in press-b.

[38]Baccha Singh researches the treasures hidden in *Ālhā*, including diamonds at Khajuraho. Note that Prānnāth tells Chatrasal Bundela, "God has given you a land which abounds in diamonds. . . . [B]y no other race shall this blessing and inexhaustible source of wealth be enjoyed" (Pogson [1828] 1971, 102). Recall also Cunningham's Kurukṣetra account linking the *Mbh* with a disappearance of the Koh-i-nûr diamond.

Babrīk—one name, by the blessings of Kṛṣṇa Bhagavan." The response includes three answers relating to Kṛṣṇa and Ūdal. Baccha Singh states that "Ūdal was from the aṃś of Kṛṣṇa." But when I ask whose avatar Babrīk is, Charan Singh intervenes: "Said to be Ūdal's," to which Baccha Singh reiterates, "With Kṛṣṇa's blessing." At this point I was confused. Thinking I was about to hear of Babrīk appearing in *Ālhā* itself, I was asking whom Babrīk incarnated *from* the *Mahābhārata* rather than recognizing Babrīk as a *Mahābhārata* personage who might reincarnate in *Ālhā* as someone else. Baccha Singh seems to begin correcting me by saying, "Babrīk belonged to the *Mahābhārat* age." But Charan Singh puts things on course. Although grammatically he says that Babrīk is "said to be Ūdal's" avatar, what he means—that Ūdal is Babrīk's avatar—becomes clear when Kṛṣṇa gives Babrīk the postwar boon that will enable him to satisfy his sword-arm: "Go! And in the time of tomorrow you shall have an avatar called Ūdal." Once it is clear that Ūdal incarnates Babrīk, I can ask whether Kṛṣṇa now has any avatar and learn that he takes birth as Maniya Dev to protect Babrīk when he wields his sword as Ūdal.

What are we to make of this? First, I think we must reject any idea that the two singers knew different stories. They work together regularly. One also makes only a little headway following the terms aṃś and avatar. Combining answers, Ūdal is both an aṃś (portion, divine element) of Kṛṣṇa and an avatar of Babrīk; Kṛṣṇa has an aṃś in both Ūdal and Maniya Dev, but also takes avatar in Maniya Dev. In both cases, the term avatar seems to be more restrictive than aṃś. But elsewhere in the interview the two are used interchangeably. Seeing this as at best a partial explanation, I propose that what we meet here is a measured pace of disclosure. The two singers, giving what the audience—two out-of-town professors—can bear, are gradually inducting us not into theological mysteries but into the complexities of regional and local *Ālhā* folklores.

Baccha Singh begins with what seems the most widely held linkage, that Ūdal is an aṃś of Kṛṣṇa. As he seems to guess, we would have already heard this from "the research institute people of Bundelkhand." Indeed, two days earlier, we had asked Krishna Chaurasia and Zahir Singh about such matters, and in particular whether Kṛṣṇa's incarnation in Ūdal is widely held. And Zahir Singh had replied (in English), "It is so supposed, and many people in India believe it, because if you believe in incarnation, there is reference to that. Whoever listens to *Ālhā* believes it. It is our tradition, *parampara*." Next, when we pick up on the cryptic reference to Babrīk, the two singers seem gratified (raising their eyebrows), and Charan Singh, having already dropped the remark that Ūdal is said to be Babrīk's avatar, now, almost solemnly, tells Baccha Singh to tell the story "properly." Finally, we elicit the information that Kṛṣṇa becomes Maniya Dev as both aṃś and avatar. This was an afterthought to the singers, who considered their story finished. Here we wind up at a thoroughly local level, familiar from having just visited the shrine of Maniya Dev, guardian deity of Mahobā and here unambiguously male (see chap. 7, § E), whom Ālhā and Ūdal are said to have worshiped.

Baccha Singh and Charan Singh also give us terms with which to understand how such underground folk *Mahābhārata* circulates, and how it fuses with *Ālhā*. "I have taken this *Ālhā* story out of the purāṇas," says Baccha Singh. "It is not taken from the *Mahābhārat*. It is distinct form *Mahābhārat*." Baccha Singh, who does not know Sanskrit, is certainly not cribbing from Sanskrit Purāṇas.[39] Rather, "purāṇa" suggests here the type of "old story" that allows Kṛṣṇa to go on playing the same old tricks and making the same old alibis, from south to north. We should not ignore Baccha Singh's claim that he has "made comparisons (*milake*)" that link this "*Ālhā* story out of the purāṇas . . . with *Mahābhārat*." According to Gyan Chaturvedi, *milake* is colloquially "comparisons" here, and not "[what is] joined," or "connections." But these more ordinary meanings are also suggestive of the singers' "comparative method."[40] By comparing and connecting "purāṇic" folk *Mahābhārata* with *Ālhā*, has Baccha Singh actually fused the two himself, as he seems to imply? Or is he placing himself in wider oral networks in which such comparing and connecting would be part of an *Ālhā* singer's technique, and the story a variant within an oral *Mahābhārata* repertoire that is primarily his to process? I think the latter. We should not underestimate Baccha Singh's penchant for research or invention,[41] but I doubt that Charan Singh would have given such importance to this story if Baccha Singh had made it up.

We can safely say that north Indian folk *Mahābhārata* Barbarīka stories have circulated primarily in Rajput milieus, and especially among "littler" Rajput clans and populations.[42] Barbarīka makes an exemplary Rajput hero: ready to fight for either side, but especially the underdog; inordinately proud of his strength, yet willing to sacrifice its use; firm in his adherence to the Rajput code of honor,[43] even when God violates it,

[39]The *BhvP*, apparently the only purāṇa to tell an *Ālhā*, says nothing about Barbarīka, and as far as I know, no other Sanskrit purāna mentions him either.

[40]See Hiltebeitel [1976] 1990, 359-60, proposing that a similar "comparative method" is at work in the composition of *Mbh*.

[41]See Schomer 1984, 9, on *Ālhā* singing as "a classical Lordian tradition of composition-in-performance."

[42]Baccha Singh and Charan Singh are Bundelas. Garhwali Rajputs are out of the high status Rajput loop (Sax 1994). Rajasthan folk *Mbh* seems to have low status Rajput connections like *Pābūjī* (Smith N.d.). Sharma and Justa describe no social background. See below on Bōyas in Andhra.

[43]Belala Sena's indignation over the dishonorable imputation that he might ask back his head

and his parents' adherence to it is empty; willing at a flash to become a severed head. In our Mahobā version, he even becomes a kind of inverse jhūjhar. Rather than a body that goes on fighting after the head is severed, he is a head that will get his sword-arm back to go on fighting with in the next life—to complete the unfinished business of the *Mahābhārata*.

C. A Permeable Divide

As to Barbarīk in Andhra, we come to the point where we must ask whether he is further evidence of rajputizing influences there, or has some "transitional" connection with what one finds across the Tamil border. Here is Chandmal Agarwal's Marwari account:

> The Rākṣasī Hiḍimbā fell in love with Bhīma after he had slain her brother Hiḍimba. Bhīma agreed to marry her on condition that their wedlock be in force for only one year. Their son Ghaṭotkaca was born without hair on his body. Ghaṭotkaca married Ahilyavatī, who gave birth to Barbarīk with a lot of hair on his body. He was called Barbarīk because of his body-hair, which resembled the hair of a *barbarīk* lion (*sher*).[44] He was taken to Kṛṣṇa for initiation and instruction. The boy and Kṛṣṇa looked at each other mysteriously laughing. After initiation, Kṛṣṇa advised Barbarīk and his people to stay in the forest and look after Ṛṣis and good people, and to live pursuing invincibility (*ajeya*) and immortality (*amara*). Barbarīk worshiped Aṣṭadevī and received three invincible arrows able to destroy everything.
>
> Having lost the dice match, the Pāṇḍavas came to Barbarīk's area in the forest. Bhīma stepped into a tank and Barbarīk objected. Not knowing each other, they fought at length, grandfather against grandson, until people who had gathered recognized them. Barbarīk was distraught to know he had fought his grandfather, and prepared to commit suicide as penance. But Kṛṣṇa intervened and convinced him to wait until his ultimate sacrifice would be useful to his grandparents.
>
> When war was about to break out between the Pāṇḍavas and Kauravas, Barbarīk set forth with his mother's consent to watch it. She cautioned him not to take sides, since both parties were their relatives. But Barbarīk decided to help the loser. On the way he met Kṛṣṇa disguised as a Brahman. When the latter heard that Barbarīk wanted to be on the loser's side, he asked to see his strength, since Barbarīk

---

has also such a Rajput echo.

[44]Having a body covered with hair except for the paws, according to M. V. Krishnayya's follow-up interview with Chandmal Agarwal (personal communication, 2/23/98). One senses here that there is something of Durgā's lion in Barbarīk.

had only three arrows in his arsenal.

Barbarīk told the Brahman that one arrow would be enough to destroy the enemy, and would suffice for the test. The Brahman plucked five leaves from a pīpal tree, concealed them under his feet, showed Barbarīk the tree, and asked him to knock down all the leaves. When Barbarīk shot, the arrow destroyed all the leaves and stood before the Brahman's feet where the leaves were hidden. Barbarīk asked the Brahman to move a step so he could finish his task. The Brahman accepted Barbarīk's power and praised him, but told him he was not yet a complete hero, and wouldn't be so unless, in addition to his other two qualities, he became a hero of the gift (*dāna vīra*) by offering his head as the gift (*dāna*). Barbarīk agreed to offer his head if he could watch the *Mahābhārata* war which he had set out to see. The Brahman promised to help him watch the war, but Barbarīk demanded proof. Then the Brahman revealed that he was Kṛṣṇa and showed his Viśvarūpa or universal form, and Barbarīk severed his head as dāna to the Brahman. Pleased, Kṛṣṇa blessed Barbarīk that he would be worshiped in the Kali yuga by the name of Śyām Bāba and would bestow all benefits to his devotees.

After the war, when Bhīma and Arjuna argued over their contributions to the victory, Kṛṣṇa told them to consult Barbarīk's head, which saw the entire war from a mountain cliff. Barbarīk's head spoke: "All I saw was Kṛṣṇa's discus cutting the warriors' throats, Kāli's skull bowl collecting the blood, and Draupadī drinking the blood."

In time, Barbarīk's head was buried in the earth. Once in Rajasthan during the Kali yuga, a cow shed milk from her udder on a mound. Surprised, the villagers dug and found Barbarīk's head inside the mound in the form of a stone, which demanded consecration and daily worship. A temple was built for the head near Jaipur at Khautu, while his trunk is worshiped at Ringus fifteen miles away, and his feet at Patala.[45] Śyām Bāba is a childlike god, at once both demanding and fully loving. His worship has its risks, as it may misfire and bring misfortune. When compassionate, he showers immense material benefits. (Krishnayya 1997; personal communication, February 23, 1998)

Clearly, there are some novelties in this story: Ghaṭotkaca's hairlessness, Barbarīk's mother Ahilyavatī, his lion-like hair, his protection of forest sages, the divine source of his three arrows, his fight with his

[45]Khautu, at which Marwari children undergo their first hair-removal, is evidently Kāt Śyām. Chandmal Agarwal is from Ringus (Krishnayya, personal correspondence, 2/23/98). Parts of Kūttāṇṭavar's body also come from different villages for assemblage with his head at Kūvākkam and are returned to them after his kalappali (Hiltebeitel 1995b, 459, 464).

grandfather Bhīma, his near-suicide as Kṛṣṇa's pretext for demanding his sacrifice, and the cow that reveals his buried head. Equally striking are some recurrences with new twists: Kṛṣṇa's Brahman disguise, the leaf test with the devotionally poised arrow,[46] the head's description of how the war was won. Barbarīk has three qualities (invincibility, immortality, and heroic giving) rather than three boons. And whereas dān as giving to Kṛṣṇa seems in some versions to be a separate strand from bali as sacrifice to the goddess, here the two coexist: Barbarīk worships the goddess to receive his arrows, makes his head-offering to Kṛṣṇa's Viśvarūpa, and sees that Kṛṣṇa, Kālī, and Draupadī together have severed all the heads and drunk all the blood—including, we must finally realize, his own.

The burrakatha story of rural Andhra lacks these specific novelties and twists, but introduces some of its own. Above all, it is the clearest of all accounts regarding Barbarīk's relation to the goddess.

> Murāsurudu, a general of Narakāsura, ruled Prāgjyotiṣpuram. By the blessings of Durgā, he had six sons and a daughter Maurvī. Attacking Narakāsura's fort, Kṛṣṇa killed Murāsurudu and his sons. Seeking revenge, Maurvī fought Kṛṣṇa until Durgā intervened, and demanded Kṛṣṇa protect the destitute girl by getting her married. Kṛṣṇa told the Pāṇḍavas to marry Ghaṭotkaca to her, and Bhīma consented, overruling Dharmarāja. But Kṛṣṇa said Ghaṭotkaca must win her by strength and skill, lest she kill him. Maurvī fought Ghaṭotkaca for fifteen days, from full to new moon. With the demons getting stronger under these conditions, Kṛṣṇa, fearing for Ghaṭotkaca, told the pair they should now marry. In nine months, a beautiful son was born. Maurvī left the child with Durgā to be raised to kill Kṛṣṇa. Durgā named him Barbarīk for his body full of hair, and trained him in all kinds of archery. When the *Mahābhārata* war was to begin, Barbarīk was willing to make any kind of sacrifice. He requested Durgā's leave and blessings. She gave him three invincible arrows. Disguised as a Brahmin, Kṛṣṇa stopped him and cajoled him to show his strength for the war. With the first two arrows, Barbarīk exhausted both earth and sky, and said he reserved the third to be used on anyone Durgā asked. Thinking this would prevent the Pāṇḍavas from completing their tasks, Kṛṣṇa wanted to kill Barbarīk. Putting on a sad face, he told Dharmarāja he needed a prewar sacrifice (bali) of a great warrior: either himself or Arjuna. Barbarīk then arrived to offer himself, even though he knew it was Kṛṣṇa's trick. Granted a last wish, Barbarīk chose to see the war. (Brahmanandam 1992; Krishnayya 1998)

[46] The Himachal Pradesh and Kuruksetra versions reverse the order of these episodes.

Kṛṣṇa's death would be enough to keep the Pāṇḍavas from completing their tasks—the pretext he admits to. But he must also divine that should Barbarīk do what Durgā asks, she could ask his own life. Yet note that Durgā never does ask, but only completes the boy's training to be *able* to kill Kṛṣṇa, as requested by her protege Maurvī. The goddess and Kṛṣṇa are never at odds, and the victim is as compliant to the instructions of the one as he is to the tricks of the other. Indeed, Kṛṣṇa's tricks guarantee Barbarīk's sacrifice for a prewar āyudha puja (Brahmanandam 1992, 9)—the "sacrifice of weapons" that is normally part of the goddess's worship at Dasarā. It is the same story in the chapbook version of Aravāṉ's kaḷappali (Hiltebeitel 1988a, 321).

Subba Rao gives another glimpse of the story known to Andhra "village folk" in which Barbarīk offers his head to "the Goddess of War" (1976, 269, 273). Intercepting Barbarīk on the way to Kurukṣetra, Kṛṣṇa is in his usual disguise:

> Old Brahman:—"How can you kill the dreadful foes with merely three arrows in your quiver?"
>
> Barbareeka:—"These three are more than enough. I can smash all the armies of the foes with one arrow. I can destroy all the valiant heroes on the Kaurava side with the second one."
>
> Old Brahman:—"Then what for the third one?"
>
> Barbareeka:—"Surely this is an extra one! I am keeping this extra arrow with a purpose. I have come to know that there is a cunning person named Sri Krishna. I could not decide which side he would take. This third arrow is for that unpredictable person!"

Again, the three arrows' new powers seem to have made the leaf test superfluous. Rather than "earth and sky," the "foes" lined up for the first two arrows are the Kauravas and, one must assume, the Pāṇḍavas. This would be enough to challenge Kṛṣṇa in any other version. But now Barbarīk threatens Kṛṣṇa's own life with the third arrow himself,[47] rather than saying he holds it anticipating the request of the goddess. "Terribly afraid of this tremendous brave boy, the sagacious Krishna immediately rushed to Dharma Raja" to convince him to "sacrifice a young hero on your side to the Goddess of War" (273). Once again, god and victim seem to wink at each other while we envision their roles reversed. Here Barbarīk favors neither side; he is just monstrously destructive in a totally neutral way.

The short news item in "Eenadu," titled "Śyām Bāba Celebrations

[47]One may be reminded of Rāja Desing raising his hand against Ranganātha.

with Bhakti and Śrāddha," also makes a novel disclosure: "In Kali yuga, the head of Barbarīk on the name of Śyām Bāba receives importance and devotion representing Śrī Kṛṣṇa." With this, we can perhaps approach one or two more mysteries. All along, we have met variations on the convoluted bonds that link the god and the victim, who, as just seen, seems to "know" the god's "tricks." We have not even mentioned the best-known of such bonds: that around Kūvākkam, Aravāṉ's short-notice demand for a bride before he dies is solved by Kṛṣṇa's marrying him as "the Deluder" Mohinī—a woman to most, and to Alis or Tamil trans-sexuals, Kṛṣṇa's Ali avatar (Hiltebeitel 1995b; in press-b). We have, however, noted that at Mahobā, Baccha Singh combines "Balrao, Babrahon, Babrīk—one name, by the blessings of Kṛṣṇa Bhagavan," and further tells that Kṛṣṇa has an aṃś in Ūdal and in Maniya Dev, in whom he also takes avatar, while Maniya Dev will protect Ūdal, who will himself be an aṃś of Kṛṣṇa and more cryptically an avatar of Babrīk! Now we have a version in which the convolution spins out from a hidden identity: Barbarīk as Śyām Bāba "representing Śrī Kṛṣṇa" is the "Dark (*śyām*) Lord," the quirky "childlike god," in the form of his own victim's severed head. It must be over such conundrums as these that Barbarīk and Kṛṣṇa mysteriously laugh when they meet in Chandmal Agarwal's story, and perhaps in Baccha Singh's narration when Babrīk's head laughs so powerfully that it momentarily forces Arjuna's chariot backward when the Kauravas start to lose. It would be Kṛṣṇa at the reins of Arjuna's chariot.

The "Eenadu" article also tells that "Marwari families of the town celebrated Shyam Baba Utsav [festival] on Saturday" [November 8, 1997] at a temple that was built for Śyām Bāba at Kachiguda in Hyderabad, and that it was the first anniversary of the Śrī Śyām Bāba Parivār (household) there. Krishnayya comments: These "Shyam Baba festivities" are "celebrated right after Navarātri, Dasarā, or Durgā Pūjā."[48] Clearly, Marwari merchants, from Rajasthan but living in Visakhapatnam,[49] have carried at least *their* version of the Rajput story and cult of Barbarīk from his temple at Khautu or Kāṭ Śyām near Jaipur, where Śyām Bāba, worshiped at the same fall festivities, is one of Barbarīk's names.[50]

Although the burrakatha and Marwari stories both link Barbarīk's sacrifice with Dasarā, it is not clear how deeply they are related. We do not know when or even whether Marwari-carried stories of Barbarīk ever impacted on Andhra folklore, or whether earlier Rajput traditions about

[48]Personal correspondence (follow-up E-mail), 1/2/1998.

[49]Krishnayya writes that preliminary inquiries indicate that Marwaris in Rajahmundry appear *not* to have heard of Barbarīk (personal communication, 1/2/98).

[50]On close ideological ties between Marwaris and Rajputs in Rajasthan, and the Marwari diaspora, see Weinberger-Thomas 1996, 164-88.

Barbarīk preceded them into Andhra. As indicated in discussing Barbarīk's mother, one senses that rural Andhra knows different traditions about Barbarīk. Nonetheless, the rural stories seem sufficiently rajputized. Nagaraj indicates that Barbarīk stories are recited in Anantapur and Kurnool Districts by Bōyas who served as "mercenaries" for landed dominant castes.[51] In the story he recalled, the Pāṇḍavas, tricked by Kṛṣṇa, kill Barbarīk in a prewar fight without knowing that he is their relative. When they realize this and blame Kṛṣṇa, he justifies his role as one that protects the Pāṇḍavas and makes amends to Barbarīk by placing his head with the cloudlike hair on the mountain.

When we move into Tamilnadu, however, we cannot very easily make Aravāṉ a Rajput. His main story goes back to the oldest surviving Tamil *Mahābhārata* by the ninth-century Pallava poet Peruntēvaṉār, who wrote during a period that also supplies the beginnings of temple recitation of the *Mahābhārata*, possibly to instil a martial spirit (Hiltebeitel 1988a, 14); the development of temple iconography of head offerings and other forms of dismemberment to Durgā (318-20); and the emergence, clear already in Peruntēvaṉār and intensified in tenth- to twelfth-century *Paraṇi* poems, of Kālī as Tamil goddess of the battlefield.[52] From a low and outlying figure, Aravāṉ becomes the focus of a new martial spirit linked with devotion to the goddess, and a dedication to royal superiors so noble and complete that he is willing to sacrifice himself painfully for the victory of either side's kings (Hiltebeitel 1995b, 451). Holding the balance of victory in his sacrificial hand, he does not, however, favor the underdog. Indeed, there is something "imperial" about Pallava images of the Pāṇḍavas that carry over to the portrayal of Aravāṉ's dutiful self-subordination to either side. Here too he differs from Barbarīka, especially as we find the latter in Mahobā, where he, the Pāṇḍavas, and their incarnations are tied up in the much more ambiguous world of *Ālhā*, in which the imperium falls into Muslim hands as the outcome of the story, and into British hands in the course of the story's history. In this world, fighting for losing sides is ennobled.

In fact, features of Aravāṉ's mythology reappear in two very different north Indian cycles: one linked with Barbarīka, champion of lost causes; the other with the greatest of legendary emperors. In a medieval adaptation, Vikramāditya's thirty-two marks—"which characterize universal emperors who rule the world"—make him the ideal person to offer his head to the goddess Kāmākṣī of Kañcipuram to get quicksilver for a supplicant Brahman:[53] "The magic quicksilver shall be obtained when an offering

[51]Cf. Roghair 1982, 374: Bōyas are "fighting men" in *Palnāḍu*.

[52]Nagaswamy 1982, 22-28; Hiltebeitel 1991a, 312-13.

[53]As in the Mahobā, Himachal Pradesh, Kuruksetra, and Andhra stories, where the Brahman

is made to the directions with blood coming from the neck of a man bearing thirty-two superior marks," says this goddess of the Pallava (and later the Draupadī and Kūttāṇṭavar cult) heartland to the great pilgrim-emperor from Ujjain.[54] As in all thirty-two tales of the throne, the deity, appreciating Vikramāditya's willing supplication, relents and fulfills his wish without the violent offering.[55] Another Vikramāditya tale has him perform a variant of the rite of cutting the body in nine places (Tamil, *navakaṇṭam*: he offers to cut his body in eight places for the eight Bhairavas and his neck for the goddess). Navakaṇṭam is a prototype for Aravāṉ's sacrifice, with parallels to be noted also in Andhra and Bengal (Hiltebeitel 1988a, 318-19; 1991a, 302-8). It is probably also of Pallava-period south Indian origin, being first mentioned in a tenth-century Nellore District inscription (1991a, 306, n. 31). Finally, having offered his head one last time, the magnanimous Vikramāditya gets the goddess's promise to end human sacrifice.[56] Of course, the Buddha too has the imperial (Cakravartin) trait of thirty-two marks, and a willingness to offer his body many times through his different lives. But unless I have missed some Vajrayāna exceptions, he never offers the goddess his head.

Aravāṉ thus has a classical textual emergence that differentiates him from the largely oral and entirely nonclassical Barbarīka. This classical tradition seems to be rooted in the plains areas where the Draupadī and Kūttāṇṭavar cults are strongest: that is, especially in the original Pallava Toṇṭaimaṇṭalam area (Chingleput and the Arcots) and also (for Draupadī only) in Thanjavur District. Yet elsewhere, Aravāṉ's profile is not so different. Where it is possible to suspect inland connections through mountainous regions, one finds him more rajputized. In Dharmapuri District, which would lie pivotally on such a route, the Kuḷiyaṉūr (Dharmapuri Taluk) Draupadī temple pūcāri Murugan tells that Kṛṣṇa urges Dharmarāja to bring Aravāṉ down from the mountain because "if he were to slap his thigh and laugh (*kokkari*: a derisive laugh of triumph), a crore would die on the battlefield." In Coimbatore,[57] the Pāratiyār at the 1995 Singanallur Kūttāṇṭavar festival knew of Kṛṣṇa's testing Kūttāṇṭavar's prowess as an archer, but with a Tamil bhakti twist. On his way to meet

---

is Kṛṣṇa in disguise. Cf. further the almanac-bearing Brahman in *Palnādu, Elder brothers*, etc. (chap. 3, sequences 6 and 7; chap. 10, § D).

[54]See Sircar 1969, 107 on Vikramāditya as "Sāhasāṅka (literally, 'one whose characteristic mark is the daring courage')"; 115, 141-42: a new type of emperor-adventurer-hero.

[55]See Edgerton 1926, xciii, 182-86; quotes 184.

[56]These tales, numbers 22, 27, and 28 of the "thirty-two tales," concentrate themes found in others: 8 and 25 link the thirty-two marks with blood offerings; 2 and 7 offer his head to the goddess; 9 has him go to Kāñci.

[57]S. Ravindran (August 1998) suggests that immigrant Naidus and Bōyas from Andhra, both numerous in Coimbatore, could have played a role in carrying such traditions.

the Pāṇḍavas before the war, Kṛṣṇa sees a youth astride two mountains with one leg on each and sharpening an arrow on a third. Learning who it is, he invites Aravāṉ to show his power, and points to a banyan tree, asking him to shoot so that the arrow pierces every leaf. When "Kūttāṇṭi" shoots, he pierces all the leaves but one. This one he saves for "Kaṇṇaṉ who is on the banyan leaf" at the end of the Kali yuga. Turning the test into a gesture of noncompliant devotion, Kūttāṇṭi recalls the purāṇic Kṛṣṇa who lies as a baby on a banyan leaf floating on the cosmic ocean during the world's dissolution. At the Mannarkad Draupadī temple on the Kerala side of the ghats near Coimbatore, the story is that Kṛṣṇa finds Aravāṉ astride two mountains while using a third peak to sharpen his sword on just one edge—which, he says, will be more than enough to win a "small war" for the losers.[58] In these stories, Kṛṣṇa connives to keep Aravāṉ from depriving the Pāṇḍavas of their fame.

It is precarious to posit a split between the two Tamil cults. Yet there are some hints that Barbarīk is closer to Kūttāṇṭavar. *Mahābhārata*-recital at Kūttāṇṭavar's Kūvākkam festival is performed by three standing singers who approximate the burrakatha style;[59] at Draupadī festivals Pāratiyārs sing seated. Barbarīka stories place his severed head in a tree to watch the war (as in Himachal Pradesh, with a variant in Garhwal), just as Kūttāṇṭi at Singanallur watches it from the top of an ātti tree.[60] Finally, Kūttāṇṭavar's associations with mountains may carry over into Tamilnadu from Barbarīka's mountain connections in Andhra, Bundelkhand, and Himachal Pradesh. Whereas Barbarīka sees the whole war from the mountain top or cliff-side in Andhra, and part of it in Mahobā, Kūttāṇṭavar descends before the war to watch it at his Tamil temples.[61]

But we cannot derive Aravāṉ from the Rajput world of Barbarīka. And we cannot very well derive Barbarīka from Aravāṉ. Aravāṉ's story clearly has older texts, but its relation to Barbarīka stories has no convincing explanation. The case has the shape of a multiple crime, but we cannot solve it where it is most fundamentally doubled. Yet if tracing themes from Barbarīka to Kūttāṇṭavar takes us from north to south, the parallel between Aravāṉ and Vikramāditya suggests that there is also much to learn from looking in the opposite direction, from south to north.

[58] A Draupadī festival Pāratiyār from near Tirunelveli knew much the same story.

[59] See above, n. 13. They say it commemorates Kūttāṇtavar's standing posture for kalappali.

[60] See nn. 29 and 30 above, and chap. 11 at n. 94.

[61] Kūttāṇṭavar seems to have late Vijayanagar rather than Pallava connections (Hiltebeitel 1995b, 467). See also n. 34 above on the likelihood that Aravāṉ's third boon—that of marrying before his battlefield sacrifice—originates within the Kūttāṇṭavar cult.

13 The Myth of the Agnivaṃśa

The "red herring" of the "real historical origin" of the Rajputs has been "dragged about in historical writings on early medieval and medieval India," says Chattopadhyaya (1994, 161). Scholars scenting a solution to this "riddle" could not fail to theorize about the origin myth of the Agnikula Kṣatriyas. One finds three positions, each driven by the conviction of one answer, as if the myth required a unitary explanation.

First are those for whom Rajputs originate from invaders and/or tribals. For them, the myth explains how Brahmans concealed such parvenus' real origins by legitimizing them as Hindus at the caste level of Kṣatriyas. Most who argued this did so with more than a whiff of opportunism—their intimations of concealed purposes not only betraying the obvious colonial purpose of delegitimizing native ranks and titles, but of legitimizing their own colonizing invasion. Tod set such theories in motion by arguing for "Scythian" origins (1877, vol. II, 384-85), viewing this pedigree as honorable for his "feudal" Rajputs.[1] But when indigenes and foreign "hordes" (notably Gujars) replace Scyths in "tribal" (rather than "feudal") turn-of-the-century explanations, denigrations become palpable. Thus Baden-Powell: "the origin of the chief 'Rājput' tribes . . . is indicated (or concealed?) by the story of the 'Agnikula'" (1899, 544), that origin being largely foreign and post-Aryan" (1899, 298), their name given by "the Brahmanic directors of social usage" who were "driven to find some designation which would embrace the various ruling clans and houses, the greater part of whom would only by a great stretch of fancy be connected with the long extinct or decayed tribes of old Kshatriya stock" (533).[2] R. B. Singh considers the "mission" of the "imperialist historians" one of "despoiling the history of the subject country," and scolds "Indian scholars of successive generations [who] failed to see

[1]See chap. 10, n. 71, and Peabody 1996.

[2]Cf. Oppert 1893, 89-94 (positing "Turanian" origins of Rajputs); Crooke as cited in chap. 9, n. 50. On other British authors, see Asopa 1976, 1-3.

through their subtle game" (1975, ii, 1v). The main Indian to promote foreign origins was Bhandarkar (1911), whom Vaidya criticized for his "Pickwickian method" (1924, 35) while nonetheless accepting an "Aryan invasion" himself to explain the solar and lunar "races" as "two hordes of Aryan invaders" whose "colonization" of India occurred at different times (7, 276). For Vaidya, Gujars "are not foreigners but are anthropometrically Aryans with the best Aryan noses and are historically the Vaiśyas."[3]

Vaidya and Singh lead a second group, for whom Rajputs carry on directly from Vedic and epic Kṣatriyas. Vaidya sees "the Rajputs as undoubtedly descendants of Vedic Aryans of the solar and lunar race, and there was no third race or Vaṃśa, according to our view (namely the Agnivaṃśa)" (1924, vii). For Singh, the Agnikula myth rejuvenates a longstanding heroic tradition of indigenous origin, but one which, by its lateness, reflects that tradition only superficially. These authors' motives for affirming, in Singh's words, "an unbroken continuity of martial ideals from the Rāmāyaṇa and the Mahābhārata down to the present age and therefore the Rajput age," and genuine solar origins behind fabricated fire origins,[4] are transparently anticolonialist and nationalist.[5] For Singh (1975, 45), "The rank and file of the Hūṇas or their associate tribes, if any, who were definitely much inferior to the Hindus in cultural attainment, must have been absorbed in their counterparts of the Hindu population, but certainly not in the Brāhmaṇa or the Kshatriya class who occupied a high place in the social order, and who would not allow an inferior stuff to mix up with them and thus lower their dignity from [a] social point of view."[6]

Chattopadhyaya (1994, 161) tweaks Vaidya for his argument that medieval Rajputs' heroism shows they "cannot but have been the descendants of Vedic Aryans. None but Vedic Aryans could have fought so valiantly in defense of the ancestral faith" (1924, 7). Nonetheless, what Vaidya has to say about affinities between epic Kṣatriyas and medieval Rajputs is often of interest. The Pāṇḍavas, Draupadī, and Kuntī

[3]1924, 31; cf. 10. See also 1907, 1-4, 29-47. On Vaidya's theories of empires and invasions in relation to the formation of both Sanskrit epics, see Hiltebeitel in press-g.

[4]R. B. Singh 1964, 23 (quote); cf. 1975, 21. On Agnikula clans having prior solar myths, see Vaidya 1924, 13-14. Cf. R. B. Singh 1964, 24, 44; 1975, 9-15, 86, 148, 158-60.

[5]See Singh 1975, 5, 8-9, 13, 29, 39. Contemporary with Vaidya, Maharaja Jai Singh of Alwar (1828-1927), drawn into nationalist, colonialist, and orientalist discourses, is said in Meo folklore to have denied Meos' Rajput (including Agnivaṃśa) identity claims (Mayaram 1997, 54-71, 131; see chap. 8, n. 43).

[6]Cf. ibid., 83 and Vaidya 1924, 26: Hūṇas were never considered Rajputs. Gahlot and Dhar 1989, 66-67, 78, 80 in similar vein. On the contrary regarding the Hūṇas, see chap. 9, n. 53.

speak and act "in true Rajput fashion," he tells us;[7] "And what should we think when we are told that Kausalyā killed by her own hands the sacrificial horse with three sword strokes. . . . She must have been very strong and a true Rajput lady indeed."[8] These claims cannot be reduced to mere rhetoric. But the affinities do not point to an unbroken continuity between an ancient "epic period" in the Vedic past (3,500-3,000 B.C., according to Vaidya) and the great Rajput tradition that begins in sixteenth-century Rajasthan.[9] Rather, they raise the question of similarities between the epics' (and especially the *Mahābhārata*'s) allusions to Vedic Vrātya warbands and the lifestyles of earlier medieval "low status Rajput" clans. Vaidya's nationalism, or better, patriotism, evokes "The Ninth and Tenth Centuries, A.D.—The Happiest Period in Indian History" (a chapter title) as having had one religion (Hinduism: Buddhism "entirely supplanted" and Islam yet to get beyond Sind), one race (Aryan, avoiding mixture with Śūdras who "represented the Dravidian race"), more fluidity and commensality among Aryan castes, no foreign domination, and wars that were good because (1) they were "between peoples of the same race, the same religion, and the same civilization and were never carried on with racial animosity or motives of seizure of territory"; (2) they could "prevent the people from becoming effete and effeminate" and "aid the progress of humanity on its onward march to civilization"; and (3), in that "India need not and could not be one state," they restored kings to their thrones and left kingdoms intact.[10]

A third group, considering Rajputs as originally Brahmans who became kings, has its most recent spokesman in Asopa, who seeks (contrary to Singh) to antiquate the Agnikula myth by tracing it to Brahmans' early connections with Agni.[11] Imputing Brahman origins to

[7]N.d., 53 (Kuntī's "stirring call to fight"); cf. 1907, 182 (the Pāṇḍavas' demand for five towns). Draupadī is also "a Rajput woman with a Rajput's bravery and determination illuminating her face" (N.d., 53).

[8]Vaidya [1906] 1972, 9. Goldman's translation, "Kauśalyā . . . with the greatest joy cut [the horse] with three knives" (1984, 151; cf. 306), would hardly invalidate Vaidya's assessment. Cf. Vaidya [1906] 1972, 146, on changes in the text, and [1906] 1972, 94, on recitation of lineages at Rāma and Sītā's wedding "in true Rajput fashion." Let us recall that Kaikeyī also rescued Daśaratha in a battle with Asuras (*Rām* 2.9.9-13).

[9]For the dating, see Vaidya 1907, v, 4-11, 21, 28; N.d., 65-110; [1906] 1972, 7-43, 62-67. Vaidya's Rajasthan was a "central tract" or "middle country" connecting Ksatriyas with medieval Rajputs: remaining Ksatriyas who had not become Buddhists left "their ancient homes in the Panjab and the Gangetic valley" under "pressure of foreign invasions" and "took shelter in the sands of Rajasthan" to reemerge as Rajputs (1924, 43-48, 66-69 [quotes 43, 68]). On his and others' views of "epic periods," see Hiltebeitel in press-g.

[10]Vaidya 1924, 247-58; cf. 1907, 180-81, 245.

[11]Kennedy 1908, 308-9 (unavailable to me; as cited by Asopa 1976, 11, n. 13); Bhandarkar 1911, 24, 27; and D. Sharma 1959, 7-10 also underwrite Brahman origins. Asopa (91) and

the Agnivaṃśa (while tracing the solar and lunar dynasties to Central Asia), he informs us that "[T]he beautiful race of North-Western India stood for Āryanisation of the whole world." Brahmans are thus placed at the very heart of the primal freedom struggle, having been the original Rajputs.[12] This exemplary "Āryanisation" is a "progressive" "proselytizing process" said to have been possible up to the early medieval period when there was still "enough fluidity" between Brahmans and kings; then in the thirteenth century Rajputs rigidified as a caste in retreat from Muslim aggression.[13]

With such one-track arguments and contrived evidence[14] distributed more or less evenly between these views, one can only retrace some of their authors' more useful steps toward different objectives.

A. Variants

My objective is to nudge discussion of the Agnikula myth along.[15] Where the debating authors have attempted to be myth interpreters, their consuming interest in origins has taken them on familiar routes to trivial conclusions. They have allegorized the myth,[16] etymologized it by linking it with far-fetched gods and peoples,[17] literalized it as an historically absurd "theory,"[18] or exposed its "contradictions."[19] Sircar, who nicely

---

R. B. Singh (1975, 46) take opposite affirmative and negative views respectively on whether foreigners could have been accepted into the highest castes.

[12]Asopa 1976, 7 (quote), 17-18, on Central Asian origins of Solar and Lunar vaṃśas; 21-30, 39, 52-54, 68-72, 89, 94-95, 98, on Brahman origins of each Agnikula clan, not to mention the Chandēls (213-15). Cf. Asopa 1972.

[13]Asopa 1976, 7-10; cf. 91, 98.

[14]Five types of evidence are prominent: (1) "hard evidence" of biology (head shape, nose, color, height, race); (2) cultural stereotypes (beautiful, ugly; pure, impure; tribal, barbaric, civilized; indigenous, nonindigenous); (3) similar-sounding names (especially Gujar-Khazar); (4) cultural traits (martial practices); (5) Sanskrit etymology, especially to misread and antiquate the Agnivaṃśa (Asopa 1972, 1976, 1, 11, nn. 3-5) or the "solar and lunar races" (Vaidya 1924, 259-300). Attempts to trace Agnivaṃśa Rajputs directly from Vedic and epic sources (e.g., Vaidya 1924, 7; Asopa 1972, 1976, 21-24) are unconvincing, and Asopa's epic references (1972, 1976, 11) are either far-fetched or unintelligible.

[15]Beyond my discussion in 1988a, 35-38.

[16]Hoernle 1905, 30: "by providing them with respectable places in their caste system," the Brahmans "naturalized" those "foreigners who intermarried with natives and were naturally disposed to favor and even adopt Brahmanism"; Crooke as cited in n. 2; R. B. Singh 1975, 158-59: back-reading the myth not as an allegory of early encounters with Buddhism, but later sixteenth-century ones with Islam. But note Singh 1975, v, rejecting Crooke's allegorical notion as "a silly suggestion!" On Tod, see below.

[17]Asopa, as cited in n. 14 above, on Agni; Oppert 1893, 89-94, linking names of peoples.

[18]Vaidya thus "explodes" the myth: "this tradition or myth of the Agnikulas is indeed a myth, a creation and modern creation of a poet's brain"; Chand has been misinterpreted since "he did not intend to convey that these warriors were heroes *newly created* by

dispels the notion that the myth has some unifying explanatory power and sensibly advocates a multiple-origins approach, shows that each theory of origins offers something in specific cases, but not all. Thus, "the Parihārs were foreigners," "the Paramāras were probably a sept of the Mālava people of ancient India," and the Caulukyas "were Kannaḍigas of the Dravidian stock" whose earlier *solar* dynasty myths parallel those that another Rajput clan, the Guhilas, used to replace earlier accounts of their descent from Brahmans.[20] But when it comes to the Agnikula myth, Sircar joins the trivializers: "this folktale of little value has received more attention of writers on Rajput history than it deserves."[21] His next six pages belie the point, since he writes Rajput history while saying more himself. The issue that cries out for better treatment is the relation of Rajput history to Rajput folklore. Baden-Powell (1899, 546-47) was apparently the first to observe that the Agnikula myth's most striking feature, birth of a warrior clan's ancestor from a firepit, appears to be connected with the Paramāras before any of the other three Agnikula clans.[22] Hoernle, whose contributions as the first to look far enough beyond "origins" to open a discussion of themes and variants,[23] adds: "Their claim can be traced back . . . to the year 1060 A.D." to two *praśastis* (eulogistic inscriptions) "which belong to the junior and senior branches respectively of the royal line of Parmars of Malwa." One of these says:

Vaśishṭha (sic). He simply wanted to convey that four warriors out of the already existing clans came out of the fire at Vaśishṭha's bid to fight the Rākshasas" (11, 16, 11-17). As elsewhere (see nn. 4, 6) Vaidya creates one myth to dispel another. R. B. Singh (1964, 18-28; 1975, 1-47) and Asopa (1976, 37, 89, etc.) treat the myth as a "theory" or "conjecture" on a par with others that might be arguable on an evidential basis. For Singh, "the theory of the fire-origin of these clans is a myth, . . . and it is altogether an absurdity from the view point of their origin, or factors leading to their origin" (1976, 15).

[19]Against implications that the "purified" barbarian or tribal Rajputs would have fought impure "barbarian" ones, R. B. Singh relieves Rajputs of the charge of fighting among themselves (as if they never did) by critiquing Tod's "apparent contradiction" that makes converted "Scythians" fight against demonized "Scythians" of their own "people": "This leads us to the irresistible conclusion that the regenerated warriors and the demons were one and the same people, and through the instrumentality of the Brāhmanas, they were made to kill each other" (1975, 20). Bingley raised this implication to a "probability," that the "four agnicular or fire tribes were . . . really Scythian mercenaries who assisted the Brahmans against their own people" ([ca. 1870] 1979, 115).

[20]Sircar 1965, 1-20 (quotes 18). Cf. Banerjee 1962, 3-18, for similar multiple-origins conclusions, suggesting that the Paramāras branch off from the Rāṣṭrakūtas and present a "likely . . . case of migration from the south" (16-17).

[21]Sircar 1965, 17. Folktales are "unsatisfactory" for Sircar (13).

[22]Cf. Crooke 1920, xxxiii; Sircar 1965, 18-21; R. B. Singh 1975, 216-25.

[23]Hoernle, forgotten by many who continued his arguments, narrowed the invasion doctrine by arguing that all four Agnikula clans were originally Gūrjaras.

> At one time on Mount Abū, Viśvāmitra forcibly took away the cow of Vasishṭa; thereupon the latter caused a hero to arise from the fire-pit (*agni-kuṇḍa*); that hero slew the enemies, and recovered the cow; in reward thereof the sage gave him the name *Para-māra* or slayer of enemies.[24]

Actual reference to a "fire lineage," which is "implied in the legend of these two *praśastis*" but unmentioned, is then supplied in "the slightly later Nagpur *praśasti*" of 1104 "in the form *vahni-vaṃśa*, not *agni-kula*" (1905, 21-22). The form "Vahni = Agni + vaṃśa" parallels the usages "Sūryavaṃśa" and "Candravaṃśa," and thus hints at parity with those two traditionally recognized vaṃśas.[25] Hoernle was, however, apparently unaware of the Sanskrit *Navasāhasāṅka Carita*, a "popular epic about one of the Paramāra kings of Malwa" (R. B. Singh 1975, 220) by the Paramāra court poet Padmagupta Parimala. Padmagupta, who was appointed by the expansionist Paramāra king Vākpati (or Muñjarāja) (ca. 973-97 A.D.) and composed his poem under his successor Sindhurāja (ca. 997-1010),[26] has an earlier version than any of these praśastis:

> There (on Mount Arbuda) the wise chaplain of the house of Ikshvāku (Vasiṣṭha) made a sage's grove, rich in wild rice, fruit, roots, firewood, and kuśa grass. His wish-granting cow was once stolen and carried away by the son of Gādhi (Viśvāmitra), like that of Jamadagni by Kārtavīrya Arjuna.[27] Arundhatī (Vasiṣṭha's wife), upon whose bosom the bark garment was bathed with streams of tears, became the sacrificial firestick (*samidh*) for the fire of her husband's wrath. Thereupon, the first of the knowers of the Atharva [Veda] (Vasiṣṭha) gave an offering with mantras into the fire, which, expanding with broad flames, became like an ascetic's hair. Quickly a man sprang out of the fire with bow, crown, and golden armour. He forcibly wrested the cow from Viśvāmitra and restored it to Vasiṣṭha. . . . From the grateful owner (Vasiṣṭha) he received the fitting name of Paramāra, "slayer of the enemy," and a ruler's power over the globe, before whom all the parasols of other kings were shut. . . . From him, who resembled the ancient king Manu, sprang a vaṃśa that obtained high-

[24]Hoernle 1905, 21; R. B. Singh 1975, 217, gives a more complete and detailed translation.

[25]*Vahni*, "[oblation] bearer," is a name for Agni, and stands behind the Tamil form *va<u>nn</u>i* for the śamī tree, and the caste name Va<u>nn</u>iyar for Draupadī's chief worshipers, who use the names Vahnikula and Agnikula interchangeably (Hiltebeitel 1988a, 35-38).

[26]R. B. Singh 1975, 216; Asopa 1976, 25, 93; Vaidya 1924, 121-23.

[27]*Hṛtā tasyaikadā dhenuḥ kāmasūr-gādhisūnunā/ kārtavīryārjuneneva jamadagneranīyata.*

esteem from virtuous kings.[28]

Note that Padmagupta links Vasiṣṭha with the *Atharva Veda*, the Veda associated with "black magic" *abhicāra* sacrifices performed to kill an enemy.[29] Singh says it is this version that "finds its echo in various inscriptions of the family," mentioning the same praśastis as Hoernle and five more besides, which "tally with each other" and with Padmagupta's narrative. Appreciating that "the fire-origin of the family was thus maintained unbroken from about 1000 A.D. to 1300 A.D. in the records of the Paramāras of different branches," Singh nonetheless stays on his literalist course in pursuing origins: "this story, repeated as it is, does not help us at all in the solution of the problem for the simple reason that Paramāra, the founder of the family, cannot be taken to have been sprung from fire" (1975, 216-18). It is, however, the Paramāra Bhojarāja, Vākpati and Sindhurāja's "legitimate" Agnivaṃśa successor, whose story enriches the mythic material by which the bhaviṣya paurāṇika threads the Agnivaṃśa into the pasts of Vikramāditya and Śālivāhana and the "future" of the "little kings."[30]

Moving on from Paramāra praśastis, Hoernle observes that one finds "substantially the same story" in the *Pṛthvīrāj-rāsau*, but without mention of abducting a cow. As Chand tells it, the first three clan heroes emerge after Vasiṣṭha has "offered a *homa*." Only after these three fail to defeat the Rākṣasas does Vasiṣṭha make "a fire in the fire-pit. . . . Then there arose from the fire the Chāhuvān, four-armed, holding a sword in each arm." Hoernle observes two useful distinctions. In favoring the Chauhān (Chāhuvān) over the other three clan eponyms, Chand "appears to have appropriated to the Chohans a peculiar claim of the Parmars" (1905, 19-22). Second, "the fire-birth is distinctly ascribed to the Chohans, but to them only." This distinction seems significant, in that Chand gives non-fiery etymologized origins to the other three clans:

> Performing meditation, he offered a *homa* in the midst of the altar in the presence of the Suras [gods]. Then there appeared the Pratihāra ["Door-keeper"]: him he placed on the road to the palace. Next there appeared the Chālukka: him Brahma brought forth from his hallowed

[28]I largely follow R. B. Singh's translation (1975, 216), with some minor changes, working from *Navasāhasāṅka Carita* 11.64-75 (verses 64-68 and 75 are those fully translated) in the edition of Bhāratīya 1963, 170-72 (rather than 9.65-76 in the edition Singh cites). The previous verses (9.49-63) are about Mount Arbuda.

[29]On abhicāra in Vedic and popular usages, see Hiltebeitel 1991a, 138-65; in the Sanskrit epics, see Hiltebeitel forthcoming. See also Türstig 1985 on its Atharvanic links and tantric usages.

[30]See chap. 9 following n. 35.

> palm [*cālu*]. The Pāvāra (Parmar) (now) appeared, the excellent hero: him the sage called blessed as the "Slayer of the enemy" (*para-māra*). (Hoernle 1905, 20)

The Paramāras still have their old etymology, but no longer their fiery birth. It seems that Chand uses traditional etyma and myths to draw his distinction in the other two cases as well. Pratihāra is straightforward as "Door-keeper."[31] And the Caulukya ancestor's birth from Brahmā's palm is mentioned in Caulukya praśastis from as early as 1018 in a story that, according to Sircar, "seems to have been borrowed from the Cālukyas of Kalyāṇa," whose origin is referred variously to a water pot or a palm holding water of either Brahmā, the sage Hāriti Pañcaśikha, or the *Mahābhārata*'s Droṇa (1965, 19-20)—with no reference in these cases to birth from fire (23).[32] Other authors who summarize Chand's account do not observe this distinction, and attribute birth from fire to all four eponymous heroes.[33] These accounts appear to be influenced by Tod's trend-setting versions, which purport to be based on Chand. Singh, however, alerts us to additional features in Chand's account, ones that Hoernle omits with his ellipses. First, the Ṛṣis' sacrifice attracts the ire of Daityas or Rākṣasas, who befoul it with flesh, blood, bones, urine, and other impurities. Then, after the first heroes prove "unequal to the task" of defeating the Rākṣasas,

> The great Rishi [Vasiṣṭha] then dug a new Yajña-kuṇḍa and, praying [to] the four-faced Brahmā, he put the "Ahuti" in the fire-fountain.[34] At once a four-armed man, holding in his hands bow and arrow, sword and shield, appeared from the Yajña-kuṇḍa. Vasishtha called him Chāhavāna and after having performed his coronation with Vedic hymns, he asked him to fight the demons. In order to help his hero he remembered the goddess Āśāpurā and sent her to the field of battle.

[31]See Sircar 1965, 20: "apparently derived from the official designation meaning 'the officer in charge of defending the gates of the royal bed chamber, palace or capital city.'" The imperial Pratīhāras of Kanauj "tried to enhance its prestige" by claiming solar descent from Lakṣmaṇa as the *pratīhāra* of Rāma (20-21).

[32]On *cālu* (Sanskrit *culuka*, water pot or hand hollowed to hold water; cf. *caluka*, small pot) and variants, see Hoernle 1905, 19, n. 1; Sircar 1965, 15, 20. However, a bardic account recorded by Cunningham (*Archaeologic Survey of India* 2, 255: unavailable to me; cf. Elliot 1878, 68-69) has the Caulukya as the only one born from fire (Asopa 1976, 48).

[33]See Tod [1929-32, 1920] 1990, 112-13; Bingley [ca. 1870] 1979, 114; D. Sharma 1959, 3-4; Asopa 1976, 46-47; R. B. Singh 1975, 10-12, 221-2.

[34]Tod's translation of "*agnicoonda*" (*agnikuṇḍa*) and "*anhul-coond*" (*analakuṇḍa*), both meaning "fire-pit," as "fire-fountain" ([1829-32] 1972, 1:79; 2,356) seems to have stuck; see Singh 1975, 219.

> Chāhuvāna killed Yantraketu while Dhūmraketu was destroyed by the goddess herself. The rest of the demons, frightened and leaderless, took to their heels. The goddess Āśāpurā, pleased by the valour of the hero, agreed to be the family deity of the Chāhuvāna race and then she disappeared. In the family of this Chāhuvāna was born Prithvīrāja, the hero of the epic.[35]

It seems that the second pit is successful because it has not been defiled. In any case, Chand draws the goddess into his account. After Vasiṣṭha has consecrated the fire-born Chauhān for combat, he remembers the goddess Āśāpurā, "Fortress of Hope."[36] He had not remembered any goddess(es) for the other three clan-ancestors' combat. It does not say that Āśāpurā comes from the fire, only that she is remembered before battle, as at a Dasarā. After their victory, she becomes the Chauhāns' family deity, kuladevatā.

Now we come to a text-historical problem. Hoernle (1905, 19) follows Tod in thinking that "Chand lived about 1190," and speaks of Chand's account as if it were from shortly after the early Paramāra praśastis. Singh's more credible argument is that the passage in question is from the sixteenth or early seventeenth century.[37] In what is considered the earliest known recension of the *Rāsau*, kept at the Fort Library at Bikaner and "presumably from the 15th century," there is "only a passing reference to the origin of the Chāhamānas": "From the sacrifice (*jaga*) of Brahmā was born the first valiant Chauhān Mānikya Rai."[38] Singh thus contends that up to "the 15th century the people, as also the bards, were altogether ignorant of any thing like the fire-origin of these clans."[39] Singh ignores the Paramāras here and seems to regard the people and bards as a class apart from those who, before the fifteenth century, would have recounted the praśasti myths and court epic. Perhaps he supposes that the Paramāras left no influence, or that kings and court poets spoke only to each other, and not to the people or bards. Similarly, Hoernle

[35]R. B. Singh 1964, 14-15; 1975, 11-12; cf. D. Sharma 1959, 4-5.
[36]Tod ([1829-32] 1972, 1:80) treats the name as Asapoorna, i.e., Āśāpurṇā, "full of hope" (cf. 2,357: "Asápúraná"), but Āśāpurā or Āśāpurī (Somani 1981, 11) seems to be correct.
[37]1964, 14 (date); cf. 1975, 10 ("looks like a composition of the 16th century"). On the text's four extant recensions, see McGregor 1984, 17-19: "a considerable repertoire of verses was probably in existence by 1470"; the shortest recension "contains at least some of the unhistorical references of the other recensions, and must, like them, post-date Pṛthvīrāj by an appreciable time"; "the main expansion" must have taken place "chiefly in Rajasthan" in the sixteenth through seventeenth centuries.
[38]R. B. Singh 1975, 10-11 (date); 1964, 13 and n. 11, with the Hindi and a "15th or early 16th century" dating. He draws on D. Sharma 1940. Cf. Vaidya 1924, 18-21.
[39]R. B. 1975, 11; similarly Ray [1931-36] 1973, 1052.

observes that the earliest Paramāra and Chauhān references to miraculous births occur only in praśastis and not in "official charters," and infers that initially "no credence, or at least no importance, was attached to it [the myth] officially" (1905, 22). Both arguments overstate their cases, but make important points.

It is, however, highly credible that the *Prṛthvīrāj-rāsau*'s full account is a sixteenth-century creation. As Singh sees it,

> The four clans, branded as "Agnikulas," fought incessant battles from the very beginning of their political career on the map of India to their end as independent powers against the Muslim invaders . . . to save their country and its ancient culture and civilization from "Mlechchhas", and this noble endeavour found its culmination in the person of Prithivīrāja, the hero of the Rajputs. . . . The same struggle was once again revived in the last quarter of the 16th century A.D., when Mahārāṇā Pratāpa, the Rajput hero of Mewar, took up arms against the mighty Mughal Emperor Akbar. . . . It was perhaps on this occasion that the theory of the heroic descent from the fire-fountain was set in motion by some unknown bard. (1975, 13; cf. 1964, 17)

The sixteenth century was a period of heightened descent-consciousness among western Rajputs under the Mughals, and in particular under Akbar.[40] The "Rajasthani aspect of the language of the later *Pṛthvīrāj-rasāu* suggests its place in the literary culture of north India as a poem prized, during the middle and even late centuries of Muslim dominance, for its tale of Rajput romance and heroism" (McGregor 1984, 19). This account would reflect this interest and also have been articulated as an accolade for centuries of resistance.[41]

From this point, variants of the myth "apparently based on" the *Rāsau*, and supposing it to have been authored by a contemporary of Pṛthvīrāj, continue to claim fire-birth for all four Agnikula clans. A "similar story," as Singh notes, found in the *Hammīra Rāso* composed by Jodharāja, court poet of prince Candrabhāna of Nīmarānā in 1728, is especially revealing:[42]

> Paraśurāma slaughtered the Kṣatriyas twenty-one times. None

[40]See, e.g., Sircar 1965, 4-5: "There is no early record mentioning the Guhilas as belonging to the solar race. From only about the sixteenth century A.D., [have] the Guhila Rāṇās of Mewar" claimed Sūryavaṃśa descent from the Ikṣvākus of Ayodhyā.

[41]Cf. Banerjee 1962, 13-14.

[42]R. B. Singh 1975, 12 (quotes and dates); cf. 1964, 15. On an apparently earlier mid-fourteenth-century version by Śārṅgadhara, see McGregor 1984, 19.

escaped but those "who held a stalk of grass by the teeth in token of submission, and who took the guise of women. Boys, eunuchs, old men, and those who put ten fingers within their mouths, those who left their swords and fled away, and those who fell down at his feet."

"For a time there were no Kshatriyas. . . . Rákshasas increased in number, the Vedas were trampled under foot, and every form of Hinduism was forgotten." The sages went to Paraśurāma's cave on Mount Abu. All the gods, men, and Nāgas assembled and "devised a plan to extirpate the Rákshasas." Vasiṣṭha erected a fire altar. Śiva appeared and the sages worshiped him. But the Rākṣasas threw "blood, flesh, grass and other rubbish" on the altar. "Then all the holy sages—Dvaipáyana, Dálbhya, Jaimini, Lomaharshan, Bhrighu, Pulaha, Áttreya, Gautama, Garga, Sáṇḍilya, Bhardváj, Bálakhilya, Márkaṇḍeya, Ushaṇá, Kaushika, Basant, Mudgala, Uddáláka and Mátanga, with Vaṣishṭha at their head, complained to Brahmá and Śiva. Again, an altar was erected, a *kund* dug and purified, fire kindled, and every rite of sacrifice begun. Hymns of the Sáma Veda were sung. All of a sudden sprang four warriors with swords in hand from the *kund*. These fought with the Rákshasas and defeated them." The sages went to Paraśurāma's cave and "asked his benediction on the newly created heroes." He blessed them. Śakti was invoked and also blessed them. "Their energy was like fire, their eyes red like the rising sun shot forth courage, their foreheads shone like flames, and their crowns sparkled. They frowned, and the devils shook with fear."

One, "Chohán," had four arms, holding a sword, bow, dagger, and knife. He asked Brahmā why he was created. Brahmā told him to do as Bhṛgu instructed. Bhṛgu told him to kill Rākṣasas, and that Śakti would protect him. "In times of peril, Ṣakti protected the Hindu champion from all dangers. Every time he fell at her feet, his strength and energy were doubled, and he rushed at the ranks of the devils and put them to the sword. The goddess is called Áṣápúrí, because she filled the hope of the holy sages, and by that name is worshipped by the Choháns to this day." (Bandopadhyaya 1879, 186-88)

The goddess first appears to bless all four clans after they defeat the Rākṣasas, but then the Chohān gets her special protection and begins the Dasarā routine of invoking her *before* battles. Let us also note that Singh, who summarizes this story twice, mentions the extinction of the Kṣatriyas only in his first account (1964, 16; 1975, 12). Perhaps he recalled that he maintains their "unbroken continuity."[43] In any case, it is but a short

[43]Similarly, Vaidya takes as "questionable" the "statement in the Purāṇas to the effect that in the Kali age there would remain no Kshatriyas." See above, n. 9.

step to Tod's 1829-32 accounts, of which there are two, and to the version in *Bhaviṣya Purāṇa*, which is probably from around the same time as Tod, or a little after.

As Crooke puts it, Tod's two versions represent "local tradition in Rājputāna so vague that in one version of the story Vasishtha, in the other Visvāmitra, is said to have been the officiating priest."[44] According to Singh, by the time Tod "borrowed the idea from the popular epic" (the *Pṛthvīrāj-rāsau*), the "fire-pit origin of the four clans" had become "popular mythology." Seeing grist for his argument that the Agnikula clans were Brahmanized Scythians, Tod, "in his own inimitable style, . . . made it [the myth] all his own" (1975, 16). Yet Tod must have made use of varied sources. Like Jodharāja in his *Hammīra Rāso*, Tod's second account (the one we will now follow) begins with the Kṣatriyas' extinction:

> When the impieties of the kings of the warrior race drew upon them the vengeance of Pursarāma, who twenty-one times extirpated that race, some, in order to save their lives, called themselves bards; others assumed the guise of women; and thus the *singh* (horn) of the Rajpoots was preserved, when dominion was assigned to the Brahmins. The impious avarice of Sehsra Arjuna, of the Hya [Haihaya] race, king of Mahéśwar on the Nerbudda,[45] provoked the last war, having slain the father of Pursarāma.

As we shall see, in *Mahābhārata* versions of this story, Bhārgava Rāma [Paraśurāma] is provoked to killing Kārtavīrya Arjuna's ["Sehsra Arjuna's"] sons not only by the slaying of his father Jamadagni, but by the prior theft of the calf of Jamadagni's cow. Tod makes no mention of the calf or cow theft in either version.[46] But one may glimpse something of the "popular mythology" he could have encountered from his contemporary (and slight literary predecessor) Ward, who heard a similar version of the Viśvāmitra-"Sahasra Arjuna" story.

> Urjunoo was a Kshutriya king with a thousand arms, who overcame the greatest monarchs, and made dreadful havoc in the world. He beat Ravunu, and tied him to the heels of his horse; but Bruhma delivered

[44]Crooke 1920, xxxiii; Tod [1829-32] 1972, 1:79-80 (Vasiṣtha version); 2, 355-57 (Viśvāmitra version). Cf. Asopa 89; R. B. Singh 1975, 16-20, 221-23, with further variants from Rajasthani "bardic tales," in which Vasistha alternates with Viśvāmitra as sacrificer.
[45]The Narmada. See chap. 5, § D and n. 51; chap. 10, § B at n. 64.
[46]In the Vasiṣtha version, one learns only that "the Moonis . . . drew support form the cow, from roots, fruits, and flowers" (Tod [1829-32] 1972, 1:79).

> him, and reconciled them again. One evening Urjunoo being in the forest, took refuge in the hut of Jumudugnee, the learned ascetic. He had with him an army of 900,000 men: yet Jumudugnee entertained them all. Urjunoo astonished, enquired of his people how this sage, living in a forest, was able to entertain so many people! They could not tell. They saw nothing except a cow Bruhma had given him. . . . Its name was Kamu Dhenoo, or the earth personified. Urjunoo offered Jumudugnee his kingdom for the cow, and on his refusal made war with him, and destroyed him and his whole army. Purushoo Ramu, hearing of the death of his father Jumudugnee, went to the residence of Urjunoo, and killed him.[47]

The calf of Jamadagni's cow has been replaced by the cow itself, making Jamadagni's cow the equivalent of Vasiṣṭha's cow. Clearly Ward had clever sources. Earth-as-"cow" (*go*), a Cow of Wishes that feeds an army of nine lākhs of men, is a recognizable symbol of the Brahman's right to the earth under protection of a dharmic king. One could say that when Kārtavīrya Arjuna and his sons violate Brahmans and steal the earth, it doesn't matter whether a cow is mentioned or not.

Tod thus makes a turn on a point that has been latent in the Agnikula myth since Padmagupta first unfurled it for the glory of the Paramāras. As Padmagupta sets the scene, he leaves a note of indeterminacy. It is clearly Vasiṣṭha's cow that is stolen from his hermitage on Mount Abu by Viśvāmitra. But Padmagupta mentions the theft of Jamadagni's cow in the same breath: Vasiṣṭha's "wish-granting cow was once stolen and carried away by the son of Gādhi (Viśvāmitra), like that of Jamadagni." Padmagupta does not imply that Viśvāmitra also stole the cow of Jamadagni. He only alludes to the obvious parallel between the two cow-theft-from-Brahman stories, which for him would have been equally famous from their tellings in the Sanskrit epics and impossible to collapse or confuse. In one, it is Vasiṣṭha's cow that gets stolen by Viśvāmitra, and once the cow defends herself against him, Viśvāmitra determines to transform himself from a Kṣatriya into a Brahman. In the other, it is the calf of Jamadagni's cow that is stolen either by Kārtavīrya Arjuna or his sons, and when the theft further results in the sons' killing Jamadagni, it provokes Jamadagni's son Paraśurāma to annihilate the Kṣatriyas twenty-one times over.[48] We must look at the Sanskrit epic versions of these two stories more closely, but for the moment we may say that Tod has

[47]Pogson [1828] 1971, 5, n. 1, citing Ward [1882] 1970 (first edition 1817-20) without the reference, which I cannot find.

[48]Summarizing *Mbh* 3.116-17 (where Kārtavīrya steals the calf; 116,21); 12.49-50.4 (where Kārtavīrya's cruel [*nṛśamsās*] sons steal it; 49.39-40).

simply changed the background of the birth of the Agnikula clan ancestors from the one cow-theft setting to the other—without, however, mentioning the cow!

This shift cannot be innocent. If it is Vasiṣṭha's cow, the fire-birth does not follow from a subsequent annihilation of the Kṣatriyas, as it does if it is the killing of Jamadagni, or his calf or cow. As noted, in preferring the annihilation option, Tod has the precedent of Jodharāja's *Hammīra Rāso*, which not only mentions the annihilation of the Kṣatriyas, but brings Paraśurāma forth from his cave on Mount Abu to bless the Agnikula Kṣatriyas who regenerate them.[49] Tod would find no such precedent in Chand, whom he claims to retell. To this point, we may agree with Singh that Tod has made the myth "all his own" to serve his argument for the Scythic origins of the Rajputs. Yet as Hoernle observed, in Chand's account, Vasiṣṭha is also not robbed of his cow. As Chand has eliminated Vasiṣṭha's cow, so Tod has eliminated Jamadagni's cow or calf. Each has replaced the despoiling of a cow by a despoiling of the earth.

But this, as we have just seen, cannot be taken to indicate that Tod invented this, or any other, part of his account. As Ward's contemporary telling shows, Singh is probably right that Tod retold a "popular mythology." Once the fire-birth of the Agnikula ancestors follows Paraśarāma's annihilation of the Kṣatriyas, we find Tod continuing his second version with other instructive changes. Without Kṣatriyas, Brahmans rule. But their chief weapon, the curse, is unable to prevent the "monstrous brood" of demons and infidels from scourging the land. With the "sacrificer" no longer Vasiṣṭha, or even Paraśurāma, but Viśvāmitra, the former would-be cow-thief-turned-Brahman now replaces Vasiṣṭha, whose cow he tried to steal, as the performer of the fire-birthing sacrifice:[50]

> In this exigence, Viśvamitra, the instructor in arms of Bhâgwân [i.e., Rāma], revolved [sic] within his own mind, and determined upon the re-0creation of the Chetris [Kṣatriyas]. He chose for this rite the summit of Mount Aboo where dwell the hermits and sages.

As an achieved Brahman, Viśvāmitra, of course, retains Kṣatriya aptitudes and dispositions. He also has to "choose" Mount Abu, since, unlike Vasiṣṭha and Paraśurāma, he apparently has neither a hermitage nor a

[49]According to Singh's summary of the *Hammīra Rāso* passage cited above, "In this sacrifice Brahmā played the Creator, Bhrigu, the Hotā, Vaśishṭha, the Āchārya, Vatsa, the Ritvika, and Paraśurāma the Yajamāna" (Singh 1964, 15)!

[50]In the *Hammīra Rāso* (cited above) Viśvāmitra has only the supportive role of *ācārya*.

cave there. Tod also introduces expanded roles for the gods. Viṣṇu, lying on his serpent bed, receives the sages, requests them "to regenerate the warrior race," and returns with them to Mount Abu to participate in the sacrifice along with Indra, Brahmā, and Rudra. After "expiatory rites were performed," each of the four gods in turn throws an "image" into the fire-pit and brings forth one of the clan eponyms: Indra the Paramāra, with the words "'Mar! Mar!' (slay, slay)"; Brahmā the Caulukya; Rudra the Pratihāra; Viṣṇu the four-armed Chauhān. The warriors fight the "infidel" demons, who had been observing the rites, but they soon face a predicament that all scholars who summarize Tod ignore.

> But as fast as the blood of the demons was shed, young demons arose; then the four tutelary divinities, attendant on each newly created race, drank up the blood, and thus stopped the multiplication of evil. These were—Asápúraná of the Chohan. Gâjun Matá of the Purihar. Keonj Matá of the Solanki. Sanchair Matá of the Pramara.

Apparently expanding on Chand and Jodharāja, who have only Āśāpurā present to kill the demons, especially for the Chauhāns, Tod now has all four clan goddesses present. Moreover, they now renew Kālī's tactic of devouring the "blood-seed" demon Raktabīja in the *Devī Māhātmyam.*[51] Tod then closes with the statement that, according to Chand, of all the thirty-six Rajput "races," "the *Agnicúla* is the greatest; the rest were born of woman, these were created by the Brahmans."[52] The account accentuates Brahmans: like the *Bhaviṣya Purāṇa* version, which cites the specific Vedas whose mantras produce each of the four ancestors. But in that account the four clans are brought forth not to oppose infidel demons, but Buddhists.

B. Themes

Taking stock of this myth's variants, we can identify certain recurrent elemental themes, and, in some cases, differences in the ways they are narrated.

1. Cow theft (consistent, except for Chand and Tod, from Padmagupta on):
   It is Vasistha's cow (first in Padmagupta); it is also reminiscent of Jamadagni's cow or calf (first alluded to explicitly by Padmagupta, and implicitly by Tod).

[51]His first version only has "Sacti-devi"-"Asapoorna"-"Kalka" (Kālikā?) come armed on her lion in answer to Vasistha's "hope" for help. There is nothing about how she helps the first Chauhān against the demons, whom he defeats ([1829-32] 1972, 1, 80).
[52]Tod (1929-32) 1972, 2:356-57.

2. Retaliatory sacrifice performed by a Brahman (or by Brahmans):
   By Vasiṣṭha (first in Padmagupta); by Viśvāmitra (first in Tod).

3. The Brahman has (Brahmans have) divine assistance:
   The gods are merely present with the Rsis (first in Chand); Viṣṇu creates the four-armed Chauhān (first in Chand); Brahmā creates the Caulukya from his palm (first in an eleventh-century praśasti); each clan ancestor is created by a different god (Tod), or from a different Veda (*BhvP*).

4. Birth from fire (consistent from Padmagupta on):
   Of first Paramāra (in Padmagupta); of first Chauhān (in Chand); of four clan eponyms (in Jodharāja); of first Caulukya.[53]

5. Goddess (goddesses) manifest(s) as family deity (deities) to help the hero(es)
   Of the Chauhāns (first in Chand, then in Jodharāja); of all four clans (Tod).

6. The enemies are defeated:
   They are "enemies" (Padmagupta, early praśastis); Rākṣasas (Chand, Jodharāja); "infidel" Daityas, Asuras, and Dānavas (Tod); Buddhists (*BhvP*); "Buddhism, Jainism, and other heresies" (Crooke);[54] Muslims (R. B. Singh).

The references to Cunningham and especially Tod, Crooke, and Singh show, of course, that scholars have added to the mythmaking. At every point, we also see that the myth has been highly elastic. Looking at all six points, there is consistency and structure, with significant oppositions and complementarities. It would be hard to argue that there is no Agnikula myth, that it is merely a scholarly fiction.[55] Yet it is also clear that the versions we have tell us nothing of the myth's origins, much less the origins of the Agnikula Rajputs. At most, one can only say that at some time, "all four dynasties connected by tradition with the *Agnikula* story were associated geographically with the Abu region," and that "[t]he importance which is accorded uniformly to 'Arbuda' in different versions of the story might have some historical basis" (Banerjee 1962, 12).

Nayakar, in his thoughtful 1891 work advocating Kṣatriya status for Tamil Vaṉṉiyars, studied such myths (including Tod's) in an attempt to influence British census categories which identified the Vaṉṉiyars as Śūdras. He observes that there are three ways that Kṣatriyas have originated: from Brahmā [i.e., Puruṣa], in the beginning of creation; by creation after a deluge; and by creation to effect a certain special object (1891, 7-8). Agnikula Kṣatriyas emerge in both the second and third contexts, in different ways, and in different times and places. Their

[53]In Cunningham: see n. 32.
[54]As cited at chap. 9, n. 50, and above n. 2.
[55]One may recall Lévi-Strauss's dictum (1963, 217) that a myth remains one so long as it is "felt as such," even, in the case of the Oedipus myth he is discussing, from the Greeks to Freud. I use "elemental themes" here with his "gross constituent units" in mind.

careers have "late," postcosmogonic beginnings and may also, as in the *Bhaviṣya Purāṇa*, find authors who would imagine their time limited to the completion of the special ends for which they were created. Indeed, a background feature of all Agnikula myths is that Agnivaṃśa Kṣatriyas are born when the solar and lunar dynasties have either been eliminated or depleted, or have defaulted in their maintenance of dharma. Here Agnikula myths build upon a persistent purāṇic genealogical myth. With Paraśurāma's holocaust as precedent, the end of the *Mahābhārata* war and the onset of the Kali yuga marks another destruction of lunar and solar dynasty Kṣatriyas.

As Thapar sees it, setting this myth in a rich interpretative discussion, the royal genealogical lists (*vaṃśānucaritas*) of the purāṇas provide three major "time markers":

(1) The deluge, which ends the period of cosmological origins and marks the beginning of the solar and lunar dynasties;

(2) The *Mahābhārata* war, which ends the period for which purāṇic authorship "constructs a record of what was perceived as the lineages of the ruling clans," relying on the stories of the two Sanskrit epics, which themselves "appear to reflect a clan or lineage-based society prior to or in transition to the formation of states." Through their *Rāmāyaṇa-Mahābhārata* sequence, the lists bring the solar and lunar dynasties to a cataclysmic end, or alternately to a profound rupture.[56]

(3) The emergence of Magadha as the beginning of the monarchical metropolitan state, to and through which the genealogies may be traced into the "futures" of current (including Rajput) histories.[57]

Buddhists and Jains treat some of the Magadha dynasties as Kṣatriya, but purāṇic genealogies consider them otherwise (low or Brahman). The

[56]On the *Mbh* war as a "terminal event" marked by a switch to the future tense, see Thapar 1992, 159; cf. 1978a, 332-35; 1984, 47, 138, 140-41; 1992, 150, n. 17. The purāṇas list a few further descendants of the solar and lunar lines, "but more now as a rounding off of descent groups" (1991, 21), leaving new links with the solar and lunar dynasties to be forged in the post-Gupta period (1992, 157). Thapar even detects this rupture within the *Mbh*'s own "symbolic" story in the suggestion "that the two contenders for the right to rule the kingdom, the Kauravas and the Pāṇḍavas, are neither of them related by blood to the Pūru lineage," which "ends with Bhīṣma. Both Dhṛtarāṣṭra and Pāṇḍu are of lesser stock," claiming a Pūru connection only through their fishergirl grandmother Satyavatī (1978a, 351; cf. 334; 1991, 17).

[57]On these three markers, and for the quotations above, see Thapar 1991, 3. For Thapar's fuller discussion, see ibid., 12-23; 1978a, 332-36; 1984, 138-47; 1992, 158-60. On bardic Agnikula myths, Thapar observes their heightening of chivalry, heroism, loyalty, royal courts focused on the king, and "a well-defined geographical area which constituted the kingdom" (1992, 168). See also Hiltebeitel in press-g.

Nandas, considered Śūdras, are said to "exterminate" the Kṣatriyas, and Mahāpadma Nanda in particular is called "finisher of all the Kṣatriyas," and compared to Paraśurāma.[58] Asking whether paurāṇikas denied Kṣatriya status to the Magadha kings because such kings favored heretics, did not seek Brahman legitimation, did not cater to the traditional clan system, or because Brahmans felt a "disapproval of monarchical states" for "encouraging competition among *brāhmaṇas* and other sects for patronage" (and suggesting all these factors), Thapar remarks that "[t]he brahmanical imprint on this section is apparent. As a projection of the decline of an earlier aristocracy and the moving in of upstarts, no statement could be more explicit."[59] It would also seem to evidence a Brahmanical purge of the Ikṣvāku-"solar" genealogy by exorcising Buddhist kings from it, making Rāma its culmination and elevating its grandeur to a hoary past (the Tretā yuga), and leaving the lunar dynasty, more palpably grounded in Vedic names and places, to run its more "segmented" course across most of real north India through the intermediate Dvāpara yuga.[60]

In any event, the lunar and solar vaṃśas must be studied as a double "dynastification" of the past: one that was purposefully fabricated by the epic and purāṇic poets from Vedic and heterodox bits and pieces to imagine a "Hindu" past that had, for the present, at least temporarily exhausted itself.[61] Following on their descriptions of these "epic age" exterminations, purāṇic authors prophesy that the solar and lunar vaṃśas will each have one descendant "endowed with great yogic powers" who will stay in a village called Kalāpa, from which the pair "will revive the Kṣatriya race when the kṛta age will start again after the present kali age comes to an end, and that some kṣatriyas exist on earth like seed even in the kali age."[62] While such passages pronounced Kṣatriyas' (virtual) extinction, representing a Brahmanical judgment on the decline of their "dynasties," Brahmanical legislative texts (*smṛtis* and *nibandhas*)

[58] Wilson [1840] 1972, 374; *Viṣnu Purāna* 4.24.20 (Gītā Press edition); cf. Sircar 1969, 150; Pargiter [1913] 1962, 58; Raychaudhuri 1967, 11-26; Thapar 1991, 22. Chatterjee 1995a, 79, treats the recapitulation of this history by the early nineteenth-century Mrityunjay, according to whom "[t]he Rājput jāti started with this Nanda"!

[59] Thapar 1991, 29; cf. Sircar 1969, 51, 54.

[60] According *Mbh* 6.11.10, the Tretā yuga is a time when there were "heroic Ksatriyas who were emperors (*cakravartins*)"; see Hiltebeitel in press-g. See chap. 7, n. 43, on lunar dynasty "segmentation."

[61] I employ Henige's (1975) sense of "dynastification." Vaidya's efforts to give Vedic credibility to the two dynasties run aground on the embarrassments that they never list genealogical sequences for more than five generations, that the lists vary, and that the same kings end up in both dynasties (1924, 274-76). See further Hiltebeitel forthcoming.

[62] Kane [1930-62] 1975, 2,1:380-82; 3:873; see *Brahmānda* 1.1.164; *Visnu* 4.24.44; *Vāyu* 1.32.39-40; *Matsya* 273.56-58; *Bhāgavata* (12th Skandha).

continued to prescribe Kṣatriyas' privileges and duties among the four varṇas, presumably recognizing that reigning kings would appreciate recognition as Kṣatriyas if they were to support the Brahmanical system.

Yet Brahmans were of two minds on this issue. Vaidya traces a fascinating debate in commentarial literature over the validity of the "oft-quoted" dictum, attributed untraceably to "some purāṇa," that there would be only two varṇas (Brahmans and Śūdras) left in the Kali yuga. He shows that the dictum probably dates from only the thirteenth or fourteenth century under conditions of Muslim rule in which claims to Kṣatriya status could be judged illegitimate by some Brahmans because the aspirants to that status, as well as to Vaiśya status, no longer studied the Veda, and that it probably comes from the east and south (where it remains axiomatic today that there are only two varṇas, Brahmans and "caste Śūdras"). In these circumstances, other champions of Kṣatriya continuity like the members of the Bhaṭṭa family "who crowned Śivaji with Vedic rites, believing him to be a good Kṣatriya," and like Vaidya and Kane themselves—Kane cites the Agnivaṃśa myth as evidence for Kṣatriyas' continuity ([1930-62] 1975, 2, 1:381-82)—could take one side, while "rigidly orthodox writers of extreme views" could pronounce extinction on the other.[63] The bhaviṣya paurāṇika is singular in this regard, carrying forward the "rigidly orthodox" position through the medium of purāṇic narrative. Having set the birth of the four Agnivaṃśa clan ancestors from the fire-sacrifice on Mount Abu against the background of the founding of Magadha, the emergence of Buddhism, and the era of Vikramāditya, this likely "easterner" with "north central" ties then updates the extinction narrative to the beginning of the thirteenth century, the very period when debate probably revives over the issue of whether only Brahmans and Śūdras remain, and applies it not only to the reextinction of the solar and lunar lines but the obliteration of the Agnivaṃśa. He also considers caste mixture entrenched south of the Vindhyas (see chap. 9, § A). Similarly, Thurston and Rangachari could cite the Madras Census Report of 1891 as recording that "the term Kshatriya is, of course, wholly inapplicable to the Dravidian races, who might with as much, perhaps more, accuracy call themselves Turks. . . . It is noted, in the Madras Census Report, 1901, that 'Parasurāma is said to have slain all the Kshatriyas seven times over but 80,000 persons have returned themselves as such in this Presidency alone'" ([1904] 1965, 4:79). Such was the mindset facing Nayakkar's 1891 argument about Agnikula Kṣatriyas.

Chauhān traditions reflect stages in these debates. According to one

[63]Vaidya 1924, 312-17, quoting from Kane [1930-62] 1975, 2, 1:381, who traces the continuation of this debate into British Indian courts (382).

inscription, "the first Chauhān was created after the solar and lunar dynasties had become extinct. His services were needed to put down the *asuras* interfering with the rites of the sage Vatsa. The Agnikula myths centre round a similar core. . . . The myths of [the Chauhāns'] solar origin regard Chāhamāna as a Kṣatriya created in Kaliyuga. He was produced, they say, to wipe out the *Mlecchas*." Sharma concludes from these myths that "the Chauhāns probably gained recognition as Kṣatriyas rather late in history, and most probably by fighting for Hinduism against non-Hindus." Sharma is clearly thinking of Muslim "non-Hindus" rather than Buddhist ones.[64]

Thus if anything is evident, it is that the Agnikula myth cobbles themes together from multiple sources. In items 1 to 3 and 6—that is, in matters having to do with cow theft, retaliatory sacrifice, divine assistance, and defeat of enemies—the myth clearly builds on epic and purāṇic sources. In addition to those already noted, a prominent one has been noticed by Sharma, who argues that the myth's earliest Paramāra instances are based on the *Rāmāyaṇa*'s version of the Vasiṣṭha-Viśvāmitra story.[65] When Vasiṣṭha's cow Kāmadhenu is dragged away by the all-conquering Kṣatriya Viśvāmitra, who has just seen her feed his entire army, Kāmadhenu obtains Vasiṣṭha's permission to retaliate. She routs Viśvāmitra's hosts by creating dreadful Pahlavas, Śakas, Yavanas, and Kāmbojas from her "roar" or "bellow" (1.54.17; 55.2); more weapon-bearing Pahlavas then come from her udders, Yavanas from her vulva, Śakas from her anus; Mlecchas, Hāritas, and Kirātas from the pores of her skin; finally Vasiṣṭha burns the remaining warriors to ashes with the syllable "*Hum.*"[66] Sharma remarks, "great indeed, would have been the astonishment" of the Chauhān bards who "adapted" the story from the Paramāras if they had known that the latter's story was "based on a similar legend in the *Rāmāyaṇa*" in which "non-Aryan tribes are said to have been created by Vasiṣṭha" (1959, 4). The unsavory (even if bovine) emanation of these non-Aryans might also have been astonishing.[67]

The *Mahābhārata*, however, tells much the same story while making it further clear that the non-Aryans are defined not just by the orifices that exude them but by what those orifices normally secrete. The "cow of plenty" (*kāmadhugdhenu*), here called Nandinī, begins her retaliation by creating Pahlavas from her tail or "arse" (*pṛcchāt*), Śabaras and Śakas

[64]D. Sharma 1959, 5-6 (quotes), xxv-xxvii.

[65]D. Sharma 1959, 4-5; cf. Banerjee 1962, 13.

[66]See *Rām* 1.50-54, and 53.16-54.7 for the details just cited; also Goldman 1984, 226-27.

[67]Singh and Asopa endorse Sharma's argument, ignoring such problems: for Asopa, birth from cow dung or urine represents caring for *artha* while birth from fire represents dharma or religion (1976, 94-95).

from her dung, Yavanas from her urine, and Puṇḍras, Kirātas, Dramiḍas, Siṃhalas, Barbaras, Daradas, and Mlecchas from the foam of her mouth; but here, once the superiority of Brahman forbearance (*kṣama*) is established over Kṣatriya strength (*bala*), Vasiṣṭha confirms the former by letting all Viśvāmitra's soldiers live.[68] Sharma gives no importance to this variant, but he would seem to need both for the analogy to work: the *Rāmāyaṇa*'s to make the Paramāra an actual "slayer," and the *Mahābhārata*'s to keep the cow-born warriors alive to become Rajputs.[69] The analogy relies on the very point where the two versions contradict. The *Mahābhārata* also knows Vasiṣṭha as having a hermitage on Mount Arbuda, which is called a "son of Himavat," who fills a place where "there was formerly a hole in the earth" (3.80.74-74). Citing this passage, Vaidya notes that the *Skanda Purāṇa* elaborates it to have Vasiṣṭha's cow fall in this hole; Vasiṣṭha must then persuade Himālaya to give one of his sons to fill it (1924, 67-68). The story clearly parallels the loss of Vasiṣṭha's cow in the Agnikula myth.

But the theft of Vasiṣṭha's cow cannot be the origin of the fire-birth myth simply because it has nothing to do with birth from fire, which is, after all, a *sine qua non* of the myth.[70] Rather, it is *drawn into* the fire-birth myth because it provides variants of some of its other themes. These, which affect everything that builds up to the fire-birth (themes 1 to 3 above), are also present in variants where it is not Vasiṣṭha's cow but Jamadagni's calf. In brief, when Kṣatriyas violate their dharma, oppress Brahmans, steal cows, and ravage the earth, Brahmans can retaliate. As noted, these more basic themes are played out differently in the two cow-theft stories.[71] If it is Vasiṣṭha's cow, barbarian warriors are momentarily created to teach the errant Kṣatriya (Viśvāmitra) a lesson. The Kṣatriya not only survives; he determines to become a Brahman. From this, all that can key itself into the fire-birth myth is that the Brahman and his cow can create special warriors to defend the

[68]*Mbh* 1.165.9-44, with the details at 34-35—to which the Southern Recension and certain northern texts make further additions, including (as in *Rām*), Yavanas from her womb (*yonideśāt*; 1.1768*). *Ksama* is one of the high *Mbh* virtues, exemplified by Yudhiṣthira (see Hiltebeitel forthcoming).

[69]Sharma had earlier considered Chand's "Agnikula myth" a "late forgery" and "an adaptation of some very old stories found in the *Rāmāyaṇa* and the *Mahābhārata*" (1940, 746-47). Why he dropped the latter is unclear.

[70]In an earlier note, D. Sharma (1934-35, 159) traces the story further, unconvincingly, to a *Brhatsamhitā* verse where Vasistha is said to slay certain Mlecchas directly, without aid of either fire or cow: "Saying that the sage destroys these, not himself, but through the agency of warriors born from his fire pit, is the first and most natural step forward in the development of the myth."

[71]See further on these two stories Hiltebeitel in press-g.

Brahmanical order, and that Vasiṣṭha, who has already done this in both Sanskrit epics, now knows, as it were, how to do it again.

If, however, it is Jamadagni's cow, it is a different matter. As we have seen, Paraśurāma empties the earth of Kṣatriyas twenty-one times. But the job is never complete. Yudhiṣṭhira, who has heard the story once in the forest, hears it a second time after the war from Kṛṣṇa, who tells it to deter him from disavowing his hard-won kingdom and giving the earth to Brahmans all over again.[72] At first, says Kṛṣṇa, Śūdras and Vaiśyas united with Brahman women to produce a kingless condition in which the strong ruled the weak.[73] Unprotected by Kṣatriyas, Earth (Pṛthivī) entered the netherworld (*rasātalam*), until the Brahman Kaśyapa bore her on his thigh and listened to her. She told him where she had concealed Kṣatriyas in strange places, and implored him to reinstate them as kings to protect her. As Kṛṣṇa tells it (49.66-75), Kṣatriyas were raised by cows, ocean, apes, and bears. The Ṛṣi Parāśara helped with some raised by cows in the forest (70), while the Ṛṣi Gautama helped with others on the bank of the Gangā who were further raised by apes on the Vulture Peak.[74] Of those protected by Ocean, some northern texts add that they lived among blacksmiths, goldsmiths, and such (*vyokāra-hemakārādi*; 75 and 114*). When the amazed Yudhiṣṭhira now realizes how the very Kṣatriyas who fought at Kurukṣetra, and those still extant, were thus regenerated, he responds (let us say, with a wink): "The scions of Kṣatriyas, troubled with the fear of [Bhārgava] Rāma, were concealed by cows, Ocean, monkeys,[75] bears, and apes! Ah! This world is rich indeed, and men on Earth fortunate, where a feat so righteous as this was performed by a Brahman" (50.3-4). Kṛṣṇa's clarification is decisive, since immediately after it, he and Yudhiṣṭhira go directly, in the very next verse, to Bhīṣma's bed of arrows for the lengthy completion of Yudhiṣṭhira's royal education.

In this myth, there is no creation of special warriors by a Brahman, but a regeneration of the entire Kṣatriya caste by the goddess Earth, with a Brahman as her instrument. What gets keyed into the Agnikula myth is the default of older Kṣatriyas and the regeneration of new ones, and maybe the Earth's coregeneration with her new kings. But since neither Paraśurāma nor Viśvāmitra ever brought forth special warriors before,

[72]Goldman 1970 discusses contrasts between these two versions, taking off from Sukthankar 1936, 8, 46-48.

[73]12.49.61-62. The Southern Recension adds that Brahmans abandoned their dharma and turned to heresies (*pāṣaṇḍān*; 111* line 4 following 49.62).

[74]Gṛdhrakūṭa (12.49.73): the one of Buddhist fame? The combination of vulture, monkeys, and bears evokes the types of "warriors" who come to Sītā and Rāma's rescue in *Rām*.

[75]Kṛṣṇa had not mentioned monkeys.

and could not have learned the trick from the calf of Jamadagni's cow, we may say that they had to learn it from Vasiṣṭha. It is thus no accident that Padmagupta tells the fire-birth of the first Paramāra not only by recalling the theft of Vasiṣṭha's cow, but by alluding to the theft of Jamadagni's. The new Agnikulas are a special creation, on analogy with the special warriors born from Vasiṣṭha's cow. But they are needed because of the default of the older Sūryavaṃśa and Candravaṃśa Kṣatriyas, whose prior annihilation—provoked by the theft of Jamadagni's cow or calf—is encapsuled in Padmagupta's bare allusion to that theft.[76]

Thus even in Padmagupta's oldest north Indian account, there appears to be no original myth behind the Agnikula myth, but a combination of analogy and allusion to other myths. Nor do the analogies and allusions stop with the two cow-theft myths. The *Rāmāyaṇa* tells how the very same Vasiṣṭha cooperates with another Brahman, Ṛṣyaśṛṅga, to produce four special Kṣatriyas, Rāma and his brothers, to rectify the default of the Kṣatriyas that occurs when the world begins to be overrun by the Rākṣasa hordes of the Brahman-King Rāvaṇa. And the *Mahābhārata*, as noted, tells not only of the regeneration of Kṣatriyas after their extermination by Paraśurāma, but provides by its war the "time marker" from which the purāṇas trace the near-annihilation and bare continuance of solar and lunar genealogies into the "future." These larger analogies and allusions are likely to have been in the epic repertoire of Padmagupta. They are certainly in that of the author of the *Bhaviṣya Purāṇa*'s *Pratisarga Parvan*, who also knows an inverse story about the Mlecchayajña of Pradyota (see chap. 9, § A) in which Veda-knowing (and probably Kṣatriya-distrusting) Brahmans destroy all the Mlecchas by pulling them into a sacrificial fire rather than creating Kṣatriyas from fire to kill them.

We have also met a spinoff from this myth that becomes clearer from the myth's analysis. As we have seen,[77] it is the sins committed by Kārtavīrya Arjuna—"murdering children, sages, and cows"—that lie seven generations behind the migration from north India of the people of Palnāḍu.[78] The penance required by their Brahmans is not only the

[76]Goldman 1977, 78-79, with a different perspective, remarks that no epic source motivates or explains the calf theft. Perhaps the stolen calf is equivalent to the princes who are the first Kṣatriyas that Paraśurāma kills in revenge for the calf's theft. The prince-calf analogy is made for the Ksatriyas hidden away by Earth after Paraśurāma's slaughter: King Pratardana's son Vatsa ("Calf") was brought up among calves (*vatsas*) in a cowpen (*Mbh* 12.49.71). The motivation of the calf theft could then be answered by asking what the calf theft motivates: retaliation against Ksatriyas who do not act like the calves of Brahmans.

[77]In chaps. 3, sequence 8 at n. 79; 10, § B.

[78]The murder of a sage and the theft of a cow has not only been pluralized, but extended to the murder of cows and children—perhaps as an extension of the analogy between calves and children (see n. 76).

people's pilgrimage to the south, but a rebirth into their Brahmans' absolving presence through the womb of a golden cow.

C. Agnikulas, North and South

Insofar as one can trace the Agnikula myth through north Indian variants and to classical Sanskrit sources, we have, it seems, come to both the beginning and end of the road. But other trails connect north India to south, Sanskrit classics to Tamil ones, and perhaps north Indian beginnings to earlier south Indian ones. Naturally, it is a question of what Padmagupta could not have found in cow-theft myths of the Sanskrit epics: Kṣatriya births from fire.

Taking stock of Hoernle's "interesting contributions," Krishnaswamy Aiyangar contended that "the legend could be traced to an earlier period than that of the Paramāras of Mālva," and that "a reference to the same legend" of "a family of ancient chiefs who claimed descent from the sacrificial fire" can be found "in the early classical literature of the Tamils" (1911, 390). The *Puṟanāṉūṟu*, one of the eight Caṅkam anthologies of early Tamil poems, relates a legend about "the Last Seven Patrons of Letters," the most esteemed of whom, Pāri of Paṟampu, was a lifelong friend of a celebrated Brahman poet named Kapilar. The "power and prosperity of Pāri as a patron of poets" aroused such jealousy in the "three crowned kings of the South"—the Cēra, Cōḻa, and Pāṇṭiya—that they jointly attacked his hill-fort and killed him. Kapilar then sought to get Pāri's two daughters, both poets, suitably married. When he came to a chief named Pulikaṭimāl[79] Iṟuṅkōvēḷ of Aṟayam, a city and area in the western hill country around Mysore, he addressed him as follows:

> "Having come out of the sacrificial fire-pit of the Rishi—having ruled over the camp of Dvārapati, whose high walls looked as though they were built of copper—having come after forty-nine generations of patrons never disgusted with giving—thou art the patron among patrons." (1911, 391)

Iṟuṅkōvēḷ refused the marriage and insulted the social standing of Kapilar's patron, the girls' father. Says Krishnaswamy Aiyangar, "The allusion to the coming out of the sacrificial fire of the sage cannot but refer to the same incident as the other versions discussed by Dr. Hoernle."[80]

[79]"Tiger-slayer": Iṟuṅkōvēl killed the tiger to "save a saint absorbed in meditation" (Krishnaswamy Aiyangar 1911, 341-43, 358-59).

[80]Krishnaswamy Aiyangar 1911, 390-91, citing *Puṟanāṉūṟu* 200-2 in Swaminatha Iyer's

It is remarkable that Iruṅkōvēl is what Krishnaswamy Aiyangar calls a "petty chief" and that he rejects a marriage to the daughter of another such chief slain by the "three crowned kings." Once again we are dealing with marriages between "little kings" and rivalries between such little kings themselves and their "imperial" overlords (1911, 342). Indeed, the rivalry here in question ends an age when little kings from the hill country were greater patrons of letters than the great ones from the big royal capitals.[81] Iruṅkōvēl's fire-origins go back forty-nine generations to "the ruler of 'Tuvarai,' who was born from the sacrificial fire." Tuvarai, according to Krishnaswamy Aiyangar, "may be either Dwaraka in Guzerat or Dwāravati or Dwārasamudra of the Hoyśālas." He leans toward the latter connection by noting the "considerable similarity" between Iruṅkōvēl's title "Tiger-slayer" (see n. 79) and "the origin story of the Hoyśālas in inscriptions of a later time" (1911, 342). But he recognizes that "the name Tuvarai in classical works is always taken to mean Dvāraka."[82]

Krishnaswamy Aiyangar thus argues that although the "three crowned kings" are not named, the fire-born Iruṅkōvēl's contemporaneity with Kapilar and the Last Seven Patrons of Letters "takes the Agnikula tradition to the age of" the *Cilappatikāram* by bringing him into the same time frame as the Cēra Ceṅkuṭṭavaṉ and king Gajabāhu of Laṅkā. Both figure in *Cilappatikāram*, Gajabāhu with approximate second-century

---

edition, and followed by Crooke 1920, xxxiii, n. 1; Sircar 1965, 22-23; and Asopa 1976, 24-25. Marr differs: "You are the Vēḷ, descended from the forty-nine Vēḷir who, with great liberality, ruled Tuvarai whose walls shown like the metal vessel in the sacrificial pit of the northern sage" (1985, 232). But Shulman (personal communication, May 1996) comments, "the critical word is the non-finite *toṟi* at the end of line 8. Its appearance here precludes the meaning that Marr gives in his translation 'like the metal vessel in the sacrificial pit of the northern sage' etc.—the point is that there is no reason to imagine the *cempu* vessel simply 'appearing' in the sacrificial pit. Much better, I am sure, is the gloss of Turaicāmippillai, who breaks after *toṉṟi* and then starts over: the 49 generations of Vēḷir who first appeared in the sacrifice of the northern sage, who ruled over Dvāra with its walls like [burnished] copper, who never turned away from giving gifts etc. In other words, one imagines the first ancestor coming out of the fire, then 49 generations at Dvara."

[81]Kapilar seems "to have been a specialist in composing poems relating to *Kuriñji*, i.e., the hill-country" (Krishnaswamy Aiyanger 1911, 341-42, 392). Iruṅkōvēl and most of the other Seven Patrons were from the "frontier 'buffer-states'" in the hilly areas between the three kingdoms which the latter frequently fought over (370-71).

[82]Krishnaswamy Aiyangar 358, n. 1. Shulman thinks Dvāra most likely means Dvārakā in Gujarat (personal communication, see n. 80). Marr observes that since Dvārakā is connected with the Yādava Kṛṣṇa and the Hoysalas of Dvārasamudra claimed Yādava descent, Kapilar "was indirectly claiming Yādava kinship for Iruṅkōvēl also" (1985, 234). Yādavas are "lunar," but are sometimes considered as a fifth Agnikula in north India (Baden-Powell 1899, 544-49). Double and triple origin claims are quite ordinary.

A.D. dates.[83] We may call this the legendary time frame, while *Puranāṉūṟu*'s time of composition could well be the second or third century A.D. and could not, as Krishnaswamy Aiyangar shows, be later than the sixth century (1911, 391-95). In any case, it is well before Padmagupta (cf. Sircar 1965, 23).

Since Krishnaswamy Aiyangar's opening, more Agnikula-type references have been spotted south of the Rajputs, but from medieval times when Rajput influence might be suspected. But that is not necessarily the most persuasive argument. Sircar mentions an inscription from Hottal in Nanded District, Maharashtra, that describes a family of chiefs loyal to the Cālukyas of Kalyāṇ in the third quarter of the eleventh century. The chiefs style themselves Agnikula and Vahnikula, and tell the following story about their family hero:

> It is said that the sage Agastya had his hermitage in the valley of Mount Kailāsa in the Himālaya. The sage's *Kāmadhenu* (wish-fulfilling cow) was snatched away by certain rulers and he offered in a great rage an oblation in to the blazing fire without uttering a curse. The result was the birth of a great hero from the fire-pit, who, after having killed those rulers, brought back the *Homa-dhenu* to Agastya as if it were the sage's *mana-siddhi* (restoration of prestige) incarnate. By his prowess, 'the son of fire,' who became known as Munimānasiddhi (restorer of the sage's prestige), became a powerful ruler after conquering all the enemies in the three worlds. (Sircar 1965, 21; Asopa 1976, 25)

Probably, as Sircar says, "The author of the Hottal *praśasti* thought fit to connect the name of Agastya, famous in legends as one who first went to the south beyond the Vindhyas and settled there for the rest of his life, with the origin of the ruling family of the Deccan. But it is difficult to understand why Agastya's hermitage was not located in south India. The intention was probably to indicate the northern origin of the fire family of Hottal" (1965, 22). Yet one cannot easily trace this variant to the Paramāras, who had Vasiṣṭha as sacrificer rather than Agastya, or, for that matter, to the Cālukyas, south or north, since at this time they had apparently not yet adopted the Agnikula myth.

[83] 113-35 A.D. based on Sri Lankan chronicles; 162-91 A.D. from conventional dating of the Buddha's nirvāṇa: see Krishnaswamy Aiyangar 1911, 363-67 (redeeming history from the "Gajabāhu connection"), 394-95. Kapilar is linked further to the Cēras by having written ten poems in praise of the Cēra king Cēlvakkaṭuṅko and having another of his works brought out by a Cēra prince (392). On Ceṅkuṭṭavaṉ's reign as pivotal in the patronage of early Caṅkam poetry, see ibid., 337-43, 355-71.

Further south, but again with possible northern connections, the Ṛṣi Kaśyapa takes a turn in the priestly role. As Sircar puts it: "Indeed the fire-pit of any sage would serve the purpose of the seekers of social prestige just as the *culuka* of Brahman, Pañcaśikhin or Droṇa or anybody else would explain the origin of the Cālukyas" (1965, 23). According to Nilakanta Sastri, an inscription from the period of Kulōttuṅka Cōḻa III (1178-1216) "gives the earliest account so far known" of the origin of left-hand, as opposed to right-hand, castes.

> The left-hand castes claim to "have been created from the *agnikuṇḍa* (fire-pit) for the protection of the sacrifice of Kaśyapa, and to have settled in the Cōḻa country in the time of the emperor Arindama; this emperor imported a large colony of holy Brahmans from Antarvēḍi (sic), and the Iḍangai [left-hand] classes accompanied these Brahman colonists as the bearers of their slippers and umbrellas. They got some lands in five villages, all of them now in the Trichinopoly district, and had long lost the memory of their origin when they recovered it about A.D. 1128. They then entered into a compact among themselves to the effect that they should thenceforth behave like sons of the same parents." ([1937] 1975, 551)

Through this "recovered memory" of a common ancestry and fire-birth descent, the left-hand castes determined to claim their rights "till we establish them." Their opponents are unnamed, but come into view in a later inscription which records the left-hand castes' hardships "at the hands of Vanniya tenants and the Brāhmaṇa and Veḷḷāla landlords, backed by [Cōḻa] government officials" (551-52). Migrations of Brahmans and their attendants from the Ganges-Yamuna Doab (Antarvedi[84]) are, of course, plausible. But Sircar, noting that such stories are also found in Karnataka and Bengal, suggests, without quite saying so, that they are probably invented to confer on Brahmans outside the Antarvedi the prestigious pure origins of that ritual center (Sircar 1965, 22). Nor does their importation by "the mythical emperor Arindama" help with dates.[85] The left-hand castes' recollection of this story in about 1128 could mean that when they came south as attendants of Antarvedi Brahmans, they were originally northern Agnikula Rajputs. But one would have to explain the transformation of Rajputs (who would normally fit a right-hand land-oriented profile) into a left-hand (mainly merchant and artisan) community, and what their attendant relation to the Brahmans would have

[84]As referred to in chap. 11, n. 135, this is a curious case where a modern Tamil author substitutes a retroflex "ḍ" for a dental "d" (see quoted passage above).

[85]Ibid. Meaning "Foe-Tamer," Arindama is a suspiciously generic name.

been. The presence of Vaṉṉiyars, perhaps already fire-born themselves, in the right-hand opposition suggests the group in question may have sought parity with them. As is typical of such right-left rivalries, there were Brahmans on both sides. Perhaps the Brahmans "from the north" helped jog their "former attendants'" memory of "imperial" service in their past.

Fire-born merchant and artisan castes are also known in modern south India. Thurston and Rangachari describe three merchant castes (Balijas and their offshoots, Kavarais and Janappans) and a weaver caste (Togatas) whose ancestors were born from sacrificial fires. All speak Telugu, and the merchants are all found in both Andhra and Tamilnadu. Togatas originated when their goddess Chaudēsvari "threw some rice on to the fire, from which sprang a host of warriors, whose descendants they are" (Thurston and Rangachari [1904] 1965, 7:170). Janappans have Kāmākṣī and Damayantī (!) as "caste deities," and spring "from a yāgam (sacrificial rite) made by Brahma." The merchants of the country needed something to carry their wares, and asked the Janappans' fire-born ancestor to provide it, whereupon he took seeds from the fire to grow hemp, and used the hemp (which gives the caste its name) to make gunny bags (1904, 2:448-50). The name of the Kavarais of Tamilnadu, often bangle-sellers, "is said to be a corrupt form of Kauravar or Gauravar [Kauravas], descendants of Kuroo [Kuru] of the Mahābharatha (sic)." They connect their fire-birth with their Balija origins, deriving it "from bali, fire, jaha sprung, i.e., men sprung from fire." Among their exogamous septs are some with martial names like "tupāki (gun), jetti (wrestler)," and some Kavarais adopt the "viceregal" title Nāyakkar, as do Vaṉṉiyars (3:263-66).

Balijas variously claim Kaurava, Nayak, or lunar dynasty ancestry (Thurston and Rangachari [1904] 1965, 1:134-35), and also have a "Tupākal, musket" sept (141). They also provide the *bali-ja* etymology for their name,[86] and this myth:

> Parvati was not satisfied with her appearance when she saw herself in the looking-glass, and asked her father to tell her how she was to make herself more attractive. He accordingly prayed to Brahma, who ordered him to perform a severe penance (thapas). From the sacrificial fire, kindled in connection therewith, arose a being leading a donkey laden with heaps of bangles, turmeric, palm leaf rolls for the ears, black beads, sandal powder, a comb, perfumes, etc. From this Maha

[86]It would literally be "sprung from sacrifice," or "sprung from that which is offered into the sacrifice" rather than the fire itself. Cf. Thurston and Rangachari [1904] 1965, 1:137: the Balijas are said to derive their name "from the Sanskrit bali (a sacrifice) and born (ja)."

Purusha who thus sprang from a sacrifice (bali), the Balijas derived their origin and name. (1:137-38)

Nothing indicates that any of these communities claim to be Agnikula Kṣatriyas. Their epic associations are not those of Vaṉṉiyars, who side more with the Pāṇḍavas than with the Kauravas, and with Draupadī rather than Damayantī, who actually joins a merchant caravan during her estrangment from her husband Nala (Mbh 3.61.106-62.16). Yet their martial traits are evident. Balijas even claim to belong to the right-hand division rather than the left (138, 145).

Finally, there are the Vaṉṉiyars themselves, whom no one but Oppert, Nayakar, and I have brought into the discussion of Agnikula Kṣatriyas.[87] Late nineteenth- and early twentieth-century accounts tell variants of the following story. Two demons, Vātāpi and Māhi (or Entapi), obtained from Brahmā the boon of invincibility against everything but fire, which they forgot to include in their request. They ravaged the countryside. Vātāpi swallowed the wind and Māhi the sun. The earth became still and dark. The terrified gods appealed to Brahmā, who directed them to ask the Ṛṣi Jāmbava Mahāmuni (or in variants Śambhu, Campuva, Campuha) to perform a fire sacrifice.[88] Rudra Vaṉṉiya Mahārāja (alternately Vīra Vaṉṉiyaṉ, Vaṉṉi Rāja, or Bannirāya) was thus born from the flames along with a host of armed horsemen. Having destroyed the two demons and released the wind and sun, this first Vaṉṉiyar governed the country, and sired five sons who became the ancestors of the subdivisions of the Vaṉṉiyar caste.[89] A chapbook version of a Terukkūttu-style drama (Saṇmukam Upāttiyayār n.d.) tells a variation. Vātāpi Cūraṉ alone has the boon from Śiva. He makes the gods shiver and threatens to capture Indra, rule Devoloka, and make the gods his servants (3-4). He captures and imprisons them. Campumuṉi then prepares a sacrificial enclosure (*yāka-cālai*) and prays to Śiva for instructions. Following these, he makes the fire in such a way that Śiva starts to sweat (*viyarvai tōṟṟa*). Then with yoga, bhoga (*pōkam*: pleasure), and Veda mantras, Campumuṉi offers the sweat into the *yākam* (sacrifice, i.e., the fire), and Vīravaṉṉiyaṉ "rises with a horse (*kutiraiyōṭu utittu*)" (26-27). With his wife Mantiramālai he

[87]Oppert (1893, 89-94) argues that the Vaṉṉiyars signified a non-Aryan "Turanian" element among Rajputs.

[88]Shulman adds to his note on the *Puṟanāṉūṟu* (see n. 80): U. Ve. Cāminātaiyar in his commentary "thinks the sage is Jambumuni (this on the basis of two medieval citations, from Irattaiyar and a text called Vicuvapurāṇacaram)."

[89]This account, summarized from Cox (1881, 280-91), is found along with others in Thurston and Rangachari [1904] 1965, 6:4-6. It is the only one telling of the birth of horsemen along with the first ancestor. Cf. Nayakar 1891, 14; Nanjundayya and Iyer 1928-35, 4:609; Hiltebeitel 1988a, 36-37.

then has four sons: Akkiṉi Vaṉṉiyaṉ, Kiruṣṇa Vaṉṉiyaṉ, Pirama Vaṉṉiyaṉ, and Campu Vaṉṉiyaṉ. Together, with help from Durgā (Turkaiyammaṉ, 48-52), they destroy Vātāpi Cūraṉ and his generals.[90]

The eponym's name, particularly in the form Vaṉṉi Rāja or Banniraya, suggests a connection with the śamī (Tamil *vaṉṉi*, Kannada *banni*) tree. I was also told a different story by the Vaṉṉiyar caste swami at the Śrī Kailas Ashram near Bangalore: The Vaṉṉiyars descend from the dvārapālakas, or "gate guardians," of the vaṉṉi tree where the Pāṇḍavas hid their weapons before entering the kingdom of Virāṭa "in the Punjab"; henceforth they worshiped Draupadī, and later migrated to Kanchipuram to serve as warriors under the Pallavas (1988a, 36). The first Vaṉṉiyar or Vaṉṉiyars thus either bear the śamī in their name before going into battle, or come from the tree itself before becoming soldiers. As with similar features in the migration of the people of Palnāḍu, both stories would seem to evoke the śamī as a feature of a prewar Dasarā.

Keeping these two main variants in view, one finds that the Vaṉṉiyars' Agnikula mythology is close to that of Chand Bardai. As in Chand's account, where Vasiṣṭha remembers the goddess Āśāpurā before the first Chauhān's combat with demons, there is a likely evocation of Dasarā as preliminary to war, which in the drama begins with Vīravaṉṉiyaṉ's homage to Durgā. Like Chand's Chauhāns, the Vaṉṉiyars are born from fire like (if not with) their kuladevatā Draupadī, who we might even say is reborn in Gingee like a "Fortress of Hope." Like Chand's Pratihāras, the Vaṉṉiyars were originally "gatekeepers." As with Chand, there are (usually) two world-ravaging demons who must be destroyed. And, as with Chand, there is no stolen cow. Indeed, of the various "southern" accounts, only one mentions a cow theft, and that is the least southern one from Maharashtra. This suggests another reason why Sanskrit epic stories of the theft of Vasiṣṭha's cow cannot provide an originating impulse to Agnikula myths. In all likelihood, there is no cow in any "original" Agnikula myth. The cow would seem to have been introduced into the myth, perhaps by Padmagupta, just as she is reintroduced by Ward, as an equivalent of the stolen earth. For Padmagupta, the mention of two cows forges credibility by way of a double epic allusion.

Leaving aside the *Puṟanāṉūṟu* passage for its uncertainties, south India still offers an impressive consistency of medieval and modern fire-birth myths that is difficult to trace from north India. Considering the overlapping complexities and convergences between Chand's version and those of the Vaṉṉiyars, it is possible that a prototype Agnikula myth has traversed south and north India. Certain details like the goddess's

[90]The detail of the sweat borrows from stories of Śiva's production of Vīrabhadra. I thank S. Ravindran for his help with this text.

association with forts, the Vaṉṉiyars' and Pratihāras' connection with "gatekeeping," and evocations of Dasarā, must be parallels that flow from the myth's unfolding in different but not *so* different conceptions. Dhumraketu ("Smoke-banner"), the demon destroyed by Āśāpurā, could achieve something of the destructive capacity of the sun-swallowing Māhi, or be so named for evoking the dark smoke from animal (and implicitly human) sacrifices that would pollute the Ṛṣis' sacrifice as well as darken the sky. But I do not think the myth relies much on cosmological allegories. In harking back to the Pallavas, both Vaṉṉiyar myths are instructive for their ties with distinctive south Indian imperial histories. In one, the Vaṉṉiyars come south to serve the Pallavas. In the other, Vātāpi, conquered by Vīra Vaṉṉiyaṉ, is none other than the demon whose defeat gives his name to the Cālukyan fort-capital of Vātāpī-Bādāmi, which Narasiṃhavarman Pallava defeated around 643 A.D.[91]

The Cālukya-Caulukyas, in their southern and northern extension, also provide an imperial history within which to consider possible linkages between Agnikula myths. As Sircar says, there is no reason to think that the early Cālukyas were anything but "Kanniḍigas of the Dravidian stock" (1965, 18), even though some of their offshoots would eventually claim to come from the north (12-15). But although they connect south and north (cf. Hanumantha Rao 1973, 323-24), it is never they themselves who are born from fire in connection with early Agnikula myths. Before they claimed birth from a palm or water pot, the Cālukyas of Badami professed no known special origin in their early mid-sixth to eighth century history, and later their origin was traced to Manu, the nourishment of the Seven Mothers, and the protection of Kārttikeya-Skanda (Sircar 14; 1954, 229). Their offshoots at Vengi and Kalyāṇ claimed to be solar and lunar (from Ayodhyā!) respectively (1965, 13-15). The Caulukya Rajputs of the north, first born from Brahmā's palm, were then not included among those born from fire until after Chand. The Cālukyas of Kalyāṇ have Agnikula chieftains but are not Agnikula themselves. And in the Vaṉṉiyar myth, it is, if anyone, the Pallavas who use Agnikula warriors to conquer the Cālukyas of Badami, not the Cālukyas themselves. Nonetheless, one repeatedly finds Agnikula warriors among Cālukya feudatories or as the warriors of their opponents. Finally, once past their phase of imperial power in north India, they become Agnikulas themselves. Considering the *Puṟanāṉūṟu*'s praise of king Iṟuṅkōvēḷ, it is curious that the *Tamil Lexicon* gives "Cāḷukya king"

[91]Sircar 1954, 231; Hiltebeitel 1988a, 14, 36; Narasimhavarman gives his name to Mahabalipuram, and "was known as Vātāpi Konta Narasingapottaraiyan" (Thurston and Rangachari [1904] 1965, 6:5), "The Man-Lion Pōttarāyaṉ who seized Badami." On Pōttarāyaṉ (equivalent to Pōttu Rāja) in this usage, see Hiltebeitel 1988a, 15-16.

and "Petty ruler, chief" as later meanings for *vēḷ*, and "The Cāḷukyas" and "Petty chiefs" as later meanings for *vēḷir*. Perhaps these early "Agnikulas" were early Cālukyas; perhaps the later Caulukyas only "recover" that former status when they revert to being "little kings"—like the Vaṉṉiyars who "served the Pallavas."[92]

Not only the Cālukya-Solaṅkīs, but the Rāṣṭrakūṭa-Rāṭhoṛs, are Rajputs with south Indian connections (Sircar 1965, 17). Some northern Rajput clans, including the Guhilas and Caulukyas, seem to have had their praśastis, their inscripted myths of origins, "fabricated" by Deccanese Brahmans at their courts (4, 25). Sircar, referring to the *Puṟanāṉūṟu* passage discussed above, even suggests such a connection for the Agnikula myth, although he drops it to a footnote: "The Agnikula story seems to have been fabricated for the Paramāras by . . . Padmagupta. . . . This author may have been a South Indian at the Paramāra court . . . since similar stories were prevalent in that region at an earlier date" (8, n. 3). Padmagupta's first patron and "friend" Vākpati-Muñjarāja made southern conquests of the Rāṣṭrakūṭas, Karaṇātas, Cholas, and Keralas (Vaidya 1924, 120-21).

But even without this uncertainty, and with or without speculation on the mythic origins of the Cālukyas of Badami, we have seen three reasons to entertain the proposition that the myth of the Agnikula Kṣatriyas has a south Indian origin:[93] the cumulative nature of the south Indian origin myths of fire-born lineages; the Cālukya-Caulukya connections from south to north; and the similarities between the Agnikula origin myths of Chand Bardai and Tamil Vaṉṉiyars, which do not rely on Padmagupta for their parallels, and which "recall," in the Vaṉṉiyars' case, an early south Indian history connected with Cālukyas.

To these we should add a fourth. The Agnikula myth seems to be only one element of a larger complex of myths, iconographies, and rituals connected with the goddess, and also Śiva, that goes back to Pallava-Cālukya times, continues into the Chola period, and appears in the north toward the end of this period in connection with the emergence of Rajput culture. This complex includes head-offerings and other bodily mutilations, and what Weinberger-Thomas calls "suicides of fidelity" related to satī. As Weinberger-Thomas shows, "epigraphy allows us to situate these rites in their geographic, historical and religious context. They seem to have prevailed in south India." Indeed, prior to the Pallavas and Cālukyas, "Tamil Sangam poetry teems with references to heroic and devo-

[92]My interpretation of a "little king" background to these lineages differs from that of Asopa, who reviews all the instances discussed so far to unconvincingly argue that the original "social milieu" of these clans "may" originally have been Brahman (1972, 341-43).

[93]Krishnaswamy Aiyangar and Sircar (1965, 21-23) also lean in this direction.

tional sacrifices," not to mention heroes who must never show their back in battle.[94]

This is not to say—though one cannot rule it out—that Vaṉṉiyars have been Agnikula Kṣatriyas since the time of Narasiṃhavarman Pallava. But they would seem to have been so for long enough to be considered in the history of the Agnikula myth. As suggested, those who formed themselves as left-hand castes in the time of Kulōttuṅka Cōḻa III (1178-1216) by "recovering" their fire-born origins had Vaṉṉiyars prominent in their opposition; if the latter were already Agnikulas, it could have provoked such a countermove from the left. More solidly, as Nayakar observes, Villipūttūr Āḻvār makes three references to the Agnikula in his Tamil *Mahābhārata*. When Yudhiṣṭhira, at his Rājasūya sacrifice, must offer the "guest-gift" to the most honored person present, he asks Bhīṣma whether the honor should go to kings of the Solar, Lunar, or Agni vaṃśas (2.1.111). Śiśupāla then vents his outrage over the choice of Kṛṣṇa, and asks how a shepherd could be chosen over Solar, Lunar, and Fire lineage kings (115). As in *Ālhā*, the *Mahābhārata* scene is a locus classicus for ranking Kṣatriyas old and new.[95]

But most important, when Draupadī's governess or foster mother (*cevilittāyar*; 1.7.34) tells her about the kings who have come to her svayaṃvara, the last three suitors she mentions are a solar dynasty Cōḻa king, a lunar dynasty Pāṇṭiyaṉ, and a "Cēra, famous through the fourteen worlds, from the ancestral line (*marapu*) of the red-glowing one (*cen taḻalōṉ . . . cēraṉ*)"—that is, from the Agnivaṃśa.[96] This means that by around 1400, the time of Villiputtūr, two important things have happened. The ancient Cēras have been identified as Agnivaṃśins. And Villi is writing for an audience for whom this is important. This is clear by his indication that Agnivaṃśa kings are among those whom Yudhiṣṭhira might credit with the highest dignity, and by his closure of the list of Draupadī's suitors with great praise of the Cēra-Agnivaṃśa candidate. Those in Villi's audience who would have found this important can only be Vaṉṉiyars, who thus, by around 1400, must have considered themselves, and been considered by Villi, as Agnikula Kṣatriyas. Vaṉṉiyars identify with Cēras at least to the extent of bearing emblems of the bow (the Cēra insignia) as well as the tiger (the Cōla insignia) on their funeral biers.[97]

[94]Weinberger-Thomas 1996, 29 (quote) and 221, nn. 28-29.

[95]See chap. 6 following n. 24.

[96]1.7.45. Tamil *akkiṉi vaṃśam* in the commentaries of Rājakōpālāccāriyār 1970, 1, 307-8 (the *carukam* arrangement cited here) and Kōpālakirusṇamācāriyar 1976, 1, 298-299 (in which this is 1.5.45).

[97]Nayakar 1891, 42-43. On the Cēra bow-emblem, see Parthasarathy 1993, 218-19, 225-26.

Vanniyars must also have established this identity well enough before Villi for him to have determined to make fire, and especially Draupadī's birth from and repeated associations with fire, a major innovative theme in his poem. I have discussed several such enhancements by fire elsewhere,[98] but one sequence now proves especially revealing. When Villi has Bhīṣma recognize Draupadī's indomitability after Duḥśāsana has failed to disrobe her, he and the attendant kings in the Kaurava court join palms and praise her as "the goddess of chastity and of the ancestral line or dynasty (*karpinukku' marapinukkun teyvam*)" (2.2.250). The scene, with its virtual theophany and evocation of lineage, is enhanced in the Terukkūttu drama "Dice Match and Disrobing," where Bhīṣma calls Draupadī not only "goddess of the lineage (*kulatteyvam*)," but "goddess [or wife, *tēvi*] to the five [Pāṇḍavas], and mother to others" (Hiltebeitel 1988a, 264). We may now say with virtual certainty that Villi recognizes Draupadī as a "goddess of chastity and the lineage" not only for the Kuru Dynasty (*marapu*) for which Bhīṣma speaks, or for the Agnivaṃśa lineage (*marapu*) of the Cēras who attend her wedding, but, and above all, for Vanniyars in his audience (cf. 1988a, 264-65). Indeed, it may be the Vanniyars whose influence makes the Cēras become Agnikula Kṣatriyas after the fact.

As to the Cēras, I do not know when they begin to be identified as Agnivaṃśins, but I know of no earlier Tamil text than Villi's *Makāpāratam* to make them so.[99] They are not so identified in the *Cilappatikāram*, the classical Tamil epic whose three "books" are titled after the three ancient Tamil kingdoms, in the sequence Cōla, Pāṇṭiya, and Cēra. After providing quite ample allusion to the solar ancestry of the Cōlas and the lunar descent of the Pāṇṭiyas, the *Cilappatikāram* leaves us absolutely in the dark about the origin of the Cēras.[100] The probably seventeenth-century *Tiruviḷaiyāṭarpurāṇam*, "The story of the sacred games" of Śiva at Madurai, does, however, inform us further. In its account of the forty-ninth of Śiva's "sacred games," Brahmā, "after a deluge," recreates the world as before, with three Tamil kings, the "Chera, Chola, and Pandya, . . . who were descendants of the Fire, the Sun and the Moon respectively."[101] Would that we were told more

[98]1988a, 194-95 (Villi on Draupadī's birth from fire), 198, 438 (on her "firewalk" and marriage fire, whose "diversified" and "intensified" symbolism in Villi suggests Draupadī cult familiarity); 271, n. 31 (Draupadī's heated body during Duḥśāsana's attempt to disrobe her, inflaming her husbands and capable of burning the Kauravas).

[99]The *Tamil Lexicon* mentions the *akkinikulam* along with the other two as "Races of kings of ancient India," but gives no sources.

[100]On the Cōlas as solar and the Pāṇṭiyas as lunar, see Parthasarathy 1993, 74 and 258 (former), 110, 130, and 243 (latter).

[101]Nayakar 1891, 8; Harman 1989, 38-39 (the lunar king's name Vaṃśaśekhara Pāṇḍya,

about how Brahmā created them. The deluge leaves the Tamil land without Kṣatriyas. As such, it is equivalent, as an endangerment of the earth, to the thefts of Vasiṣṭha's or Jamadagni's bovine. Indeed, this southern story returns us to a point that has been trying to surface all along: that it is not floods, or particular Vedic Brahmans or their cows, that define the myth of the Agnikula Kṣatriyas, but the Earth's requirement of new Kṣatriyas to defend her.

Let us return with this thought to Villiputtūr Ā<u>l</u>vār's *Makāpāratam*, and consider what it might mean that Villi, like the author of the *Kṛṣṇāṃśacarita*, has rethought the *Mahābhārata* in relation to the myth of the Agnikula Kṣatriyas. Unlike the bhaviṣya paurāṇika, who brings the Agnivaṃśa to a *second* Kurukṣetra to finish the *Mahābhārata*'s unfinished business, Villi imports the Agnivaṃśa right into the *Mahābhārata* itself. In so doing, when he makes Draupadī the "goddess of chastity and the lineage," he fills the text with echoes. In his *Makāpāratam*, Draupadī is born from fire along with her brother Dhṛṣṭadyumna, the Kṣatriya incarnation of Agni. Indeed, all along, although Dhṛṣṭadyumna has no offspring and his Pāñcāla line becomes extinct by the end of the *Mahābhārata* war, his birth from fire has been another prototype of the Agnikula myth. Now Villi fills out the prototype by having not only Dhṛṣṭadyumna be born from fire, but Draupadī, who in the Sanskrit epic is born instead from the earthen sacrificial altar or vedi.[102] Yet as we have seen, Villi's description registers Draupadī's status as a lineage goddess and goddess of chastity not only for the Kaurava family of lunar dynasty Kṣatriyas and the audience families of Agnivaṃśa Va<u>nn</u>iyars, but the Agnivaṃśa Cēras. Here Villi is echoing the *Cilappatikāram*, whose Cēra king he must consider an Agnivaṃśin even if the *Cilappatikāram* does not. It is the Cēra king Ceṅkuṭṭuva<u>n</u> who establishes the heroine Kaṇṇaki as the goddess of chastity. And although she does not explicitly become his lineage goddess, it is he and his queen who determine to honor Kaṇṇaki by bringing back a stone from the Himalayas for the carving of her image. Moreover, it is through this northern campaign and its aftermath that Ceṅkuṭṭuva<u>n</u> brings the Cōla and Pāṇṭiya kings, the (presumably) Buddhist king Gajabāhu of Sri Lanka, and, among the northern kings he has conquered and imprisoned, even the Mālva king (from the land of the future Paramāras) to worship Kaṇṇaki as their goddess of chastity as well.[103]

"Crown of the Vaṃśa," is transparent); cf. Dessigane, Pattibiramin, and Filliozat 1960, 75-76; Shulman 1980, 69-75, on the wider flood themes and variants in this text; Harman 27 and n. 10 on the text's dating.

[102]See Hiltebeitel forthcoming. This is not to say that Villi invents this theme. By his time, Va<u>nn</u>iyars have perhaps already made the fire-born Draupadī their kuladevatā.

[103]Parthasarathy 1993, 223, 273; see Obeyesekere 1984 on Kannaki in Sri Lanka.

On analogy with other myths we have discussed, the *Cilappatikāram* is an Agnikula myth waiting to be realized. The three Tamil kingdoms are beset by Yavanas with "strange tongues" and "weird speech" (Parthasarathy 1993, 62, 266). The Yavanas form enclaves in the Cō<u>l</u>a port-capital of Pukār and even guard the fortress gates (like Pratihāras) in Madurai. There is something implicitly wrong here. Only a Cērā, one of Ceṅkuṭṭuvaṉ's ancestors, has made a challenge, entering "the fertile kingdom in the high mountain of the ill-bred Yavanas" (254). Ceṅkuṭṭuvaṉ establishes Kaṇṇaki as goddess of chastity after something has gone wrong, more specifically, in her human life in the other two kingdoms. In the Cō<u>l</u>a capital of Pukār, her husband Kōvalaṉ falls in love with a courtesan, loses all his wealth, and forces their departure for Madurai. It is never the Cōlaṉ's fault,[104] but curiously, as if the narrative eclipses him, we never hear who he is, and Pukār is next heard of as having been ruined by a flood, and the capital moved inland to U<u>r</u>aiyūr,[105] through which Kaṇṇaki and Kōvalaṉ travel on their route to Madurai. At Madurai, where king Neṭuñcē<u>l</u>iyaṉ orders the falsely accused Kōvalaṉ executed without examining the charge, everything is this Pāṇṭiyaṉ's fault, who dies accordingly, seeing the disheveled Kaṇṇaki's derangement, leaving her to destroy his city by fire. The Cō<u>l</u>a and Pāṇṭiya kings have thus defaulted. With suitable cosmological inversions and eschatological echoes, the solar king's capital is destroyed by water and the lunar king's capital by fire. The Cēra king is thus left to rectify matters by establishing the worship of the goddess of chastity, who, in conjunction with Agni, burns Madurai with fire from her left breast. An elaborate symbolism involving the sun, moon, and "Mother Earth" can be traced in Kaṇṇaki and Kōvalaṉ's movements through the Cō<u>l</u>a and Pāṇṭiya lands.[106] The Pāṇṭiyaṉ "gave up his life on the throne itself to reassure Mother Earth that his rule was just" (195). Kaṇṇaki is Mother Earth's protege. But Kaṇṇaki's connection with fire stops in Madurai; the Cēra king does not pick it up.

How much of this Villiputtūr echoes by allusion, and how much we see only by irresistible analogy (Bourdieu 1990), is guesswork. My guess is that Villi's allusion and my analogy divide at the beginning of the last paragraph. But I do think that Villi connects Draupadī and Kaṇṇaki by way of literary allusion, and that this recognition lets us see the relation of these two ultimately literary goddesses properly. It begins not with the

[104]Though he does purchase the courtesan's garland and make it available for Kōvalaṉ to purchase, thus launching their affair.

[105]As background, see Krishnaswamy Aiyangar 1911, 348-52.

[106]See especially Parthasarathy 1993, 30, 41, 45-46, 6, 77-78, 80, 92, 109-10, 130-31, 181-83.

Draupadī cult replacing the Kaṇṇaki cult, as some have thought,[107] but with literary allusions—first by Villi and then by modern scholars—to similarities between two heroine-goddesses whose cults never overlapped, but did, as I have shown,[108] develop analogous themes in their own rites and folklore, in different times and places. Yet, this is not to say that Villi's description of Draupadī as "goddess of chastity and the lineage" is exhausted by literary allusions to the *Mahābhārata* and *Cilapatikāram*. There are also cultural and even cultic allusions: not only to Vaṉṉiyars via the Cēras as fire-born kings, but to other fire-born goddesses via Draupadī. The Tamil country gives virtually every goddess a mythic and iconographic birth from fire, often with Brahman sages attending the firepit.[109] By Villi's time it was probably already a cultic cliché.[110]

This brings us back to the similarities between the Agnikula myths of Chand Bardai and the Vaṉṉiyars. I have argued that Agnikula myths are composed of elemental themes, and have no original Agnikula myth as their prototype. Two of the six themes outlined look especially south Indian: number 4, the eponymous hero's birth from fire, and number 5, the manifestation of a goddess to fight beside him, who becomes his clan's family deity. In Chand's and Jodharāja's accounts, the goddess only appears; she is not born from fire like her Chauhān hero. Indeed, the only place where we find a warrior and clan goddess born from the same sacrificial fire is in the *Villipāratam*, and there, while Draupadī becomes a chaste lineage deity for Agnivaṃśins, her brother Dhṛṣṭadyumna is not an Agnivaṃśin himself. Villiputtūr holds these elemental themes together by combining the fire-birth of the goddess with the fire-birth of the Vaṉṉiyars by way of allusion to the fire-birth of the Cēras. Chand's circa sixteenth-century Agnikula myth of the double-manifestation of hero and goddess probably has the same south Indian matrix behind it as the late fourteenth- or early fifteenth-century *Villipāratam*, just as earlier Agnikula myths seem to have southern roots, and be part of a complex connected with worship of the goddess by "little king" feudatories of the Pallavas and Cālukyas. The myth would thus seem to have been transmitted northward among the strong influences—but certainly not the only ones—on the "origins" of the Agnikula Rajputs.

[107] Dikshitar 1939, 371; Obeyesekere 1984, 3; Frasca 1984, 134.

[108] Hiltebeitel 1988a, 149; 1991a, 359-63, 366-68, 379, 428.

[109] Durgā, Māriyammaṉ, Aṅkāḷammaṉ (Hiltebeitel 1988a, 390-91 and n. 20), to whom one can add Mīnākṣī, Kālī, and many others.

[110] See Stein 1977 on the proliferation of goddess temples in the early medieval period, at least according to data viewed from the 1961 Madras State census volumes on temples.

14 Draupadī Becomes Belā, Belā Becomes Satī

Draupadī's firewalk calls for her to put up her hair before she crosses the fire. Once she has fulfilled her vow of oiling her hair with blood from Duryodhana's thigh, her hair is rebound with flowers like that of an auspiciously married woman (or goddess) for her to cross the coals. Yet while Draupadī crosses the coals with her hair up, women who follow behind her icon, performing the firewalk ritually, ordinarily cross the coals with their hair loose.

A. Disposing of the Kaurava Widows

There are several ways to contextualize this contrast within Draupadī cult myths and rituals. One is paradoxical: although Draupadī's icon crosses the coals with her hair up and adorned, firewalkers may envision her protecting them by spreading her loose incombustible hair over the coals (Hiltebeitel 1988a, 437). Here women firewalkers would have two simultaneous Draupadīs: one coiffured to lead them and one disheveled to protect them. Another is a sequential formula: As Draupadī fulfills her vows through the eighteen-day war, so she inspires others to fulfill theirs by crossing the firepit. From this standpoint, there is an equivalence between the battlefield (paṭukaḷam) and the firepit, and the women are like Draupadī.

But from a third standpoint, the firepit is a special part—indeed, an epitome—of the battlefield. It is its cremation ground.[1] In *Mahābhārata* terms, it is where the warriors have died, and where the women, most notably their wives, weep for them before they are cremated in the epic's *Strī Parvan*, the "Book of the Women." Rather than being where Draupadī fulfills her vow, it is where she fulfills her curse.

[1]On the firewalk as a crossing of the cosmic cremation ground of the *pralaya*, see Hiltebeitel 1991a, 470; Biardeau 1989b, 284. On Kurukṣetra as a cremation ground, Witzel notes that as an "altar of the gods," Kurukṣetra tips the wrong way for a Vedic altar, presenting the declivity of a cremation ground, from northeast to southwest (1984, 220, 248, n. 50).

In the Sanskrit epic, Draupadī makes this curse when she goes into exile after her humiliations at the dice match. As Vidura tells Dhṛtarāṣṭra:

> Wearing a single garment, weeping, her hair loose, menstruating, her wet garments stained with blood, Draupadī spoke this word: "Those on account of whom I have reached this condition, their wives, in the fourteenth year, with their husbands slain, their sons slain, their relatives and dear ones slain, their limbs smeared with the blood of their relatives, hair loose, menstruating (*rajasvalāḥ*), having thus offered water to the dead, will enter Hāstinapura." (*Mbh* 2.71.18-20)

Draupadī's vow to remain disheveled after the dice match and her curse that the Kaurava women will become disheveled after the war are clearly complementary. But historically, the curse and vow become complementary only in *Mahābhārata* folklores. Textually, the curse, as expressed in the Sanskrit epic, is older than the vow, which both the epic and the early eighth-century drama, the *Veṇīsaṃhāra* or "Binding of the Braid" by Bhaṭṭa Nārāyaṇa, seem to echo, but without ever making it explicit that Draupadī ever made such a vow herself.[2]

Vyāsa, however, does not forget about the hundred Kaurava widows. Once Bhīṣma dispels Yudhiṣṭhira's grief through the *Mahābhārata*'s lengthy twelfth and thirteenth books, and an Aśvamedha expiates Yudhiṣṭhira's sins in the fourteenth,[3] the Pāṇḍavas settle down in Hāstinapura until their elders—Kuntī, Vidura, Dhṛtarāṣṭra, Gāndhārī, and Sañjaya—leave for the forest to close out their lives. Again grief wells up and descends on the all the people of Hāstinapura. The Pāṇḍavas in particular, worried about Kuntī, "took pleasure neither in rule, women, nor Veda recitation" (15.28.1-10). Seeing Yudhiṣṭhira's grief, Sahadeva waits for a fitting time to tell him they may visit the elders in the forest (29.11),[4] and Draupadī adds that the womenfolk are ready to go with the balls of their feet (17). Yudhiṣṭhira orders provisions for his army and the women, and a vast exodus heads for the forest. In the lead, surrounded by Brahmans and bards (30.7) and with the ladies behind riding in litters (*śibikā*; 12), Yudhiṣṭhira "descended (*avātarat*) into Kurukṣetra, and gradually crossed (*krameṇottīrya*) the Yamuna"; only then do they see the elders' ashram "at a distance" (16-17). Since they leave Hāstinapura,

[2]See Hiltebeitel 1981, 179-201, on treatments of the curse and vow in these sources. The drama has Bhīma make the vow *for* Draupadī. Curiously, Bhaṭṭa Nārāyana is said to have hailed from Kanauj.

[3]14.70.15-19; 90.13-14; 191.4; see Hiltebeitel [1976] 1990, 292-93.

[4]Sahadeva seems to act like an astrologer here, something I have not noticed him doing elsewhere in the Sanskrit *Mbh*.

which is on the Ganges, and must travel northwest across the Yamuna to Kurukṣetra before they can "descend into" Kurukṣetra and head northeast to "cross" the Yamuna *again*, they take a roundabout route. Considering that this episode's destination is the Ganges as a river that opens a way to heaven, it is more than a coincidence that in crossing Kurukṣetra and the Yamuna, Yudhiṣṭhira replicates parts of an earlier journey by Balarāma. When the end of Balarāma's forty-day pilgrimage up the Sarasvatī coincides with the end of the *Mahābhārata* war, he passes through Kurukṣetra to reach the Yamuna and then returns to Kurukṣetra to see the final mace duel between Bhīma and Duryodhana. As I show elsewhere (forthcoming), Balarāma traverses a Vedic route to a point where one may see through the door of the starry heavens, and along the way he hears that the Ṛṣis of the Naimiṣa Forest have several times preceded him on the route. In what follows, we must thus once again keep these Naimiṣa conventions in mind.[5]

When the Pāṇḍavas and the "wives of the foremost Kauravas (*striyaśca kurumukhyānām*)" find their elders, they are on a bank of the Yamuna (15.31.2, 6). Shedding tears with the rest, Dhṛtarāṣṭra "approached the ashram frequented by Siddhas and Caraṇas, crowded by those desirous of seeing him like the firmament with hosts of stars (*didṛkṣubhiḥ samākīrṇaṃ nabhas tārāgaṇair iva*)" (31.20). The blind king with "radiant lotus eyes" (32.1) asks Sañjaya to describe his visitors, and the Sūta, after rich descriptions of the Pāṇḍavas and their wives, ends with what interests us: "These ladies, whose hair has only a part, wearing white upper garments, wives of kings, known as more than a hundred, without husbands, whose lords and sons are slain, are the daughters-in-law of this old king" (32.15). Long after they would have entered Hāstinapura with their "hair loose, menstruating (*rajasvalāḥ*), having offered water to the dead," the Kaurava widows now wear inauspicious white and nothing ornamental but the part of their hair.[6]

After the emaciated Vidura dies unblinking (*animiṣa*) with a steadfast gaze while leaning against a tree, transmitting his energies into Yudhiṣṭhira by the power of yoga (15.33.24-27), all the rest pass an "auspicious night furnished with constellations" (34.1). The Pāṇḍavas complete their morning rites, and just as they sit down with Dhṛtarāṣṭra and the great Ṛṣis of Kurukṣetra, "the lord Vyāsa, worshipped by the

[5]See chaps. 4, n. 7; 9, §§ A and C and n. 12. Cf. chap. 9 at nn. 12 and 77-87.

[6]Taking *sīmantaśiroruhā* like Nīlakaṇtha as *sīmantamātreṇa upalakṣitā*, "characterized by a part but nothing more, with no adornments or the like," to which he adds, "The reading '*asīmanta* having no part (in the hair)' is also fine (*yuktah*)" (Kinjawadekar 1929-33, vol. 6, book 14, p. 28, with thanks to James Fitzgerald for this translation). Cf. Ganguli [1884-96], 1970, 12:228. Perhaps the part is not adorned with vermilion, as would befit a widow.

hosts of divine Ṛṣis, showed up (*darśayāmāsa*), surrounded by his disciples" (34.22). Vyāsa explains the manner of Vidura's death and tells Dhṛtarāṣṭra he will perform a wonder never before accomplished by any of the great Ṛṣis. What does Dhṛtarāṣṭra wish to see, touch, or hear? he asks (35.24-25). Other celestials (including Nārada) join the throng to hear Vyāsa tell his "most virtuous heavenly stories" (36.14).

Soon, however, getting no answer from Dhṛtarāṣṭra, Vyāsa says he knows what is in the old king's heart, as also the hearts of Gāndhārī, Kuntī, Draupadī, and Subhadrā (36.16-18): their grief for their sons. Dhṛtarāṣṭra says he does indeed mourn his sons and wonders what way they have gone (30). And Gāndhārī and Kuntī deepen the grief. Gāndhārī laments her hundred sons in the company of their hundred widows, who now surround her with their repeated and increasingly insistent mourning (37.12). And Kuntī is reminded of Karṇa (38). Without anyone saying what they'd like to see, touch, or hear, this is enough to bring Vyāsa to reveal the resolve that was already in *his* heart before they spoke (39.3): he will show them all their sons and other loved ones slain in battle. Disclosing the celestial and demonic origins of both the dead and living heroes, he tells the gathering to proceed to the Ganges (18)—which, as noted, cannot be very near (it would be at least sixty miles from the Yamuna).

Once at the Ganges, the "ocean of folk (*janārṇava*)" (39.21) waits till night for a day that seems like a year (23). Their evening rites finished, all sit—the men around Dhṛtarāṣṭra, the women with Gāndhārī (40.1-3). "Then the great Muni Vyāsa of great energy, having plunged into the meritorious water of the Bhāgīrathī, thereupon summoned all the lokas—the warriors of the Pāṇḍavas and Kauravas collectively, including great-fortuned kings who had lived in various countries. Then a tumultuous sound arose within the water, O Janamejaya, from the armies of the Kurus and Pāṇḍavas, just as it was before" (4-6). As the dead rise from the Ganges with celestial bodies and apparel, Vyāsa, gratified with Dhṛtarāṣṭra, gives him celestial sight to see them, while Gāndhārī, apparently with her blindfold still on, sees them with the power of her celestial knowledge (17-18).[7] The living delight with the dead for the whole night as if they were heaven-dwellers (41.8). And then in a moment or twinkle (*kṣaṇena*) Vyāsa dismisses (*visarjayāmāsa*) the dead to reenter the auspicious triple-pathed river and return to the (starry) worlds from which they came (12-13).

Having fulfilled this high and stated purpose of "*his* heart," the author now turns to a purpose he hasn't admitted:

[7]See the nice handling of this scene in Carriere and Brook 1987, 232-34, and my discussion (1992b, 147-49).

When they were all gone, the great Muni of righteous conduct and great energy, ever the Kurus' benefactor, standing in the water, then said, "All those Kṣatriya women whose lords are slain, those foremost women who desire the worlds won by their husbands, unwearied, let them quickly (*kṣipram*) plunge into the Jāhnavī's (Ganges') water." Hearing his words, having faith, taking leave of their father-in-law [Dhṛtarāṣṭra], the beautiful women entered the water of the Jāhnavī. Released from human bodies, these chaste women all came together with their husbands, O king. Women of good conduct, women of the family,[8] they all in course, having entered the water, were released, and obtained residence in the worlds of their husbands. Endowed with heavenly forms, adorned with heavenly ornaments, wearing heavenly garlands and garments, as they were, so were their husbands. (41.17-22)

Coming at the end of the *Putradarśana Parvan*, the "Book of Seeing the Sons," the removal of the widows to heaven is both that episode's culmination and a major moment in the series of stories that finish the epic with the deaths of the war's survivors. The "author's" intervention might indeed cause wonder, for it is more than a little bit troubling.[9] Through this episode, the Pāṇḍavas dispose of grief for their elders. The elders dispose of grief for their sons. But the Kaurava widows' grief for their husbands is a surplus that is disposed of by Vyāsa. We cannot precisely say that he makes them satīs. That possibility would have existed in the *Strī Parvan*. Now their husbands are too long dead. But like the author of the *Kṛṣṇāṃśacarita*, who clearly follows him, and for whom the Kauravaṃśa widows are defective women to begin with and moreso for outliving their husbands (see chap. 8, § A), Vyāsa hints that the Kaurava widows are delinquent in becoming satīs. Even Gāndhārī seems to find their mourning overbearing. Satī is evoked by analogy here, but the *Mahābhārata* knows it: by the precedent of Mādrī who joins Pāṇḍu on the pyre; and by the sequel satīs of some of the wives of Kṛṣṇa—scenes to be noted further. The Kaurava widows are invited to enter the water as Kṣatriya women, and do so as *sādhvīs* ("chaste women, faithful wives, lady sādhus") and "women of the kula" (as I see it, taking this action through their marital ties rather than their natal ones). All of this befits a language of satī that the epic clearly makes familiar.[10]

[8]Or "good family," "of good conduct": *kulastriyah*.
[9]See Hiltebeitel forthcoming on the Mbh's conventions of authorship.
[10]See Shah 1995, 85, 91-93, for other instances and echoes of satī in the *Mbh*, e.g., the demands of Kīcaka's relatives that Draupadī be cremated along with him (4.22.6-8). The same can be said of the *Rām*, on which satī folklores are also built (see chap. 12, n. 2). Cf.

Yet even saying "quickly," Vyāsa doesn't quite encourage one to think that he lures the widows with a trick. The great "wonder-worker" (*Mbh* 1.1.16) simply stands in the river that flows between the worlds of his stories. It is never said that Yudhiṣṭhira finds these inauspicious women a deterrent to his rule. Nor does anyone say anything to remind us that the widows inauspiciousness follows from the fulfillment of Draupadī's curse. She herself seems quite congenial to these widows by now. But Draupadī cult stories build on these dark openings.

In Draupadī cult folklore—but only, as noted, in the "rajputized" Gingee core area (see chap. 10, § B)—the vow-curse complementarity finds expression in a distinctive myth. When the wailing women disturb Yudhiṣṭhira by their battlefield laments for their husbands and sons, Kṛṣṇa tells Draupadī to create a sacrificial fire and lure the women into it:

> "Ordinarily people won't walk through fire, but knowing that you were born in fire, if you say they will get back their children, husbands, etc., they will follow you, believing that by doing so they will get their loved ones back, that those whom they lost in battle will come back to life." . . . They all die in the fire. Only Pāñcāli-Śakti comes out. So now there are no more voices of wailing and weeping, nothing to deter Dharma from becoming king. This is another aspect of Kṛṣṇa's trick. . . . And the ones who died did rejoin their loved ones, but in heaven. Their bodies, flesh and blood, were destroyed by the fire, but their souls were released. (Hiltebeitel 1988a, 440-41)

This myth introduces a mass satī for the weeping women of the *Strī Parvan*, where no woman becomes a satī at all. According to one Pārati-yār, the women in question are precisely the widows of the hundred Kauravas (ibid., 441). Their removal to heaven in the epic's *Putradar-śana Parvan* is thus preponed to the end of the war. Satī by fire replaces salvation by water. The deity replaces the author, with it clear that he lures the widows with a "trick." Draupadī becomes the means to fulfilling her own curse. And Yudhiṣṭhira is relieved of the Kaurava widows explicitly because they are inauspicious, not as the aftereffect of the author's response to a collective grief.

Involuntary as these satīs are, Kṛṣṇa and Draupadī devise for them a satī's typical reward: reunion with the loved one in heaven, and release of her soul. Typical Rajput motivations for satī, love for the deceased and the desire to join him in heaven (Weinberger-Thomas 1996, 123-34), thus

---

Hawley 1994, 12: "a sati is a good woman (*sadhvi*), a woman devoted to her husband."

provide the very heart of the Tamil story. But there is something unsettling. It is almost as if these Tamilized Kaurava widows haven't fully absorbed this ideology, and *have* to be deceived into taking the necessary steps. Through all this Draupadī lives on, and does not become a satī herself. Why should she? Although she laments her sons, her husbands are still alive.

B. Draupadī Becomes Belā

Yet by becoming Belā, Draupadī does become a satī. It is through Belā, a "portion of Draupadī," and particularly through Belā's hair, that Draupadī's fiery nature finally self-combusts. Nor does Belā burn alone. In the *Kṛṣṇāṃśacarita*, she is the "Velā-fire (*velāgni*)" that consumes big and little kings alike (24.12). In *Ālhā*, a mass satī combines with a folklore of vows and curses. Belā makes no vow concerning her hair, but it is her hair that fulfills her vow to become a satī. And when she makes that vow upon learning of Brahmā's imminent death,[11] she "prophesies that in three months and seventeen days Delhi will be sacked, and every married woman there" will be widowed like her (W&G 263). Once Belā has become satī, "Sunwā and all the other widows . . . throw themselves into the great blazing pit which had formed Bēlā's funeral pyre" (273). The only satīs mentioned are from the Mahobā party: consistent with other reversals, the Delhi widows are too lax to become satīs, as is implied by Brahmānanda's censure of the surviving Kauravāṃśa widows.[12] Whether it is because they are wives of Pāṇḍavāṃśas or just because they are north Indian, those who do become satīs do not have to be deceived into doing so. Yet we should be more precise when we say "north Indian." Pīr Shams's ginān on Draupadī and the ghaṭpāṭ ceremony takes things in a different direction: the suffering Draupadī, "upon whom posterity may shower such great praise," is a model of satī and a model for satīs. But she does not *become satī* herself and neither do her Satpanth satī followers—either the men or women among them.[13] In contrast, the Tamil Draupadī and the north Indian Belā are both provided with Rajput myths to explain the jauhar-like mass satīs of other widows who follow

[11]It is not a case of "ambition" to become a satī before Brahmā's death, which would be "to will that her husband's death precede hers" (Harlan 1996, 235). It is Brahmā's request.

[12]Kishan Sharma of Agra makes the point that "All the women of Ālhā's family become satīs." That Sunwā does so in particular is instructive, since Ālhā never dies, but goes to the forest of immortals. The Delhi court's lax attitude toward satī is also evidenced by Agmā's counsel to Belā to forget satī and marry someone else, e.g., as Belā infers in rejecting the advice, a "Musulmān Mughul" (W&G 263).

[13]See chap. 10 at nn. 169 and 173. I do not press the point that Draupadī's Tamil followers, usually both men and women (Hiltebeitel 1991a, 441-46), have this Satpanth precedent.

them. And *Ālhā* tells further how Draupadī fulfills her destiny as a Rajput by becoming Belā, who closes Draupadī's cycle of seven lives. We must at last look more closely at what it means for Draupadī to have become Belā.

It appears as if much that Belā carries forward from her previous life as a folkloric version of Draupadī is oriented toward satī: not only Draupadī's vows and curses, but her hair, Kālīrūpā, jewels, and fire-born body. If Draupadī's hair is incombustible (birth from fire with long black hair would suggest this even without south Indian firewalking myths), Belā's hair becomes the means of her burning, at least in the Elliot *Ālhā*. One informant questioned at Bairāgarh (see below) knew of Belā's satī-fire starting from her hair. But denying this, Baccha Singh said, "She sits cross-legged on the wooden pyre with her husband on her lap, and closes her eyes. Ghee is put on the pyre. People around chant 'Satīmātā ki jai' ('Victory to Satī-mother') and the Agnidevatā (Fire-god) is pleased. Naturally and automatically the fire starts leaping. She is talking up to the moment the flames reach her throat, giving blessings (*āśīrvāda*). Then her head slumps and she is engulfed in fire and can talk no more." But he adds, "Letting down the hair is a sign of fire. When she goes and sits on the pyre, the hair is tied up. When it is let down, because it would be touching the fire down below her back, the fire would catch there. So it would seem the hair lights of its own. The wind lifts it up and it appears to be burning very quickly. But the fire starts by itself and catches the hair first." Kishan Sharma recounts, "Belā said, 'No one is going to light my fire.' So she sat there and worshiped Devī, and because of this the flames started leaping all by themselves. Because of Devī's blessing, the flames leapt."

Such variants thus follow Rajput ritual and iconographic conventions by which a satī may light her pyre from her hair after oiling it (Weinberger-Thomas 1996, 104, 199); be represented with the sun god or a goddess lighting the nimbus around her hair;[14] or with hair that bursts toward the sky like "a kind of mane, a nimbus of flames, evoking the 'terrible' aspect" of such goddesses as Kālī or Cāmuṇḍā.[15] Draupadī is identified with Kālī not only in the Draupadī cult and in Andhra (Hiltebeitel 1988a, 289-95), but in north Indian *Mahābhārata* folklores—linked in each case with rural Rajputs (among others)—in Garhwal and Rajasthan.[16] Belā does not seem to carry this Kālī-identi-

[14]Weinberger-Thomas 1996, fig. 5; Sunder Rajan 1993, 27-28.

[15]Weinberger-Thomas 1996, 141-43 and figs. 25, 26.

[16]For Rajasthan, see J. D. Smith 1991, 97-98, on the *Pābūjī* song about the world mother who swings from the hollow khejaṛī (śamī), and who is both Kālī and Draupadī who "duped [or destroyed, *chal*] the Kauravas and Pāṇḍavas" (cf. 1990, 13); cf. Smith n.d., 67, on

fication forward in the Elliot *Ālhā*, at least explicitly; but in the *Kṛṣṇāṃśacarita*, the four as-yet-unwidowed Kauravāṃśa wives say, "Velā, possessing the form of strife, is Kālī herself" (31.25). Belā takes her jewels—surely including those that were Draupadī's—when she leaves Delhi for her tragic "homecoming" (W&G 263), and puts them all on when she mounts the pyre in full bridal array (271). From known practice, a satī may retain her jewels, remove them and break her bangles, or give them to a Brahman and his wife, keeping her nose-ring as a symbol of marriage (see plate 14).[17] It is as if the folklore, once it has given Draupadī a birth from fire rather than from the earthen fire altar, requires that her body return to the element from which it came.[18] The fire of her birth can become a satī pyre because Agni is the devourer of corpses.

Nor is this momentum toward satī limited to only two successive lives. When Belā, leaving Delhi, prepares herself for this destiny, she recalls that this is the seventh life in a row, beginning with one as a pair of fish (followed by births as snakes, *chakwā* birds, deer, and swans), that she has passed with the same husband (and in the last life with four other husbands as well), and that in each such life she was left un-"satisfied" (see chap. 6, § E). In the *Kṛṣṇāṃśacarita*, rather than recall her own successive dissatisfactions, Velā recites just the seven lives of her husband, telling "the story of Brahmānanda's seven births" (the text gives no details) as her last word upon entering the pyre: "Having told the story of her husband's seven births, she burned."[19]

Neither text says anything about Belā ever having been a satī before, which would be difficult considering what we know of the previous six lives. But in recounting all seven, and, in *Ālhā*, making it clear that it is a question of seven marriages, both texts would appear to be familiar with the practice by which satīs announce—sometimes verbally, sometimes by holding up two sets of fingers—how many times they have become satī with the same husband, and how many times are left, on the way to the full total of seven that will bring the couple their final deliverance.[20] If not seven times a satī, Belā would appear at least to be

---

Draupadī as a destructive form of Śakti in the Rajasthani folk-*Mbh*; Kothari 1989, 114: "Draupadī appeared to kill the Pāṇḍavas." For Garhwal, see Sax 1986, 6; 1995b; Zoller 1993. Sāralādāsa's Oriya Draupadī, "a woman of incredible beauty with more than a touch of terror in her makeup," is "the incarnation of Ketuka Candi" (Boulton 1976, 21).

[17]See discussion in Weinberger-Thomas 1996, 101, 104, 122, 133, 152.

[18]Other folklores about Draupadī, in Himachal Pradesh (B. R. Sharma 1993, 38) and Andhra (Chary 1993, 208), also seem to make this connection. So too Sītā, whom the *Rām* brings forth from an earthen furrow, returns to an earthen pit.

[19]*Saptajanmakathāṃ kṛtvā svapates tu dadāha vai*; 32.208.

[20]Weinberger-Thomas 1996, 146, 208; Hawley 1994, 180; Harlan 1996, 228.

seven times a virgin, seven times a pativratā, and thus a woman who has amassed considerable sat through seven lives. That it is in each text a matter of seven suggests that Draupadī, in becoming Belā, and Arjuna, in becoming Brahmā, may have reached the limit that brings deliverance.[21]

In providing the additional myth in which Draupadī, by becoming Belā, becomes a satī herself, returns to the element from which she came, and reaches with her husband the possible limit of their deliverance, *Ālhā*, I believe, fashions an astonishing fusion between etymology and narration.[22] Weinberger-Thomas has assembled the relevant etymological dossier. Hindi *belā*, in "very current usage" as "'time' or 'moment taken to do something,'" derives from Sanskrit *velā* as "limit, frontier, terminus (term); time limit, period, hour" (1996, 29). Sanskrit *velā*, which is of course the heroine's name in the *Bhaviṣya Purāṇa*, has such early meanings as "limit, boundary, time" in the *Śatapatha Brāhmaṇa* and "flood-tide" in *Maitrī Upaniṣad* (R. L. Turner 1966, 702). It also means "the last hour, hour of death" (Monier-Williams [1899] 1964, 1018). Belā herself stipulates a satī's time limit when she says a satī has only seven days. Three of hers having already passed, she demands her father's sandalwood pillars before her time as a satī runs out (W&G 268).

Weinberger-Thomas also adduces the Kannada term *veḷevāli* (or *veḷevāḍica*), which describes a warrior "whose vocation toward death constitutes the rule of life" (1996, 25-26). Glossed as a compound of *veḷe* (from Sanskrit *velā*, "time limit") + *pāli* (from Sanskrit *pāla*, "one who guards, defends, or protects"), a veḷevāli is "'one who acquits himself of his vow or his promise once the moment comes' (at the death of the master)" (28). Or according to Settar and Kalaburgi, "*Veḷe* means time or occasion, *pāḷi* means duty or obligation; the principle and philosophy of the *veḷavāḷis* were to do their duty and fulfil their obligation whenever they were called upon." They "regarded themselves as the sons of their master, or their master's wife; and, identifying with the master's sentiments and sensibilities, they never hesitated to sacrifice themselves or their family" (1982, 31-32). According to Weinberger-Thomas, "The *veḷevāli*'s entire field of existence is occupied with active devotion through which he proves to his master what is translated by the expression 'vow of the *veḷe*.' When his master dies, he chooses to follow him

[21]Cf. Weinberger-Thomas 1996, 208, hypothesizing that the seven lives ending together in fire replicate the seven circumambulations around the marriage fire; 89: a satī purifies three lines for seven generations: her father's, her mother's, and her husband's; 105: a woman can accumulate sat through previous lives; Harlan 1994, 84: a satī's curse lasts seven generations.

[22]Parts of the following two sections are condensed in Hiltebeitel in press-d.

in death as he has vowed. Thus Marco Polo reports . . . : 'And you must know that when the King dies, and they put him on the fire to burn him, these Lieges cast themselves into the fire round about his body, and suffer themselves to be burnt along with him.'"[23] Their modes of suicide include not only "plunging into a pyre," but live burial, offering one's head on a spring device, "falling from a height, allowing oneself to be skinned etc."[24] The *bela-veḷe* cognate reminds Weinberger-Thomas that satī is only one of several forms of funerary ceremony entailing the voluntary death of survivors who immolate themselves (individually or en masse) at obsequies of the higher ranked:

> This can be a sovereign, a master, or a husband. The belief which animates the ensemble of these suicidal practices (altruistic, according to Durkheim) is that the deceased must enjoy in the world beyond the same goods, the same services, as in his terrestrial life. He will need his horse and weapons to make war, food to satisfy his hunger, ornaments to enhance his beauty and glory. In the same manner, he must be accompanied by his servants, his councilors, finally his wives. The dominant idea of 'to follow in death' is the payment of a debt of obligation and love (the two things go together) that bind the different parties involved to the common master.[25]

Pābūjī's three surviving retainers are veḷevālis in all but the name when they vow to behead each other upon the death of Pābūjī.[26]

All the more remarkable, then, that in Hindu Bali, a bela is a satī (Balinese *satia*). The two terms are often used interchangeably; or, where

[23]Weinberger-Thomas 1996, 25-26; Polo 1969, 257 (unattributed translation). Cf. Tarabout on two Kerala festivals recalling wars lost by the Cēras to Tamil kingdoms that may devolve elements from this complex. In one, representing the sacrifice of an army, *cāvēṟu* warriors, "those who rush to their death" sworn to die fighting after the fall of their king, recall an eleventh-century hundred-year Cēra-Cōḻa war said to have instituted the *kalari* military training system (1986, 413-21). In the other, the god Tampuran, representing the Cēras and the goddess against the Pāṇṭiyans and Śiva, throws himself on his sword after his twelve-year rule, and his wives and mother become satīs—represented, along with his palace, by huge cones made of dried palm matting called *kampam* ("pillar, post," from Sanskrit *skambha*) which become pillars of fire (Tarabout 1986, 192-202, 665).

[24]Settar 1982, 197. In *Palnāḍu*, the sixty-six heroes of Kārempūḍi—whom Jaffar and Farīd bury themselves to join (see chap. 3, 7)—offer their heads with a giant shears after losing a dice match with Kṛṣna (Roghair 1982, 143, 145, n. 23, 207).

[25]Weinberger-Thomas 1996, 25 (my translation), citing Lincoln 1991 on Scythian royal funerary practices, who argues that the postmortem interpretation is "facile" when "forced" upon the Scyths (191, 195; cf. Boon 1990, 43-44). But it is the rhetorical dismissal that seems forced and facile. A postmortem exegesis is, in any case, not facile for India.

[26]J. D. Smith 1991, 445-51; above, chap. 4, sequence 6.

they are differentiated, a bela is a satī of a certain kind. Distinctions, where found, are consistent in imputing higher dignity and rank to the satia: she burns in her husband's cremation fire, the bela only in a separate pit; she submits to death by a *kris* (dagger) before being burnt, the bela only leaps into the flames (Weinberger-Thomas 1996, 24); she is a wife, the bela "a concubine, slave, or other domestic."[27] But there is no consistency in these usages: a bela may choose the kris, be of noble origin, and be a wife of the deceased (van der Kraan 1985, 102, 119). Reading the descriptions, it looks as if bela is the operative term, and that the more recognizably Sanskritic satia is kept for whatever higher distinction best suits the occasion.

Nineteenth-century European etymologies for belas' rituals are revealing. One derives *bela* "from the Sanskrit '*wela*' (sudden and easy death)," since it refers "to a woman who at the cremation of her husband or master jumps alive into a blazing pit."[28] Monier-Williams does give "easy or painless death" as one of the meanings of Sanskrit *velā*. As among advocates of both sides of nineteenth-century India's satī debates, the quickness and painlessness of satī are considered axiomatic (Sunder Rajan 1993, 16-24). But it is also a sophisticated discourse: such an obscure Sanskrit etymology is likely to have come from Brahman paṇḍit exegetes of the Balinese bela rituals.[29] Friederich says *bela* "is also used to denote all those men, women, and children who elect to die with their lord in a mass suicide attack (*puputan*)."[30] A practice like that of the Kannada *veḷevāli* thus reappears in a Balinese exegesis for *bela*. Crawfurd, as if in confirmation, glosses *bela* as "retaliation" or "retribution."[31] One wishes for his explanation. It is easiest to imagine it connected with a satī's power to curse. But it could also be that a bela embodies "retaliation" against those who are, or might be, her deceased master or husband's rivals, and thus also of the rivals of his successor,

[27]Crawfurd [1820] 1985, 241. The velevāḷi is also a "servant" (Settar 1982, 196).

[28]Friederich 1850, as translated in van der Kraan 1985, 102, n. 21, according to whom Friederich was "a German Orientalist and linguist, specialized in Hinduism and with a good knowledge of Sanskrit," who "published the first really scholarly account of Bali," which includes his account of a royal cremation with belas that van der Kraan translates (116-17).

[29]On the imposing and controlling presence of the Brahmans in these ceremonies, see van der Kraan 1985, 97-98, 102, 113.

[30]van der Kraan 1985, 116, 102, n. 21, translating from Friederich 1850, 10. For *puput-an*, Barber 1979, 620, has "bringing to an end, conclusion; the word is used for the final battle of the B[alinese] nobility and their slaughter by the Dutch in 1906"; from *puput*, "complete, finish off, bring to an end, perfect." Cf. Harlan 1996, 240, on "what the Rajasthanis term a *saka*—an unwinnable bloody battle."

[31]Crawfurd [1920] 1985, 241: "When a wife offers herself, the sacrifice is termed *Satya*; when a concubine, slave, or other domestic, *Bela*, or retaliation." I take it that a seeming reversal of the distinction on the next page is a mistake.

his son the next king. Indeed, we have seen these two explanations converge in Pāvalar's version of the nawab's fear of Rāṇiyammāḷ's satī after the death of Desing.[32] Like warriors who fulfill their vow to fight to the death after a king's fall, each bela is the ultimate pyrrhic victory for her deceased lord and master, and for those who succeed him if his kingdom and family survive him, or continue resistance against his opponents.

Given the stakes of marital exchange, a bela's father and brothers would theoretically have a place among such potential rivals. Elsewhere (in press-d) I attempt an interpretation of hidden antagonisms between satīs and their fathers, and Belā is one of the key examples. Suffice it to say that in both *Desing* and *Ālhā*, the princesses' predicaments are traceable to their being married off by their fathers, two Delhi emperors, to two low status princes who become their fathers' rivals. In *Ālhā*, with Mahobā decimated and its princes dying, Belā is left not only to symbolize Chandēl revenge by her satī but to exact it by killing her brother and demanding her father's sandalwood pillars. Indeed, she might have her own motivations for fighting this father who has ruined her marriage, although, as we shall see, it is a difficult question.

While Weinberger-Thomas finds Indian counterparts to Balinese belas, she asks (1996, 24-25) whether India knows anything comparable to the satia's death by stabbing, which can distinguish her as a wife from the lower status bela. Again an oral regional martial epic provides an answer from its satī scenes of revenge. When the widows of the Rāṭhoṛ heroes of Koḷū are about to immolate themselves in *Pābūjī*, "The other *satīs* toyed with tufted coconuts, (but) Gailovat toyed with a fine dagger." With this dagger, the queen and chief satī, wife of Pābūjī's elder half-brother Būṛo, opens her belly to deliver the baby Rūpnāth; then she apparently becomes satī on the pyre with the others (J. D. Smith 1991, 458-59). Again, the satīs both symbolize and result in revenge: Rūpnāth will avenge the Rāṭhoṛs against the Khīcīs, who destroyed Koḷū. Bundela history also supplies an example of apparent satī by sword rather than fire when the wife of Champat Rai (father of Chatrasal) stabs herself to death upon seeing her husband fallen.[33]

[32]See chap. 11 at n. 123. Indeed, all the versions suggest such concerns. Rāma's prevention of Mandodarī widowhood by having Hanumān forever stoke Rāvaṇa's cremation fire also seems to gloss such a notion, although Mandodarī (like the Kaurava and Kauravāṃśa widows) does not become a satī (see chap. 12, n. 2).

[33]Pogson [1828] 1974, 43; cf. Gupta 1980, 13. Jujhar Singh and his band, before capture, also "tried to stab their women, in order to save their honor"—unsuccessfully, with the result that Shahjahan "admitted them into the imperial seraglio after conversion" (B. D. Gupta 1980, 7). One also finds a reverse tradition that the son of Prithīrāj, ruling Ajmer after his father's death, "sacrificed himself in the flames of a pyre" before his fort was

Such retaliatory acts help explain why Prithīrāj fights to oppose Belā's becoming a satī,[34] and even more so his opposition to Gajmōtin's satī in Kishan Sharma's account (Agra, December 11, 1995):

> After Prithīrāj kills Malkhān, Gajmōtin wants to become satī. Prithvīrāj orders his army to prevent it. She is protected by a "*Lakshman rekhā*" (a boundary line of fire such as Lakṣmaṇa creates to protect Sītā in popular versions of the *Rāmāyaṇa*'s abduction scene); it will burn anyone to death who crosses it entering her palace. She sends to Mahobā for help. Ūdal arrives, crossing the *rekhā* on his flying horse. The pyre is ready in the garden. He orders it lit. Just as Gajmōtin is about to enter, Prithīrāj's army breaks in. Palace women hand firebrands from the pyre to the soldiers, and they fight Prithvīrāj's army with the brands as weapons.[35] Prithvīrāj is defeated and the satī completed.

In this account Brahmā's death and Belā's satī come in an earlier battle, leaving the ending to approximate the *Pṛthvīrāj-rāsau*, in which Belā does not appear, but with Gajmōtin's satī now raised to the importance of Belā's. Here Prithīrāj's attempted prevention has nothing to do with a daughter of his own; rather, he attempts to suppress a retaliatory act which launches the final cycle of further retaliations as its outcome. The same motives are only clearer in the fight over Belā's satī, in which Belā delivers the Chandēls' retaliatory blows against the same king, her father, and her brother.

One must be cautious in tracing an etymon through irregular appearances in such rarely linked places as north India, Karnataka, and Indonesia. *Bhargava's illustrated dictionary* glosses Hindi *belā* (masculine) as "a jasmine flower, wave, a cup, a bottle of leather, seashore, time, a violin, fiddle" (Pathak 1967, 800). Among these meanings, only "time, wave, and seashore" are derived from Sanskrit *velā*, whose first and most generative meaning is always "limit, boundary," whether of time or tide, land or sea, or life itself.[36] "Jasmine" seems to be the regular folk etymology for the heroine's name, but Zahir Singh, one of several informants to provide it, also relates her epic role to a harsh proverb: "When there is devastation, it is said, 'You have entered this

taken by Kutubuddin (Vaidya 1926, 341).

[34]On the theme of Belā's revenge, see Schomer 1989, 148.

[35]Such firebrands are by implication impure weapons used in extremis; cf. Gupta 1987, 61.

[36]Monier-Williams [1989] 1964, 1018, begins with such definitions, leading to "coast, shore, hour of death, etc." and mentions Velā "personified as the daughter of [the cosmic mountain] Meru and Dhāriṇī, and the wife of Samudra [Ocean]."

house as a Belā' (*jab kahin vināś hotā hai to kahajata hai ki tum belā bankar ā ho is ghar mein*)." According to Zahir Singh, jasmine is used in pūjās to goddesses. Belā is also "Jasmine" in Gandhi's dictionary of Indian names: "the jasmine creeper (*Jasminum sambac*); wave; time" (1992, 54).

One circles around satī in these meanings. But it would appear that *Ālhā* evokes satī through such connotations. Medieval Kannada poets knowingly compact the same metaphors while referring to veḷevāḷi heroes. For the tenth-century Pampa, "like the jasmine in full bloom which reminds the lovers of their love, the brave appeared to have taken a *veḷe*-vow to their loves"; "the army of heroes . . . like the waves merging into the ocean, the *veḷes* terminated the fight for the day and retired to their camps"; the thirteenth-century Panna says those who follow "the *veḷe dharma*" are "like the waves of the surging sea at whose roaring approach, the stars (enemy soldiers) fall, like withering stalks" (Settar and Kalaburgi 1982, 32-33). Lingāyat *Vacana* poets also knew the term and adapted it to their mission: Basava, for instance, declared himself "not a *joḷavāḷi* (slave of subsistence) but a *veḷavāḷi* (a slave of conviction)" (33).[37] But while "the *Vacanakāras* accepted the concept of *veḷe*, (for they agreed to be dedicated not to a master but the Supreme Master of all), they seem to have disapproved of it as a social institution" (34).

For old Javanese, *bela* has what Weinberger-Thomas calls an "obscure etymology" and "complex semantic biography" as it passes into Balinese and Indonesian.[38] She finds that "a common notion emerges from all its particular usages: *bela*, that is, to follow in death and by metonymy, those who accompany their deceased husband into his celestial abode. *Bela*, the servants of a prince who immolate themselves the day of his obsequies. *Bela*, the warriors who run *amok* if their chief has been defeated in combat. *Bela*, again, the women burned or stabbed by the kris at the time of grandiose cremations reserved for members of the royal castes" (1996, 23).

In Bali, it is not just terms but images that remind one of Belā. Following the processional tower bearing the body of the king, three belas "[d]ressed in white, their long black hair partly concealing them, with a mirror in one hand and a comb in the other, . . . appeared intent only upon adorning themselves, as though for some gay festival." "The victim sat in the little house on the bridge, accompanied by a female

[37] A joḷavāli lives on *joḷa*, millet, received from his master. Karṇa, Drona, and Bhīṣma are exemplary joḷavālis for classical Kannada poets (Settar and Kulaburgi 1982, 33-34).

[38] Barber (1979, 27) has "*béla* n. sacrifice; *béla* i[n]tr[ansitive]: commit sati, die on a husband's funeral pyre, kill o.s. as a sign of loyalty."

priest and her relatives. They all spoke to her of the happiness which she would soon enjoy. She groomed herself; combed her hair, looked into her mirror, rearranged her garment, in short, she arranged herself as if she were going to a party. Her dress was white, her breasts were covered with a white *slendang*, and her hair had been made up in such a way that it would continue to hang down during the jump into the fire." Adorned in the little house on the bridge, the bela "is dressed in white from the bosom to her knees, while her hair, curiously arranged, is decorated with flowers"; following a "trance-like dance," she then nears the end of the plank that extends from the bridge over the fire, "loosens her hair and lets it fall over her shoulders."[39] The mirror, comb, flowers, approach to fire, and the atmosphere itself, might remind one of a Draupadī festival,[40] or, except for the mirror, the satī of Rāṇiyammāḷ in the ballad of Rāja Desing.

C. High and Low Satīs

To these Balinese, Kannada, and other usages, we must add the *Ālhā* heroine. I propose that a "limit" situation defines them all, and that it must apply specifically to the limit situation of royal suicide squads and satīs, especially royal satīs (or their lower status bela substitutes), who mark the limit of a reign, and in Belā's own case, the end of an era. Indeed, Belā is the spectacular and exemplary satī who completes the career of Draupadī at its "limit" of seven lives. Her *velāgni* is the "fire of the limit." The tenth to fifteenth centuries look like the earliest period one could consider for these usages to have gained force and currency, with the Kannada veḷevāli, linked with epic poetry and Lingāyat spirituality, marking a field from which one could plausibly propose further flowerings in north India and Bali. But if this period provides grounds for these seeds to flower, one must also ask what conditions give them their spectacular form. As Boon says of Bali, "Evidence of the frequency and extent of actual *satia* and *bela* across periods of Balinese history is obscure by its very nature. . . . Balinese may have fixated on *doing* sacrifices for reasons connected to those that make Europeans fixate on *describing* them. Did incentives develop for courts to 'play to' this intense ritual image, as forces in local rivalries, colonialist encroachments, Islamization, and trade continued unfolding?"[41]

[39]Van der Kraan 1985, 113, 104, 117, translating reports from Ludwig Verner Helms (1847, Dutch), R. Th. Friederich (Dutch, 1847), and Pierre Dubois (1829, French).
[40]See Hiltebeitel 1991a, 334-38, 439-75.
[41]Boon 1990, 42. Boon also asks, "Was the pulse of sacrifices regular, or were sacrifices 'critical' responses to pressures perceived as external?" While the question of such "perception" is important, it borders on the cosmetic and insupportable argument of Nandy

Such questions should also be asked of *Ālhā*, but with a difference.[42] In the one case, it is court ritual that "plays to" the rivalries and insecurities of what Geertz calls a "theatre state" (1980, 98-120) by staging leaps into firepits of belas who, if they are differentiated from satias, are the deceased's female slaves or low status concubines (van der Kraan 1985, 119-21). In the other, it is a story—one that recalls *the* formative era in the history of Rajput rivalries and insecurities—that "plays" not to Rajput courts aspiring to keep or obtain high status, but to countryside audiences of low status Rajputs, and others beholden to them, who know that Belā is somehow one of their own. This they know because her story is one that tells how her father, the last Rajput king of Delhi, refuses to ever finalize her marriage after he is forced to marry her "down" to a Chandēl prince of low enough Rajput status of his own, who is, moreover, the "brother" of the even lower status Banāphars who have won Belā for him. It is these "brothers" of Belā's husband, the great heroes of *Ālhā*, portions of Pāṇḍavas, and, according to some, of Kṛṣṇa, who escort Belā on her homecoming to Mahobā and attend her as she fights her way to the pyre.[43] Indeed, when she asks Ūdal to light the pyre, "her father cannot allow it because of the Banāphars' low status" (Schomer 1989, 151; cf. 153). So she lights it with her hair. Let us recall that Belā, who makes no appearance among Brahmā's wives or Pṛthvīrāj's daughters in the *Pṛthvīrāj-rāsau* or the *Parmāl-rāsau*, seems to be an *Ālhā* creation (see chap. 5, § A). She also, as we have noted (chap. 6, § A), has a parallel destiny as heroine of a "tribal" *Ālhā*, and it now seems rather natural that tribals would have been drawn to her. The heroine and the heroes ultimately find themselves and their audiences at the same low levels. Note also that in Kishan Sharma's Agra version, the culminating satī is Gajmōtin, wife of the Malkhān, the lowest of all the Banāphars and *Ālhā*'s rough exemplar of an LSRSC.

Although Belā is not contrasted with any higher status co-wife, her lowness and common cause with others like her is thus understood. *Ālhā* knows her as Brahmā's only wife, and only *Ālhā*s tell her story. Indeed,

---

(1980, 3-4) and others that satī can be deproblematized as a result of "epidemics" provoked by Islamic and colonial influences. For a critique of "epidemic" theories, see Weinberger-Thomas 1996, 183-84; 226, n. 99, 253, nn. 24-26; Hiltebeitel in press-d.

[42]They can also be asked of more recent satīs: cf. Sunder Rajan 1993, 25: "a sati, by virtue of being a publicly witnessed event, is at once a 'production,' here the staging of a 'miracle', a show of strength by believers, and a defiance of the state as repressive 'other.'"

[43]On brothers especially among the relatives helping their sisters become belas in Bali, see van der Kraan 105, 109, 115, 120-21. Note that Belā puts not only Ālhā to a test but Ūdal (W&G 263), in each case baiting them with challenges that will prove they are not acting out of desire for her or for the kingship that comes with her: Ālhā on her homecoming to Mahobā (266), Ūdal in the fight for the sandalwood pillars (268). See chap. 6, §§ E and I.

such lowness as a satī has the precedent of the *Mahābhārata*, in which the women who become satīs are co-wives of low rank. It is the inferior junior wife Mādrī rather than the higher status chief wife (*mahiṣī*) Kuntī who joins Pāṇḍu on the pyre to continue their lovemaking in heaven.[44] And when Kṛṣṇa dies, Satyabhāmā, his chief queen (*mahiṣī*),[45] leads the widows who retire to the forest, while the group of five that enters fire is led by his "favorite," Rukmiṇī, and includes Jambavatī, daughter of the king of bears![46] As to those delinquent satīs, the Kaurava widows, their marriages are so uninteresting that the *Mahābhārata* never tells us whether they are of high status or low. But their successors, the widows of the Kauravāṃśas, more than make up for this by being so outlandishly the lowest of the low that they never become satīs.

This pattern of the low status wife or concubine becoming a satī while the chief wife refrains also has a remarkable recurrence at Gingee. Thereabouts, one hears that an ancient Gingee king had some trouble over the question of whether Draupadī's stone temple icon could have hair. Every day the temple pūcāri would bring the flowers he had placed on the icon to the king. But one day the pūcāri's concubine ("keeper") had playfully put them in her hair, and when the queen received the offerings, she raised a doubt: Can a stone deity have hair? This drew the pūcāri and the king into a dramatic test of faith in which Draupadī saved the believing pūcāri's head and temporarily blinded the disbelieving king with a flash of hair from her stone icon (Hiltebeitel 1988a, 93-95). As I observed, there is "a tacit contrast between the queen and the pūcāri's concubine." The queen "is punctilious" in spotting the defiling hair while the concubine "is carefree" and probably exhibits loving devotion in playing with the goddess's flowers (97-98). Each gets her man in trouble—the pūcāri with the king, the king with Draupadī—but neither, at least as far as this story goes, draws any punishment on herself.

[44]*Mbh* 1.116. Consider too that in Draupadī cult folklore, when Mādrī becomes satī on Pāṇdu's pyre, Kṛṣna saves the embryo from their brief union and has it raised in a sea conch by Sumudrarāja, king of the ocean. Kṛṣna then makes Caṅkovati-Cankotari-Caṅkāmirtam, the Pāṇdavas' younger sister, the wife of the Pāṇdavas and Draupadī's servant Pōrmannaṉ-Pōttu Rāja (or, in the Thanjavur region, Vīrapattiraṉ) (Hiltebeitel 1991a, 29, n. 26; 405-22). The Pāṇḍavas thus marry down their sister, daughter of the lower status mother, to one of far lower status than themselves. The saving of the embryo from the satī fire may remind one of Gailōvat's extraction of Rūpnāth before her satī.

[45]*Mbh* 3.222.3, 10; 224.16; 4.8.17.

[46]*Mbh* 16.8.71-72. Oldenburg 1994, 163, is surely right, considering the Rukmiṇī story's northwest setting and the lurking dangers to the women from Dasyus and Mlecchas, to suggest that this group-satī describes something like jauhar; but this does not exclude reference to satī. Dehejia's statement (1994, 52) that Madrī and Rukmiṇī's satīs are from "the latest parts" of the *Mbh* is groundless, since both are found in the Poona Critical Edition. Arguments for interpolation beyond this "archetype" are necessarily suspect.

Yet if the story revolves around lack of faith, it is the queen who sows the doubt that grows in the king's mind. As noted, "a sequel story . . . further accentuates the deficiencies of the queen in contrast to a different concubine"—that of the king himself. When the king died and was being cremated, "the suttee who 'entered the fire' was not his wife, the queen, but his own 'keeper': a Telugu-speaking Nāyuṭu lady named Kṣatriya Maṅkapāy." These events are commemorated at Mēlaccēri at a temple called Tī Pañcan̲ Kōvil, the "Fire Entry Temple"—or, more vividly, the "Fire Diving" or "Fire Springing Temple"[47]—about two hundred yards southeast of "the original" Draupadī temple. It is an open-air cupola on four pillars over a satī stone showing the king and the concubine (see plate 15). Adjacent to the north a satī platform embeds five plaques, each with a set of footprints. And in back, on the west side, is an overgrown and dilapidated bathing pool that the king dedicated to the devoted concubine. Such were the stories I heard in the 1980s.[48]

In January 1997, however, Krishnan Singh told me that the Tī Pañcan̲ Kōvil is, along with the Bhairava temple, one of three that he serves as pūcāri.[49] Krishnan Singh, it will be recalled, is the pūcāri for the "Singh"-Bundela community of what he estimates to be fifteen Singh families still resident in Mēlaccēri who claim descent from Rāja Desing.[50] By his account, when the king of the story died, the queen was not ready to become satī.[51]

> Then, you know about these arrack sellers? The king had a concubine (*kūṭṭiyā*) from that community. The concubine immediately adorned herself with a yellow cloth (*mañcaḷ tuṇi*) and climbed (*erittār*) [on the pyre]. The Rāṇi did not climb (*era illai*). But they beat the drums and pushed the Rāṇi in.

It was members of the king's own clan or line (*paramparai*) who pushed in the Rāṇi. Krishnan Singh did not know a name for the concubine or the king. M. Rangaswamy, contributing to the interview,[52] exonerated him by saying the king was just a "little king" (*cir̲r̲a rācan̲*). But

[47] *Pañcan̲*, from *pāy*, "to dive, spring into fire, as with a tiger that springs" (S. Ravindran), recalls the "leap" of Rāṇiyammāḷ, wife of Rāja Desing.

[48] See Hiltebeitel 1988a, 97-98. I add the detail about the five sets of footprints, said to be stones commemorating the feet of the satīs who burned here, but with a shrug as to how one reaches the number five. Four of the plaques are round, the fifth, in the middle, square.

[49] The other is a forest Paccaivāḻiyamman̲ temple between the Draupadī and Bhairava temples.

[50] See chap. 11, § A.

[51] Again, "to climb as a log/body with (*utan̲ kaṭṭai erutal*)"; cf. chap. 11, n. 115.

[52] See chap. 11, n. 12.

Krishnan Singh did know the concubine's jāti or "caste": "Pāḷaiyakkārar (poligar), Nayakar. They had some link to the arrack profession." The Telugu-speaking Nāyuṭu lady named Kṣatriya Mañkapāy is now from a poligar family of the Nāyakar community—and by "Nāyakar" Krishnan Singh meant "Vaṉṉiyar." One could plausibly reconcile most of this information by equating "Kṣatriya" and "poligar," and observing that Nāyuṭu and Nāyakar can be interchangeable. That would leave us with a Telugu-speaking Vaṉṉiyar, which might be a useful combination in the arrack profession. But the important points in Krishnan Singh's story are the following. Poligars are local chiefs, and in this story the one in question, the concubine's arrack-selling father, would be subordinated to a "little king" commemorated at a satī temple with a Rajput pūcāri. Moreover, the king's poligar concubine, who is from a low status liquor-selling Vaṉṉiyar family, is a more dedicated satī than the "little king's" queen. If we cannot say for sure that the little king and queen are Rajputs, we can say without hesitation that their story has been rajputized. And since it is the same queen who has doubts about the hair of Draupadī's stone icon, it is tempting to think that both of these intertwined stories come from Gingee's Rajput folklore. Indeed, although informants usually knew the king in the story as Cunītaṉ, a descendant of the Pāṇḍavas, one interviewee, the Draupadī temple's chief trustee, called him Pirutivirāja (Hiltebeitel 1988a, 99). Possibly the *Ālhā* king of Delhi has lent his name to a version of this story, with which parts of his own story—his mistreatment of an embodiment of Draupadī, his blindness[53]—could have been felt to overlap. Just as the king of Gingee does not believe a stone Draupadī can have hair, Prithīrāj does not foresee the ability of his daughter Belā, Draupadī incarnate, to light her satī pyre with fire from her own hair.

D. Belā Becomes Satī

"Was Bēlā angry at her father for preventing her wedding?" When I asked Baccha Singh this question, which seemed go to the heart of Belā's lowered treatment and her drive for revenge, he seemed to respond only obliquely:

> When Ālhā was thirteen years old, the Mughals attacked Delhi. Sixty lākhs of Mughals attacked Delhi. All these people, Ālhā, Parmāl, were called to defend Delhi. The bīrā (role of betel) was kept for the one who would fight the Mughals. Ālhā picked it up, saying, "I am going to fight the Mughals." Ālhā fought the sixty lakhs of

[53]See chaps. 8 at n. 38 and ff.; 10, n. 57.

Mughals and defeated them. Prithīrāj was so happy, he said, "I am going to marry Belā to you." But Ālhā said, "No, at the moment I have the rank (*padavī*) of a *naukar* (retainer). You should marry Belā to Brahmā." So the marriage was performed between Belā and Brahmā. Belā was the avatar of Draupadī. Belā had also come back to fulfill a boon (varadān) because her (Draupadī's) full work had not been done.[54] She has taken the form of Belā, the avatar of Belā, in order to complete the incomplete (*adhūri*) task of Draupadī. She has not taken this avatar for any indulgence.[55]

AH: What was incomplete about Draupadī's life?

What remained incomplete was that the five Pāṇḍavas could not be killed in *Mahābhārat*. They had not been killed. The life-cycle (*khappar*) was not complete, and they have to be killed. Therefore they take these incarnations in which they are properly killed. By getting killed their cycle is complete.

AH: That is what was incomplete about the Pāṇḍavas' life, but what about Draupadī's?

Her condition (*shart*: term of agreement, stipulation) had not been completed as Draupadī, and that condition is now complete. Draupadī had two dissatisfactions, one in the past life and one in this: [when she was Draupadī] the Pāṇḍavas had not been killed, and [as Bēlā] her condition for marriage had not been fulfilled. During her svayaṃvara, Belā set a condition. A pillar (*kambh*) made of eight metals weighing eighty maunds was planted in the ground, and the condition was that she would marry any warrior able to pierce this pillar with his arrow. Ālhā completed this condition, but actually the marriage takes place with Brahmā. This was the great condition for the dissatisfaction (*asaṃtosh*), that whereas she should have been married to Ālhā, she was married to Brahmā. She had no satisfaction (*saṃtosh nahī*).

AH: Now we know why Belā was dissatisfied, but why was Draupadī dissatisfied about the way the Pāṇḍavas died?

Because the Pāṇḍavas were not killed, therefore their blood couldn't be utilized to propitiate Devī. Like Sītā, Draupadī was also the avatar of Mahādevī. The blood of the five Pāṇḍavas had to be utilized to propitiate Mahādevī, who was Draupadī herself. But this could not be fulfilled because the Pāṇḍavas were not killed. And therefore she remains dissatisfied as Draupadī, and comes as Belā. And again, as Bēlā, rather than marrying Ālhā, she marries Brahmā. So she remains dissatisfied again.

[54]*Pūra kām nahī ho pāyā tha*. That is, the full karma of her life as Draupadī had not been completed.

[55]Indulgence in carnal pleasures or gratification, Urdu *aish*.

AH: So, does she resent her treatment by her father?

She had no feelings toward her father. Prithvīrāja runs away. She took Brahmā and became satī. And so the *Ālhā* story comes to an end. Muhammad Ghori comes again. But that's another story.

This wrap-up (heard toward the end of my Mahobā fieldwork) floods us with unexpected themes and details: more anachronisms carried backward into *Ālhā*'s time-frame; more unfinished business brought forward from the *Mahābhārata*; another confirmation of Kolff's thesis that, in fighting for the Chandēls, *Ālhā*'s Banāphar heroes reflect early naukarī traditions of the Hindustani military labor market;[56] and some new questions about Draupadī and Belā's dissatisfactions.

When Belā tells of her marital dissatisfactions through seven lives in the Elliot *Ālhā*, it is in different terms (*aghāy*, modern Hindi *aghāna*,[57] rather than *saṃtosh*), and the dissatisfactions are different. In the Elliot *Ālhā*, Draupadī's dissatisfaction is understated: that "five men were called my husbands" probably suggests that one would have been preferable, as statements about her polyandry often imply elsewhere.[58] But Belā's dissatisfaction is vividly clear: "My father became my enemy and got my husband murdered."[59] This is very different from saying, "She had no feelings toward her father"—and that, only in response to my second asking of the question. It is almost as if Baccha Singh's stories of Draupadī's and Belā's dissatisfactions are a detour around the initial question of whether Belā was angry at her father for preventing her marital homecoming. There seems to be a tendency to deny or censor open admission of a satī's anger at her father, despite the fact that the goddess Satī makes it painfully clear that it *is* anger at Dakṣa, her father, that leads her to become a primal satī even though Śiva, her husband, hasn't died.[60] One also senses such denial at work variously in *Desing*: in the printed ballad, where one hardly realizes that Rāṇiyammāḷ is the padshah's daughter at all; in Srinivasan's version, where the padshah gets the last and only word on his own daughter's satī; and in versions where the nawāb intervenes as the padshah's proxy.[61]

One cannot, however, easily square all the dissatisfactions. In Draupadī's case, the implied dissatisfaction of having four husbands too

[56]On naukarī, see chap. 10, n. 23.

[57]Lutgendorf 1997. See chap. 6 at n. 34.

[58]See chap. 11 at nn. 162 and 163.

[59]See chap. 6 at n. 35.

[60]See Hiltebeitel in press-d, with other examples of such denial and a psychoanalytic interpretation.

[61]See at n. 32 above.

many is not commensurate with the expressed dissatisfaction of not receiving the blood of all five. And Belā's dissatisfaction with her father's having had her husband murdered is not the same as her dissatisfaction at being married to Brahmā rather than Ālhā, to whom her father offered her, according to Baccha Singh. In the latter case, had Belā married Ālhā rather than Brahmā, not only would Prithīrāj have condoned the marriage; even if he hadn't, he couldn't have killed her husband because Ālhā is immortal. One is thus led to a further question. If one thinks of Draupadī having a preference, it is usually for Arjuna. Even Yudhiṣṭhira has such thoughts. When Draupadī is the first to fall on the Pāṇḍavas' ascent to heaven, he explains that it was because of her "great partiality for Arjuna" (*Mbh* 17.2.6). But there is another strain of Draupadī's continued frustrations with Yudhiṣṭhira. The dissatisfactions of Draupadī and Belā imply a reversal. In the *Mahābhārata*, Draupadī seems to want to be married to Arjuna alone, but has to also marry Yudhiṣṭhira.[62] In *Ālhā*, Belā wants to be married to Ālhā, Yudhiṣṭhira incarnate, but has to settle for Brahmā, incarnation of Arjuna.

That Pṛthvīrāj, about a decade after the last battle of *Ālhā*, defeated Shihāb al-Dīn (Muhammad Ghuri) at Tarain, near Kurukṣetra, in 1191 before they reversed their fortunes there in 1192, is probably history. It has been recounted by enough Persian, Sanskrit, and Hindi authors for modern writers to argue over the conflicting details. Did Prithvīrāj capture Shihāb al-Dīn and then release him? Did Shihāb al-Dīn capture Prithvīrāj in turn? How did Prithvīrāj die? Under what circumstances did the Rajputs first win and then lose? How many times did Prithvīrāj capture Shihāb al-Dīn? How many times did he defeat him before the tables finally turned: one, three, seven, twenty?[63] For battles to turn at "Kurukṣetra" is, of course, a recurrent theme.

It is likely that Muslim, Hindu, and Jaina authors "debated" over oral epic sources for their contending histories of these events. It is thus not surprising to find these incidents fused into Baccha Singh's oral *Ālhā*. Historians would recognize the initial battle with Shihāb al-Dīn, but dismiss the Mughal identity of the invader.[64] And they would recognize

[62]On this point, see Hiltebeitel forthcoming. The *Mbh* never has Draupadī actually say this, but I believe a recent novelist (P. Ray 1995) and poet (Varma 1996) are right to read it between the lines, and that one may make the same inference as Baccha Singh's *Ālhā*.

[63]Vaidya 1926, 323, 332; D. Sharma 1940, 741-48; Somani 1981, 65-71; Ganguly 1940, 568; Majumdar 1957, 109-131; Pritchett 1980, 60, 71 (three times in the *Pṛthvīrāj-rāsau* in the edited version studied).

[64]If the Mughals stand for Shihāb al-Dīn and his forces, it raises some interesting ahistoric possibilities for *Ālhā* folklore. Either it implicates Pṛthvīrāj and Shihāb al-Dīn as opponents before they ever were so by having Ālhā fight Shihāb al-Dīn's "Mughal" substitutes during the latter's earlier (1175) invasions of Multan and Sind (when Ālhā would have supposedly

Prithīrāj's initial victory under one of his prominent generals, but reject that the latter could be Ālhā.[65] Folklorists, however, should not be surprised to find Prithīrāj so happy with Ālhā's victory that he would offer him Belā, since they would now know something similar in the story of Rāja Desing. And no one should be surprised to find one more confirmation that Ālhā is his story's "hidden king."

As to Belā, the folklorist might be surprised at her dissatisfaction with Brahmā, since other sources have not given her much voice in this matter. But the reason for her dissatisfaction cannot be surprising. It results not so much from a preference for Ālhā as a karmic and theological burden that lands on her from her previous life as Draupadī, and is reiterated by Velā in the *Kṛṣṇāṃśacarita* when she tells her father she wants a husband who will win her through waterfalls of blood.[66] We know from Draupadī cult sources that from the time she is disheveled, Draupadī "nightly takes on the 'form of Kālī' (Kālīrūpa), her 'universal form' (Viśvarūpa)," eats live creatures in the forest, drinks the blood of the slain at Kurukṣetra, and constitutes a continuous threat to the lives of her Pāṇḍava husbands that only Kṛṣṇa prevents from ending in disaster (Hiltebeitel 1988a, 291-92). A Telugu variant provides background: "Draupadī is the primal Śakti, who had once been promised by Viṣṇu that in a future birth she would have enough human flesh to satiate her. To achieve this, Kṛṣṇa has taken human birth to engineer the *Mahābhārata* war and provide corpses for Draupadī to devour during nighttime ravages on the battlefield" (291). Indeed, as mentioned in chapter 6, Draupadī plays dice herself in a Telugu folk *Mahābhārata*. Opposing Duryodhana, playing behind a screen and throwing the dice with her toes, she wins back the kingdom that Yudhiṣṭhira has just lost; but the Pāṇḍavas, like good Rajputs, then refuse to accept a gift won by a woman, and determine to conquer it directly and on their own in battle after the agreed-upon period of exile (Rama Raju 1982). The chapbook version of the pivotal Draupadī festival drama "Dice Match and Disrobing" knows a variant (Irāmaccantira Kavirāyar [1857] 1977, 91-98), which it gets from Villiputtūr's Tamil *Makāpāratam*—that Draupadī insists on the final throw, but turns the betting over to Yudhiṣṭhira who wins this time because Draupadī tells him to pray to Kṛṣṇa (Hiltebeitel 1988a, 238).

---

been "thirteen"); or it requires Ālhā, Brahmā, and Belā to survive *Ālhā*'s final battle (in 1182) by nearly a decade to include them in the real wars between Pṛthvīrāj and Shihāb al-Dīn in 1191-92. In the first case, Ālhā and the other Banāphars would have been natural allies of the Ismā'īlīs Shihāb al-Dīn massacred; in the latter case of their survivors.

[65]Some sources mention a great general named Skanda who enabled Pṛthivīrāj to win the first battle, but was away for the second (Ganguly 1940; Majumdar 1957, 110-11).

[66]See chap. 6 at n. 11.

The Draupadī who plays with her toes behind a screen is certainly still the menstruating Draupadī who was just gambled and lost. And indeed, we have already met intimations of such a Draupadī in Srinivasan's version of *Desing*, in which the Rāṇi—yet to learn she will become Draupadī in her next life—plays dice and makes her period of confinement after menstruating her reason for setting up seven curtains to separate her from Desing in their final meeting. Clearly, there is a rich tradition of women and goddesses gambling for high stakes, and intimations that the outcomes can be disastrous.[67] For both Draupadī and Belā, there is a gambling with disrobing that precedes the final war.[68] And for both Draupadī and the Rāṇi, dicing combined with menstruation is a sign that the game has gone beyond what the males can control.[69] The Draupadī who can be satisfied with the Pāṇḍavas' blood in her next life as Belā—who will also play dice to tempt Ālhā in the desolation of Mahobā—is not very different from the future Draupadī who will have been left unsatisfied at the death of Rāja Desing. But whereas the Rāṇi will get the pleasures she missed when she becomes Draupadī, the Draupadī who becomes Belā "has not taken this avatar for any (carnal) indulgence." Complementing the Rajput husband ascetically away for war, the Rajput Draupadī is on a cycle of virginity and indulgence, which the Rāṇi extends to a cycle of unconsummated wedlock and sexual overcompensation.[70] The Tamil Draupadī cult resolves such tensions in one person, favoring virginity and nonconsummation.

These stories thus continue to explain each other, and not only regarding Draupadī's sexuality but her taste for blood. Evidently Draupadī, or the supreme Śakti (also known as Mahādevī) in becoming Draupadī, did not have enough human flesh and blood to satiate her. Her "condition" went unfulfilled because the Pāṇḍavas' could not be "utilized to propitiate Mahādevī, who was Draupadī herself." *Ālhā*'s vast turning of the tables has now one more explanation. The unfinished business of the *Mahābhārata* is the "condition," left unfulfilled, of the Great Goddess's birth as Draupadī, that she will be able to satisfy herself with blood. Although Viṣṇu provides her with the immense slaughter of Kurukṣetra, he does not provide the Pāṇḍavas for her cup. Now in *Ālhā*, Draupadī's condition can be satisfied through Belā with the deaths of the

[67] See Handelman and Shulman 1997, 17-25, 61-96. On the goddess's dicing with Śiva as a kind of strip poker, see ibid., 88; O'Flaherty 1973, 204, 207; Hiltebeitel 1987; 1988a, 238. Cf. Flueckiger 1996, 69, 72, 161-68, and the caupar game between Sonā and Vāghelī in Naiṇasī (chap. 4 at n. 72). Pārvatī and Śiva are also playing dice while Śiva curses the five Indras to be born as the Pāṇḍavas (*Mbh* 1.189).

[68] See chap. 6 following n. 101.

[69] Cf. Handelman and Shulman 1997, 106-8.

[70] See chap. 11, n. 163, and above, n. 58.

Pāṇḍavas' portions, even though this requires that Belā must now be unsatisfied to motivate the destruction. Thus it is Draupadī, not Belā, who is satisfied through *Ālhā*, and not only by the Pāṇḍavas' blood, but some of Kṛṣṇa's blood (since Ūdal is a "portion" of Kṛṣṇa). Indeed, following Baccha Singh's narrative, Ūdal is also an avatar of Babrīk, who, in his fuller north Indian as well as Telugu mythology, is like Aravāṉ in satisfying the goddess with his own blood, and in announcing after the war that Draupadī has thirsted on virtually everybody's blood *except* her husbands and Kṛṣṇa's.

But what can this mean? Two new questions now arise. The first flows from the rather exasperating relationship of Draupadī and Yudhiṣṭhira, which gets carried over to Belā's dissatisfaction at not being able to marry Ālhā. We now know that Dharma is incarnate in Yudhiṣṭhira, that Yudhiṣṭhira is incarnate in Ālhā, that neither Yudhiṣṭhira nor Ālhā ever really dies, and that, at least in the Elliot *Ālhā*, milk rather than blood flows from Ālhā's wounds.[71] Will Draupadī-Mahādevī ever get to drink the blood of Yudhiṣṭhira? It seems she is getting shortchanged once again, and that another epic will have to follow. Yet perhaps, as in Aeschylus' *Eumenides*, the bloodlust cycle does come to an end. If one Pāṇḍava has milk instead of blood, Draupadī can still satisfy herself with all the blood that the Pāṇḍavas' portions have. As we shall see, these issues reappear in another folk *Mahābhārata* tradition, where they leave us with similar questions. In the present case, I assume there is something incorporeal, or, if corporeal, finally milk-like and nurturing rather than blood-like and violent, about the dharma that flows through Ālhā's veins.[72]

E. Bairāgarh

The second question is, *how* does Draupadī satisfy her "condition" through Belā? Baccha Singh provides another lead, once again dropping a gem in responding to what he must have seen as a less interesting question, this time one about the career of Chauṉrā:

> Chauṉrā was killed in the battle of Bairāgarh, which is near Urai—not a village but a battlefield, a place that is worth a visit. There are small platforms commemorating the deaths of the heroes and satī chabūtrās. The last battle begins from the Betwa and ends at Bairāgarh. It is where Belā becomes satī.

[71] W&G 273. I regretfully did not ask Baccha Singh about this seeming exception of Ālhā.

[72] Ālhā did not, however, inherit this trait from Yudhiṣṭhira, whose nose bleeds in the scene where Draupadī collects blood from the nosebleed; had it touched the earth, it would have brought destruction to Virāta's kingdom (*Mbh* 4.63.46-47).

The last battlefield of *Ālhā*, the place of Brahmā's dying and Belā's satī: I had all but given up. A few days earlier, Zahir Singh had said the last battle began at the Betwa, but he could not remember where Belā became satī: "It was on the way from Delhi to Mahobā . . . We can look it up in *Ālhā*." But which *Ālhā*? Not Waterfield and Grierson's Elliot *Ālhā*, which tells us no more than Zahir Singh: that the spot must be between Delhi and Mahobā. Farther afield, Kishan Sharma places Brahmā's end and Belā's satī outside Delhi, but, as we have seen, considers this an earlier sequence; for him, the final battle begins with the fall of Sirsā and the satī of Gajmōtin, and ends at Mahobā with its devastation. One thing is clear: only the bhaviṣya paurāṇika thinks it all happened at "dear Kurukṣetra," ignoring the inconvenience that Kurukṣetra is on the other side of Delhi from Mahobā.

Drawing on "the account of Mahoba Khand and Alha Khand," it seems that only Somani has put us in the right area: the Chandēl army camps "on the bank of the Betawa," and the "decisive battle was fought at Urai" (1981, 47-48). But to visit the large town of Urai, home of the treacherous Māhil, is not to have found Bairāgarh, which is about fifteen kilometers west of Urai, ten north of the Betwa on the river's Delhi side, and twenty-five from Urai when approached by road via Ait.[73] Nearing Bairāgarh, before one sees the temple and other details, it appears to be no more than a rectangular plot lined with trees and surrounded by nothing but miles of fields. My arrival on December 9, 1995, a Saturday, found only one helpful informant, Hariprakash Dwivedi of the nearby village of Vīrgaon, who said the chief elderly priest, who could have said more, was away. The priest's replacement, and others milling about, insisted they did not know much.

Baccha Singh provided another detail: Ālhā and Ūdal planted a victory flag at Bairāgarh on top of the temple. "When the sun goes down it tips a wee bit, and when the sun comes up it tips to the other side. Otherwise you can't see the tilt. It represents Ālhā's victory over Prithīrāj, who flees to Delhi after his last fight with Ālhā." On the day I visited, there was no flag on the temple, or, for that matter, in the adjacent banyan tree. But Hariprakash Dwivedi knew a variation: "The last battle fought here is also known as *Jaitkambh*. The war took place when the victory flag/pillar was planted by Ālhā and Ūdal. Ālhā and Ūdal were victorious over Prithīrāj at the end." Here it seems to be a question of a pillar planted in the ground, with the temple built later in commemoration. Meanwhile, Kishan Sharma, who relocates *Ālhā*'s final battles to Sirsā and Mahobā, has another variant, now predictable in its differences:

[73]As Baccha Singh recommended. Ait is southwest of Urai, which is on national Highway 28 between Kanpur and Jhansi.

> . . . So now Prithīrāj's army was at Sirsā, seeking to prevent Gajmōtin from becoming satī. She sent a messenger to Mahobā with the message that "Prithī's army is preventing me from becoming sati." Ūdal was dispatched to Sirsā in order to facilitate the satī. Meanwhile, in Mahobā it was decided that they would continue to fight: a symbolic fight, like an Aśvamedha—"So we will continue to fight to win the Jaitkambh. Whoever wins it will have the whole world."

"A symbolic fight, like an Aśvamedha." The comment, a Brahman's, draws a valuable and precise analogy, reminding us that our investigation of *Ālhā* began with a recognition that Dasarā, like the Aśvamedha and Rājasūya, can provoke wars between kingdoms over symbolic objects. Whether it is the Aśvamedha horse, the nine-lākh chain, or the pillar of victory, "Whoever wins it will have the whole world." At Bairāgarh, ultimate victory is with Ālhā, or with Ālhā and Ūdal. Ūdal's beheading by Chauṉṛā at the final battle does not seem to weigh into these recollections.

So Bairāgarh is a ritual battlefield, associated with a victory flag or pillar of victory that can tilt to the movement of the sun, and, I suspect, to the tides of battle.[74] As a ritual battlefield, it has one striking feature in common with others (see Hiltebeitel 1991a, 239-41, 310-19): the ritual ground is the extension of a north-facing goddess temple, a temple—as one would expect from her *Ālhā* associations—of Śāradā Devī, as is shown in map 3.

According to Hariprasad Dwivedi, Bairāgarh is the site of a festival (melā) during Rām Navamī in Cait (March-April) that attracts sixty lākhs of people. He could not recall the ceremonies, but the new temple to Hanumān at the position of the goddess's left hand might suggest that *Rāmāyaṇ* is replacing *Ālhā* as the site's claim to fame.[75] *Ālhā*, he says, is performed there only in Śrāvaṇ (July-August), in the monsoon season. At that time *Ālhā* singers arrive, "but they perform better in the villages." He did not know what portions of *Ālhā* they sing. He and others identified Belā's satī chabūtrā near the center of the open area: a simple square masonry platform with a conical linga-shaped stone rising from it (see plate 16). There were a few other such platforms without offering

[74]Cf. Zoller 1993, 204, 201-13: the Garhwali ball game, with local variants in *Mbh* folklore (see chap. 12), is played typically at Makara Saṃkrānti, the winter solstice, with banners planted (204, 213), and with the ball as a head-trophy.

[75]The left-hand position is that of a nirmālyadevatā, a god who receives the main deity's "residue of offerings"; it is to northeast of an east-facing temple or, by axial rotation, northwest of a north-facing temple (Hiltebeitel 1988a, 127; 1991a, 157-58). Cf. chap. 3 at n. 67. On Hanumān in Rajput connections, see chap. 10, n. 34.

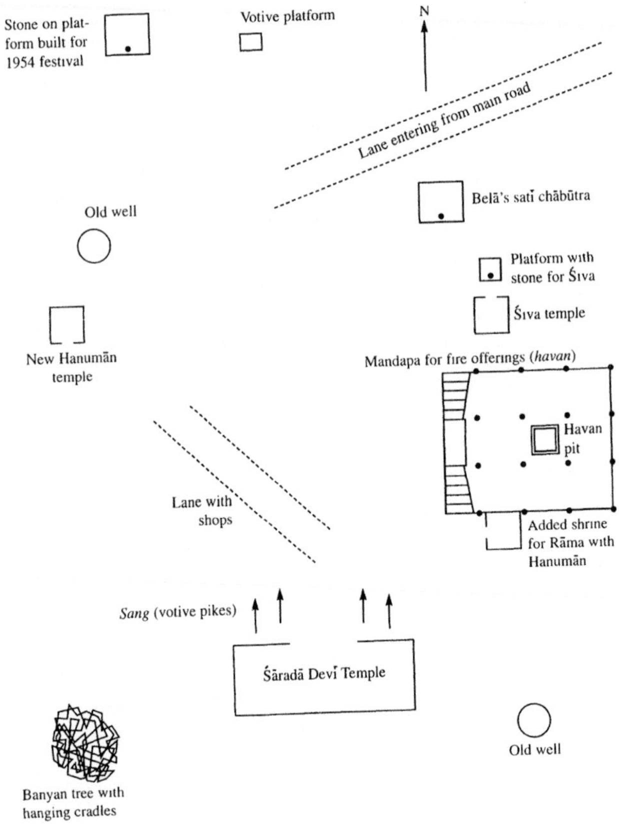

Map 3. Bairāgarh battlefield ritual sites

stones and other rough monuments on the grounds, but no one present could identify any with figures from *Ālhā*. To either side of the Śāradā Devī temple's entrance, tall colorfully decorated spears or pikes, called *sang*, point upward (see plates 7, 8, 17, and 18).[76] These, he said, are erected when the goddess has fulfilled a devotee's wish. The only one with an explicit *Ālhā* connection shows the head of "Chand Muṇḍ" (Cāmuṇḍa, Cauṉṛā) that was "severed by Śārada Devī" (see plate 8). Again, *Ālhā* seems a dimming memory: in the Elliot *Ālhā*, Chauṉṛā dies

[76]The terms "*sanga* or *sanka*" caption a spear of this type in Hoernle's edition of Chand Bardai 1873-86, 1886 fascicle, plate 3. The up-standing end has a long spear-point with a disc at its base, while the bottom has a smaller tapered point that could stick into the ground. *Ālhā* uses *sāṃgi* for the spears that kill Malkhān (chap. 6, n. 59). Muhammad Khan Bangash uses a "steel javeline (*sáng*)" against Chatrasal Bundela (Irvine 1878, 293).

when Ālhā squeezes him to death to prevent his blood from touching the ground (W&G 272). Perhaps these implanted sang are votive counterparts to the victory flags implanted by Ālhā and Ūdal. There are two icons in the sanctum: Śāradā Devī in the main central shrine and a smaller deity to her left who could not be identified during my visit. Baccha Singh later indicated by post that the little one was probably Kusumī Devī, the statue having been established and worshiped by Ūdal before one of the wars. Kusumī Devī is the wife of Lākhan. As we noted in chapter 7, § E, the *Bhaviṣya Purāṇa* calls her Padminī and seems to link her with Maniya Deo/Devī. Her connections would seem to make her a link between Mahobā and Kanauj, while her names, meaning "lotus," might suggest that she would be an auspicious counterpart to the more ferocious Śāradā.

There is obviously more to learn. But on one point Hariprasad Dwivedi's local knowledge was stunning. Baccha Singh offered no clarification of the name Bairāgarh other than to point out that I had misheard his initial pronunciation: it could have nothing to do with Bhairava/Bhairõn, since it is not "Bhairõn-garh" but "Bairā-garh."[77] Hariprasad Dwivedi had this to say: "It is firstly linked to *virāṭ*. *Virāṭ* means 'huge, big.' And this is because not just Bēlā satī, but a number of women became satīs in this place. So it is 'huge, big.'[78] Also, Ālhā and Ūdal took *vairāgya* here after the battle. They became Bairāgīs at this place."[79] I do not think there will be major improvements on this double etymology.[80] It fits the end of *Ālhā* beautifully:

> . . . the armies join battle in what is the Armageddon of Mahōbā. While it progresses, fire bursts from Bēlā's hair and sets the pyre alight, and she is consumed with Brahmā's body. The fight is terrific. Thousands of soldiers on both sides are slain. . . . The news reaches Mahōbā, where all the wives of the knights of the army find themselves widows. Headed by Sunwā, Ālhā's wife, and Phulwā, Ūdal's widow, they hasten, weeping, to the battlefield and search among the corpses each for her husband. Sunwā finds Indal, her son, alive, and

[77]A Śaivite "Gosain fort or monastery of Bhairoṅgarh" overlooks the river Siprā near Ujjain, where a rain of the Gosains' arrows killed a group of peacefully bathing Bairāgis, provoking the latter to regiment themselves. Orr adds that "surviving [Kānphaṭa] Yogi temples and monasteries throughout Rajputana more closely resemble miniature fortresses than places of worship and meditation" (1940, 88, 93).

[78]*Bhargava* glosses Hindi *virāt* as a masculine noun meaning "a Kshatriya, splendour, light, the embodied spirit, beauty," and, as an adjective, "very big, weighty, gigantic, enormous" (Pathak 1967, 996).

[79]Hindi has both *vairāgī* and *bairāgī*, "renunciant," from Sanskrit *vairāgya*, "renunciation."

[80]Jayati Chaturvedi suggests *vaira-garh*, "the enemy fort," which might be interesting within a set of temple-battlefield-fort analogies; but it doesn't allow for *vairā-* rather than *vaira-*.

> in the agitation of the moment asks him where Ālhā is, mentioning him by name in the presence of her son, a thing which is forbidden by one of the strongest Rājpūt taboos. Ālhā hears this, and bids her farewell for ever. Accompanied by Indal, he sets out for the mysterious Kajarī-ban. . . . Sunwā, Phulwā and all the widows then throw themselves in the fiery pit which forms the remains of Brahmā's funeral pyre. (W&G 19-20)

The fire is "huge, great": for as long as it takes for news to reach the widows in Mahobā and for them to reach Bairāgarh and search the battlefield, Belā's satī fire burns strong enough to consume them. And at the same spot, as part of the same closing sequence, Ālhā and Indal[81] renounce the world to become Bairāgīs and go to the Plantain Forest or Forest of Lampblack. Indeed, we might have found intimations of such a final world-abandonment from the very beginning, in the young Banāphars' first Jōgī-musician disguises:

> To Jambay's son did the messenger run,
>   And cried in the palace there;
> "At the gate there stand a Bairāgī band,
>   No tongue can say how fair.
>
> "These youths shall I bring to my lord the King?
>   They must show a merry game."
> Quoth Anūpī,[82] "Yea, let us see their play;"
>   So into the hall they came. (W&G 81)

Once again, the Bairāgī disguise covers not only the young Banāphars but their mentor Mīrā Tālhan, Saiyid of Banaras.

As we would expect, it is no ordinary fire that Belā has inherited from Draupadī. Her satī fire is lit at a boundary between Mahobā and Delhi. As a "fire of the limit," it is analogous to the fire-containing śamī at the boundary of a kingdom, which can both define a cremation ground and "function as the goddess of the limit (la déesse de la limite), the complementary aspect of the goddess who protects royal lineages who habitually resides in the palace at the heart of capital" (Biardeau 1989a, 300). Belā's homecoming is the story of her nonresidence at the heart of Mahobā. As such she combines traits of the two heroines of *Pābūjī* who will never reside in Koḷū: Sonā's link with the śamī and Phulvantī's virginal satī. Emptied kingdoms leave only traces of their Dasarās.

[81]Not Ālhā and Ūdal: Hariprasad Dwivedi is consistent in having Ūdal survive the war.
[82]Anūpī, "Marshy," the second of Jambay's three sons.

Belā's fire would also be "huge" if one thinks of the *Kṛṣṇāṃśacarita*, where Velā is Kālī incarnate, and where her name itself means the "limit." The bhaviṣya paurāṇika completes the unfinished business of the *Mahābhārata* by having Draupadī be reborn into the Agnivaṃśa as the "limit fire" that consumes not only the satīs at Kurukṣetra, but the entire Rajput-Kṣatriya world. *Virāṭ*, not just "huge," carries the same connotations of the doomsday fire that it has in connection with Kṛṣṇa's *virāṭ rūpa*: the flaming form of universal destruction, also known as Viśvarūpa, which Kṛṣṇa reveals to Arjuna in popular oleographs of the eleventh chapter of the *Bhagavad Gītā*, and to Barbarīk in the Marwari narrative of Chandmal Agarwal.

But finally, let us picture this fire one last time from the angle of a parallel oral *Mahābhārata*. The Pāṇḍav Līlās of Garhwal have rich variations on many of the themes we have been discussing, beginning with the following song that summons Draupadī-Kālī into a ritual performance:

> In Dwapar Yug, you incarnated as Draupadi
> in the home of Drupad raja.
> You were born from the fire pit
> and you wear a burning headcloth
> and in Kaliyug you are incarnate as Kali.
> The mother of four yugas and
> the dangerous woman (*dūranārī*) of five brothers. (Sax 1995b, 3)

In Garhwal, the Pāṇḍavas also learn (though not from Kṛṣṇa) that Draupadī eats corpses and craves blood. Explicitly, it is only the Kauravas she wishes killed. But she drinks Kṛṣṇa's blood before binding his wound when he once cuts his finger with a sword.[83] And one of the Pāṇḍavas must offer his blood as well: After Draupadī has seen her five sons killed at the end of the eighteen-day war, she says, "The fire in my heart will be quenched only by blood." Bhīma protests, "A second *Mahābhārata* can't be fought; where will the blood come from?" Answering with his own blood, he throws his club up in the air, receives it on his chest,[84] and lets the blood rush from his mouth into the firepit from which Draupadī had been born, "which had burned continuously until that moment." The fire goes out.[85] Again the bloodlust cycle is brought to

[83]A variant of her using the endpiece of her sari to stanch the finger Kṛṣṇa cuts after releasing his cakra to kill Śiśupāla. For south and north Indian (including *Ālhā*) variants, see chap. 6, § D.

[84]As we have seen Rāja Desing do with his sword.

[85]Unlike Rāvaṇa's cremation fire; see n. 32 above and chap. 12, n. 2.

an end, while the story can be ritually reenacted by offering Draupadī a goat (4-8).

In quenching the awesomely durable fire of Draupadī's birth, which has mysteriously relocated from Pāñcāla to Kurukṣetra, with blood sufficient to her demand, Bhīma eliminates the "condition" that would produce "a second *Mahābhārata* war." No reincarnations are necessary, no satīs are to be their result; there will be no "*Mahābhārata* of the Kali yuga," no *Ālhā*. Draupadī becomes Kālī in the Kali yuga. She does not become Belā. But once again, we might wonder whether she has been shortchanged. Can her fire really be satisfied by just the blood of Bhīma?

F. Questions, Questions

Draupadī asked certain questions herself. By her most famous one in the *Mahābhārata*—did Yudhiṣṭhira bet himself first before he wagered her?—she saves herself and her husbands by stumping everybody in the Kaurava court. In her folklore, Kṛṣṇa tells her and the Pāṇḍavas to take a question they have raised to Aravāṉ or Barbarīk: Who really won the war? This question invites us to think of her as a woman who takes extraordinary pride and satisfaction in an outcome of violence. Many ask questions of her. In the *Villipāratam*, Kṛṣṇa asks about her innermost secret "truth" and learns, along with her husbands, that she yearns for still one more man.[86] In the Sanskrit epic, Kṛṣṇa's wife Satyabhāmā asks her how she manages five husbands with her "famous sexual power (*yaśasyaṃ bhagavedanam*)."[87] And when Jayadratha, in a marrying mood, finds her unprotected in the forest, he and his men wonder whether she is an Apsaras, a divine maiden, or an illusion fashioned by the gods (*māyā vā devanirmitā*);[88] and his henchman, like a jackal approaching a tigress, asks her, "Who are you, bending a kadamba branch, staying alone in a hermitage, radiant like a fiery flame burning the night? . . . A goddess? A Yakṣī? A Dānavī? An Apsaras? Or a Daitya beauty? A lovely serpent maiden? Or a forest-roving woman night-stalker? Perhaps the wife of king Varuṇa, or of Yama, Soma, or Kubera?" (3.248.6-249.3).

Oral regional martial epics and regional *Mahābhārata* folklores like that of the Draupadī cult do not so much ask questions of Draupadī as answer ones that they raise implicitly by telling more stories. Scholars,

[86] *Villipāratam* 3.7.21; Hiltebeitel 1988a, 288-89. The story is also known in Sāralādāsa's Oriya *Mbh* (Swain 1993, 179-80; Mishra 1993, 159).

[87] *Mbh* 3.222-23, especially 222.7. Note Shah 1995, 82: "that fearless lady Draupadī with a mind of her own suddenly indulges in a vapid innane (sic) dialogue with Satyabhāmā talking at length about the religion of a *pativratā*."

[88] Draupadī was "fashioned by the trident-bearer" (*nirmitā śūlapāninā*; *Mbh* 18.4.10) Śiva.

on the other hand, usually raise questions explicitly and answer them by argumentation. But the answers must often leave the ambiguities. Shah, for instance, asks of Draupadī's polyandry: "Did Draupadī really desire that? We cannot say" (1995, 78). As Shah shows, the text gives us both answers. I have left three questions, the first, one of this type.

As we have seen, when Draupadī is born in the Sanskrit epic, a heavenly voice announces she will be the destruction of the entire Kṣatra class. If the gods are born to lift the burden of the earth, this is a heavy burden on the dark heroine who embodies the earth. As one works one's way through the literatures that tell her story, one may thus ask whether that burden is ever lifted. Does Draupadī represent throughout her life the agonistic principle of sacrifice that gives her birth, or is she "transformed?" I think there is room to say she is transformed in the Sanskrit *Mahābhārata*, in large part from putting up with the exasperating Yudhiṣṭhira. Draupadī and Yudhiṣṭhira are each other's mutual education. If she is a tapasvinī, one who suffers and undertakes long penances, it is primarily in relation to him. Her life as a dharmacariṇī and "lady pundit" (Karve 1974, 90) is nurtured through a marriage with this Brahmanical husband who comes to understand at least some things about her. As we noted, when the Kaurava widows she had cursed finally go to heaven, she seems to be their friend.

But if this is the direction of her transformation in the Sanskrit text, there is an entirely different transformation in rajputized folk traditions about her. Here the violent, agonistic, and sacrificial dimensions of her character rise again to the fore in new and powerfully reimagined forms. Instead of coming to an end, the cycles of violence only become vaster and potentially unending. Dissatisfied with the blood she obtained in her life as Draupadī, she must be reborn as Belā to get what she missed. Even as Belā, we are left unsure whether she has had enough. And then there is another Draupadī yet to come: the reborn Rāṇi of Rāja Desing. One can only wonder what dissatisfactions will motivate this new Draupadī named Yākajōti, reborn from a Rāṇi who became satī through "no sin" of her own. Both backward in time and forward in time, we cannot glimpse the end of such Draupadīs.

Yet there could be no greater mistake than to conclude from this that these two types of transformation are best understood apart. The epic poets imagined Draupadī against the background of an agonistic "Vrātya" world of the Vedic past that has many similarities *and continuities* with the low status Rajput or Rajputized worlds in which regional martial oral epics and the Draupadī cult *Mahābhārata* reimagined her.[89] I have tried

[89]It is perhaps on the nature of such continuities that one will be able to best consider the question raised by Zoller (chap. 10, n. 3).

to show that these two transformations of Draupadī answer to each other in a complex intertextual situation, and that neither goes entirely in one direction or the other. As just observed, the Sanskrit *Mahābhārata* does not let one forget that Draupadī can seem a tigress. Similarly, the Draupadīs reimagined through Belā, Māncāla and her parrot, Taṅkāḷ, and Rāṇiyammāḷ, who have so much in common with the Draupadī of the Tamil Draupadī cult, are always sympathetic figures who confront unbearable obstacles with resilience and intelligence.

Second, I have not offered an explanation of how it comes about that, with all the similarities between such Draupadīs, the Gingee area produced an "iconic" regional folk *Mahābhārata* cult, the Draupadī cult, while other regions developed hero cults around regional oral epics that "indexically" reenplot the *Mahābhārata* or *Rāmāyaṇa*. This question is rather too vast to answer comparatively, since it would require more research on other regional "iconizing" *Mahābhārata* traditions like the Pāṇḍav Līlā in Garhwal, Pāṇḍvānī in Chhatisgarh, the Rajasthani *Mahābhārata*, and the popular Mahābhārata of Sind that must have preexisted the ginān̄s of Pīr Shams.[90] Suffice it to say that for the Gingee area, I content myself with the tentative explanation that the region was imbued since Pallava times with texts (Peruntēvaṉār's *Pāratam*), iconography, and other practices that popularized the *Mahābhārata* in relation to the goddess in ways that set a foundation for the Draupadī cult to recuperate by at least the time of Villiputtūr (Hiltebeitel 1988a, 13-16, 318-20).

Finally, I have left from earlier chapters the question of whether it makes any difference whether an oral regional martial epic spins out the unfinished business of the *Rāmāyaṇa* or the *Mahābhārata*. Certainly, chapters 3 and 4, with their same eight "functions," might lead one to think that it does not. And to a very basic extent, that is the case: at least from the perspective of these epics' regional expressions with regard to land, status, the goddess, and the repeated importance of Dasarā. But there is a difference in the way these originally Sanskrit texts and their regional folklores are felt. The unfinished business of the *Rāmāyaṇa* is not only found in the karmic destiny of Lakṣmaṇa, Śūrpaṇakhā, and Rāvaṇa, but in the sealing off of their hidden sexual and vengeful motivations to effect the continued purification of the innocent god Rāma and the chaste Sītā. A cycle of violence is resumed and ended, but its end is brought about as a kind of punishment for hidden motives in the *Rāmāyaṇa*—Lakṣmaṇa's attraction to Sītā, Śūrpaṇakhā's attraction to Rāma—that violate the purity of the divine couple, who are left entirely

[90]See chap. 1, n. 3, and the beginning of chap. 12.

out of and *above* the story of *Pābūjī*.[91] This is a very different project from the unfinished business of the *Mahābhārata*, which, to take *Ālhā* and Srinivasan's oral version of *Desing* as our richest examples, are about fulfilling rather than suppressing unfulfilled yearnings: Yudhiṣthira's desire for Draupadi's trust; Arjuna's desire for more fighting; Draupadī's marital dissatisfactions; her rage at Karṇa, who dies as her next-life-brother; her anger at Duryodhana, who as Prithīrāj becomes her manipulative father; Duryodhana's resentment at Draupadī, whom he repays by preventing the completion of Belā's marriage; Draupadī's anger that her husbands didn't die—perhaps rather than her sons or brothers or father; her thirst for blood; Rāṇiyammāḷ's desire for a more sexually fulfilling marriage. And so on. Here, too, cycles of violence are resumed and possibly ended, but not to punish these motives or insulate the deity. Rather, the motives are just as good as ever in the new lives turned upside down. And the deities remain hidden in the action, working things out yet also leaving things open as darkly and notoriously as ever.

[91]One could formulate these differences in relation to Shulman's contrast between the *Rām* as a "poetics of perfection" and the *Mbh* as a "poetics of dilemma" (1991, 19). While Rāma and Sītā's perfection *and purity* is safeguarded in *Pābūjī*, *Mbh* folklores roll on with the dilemmas. Cf. chap. 12, n. 2, on Rāma's exemption from the Shāh's army in the ginān s.

Abbreviations

Indian Texts

AV	*Atharva Veda*
BĀUp	*Bṛhadāraṇyaka Upaniṣad*
BhG	*Bhagavad Gītā*
BhvP	*Bhaviṣya Purāṇa*
ChUp	*Chāndogya Upaniṣad*
DM	*Devī Māhātmyam*
HV	*Harivaṃśa*
Mbh	*Mahābhārata*
Rām	*Rāmāyaṇa*
ṚV	*Ṛg Veda*

Bibliographical Entries

ABORI	*Annals of the Bhandarkar Oriental Research Institute*
BEFEO	*Bulletin de l'Ecole Française d'Extrême Orient*
BSOAS	*Bulletin of the School of Oriental and African Studies*
CIS	*Contributions to Indian Sociology*
HR	*History of Religions*
IA	*Indian Antiquary*
IHQ	*Indian Historical Quarterly*
IIJ	*Indo-Iranian Journal*
JAOS	*Journal of the American Oriental Society*
JAS	*Journal of Asian Studies*
JASB	*Journal of the Asiatic Society of Bengal*
JIH	*Journal of Indian History*
JIP	*Journal of Indian Philosophy*
JRAS	*Journal of the Royal Asiatic Society*

Bibliography

Works in Indian languages

Bhāratīya, Shastrī Sitendrachandra. 1963. *The Navasāhasāṅkacharitam of Āchārya Parimala Padmagupta*. Vidyabhawan Sanskrit Granthamala 66. Varanasi: Chowkhamba Vidyabhawan.

Bhatt, G. H., and U. P. Shah, gen. eds. 1960-75. *The Vālmīki Rāmāyaṇa: Critical edition*. 7 vols. Baroda: University of Baroda.

Brahmanandam, Devadula. 1992. *Madhava Vijayam anu Vīra Barbarīka*. Peddapuram, Andhra Pradesh.

Caṇmukacuntaram, Cu., ed. 1984. *Tēciṅku Rājaṉ Katai*. Madras: Pumpukār Piracuram Press.

Cēṣāttiri, E. Kē. 1994. *Ceñcik kōṭṭai*. Chennai: Cēkar Patippakam.

Dikshitar, V. R. Ramachandra, ed. 1952. *Karnaṭaka Rājākkaḷ Cavistāra Carittiram*, by Nārāyaṇaṉ Piḷḷai. Madras: Government Oriental Manuscripts Library.

Elliot, C. A. [1881] 1992. *Ālhakhaṇḍa*. 3d ed. Fatehgarh 1881. Microfilm, British Library Oriental and India Office Collections. London: British Library.

Irāmaccantira Kavirāyar, Irāyanallūr. [1857] 1977. *Śrī Makāpāratavilācam Cūtu-Tukilurital*. Madras: Irattiṉa Nāyakar and Sons.

Islāmiyak kalaikkalañciyam (Islamic encyclopedia). 1980. 3 vols. Madras: Universal Publishers.

Karuṇāṉantacuvāmi, Citamparam. 1875. *Ceñcimānakaram Tēciṅkurājankatai*. Cintāttirippēṭṭai: Nārāyaṇacāmi Mutaliyar, Pirapākara Accukkūtam.

Kāśīnātha Upādhyāya. 1968. *Dharmasindhu*. Kashi Sanskrit Series, 183. Varanasi: Chowkhambha.

Kinjawadekar, Ramachandra, ed. 1929-33. *Mahābhāratam with the commentary of Nīlakaṇṭha*. 6 vols. Poona: Chitrashala Press.

Kiruṣṇacāmippāvalar, Tē. 1917. *Tēciṅku Rājaṉ*. Chennai: Caccitāṉantan Press.

Kōpālakiruṣṇamācāriyar, Vai. Mu., ed. 1976-78. *Villiputtūrār Iyaṟṟiya Makāpāratm, with commentary*. 9 vols. Madras: Kuvaippalikēṣaṉs.

Muṉicuvāmi Upāttiyāyar, K. N.d. *Akṣaya Pāttira Makuttuvam eṉṉum Tūrvācar Viruntu Nāṭakam*. Tiruppātirippuliyūr (Cuddalore): Śrī Vāṇi Vilāca Press.

Pukaḻēnti Pulavar. 1980. *Pañcapāṇṭavar vaṉavācam*. Madras: Śrīmakaḷ Com-

pany.
Pukaḻentippulavar. N.d.-a. *Periya eḻuttu Tēcinkurājaṉ Katai*. Madras: Irattiṉa Nāyakar and Sons.
———. N.d.-b. *Āravalli Cūravalli Katai*. Irattiṉa Nāyakar and Sons.
Rājakōpālācāriyār, Ko., ed. 1970-71. *Villi Pāratam*. 2 vols. Triplicane, Madras: Star Publications.
Ṣaṇmukam, Mu. N.d. *Muttālrājaputtiraṉ-Pōrmaṉṉaṉ Caṇṭai Nāṭakam*. Tiru-pātirippuliyūr: Śrī Vāṇi Vilāca Press.
Ṣaṇmukam Upāttiyāyar, S. N.d. *Vātāpi Cūra Cammāram eṉṉum Vīra Vaṉṉiyar Nāṭakam*. Madras: Ṣaṇmukāṉanta Puttakacālai.
Śarmā, Śrīrāma. 1968. *Bhaviṣya Purāṇa*. 2 vols. Bareli: Saṃskrti Saṃsthāna.
Sharma, R. N., ed. 1984-85. *The Bhaviṣyamahāpurāṇam*. 3 vols. Delhi: Nag Publishers.
Shastri, J. L., ed. 1973. *Brahmāṇḍa Purāṇa*. Delhi: Motilal Banarsidass.
Sukthankar, V. S., et al., eds. 1933-70. *Mahābhārata: Critical edition*. 24 vols. with *Harivaṃśa*. Bhandarkar Oriental Research Institute.
Turaicāmi Piḷḷai, Auvai, ed. 1947 and 1951. *Puṟanāṉūṟu*. 2 vols. Madras. South India Śaiva Siddhanta Works Publishing Society.
Viṣṇu Purāṇa (Śrīśrīviṣṇupurāṇa). N.d. Gorakhpur: Gītā Press.
Viśvambhara Nātha "Vācāla." 1986. *Asalībaḍā Ālhakhaṇḍa*. 1986. Allahabad: Śrī Durgā Pustaka Bhaṇḍāra.

Secondary Sources

Abu Sail, Haled. 1998. Women of paradise, I: The black woman. *Islamic voice* (Bangalore). No. 138 (July):17.
Alavi, Seema. 1995. *The sepoys and the company: Tradition and transition in northern India* 1770-1830. Delhi: Oxford.
Allana, G. 1984. *Ginans of Ismaili Pirs*. Vol. 1. Karachi: His Highness Prince Aga Khan Shia Imami Ismailia Association for Pakistan.
Andhare, B. R. 1984. *Bundelkhand under the Marathas*. Nagpur: Vishwa Bharati Prakashan.
Arora, Raj Kumar. 1972. *Historical and cultural data from the Bhaviṣya Purāṇa*. New Delhi: Sterling Publishers.
Arunachalam, M. 1976. *Peeps into Tamil literature: Ballad poetry*. Tiru-chitrambalam: Gandhi Vidyalayam.
Asani, Ali S. 1991. The Ginān literature of the Ismailis of Indo-Pakistan. In Diana L. Eck and Françoise Mallison, eds. *Devotion divine: Bhakti traditions from the regions of India. Studies in honour of Charlotte Vaudeville*. 1-18. Groningen: Egbert Forsten; Paris: École Française d'Extrême Orient.
Asopa, Jai Narayan. 1972. History of the myth of fire origin. *Journal of the Oriental Institute of Baroda* 21:336-43.
———. 1976. *Origin of the Rajputs*. Studies in Rajput History and Culture

Series, 1. Delhi: Bharatiya Publishing House.

Assayag, Jackie. 1992. *La colère de la déesse décapitée: Traditions, cultes et pouvoir dans le sud de l'Inde*. Paris: CNRS Éditions.

———. 1995. *Au confluent de deux rivières: Musulmans et hindous dans le Sud de l'Inde*. Paris: Presses de l'École Française d'Extrême-Orient.

Aufrecht, Theodor. 1903. Über das Bhaviṣyapurāṇa: Ein literarischer Betrug. *Zeitschrift der Deutschen Morgenländischen Gesellschaft* 57:276-84.

Babb, Lawrence. 1975. *The divine hierarchy: Popular Hinduism in central India*. New York: Columbia University Press.

Babu, P. Ranjan. 1996. *Palanati Vira Charitra (A heroic ballad sung by Malas and Dalits of Palanadu): A socio-cultural study*. Ph.D. dissertation. Department of History, Nagarjuna University. Nagarjunanagar, Guntur, Andhra Pradesh.

Baden-Powell, B. H. 1899. Notes on the origin of the "lunar" and "solar" Aryan tribes, and on the "Rājput" clans. *JRAS*, 295-328, 519-63.

Baker, D. E. U. 1993. *Colonialism in an Indian hinterland: The Central Provinces 1820-1920*. Delhi: Oxford University Press.

Bakhtin, M. M. [1981] 1990. *The dialogic imagination*. Ed. Michael Holquist. Trans. Caryl Emerson and Michael Holquist. Austin: University of Texas.

Bandyopadhyaya, Brajanatha. 1879. Hamír Rásá, or a History of Hamír, prince of Ranthambor. Translated from the Hindi. *JASB* 48:186-26.

Banerjee, Anil Chandra. 1962. *Lectures in Rajput history*. Calcutta: Firma K. L. Mukhopadhyay.

Barber, C. Clyde. 1979. *A Balinese-English dictionary*. Aberdeen: Aberdeen University [trans. and re-ed., R. van Eck, Eerste Proeve van een Balineesch-Hollandsch Woordenboek. Utrecht: 1876].

Barnett, Richard B. 1980. *North India between empires: Awadh, the Mughals, and the British 1720-1810*. Berkeley: University of California Press.

Basham, A. L. 1967. *The wonder that was India*. New York: Grove Press.

Bayly, C. A. 1990. *Indian society and the making of the British empire*. Cambridge: Cambridge University Press.

Bayly, Susan. 1989. *Saints, goddesses and kings: Muslims and Christians in south Indian society 1700-1900*. Cambridge: Cambridge University Press.

———. 1993. The limits of Islamic expansion in south India. In Anna Libera Dallapiccola and Stephanie Singel-Avé Lallement, *Islam and Indian regions*. Stuttgart: Franz Steiner Verlag.

Beach, Milo Cleveland, Ebba Koch, and Wheeler Thackston. 1997. *King of the world: The Padshahnama, an imperial Mughal manuscript from the Royal Library, Windsor Castle*. Washington, D.C. Smithsonian Institution.

Beck, Brenda E. F. 1975. *The story of the brothers: An oral epic from the Coimbatore District of Tamilnadu, collected in 1965*. Mimeographed and privately circulated by the author.

———. 1978. The personality of a king. In Richards 1978:168-91.

———. 1982. *The three twins: The telling of a South Indian folk epic*. Bloomington: Indiana University Press.

———. 1989. Core triangles in the folk epics of India. In Blackburn, Claus, Flueckiger, and Wadley 1989, 155-75.

———. 1992. Collector and trans. *Elder brothers story. Aṇṇanmār Katai (An oral epic of Tamil)*. 2 Parts. Folklore of Tamilnadu Series, 4. Madras: Institute of Asian Studies.

Belvalkar, Shripad Krishna. 1959. Introductions and apparatus. In Sukthankar et al. 1933-70.

Benson, Larry D. [1966] 1990. The literary character of Anglo-Saxon formulaic poetry. In John Miles Foley, ed. *Oral-formulaic theory: A folklore casebook*. 227-42. New York and London: Garland.

Bhabha, Homi K. 1994a. *The location of culture*. London: Routledge.

———. 1994b. Representation and the colonial text: A critical exploration of some forms of mimeticism. In *The theory of reading*. Frank Gloversmith ed. 93-112. Sussex and New Jersey: Harvester Press and Barnes & Noble Books.

Bhandarkar, D. R. 1911. Foreign elements in the Hindu population. *IA* 40:7-37.

Bhardwaj, Surinder Mohan. 1973. *Hindu places of pilgrimage in India: A study in cultural geography*. Berkeley: University of California Press.

Biardeau, Madeleine. 1969. La décapitation de Reṇukā dans le mythe de Paraśurāma. In Jan C. Heesterman, ed. *Pratidānam. Indian, Iranian and Indo-European studies presented to F. B. J. Kuiper on his sixtieth birthday*. Janua Linguarum, Series Major, 34. 563-72. The Hague: Mouton.

———. 1976. Études de mythologie hindoue: 4. Bhakti et avatāra. *BEFEO* 63:87-237.

———. 1978. Études de mythologie hindoue: 5. Bhakti et avatāra. *BEFEO* 65:111-263.

———. 1981. L'arbre *śamī* et le buffle sacrificiel. In Biardeau, ed., *Autour de la déesse hindoue*. *Puruṣārtha* 5:215-44.

———. 1984. The *śamī* tree and the sacrificial buffalo. *CIS*, n.s. 18,1:1-23.

———. 1989a. *Histoires de poteaux: Variations védiques autour de la déesse hindoue*. Paris: École Française d'Extrême Orient.

———. 1989b. *Hinduism: Anthropology of a civilization*. Delhi: Oxford University Press.

Biardeau, Madeleine, and Jean-Michel Péterfalvi. 1985. *Le Mahābhārata, Livres I à V*. Paris: Flammarion.

———. 1986. *Le Mahābhārata, Livres VI à XVIII*. Paris: Flammarion.

Bingley, A. H. [1870] 1979. *Caste, tribe and culture of Rajputs*. K. P. Bahadur ed. Delhi: Ess Ess Publications.

Blackburn, Stuart H. 1981. Oral performance: Narrative and ritual in a Tamil tradition. *Journal of American Folklore* 94:207-27.

———. 1985. Death and deification: Folk cults in Hinduism. *HR* 24, 3:255-74.

———. 1986. Performance markers in an Indian story-type. In Blackburn and

Ramanujan 1986, pp. 167-94.

———. 1988. *Singing of birth and death: Texts in performance*. Philadelphia: University of Pennsylvania Press.

———. 1989. Patterns of development for Indian oral epics. In Blackburn, Claus, Flueckiger, and Wadley 1989, 15-32.

Blackburn, Stuart H., Peter J. Claus, Joyce B. Flueckiger, and Susan S. Wadley, eds. 1989. *Oral epics in India*. Berkeley: University of California Press.

Blackburn, Stuart H., and Joyce Burkhalter Flueckiger. 1989. Introduction. In Blackburn, Claus, Flueckiger, and Wadley 1989, 1-11.

Blackburn, Stuart H., and A. K. Ramanujan. 1986. *Another harmony: New essays on the folklore of India*. Berkeley: University of California Press.

Bonazzoli, Giorgio. 1979a. Christ in the Bhaviṣya Purāṇa (a methodological approach to Bhav. P. III.3.2.21-32). *Purāṇa* 21:23-39.

———. 1979b. The dynamic canon of the purāṇa-s. *Purāṇa* 21:116-66.

———. 1980. A devī in form of liṅga. *Purāṇa* 22:221-31.

———. 1981. Places of purāṇic recitation according to the purāṇas. *Purāṇa* 23,1:48-60.

Boon, A. 1990. *Affinities and extremes: Crisscrossing the Bittersweet ethnology of East-Indies studies, Hindu-Balinese culture, and Indo-European allure*. Chicago: University of Chicago Press.

Bose, Nemai Sadhan. 1956. *History of the Candellas of Jejakabhukti*. Calcutta: K. L. Mukhopadhyay.

Boulton, J. V. 1976. Sarala Dasa: His audience, his critics, and his Mahabharata. *Image (Balasore)*, 1-24.

Bourdieu, Pierre. 1990. *The logic of practice*. Richard Nice trans. Stanford: Stanford University Press.

Bowra, C. M. 1952. *Heroic poetry*. New York: Macmillan.

Bradnock, Robert, ed. 1995. *1995 India handbook with Sri Lanka, Bhutan and the Maldives*. 4th ed. Chicago: Passport Books.

Briggs, George Weston. [1938] 1989. *Gorakhnāth and the Kānphaṭa Yogīs*. Delhi: Motilal Banarsidass.

Brown, C. Mackenzie. 1990. *The triumph of the goddess: The canonical models and theological visions of the Devī-Bhāgavata Purāṇa*. Albany: State University of New York Press.

Brückner, Heidrun. 1987. Bhūta-worship in Coastal Karnāṭaka: An oral Tuḷu myth and festival ritual of Jumādi. *Studien zur Indologie und Iranistik* 13/14: 17-38.

———. 1993. Kannālāye: The place of a Tuḷu pāḍdana among interrelated oral traditions. In Brückner, Lutze, and Malik 1993, 283-334.

Brückner, Heidrun, Lothar Lutze, and Aditya Malik. 1993. *Flags of fame: Studies in South Asian folk culture*. South Asian Studies, 27. South Asia Institute, New Delhi Branch, Heidelberg University.

Brückner, Heidrun, and Narasimha Poti. 1992. "Dhūmāvati Bhūta": An oral

Tuḷu-text collected in the 19th Century edition, translation and analysis. *Studien zur Indologie und Iranistik* 16/17:13-64.

Burghart, Richard. 1978a. The disappearance and reappearance of Janakpur. *Kailash* 6:256-84.

———. 1978b. The founding of the Ramanandi sect. *Ethnohistory* 25:120-39.

Burnell, A. E. 1894. The devil worship of the Tuluvas: The song of Koti and Channayya, *IA* 23:29-49, 85-91.

———. 1895. The story of Koti and Channayya, *IA* 24:114-21, 141-53, 211-15, 242-44, 267-72.

———. 1886. The devil worship of the Tuluvas: The origin of the Beiderlu (Mr. Männer's variants), *IA* 25:295-310, 328-42.

Burrow, T., and M. B. Emeneau. 1961. *A Dravidian etymological dictionary*. Oxford: Clarendon Press.

Caland, Willem. [1931] 1982. *Pañcaviṃśa-Brāhmaṇa: The Brāhmaṇa of twenty five chapters*. Bibliotheca Indica, No. 255. Calcutta: Asiatic Society.

Callewaert, Winand M. 1980. *Early Hindī devotional literature in current research*. Proceedings of the International Middle Hindī Bhakti Conference (April 1979). Orientalia Lovaniensia Analecta, 8. Department Oriëntalistiek: Catholic University of Leuven; New Delhi: Impex India.

Campbell, Joseph. [1949] 1956. *The hero with a thousand faces*. Bollingen Series, 17. Princeton: Princeton University Press.

Caputo, John D. 1997. *The prayers and tears of Jacques Derrida: Religion without religion*. Bloomington: University of Indiana Press.

Caroe, Olaf. 1964. *The Pathans: 550 B.C.—A.D. 1957*. London: Macmillan; New York: St. Martin's Press.

Carriere, Jean-Claude, and Peter Brook. 1987. *The Mahabharata*. Trans. Peter Brook. New York: Harper and Row.

Carrington, C. E. 1955. *The life of Rudyard Kipling*. Garden City, N.Y.: Doubleday and Company.

Carstairs, Morris. 1961. *The twice-born: A study of a community of high-caste Hindus*. Bloomington: University of Indiana Press.

Chand Bardāī. 1873-86. *The Prithirāja Rāsau*, ed. by John Beames (1873 fascicle) and A. F. R. Hoernle, and in part trans. by Hoernle (1881 fascicle). Bibliotheca Indica. Calcutta: Baptist Mission Press.

Chandra, Satish. 1994. *Mughal religious policies: The Rajputs and the Deccan*. New Delhi: Vikas.

Chandra Sekhar, A. 1961. *Fairs and festivals* (6. *Guntur District*). Part 7B of *Census of India 1961*, Vol. 2, *Andhra Pradesh*. Delhi: Manager of Publications.

Chary, P. Subha. 1993. The Pandavulu and Mahābhārata tradition. In K. S. Singh 1993, 202-10.

Chatterjee, Partha. 1995a. *The nation and its fragments: Colonial and postcolonial histories*. Delhi: Oxford University Press.

———. 1995b. History and the nationalization of Hinduism. In Dalmia and von Stietencron 1995, 103-28.

Chattopadhyaya, B. D. 1976. Origin of the Rajputs: The political, economic and social processes in early medieval Rajasthan. *Indian Historical Review* 3, 1:59-82.

———. 1994. The emergence of the Rajputs as historical process in early medieval Rajasthan. In Schomer et al. 1994, 161-91.

Chinnian, P. 1982. *The Vellore mutiny, 1806*. Madras: Capricorn Printing House.

Claus, Peter J. 1973. Possession, protection and punishment as attributes of the deities in a south Indian village. *Man in India* 53:231-42.

———. 1975. The Siri myth and ritual: A mass possession cult of south India. *Ethnology* 14,1:47-58.

———. 1982. The significance of variation in the performance context of the Kordabbu epic. Paper presented at the Conference on Indian Oral Epics, Madison, Wisconsin.

———. 1989. Behind the text: Performance and ideology in a Tulu oral tradition. In Blackburn, Claus, Flueckiger, and Wadley 1989, 55-74.

Claus, Peter J., and Frank J. Korom. 1991. *Folkloristics and Indian folklore*. RRC Publications in International Folkloristics, 1. Udupi: Regional Resources Centre for Folk Performing Arts, Mahatma Gandhi College.

Cohn, Bernard S. 1990. *An anthropologist among the historians and other essays*. Delhi: Oxford University Press.

Corbin, Henry. 1983. *Cyclical time and Ismaili gnosis*. London: Kegan Paul International and Islamic Publications.

Courtright, Paul B. 1995. *Satī*, sacrifice, and marriage: The modernity of a tradition. In Harlan and Courtright 1995, 184-203.

Cox, J. F. 1881. *A manual of the North Arcot District*. Madras: Government Press.

Crawfurd, J. [1820] 1985. *History of the Indian archipelago, containing an account of the manners, arts, languages, religions, institutions, and commerce of its inhabitants*. 3 vols. London: Frank Cass.

Crooke, William. [1896] 1968. *The popular religion and folklore of northern India*. Delhi: Munshiram Manoharlal.

———. 1914. Gurkhā, Gorkhā and Indian charms and amulets. In James Hastings, ed. *Encyclopaedia of religion and ethics*. 6:456-57 and 3:446-47. Edinburgh: T. & T. Clark.

———. 1915. The Dasahra: An autumn festival of the Hindus. *Folklore* (London) 75, 28-59.

———. 1920. Introduction to Tod [1829-32, 1920] 1990.

———. 1926. *Religion and folklore of northern India*. Oxford: Oxford University Press.

Cunningham, Alexander. 1970. *Report on a tour in the Punjab in 1878-79*. Archaeological survey of India, Vol. 14. Varanasi: Indological Book House.

———. 1880. *Report of tours in the Gangetic provinces from Badaon to Bihar in 1875-76 and 1877-88*. Archaeological Survey of India, 11. Calcutta: Office of the Superintendent of Government Printing.

Daftary, Farhad. 1990. *The Ismā'īlīs: their history and doctrines*. Cambridge: Cambridge University Press.

Dalmia, Vasudha, and Heinrich von Stietencron, eds. 1995. *Representing Hinduism: The construction of religious traditions and national identity*. New Delhi: Sage Publications.

Dandekar, R. N., ed. 1990. *The Mahābhārta revisited*. New Delhi: Sahitya Akedemi.

Das, Rahul Peter. 1991. On the subtle art of interpreting. *JAOS* 111, 4:737-67.

de Bruin, Hanna M. 1994. Kaṭṭaikkūttu: The flexibility of a south Indian theatre tradition, with supplement, Karṇa's death: A play by Pukaḻēntippulavar, *Karṇa Mōksham*. Ph.D. dissertation. University of Leiden.

Deb, Raja Binaya Krishna. 1905. *The early history and growth of Calcutta*. Calcutta: Romesh Chandra Ghose.

Dehejia, Vidya. *Comment*: A broader landscape. In Hawley 1994. Pp. 49-53.

Dessigane, R., P. Z. Pattabiramin, and J. Filliozat. 1960. *La légende des jeux de Civa à Madurai d'après les textes et peintures*. Publications de l'Institut Français d'Indologie, No. 19. Fasc. 1: Text; Fasc. 2: Plates. Pondicherry: Institut Français d'Indologie.

de Vries, Jan. 1963. *Heroic song and heroic legend*. B. J. Timmer trans. London: Oxford University Press.

Dey, Nundo Lal. [1899] 1927. *The geographical dictionary of ancient and mediaeval India*. 2d ed. Calcutta Oriental Series, No. 21. E 13. London: Luzac & Co.

———. 1927. *Rasātala or the under-world*. Calcutta Oriental Series, No. 20. E. 12. Calcutta: Calcutta Oriental Press.

Diehl, Carl Gustav. 1981. The passage III, 3.2.21-33 in Bhaviṣya-Purāṇa. *Purāṇa* 23:73-77.

Dikshit, R. K. 1977. *The Candellas of Jejākabhukti*. Delhi: Abhinav Publications.

Dikshitar, V. R. Ramachandra, trans. 1939. *The Silappadikaram*. Madras: Oxford University Press.

Dimmitt, Cornelia, and J. A. B. van Buitenen, trans. 1978. *Classical Hindu mythology: A reader in the Sanskrit purāṇas*. Philadelphia: Temple University Press.

Dirks, Nicholas B. 1979. The structure and meaning of political relations in a south Indian little kingdom. *CIS*, n.s. 13, 2:125-57.

———. 1982. The pasts of a Pāḷaiyakārar: The ethnohistory of a south Indian little king. *JAS* 41:655-83.

Dixit, R. S. 1992. *Marketing geography in an urban environment*. Jaipur: Pointer Publishers.

Doniger, Wendy [see also O'Flaherty]. ed. 1993. *Purāṇa perennis: Reciprocity and transformation in Hindu and Jaina texts*. Albany: State University of New York Press.

Dumézil, Georges. 1969. *The destiny of the warrior*. Trans. Alf Hiltebeitel. Chicago: University of Chicago Press.

———. 1971. *Mythe et épopée, 2. Types épiques indo-européens: Un héros, un sorcier, un roi*. Paris: Gallimard.

———. 1973. *The destiny of a king*. Trans. Alf Hiltebeitel. Chicago: University of Chicago Press.

Dundes, Alan. 1989. *Folklore matters*. Knoxville: University of Tennessee Press.

Dunham, Deborah, and James W. Fernandez. 1991. Tropical dominions: The figurative struggle over domains of belonging and apartness in Africa. In Fernandez 1991, 190-210.

Dwivedi, Ram Awadh. 1966. *A critical survey of Hindi literature*. Delhi: Motilal Banarsidass.

Dymock, W. 1890. On the use of turmeric in Hindoo ceremonial. *Journal of the Anthropological Society of Bombay* 2:441-48.

Eaton, Richard M. 1978. *Sufis of Bijapur, 1300-1700*. Princeton: Princeton University Press.

Edgerton, Franklin. 1926. *Vikrama's adventures or the thirty-two tales of the throne*. Harvard Oriental Series. Cambridge: Harvard University Press.

Edwardes, S. M. 1926. *A manuscript history of the rulers of Jinji*. *IA* 55:1-3.

Elliot, Henry M. 1879. *Memoirs on the history, folk-lore, and distribution of the races of the North Western Provinces of India; being an amplified edition of the original supplemental glossary of Indian terms*. Ed. John Beames. 2 vols. London: Trübner and Company.

Elmore, Wilbur Theodore. 1915. *Dravidian gods in modern Hinduism: A study of the local and village deities of southern India*. Lincoln: University of Nebraska.

Erndl, Kathleen. 1991. The mutilation of Śūrpaṇakhā. In Richman 1991, 67-86.

Erndl, Kathleen, and Alf Hiltebeitel, eds. Forthcoming. *Writing goddesses: Is the South Asian goddess a feminist?*

Fabricius, Johann Philip. 1972. *Tamil and English dictionary*. 4th ed. Tranquebar: Evangelical Lutheran Mission Publishing House.

Farquhar, J. N. 1925. The fighting ascetics of India. *Bulletin of the John Rylands Library* 9:431-52.

Fernandez, James W. 1986. *Persuasions and performances: The play of tropes in culture*. Bloomington: Indiana University Press.

———, ed. 1991. *Beyond metaphor: The theory of tropes in anthropology*. Stanford: Stanford University Press.

Flueckiger, Joyce Burkhalter. 1983. Bhojalī: Song, goddess, friend—a Chhatisgarhi women's oral tradition. *Asian Folklore Studies* 42:27-43.

———. 1989. Caste and regional variants in an oral epic tradition. In Blackburn, Claus, Flueckiger, and Wadley, 33-54.

———. 1996. *Gender and genre in the folklore of middle India*. Ithaca: Cornell University Press.

Flueckiger, Joyce Burkhalter, and Laurie J. Sears, eds. 1991. *Boundaries of the text: Epic performances in South and Southeast Asia*. Michigan Papers on South and Southeast Asia, 35. Ann Arbor: Center for South and Southeast Asian Studies, University of Michigan.

Foley, John Miles, ed. 1981. Introduction: The oral theory in context. *Oral traditional literature: A Festschrift for Albert Bates Lord*. 27-122. Columbus, OH: Slavica Publishers.

Frasca, Richard. 1984. The Terukkūttu: Ritual theatre of Tamilnadu. Ph.D. dissertation. University of California, Berkeley.

———. 1990. *The theatre of the* Mahābhārata: *Terukkūttu performances in south India*. Honolulu: University of Hawaii Press.

Freud, Sigmund. 1961. *The interpretation of dreams*. Trans. and ed. by James Strachey. New York: Science Editions.

Gaborieau, Marc. 1975. Légende et culte du saint musulman Ghâzî Miyâ au Népal occidental et en Inde du nord. *Objets et Mondes* 15, 3:289-318.

Gadamer, Hans-Georg. 1993. *Truth and method*. 2d. rev. ed. Trans. J. Weinsheimer and D. G. Marshall. New York: Continuum.

Gahlot, Sukhvir Singh, and Banshi Dhar. 1989. *Castes and tribes of Rajasthan*. Jodhpur: Jain Brothers.

Gandhi, Maneka. 1992. *The penguin book of Hindu names*. New Delhi: Viking.

Ganguli, Kisari Mohan, trans., and Pratap Chandra Roy, publisher. [1884-96] 1970. *The Mahabharata*. New Delhi: Munshiram Manoharlal.

Ganguly, D. C. 1940. A new light on the history of the Cāhamānas. *IHQ* 16,3: 567-73.

Geertz, Clifford. 1980. *Negara: The theatre state in nineteenth-century Bali*. Princeton: Princeton University Press.

Gehrts, Heino. 1975. *Mahābhārata: Das Geschehen und seine Bedeutung*. Bonn: Bouvier Verlag Herbert Grundmann.

Ghurye, G. S. 1964. *Indian sadhus*. Bombay: Popular Prakashan.

Gibb, H. A. R., and J. H. Kramers, eds. 1953. *Shorter encyclopaedia of Islam*. Ithaca: Cornell University Press.

Gill, Harjeet Singh. 1986. The human condition in Puran Bhagat: An essay in existential anthropology of a Punjabi legend. In Veena Das, ed. *The word and the world: Fantasy, symbol and record*. 133-52. New Delhi: Sage Publications.

Gold, Ann Grodzins. 1992. *A carnival of parting: The tales of king Bharthari and king Gopi Chand as sung and told by Madhu Natisar Nath of Ghatiyali, Rajasthan*. Berkeley: University of California Press.

Goldman, Robert P. 1970. Akṛtavraṇa vs. Śrīkṛṣṇa as narrators of the legend of Bhārgava Rāma *à propos* some observations of Dr. V. S. Sukthankar. *ABORI* 53:161-73.

———. 1977. *Gods, priests, and warriors: The Bhṛgus of the* Mahābhārata. New York: Columbia University Press.

———. 1978. Fathers, sons, and gurus: Oedipal conflict in the Sanskrit epics. *JIP* 6: 325-92.

———. 1980. Rāmaḥ sahalakṣmaṇaḥ: Psychological and literary aspects of the composite hero of Vālmīki's *Rāmāyaṇa*. *JIP* 8:149-89.

———, ed. and trans. 1984. *The Rāmāyaṇa of Vālmīki*, Vol. 1: *Bālakāṇḍa*. Princeton: Princeton University Press.

———. 1997. *Eṣa dharmaḥ sanātanaḥ*: Shifting moral values and the Indian epics. In P. Bilimoria and J. N. Mohanty, eds. *Relativism, suffering and beyond*. 187-223. Delhi: Oxford University Press.

Gopinatha Rao, T. A. 1971. *Elements of Hindu Iconography*. 2d ed. 2 vols. Varanasi: Indological Book House.

Gordon, Stewart. 1994. Marathas, marauders, and state formation in eighteenth-century India. Delhi: Oxford University Press.

Gover, Charles E. [1871] 1959. *The folk-songs of southern India*. Tirunelveli: South India Śaiva Siddhanta Work Publishing Society.

Grierson, Sir George A. 1879. Some further notes on Kálidása. *JASB* 48:32-48.

———. 1885a. The song of Alha's marriage: A Bhojpuri epic. *IA* 14:209-227.

———. 1885b. A summary of the Alha Khand. *IA* 14:225-60.

Griffiths, Walter G. 1946. *The Kol tribe of central India*. Calcutta: Royal Asiatic Society of Bengal.

Growse, F. S. 1879. The sect of the Prán-náthís. *JASB* 48:171-80.

Guha, Ranajit. 1997. *Dominance without hegemony: History and power in colonial India*. Cambridge: Harvard University Press.

Gupta, Bhagwan Das. 1980. *Life and times of Maharaja Chhatrasal Bundela*. New Delhi: Radiant Publishers.

———. 1987. *A history of the rise and fall of the Marathas in Bundelkhand (1731-1804)*. Delhi: Neha Prakashan.

Halbfass, Wilhelm. 1988. *India and Europe: An essay in understanding*. Albany: State University of New York Press.

Halder, R. R. 1927-28. Some reflections on Pṛthivīrāja Rāsā. *Journal of the Royal Asiatic Society, Bombay Branch*, n.s. 3-4:203-11.

Handelman, Don, and David Shulman. 1997. *God inside out: Śiva's game of dice*. New York: Oxford.

Hansen, Kathryn. 1992. *Grounds for play: the Nauṭaṅkī theatre of north India*. Berkeley: University of California Press.

Hanumantha Rao, B. S. L. 1973. *Religion in Āndhra*. Guntur: Tripurasundari.

Harlan, Lindsey. 1992. *Religion and Rajput women: The ethic of protection in contemporary narratives*. Berkeley: University of California Press.

———. 1994. Perfection and devotion: Sati tradition in Rajasthan. In Hawley 1994, 79-99.

———. 1996. The story of Godāvarī. In John Stratton Hawley and Donna

Marie Wulff, eds. *Devī: Goddesses of India*. 227-49. Berkeley: University of California Press.

———. In press. Heroes alone and heroes at home: Gender and intertextuality in two narratives. In Julia Leslie, ed. *Religion, gender and social definition*. Personal communication.

Harlan, Lindsey, and Paul B. Courtright, eds. 1995. *From the margins of Hindu marriage*. New York: Oxford University Press.

Harman, William P. 1989. *The sacred marriage of a Hindu goddess*. Bloomington: University of Indiana Press.

Hawley, John Stratton, ed. 1994. *Sati, the blessing and the curse: The burning of wives in India*. New York and Oxford: Oxford University Press.

Hazra, R. C. 1936-37. Our present Bhaviṣya Purāṇa. *Indian Culture* 3:223-29.

———. [1940] 1975. *Studies in the purāṇic records on Hindu rites and customs*. Delhi: Motilal Banarsidass.

Heesterman, Jan. 1957. *The ancient Indian royal consecration: The Rājasūya described according to the Yajus texts and annotated*. The Hague: Mouton & Co.

———. 1985. *The inner conflict of tradition: Essays in Indian ritual, kingship, and society*. Chicago: University of Chicago Press.

———. 1993. *The broken world of sacrifice: An essay in ancient Indian ritual*. Chicago: University of Chicago Press.

Henige, David P. 1975. Some phantom dynasties of early and medieval India: Epigraphic evidence and the abhorrence of a vacuum. *BSOAS* 38.3:529-49.

Heras, Henry. 1926. The city of Jinji at the end of the sixteenth century. *IA* 55:41-43.

Hiltebeitel, Alf. 1975. Comparing Indo-European "Epics." *HR* 15:90-100.

———. [1976] 1990. *The ritual of battle: Krishna in the Mahābhārata*. Albany: State University of New York Press.

———. 1977. Review of Gehrts 1975, in *Erasmus* 29:86-92.

———. 1978. The Indus Valley "Proto-Śiva," reexamined through reflections on the goddess, the buffalo, and the symbolism of vāhanas. *Anthropos* 73:767-797.

———. 1979. Kṛṣṇa in the *Mahābhārata*: A Bibliographical Study. *ABORI* 60:83-107.

———. 1980a. Draupadī's garments. *IIJ* 22:97-112.

———. 1980b. Śiva, the goddess, and the disguises of the Pāṇḍavas and Draupadī. *HR* 20:147-174.

———. 1980c. Rāma and Gilgamesh: The sacrifices of the water buffalo and the bull of heaven. *HR* 19:187-223.

———. 1980-1981. Sītā vibhūṣitā: The jewels for her journey. *Ludwik Sternbach commemoration volume, Indologica Taurinensia* 8-9:193-200.

———. 1981. Draupadī's Hair. In Madeleine Biardeau, ed., *Autour de la déesse hindoue*. *Puruṣārtha* 5:179-214.

———. 1984a. The two Kṛṣṇas on one chariot: Upaniṣadic imagery and epic mythology. *HR* 24:1-26.
———. 1984b. Two south Indian oral epics. *HR* 24:164-173.
———. 1985a. On the handling of the meat, and related matters, in two south Indian buffalo sacrifices. In Christiano Grottanelli, ed., *Divisione della carni: Dinamica sociale e organizzazione del cosmo. L'Uomo* 9:171-199.
———. 1985b. Two Kṛṣṇas, three Kṛṣṇas, four Kṛṣṇas, more Kṛṣṇas: Dark interactions in the Mahābhārata. In Arvind Sharma, ed. *Essays on the Mahābhārata, Journal of South Asian Literature* 20:71-77.
———. 1987. Gambling In Mircea Eliade, ed. in chief, *The Encyclopedia of Religion*. 5:468-74. New York: The Free Press.
———. 1988a. *The Cult of Draupadī*, Vol. 1, *Mythologies: From Gingee to Kurukṣetra*. Chicago: University of Chicago Press.
———. 1988b. Director, "Lady of Gingee: South Indian Draupadi festivals," Parts 1 and 2. Videotape. Washington, D.C.: George Washington University. Distributed through University of Wisconsin South Asia Center.
———, ed. 1989a. *Criminal gods and demon devotees: Essays on the guardians of popular Hinduism*. Albany: State University of New York Press. Introduction, 3-18.
———. 1989b. Draupadī's two guardians: The buffalo king and the Muslim devotee. In Hiltebeitel 1989a, 339-71.
———. 1989c. Kṛṣṇa at Mathurā. In Doris M. Srinivasan, gen. ed., *Mathurā: The cultural heritage*. 92-102. New Delhi: American Institute of Indian Studies.
———. 1991a. *The cult of Draupadī*, Vol. 2, *On Hindu ritual and the goddess*. Chicago: University of Chicago Press.
———. 1991b. The folklore of Draupadī: Sarees and hair. In Arjun Appadurai, Frank Corom, and Margaret Mills, eds. *Gender, genre, and power In South Asian expressive traditions*. 395-427. Philadelphia: University of Pennsylvania Press.
———. 1992a. Colonial lenses on the South Indian Draupadī cult. In *Ritual, state and history, Festschrift for Jan Heesterman*. 507-31. Leiden: E. J. Brill.
———. 1992b. Transmitting *Mahabharatas*: Another look at Peter Brook. *The drama review* 36, 3:131-59.
———. 1993. Epic studies: Classical Hinduism in the Mahābhārata and the *Rāmāyaṇa*. *ABORI* 74:1-62.
———. 1994. Review of Doniger 1993. *JAS* 53, 2:587-89.
———. 1995a. Religious studies and Indian epic texts. *Religious Studies Review* 21, 1:26-32.
———. 1995b. Dying before the *Mahābhārata* war: Martial and transsexual body-building for Aravāṉ. *JAS* 54, 2:447-73.
———. 1995c. Draupadī cult līlās. In William Sax, ed. *The gods at play: Līlā in South Asia*. 204-34. New York: Oxford University Press.

———. 1995d. Hinduism. *The HarperCollins dictionary of religion*. Jonathan Z. Smith gen. ed. 424-40. San Francisco: HarperSanFrancisco.

———. 1997. Orders of diffusion in two Tamil *Mahābhārata* Folk Cults. *South Asian Folklorist* 1:9-36.

———. In press-a. Kūttāṇṭavar: The divine lives of a severed head. In Claus Peter Zoller, ed., *Death in South Asia*. Heidelberg: South Asia Institute.

———. In press-b. Hair like snakes and mustached brides: Crossed gender in an Indian folk cult. In Barbara D. Miller and Alf Hiltebeitel, eds. *Hair: Power and Meaning in Asian Cultures*. Albany: State University of New York Press.

———. In press-c. Reconsidering Bhṛguization. In Mislav Ježić et al., eds. Papers from the 1997 Dubrovnik International Conference on the Sanskrit Epics and Purāṇas.

———. In press-d. Fathers of the bride, fathers of *satī*: Mythologies of the self-immolating goddess. In Alf Hiltebeitel, *Hinduism and the human sciences*. Delhi: Motilal Banarsidass.

———. In press-e. Boar and twins: Comparing the Tulu Kōṭi-Cennaya *pāḍdana* and the Tamil Elder brothers story. In Aditya Malik, ed. Memorial volume for Günther-Dietz Sontheimer.

———. In press-f. The primary process of the Indian epics. In Bruce Sullivan, ed., Indian Literature Issue, *International Journal of Hindu Studies*.

———. In press-g. Empire, invasion, and India's epics. Sushil Mittal, ed. Issue on Hinduism and religious studies, *International Journal of Hindu Studies*.

———. In press-h. Conventions of the Naimiṣa forest. *JIP* 1998.

———. Forthcoming. *Rethinking the Mahābhārata: A reader's guide to the education of Yudhiṣṭhira*. Chicago: University of Chicago Press.

Hodgson, Marshall G. S. 1955. *The order of assassins: The struggle of the early Nizârî Ismâ'îlîs against the Islamic world*. The Hague: Mouton.

Hoernle, A. F. Rudolph. 1874-86. See Chand Bardai 1873-86.

———. 1905. Some problems of ancient Indian history, 3: The Gūrjara clans. *JRAS*, 1-32.

———. 1909. Some problems in ancient Indian history, 4: The identity of Yasodharman and Vikramāditya, and some corollaries. *JRAS*, 89-144.

Hoffman, Helmut. 1967. Einleitende Bemerkungen. In Hohenberger 1967, vii-xii.

Hohenberger, Adam. 1967. *Das Bhaviṣyapurāṇa*. Münchener Indologische Studien, 5. Wiesbaden: Otto Harrassowitz.

Hollister, J. 1953. *The Shia of India*. London: Luzac.

Hopkins, E. Washburn. [1901] 1969. *The great epic of India: Its character and origin*. Calcutta: Punthi Pustak.

———. 1918. *The history of religions*. New York: The Macmillan Company.

———. 1923. *Origin and evolution of religion*. New Haven: Yale University Press.

Humayuni, Sadeq. 1979. An analysis of the Ta'ziyeh of Qasem. In Peter J. Chelkowski, ed. *Ta'ziyeh: Ritual drama in Iran*. 12-23. New York: New York

University Press and Saroush Press.

Humes, Cynthia Ann. 1996. Vindhyavāsinī: Local goddess yet great goddess. In John Stratton Hawley and Donna Marie Wulff, eds. *Devī: Goddesses of India*. 49-76. Berkeley: University of California Press.

Irvine, William. 1878 and 1879. The Bangash nawábs of Farrukhábád—A chronicle, Parts 1 and 2. *JASB* 47 and 48:259-383 and 49-170.

Irving, John. 1994. *Son of the circus*. New York: Random House.

Irwin, Robert. 1995. *The Arabian nights: A companion*. London and New York: Penguin.

Jain, Ravindra K. 1975. Bundela genealogy and legends: The past of an indigenous ruling group of central India. In J. H. M. Beattie and R. G. Lienhardt, eds., *Studies in social anthropology: Essays in memory of E. E. Evans-Pritchard by his former Oxford colleagues*. 239-72. Oxford: Clarendon Press.

———. 1979. Kingship, territory and property in pre-British Bundelkhand. *Economic and political weekly* 2:946-50.

Jaiswal, M. P. 1962. *A linguistic study of Bundeli (a dialect of Madhyadēśa)*. Leiden: E. J. Brill.

Jamison, Stephanie. 1994. Draupadī on the walls of Troy: *Iliad* 3 from an Indic perspective. *Classical antiquity* 13, 1:5-16.

———. 1996. *Sacrificed wife, sacrificer's wife: Women, ritual, and hospitality in ancient India*. New York: Oxford.

Jindal, K. B. [1955] 1993. *A history of Hindi literature*. Delhi: Munshiram Manoharlal.

Joshi, Hariprasad Shioprasad. 1965. *Origin and Development of Dattātreya worship in India*. Baroda: Oriental Institute.

Justa, H. R. 1993. Temples and village gods associated with heroes of Mahābhārata in Himachal Pradesh. In K. S. Singh 1993, 56-65.

Kane, Pandurang Vaman. [1930-1962] 1975. *History of Darmaśāstra*. 5 vols. Poona: Bhandarkar Oriental Research Institute.

Kapur, Anuradha. 1995. The representation of gods and heroes in the Parsi mythological drama of the early twentieth century. In Dalmia and von Stietencron 1995, 401-20.

Karve, Irawati. 1974. *Yuganta: The end of an epoch*. New Delhi: Sangam Press.

Kassam, Tazim R. 1994. Syncretism on the model of the figure-ground: A study of Pīr Shams' *Brahma Prakāśa*. In Katherine K. Young, ed. *Hermeneutical paths to the sacred worlds of India: Essays in honour of Robert W. Stevenson*. 231-41. Atlanta: Scholars Press.

———. 1995. *Songs of wisdom and circles of dance: Hymns of the Satpanth Ismā'īlī Muslim saint, Pir Shams*. Albany: State University of New York Press.

Katz, Ruth Cecily. 1989. *Arjuna in the Mahabharata: Where Krishna is, there is victory*. Columbia, S.C.: University of South Carolina Press.

Kennedy, J. 1908. *Imperial gazetter of India, Indian empire*, Vol. 2, as cited in

Asopa 1976.

Khakee, Gulshan. 1972. The *Dasa avatāra* of the Satpanthi Ismailis and the Imam Shahis of Indo-Pakistan. Ph.D. dissertation. Harvard University.

Khan, Dominique-Sila. 1993. L'origine Ismaélienne du culte hindou de Rāmdeo Pīr. *Revue de l'Histoire des Religions* 210, 1:27-47.

———. 1994. Deux rites tantriques dans une communauté d'intouchables au Rajasthan. *Revue de l'Histoire des Religions* 211:443-62.

———. 1995. Ramdeo Pir and the Kamadiya Panth. In N. K. Singhi and Rajendra Joshi, eds. *Folk, faith and feudalism: Rajasthan studies*. 295-327. Jaipur and New Delhi: Rawat Publications.

———. 1996. The Kāmaḍ of Rajasthan—Priests of a forgotten tradition. *JRAS* 6,1:29-56.

———. 1997a. The coming of Nikalank avatar: A messianic theme in some sectarian traditions of north-western India. *JIP* 25:401-26.

———. 1997b. *Conversions and shifting identities: Ramdev Pir and the Ismailis in Rajasthan*. New Delhi: Manohar and Centre de Sciences Humaines.

Khurana, K. L. 1991-92. *The sultanate of Delhi*. Agra: Lakshmi Narain Agarwal.

Kibe, M. V. 1939. Inhabitants of the country around Rāvaṇa's Laṅkā in Amarkantak. In S. M. Katre and P. K. Gode, eds. *A volume of eastern and Indian studies presented to Professor F. W. Thomas*. 142-45. Bombay: Karnatak Publishing House.

Kinsley, David. 1975. *The sword and the flute. Kālī and Kṛṣṇa, dark visions of the terrible and the sublime in Hindu mythology*. Berkeley: University of California Press.

———. 1986. *Hindu goddesses. Visions of the divine feminine in the Hindu religious tradition*. Berkeley: University of California Press.

Kipling, Rudyard, in collaboration with Wolcott Balestier. [1891] 1905. *The naulakha: A story of east and west*. New York: Charles Scribner's and Sons.

Kirāmaṅkaḷiṉ Akaravaricaip Paṭṭi (Alphabetical list of villages). 1972. Madras (?): Tamilnāṭu Aracu.

Kloetzli, W. Randolph. 1985. Maps of time—mythologies of descent: Scientific instruments and the purāṇic cosmograph. *HR* 25, 2:116-47.

Kolff, Dirk H. A. 1990. *Naukar, Rajput, and Sepoy: The ethnohistory of the military labour market in Hindustan, 1450-1850*. Cambridge: Cambridge University Press.

———. 1995. The Rajput of ancient and medieval north India: A warrior-ascetic. In N. K. Singhi and Rajendra Joshi, eds. *Folk, faith and feudalism: Rajasthan studies*. 257-94. Jaipur and New Delhi: Rawat Publications.

Kothari, Kamal. 1989. Performers, gods, and heroes in the oral epics of Rajasthan. In Blackburn, Claus, Flueckiger, and Wadley 1989, 102-17.

Kripal, Jeffrey J. 1995. *Kālī's child: The mystical and the erotic in the life and teachings of Ramakrishna*. Chicago: University of Chicago Press.

Krishnaswamy Aiyangar, S. 1911. *Ancient India*. London: Luzac & Co.; Madras:

S.P.C.K. Depository.

———. 1930. Raja Desing of Gingee. *JIH* 9:1-22.

Krishnayya, M. V. 1997. Personal communication, November 20, including cover letter, translation of interview with Chandmal Agarwal, and translation of "Shyam Baba celebrations with bhakti and śrāddha" from the Telugu daily "Eenadu," November 9, 1997.

———. 1998. Personal communication, February 23, including cover letter and translation of Brahmanandam 1992.

Kurtz, Stanley. 1992. *All the mothers are one: Hindu India and the cultural reshaping of psychoanalysis*. New York: Columbia University Press.

Lapoint, Elwyn C. 1978. The epic of Guga: A north Indian oral tradition. In Sylvia Vatuk, ed. *American studies in the anthropology of India*. 281-308. New Delhi: Manohar.

Lath, Mukund. 1990. The concept of *ānṛśaṃsya* in the *Mahābhārata*. In Dandekar 1990, 113-19.

Lefeber, Rosalind, trans. 1994. *The Rāmāyaṇa of Vālmīki: An epic of ancient India*, 4: Kiṣkindhākāṇḍa. Robert P. Goldman, ed. Introduction and annotation by translator. Princeton: Princeton University Press.

Lévi-Strauss, Claude. 1963. *Structural anthropology*. Trans. Claire Jacobson and Brooke Grundfest Schoepf. New York: Basic Books.

Lincoln, Bruce. 1991. *Death, war, and sacrifice: Studies in ideology and practice*. Chicago: University of Chicago Press.

Lord, Albert B. 1964. *The singer of tales*. Harvard Studies in Comparative Literature, 24. Cambridge: Harvard University Press.

Lorenzen, David N. 1978. Warrior ascetics in Indian history. *JAOS* 98: 61-75.

Luard, Capt. C. E. (compiled). 1907. *The Central India state gazetteer series*, Vol. 6, Bundelkhand. Lucknow: Newar Kishore Press.

Lushington, Stephen. 1916. *Collector's report regarding the Tinnevelly Poligars 1799-1800*. Tinnevelly: Tinnevelly Collectorate Press.

Lutgendorf, Philip. 1979. The Ālhā cycle and written dimensions of a North Indian epic tradition. Courtesy of the author.

———. 1997. Personal communication, February 18.

MacLean, Derryl N. 1989. *Religion and society in Arab Sind*. Leiden: E. J. Brill.

Maindron, Maurice. [1909] 1992. *Dans l'Inde du sud: Le Carnatic et le Maduré*. Pondicherry: Kailash Editions.

Majumdar, R. C., gen. ed. 1957. *The struggle for empire. The history and culture of the Indian people*, 5. Bombay: Bharatiya Vidya Bhavan.

Malik, Aditya. 1993. Avatāra, avenger, and king: Narrative themes in the Rājasthānī oral epic of Devnārāyaṇ. In Brückner, Lutze, and Malik 1993, 375-410.

———. Forthcoming. Divine testimony: *The Rajasthani oral narrative of Devnārāyaṇ*, Vol. I, *Study*; Vol. 2, *Text in Devanāgarī*; Vol. 3, *Translation*. Personal communication.

Mallison, Françoise. 1989. Hinduism as seen by the Nizārī Ismā'īlī missionaries of western India: The evidence of the ginān. In Günther D. Sontheimer and Hermann Kulke, eds. *Hinduism reconsidered*. 93-103. Delhi: Manohar.

Mankekar, Purnima. 1993. National texts and gendered lives: An ethnography of television viewers in a north Indian city. *American Ethnologist* 20, 3:543-63.

Marr, John Ralston. 1985. *The eight anthologies. A study in early Tamil literature*. Tiruvanmiyur, Madras: Institute of Asian Studies.

Masilamani-Meyer, Eveline [see Meyer, Eveline]. 1997. The eyes of the goddess. In Alex Michaels, Cornelia Vogelsanger, and Annette Wilke, eds. *Wild goddesses in India and Nepal*. Bern: Peter Lang.

———. In press-a. "No house please!" Guardian deities of Tamilnadu's villages and wilderness.

———, trans. and ed. In press-b. The story of Kāttavarāyaṉ.

Matilal, Bimal Krishna. 1991. Kṛṣṇa: In defence of a devious divinity. In Sharma 1991, 401-18.

Mayaram, Shail. 1997. *Resisting regimes: Myth, memory and the shaping of a Muslim identity*. Delhi: Oxford University Press.

McGregor, R. S. 1984. *Hindi literature from its beginning to the nineteenth century*. Wiesbaden: Otto Harassowitz.

———. 1993. *The Oxford Hindi-English dictionary*. London: Oxford University Press.

Metcalf, Thomas R. 1995. *Ideologies of the Raj*. The New Cambridge History of India, 3, 4. New Delhi: Cambridge University Press.

Meyer, Eveline [see Masilamani-Meyer]. 1986. *Ankāḷaparamēcuvari: A goddess of Tamilnadu, her myths and cult*. Wiesbaden: Franz Steiner Verlag.

Miller, Joseph C. 1980. Current investigations in the genre of Rajasthani Paṛ painting recitation. In Callewaert 1980, 116-25.

Minkowski, C. Z. 1989. Janamejaya's *sattra* and ritual structure. *JAOS* 109, 3: 401-20.

Mishra, Mahendra Kumar. 1993. A hero of the Mahābhārata in folklore of central India. In K. S. Singh 1993, 157-69.

Mitra, Sisir Kumar. [1958] 1977. *The early rulers of Khajurāho*. Delhi: Motilal Banarsidass.

Mohanty, Jatindra Mohan. 1990. The attitude of modern creative writers towards the Mahābhārata: Oriya scene. In Dandekar 1990, 267-80.

Monier-Williams, Monier. 1863. *Indian epic poetry*. Edinburgh: Williams and Norgate.

———. [1899] 1964. *A Sanskrit-English dictionary*. Oxford: Clarendon Press.

Mukherjee, S. N. 1987. *Sir William Jones: A study in eighteenth-century British attitudes in India*. Bombay: Orient Longman.

Munshi, K. M. 1957. Foreword to Majumdar 1957.

Nagaswamy, R. 1982. *Tantric cult of south India*. Delhi: Agam Kala Prakashan.

Nagy, Gregory. 1996. *Homeric questions*. Austin: University of Texas Press.

Nandy, Ashis. 1980. *At the edge of psychology: Essays in the politics of culture*.

Delhi: Oxford University Press.

Nanji, Azim. 1978. *The Nizārī Ismā'īlī tradition in the Indo-Pakistan subcontinent*. Delmar, N.Y.: Caravan Books.

———. 1988. *Sharī'at* and *Haqīqat*: Continuity and synthesis in the Nizārī Ismā'īlī Muslim tradition. In Katherine P. Ewing, ed. Sharī'at *and ambiguity in South Asian Islam*. 63-76. Berkeley: University of California Press.

Nanjundayya, H. V., and L. Krishna Ananthakrishna Iyer. 1928-1935. *The Mysore tribes and castes*, 4 vols. Mysore: Mysore University.

Narayana Rao, Velcheru. 1986. Epics and ideologies: Six Telugu folk epics. In Blackburn and Ramanujan 1986, 131-66.

———. 1990. *Śiva's warriors: The Basava Purāṇa of Pālkuriki Somanātha*. Princeton: Princeton University Press.

———. 1993. Purāṇa as Brahmanic ideology. In Doniger 1993. 85-100.

Narayana Rao, Velcheru, David Shulman, and Sanjay Subrahmanyam. 1992. *Symbols of substance: Court and state in Nāyaka period Tamilnadu*. Oxford: Oxford University Press.

Nayakar, T. Aiyakannu. 1891. *Vannikula vilakkam: A treatise on the Vanniya caste*. Madras: Albion Press.

Nilakantha Sastri, K. A. [1937] 1975. *The Cōḷās*. 2d ed. Madras: Universitv Madras.

Nirmala Devi, R., ed., and V. Murugan, trans. 1987. *The wandering voice. Three ballads from palm leaf manuscripts*. Folklore of Tamilnadu Series, 1. Madras: Institute of Asian Studies.

Obeyesekere, Gananath. 1984. *The cult of the goddess Pattini*. Chicago: University of Chicago Press.

———. 1990. *The work of culture*. Chicago: University of Chicago Press.

O'Brien, Anthony Gordon. 1996. *The ancient chronology of Thar: The Bhāṭṭika, Laukika and Sindh eras*. Delhi: Oxford University Press.

O'Flaherty, Wendy Doniger [See also Wendy Doniger]. 1976. *Asceticism and eroticism in the mythology of Śiva*. London: Oxford University Press.

———. 1980. *Women, androgynes and other mythical beasts*. Chicago: University of Chicago Press.

Oldenburg, Veena Talwar. 1994. *Comment*: The continuing invention of the sati tradition. In Hawley 1994, 159-74.

Olsen, Alexandra Hennessey. 1987. Literary artistry and the oral-formulaic tradition: The case of Gower's *Appolinus of Tyre*. In John Miles Foley, ed. *Comparative research on oral traditions: A memorial for Milman Parry*. 493-500. Columbus, OH: Slavica Publications.

Oppert, Gustav. 1893. *The original inhabitants of Bharatavarṣa or India*. Westminster: Archibald Constable & Co.; Leipzig: Otto Harrassowitz.

Orr, W. G. 1940. Armed religious ascetics in northern India. *Bulletin of the John Rylands Library* 24:81-100.

———. 1947. *A sixteenth-century mystic: Dadu and his followers*. London:

Lutterworth Press.

Pandey, Gyanendra. 1995. The appeal of Hindu history. In Dalmia and von Stietencron, 369-88.

Pandian, Jacob. 1978. The Hindu caste system and Muslim ethnicity: The Labbai of a Tamil village in south India. *Ethnohistory* 25:141-57.

Pargiter, Frederick Eden. [1913] 1962. *The purāṇa text of the dynasties of the Kali age*. Varanasi: Chowkhamba Sanskrit Series Office.

Parker, Henry. 1909. *Ancient Ceylon*. London: Luzac.

Parpola, Asko. In press. From Ištar to Durgā: Sketch of a prehistory of India's feline-riding and buffalo-slaying goddess of victory. In *Durgā and the buffalo*. ed. Günther D. Sontheimer and M. L. K. Murthy. Heidelberg: South Asia Institute.

Parthasarathy, R. 1993. *The Cilappatikāram of Iḷaṅkō Aṭikaḷ. An epic of south India*. New York: Columbia University Press.

Pathak, R. C., ed. 1967. *Bhargava's standard illustrated dictionary of the Hindi Language (Hindi-English edition)*. Varanasi: Bhargava Book Depot.

Patnaik, Pathani. 1993. Sarala's Oriya Mahābhārata: "A vox populi" in Oriya literature. In K. S. Singh 1993, 171-76.

Peabody, Norbert. 1996. Tod's *Rajast'han* and the boundaries of imperial rule in nineteenth-century India. *Modern Asian Studies* 30, 1:185-220.

Perumal, A. N. 1981. *Tamil drama: Origin and development*. Adyar, Madras: International Institute of Tamil Studies.

Pinch, William R. 1996. *Peasants and monks in British India*. Berkeley: University of California Press.

Pinney, Thomas. 1986. *Kipling's India: Uncollected sketches 1884-88*. Houndmills: The Macmillan Press Ltd.

Pogson, W. R. [1828] 1971. *A history of the Boondelas*. 2 parts. Delhi: B. R. Publishing Corporation.

Pollock, Sheldon I., trans. 1991. *The Rāmāyaṇa of Vālmīki: An epic of ancient India*, 3: *Araṇyakāṇḍa*. Robert P. Goldman, ed. Introduction and annotation by translator. Princeton: Princeton University Press.

———. 1993. Rāmāyaṇa and political imagination in India. *JAS* 52:261-97.

———. 1994. Deep orientalism? Notes on Sanskrit and power beyond the Raj. In Carol A. Breckenridge and Peter van der Veer, eds., *Orientalism and the postcolonial predicament*. 76-133. Delhi: Oxford University Press.

Polo, Marco. 1969. *The travels of Marco Polo*. Yule edition. New York: Airmont Publishing Company.

Poole, Fitz John Porter. 1986. Toward comparison in the anthropology of religion. *Journal of the American Academy of Religion* 54, 3:411-60.

Prabhu, K. Sanjiv. 1977. *Special study report on Bhuta cult in South Kanara District. Census of India 1971, Mysore*, series 14. Delhi: Controller of Publications.

Pritchett, F. W. 1980. Prthivraj Raso: a look at the poem itself. *Indian Literature*

23, 5:56-75.

Propp, Vladimir. [1968] 1994. *Morphology of the folktale*. 2d. ed. Laurence Scott trans. Austin: University of Texas Press.

———. 1984. *Theory and history of folklore*. Trans. Ariadna Martin and Richard P. Martin; Anatoly Liberman, ed. Theory and History of Literature, 5. Minneapolis: University of Minnesota Press.

Qanungo, K. L. 1969. *Studies in Rajput history*. Delhi: S. Chand.

Quint, David. 1993. *Epic and empire: Politics and generic form from Virgil to Milton*. Princeton: Princeton University Press.

Ragam, V. R. 1963. *Pilgrim's travel guide*, Part 2: *North India with Himalayan regions*. Guntur: Sri Sita Rama Nama Sankirtana Sangam.

Raglan, Richard Somerset. [1949] 1975. *The hero: A study in tradition, myth, and drama*. Westport: Greenwood Press.

Rajan, Chandra, trans. 1995. *Śivadāsa: The five-and-twenty tales of the genie (Vetālapañcaviṅśati)*. New York: Penguin.

Rajayyan, K. 1971. *South Indian rebellion: The first war of independence 1800-1801*. Mysore: Rao and Raghavan.

Rama Raju, B. 1982. The folk versions of *Mahabharata* stories. National lecture series, Madras. Mimeograph.

Ramanujan, A. K. 1973. *Speaking of Śiva*. Baltimore: Penguin.

———. 1986. Two realms of Kannada folklore. In Blackburn and Ramanujan 1986, 41-75.

———. 1991a. Repetition in the Mahābhārata. In Sharma 1991, 419-43.

———. 1991b. Three hundred Rāmāyaṇas: Five examples and three thoughts on translation. In Richman 1991, 22-49.

———. 1993. On folk mythologies and folk purāṇas. In Doniger 1993, 101-20.

Rao, T. V. Subba. 1976. Telugu Folk Additions to Mahabharatha. *Folklore (Calcutta)* 8-9: 269-75.

Ray, Hem Chandra. [1931-36] 1973. *The dynastic history of northern India (early medieval period)*. 2 vols. Delhi: Munshiram Manoharlal.

Ray, Pratibha. 1995. *Yajnaseni: The story of Draupadī*. Trans. Pradip Bhattacharya. Calcutta: Rupa and Co.

Raychaudhuri, H. C. 1967. India in the age of the Nandas. In K. A. Nikalanta Sastry, ed. *Age of the Nandas and Mauryas*. 9-45. Delhi: Motilal Banarsidass.

Reiniche, Marie Louise. 1979. *Les dieux et les hommes: Étude des cultes d'un village du Tirunelveli Inde du Sud*. Cahiers de l'homme Ethnologie-Geographie-Linguistique, n.s. 18. Paris: Mouton.

Richards, John F. 1993. *The Mughal empire*. New Cambridge History of India, 1, 5. Cambridge: Cambridge University Press.

Richman, Paula. 1991. *Many Rāmāyaṇas. The diversity of a narrative tradition in South Asia*. Berkeley: University of California Press.

Ricoeur, Paul. 1970. *Freud and philosophy: An essay on interpretation*. Trans. Denis Savage. New Haven: Yale University Press.

Rocher, Ludo. 1986. *The purāṇas*. A history of Indian literature, Vol. 2, Epics and Sanskrit religious literature. Fasc. 2. Wiesbaden: Otto Harrassowitz.

Roghair, Gene. H. 1982. *The epic of Palnāḍu. A study and translation of Palnāṭi Vīrula Katha, a Telugu oral tradition from Andhra Pradesh, India*. Oxford: Clarendon Press.

Rose, H. A. 1911-19. *A glossary of the tribes and castes of the Punjab and North-West Frontier Province*. 3 vols. Lahore: Government Printing, Punjab.

———. 1926. Sacrifices of the head to the Hindu goddess. *Folk-lore (London)* 37:80-92.

Roy, Tapti. 1994. *The politics of a popular uprising: Bundelkhand in 1857*. Delhi: Oxford.

Rukmani, T. S. 1995. Folk traditions related to *Mahābhārata* in south India. In S. P. Narang, ed. *Modern evaluation of the Mahābhārata (Prof. P. K. Sharma felicitation volume)*. 271-81. Delhi: Nag Publishers.

Rushdie, Salman. 1990. *Haroun and the sea of stories*. London: Penguin Books.

Russell, R. V., and Hira Lal. [1916] 1993. *The tribes and castes of the central provinces of India*. 4 vols. New Delhi and Madras: Asian Educational Services.

Sachau, Edward C. 1962. *Alberuni's India*. Lahore: Government of West Pakistan.

Sankalia, H. D. 1973. *Ramayana: Myth or Reality*. New Delhi: People's Publishing House.

Santillana, Giorgio de, and Hertha von Dechend. 1969. *Hamlet's mill: An essay on myth and the frame of time*. Boston: Gambit.

Sax, William S. 1986. The Pāṇḍav-Līlā: Self-representation in a central Himalayan folk drama. Manuscript presented to the Graduate Seminar on South Asia, University of Chicago. Personal communication.

———. 1994. Playing the villains: Good guys and bad guys in a central Himalayan epic tradition. Paper presented at Madison, WI, conference on "Epics in the contemporary world." Personal communication.

———. 1995a. Who's who in the Pāṇḍav Līla? In Sax, ed., *The gods at play: Līlā in South Asia*. 131-55. New York: Oxford University Press.

———. 1995b. Draupadi and Kunti in the Pandavlila. Personal communication (forthcoming in Studia Religiosa Helvetica).

———. 1996. Babril's story. Personal communication, March.

Scheuer, Jacques. 1982. *Śiva dans le Mahābhārata*. Bibliothèque de l'École des Haute Études, Sciences Religieuses, 56. Paris: Presses Universitaires de France.

Schimmel, Annemarie. 1979. The *marsiyeh* in Sindhi poetry. In Peter J. Chelkowski, ed. *Ta'ziyeh: Ritual drama in Iran*. 210-21. New York: New York University Press and Saroush Press.

Schnepel, Burkhard. 1995. Durga and the king: Ethnohistorical aspects of politico-ritual life in a south Orissan jungle kingdom. *JRAS*, n.s. 1:145-66.

Schomer, Karine. 1984. Cycle and episode in a North Indian epic, with excerpts from *Ālhā* recording. Paper presented at the Annual Meeting of the Association of Asian Studies, Washington, D.C. Courtesy of the author.

———. 1989. Paradigms for the Kali yuga: The heroes of the Ālhā epic and their fate. In Blackburn, Claus, Flueckiger, and Wadley 1989, 140-54.

Schomer, Karine, Joan L. Erdman, Deryck O. Lodrick, and Lloyd I. Rudolph, eds. 1994. *The idea of Rajasthan: Explorations in regional identity*. 2 vols. Delhi: Manohar and American Institute of Indian Studies.

Schwartzberg, Joseph E., ed. 1992. *A historical atlas of South Asia*. 2d impression. New York: Oxford University Press.

Schwerin, Kerrin Graefin V. 1881. Saint worship in Indian Islam: The legend of the martyr Salar Masud Ghazi. In Ahmad Imtiaz, ed. *Ritual and religion among Muslims in India*. 143-61. Delhi: Manohar.

Settar, S. 1982. Memorial stones in south India. In Setter and Sontheimer 1982, 183-97.

Settar, S., and M. M. Kalaburgi. 1982. The hero cult: A study of Kannaḍa literature from the 9th to 13th centuries. In Settar and Sontheimer 1982, 17-36.

Settar, S., and Günther D. Sontheimer, eds. 1982. *Memorial stones: A study of their origin, significance, and variety*. Dharwad: Karnatak University; Heidelberg: South Asia Institute, University of Heidelberg.

Sewell, Robert. 1882. Lists of the antiquarian remains of the Presidency of Madras. *Archaeological survey of southern India*, Vol. 1. Madras: Government Press.

Shackle, Christopher and Zawarhir Moir. 1992. *Ismaili hymns from South Asia: An introduction to the Ginans*. SOAS South Asian Texts No. 3. London: University of London.

Shah, Kirit K. 1988. *Ancient Bundelkhand: Religious history in socio-economic perspective*. Delhi: Gian Publishing House.

Shah, Shalini. 1995. *The making of womanhood (gender relations in the Mahābharāta)*. Delhi: Manohar.

Sharma, Arvind. 1991. *Essays on the Mahābhārata*. Leiden: E. J. Brill.

Sharma, B. R. 1993. Impact of the Mahābhārata on folk and tribal culture of Himachal Pradesh. In K. S. Singh 1993, 32-46.

Sharma, Dasharatha. 1934-35. The Agnikula myth. *ABORI* 16:159.

———. 1940. The age and historicity of the Pṛthvīrāja Rāso. *IHQ* 16, 4:738-49.

———. 1959. *Early Chauhan dynasties (a study in Chauhan political history, Chauhan political institutions and life in the Chauhan dominions from c. 800 to 1316 A.D.)*. Delhi: S. Chand & Co.

Sherring, M. A. 1872. *Hindu tribes and castes as represented in Banares*. London: Trubner and Co.

Shideler, David William. 1987. Walking the path of Draupadī: Ritual vitalization of the *Mahābhārata* in a south Indian Draupadī amman festival. M. A. dissertation, University of Hawaii.

Shulman, David Dean. 1980. *Tamil temple myths: Sacrifice and divine marriage in south Indian Śaiva tradition*. Princeton: Princeton University Press.

———. 1991. Toward a historical poetics of the Sanskrit epics. *International Folklore Review* 11:9-17.

———. 1993. *The hungry god: Hindu tales of filicide and devotion*. Chicago: University of Chicago Press.

———. 1997. Arcot heroes: Desingu Rāja and Teyvīka Rājan̲ in text and time. Presented at the Pondicherry conference, Les Sources et le temps, sponsored by the École Française d'Extrême Orient and the Institut Français de Pondichéry. Courtesy of the author.

Singh, Bahadur. 1980. The *Bagaṛāvat*—A popular heroic narrative of Rājasthān. In Callewaert 1980, 162-67.

———. 1993. The episode of the golden Śiva image in the Bagaṛāvat. In Brückner, Lutze, and Malik 1993. 411-22.

Singh, Ganda. 1959. *Ahmad Shah Durrani: Father of modern Afghanistan*. Bombay: Asia Publishing House.

Singh, K. S. 1993. *The Mahābhārata in the tribal and folk traditions of India*. Shimla: Indian Institute of Advanced Study; New Delhi: Anthropological Survey of India.

Singh, R. B. 1964. *History of the Chāhamānas*. Varanasi: Nand Kishore & Sons.

———. 1975. *Origin of the Rajputs*. Buxipur: Sahitya.

Singh, Surajit. 1962. State formation and Rajput myth in tribal central India. *Man in India* 42,1:35-80.

Sinha, Shyam Narain. 1982. *The revolt of 1857 in Bundelkhand*. Lucknow: Anuj Publications.

Sircar, D. C. 1954. The Chālukyas. In R. C. Majumdar, gen. ed. *The history and culture of the Indian people*, Vol. 3, *The classical age*. 227-54. Bombay: Bharatiya Vidya Bhavan.

———. 1965. *Guhilas of Kishkindhā*. Calcutta: The Principal, Sanskrit College.

———. 1969. *Ancient Malwa and the Vikramāditya tradition*. Delhi: Munshiram Manoharlal.

Sleeman, W. H. 1915. *Rambles and recollections of an Indian official*. V. A. Smith ed. London: Oxford University Press.

Smith, John D. 1977. The singer or the song? A reassessment of Lord's "oral theory." *Man*, n.s. 12:141-53.

———. 1980a. Old Indian: The two Sanskrit epics. In A. T. Hatto, ed. *Traditions of heroic and epic poetry*, 1: *The tradition*. 48-78. London: Modern Humanities Press.

———. 1980b. Publications. In Callewaert 1980, 168-70.

———. 1986. Where the plot thickens. *South Asian Studies* 2:53-64.

———. 1989. Scapegoats of the gods: The ideology of the Indian epics. In Blackburn, Claus, Flueckiger, and Wadley 1989, 176-94.

———. 1990. Worlds apart: Orality, literacy, and the Rajasthani folk-*Mahābhā-*

rata. Oral tradition 5, 1:3-19.

———. 1991. *The epic of Pābūjī: A study, transcription and translation*. Cambridge: Cambridge University Press.

———. N.d. The Rajasthani folk-*Mahābhārata*. Personal communication.

Smith, Jonathan Z. 1978. *Map is not territory. Studies in the history of religion*. Leiden: E. J. Brill.

———. 1982. *Imagining religion: From Babylon to Jonestown*. Chicago: University of Chicago Press.

———. 1990. *Drudgery divine: On the comparison of early Christianities and the religions of late antiquity*. Chicago: University of Chicago Press.

Smith, V. A. 1909. The Gurjaras of Rajputana and Kanauj. *JRAS of Great Britain and Ireland*, 53-76.

Smith, V. A., and F. C. Black. 1879. Observations on some Chandel antiquities. *JASB* 48:285-96.

Somani, Ram Vallabh. 1981. *Prithviraj Chauhan and his times*. Jaipur: Publication Scheme.

Spivak, Gayatri Chakravorty. 1988. *In other worlds: Essays in cultural politics*. New York and London. Routledge.

Srinivasachari, Rao Bahadur C. S. 1943. *A history of Gingee and its rulers*. Annamalai University Historical Series, 2. Annamalainagar: The University.

Srivastava, Vinay Kumar. 1997. *Religious renunciation of a pastoral people*. Delhi: Oxford.

Stein, Burton. 1977. Temples in Tamil country, 1300-1750 A.D. In Burton Stein ed., *Special number on south Indian temples. Indian Economic and Social History Review* 14:11-46.

Stokes, Eric. 1978. *The peasant and the raj: Studies in agrarian society and peasant rebellion in colonial India*. New Delhi: S. Chand and Co. Ltd; London: Cambridge University Press.

Strenski, Ivan. 1987. *Four theories of myth in twentieth century history: Cassirer, Eliade, Lévi-Strauss and Malinowski*. Iowa City: University of Iowa Press.

Subba Rao, T. V. 1976. Telugu Folk Additions to Mahabharatha. *Folklore (Calcutta)* 8-9: 269-75.

Subrahmanyam, Sanjay. 1995. The 'infidel' within: Making the legend of Desinguraja. Duke University conference on Hinduism and Islam in South Asia. Personal communication.

———. In press. Friday's child: Or, how Tej Singh became Desinguraja. Forthcoming in J. F. Richards, ed., *The making of Indo-Muslim identity in pre-colonial South Asia*. Personal communication.

Sukthankar, Vishnu S. 1936. Epic studies, 6: The Bhṛgus and the Bhārata: A text-historical study. *ABORI* 18, 1:1-76.

Sullivan, William. 1996. *The secret of the Incas: Myth, astronomy, and the war against time*. New York: Crown.

Sundari, P. Usha. 1993. Draupadi in folk imagination. In K. S. Singh 1993, 254-

59.
Sunder Rajan, Rajeswari. 1993. *Real & imagined women: Gender, culture, and postcolonialism*. London: Routledge.
Sutherland, Sally J. M. 1990. Review of Hiltebeitel 1988a. *JAOS* 110, 2:371-72.
Swain, Pravakar. 1993. Folk-tales from Sarala's Mahābhārata. In K. S. Singh 1993, 177-84.
Tagare, Ganesh Vasudeo, trans. with annotation. 1980. *The Nārada-Purāṇa*. Part 1. Delhi: Motilal Banarsidass.
———, trans. with annotation. 1983. *The Brahmāṇḍa Purāṇa*. Part 1. Delhi: Motilal Banarsidass.
Tamil Lexicon. 1982 (1926-39). 6 vols. Madras: University of Madras.
Tarabout, Gilles. 1986. *Sacrifier et donner à voir en pays Malabar*. Paris: École Française d'Extrême Orient.
Temple, R. C. 1884-1900. *Legends of the Punjab*. 3 vols. Bombay: Education Society's Press.
Tessitori, L. P. 1916. A progress report on the work done during the year 1915 in connection with the proposed Bardic and Historical Survey of Rajputana. *Journal of the Asiatic Society of Bengal*, n.s. 12:57-116.
Thapar, Romila. 1966. *A history of India*, Vol. 1. London: Penguin.
———. 1977-78. Some aspects of the economics data in the *Mahābhārata*. *ABORI* 59: 993-1007.
———. 1978a. *Ancient Indian social history: Some interpretations*. Delhi: Orient Longmans.
———. 1978b. *Exile and the kingdom: Some thoughts on the Rāmāyaṇa*. Bangalore: The Mythic Society.
———. 1984. *From lineage to state: Social formations in the mid-first millennium B.C. in the Ganga valley*. Delhi: Oxford University Press.
———. 1991. Genealogical patterns as perceptions of the past. *Studies in history*, n.s. 7, 1:1-36.
———. 1992. *Interpreting early India*. Delhi: Oxford University Press.
Thurston, Edgar, and K. Rangachari. [1904] 1965. *Castes and tribes of southern India*. 7 vols. Madras: Government Press.
Titus, Murray T. 1959. *Islam in India and Pakistan*. Calcutta: Y.M.C.A. Publishing House.
Tod, James. [1829-32] 1972. *Annals and antiquities of Rajasthan*. 2 vols. London: Smith and Elder and Co.
———. [1829-32] 1984. *Annals and antiquities of Rajasthan*. Calcutta: S. K. Lahari.
———. [1829-32, 1920] 1990. *Annals and antiquities of Rajasthan or the central and western states of India*. Ed. with introd. by William Crooke. Delhi: Low Price Publications.
Trautmann, Thomas R. 1981. *Dravidian kinship*. Cambridge: Cambridge University Press.

Tripathi, R. S. [1937] 1989. *History of Kanauj to the Moslem conquest*. Delhi: Motilal Banarsidass.

Turner, R. L. 1966. *A comparative dictionary of the Indo-Aryan languages*. London: Oxford University Press.

Turner, Terence. 1991. "We are parrots," "twins are birds": Play of tropes as operational structure. In Fernandez 1991, 121-58.

Turner, Victor. 1974. *Dramas, fields, and metaphors: Symbolic action in human society*. Ithaca: Cornell University Press.

Türstig, Hans-Georg. 1985. The Indian sorcery called *abhicāra*. *Wiener Zeitschrift für die Kunde Südasiens* 29:69-117.

Vaidya, Chintaman Vinayak. N.d. *The Mahābhārata: A criticism*. (published with different pagination at Delhi: Mehar Chand Lachhman Das, 1966).

———. [1906] 197^ *The riddle of the Rāmāyaṇa*. Delhi: Meharchand Lachhmandas.

———. 1907. *Epic India, or India as described in the Mahabharata and the Ramayana*. Bombay: Mrs. Radhabai Atmaram Sagoon.

———. 1924. *History of medieval Hindu India*, Vol. 2, *Early history of the Rajputs (750 to 1000 A.D.)*. Poona: Oriental Book-supplying Agency.

———. 1926. *History of medieval Hindu India*, Vol. 3, *Downfall of Hindu India (c. 1000 to 1200 A.D.)*. Poona: Oriental Book-Supplying Agency.

Vanamamalai, N. 1969. *Studies in Tamil folk literature*. Madras: New Century Book House.

van Buitenen, J. A. B. 1973, 1975, 1978. *The Mahābhārata*, Vols. I:1. *The book of beginnings*; II:2. *The book of the assembly hall*; 3. *The book of the forest*; III:4. *The book of Virāṭa*; 5. *The book of the effort*. Chicago: University of Chicago Press.

van der Kraan, A. 1985. Human sacrifice in Bali: Sources, notes, and commentary. *Indonesia* 40:89-121.

van der Veer, Peter. 1989. *Gods on earth: The management of religious experience and identity in a north Indian pilgrimage centre*. Delhi: Oxford University Press.

Varma, Pavan K. 1996. *Yudhishtar & Draupadi: A tale of love, passion and the riddles of existence*. New Delhi: Viking Penguin India.

Venniyoor, E. M. J. 1981. Script. In R. Ramachandran Nair et al., eds., *Ravi Varma*. Trivandrum: Museums and Zoos and Art Gallery.

Vogel, J. Ph. 1930-1932. The head-offering to the goddess in Pallava sculpture. *BSOAS* 6, 2:539-543.

Wadley, Susan. 1976. Brothers, husbands, and sometimes sons: Kinsmen in north Indian ritual. *Eastern Anthropologist* 29:149-70.

Ward, William. [1882] 1970. *A view of the history, literature, and mythology of the Hindoos: Including a minute description of their manners and customs, and translations from their principal works*. 3 vols. Port Washington, N.Y.: Kennikat Press.

Waterfield, William, trans. and George Grierson, ed. 1923. *The lay of Alha: A saga of Rajput chivalry as sung by the minstrels of northern India*. London: Oxford University Press.

Webster, John C. B. 1994. *The Dalit Christians: A history*. New Delhi: ISPCK.

Weinberger-Thomas, Catherine. 1996. *Cendres d'immortalité: La crémation des veuves en Inde*. Paris: Éditions du Seuil.

White, David Gordon. 1991. *Myths of the dog-man*. Chicago: University of Chicago Press.

———. 1996. *The alchemical body: Siddha traditions in medieval India*. Chicago: University of Chicago Press.

Whitehead, Henry. 1921. *The village gods of south India*. Calcutta: Association Press.

Wikander, Stig. 1950. Sur le fonds commun indo-iranien de épopées de la Perse et de l'Inde. *La nouvelle Clio* 2:310-29.

———. 1957. Nakula et Sahadeva. *Orientalia Suecana* 6:66-96.

———. 1960a. Från Bråvalla till Kurukshetra. *Arkiv för Nordisk Filologi* 75:183-90.

———. 1960b. Germanische und Indo-Iranische Eschatologie. *Kairos* 2:83-88.

———. 1978. Brávellir und Kurukshetra. *Sonderdruck aus Europäische Heldendichtung*. Trans. Jörg Scherzer [from 1960a]. Darmstadt: Wissenschaftliche Buchgesellschaft.

Wilson, H. H., trans. [1840] 1972. *The Vishnu Purāṇa*. Calcutta: Punthi Pustak.

Winslow, M. [1862] 1979. *Winslow's comprehensive Tamil and English dictionary*. Delhi: Asian Educational Series.

Witzel, Michael. 1984. Sur le chemin du ciel. *Bulletin des études indiennes* 2:213-79.

———. 1987. The case of the shattered head. *Studien zur Indologie und Iranistik* 13/14:363-416.

Wright, F. N. 1873. The Chandel Thákúrs. *IA* 2:33-37.

Yule, H., and A. C. Burnell. [1886] 1986. *Hobson-Jobson*. Calcutta: Rupa and Co.

Ziegler, Norman P. 1978. Some notes on Rajpūt loyalties during the Mughal period. In Richards 1978, 215-51.

Zoller, Claus Peter. 1993. On Himalayan ball games, head hunting, and related matters. In Brückner, Lutze, and Malik 1993, 201-39.

Index